Foundation
in
Accounting | *2*

Foundation in Accounting 2

Second Edition

RICHARD LEWIS
Council for National
Academic Awards

MICHAEL FIRTH
University of
British Columbia

Prentice/Hall **PHI** International

ENGLEWOOD CLIFFS, NEW JERSEY   LONDON   MEXICO   NEW DELHI
RIO DE JANEIRO   SINGAPORE   SYDNEY   TOKYO   TORONTO   WELLINGTON

To Ron and the memory of Edna and to Pamela, Claire, Paige, Sian, Tate and Roanne.

British Library Cataloguing in Publication Data

Foundation in accounting.
  2. —2nd ed.
  1. Accounting
  I. Lewis, Richard, *1941 Sept. 30 –*
  II. Firth, Michael
  657   HF5635

ISBN 0-13-329680-6

ISBN 0-13-329680-6

Prentice-Hall, Inc., *Englewood Cliffs, New Jersey*
Prentice-Hall International, UK. Ltd., *London*
Prentice-Hall of Australia Pty., Ltd., *Sydney*
Prentice-Hall Canada, Inc., *Toronto*
Prentice-Hall Hispanoamericana, S.A., *Mexico*
Prentice-Hall of India Private Limited, *New Delhi*
Prentice-Hall of Japan, Inc., *Tokyo*
Prentice-Hall of Southeast Asia Pte., Ltd., *Singapore*
Editora Prentice-Hall Do Brasil Ltda., *Rio de Janeiro*
Whitehall Books Limited, *Wellington, New Zealand*

Printed in Great Britain by A. Wheaton & Co. Ltd, Exeter
10 9 8 7 6 5 4

Contents

PREFACE TO SECOND EDITION	**x**
A NOTE TO READERS	**xi**
TERMINOLOGY AND NOTATION	**xiii**

1. INTRODUCTION — **1**

Ancient accounting records — 2
Renaissance Italy — 2
Early forms of business structure — 3
Early influences on accounting principles — 4
The separation of ownership and management — 5
Limited companies — 6
Groups of companies — 8
Objectives of accounting — 8
The accountancy profession and its influence on accounting
    methods — 11
The Accounting Standards Committee — 12

SECTION A

2. THE ACCOUNTS OF MANUFACTURING FIRMS — **16**

Job-order cost sheets — 19
Structure of the manufacturing account — 21
Inventories — 21
Manufacturing overheads and the 'valuation' of inventories — 22
Limitations of manufacturing accounts — 24
Contracting companies — 26
Contract accounts — 27
    Retentions — 28
The recognition of profit — 28
Methods of estimating profit on uncompleted contracts — 29
The book-keeping treatment of cash received from customers — 31
Losses — 34
Appendix: The pure ledger system — 35
    Materials (direct) — 35
    Direct labour — 36
    Manufacturing overheads — 36

	Work in progress	36
	Finished goods inventory	37
	Exercises	40

3. INCOMPLETE RECORDS AND CLUB ACCOUNTS — **47**

Incomplete records	47
Unidentified payments	49
Drawings	49
Cash receipts and payments	49
Totally incomplete records	53
Incomplete records and limited companies	54
Examination technique	55
The accounts of clubs, societies and associations	60
Presentation	61
Special funds	62
Outstanding subscriptions	66
Life subscriptions and entry fees	66
Exercises	69

4. PARTNERSHIP ACCOUNTS — **77**

Capital, current and drawings accounts	78
The appropriation of profit	79
Interest on capital	79
Salaries	80
Partners' loan accounts	84
Lack of a partnership agreement	84
The peculiar problems of partnerships	85
Goodwill	86
Valuation of goodwill	87
Average profit	87
Average revenue	88
Future profits	89
Super profits	89
Treatment of goodwill on the admission of a new partner	90
Change in the profit-sharing ratio	94
Undervalued assets other than goodwill	95
The death or retirement of a partner	95
(a) Immediate payment	96
(b) Payment by instalments	97
(c) Discharge by the payment of an annuity	97
(d) Use of life policies	98
The Partnership Act 1890	98
Absence of accounts at the date of change in partnership arrangements	98
Dissolution of partnerships	99
Dissolution and the Partnership Act 1890	99
Non-cash proceeds	102
The rule in Garner *v* Murray	102
Piecemeal realization and interim distributions	103
Joint ventures	104
Appendix: An extended example of partnership accounts	108
Exercises	115

APPENDIX TO SECTION A — **123**

SECTION B

5. LIMITED COMPANIES - 1 — **132**

Formation of limited companies	133
The nature of shares and limited liability	134

Private and public companies 135
Listed and unlisted companies 135
Dividends 135
Different types of share capital 136
Preference shares 137
Ordinary shares 138
Deferred shares 138
Redeemable shares 138
Stock 139
Shares of no par value 139
The balance sheets of limited companies 139
Accounting for the issue of shares 140
Forfeited shares 143
Convertible loan stocks 144
Longer-term liabilities 145
The burdens imposed on limited liability companies 146
Restrictions on the reduction of subscribed capital 147
Profits available for dividend 149
Reserves 150
Statutory reserves 151
The share premium account 151
Capital redemption reserve 152
The distinction between the redemption and purchase
of shares 153
Acquisition of its own shares by public companies 153
Purchase out of earnings 154
Purchase out of the proceeds of an issue of new shares 155
Premium paid out of earnings 155
Premium paid partly out of the issue of new shares 156
Redemption and purchase of own shares by private
companies out of capital 157
Protection afforded to shareholders 159
Off-Market purchases 160
Market purchases 160
Protection afforded to shareholders 160
The advantages of allowing companies to purchase
their own shares 161
Unrealized profits 163
Non-statutory reserves 163
Capitalization issues 163
The redemption of debentures 166
Sinking funds 167
The basic method 167
Redemption by purchasing in the open market 168
Statutory books 169
The annual return 171
Exercises 171

6. **TAXATION IN ACCOUNTS** **177**
Income tax 177
Income tax on the profits of partnerships and sole traders 178
Value Added Tax 179
Accounting for Value Added Tax: SSAP5 180
Corporation tax 180
The adjustment of the profit disclosed by the profit and loss account 181
Capital gains 182
Rate of corporation tax 182
Date on which tax is payable 183
Capital allowances 184

Losses   184
Advance corporation tax   185
Surplus advance corporation tax   187
    ACT on proposed dividends   188
Stock relief   189
Deferred taxation   191
    Liability method   193
    Deferral method   195
    Asset revaluation   196
    First attempts at standardization   196
    Accounting for deferred taxation: SSAP15   197
    Profit and loss account   198
    Balance sheet   198
    Recoverable ACT and the deferred taxation account   198
The treatment of taxation under the imputation system: SSAP8   199
Investment incentives and government grants   202
The accounting treatment of government grants SSAP4   202
Exercises   203

7. LIMITED COMPANIES – 2: ANNUAL ACCOUNTS   **208**
The law   208
    True and fair   210
The formats   210
The balance sheet formats   211
Profit and loss account formats   213
The differences between the profit and loss account formats   216
Accounting principles and rules   217
Accounting principles   218
Accounting Rules   218
Historical cost accounting rules   219
The alternative accounting rules   221
Notes to the accounts (disclosure requirements)   222
The directors' report   233
Accounting exemptions available to 'small' and 'medium sized' companies   235
Criteria for small and medium sized companies   236
Exemptions for small companies   236
Exemptions available for medium sized companies   237
Signatures of the directors   238
Stock exchange regulations   238
Statements of standard accounting practice   239
    SSAP2: Disclosure of accounting policies   239
    SSAP6 : Extraordinary items and prior year adjustments   241
    SSAP9 : Stock and work in progress   243
    SSAP12: Accounting for depreciation   243
    SSAP13: Accounting for research and development   246
    SSAP17: Accounting for post balance sheet events   248
    SSAP18: Accounting for contingencies   250
    SSAP19: Accounting for investment properties   251
The auditor   253
    The auditor and small and medium sized companies   254
Exercises   254

8. CONSOLIDATED ACCOUNTS   **262**
Introduction   262
    The nature of the problem   262
    Consolidated accounts   264
Purchase method of consolidation   264
    Wholly owned subsidiaries   264
    The nature of goodwill on consolidation   269
    Goodwill – what should we do with it?   270

Capital reserve on consolidation or negative goodwill 272
The definition of a subsidiary company 274
Partly owned subsidiaries 275
    Consolidated balance sheets 275
    The consolidated profit and loss account 279
    Inter-company balances and trading 284
    Unrealized profits on inter-company sales 285
    Preference shares in subsidiary companies 286
    More on minority interest 286
Consolidated accounts – legal provisions 294
    Purchase consideration other than cash 297
Merger or pooling of interest 297
    The consolidated profit and loss account 300
    Criteria for the merger method 301
    Group accounts 302
Associated companies 302
Exercises 308

9. FUNDS FLOW STATEMENTS AND CASH BUDGETING **316**
Introduction 316
    Profit, cash and working capital 317
    Sources and applications of funds other than from operations 321
    The format of funds statements 322
    Sale of fixed assets 324
    Preparation of sources and application statements 324
    Uses and limitations of funds statements 329
    Statements of sources and applications of funds: SSAP 10 332
    Taxation in funds statements 335
    Other definitions of funds 336
        All financial resources 336
        Net monetary assets 337
        Cash 337
Cash flow accounting 338
Cash budgets 340
Exercises 346

SECTION C

10. CURRENT VALUE ACCOUNTING **354**
The nature and valuation of assets 357
    1. Net realizable value 357
    2. Replacement cost 357
    3. Value in use or economic value 357
Market values 358
'Economic value' 358
Deprival value 360
Valuation of liabilities 363
Balance sheets and current values 364
Gains and current value accounting 365
    Operating gain 368
    Extraordinary gain 368
    Holding gains 368
Gains and profits 368
    1. Profit = operating and extraordinary gains 369
    2. Profit = all gains 369
    3. Profit = all gains except unrealized holding gains 369
    Distinction between holding and operating gains 370
Appendix: Present values 370
Exercises 372

11. ACCOUNTING FOR CHANGES IN THE GENERAL PRICE LEVEL   **374**
Current purchasing power accounting   375
Measuring changes in the general purchasing power of money   375
   Index numbers   377
   The index of retail prices   378
   Conversion to pounds of current purchasing power   378
   CPP accounts and current values   380
   Losses and gains on holding monetary assets and liabilities   380
   Equity share capital and reserves   384
Differences between historical cost and CPP profits   387
   Time lag between the acquisition and use of an input   387
   Restatement of mid-year pounds in terms of year-end pounds   388
Exercises   391

12. CURRENT COST ACCOUNTING   **396**
   Scope of SSAP16   396
The main principles of current cost accounting   397
   The unit of account   397
   The CCA balance sheet   397
The current cost profit and loss account   398
   Current cost operating profit   398
   The three current cost operating adjustments   400
   Current cost profit attributable to shareholders   403
   The gearing adjustment   404
   Current cost profit attributable to shareholders and the gearing ratio   409
   Value to the business   410
   Fixed assets   411
      Plant and machinery   411
      Cases where the use of index numbers will not be appropriate   413
      Depreciation of plant and machinery   414
      Backlog depreciation   414
      Land and buildings   419
      Depreciation of non-specialized buildings   420
      Wasting and intangible assets   420
      Investments   420
      Goodwill on consolidation   421
      Disposal of fixed assets   421
      Entries following the recognition of a permanent diminution to below
        net current replacement cost   421
   Stock   422
   Stock subject to the cost of sales adjustment   422
      Cost of goods sold expense   423
      The averaging method   423
   Monetary working capital adjustment   430
      Calculation of the MWCA   431
      Negative monetary working capital   431
      Stock not subject to the COSA   432
   The gearing adjustment   433
   Current cost accounting and general price Level changes 449
   Development of the Sandilands model   451
   CCA and the valuation of a business   454
   Interdependent assets   455
Exposure draft 35 "Accounting for the effects of changing prices"   455
   Scope of ED 35   456
   Method of presenting current cost information   456
   The required current cost information   457
   Changes to the basic method specified in SSAP16   457
Conclusion   458
Exercises   458

SECTION D

13. FINANCIAL STATEMENT ANALYSIS   **468**
Financial ratios   469
    Liquidity and solvency ratios   472
    Short run indicators   472
        Current ratio   472
        Quick ratio   473
        Inventory turnover ratio   477
        Debtors' collection period   479
        Creditors' payment period   480
        The matching of cash flows   480
    Medium and long-term measures of solvency   482
        Coverage ratios   482
        Debt to equity ratio   483
    Profitability   486
        Profit to sales   489
        Asset turnover rates   490
        Companies engaged in more than one industry   492
        Return on shareholders' equity   492
Cross-sectional and time-series analysis of ratios   494
Earnings per share   497
        Earnings per share: SSAP 3   498
A case study   499
        Short run liquidity measures   501
        Coverage ratio   503
        Profitability   503
        Overheads   505
Summary   506
Exercises   507

EPILOGUE   **513**
Introduction   513
Objectives   513
A comparison of historical cost and current value   515
    Success   515
    Consumption   516
    Stewardship   517
    Objectivity   518
    The Corporate Report   519
    (a) Statement of value added   522
    (b) Employment report   525
    Basis of accounting measurements   526
    The European Economic Community (EEC)   526

FURTHER READINGS   **528**

INDEX   **531**

Preface to the Second Edition

In preparing the second edition we have retained the basic approach of its predecessor by introducing readers to both accounting techniques and concepts. We have, however, rewritten substantial portions of the book. This has enabled us to take account of the helpful suggestions we have received from readers and to incorporate the very many changes that have occurred since the first edition was published. In particular the book includes a comprehensive treatment of the accounting provisions of the Companies Act 1980 and 1981 as well as a detailed description of the development of current cost accounting.

Our thanks are due to Giles Wright of Prentice-Hall International for providing the motivation for the new edition and to Mrs Carol Allan for turning an untidy scrawl into a usable typescript. We have also been greatly assisted by a number of reviewers especially Greg Wales.

In addition we would like to repeat your thanks to all those who helped with the first edition of the book especially Neil Ferguson, Dylan Thomas and Ian Gillespie of the City of London Polytechnic and Professor Peter Bird of the University of Kent.

We would like to acknowledge the kind permission of the London Welsh RFC which enables us to reproduce their accounts. (May their kindness be rewarded by results on the field as well as in their balance sheet.). The Consultative Committee of Accountancy Bodies (CCAB) has also kindly allowed us to quote extracts from their publications. In addition, we would like to thank the Institute of Chartered Accountants in England and Wales, the Association of Certified Accountants and the Institute of Bankers for allowing us to include questions from their examination papers.

A Note to Readers

Since this book is the second volume in a series the authors hope that its readers will have digested, with understanding and some enjoyment, the contents of Volume 1. However, even if some have not had this pleasure, they can still use this book, so long as they are familiar with the basic principles of double-entry book-keeping and are aware of the assumptions underlying the historical cost system.

In Volume 1, double-entry book-keeping was described, and the historical cost accounting model was introduced in the context of the simplest form of business structure – a retailing sole trader. The topics of manufacturing firms, partnerships and limited companies were not included, but will be introduced *ab initio* in this book. Balance sheets and income statements (or profit and loss accounts) were introduced in Volume 1, and particular attention was paid to the realization and matching conventions. The nature of depreciation was discussed, as was the question of inventory (or stock) valuation and the associated problem of determining the cost of goods sold. Some attention was paid to the presentation of financial statements and the topics of cash discounts, doubtful debts, control accounts and bank reconciliations were covered. Finally, the technique of using a worksheet to prepare a set of financial statements from a trial balance was described. For the convenience of both old and new readers, a number of the terms used and defined in Volume 1 are summarized on pages xiii to xv.

VOLUME 2

This book is divided into four sections. Section A deals with the accounting aspects of manufacturing firms and clubs and associations. It also includes a discussion of the special accounting problems of partnerships and some space is devoted to the problem of the preparation of accounting statements from 'incomplete records'. Section B is concerned with the accounting aspects of the most important form of business structure in the private sector of the economy – the limited liability company. This section includes a chapter on the impact of taxation on the accounts of limited companies as well as one on the subject of consolidated (or group) accounts. A chapter on funds flow statements is also included in this section since it is being increasingly recognized that such statements form an important part of the accounts of limited companies.

Both Sections A and B are couched in terms of the historical cost model. A discussion of alternative methods is introduced in Section C where special emphasis is placed on 'current cost accounting'. It is in fact possible, and perhaps desirable, to study Section C before sections A and B, and there was a great temptation to arrange the book in that order. The reason for adopting the present arrangement was the wish to allow teachers to introduce the topics of the earlier sections before dealing with current value accounting. Other teachers will no doubt wish to reverse the order and emphasize the point that historical cost will soon not be the only (or even the main) basis of accounting. However, it should be noted that very much of the material included in the first two sections will remain relevant even when the historical cost model is replaced by a system based on current values.

The last section, D, provides a brief introduction to financial statement analysis. It is primarily concerned with the analysis of historical cost statements but reference is made to the changes that will result from the introduction of current value accounting. Ideally this section should be studied after Section C so that readers may be better informed of the limitations of historical cost accounts as the basis for financial statement analysis.

This book is topped and tailed by an introduction (Chapter 1) and an epilogue. In the introduction, a brief historical background of accounting is given and a tentative discussion of the objectives of financial accounting is provided. The latter subject reappears in the epilogue for an adequate treatment of this vitally important subject depends on a knowledge of the various possible accounting models. The epilogue also contains a section on likely developments including an examination of the impact on accounting practice in this country of the United Kingdom's membership of the EEC.

Terminology and Notation

In tables and examples, figures printed in brackets indicate negative figures

£K indicates thousands of pounds.

In general British terminology has been used. One exception is the use of the word inventory to mean stock (of goods). In many ways, the American usage is preferred because it avoids the confusion between stock-in-trade and capital stock, and the need to use the messy phrase 'stock of stock'. Both words are used in the book, in particular, 'stock' is used when describing the provisions of Companies Acts, Statements of Standard Accounting Practice, etc., in which that term is used.

The following terms were defined in Volume 1 and are repeated here for the convenience of readers.

Assets
A right which is of economic value to its owner, i.e. the future net cash flow to the owner will be greater by virtue of the ownership of the asset. For an asset to be recognized in the accounting records, it normally must have been acquired for a measurable cost.

Conventions (accounting)
Guidelines which appear to explain current accounting practice although they are not specified by any authority.

Current Assets
Cash and those assets (q.v.) which the firm's management intends and can reasonably expect to convert into cash, sell or consume within a year (or within the normal trading cycle of the firm if that is longer than a year).

Current Liabilities
Those liabilities (q.v.) which are repayable (or otherwise have to be discharged) either immediately or within a year.

Depreciation
   The process of converting the cost of a fixed asset (q.v.) into an expense over the life of the asset.

Drawings
   The amount of cash (or other asset) withdrawn by a sole trader (q.v.) from his business.

Expenses
   The expense for a period is the amount of assets that have been used up in the revenue-earning process.

Fixed Assets
   Those assets which are held to further the main activities of the firm and which it is not intended should be used up within a year.

Gross Profit
   Sales less cost of goods sold.

Gross Profit Percentage

$$\frac{\text{Gross profit}}{\text{Sales}} \times 100$$

Horizontal Accounts
   A method of presenting profit and loss accounts and balance sheets in which these statements have two 'sides'. In the profit and loss account, one side will record the revenue and the other the expenses. In the balance sheet one side will be the assets while the other side will be the liabilities and owner's equity. (*See* Vertical Accounts.)

Inventory
   Goods held for resale in the normal course of business.

Liability
   An amount owed by a business or individual. The liability may be an obligation to provide goods or service in the future.

Mixed Ledger Account System
   A system of book-keeping in which the same ledger account might be used to record, for example, both an expense and a liability (expense payable). (*See* Pure Ledger Accounting System.)

Net Profit
   Revenue (q.v.) less all expenses (q.v.).

Owner's Equity
   The assets (q.v.) less liabilities (q.v.) of the business. It represents the portion of the assets of the business that have been obtained from resources provided by the owner. Owner's equity is sometimes described as being the owner's 'claim' on the business.

Provision
An estimated liability (q.v.), i.e. where the existence of the liability is known but where its amount cannot be determined with a reasonable degree of accuracy.

Pure Ledger Accounting System
A system of book-keeping in which each ledger account records either an asset, a liability, revenue or an expense, etc. Thus, for example, rent expense and rent payable will be recorded in separate accounts. (*See* Mixed Ledger Account System.)

Returns
Sales returns, or returns in. Goods returned to the firm by its customers.

Purchase returns, or returns out. Goods returned by the firm to its suppliers.

Revenue
The gross (i.e. before the deduction of expenses) increase in assets that takes place as a result of selling goods or providing services.

Sole Trader
An individual carrying on a business with a view to profit with no other person sharing in the ownership of the business.

Stock
See Inventory.

Vertical Accounts
Vertical accounts do not have sides (*see* Horizontal Accounts). In a vertical profit and loss account, the expenses are deducted from revenue to arrive at the gross profit, net profit, etc. In a vertical balance sheet, the assets (usually fixed assets plus current assets less current liabilities) are shown either above or below owner's equity plus long-term liabilities.

Working Capital
The difference between current assets and current liabilities.

1 | Introduction

Accounting did not emerge like the unclothed Venus from the seas complete and perfect in every detail. Instead, it developed slowly over the centuries in order to satisfy the needs of those concerned with the conduct of business. If we are to understand the present stage in the development of accounting it is necessary for us to know something about the history of accounting. Unfortunately, it appears that many accountants have only the vaguest knowledge of how accounting practice developed over the centuries; they are thus unable to recognize that the justification of many current accounting practices is based on the needs of the past and may not be relevant to the circumstances of the present. We do not have sufficient space to provide anything more than the merest glance at the history of accounting but we hope that our readers will have the opportunity, and the wish, to study this topic in greater depth.

In this chapter we shall trace the history of accounting and devote some attention to the different types of business entities that have been developed. This latter subject has a particularly important bearing on the later chapters of this book of which a considerable portion is concerned with the problems of accounting for the different types of business entities. We shall also consider the objectives that accounting has served over the centuries and compare them with the functions that accounting is nowadays seen to serve. We shall also discuss the institutional influences on the development of accounting practice – governments, professional institutions, etc. – and pay special attention to those that are currently significant.

In later chapters we shall introduce certain alternatives to the historical cost method and, hence, will postpone a detailed discussion of the extent to which the various accounting bases satisfy accounting objectives to the epilogue at the end of the volume.

Ancient Accounting Records

Some of the earliest written records known to us today are accounting records. They come from the Middle Eastern civilizations of Mesopotamia, Egypt, Crete and Mycenae. The earliest records were in physical quantities rather than money but once money was 'invented' it was recorded and so the Greek and Roman records were expressed in terms of money and other goods.

The ancient documents appeared to serve two functions that are still relevant to the needs of the present day. They helped people to keep track of their assets and made it easier to exercise control over those who had been entrusted with other people's money and property. This latter purpose is termed the *stewardship* function of accounting.

The basic form of accounting statement used in both the ancient world and the Middle Ages to fulfil the stewardship function was based on the charge and discharge principle. A charge and discharge statement covered a period of time and was in two parts. One part of the statement, the 'charge', showed the cash and goods held by the steward on behalf of the owner at the start of the period together with the cash and goods collected by the steward during the period. The 'discharge' part of the statement showed the cash and goods expended by the steward on behalf of the owner as well as the assets transferred to the owner. The balancing figure was the amount owing to the owner at the end of the period. The charge and discharge statement has survived over the years and is now to be found in the form of receipts and payments accounts (see Chapter 3) which are produced by, amongst others, treasurers of sports and other clubs.

Renaissance Italy

The Italian city states of the thirteenth and fourteenth centuries produced the next significant advance in accounting technique – the evolution of double-entry book-keeping. The need for better systems of book-keeping was created by the considerable developments in trade, banking and manufacturing which occurred in this period. The increased size of firms and the more widespread use of credit meant that it was even more necessary to have a satisfactory method of keeping track of assets and liabilities.

It is not known when or where double-entry book-keeping was first fully established. It probably developed in a number of cities – possibly Florence, Venice and Genoa – between 1250 and 1350. It is generally accepted that the earliest surviving set of completely balanced books based on double-entry principles were those for the year 1340, of the stewards of the commune of Genoa, and it seems that by 1400 double-entry was in general use by Italian firms.

The earliest known textbook describing double-entry book-keeping was written by Luca Pacioli, a Franciscan friar and mathematician, and was published in 1494 at Venice. The book had the modest title of *Summa de Arithmetica, Geometria, Proportioni et Proportionalità* (Everything about arithmetic, geometry and proportion). The book was essentially a mathematics textbook but it included a section on book-keeping called *De Computis et Scripturis* (of reckonings and writings). Pacioli stated his reason for including a book-keeping section in a mathematics book in the preface: 'In order that the subjects of the most gracious Duke of Urbino may have complete instructions on the conduct of business, I have determined to go outside the scope of this work and add this most necessary treatise'. (Pacioli was living in Urbino when he completed his book.)

Pacioli did not claim to have originated the principle of double-entry book-keeping; he stated that he had followed the method then used in Venice. However, Pacioli's contribution was immense, for *De Computis*, the book-keeping section, was separately reprinted in 1504 and was translated and imitated in many languages; thus it was largely responsible for the spread of the method throughout Europe. Although the adoption of the method took place at the same time as the growth in the scale of business activity it was not universally adopted even by all large firms for a number of centuries. For example, the Capital and Counties Bank, a sizeable concern, used a 'single entry' form of book-keeping until it merged with Lloyds Bank in 1918. Even now many small firms do not use a complete double-entry system (*see* Chapter 3).

The method outlined by Pacioli would not seem strange to a modern student of accounting. Three main books of account are described: the memorial (or memorandum or waste book), the journal, and the ledger. The memorial was used to make rough notes of all transactions in chronological order. The journal and ledger performed the same functions as they do today.

So far as the development of accounting principles is concerned, it is of interest that, in the examples provided by Pacioli, private transactions were recorded in the same set of books as the business transactions and that no attempt was made to determine the profit for a period. The distinction between private and business transactions was considered unimportant in the case of sole traders. Partnerships did exist in this period, but they were often formed for a specific purpose and for a short duration – what we would now call joint ventures (*see* Chapter 4) – and the *De Computis* did not deal with the accounting for permanent partnerships. Trading at this time was seen as a series of separate ventures and the profit on a venture was not calculated until its conclusion. Hence, Pacioli did not deal with the problem of dealing with uncompleted transactions, and his text did not call for an annual balancing of the books, although it was the practice in parts of Italy other than Venice to balance the books at regular intervals.

Early Forms of Business Structure

Trading was first carried out by people trading on their own account (sole traders). The traders may have been formed into guilds, but these were what we would now call trade protection societies or professional associations. That is, the guild would regulate the activities of its members and obtain a charter from the Crown enabling them to exercise a monopoly in a particular trade. However, the trade was carried out by the members and not by the guild.

Two forms of partnership existed in medieval times known as *commenda* and *societas*. The first was a partnership between a financier (or sleeping partner) and an active partner. The financier advanced a sum of money to his partner and received a share of any profit. However, he did not incur any liability over and above the amount advanced. The partnerships were usually of a limited duration and for a specific venture, for example, to engage in a voyage to the Indies. The active partner would equip an expedition and sail away. If he returned, the profit would be shared with the financier. The determination of the profit would be a simple matter since it would be based on a completed venture and would be the difference between the cash received from the proceeds of the voyage and the cash required to equip and carry out the expedition. This form of partnership had a considerable influence on the development of business structures on the continent of Europe but it did not take root in Britain. The closest modern British equivalent is the (rare) Limited Partnership which was not granted legal recognition until 1907. The other type of partnership, the *societas*, was a more permanent form of association which developed into the partnerships we know today. However, the full implications of this form of partnership were not worked out by the courts until the eighteenth and nineteenth centuries.

The British chartered companies, of which the best known example is probably the East India Company (which received its first charter in 1600), were based on similar principles to the domestic guilds. A group of individuals was granted a charter which gave them the exclusive right to trade in a particular part of the world. As in the case of the guilds, the members of the chartered company were able to trade on their own account but the members of the East India Company also had the opportunity of sharing in the financing of 'joint stock', i.e. a number of members could agree to finance a voyage. At the beginning of the Company's life, each venture was dealt with in isolation, and the capital was returned and profit distributed at the end of each voyage. But from 1614 the joint stock was subscribed for a given number of years, and this situation continued until 1653 when a permanent interest in the joint stock could be obtained. The opportunity to engage in private ventures was not prohibited until 1692.

Limited companies (*see* Chapters 5 and 7) are still sometimes called joint-stock companies and this name is derived from the above concept of the joint financing of 'stock in trade' and has nothing to do with the capital stock of a company as in 'stocks and shares'.

Early Influences on Accounting Principles

This seems to be a convenient point at which to step back and look at the early influences on accounting principles. The charge and discharge system of accounting for stewardship survived into the seventeenth century and beyond but did not result in the calculation of a profit figure. Until the eighteenth century, trading and manufacturing were generally carried on by individuals on their own account, even if under the aegis of a chartered company. Accounting was often a case of 'do it yourself' or, at least, 'done for yourself'. The owners were themselves engaged in their businesses on a day-to-day basis and did not generally require their accounting systems to generate information about how well the business was doing. Their main need was to have records of their assets and liabilities both to check the honesty and accuracy of their clerks – internal control – and to help them collect their debts. The concept of periodic profit, which has come to dominate the problems of present-day accounting, was not seen to be important, and hence early accounting practice was not concerned with the problem of valuation.

The Separation of Ownership and Management

The general advance of the economy and the growth in technology meant that many businesses grew larger. It thus became more difficult for a single individual to provide sufficient finance for a business.

Partnerships (see Chapter 4) became increasingly important, although this type of business structure has certain limitations. It requires that each partner must be able to trust the others. Each partner is liable for the actions of all the others, so long as they are apparently acting in the ordinary course of business, and they are all personally responsible for the debts of the partnership. A partnership is thus only a suitable vehicle for business when all the partners can take a part in its management. There is clearly a limit to the number of people who can effectively share in the decision-making, and under present laws, with certain exceptions, twenty is the maximum number of partners. A further disadvantage in partnerships is that it is fairly difficult to transfer a share in their ownership.

Thus, there was an obvious need to establish a form of business entity which, in the eyes of the law, existed independently from its owners. There was also a desire to establish an entity which afforded limited liability to investors. That is, one which enabled them to invest in it in exchange for a share in the profits without being personally liable for the debts of the business.

Although the chartered companies were available for this purpose, obtaining a charter was a slow and tedious business. There was, for a time, a trade in the charters of moribund companies but this practice was stopped in 1720. It was also possible to form statutory companies which required an Act of Parliament, but this too was a time-consuming process.

Neither chartered companies, statutory companies nor partnerships were really suitable forms of business entities, especially in the period of rapid growth which the economy experienced in what we now call the Industrial Revolution. The next important step in Britain was the passing in 1844 of the Joint-Stock Companies Act. This Act allowed the establishment, or incorporation, of companies by a comparatively simple process of registration with the Board (now Department) of Trade. The Act did not allow the investors, or shareholders, to have limited liability and for this right the business community had to wait until the passing of the Limited Liability Act of 1855.

In a sense we have now arrived at the present, for the limited companies which are incorporated under the provisions of the successors of the above Acts are the entities which are now responsible for most commercial and industrial activity in the private sector. We shall deal with limited companies in some detail in Chapters 5 and 7 and so at this stage we shall confine ourselves to a brief discussion of their nature so that we can discuss the influence of the separation of ownership and management and the existence of limited companies on accounting principles. A brief history of company legislation since 1844 will be provided in an appendix to Chapter 7.

Limited Companies

For our present purposes it is sufficient to note the following.

1. The ownership of a company is divided into shares.

2. These shares can be traded either easily on a stock market (listed public companies) or with some difficulties (unlisted public companies) or with difficulties and some restriction (private companies).

3. The prices at which the shares are traded are not based exclusively on the information disclosed by the company's accounts, but this information does have an effect on the price of the shares.

4. The transfer of shares from one shareholder to another is not an event which affects the existence of the company, nor is it recorded in the company's accounts.

5. The liability of the shareholders is limited. That is, if the company cannot pay its debts the shareholders will not be required to satisfy the creditors from their private assets.

The vast majority of limited companies are owned by one person or by a small number of people, and generally in such cases the owners manage their own companies. However, in most of the very large limited companies the position is different. These companies may have many thousands of shareholders, so that a clear distinction may be made between those who own the company (the shareholders) and those who manage it on their behalf (the directors).

The advent of limited companies meant that the calculation of periodic profit became important. One reason for this was the possible separation of ownership and management. It could no longer be assumed that the owners were in day-to-day touch with the business. They had to rely on the company's accounts when judging its progress and the annual profit figure came to be regarded as the main indicator of the company's success. Thus the reporting of a company's annual profit came to be regarded as an important feature of the stewardship role of accounting.

The second reason was that it became the practice, later enshrined in law, to require that the amounts paid to shareholders (dividends) should not exceed the profits earned by the company. Such a restriction did not apply to partnerships. The reason for this restriction was to provide some protection for creditors. We shall discuss this point in more detail in Chapter 5.

The determination of the profit for a period involved coping with the problem of dealing with uncompleted transactions, that is, the accountant had to 'value' assets such as inventory and fixed assets. This task is far more difficult than the one faced by medieval merchants of measuring the profit on completed voyages.

The calculation of periodic profit involves, as we showed in Volume 1, the making of estimates and, since the middle of the last century, the making of the necessary estimates has been influenced to a considerable extent by the attitude of conservatism. Conservatism is the view that it is better, when making accounting measurements, to err on the side of caution and under-state rather than overstate assets and profits, and correspondingly overstate rather than understate liabilities. Thus the accountant anticipates possible losses but does not recognize profits until they are realized.

Conservatism was not a feature of medieval accounting nor was it much in evidence before the mid-nineteenth century. In many ways, it was the reverse. For example, there were a number of railway companies which deliberately overstated their profits in order to justify the payment of large dividends. This habit often resulted in the collapse of the company. These scandals and the new company legislation helped to create a new attitude, and emphasis began to be placed on safety. The principle adopted was to ensure that profits were not overstated and to avoid the danger of paying dividends out of capital. The conservative attitude was thus justified because of the protection it was seen to afford to creditors; for it should be noted that in the nineteenth century limited liability companies were considered to be very dangerous novelties.

Of course, conservatism may harm the position of an existing share-holder who wishes to sell his shares. The production of a conservative set of financial accounts which understates the worth of a company is likely to result in a lower price being received from the sale of shares than would have been paid if the accounts had been more realistic. It may seem strange that general approval was accorded to procedures which tended to favour potential owners at the expense of existing owners. One of the main reasons for this was that limited companies were seen as being basically an extended form of partnership. That is, shareholders were expected to hold their shares for a considerable period. Thus, the emphasis was placed on the preservation of their investment rather than on the provision of information which would be relevant in decisions concerning the valuation of shares.

An extra dimension was added to conservatism in the second half of the nineteenth century and in the first few decades of the twentieth. This was the practice of creating secret reserves. A secret reserve is the result of a deliberate understatement of an asset or overstatement of a liability. The provision against doubtful debts may be used as an example to show the difference between the application of conservatism and the creation of a secret reserve. Suppose that an accountant believes that between 5 and 10 per cent of the year-end debtors will prove to be bad. If he bases his provi-

sion on 10 per cent, the most gloomy possible estimate, he is being conservative. If, on the other hand, he bases his provision on, say, 25 per cent of the
year-end debtors he has created a secret reserve.

It was accepted that, so long as it was done in good faith, the setting up
of a secret reserve was an acceptable practice which was in the best interests
of the shareholders. One reason for this view was that the understatement of
profit made it easier for the directors of companies to restrict dividends. For
example a prominent company chairman of the 1930s is quoted as saying
that it is better not to show more (profit) and run the risk of exciting
appetites.* A further reason was that companies could reduce their secret
reserves in years in which they experienced a fall in profits, and hence dis-
guise the full extent of the decline.

The use of secret reserves is now much reduced and the emphasis is
now, subject to conservatism which is still with us, on presenting accounts
which disclose a more realistic view of the company's position. However,
company legislation still permits certain types of companies such as banks
and discount houses to maintain secret reserves. The argument for their
exemption from the normal rules is the not very good one that if, say, a bank
disclosed a severe reduction in profits the resultant panic would lead to the
demise of the bank causing much harm to the depositors. It was thus argued
that it was in the public interest to give banks the opportunity of disguising
the extent of the reduction by drawing on their secret reserves. However, it
should be noted that, since 1969, the London clearing banks and the Bank of
England have waived their rights, and now publish accounts based on
generally accepted accounting principles which preclude the creation of
secret reserves. Other banks and discount houses, however, still take advantage of the rights allowed to them.

Groups of Companies

While the limited company remains the most important form of business entity in the private sector of the economy, there is one further development which we should mention at this stage. That is the practice of forming a
group of companies. A group of companies is created when one company
(the **parent** or **holding** company) purchases all, or the majority of, the shares
in another company (the **subsidiary** company). This development was recognized in the 1948 Companies Act which calls for the publication of group
accounts. We will provide an introduction to this topic in Chapter 8.

Objectives of Accounting

In this section we shall summarize some parts and expand other parts
of the introduction to accounting we provided to Volume 1. In that volume
we said that accounting is concerned with:

* Mr Arthur Chamberlain quoted by Yamey in 'Accounting in England 1500–1900', in **Studies in Accounting Theory** edited by Baxter and Davidson, page 42.

the provision of information in financial* terms that will help in decisions concerning resource allocation, and the preparation of reports in financial terms describing the effects of past resource allocation decisions.

Thus accounting involves providing information on the inputs and outputs of an entity† which can aid decision-making. We can identify two major users of this information at the present stage; they are (1) internal parties (managers and other people employed by the entity) and (2) external parties (shareholders, creditors, customers, government bodies and society at large). Internal parties can receive accounting information in a variety of forms depending on the question under consideration (e.g. what selling price to charge for a product, whether a project should be undertaken). This type of information is usually termed management accounting. Our book, however, is concerned with financial accounting, that is with the provision of information to external parties. The information provided in financial accounts is of a far less detailed nature than that contained in management accounts and is reported at much more infrequent intervals. Originally financial accounts of profit-making businesses were prepared mainly for existing shareholders and creditors although there is now a growing recognition that there are many other people who have a legitimate interest in the financial affairs of these entities. Likewise, there are a multitude of people who are interested in the activities and efficiency of other entities (nationalized industries, hospitals, educational bodies, local authorities, non-profitmaking organizations).

We shall now consider briefly who might be interested in the financial accounts of a limited company and how they might use the information contained therein in their decision-making. Starting with the latter, the information contained in financial accounts summarizes the position of the firm in monetary terms at one point in time and shows how this position has been reached over various periods. By using this information together with any other data they can obtain, the users of the accounts can make estimates of the future performance and position of the firm. From this, various decisions can be made, e.g. to buy shares in, or lend money to, the firm, or to take up employment in it. Additionally, a user of accounts may form an expectation about the future state of the company which is not to his liking and may try to force changes in the firm or in its environment (e.g. change the directors, mobilize public feeling, such as against activities which they consider anti-social).

The major users of accounts of business firms include:

1. *Existing Shareholders*   In larger firms the shareholders take no part in the day-to-day running of the business and so they have to rely on the information contained in the accounts. Typical decisions that these shareholders

---

* There is, however, an increasing recognition that attention should also be paid to the resource inflows and outflows which cannot be measured in monetary terms. The reporting of this information may require skills other than those normally associated with an accountant.

† An entity may be said to be a set of assets which are subject to a common management in order to achieve one or more objectives.

face include (i) whether to sell, keep or increase their shareholding; (ii) the annual voting on the re-election of directors, acceptance of the accounts, fixing the remuneration of the auditors, the declaring of the dividend (sometimes called the consumption decision, i.e. how much of the resources should be taken out of the business in the form of dividends); (iii) whether to call special meetings of the shareholders to remove the directors and bring in new management with more acceptable business policies or abilities.

2. *Potential Shareholders*   Stock market investors are continually appraising stock exchange quoted firms to see if their shares are 'cheap' and therefore worth buying. The financial accounts of a firm provide perhaps the most important of the basic information used by investors in analysing companies. Financial accounts also provide the basic data in ascertaining the value to be placed upon unquoted shares.

3. *Creditors*   Banks and other lending firms use the data contained in financial accounts to help forecast the future profitability and liquidity of the firm. On the basis of this assessment the bank or lender can reach decisions as to whether to lend money and on what terms and conditions. In some cases the bank or lender may be able to get more detailed accounting information from the firm than is published generally.

Trade creditors may also utilize a firm's accounts in assessing their creditworthiness. This is most likely to happen when a supplier contemplates giving credit to the firm for the first time.

4. *Investment and Credit Analysts*   These analysts work for investors and creditors and hence they use accounts in the same way as described above. Because the analysts are usually highly trained they are able to make fairly sophisticated interpretations of accounting information.

5. *The Government*   The government has a direct responsibility for the control of the economy and in carrying this out it obviously requires as much relevant information as possible. The civil service extracts information from the accounts of companies, and from this various conclusions are reached regarding the growth, liquidity, profitability, etc., of industrial sectors and private enterprise industry as a whole. By using this accounting data in conjunction with other economic information, the government can then make its economic policies and decisions. Decisions which may be directly influenced by accounting data include corporate taxation rates, price regulations (e.g. prices and incomes policies), investment incentives, import controls to help declining industries which face stiff international competition, credit policies (e.g. hire-purchase controls).

6. *Taxation*   Taxes of business enterprises are usually based on annual financial accounts although these are modified slightly from the accounts that are sent to shareholders (see Chapter 6).

7. *Employees*   Recently, employees, especially through their trade unions, have been taking a growing interest in the financial accounts of their firms. The accounts give information which the employees, or their trade unions, use in forecasting the future of the business. From this employees will assess such items as employment prospects and whether the firm will be able to pay increased wages. In many firms financial accounting information of a more detailed nature is given, in confidence, to the employees or their representatives. The more detailed accounting information may consist of, say, monthly accounting information for each major division of a firm.

8. *Society at Large*   The financial accounts often represent the only significant information that is made publicly available by a company (obviously consumer-oriented firms are an exception because of their advertising). From this information, public opinion may be turned against or in favour of a firm, and the pressure may be severe enough to make the company change its policies, etc.

Whilst the objective is stated as being that of providing information which will improve decision-making, there are some caveats to this in practice. Amongst the principal ones are: (1) The cost of producing financial accounts can be significant. This argument has been given as a reason for not producing accounts more frequently – more frequent accounts being likely to give better information to the various users of accounts. (2) Making 'better' accounting information publicly available means that competitors are likely to gain a greater commercial understanding of the firm. Although this is the same for all companies, it is still used as a reason against greater disclosure of accounting information.

Recent trends in company accounting and financial reporting have been moving towards the idea of publishing more relevant data for decision-making; this has been and is continuing to be a long-drawn-out process.

The Accountancy Profession and its Influence on Accounting Methods

A major development in the nineteenth century was the growth of the accountancy profession and the formation of the first association of professional accountants. The forerunner of the Institute of Chartered Accountants of Scotland was established in 1854, while the Institute of Chartered Accountants in England and Wales was formed in 1880. These developments led to an improvement in accounting methods but for many years the professional accountancy bodies gave no specific guidance in such matters.

From the very start, the chartered bodies required prospective members not only to pass examinations but also to serve a specified period of articled clerkship with a practising accountant. Thus, the intending accountant learned the 'received wisdom' of the time by both formal study, usually by means of correspondence courses, and by observation during the required period of experience.

It was not until 1942 that the Institute of Chartered Accountants in England and Wales began to publish *Recommendations on Accounting Principles*. However, these were little more than descriptions of those methods which the Institute judged, on a highly subjective basis, to be 'best practice', for there was not then (nor is there yet) any coherent body of accounting theory which could be drawn on when adjudicating between alternative methods. In some cases the *Recommendations* did not specify a single method. Some listed a number of alternatives and then gave the 'helpful' advice that the method should be the one that was 'appropriate in the circumstances'. The statements were only recommendations and the members of the Institute were under no obligation to follow them. There was, at the end of the 1960s, a flurry of *causes célèbres* – AEI and GEC, Pergamon Press, etc. Basically, the situation was that the public became aware of the problem, that had always existed, that accountants could not agree on what figure of profit should be disclosed in a given set of circumstances. It appeared, for a time, that there was the 'danger' (from the point of view of the accountancy profession) that the government might step in and regulate accounting methods. This did not take place but, mainly as a result of the disquiet, the various professional accountancy bodies began to take a far more active role in the development of accounting practice.

The Accounting Standards Committee

The Accounting Standards Committee (ASC)* was set up in 1970 by the principal United Kingdom professional accounting institutions. Its brief is to prepare statements of best accounting practice or, as they are called *Statements of Standard Accounting Practice* (SSAP). Accountants are expected to ensure that the methods specified in the SSAPs are used in the preparation of accounts. If the specified method is not used, the fact and the reason for the adoption of the 'non-approved' method must be stated. The financial effect of using the non-approved as compared with the specified method should be disclosed unless to do so would be impracticable or misleading. If the financial effects are not stated, the reason for the omission must be disclosed. The councils of the professional bodies represented on the ASC require that their members observe the accounting standards when preparing and auditing accounts or, if they do not, that they should act in the manner described above. Otherwise, the members may be subject to the disciplinary procedures of the appropriate professional institution.

The ASC's mode of operation is first to issue an *exposure draft* (ED) 'for comment by persons interested in financial reporting'. The ASC then considers the comments before it issues the SSAP. We shall discuss some of the SSAPs in the chapters that follow.

* Formerly known as the Accounting Standards Steering Committee (ASSC).

Apart from the ASC, the main British accounting bodies have also joined together in forming a Consultative Committee of Accountancy Bodies (CCAB). The CCAB acts as a joint voice of the accountancy profession in commenting on and influencing matters of current interest. It has been particularly active in matters that are the subject of current legislation or political discussion, e.g. the annual finance bills.

There is also an international organization which represents the major national professional accounting bodies known as the International Accounting Standards Committee (IASC). It issues exposure drafts and accounting standards with which the members of the constituent bodies are expected to comply.

SECTION A

2 | The Accounts of Manufacturing Firms

In Volume 1 we confined ourselves to simple sole traders. Now while Britain may be a nation of shopkeepers we would be a very hungry nation if no one actually made things. So let us now consider the problems of preparing financial accounting statements for manufacturing firms.

The most obvious difference between a manufacturing and a trading firm is that the former has many more different types of expense. The purchases of the trading firm are replaced by the myriad expenses that arise when, for example, a tree is converted into a cricket bat. The traditional way of showing the cost of goods produced is the *manufacturing account*. In order to understand the way in which a manufacturing account is laid out it is necessary, as ever, to learn some terminology as well as some of the basic features of *cost accounting*.

Cost accounting is essentially concerned with determining the cost of production of each unit (or batch of units) produced. A detailed discussion of cost accounting is outside the scope of this book but we shall have to outline some of the problems involved.

The first task is to classify and group expenses of similar type. The aim is that readers of the accounts should gain greater insight into the business and be better able to make economic decisions, one of the main purposes of accounting. The classification of expenses will of course require some subjective judgement on the part of the accountant who prepares the accounts.

Typical major expense classifications are:

> Manufacturing expenses
> Administration expenses
> Financial expenses
> Selling and distribution expenses

Administration expenses are those expenses that are incurred in running the firm as a whole and that are not directly related to the manufacturing or selling and distribution functions. If the *financial expenses* of a firm are comparatively small, they may be included with administration expenses.

Selling and distribution expenses are the expenses incurred in advertising and other promotional activities, and those concerned with delivering the goods to customers.

However, it is to *manufacturing expenses* that we must direct our attention, and these are subdivided into *direct* and *indirect expenses*.

Direct expenses are those which can be conveniently assigned to a particular unit of production while indirect expenses, which are also called *manufacturing* or *works overheads*, are those which cannot be so conveniently assigned.

It may help if we present a simple example of a manufacturing process to illustrate the classification of costs.

Fred Chippinwhite owns a firm of cabinet and furniture makers. The following figure illustrates the layout of his premises, and shows the number and type of employees.

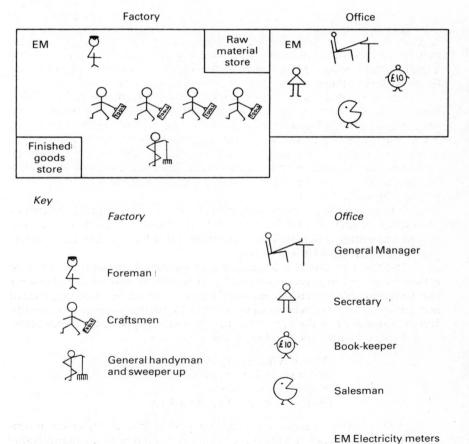

We list below some of the expenses of the firm, including some whose classification is not self-evident.

	Expense	Classification	Comments
(a)	Wood	Direct manufacturing	When a job is started the wood is charged out against the particular job.
(b)	Glue, varnish, etc.	Indirect manufacturing	It is too time-consuming to record the amount of glue and varnish used on each job.
(c)	Wages of foreman	Indirect manufacturing	Some of the foreman's time is spent on general matters and it is too time-consuming to record how much of it is spent on each individual job.
(d)	Wages of craftsmen	Direct manufacturing	Since each craftsman spends a number of days on each job, it is considered worth while recording the amount of time he spends on each. The craftsmen's wages are then assigned to the various jobs.
(e)	Wages of sweeper-up	Indirect manufacturing	It is not possible to allocate the benefit of his efforts to the various jobs.
(f)	Licence fees	Direct manufacturing	Many of Fred Chippinwhite's products include a novel lock designed by Chippinwhite's cousin Yoko Chippinwhite of Tokyo. Fred pays Yoko £1 for each product manufactured which includes the lock.
(g)	Rent and rates	Indirect manufacturing/ Administrative	Since the expense is related to the premises as a whole, it has to be apportioned on some

			basis (e.g. floor area) between the two classifications.
(h)	Electricity	Indirect manufacturing/ Administrative	As there are separate meters for the factory and the office, the appropriate electricity expense can be assigned to each area.
(i)	Sundry expenses	Indirect manufacturing/ Administrative	This is often apportioned by some rule of thumb.
(j)	Salary of general manager	Administrative	The general manager spends some time on all aspects of the firm's operation, and it is customary to treat his salary as an administrative expense.
(k)	Wages of secretary and book-keeper	Administrative	As (j) above.

It can be seen that there are two reasons for treating some manufacturing expenses as indirect. Firstly, it may be possible to assign an expense to each unit of production but only at a considerable expenditure of time and effort. Assigning the cost of glue to each job is a good example of what is possible but very expensive to carry out. The key here, as in many other similar problems, is to stop when the cost of obtaining the information exceeds the benefits that flow from having it. The second reason is that it may not be possible to identify any direct link between the expense (e.g. the rent and rates) and the various jobs.

We have used the words *allocate* and *apportion* in our example. These words are often treated as synonyms, but they have different meanings in cost accounting, and the difference is worth preserving. Allocation means that the assignment can be done with exactitude, e.g. in the above illustration, separate meters could be used to allocate the electricity expense between the office and factory. By contrast, apportionment implies that a degree of estimation is involved. Rent and rates is apportioned on the basis of floor area in the above illustration, but this is only one possibility since, for example, we could take account of the fact that the office is better built than the factory and should carry a greater rent and rates charge per square foot.

Job-Order Cost Sheets

We describe below one way in which a firm like Chippinwhite's might work out the cost of each piece of furniture produced. For a detailed description of this method and some alternatives we would refer you to a cost accounting text.

When a job is started a job-order sheet is issued (*see* Figure 2.1). All the direct materials for that job are booked against the job and recorded on the sheet.

The amount of time spent by each craftsman on each job is recorded and the times are converted to expenses by reference to an hourly rate which should take account of such items as the employers' contribution to National Insurance besides the wages paid to the workers. Thus the direct labour section of the job-order cost sheet can be completed. If there are any direct expenses these are added to the sheet.

The total of the direct expenses is known as the *prime cost*.

Deriving the prime cost is a relatively simple clerical exercise, for direct expenses have been defined as those expenses which can be conveniently assigned to the various units of production. We now have to deal with those manufacturing expenses which cannot be conveniently assigned, i.e. the manufacturing overheads. There are a number of ways of assigning them, and the method which we shall describe is one which might well be used by firms like Chippinwhite's. Under this method the manufacturing overheads charged against each job are based on the number of direct labour hours that have been expended on it.

```
┌─────────────────────────────────────────────────────────────────┐
│                      FRED CHIPPINWHITE                            │
│                                                                   │
│                   Job-Order Cost Sheet                            │
│                                                                   │
│  Job Order No. Y.43                                               │
│  Date started 1 Apr X5          Date completed 10 Apr X5          │
│                                                                   │
│                                              Total                │
│                                                                   │
│  Direct materials                        £      £                 │
│    1 Apr X5                              20                       │
│    6 Apr X5                              30      50                │
│                                         ────                      │
│                                                                   │
│  Direct labour @ £3 per hour                                      │
│                        Hours                    £                 │
│    7 Apr X5         40      120                                   │
│   10 Apr X5         15       45                165                │
│                     ──      ──                                    │
│                     55                                            │
│                     ──                                            │
│                                                                   │
│  Direct expenses                                                  │
│  Lock                                           1                 │
│                                                ──                 │
│  Prime cost                                    216                │
│  Manufacturing overheads                                          │
│  55 hours @ £2 per hour                        110                │
│                                                ──                 │
│  Works or Factory Cost                        £326                │
│                                                ══                 │
└─────────────────────────────────────────────────────────────────┘
```

Figure 2.1

For example, suppose that in 19X5 the manufacturing overheads amounted to £16,000 and 8,000 direct labour hours were worked. Then the appropriate *overhead recovery rate* would be £2 per hour, and hence a job taking 20 direct labour hours would be considered to have incurred a manufacturing overhead expense of £40. This is all very well if one were prepared to wait until the end of the year. However, the information would then be too late to be of help in, say, fixing the price of the product.* So in practice both the total manufacturing overheads for a year and the number of direct labour hours to be worked in that year are estimated, and the overhead recovery rate is based on those estimates.

Prime cost plus the manufacturing overhead charge gives us the *works or factory cost* (also known as full cost).

Structure of the Manufacturing Account

The manufacturing account is simply a list of the manufacturing expenses, both direct and indirect. The order of the manufacturing account is important and follows from the cost accounting method described above. The order can be summarized as follows:

	£
A. Direct materials	15,000
B. Direct labour	20,000
C. Direct expenses	7,000
D. *Prime cost*	42,000
E. Manufacturing overheads	18,000
F. *Works cost*	£60,000

The works cost of the goods produced in the period is then carried to the trading account where it replaces or complements the purchases figure (i.e. where a firm sells goods manufactured by others as well as its own products).

Inventories

A trading firm has its inventory in only one form – goods held for resale – while a manufacturing firm has its inventory in three forms – direct materials, work in progress, and finished goods.

DIRECT MATERIALS are those that have not yet been issued to production, i.e. the materials which are held in the materials store.

WORK IN PROGRESS consists of partly completed goods.

FINISHED GOODS INVENTORY consists of completed but unsold items.

---

* The works or factory cost is one basis that is quite often used in practice in helping set sales prices although many arguments can be advanced against the procedure.

Manufacturing Overheads and the 'Valuation' of Inventories

Since we are concerned with historical cost accounting, the inventories must be stated at cost, but what are the costs of the partly, and of the completely, finished goods?

The basic principle is that inventories should be stated at the costs which are incurred in bringing the products to their present form. The main difficulty is how we should treat manufacturing overheads for it is obvious that the prime costs should be included in the computation of cost, while administration, selling and distribution expenses should not be included, since they are, by definition, not related to the manufacturing process.

Some accounting theorists argue that only the prime costs should be included but the general view which is supported by the Accounting Standards Committee* is that manufacturing overheads should also be included. However, since there are a number of ways of dealing with manufacturing overheads and because these methods involve a degree of estimation, there is no uniformity in the ways in which they are included.

Example 2.1

We will now present an example of a manufacturing account which is based on the 'mixed ledger' system. The appendix to this chapter is concerned with the way in which the 'pure ledger' system deals with manufacturing expenses. The topic is introduced in the appendix because knowledge of it is not required for an understanding of the remainder of the chapter.

The following is an extract from the trial balance of Fred Chippinwhite as at 31 December 19X5. It shows only those items that are relevant to the manufacturing, trading and profit and loss accounts.

Debits	£	*Credit*	£
Advertising	900	Sales	80,000
Audit fees	300		
Carriage in	600		
Carriage out	2,200		
Depreciation expense			
– Office equipment	500		
– Plant and machinery	1,000		
– Salesman's car	800		
Direct labour	9,300		
Direct materials	19,400		
Electricity			
– Office	200		
– Factory	800		
Indirect labour	6,000		
Indirect materials	2,800		
Inventories at 1 January 19X5			
– Direct materials	1,700		
– Work in progress	1,900		
– Finished goods	3,200		
Legal fees	200		
Licence fees (i.e. direct expenses)	130		
Rent and rates	5,000		
Salaries	14,000		
Salesman's expenses	1,400		
Sundry expenses	6,000		

* Statement of Standard Accounting Practice 9: *Stocks and Work in Progress*

The following information is also relevant.

1. Inventories, at cost, at 31 December 19X5

Direct materials	1,800
Work in progress	1,750
Finished goods	4,100

2. Sundry expenses are to be apportioned between the factory and the office in the ratio of 1 to 2 while rent and rates are to be apportioned in the ratio of 3 to 2. Of the salaries expense of £14,000 shown above, £3,000 is in respect of the salesman while the remainder was paid to the general manager and the office workers.

FRED CHIPPINWHITE

Manufacturing, Trading and Profit and Loss Account
Year ended 31 December 19X5

	£	£
Inventory of direct materials 1 January 19X5		1,700
Purchases of direct materials (see note 2)		20,000
		21,700
less Inventory of direct materials 31 December 19X5		1,800
Direct materials consumed		19,900
Direct labour		9,300
Direct expenses (i.e. licence fees)		130
Prime cost		29,330
Manufacturing overheads		
Indirect labour	6,000	
Indirect materials	2,800	
Rent and rates	3,000	
Electricity	800	
Sundry expenses	2,000	
Depreciation of plant	1,000	15,600
		44,930
add Work in progress 1 January 19X5		1,900
		46,830
less Work in progress 31 December 19X5		1,750
Works Cost of Goods Produced		£45,080
Sales		80,000
Finished goods inventory 1 Jan 19X5	3,200	
Cost of goods produced	45,080	
	48,280	
less Finished goods inventory 31 Dec 19X5	4,100	
Cost of goods sold		44,180
Gross Profit		35,820

	£	£	£
Gross Profit (c/f)			35,820
less *Administrative expenses*			
Salaries	11,000		
Rent and rates	2,000		
Electricity	200		
Audit fees	300		
Legal fees	200		
Sundry expenses	4,000		
Depreciation of office equipment	500	18,200	
Selling and distribution expenses			
Salaries	3,000		
Salesman's expenses	1,400		
Advertising	900		
Carriage out	2,200		
Depreciation of salesman's car	800	8,300	26,500
Net Profit			£9,320

Notes

1. Direct materials are often called raw materials. The latter is not a good description since the indirect materials included as overheads are also raw materials in the sense that they are necessary ingredients in the production of the goods. Direct labour may also be described as productive wages.
2. Carriage in has been included in the purchases of direct materials.
3. The profit and loss section of the above statement (the part showing the expenses deducted from gross profit to arrive at net profit) will often have more than the two classifications shown, e.g. financial expenses are often shown under a separate heading.
4. The three different types of inventory should be shown separately on the balance sheet and their basis of valuation stated.

Limitations of Manufacturing Accounts

The manufacturing account is an essential one in that the total of the manufacturing expenses has to be found. But how useful is it in providing information about the efficiency of the firm's productive processes? We fear that the answer is often 'very little', and there are two main reasons for this.

The first comes from the degree of aggregation in the accounts involved. The expenses are the total for the period, i.e. they relate to a large number of units produced and, in many cases, to a wide range of different products.

In order to use financial, and other, information to study performance, it is necessary to have a yardstick against which comparisons can be made. The amount of aggregation involved in the preparation of manufacturing accounts means that they are not usually helpful yardsticks. For even a comparison with the results of the previous period will be of little use if there has been any significant change in the number and type of products manufactured. A suitable yardstick could be a budget which shows the expected expenses, on the basis of reasonable estimates of efficiency, etc.

for the actual mix of goods produced. Such a budget, if prepared, would only be available to the management of the firm and does not form part of the financial statements. However, management cannot wait until the manufacturing account has been prepared, and it is one of the tasks of the management accountant to provide *timely* information about the *efficiency* of the firm. This should be done on a product-by-product basis using, amongst other things, the information obtained from the job-order cost sheets or their equivalent.

The second reason for the comparative uselessness of the manufacturing account as an indicator of the firm's productive efficiency is that the first point where expenses are compared with revenue is in the trading account, i.e. in the computation of gross profit. This means that the productive efficiency and the trading efficiency of the firm are mixed together in calculating the gross profit. Managers will find it useful to differentiate between these efficiencies – for example it may help them decide whether the firm should make or buy its products.

If it is possible to estimate how much the goods would have cost if they had been purchased from an outside supplier, the difficulty can be overcome. The trick is to transfer the market value,* instead of the cost, of the goods produced from the manufacturing account to the trading account. This will leave a balance in the manufacturing account, hopefully a profit, representing the difference between the market value and the cost. This manufacturing profit will then be carried to the profit and loss account together with the revised, lower, gross profit from the trading account.

However, there is a minor complication in using this method as the 'manufacturing' profit on unsold goods must not find its way into the overall profit for the period, for this would not accord with the historical cost principle. We use a provision account to remove the unrealized profit which, mechanically, works exactly like a provision against doubtful debts account. The balance on the provision against unrealized profit account is the manufacturing profit on the unsold items. There will be a debit or a credit to the profit and loss account depending on whether the unrealized profit on the closing finished goods inventory is greater or less than the unrealized profit on the opening inventory.

Example 2.2

The facts are as in Example 2.1 except:

	Market value £	Cost £
Goods produced during the year	60,000	45,080
Finished goods inventory 1 January 19X5	5,000	3,200
Finished goods inventory 31 December 19X5	6,400	4,100

If the transfer between the manufacturing account and the trading account is made at market value then, in outline, the manufacturing, trading and profit and loss account becomes:

---

* There are a number of interpretations of market value (see Chapter 10). Here we refer to the price which the firm would have had to pay for the goods, i.e. their replacement cost.

	£	£
Works cost of goods produced (from Example 2.1)		45,080
Manufacturing profit		14,920
Market value of goods produced		£60,000
Sales		80,000
Finished goods inventory 1 January 19X5	5,000	
Market value of goods produced	60,000	
	65,000	
less Finished goods inventory 31 December 19X5	6,400	58,600
Gross profit on trading		£21,400
Gross profit: on manufacturing	14,920	
on trading	21,400	36,320
less Administrative expenses	18,200	
Selling and distribution expenses	8,300	
Increase in provision for unrealized profit (see below)	500	27,000
Net profit		£9,320

Note that the net profit remains the same; the purpose of this alternative is simply to provide an estimate of how the gross profit should be apportioned between the manufacturing and trading activities.

Provision against unrealized profit account

19X5	£	19X5	£
31 Dec Balance c/d (£6,400–£4,100)	2,300	1 Jan Balance b/d (£5,000–£3,200)	1,800
		31 Dec Profit and loss account increase in provision	500
	£2,300		£2,300
		19X6 1 Jan Balance b/d	2,300

In the balance sheet the finished goods inventory would be shown as follows:

	£	£
Finished goods inventory at market value	6,400	
less Provision against unrealized profit	2,300	4,100

CONTRACTING COMPANIES

The previous section dealt with the generality of manufacturing firms but a different approach is used by firms such as shipbuilders, bridge builders, etc. which engage in large contracts. The distinguishing feature is that a large proportion of the expenses of the contracting firms can be assigned to specific jobs, and so can be treated as direct expenses. In general, the contracts last for a reasonably long period, i.e. longer than a year.

The special nature of the problems gives rise to two features that are of interest to us. The first is concerned with the way in which financial information is presented and classified, the second with the recognition of profit.

Contract Accounts

Contracting firms are more interested in the total expenses incurred on each contract rather than the totals of direct materials, direct labour, etc. for the firm as a whole. In order to enable a firm to focus on this, an account is opened for each contract and all the expenses which can be assigned to that contract are debited to that account.

The principle is a straightforward one but there are, inevitably, a number of practical difficulties. The introduction of two problems will, perhaps, suffice at this stage to illustrate the point.

Should the job be charged (i.e., the contract account be debited) with a proportion of the general expenses of the firm? If so, this can only be done on an arbitrary basis and thus it is probably best not to, even though some firms do adopt this approach.

The cost of using plant and machinery produces another difficulty. If the plant is purchased specifically for a contract the cost is debited to the contract account and, at the end of each accounting period, the depreciated 'value' of the plant is credited to the account and is carried down as an opening balance for the next period. Any proceeds that are received from the disposal of the plant will be credited to the contract account.

Some pieces of plant and machinery may be used on a number of contracts and in such cases a fairly common practice is to charge the contract account for the hire of the plant. The charge could be based on the time spent by the plant on each contract.

An example of a contract account is shown below:

Contract 57

	£		£
Wages	20,000	Balances c/d	
Materials	18,000	Materials	1,500
Hire of plant	2,000	Plant	10,000
Purchase of plant	14,000	Work in progress	49,500
Sundry expenses	7,000		
	£61,000		£61,000
Balances b/d			
Materials	1,500		
Plant	10,000		
Work in progress	49,500		

Notes

1. The contract account serves as an inventory account in that all materials which are sent to the contract are debited to the account. If there are any unused materials at the end of the period the inventory is carried forward as a balance on the account.
2. Since the plant was purchased for £14,000 and the period end balance representing the 'value' of the plant was £10,000 the depreciation recognized during the period was £4,000.
3. This contract has had, as yet, no effect on the income statement. The expenses that have been incurred are deemed to have created the asset of work in progress.

Retentions

When contracts last for an extended period the customer usually makes progress payments during the life of the project. A common procedure is that, from time to time, a suitably qualified independent person, e.g. an architect, naval architect or consulting engineer depending on the nature of the contract, visits the contract site and issues a certificate which shows his estimate of the value of the work done to date. The customer pays the contractor a proportion, often 90 per cent of the value of the certificate. The balance, which is known as the *retention*, is not paid until, say, six months after the end of the contract. The retention system enables the customer to deduct, from the final payment, amounts which could cover any defective items which are discovered and, if such a clause is included in the contract, any penalty payable for late completion.

The Recognition of Profit

There is a problem associated with the recognition of profit because it is highly probable that there will be some years when a relatively large number of contracts are completed and other years when completed contracts are few. Thus if the realization convention (profit recognized when the goods are sold or service rendered) is strictly applied, the firm's profit may fluctuate widely from year to year. So, for example, a sharp reduction in profit will not necessarily imply that the firm is operating at a lower level of efficiency, but may simply mean that only a few contracts have been completed in that period.

In order to avoid such distorted messages being transmitted by the financial statements, the realization convention is often breached, and many contracting firms recognize profit during the life of the contract. Some larger firms do not act in this way but the problems facing such firms are less since, with their larger number of contracts, the fluctuations in the number of contracts completed in each year will be less severe.

Methods of Estimating Profit on Uncompleted Contracts

In Volume 1 we examined some possible justifications of the realization convention. We came to the conclusion that objectivity was the reason why profit is recognized at the time the goods are sold. For it is at that time that the asset changes from one of uncertain value, inventory, to one whose value is considered to be sufficiently objective – the debt or cash.

When attempting to measure the profit that may be recognized on an uncompleted contract there is a reasonably objective measure that is available – the value of the certificate issued by the architect or engineer. In that sense the basic principle behind the realization convention is maintained even if the manner of application is different.

There is no statute or even any real guidance from the professional accounting bodies* as to the way in which profit on contracts should be computed, and hence there is considerable variation in practice. However, the following summary describes the usual 'standard textbook' methods which, even should you disagree with them, should be learnt, since they are used in the 'real world'.

(a)   If the contract has only just started, no profit should be recognized on it, and the asset of work in progress should be stated at cost. There is little agreement on what is meant by 'just started' but a reasonable interpretation might be that no certificate had yet been issued.

(b)   If the contract is reasonably well advanced but it is not possible to estimate future, and hence, total costs with any accuracy, the basis of the profit estimate is the difference between the value of the certificates and the expenses incurred. So the first estimate of profit, P_1, is given by:

$$P_1 = \text{Value of certificates} - \text{Cost of work in progress}$$

We will assume for the moment that there is no reason to suppose that the rest of the contract will be unprofitable. On this basis it may be thought that the task is completed, but no such luck. Prudence now enters the scene and it is argued that the first estimate of profit should be reduced to take account of the cash not yet collected. The usual justification for this adjustment is that it prevents the firm 'paying away profits' by way of dividends, drawings, etc. that have not yet been turned into cash. The arguments against the adjustment are firstly, that the method does not conform to the accrual concept and secondly, that (as we shall show in Chapter 9) measures of profitability should not, in any case, be viewed as measures of liquidity.

The second, more prudent, estimate of profit, P_2, is given by:

$$P_2 = \frac{\text{Cash received}}{\text{Value of certificates}} \times P_1$$

---

* See the provisions of SSAP 9 on page 243.

But we have not finished – for yet a further reduction in the estimate is often suggested.

P_3, an even more prudent estimate of profit, is:

$$P_3 = \tfrac{2}{3} \times P_2$$

$$= \tfrac{2}{3} \frac{\text{Cash received}}{\text{Value of work certified}} \times \frac{\text{(Value of certificate less}}{\text{Cost of work in progress)}}$$

The fraction $\tfrac{2}{3}$ is interesting. Why should it be $\tfrac{2}{3}$ and not, say, $\tfrac{11}{19}$? We do not know, but suspect that one firm (or possibly a textbook author) picked that fraction and the practice just spread.* We reiterate that all this is done even if there is no reason to suppose that a loss will be made in completing the contract. So the best estimate of profit is made and then an arbitrary reduction is made.

(c)   If the contract is reasonably complete and the future, and hence, total costs can be estimated with reasonable accuracy a different approach can be adopted.

First the total profit on the contract is estimated as follows:

		£	£
Contract price			70,000
less			
	Costs to date	45,000	
	Estimated future cost	10,000	
		55,000	
add	Contingency provision, say, 10 per cent of £10,000	1,000	
Estimated total costs			56,000
Estimated profit			£14,000

We now have to decide how much of the £14,000 can be treated as being earned to date, and hence how much will be left to be recognized in future periods.

There are two methods which can be used, one based on proportioning costs and one on revenue.

i.e. Profit to be recognized to date

$$= \frac{\text{Costs to date}}{\text{Estimated total costs}} \times 14{,}000$$

---

* We offer a $\tfrac{2}{3}$ rebate on the cost of this book to the first reader who can provide us with details of the origin of the use of this factor.

$$= \frac{45,000}{56,000} \times 14,000 = £11,250$$

or

$$= \frac{\text{Value of certificates issued to date}}{\text{Total contract price}} \times 14,000$$

$$= \frac{50,000 \text{ (say)}}{70,000} \times 14,000 = £10,000$$

In addition the above estimates could be reduced by the fraction:

$$\frac{\text{Cash received}}{\text{Value of certificates}}$$

The valuation and accounting for work in progress has been the subject of a statement issued by the ASC (SSAP 9). This is briefly summarized in Chapter 7.

The Book-keeping Treatment of Cash Received from Customers

The normal method is to credit the customer's personal account with the cash received. The face value of the certificates is not debited to that or any other account so the balance on the personal account will be a credit representing the 'payments made in advance'. This credit balance is deducted from the work in progress balance in the balance sheet.

When the contract is completed the personal account is debited with the contract price, the credit being to the contract account. The balance on the contract account is a credit (if the contract is profitable) and represents:

Contract price – cost of contract – profit already taken
= Profit to be recognized in the final year of the contract.

Example 2.3

The following details refer to Contract 58 which is for £100,000.

	Year 1	Year 2	Year 3
	£	£	£
Cost of plant	20,000	—	—
Items charged to contract account	13,000	29,000	8,000
Materials inventory at the year end	3,000	2,000	—
Cash received on sale of plant	—	—	2,000
Value of certificates issued	—	60,000	40,000
Cash received	—	54,000	46,000

Notes

(a)   Depreciation of the plant is taken to be £6,000 per year.
(b)   The company's year end is 31 December. In Year 2 the certificates issued covered work completed up to 31 November. Expenses incurred (including depreciation) in December of Year 2 are estimated to be £7,000.

Calculation of Profit

Year 1
      The contract has only just started so no profit is recognized (i.e. the first situation above).

Year 2
      It will be assumed that future expenses cannot be estimated with the required degree of accuracy, i.e. the second situation.

	£	£
Value of work certified to 30 November		60,000
Expenses to 31 December (see below)	52,000*	
less December expenses	7,000	45,000
First estimate of profit		£15,000

We will adopt the most prudent position.

$$\text{Prudent profit} = \tfrac{2}{3} \times \frac{\text{Cash Received}}{\text{Value of Certificates}} \times £15,000$$

$$= \tfrac{2}{3} \times \frac{54,000}{60,000} \times £15,000$$

$$= £9,000$$

We will use this estimate in the ledger accounts which follow, but, in order to illustrate the third method, we will now assume that future expenses can be estimated with sufficient accuracy.

	£	£
Contract price		100,000
less Expenses to date	52,000	
Estimated future expenditure	14,000†	
	66,000	
Provision against contingencies, say, 10% of £14,000	1,400	67,400
Estimated total profit		£32,600

Taking the prudent position, the profit to be recognized to date can be calculated as follows:

† This is not equal to the actual figure, but then estimates seldom are.

$$\text{Profit} = \frac{\text{Cash received to date}}{\text{Value of certificates}} \times \frac{\text{Cost of work to date}}{\text{Estimated total costs}} \times 32,600$$

$$= \frac{£54,000}{£60,000} \times \frac{£52,000}{£67,400} \times £32,600$$

$$= £22,636$$

Note:
Expenses to 31 December

	£
Items charged to contract account: Year 1	13,000
Year 2	29,000
	42,000
less Materials inventory at the end of Year 2	2,000
	40,000
add Depreciation of plant expense: Year 1	6,000
Year 2	6,000
	£52,000

Contract 58 Account

Year 1	£	Year 1	£
Plant	20,000	Closing balances c/d	
Other items	13,000	Plant	14,000
		Raw materials	3,000
		Work in progress	16,000
	£33,000		£33,000
Year 2		**Year 2**	
Opening balances b/d		Closing balances c/d	
Plant	14,000	Plant	8,000
Raw materials	3,000	Raw materials	2,000
Work in progress	16,000	Work in progress	61,000
	33,000		
Sundry items	29,000		
Profit to profit and loss account	9,000		
	£71,000		£71,000
Year 3		**Year 3**	
Opening balances b/d		Cash (sale of plant)	2,000
Plant	8,000	Customer's personal	
Raw materials	2,000	account (contract price)	100,000
Work in progress	61,000		
	71,000		
Sundry items	8,000		
Profit to profit and loss account	23,000		
	£102,000		£102,000

Customer's personal account

Year 2	£	Year 2	£
Closing balance c/d	54,000	Cash	54,000
	£54,000		£54,000
Year 3		Year 3	
Contract Account	100,000	Opening balance b/d	54,000
		Cash	46,000
	£100,000		£100,000

Extracts from profit and loss accounts

	Year 1	Year 2	Year 3
Profit from contract	—	£9,000	£23,000

Extracts from balance sheets

		End Year 1		End Year 2
Fixed assets	£	£	£	£
Plant, at cost	20,000		20,000	
less accumulated depreciation	6,000	14,000	12,000	8,000
Current assets				
Raw materials inventory		3,000		2,000
Work in progress	16,000		61,000	
less Cash received on account	—	16,000	54,000	7,000

Note that the work in progress figure is stated at cost plus any profit recognized to date.

Losses

If at any stage it is thought that a loss has been incurred on a contract the prudence concept requires that the full amount of the loss should be immediately recognized, i.e. the amount of the loss is charged to the income statement and the work in progress figure in the balance sheet is based on cost less the expected loss.

But we do not stop here, for prudence takes us one step further. If it is considered that a loss will result from the remaining stages of the contract full provision* against the loss should be made. As before, a charge is made against the income statement but this time the balance sheet should show, as part of the liabilities, the amount of the provision.

* A provision is an amount written off to cover a loss or liability the amount of which cannot be determined with substantial accuracy.

APPENDIX: THE PURE LEDGER SYSTEM

The method outlined in the main part of the chapter used the 'mixed ledger' approach (see Volume 1). In this appendix we shall describe the 'pure ledger' system which is perhaps less commonly used in Britain than the alternative approach.

The main feature of the pure ledger system is that assets and expenses are kept separate and, accordingly, manufacturing costs are treated as resulting in the creation of an asset – the necessary transfer to an expense account being made only when the goods are sold. A further important difference between the two systems is that the method outlined in this appendix makes use of perpetual inventory systems.

Figure 2A.1 illustrates the way in which the flow of manufacturing costs is treated.

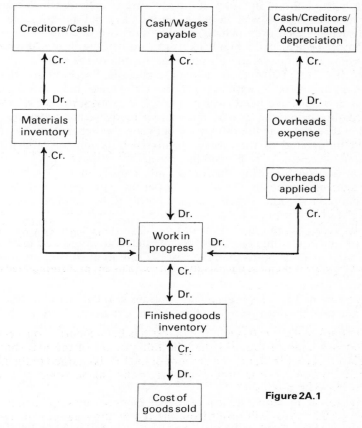

Figure 2A.1

Materials (Direct)

When the materials are purchased their cost is debited to the *materials inventory account*. The cost of the materials transferred to the factory floor is credited to the inventory account and debited to the work in progress account.

Direct Labour

Since wages cannot be stored in the same way as materials, there cannot be an inventory account for wages. When direct labour is incurred the debit is to the work in progress account, the credit being to cash or wages payable.

Manufacturing Overheads

The treatment of overheads is more complicated. Manufacturing overheads, including depreciation of manufacturing assets, are debited to an account called the *overhead expense account*. However, when overheads are charged to production, i.e. debited to the work in progress account, the credit is to the *overhead applied account*. As we explained in the body of the chapter the charge is usually based on a predetermined overhead recovery rate which is derived from estimates of both the total manufacturing overheads for the year and the total of the measure of activity which is used to charge overheads. This was, in our example, direct labour hours but other possible activity measures include direct labour costs and machine hours.

Since, in practice, it is highly likely that both of the above estimates will differ from actual results there will be, at the end of the year, a difference between the credit balance on the overhead applied account and the debit balance on the overhead expense account. If the credit balance exceeds the debit, overheads have been over-recovered or over-absorbed while if the reverse holds the overheads have been under-recovered or under-absorbed. At the end of the year the difference between the accounts will either be credited or debited to the cost of goods sold account or, alternatively, divided between that account and the finished goods inventory.

The reason for using this apparently clumsy method is that many manufacturing overheads are essentially period expenses and, if overheads were charged to production on, say, a monthly rather than an annual basis the overhead charge per unit for goods produced in a month of lower activity would be greater than the charge per unit for goods produced in months in which production is higher. Thus the cost per unit would be higher in the comparatively idle months than the cost per unit in the busier months, thus signalling that the firm was operating less efficiently in the months of low activity.

Now many firms face seasonal variations in the demand for their products, and take this into account when planning their production schedules. Thus to the extent that lower than average monthly production is planned the above signal gives an erroneous message. To avoid this, the overhead charge is worked out on an annual basis – remember the predetermined overhead recovery rate is based on annual estimates. Example 2A.1 below includes an instance of over-recovered (over-absorbed) overheads.

Work in Progress

This account accumulates all the expenses incurred in the manufacture of the goods, and when the production stage is completed the cost of the finished goods, which is derived from the cost accounting records, is credited to work in progress and debited to finished goods inventory.

Finished Goods Inventory

When goods are sold, their cost is credited to the finished goods inventory account and debited to the cost of goods sold account, thus recognizing the expense.

The entries recording the transactions will be done at regular intervals, e.g. weekly or monthly. In the example that follows they have been done monthly.

Example 2A.1

The following trial balance, as at 30 November 19X4, is taken from the books of Hank Chippinwhite Jnr whose accounting year ends on 31 December.

		Debit			Credit
		£			£
(a)	Manufacturing fixed assets, at cost	18,000	(a)	Manufacturing fixed assets, accumulated depreciation	7,000
(a)	Administrative fixed assets, at cost	8,000	(a)	Administrative fixed assets, accumulated depreciation	3,000
(a)	Inventories:		(b)	Sales	76,000
	Materials	4,000	(a)	Creditors	10,000
	Work in progress	2,000	(b)	Overhead applied account	20,000
	Finished goods	5,000	(a)	Electricity payable	500
(b)	Depreciation of administrative fixed assets expense	1,100		Capital account as at 1st January 19X4	24,400
(b)	Overhead expense account	17,000			
(b)	Cost of goods sold	42,000			
(b)	Rent (of office) expense	5,500			
(b)	Electricity (administrative expense)	800			
(b)	Other administrative expenses	4,000			
(b)	Selling and distribution expenses	2,500			
(a)	Prepaid rent	3,000			
(a)	Debtors	16,000			
(a)	Balance at bank	1,000			
(b)	Drawings	11,000			
		£140,900			£140,900

The accounts labelled (a), the asset, contra asset and liability accounts, are the balances as at 30 November 19X4 while the accounts labelled (b), the revenue and the expense accounts and the drawings account, cover the perod 1 January to 30 November 19X4. The capital account is the balance at the start of the year since the owner's equity accounts have yet to be transferred to it.

The following table shows the transactions for the month of December 19X4. The boxes on the right-hand side act as a journal indicating the accounts to be debited and credited.

Transaction	Account to be Debited	Credited	Amount £
1 Materials purchased, on credit, for £5,000	Materials inventory	Creditors	5,000
2 Materials issued to production have a cost of £5,500	Work in progress	Materials inventory	5,500
3 Direct wages are £6,000	Work in progress	Cash	6,000
4 Sundry manufacturing over-heads, all paid in cash, for the month are £2,000	Overhead expense	Cash	2,000
5 Depreciation of manufacturing fixed assets to be recognized for the month is £500	Overhead expense	Manufacturing fixed assets accumulated depreciation	500
6 Depreciation of administrative fixed assets to be recognized for the month is £100	Depreciation of administrative fixed assets expense	Administrative fixed assets accumulated depreciation	100
7 2,000 direct labour hours were worked during the month and the predetermined overhead recovery rate is £0.50 per hour	Work in progress	Overhead applied	1,000
8 Cost of goods completed during the month £12,500	Finished goods inventory	Work in progress	12,500
9 Sales for the month, on credit, are £20,000	Debtors	Sales	20,000
10 Cost of goods sold – £15,000	Cost of goods sold	Finished goods inventory	15,000
11 Rent expense for the month Factory £1,000	Overhead expense	Prepaid rent	1,000
Office £500	Rent expense	Prepaid rent	500
12 Electricity for the month Factory £300	Overhead expense	Electricity payable	300
Office £100	Electricity expense	Electricity payable	100
13 Cash receipts for the month from customers	Cash	Debtors	16,000
14 Cash payments, other than those referred to above	Creditors	Cash	5,100
	Other admin-istrative expenses	Cash	500
	Selling and distribution expenses	Cash	300
	Drawings	Cash	1,000

Note how the above table highlights the difference between the treatment of the manufacturing expenditures which are debited directly to the work in progress account or debited to the overhead expense account, while administrative and selling and distribution expenses are debited to the various expense accounts.

The 31 December balance on the overhead expense account is, debit, £20,800 while the balance on the overhead applied accounts is, credit, £21,000. The difference between the accounts is the over-recovery of overheads, and can be credited to the cost of goods sold account, i.e.

	Debit	Credit
Overhead applied account	£21,000	
Overhead expense account		£20,800
Cost of goods sold		£200

Readers are invited, as an exercise, to work through the above example and prepare an income statement and balance sheet which, hopefully, will be as follows:

HANK CHIPPINWHITE, JNR
Income Statement for the Year ended 31 December 19X4

	£	£
Sales		96,000
less Cost of goods sold		56,800
Gross Profit		39,200
less		
Rent	6,000	
Electricity	900	
Depreciation expense	1,200	
Other administrative expenses	4,500	
Selling and distribution expenses	2,800	15,400
Net Profit		£23,800

Balance Sheet as at 31 December 19X4

Fixed Assets	Cost	Accumulated depreciation	Net book value
	£	£	£
Manufacturing fixed assets	18,000	7,500	10,500
Administrative fixed assets	8,000	3,100	4,900
	£26,000	£10,600	15,400

Current Assets		
Inventories		
Materials	3,500	
Work in progress	2,000	
Finished goods	2,500	
	8,000	
Debtors	20,000	
Prepaid rent	1,500	
Balance at bank	2,100	
	31,600	15,400

	£	£	£
less *Current Liabilities*			
Creditors	9,900		
Electricity payable	900	10,800	20,800
			£36,200

	£
Capital account as at 1 January 19X4	24,400
add Profit for the year	23,800
	48,200
less Drawings	12,000
	£36,200

Under this system the ledger accounts will not reveal directly the breakdown of the cost of goods sold that was produced by the alternative method. In order to obtain that information an analysis would have to be made of the ledger accounts.

EXERCISES

2.1 Charles White owns a firm of builders and decorators. In the past most of his jobs lasted for, at the most, a few months. However, in the last few years, White has increasingly been undertaking larger jobs which are taking a couple of years to complete. At present, White's accounts are based on a strict application of the realization convention (i.e. no profit is recognized until a job is completed), but he has recently met a number of people who work for large contractors and discovered that their firms use an alternative method. He is now wondering whether he should change his method of accounting.

You are asked to prepare a report for White to explain the alternative methods and to describe their advantages and disadvantages compared with his present basis.

2.2 Jackpot started in business on 1 July 1973 as a manufacturer of a standard vending machine. The following figures were extracted from his books on 30 June 1974:

	Dr. £	Cr. £
Purchases – Raw materials	136,700	
– Tools and utensils	3,200	
Sales (15,000 machines at £30 each)		450,000
Factory plant and machinery at cost 1 July 1973	40,000	
Delivery vans at cost 1 July 1973	5,000	
Delivery van expenses	2,500	

Drivers' wages and salesmen's salaries	26,500
Rates and insurance (see note 3)	5,000
Repairs – buildings (see note 3)	10,000
– plant	5,500
Electricity and power (see note 3)	20,000
Factory wages – direct	151,000
– indirect	27,000
General administration expenses	3,000
Administration wages	9,000

You are given the following information:

(1) Closing stocks on 30 June 1974: raw materials £6,700; tools and utensils £1,200.

(2) Depreciation is to be provided at the following rates: plant and machinery 10 per cent p.a.; delivery vans 20 per cent p.a.

(3) Expenses are to be allocated as follows:

	Works	Administration
Rates and insurance	4/5	1/5
Repairs – buildings	3/5	2/5
Electricity and power	9/10	1/10

(4) The work in progress on 30 June 1974 valued at works cost (i.e. prime cost plus works indirect expenditure) amounted to £27,500.

(5) A manufacturing profit of 25 per cent on works costs was added for the purpose of transfer of finished goods to the trading account. The works manager was entitled to a bonus of 5 per cent of manufacturing profit before charging the bonus and this is to be charged in the profit and loss account.

(6) During the year 20,000 machines were completed; as prices have been stable during the year, an equal distribution of costs to machines can be assumed in valuing the 5,000 machines in stock at the year end. The basis of valuation is to be works cost plus 25 per cent for the trading account but a provision for unrealized profit is to be made in the profit and loss account to reduce to works cost for balance sheet purposes.

(7) The sales manager is to receive a bonus of 5 per cent of the gross profit on trading less the selling and distribution costs before charging the bonus.

You are required to prepare the manufacturing, trading and profit and loss account for the year ended 30 June 1974 showing prime cost and works cost of goods manufactured.
(Institute of Chartered Accountants in England and Wales, Foundation Examination, October 1974.)

2.3 Jim owns a small business which manufactures three products. He takes no part in the day-to-day management of the business and employs a general manager, Dennis, and a production manager, Len.

Jim has been presented with the following summary of the manufacturing, trading and profit and loss accounts for 19X8 together with the comparative figures for 19X7.

		19X8		19X7	
		£000	£000	£000	£000
	Raw material consumed		240		190
	Direct labour		190		170
	Manufacturing overheads		130		100
	Increase/decrease in work in progress		(30)		10
	Cost of goods produced		£530		£470
	Sales		1,000		980
less	Opening inventory	88		72	
	Cost of goods produced	530		470	
		618		542	
less	Closing inventory	114	504	88	454
	Gross profit		496		526
less	Selling and administrative expenses		216		210
	Net profit		£280		£316

Jim has made the following observations on the above.

1. I am very disappointed with the results, especially on the production side. Sales have only increased by £20,000 yet the cost of goods produced has gone up by £60,000. This means that Len's department is operating less efficiently than last year.

2. I understand that there was a substantial under-recovery of overheads (based on labour hours) in 19X8 as compared with 19X7. This is obviously another indication of slackness in the production department.

3. It seems to me that one of the problems is that Len has no incentive because no part of the profit is credited to the production department. Why don't we transfer goods from the factory at cost plus 10 per cent to give him some incentive. Better still, we could pay him a commission based on the factory profit. After all, the introduction of a commission scheme worked wonders in the sales department.

4. But, to look on the bright side, perhaps the results are not as bad as they first appear. I suppose that the profit for 19X8 would have been much higher had it not been for the significant increases in work in progress and finished goods that we planned in order to take advantage of the extra orders which will come in during the first few months of 19X9.

Required:

Comment on each of Jim's observations.

2.4 Stephen owns a small business which manufactures a single product. The product is mostly sold at Christmas but a small number are sold at other times of the year for children's parties. It is the practice of the firm to employ a small permanent workforce and to operate at a comparatively low level of production from January to June (Period 1) of each year. Extra workers are taken on from July to December (Period 2) and production is substantially increased.

The factory office has produced the following results for Periods 1 and 2 of 19X6. They can be assumed to be correct.

	Period 1	*Period 2*
Production	30,000 units	80,000 units
Sales (at £4 per unit)	15,000 units	90,000 units
	£	£
Direct materials consumed	21,000	58,400
Direct labour	37,500	94,400
Manufacturing overheads	32,000	35,000
Administrative expenses	20,000	25,000
Selling expenses	16,000	46,000

Notes

1. In both periods actual production was equal to planned production.

2. There was no opening inventory of finished goods at the start of Period 1, and there was no work in progress at the start or end of either period.

3. Manufacturing overheads mainly consists of the rent and rates of the factory.

At the end of June 19X6, the firm's manager, A. Dolt, left and was replaced by I. M. Sharpe. In January 19X7 Stephen received the following letter from Sharpe.

Dear Steve,

As you well know I feel that the firm was in an awful mess when I took over from Dolt and that you are being a bit tightfisted in only paying me the same amount you paid Dolt. It is now possible to compare the results that I have achieved in my first six months with those 'achieved' by Dolt in his last six months. I have produced the following accounts myself based on the information provided by the factory office. There is no need to bring an accountant into this. They charge too much and produce reports which are too full of jargon to be of any use to practical businessmen.

	£	£	£	£
		Dolt		*Sharpe*
Sales		60,000		360,000
Direct materials	21,000		58,400	
Direct labour	37,500		94,400	
Manufacturing overheads	32,000		35,000	
	90,500		187,800	
add Opening inventory	—		45,250	
	90,500		233,050	
less Closing inventory	45,250(a)		11,738(b)	
	45,250		221,312	
Administrative expenses	20,000		25,000	
Selling expenses	16,000	81,250	46,000	292,312
Loss for period		£21,250		
Profit for period				£67,688

Notes

(a) Half the goods produced in the period were in stock at the end of the period, so closing inventories = 50 per cent of £90,500 = £45,250.

(b) Of the 90,000 units sold in Period 2, 15,000 units were produced in Period 1 and 75,000 units in Period 2. Thus the closing inventory is $£187,800 \times \dfrac{5,000}{80,000} = £11,738$.

I think that the main reason for the dramatic turn-round must be the improvements I have made to the production side of the business. The production cost per unit in Period 1 was £3.02 $\left(\dfrac{£90,500}{30,000}\right)$ while for Period 2, I got it down to £2.35 $\left(\dfrac{£187,800}{80,000}\right)$.

I am sure that you must agree that the above figures are sufficient justification for me to once again ask you for a substantial increase in salary.

Yours sincerely,

Ian

Required:

Stephen has asked you, as his accountant, for your advice. Prepare a report for him which should include accounts for both periods which you think may be of help in assisting Stephen compare the performances of Dolt and Sharpe.

2.5 J. Builder started business on 1 January 19X3 as a building contractor. He did not obtain very much business in the first year and what business he did get consisted mainly of small repair jobs which were completed within a few weeks. He did start one large contract (Contract 1) in November 19X3 and this is expected to last until early 19X5.

His trial balance as at 31 December 19X4 was as follows:

	£	£
Capital (1 January 19X4)		50,000
Drawings	8,000	
Contract 1	30,000	
Contract 2	5,000	
Contract 3	25,000	
Contract 4	40,000	
Contrast 5	3,000	
General expenses	23,000	
Plant A (at cost)	14,000	
Plant B (at cost)	9,000	
Cash received from customers		103,000
Balance at bank	4,000	
Sundry expenses payable		11,000
Sundry prepaid expenses	3,000	
	£164,000	£164,000

Builder issues requests for payments based on the value of work certified by the customers' architects. These requests are not recorded in the books, i.e. only the cash actually received from customers is recorded.

The following information relating to the contract accounts is available.

	Contract				
	1	2	3	4	5
	£	£	£	£	£
Cost of work at 31 December 19X4 (excluding depreciation)	30,000	5,000	25,000	40,000	3,000
Value of certificates, all issued in respect of work done to 31 December 19X4	50,000	8,000	28,000	48,000	—

Contract

	1	2	3	4	5
	£	£	£	£	£
Final contract price	60,000	8,000	40,000	80,000	30,000
Estimate of final cost (including depreciation) (Actual for Contract 2)	40,000	5,000	42,000 to 50,000	60,000 to 70,000	20,000 to 26,000

The customer's architect had not visited the site of Contract 5 by 31 December 19X4.

The plant (all of which was purchased on 1 January 19X4) is to be written off on a straight line basis over four years. The following scrap values are assumed. Plant A £2,000, Plant B £1,000. Plant A was mainly used on Contract 1. However, towards the end of 19X4 the bulk of the plant was moved to Contract 5. Taking the year as a whole it is estimated that it was used on Contract 1 for 80 per cent of the time and on Contract 5 for 20 per cent of the time. Plant B was specially purchased for Contract 4. The plant used on the other contracts was hired and the hire charges are included in the above costs.

An analysis of the cash received from customers' accounts is as follows:

Contract	£
1	45,000
2	7,200
3	16,800
4	34,000
	£103,000

In the case of a contract where the final cost can be estimated with reasonable confidence (i.e. Contract 1), the profit to be recognized is to be based on the proportion of the total estimated profit by using the ratio of cost of work completed to estimated total cost. Otherwise, for those contracts on which a significant amount of work has been done, the profit is to be based on the difference between the value of the certificates issued and the cost of the work done. In all cases, only two thirds of the profit (as calculated above) should be recognized and this estimate should be further reduced by the fraction that the cash received to date bears to the value of the certificates.

Required:

(a) Calculate, for each contract, the profit or loss to be taken to J. Builder's profit and loss account for 19X4.

(b) Prepare J. Builder's profit and loss account for the year ended 31 December 19X4 and his balance sheet as at that date.

3 | *Incomplete Records and Club Accounts*

INCOMPLETE RECORDS

Depending on their experience or cynicism, readers may be surprised to learn that not all firms maintain complete accounting records. Many firms' records lack a lot or a little, and such systems are usually described as *incomplete records*.

This chapter is important because a surprisingly large number of firms rely on incomplete records. We do not have the necessary empirical evidence, but experience suggests that most sole traders, some partnerships and a good number of small limited companies have records which are more or less incomplete.

There are many kinds and degrees of incompleteness, depending on the ignorance and ingenuity of traders. At one extreme there may be absolutely nothing, while at the other the firm may have a superb set of cash books and personal ledgers and may only lack a nominal ledger.

In practice, most cases of incomplete records would be more accurately described as delayed double entry. Typically, a firm of accountants is employed, at the end of each year, to complete the double entry and prepare the accounts. This sort of activity may constitute a large proportion of the work of many small firms of accountants, and many large and medium-sized accounting firms have special departments to deal with such clients.

The procedure depends on the circumstances of each case; the following, however, represents a fairly standard framework:

1. A balance sheet as at the start of the year must be prepared if one is not already available. This may be a difficult task as more than a year would have passed since the critical date and, in particular, the evaluation of inventories often produces considerable difficulties. By using what evidence is available, the memory of the owner, and his own judgement, the accountant will try to identify the assets and

liabilities as at the appropriate date, and hence estimate the owner's equity. A balance sheet drawn up under such circumstances is sometimes called a *statement of affairs*.

2. A cash book and a petty cash book will next be prepared in conventional double-entry form. The source documents for the cash book will usually be the bank statement. Unfortunately, nowadays, most bank statements only show cheque numbers, and so reference will have to be made to the cheque counterfoils and returned cheques. However, they will only provide the names of the payees and so the accountant must delve further to find the nature of the payments. He hopes that he will find an invoice, or a statement or some other documentary evidence to support the payment. These documents, which are often called vouchers, may have been kept in good order in some cases but others may well be in an awful mess. So many such exercises start with the client presenting his accountant with a shoebox full of sundry papers and a severe headache.

The preparation of the petty cash book can present many difficulties since the vouchers may be incomplete or non-existent. The accountant will often have to undertake a considerable amount of detective work and will, of course, have to fall back on his own judgement.

To facilitate the next step in the process, posting to the ledger, it is customary to use an analysed cash book and petty cash book. An analysed cash book is illustrated in Figure 3.1. Columns are provided for the major heads of receipts and payments, and these enable the accountant to post one figure for, say, travelling expenses, instead of having to deal separately with each item. For the same reason, this form of cash book is also usually maintained by firms keeping complete records. The client firm will often keep a cash book and petty cash book itself. (It is, after all, nice to know how much money you have.) In such cases the accountant's task is reduced to checking what has been done and performing the necessary analysis.

3. The next step is to post from the cash book and petty cash book to the ledger. Depending on the circumstances, and in particular the extent of the sales and purchases made on credit, personal ledgers and control accounts may be used. Alternatively, trade debtors and creditors may be shown as balances on the sales and purchases accounts in the same way as, for example, prepaid rates.

4. The incomplete system has now been completed and the preparation of the annual accounts can follow its usual course, i.e. the extraction of the trial balance and the identification and the recording of the year-end adjustments, etc.

Computerized packages are now available to lighten the accountant's task. He can feed in the opening balance sheet, the (suitably analysed) receipts and payments, and the year-end adjustments, and so generate the firm's accounts.

We have made a number of references to the need to estimate and exercise judgement, for the necessary information may be non-existent or unclear. It may be helpful if we mention one or two of the more common problems that may be encountered.

Unidentified Payments

Although the name of the payee may be known, the voucher may be missing and the client may not be able to remember what the payment was for. Should it be treated as a drawing or as a sundry expense? The accountant may, in the circumstances, feel that it should be treated as a drawing. However, the client may well have other ideas, and insist that although he could not remember what that particular payment was for, he does know that he did not make any drawings in this way and that the payment must have been made on behalf of the business.

The client will win – for it must be recognized that he is responsible for his own accounts, and that the accountant is simply providing a service to his client. If the accountant has evidence that the client is lying, he may probably prefer to stop acting for him, but it is more usually a case of his being obliged, despite some misgivings, to rely on the memory of the client.

The accountant may also act as an auditor (*see* Chapter 7) and in this case he would have to carry out such investigations as would enable him to report that the accounts give a true and fair view of the trading results for the year and of the business affairs as at the end of the year. If he does not perform the audit function, any statement attached to the accounts will say little more than 'I prepared the accounts on the basis of the information supplied to me', – that is, 'I did what I was told'.

Drawings

Many traders make non-business payments from the business bank accounts and cash box. The accountant must be on his guard and ensure, for example, that rates for the client's house do not find their way into office expenses instead of drawings. One of the authors well remembers shivering over a client's gloomy gas fire and finding that a payment for central-heating oil had been included as an office expense. Discussion with the client revealed the 'fact' that the central-heating system had been removed part way through the year!

Cash receipts and payments

Bank transactions are comparatively easy to deal with because there is bound to be some documentation, but the problems related to cash receipts and payments can often make even the most dedicated accountant wish that he had entered some simple employment like the translation of Einstein into Ancient Greek. There are, however, some guidelines which may be of help.

Figure 3.1 An Analysed Cash Book

		Receipts								Payments					
Date	Detail	Total	Sales	Fo	Sundry Receipts	Date	Detail	Total	Purchases	Travelling Expenses	Postage	Fo	Sundry Expenses

The entries in the sundry expenses and sundry receipts columns are posted item by item.

The first step is usually to estimate the cash available to the firm. An estimate of the opening cash balance has to be made, and to this is added any cash withdrawn from the bank. The estimation of the cash received from the supply of goods and services is usually the main difficulty. The firm may have some records such as till rolls which record the amounts rung up on cash registers. If the records are complete there is no problem but, for some reason, one usually finds that some of the records are lost.

Sometimes the quality, or absence, of the records is such that indirect methods have to be used. The purchase records are often in better order than the sales records, and use may be made of this if it is believed that a reasonably reliable estimate may be made of the 'mark-up'. The mark-up is the gross profit expressed as a percentage of the cost of goods sold, and so if both the mark-up and the cost of goods sold are known or can be estimated, an estimate of sales may be made. Thus, after making the necessary adjustments for opening and closing debtor balances and for receipts from customers which have been paid directly into the bank, the amount of cash that should have been received from customers can be determined. This procedure is illustrated in Example 3.1.

Example 3.1

Relevant information about Alf is as follows:

Payments made to suppliers in 19X4	£11,600
Cheques received from customers paid directly into the bank in 19X4	£ 6,210
The mark up is 30 per cent	

	1 January 19X4 £	31 December 19X4 £
Creditors	1,200	1,800
Inventory, at cost	2,200	2,400
Debtors	450	380

(a)   Find the purchases:

Creditors' account			
	£		£
Cash	11,600	Opening balance	1,200
Closing balance	1,800	Purchases	12,200*
	£13,400		£13,400

   * Balancing figure

(b)   Cost of goods sold = Opening inventory + purchases − closing inventory
   = £2,200 + £12,200 − £2,400
   = £12,000

(c)   Sales = Cost of goods sold plus 30 per cent of cost of goods sold
   = £12,000 + 30 per cent of £12,000
   = £15,600.

(d)   Find the total receipts from customers.

Debtors' account

	£		£
Opening balance	450	Receipts	15,670†
Sales	15,600	Closing balance	380
	£16,050		£16,050

† Balancing figure

(e)   Cash received = total receipts less cheques banked
                      = £15,670 – £6,210
                      = £9,460

Sometimes, such as in an examination, use has to be made of the gross profit percentage rather than the mark-up. The gross profit percentage is the gross profit expressed as a percentage of sales.

Say that the gross profit is P per cent   Then

$$\text{Sales} - \text{cost of goods sold} = \frac{P}{100} \times \text{sales}$$

$$\text{Cost of goods sold} = \text{sales} \times \frac{(100 - P)}{100}$$

$$\text{Sales} = \text{cost of goods sold} \times \frac{100}{(100 - P)}$$

Hence if, for example, the gross profit percentage is 25 per cent. Then Sales $= \frac{4}{3}$ of the cost of goods sold.

So a gross profit percentage of 25 per cent is equal to a mark-up of $33\frac{1}{3}$ per cent.

Even if it appears that all the necessary information has been provided, the accountant will, as a check, consider the mark-up (in addition to other factors) to see whether the figure revealed by the profit and loss account is reasonable in the circumstances.

A similar approach may be used to estimate such things as the amount of inventory lost in a fire or the amount of cash stolen by an employee. The key is the trading account, which in the form of a 'T account' is as follows:

Trading account

	£		£
Opening inventory	x	Sales	x
Purchases	x	Closing inventory	x
Gross profit	x		
	£xx		£xx

or, in the form of an equation:

Opening inventory + Purchases + Gross profit = Sales + Closing inventory.

If any four of the above five items are known, the remaining item can be determined.

Having estimated the cash available to the firm, the next task is to deal with the payments that have been made in cash. A reasonably reliable petty cash book may be available, but it is the practice in many small businesses to take cash out of the till to pay certain expenses, and these may not be recorded in the petty cash book. We shall concentrate on those items which have not been dealt with through the petty cash system.

There may be some vouchers available and/or there may be a note-book or some other record showing the cash payments. However, such information will usually be incomplete, and so the accountant will have to make further enquiries. He will consider whether there are any regular pay-ments that have been made, perhaps for part-time help. He will also use his knowledge of the business to see whether there are necessary payments which have not been recorded (e.g. rent). The client should be asked for details of his drawings, and the accountant will use his knowledge of the client's standard of living and other sources of income to help him decide when to stop pressing this point. However, as has already been mentioned, the client and not the accountant is responsible for the accounts and so the accountant will usually accept the client's word.

The difference between the cash available less the cash paid out is now compared with the year-end cash balance. It should be noted that these are all likely to be estimates, even the year-end cash balance, as the accountant may not have started his work until some time after the end of the year.

The last question is then how to treat the difference – sundry expenses or drawings? The answer will depend on the circumstances.

Sometimes, but rarely, the estimated payments exceed the cash availa-ble less the closing balance. This may be due to an error in the estimation of the mark-up, but can also be caused by the client's paying business expenses out of his own pocket, throwing the vouchers into the cardboard box but neglecting to withdraw the cash. A strange way to behave, but stranger things happen in incomplete record work.

Totally Incomplete Records

Sometimes there may be no records at all. Can an accountant attempt to determine the profit in such circumstances? Surprisingly, perhaps, the answer is a, highly qualified, yes. The key is the fundamental accounting identity:

Assets − Liabilities ≡ Owner's equity

If the accountant can estimate:

Assets − Liabilities at the start of the period; and
Assets − Liabilities at the end of the period; and

The drawings made during the period;   and
Any capital introduced during the period;

then he can estimate the profit for the period by using the following steps:

1. Increase in Owner's equity = Closing assets less liabilities −
   Opening assets less liabilities

2. Increase in Owner's equity = Profit + Capital introduced − Drawings
   So Profit = Increase in Owner's equity − Capital Introduced
                                + Drawings.

We need not, at this stage, dwell on the difficulties involved in making
the above estimates.

Of course, if the above method has to be used it will not be possible to
produce a profit and loss account. The most that can be achieved is an estimate of the profit for the period.

A similar method is often used in 'back duty' investigations. These are
carried out when the Inland Revenue has reason to believe that a taxpayer
has falsified his tax returns and, in particular, has not reported all his
income. If the Inland Revenue has sufficient evidence to support such an
allegation then, in order to estimate the amount of the unreported income,
they will often require the taxpayer to employ, at his own expense, an
accountant to carry out an investigation into his affairs.

The accountant will attempt to draw up annual statements of assets less
liabilities. He will then see how the differences between the estimates of net
worth (assets less liabilities) can be explained in terms of income less expenditure. It is at this stage that it can often be seen that the only way the errant
taxpayer could have lived at the rate he did and increased his net worth by
the amount that had been achieved was to have an income which was larger
than that reported to the Inland Revenue. In back duty cases, the whole of
the taxpayer's assets and liabilities, etc., both business and private, will be
considered in the investigation.

Incomplete Records and Limited Companies

Section 12 of the Companies Act 1976 requires all limited companies to
maintain accounting records which should be sufficient to show and explain
the company's transactions. In this respect the accounting records should be
such as to "disclose with reasonable accuracy, at any time, the financial position of the company at that time"* and to enable the directors to ensure that
any balance sheet and profit and loss prepared by them gives a true and fair
view of the company's state of affairs and of its profit and loss.

In particular, the Act requires:

* Companies Act 1976 (Section 12 3(a))

Subsection 4. The accounting records shall in particular contain:
  (a) entries from day to day of all sums of money received and expended by the company and the matters in respect of which the receipt and expenditure takes place;
  (b) a record of the assets and liabilities of the company;
  (c) where the company's business involves dealing in goods, the statements mentioned in subsection 5 below.

Subsection 5. The statements referred to in subsection 4(c) above are:
  (a) statements of stock held by the company at the end of each financial year of the company;
  (b) all statements of stocktakings from which any such statement as is mentioned in paragraph (a) above has been or is to be prepared;
  (c) except in the case of goods sold by way of ordinary retail trade, statements of all goods sold and purchased showing the goods and the buyers in sufficient detail to enable the goods and the buyers and sellers to be identified.*

The accounting records of many smaller limited companies are poor and probably only just satisfy the requirements of the Act. The records must record all the necessary transactions and obviate the need to make estimates of the type we have discussed above. Delayed double entry is used by many small limited companies and if the basic records are reliable enough to enable the ledgers to be written up and the accounts to be prepared, the requirements of Section 12 would be satisfied.

Examination Technique

Incomplete records questions are very popular examination questions not only because of the large number of firms which rely on incomplete records but also because they provide a very good test of basic double-entry principles. Thus all students need to master this sort of question including those who do not expect to work for any firm smaller than General Motors.

Happily this is one type of question where good examination technique closely follows actual practice, i.e. the first steps are, usually, to prepare the opening balance sheet and the cash and petty cash accounts. However, unless the candidate can write with the speed of light, he will be unlikely to find himself with enough time to write up all the ledger accounts. The best thing is to plug in all the obvious figures into the profit and loss account and balance sheet and only use workings (the equivalent of the ledger accounts) for those items which require adjustment.

Surprisingly, considering the frequency with which these questions appear in examinations, they are mostly of pretty much the same type. We shall illustrate the basic question in Example 3.2 below. The most common variation is the situation where the cash records are incomplete and sales have to be estimated on the basis of the average mark-up (see Example 3.1).

*Companies Act 1976 (Sections 12 (4) and 12 (5))

Example 3.2

Seamus O'Foole is the proprietor of the Donaghadee General Trading Company. He approaches you in April 19X6 and asks you to prepare his accounts for the year ended 31 December 19X5. He had started business on 1 January 19X4 and the 19X4 accounts had been prepared by a friend but, due to an argument as to who was to pay for the next round, he has lost both his friend and the accounts.

O'Foole has kept a cash book which he presents to you together with some vouchers. O'Foole is not entirely unversed in the ways of business; so he can supply you with the following information:

	1 January 19X5	31 December 19X5
	£	£
Inventory at cost	2,400	3,200
Due from customers	300	450
Due to suppliers	1,100	1,320

O'Foole made certain payments from the cash received from customers, the balance of which was banked. He used to keep a float of about £20 in the till but he increased this to £30 midway through 19X5. He kept a notebook which recorded the payments made out of the takings and a summary of the information contained in the notebook is as follows:

	£
Wages	260
Suppliers	300
Sundry expenses	420
Drawings	1,872
	£2,852

The summarized cash book is:

	£		£
Amounts banked	12,500	Opening balance	200
		Suppliers	7,200
		Wages	1,800
Closing balance	700	Rates	1,600
		Insurance	800
		Fixtures and fittings	200
		Unidentified payments	1,400
	£13,200		£13,200

An analysis of the cash book and discussions with O'Foole revealed the following:

(a) O'Foole owns his shop which cost £6,000 on 1 January 19X4. O'Foole's father paid for the shop and O'Foole agreed to pay his father interest of 10 per cent per annum on the loan. O'Foole has not repaid anything to his father and the last interest payment was made on 30 June 19X4.

(b) O'Foole valued his fixtures and fittings at £800 on 1 January 19X5 and at £850 on 31 December 19X5.

(c) Wages are paid in arrears and wages payable were £30 on 1 January 19X5 and £40 on 31 December 19X5.

(d) The payment for insurance was the premium for the year ended 30 June 19X6. The premium for the year ended 30 June 19X5, which was paid in 19X4 was £640.

(e) Prepaid rates at 1 January 19X5, £350 and at 31 December 19X5, £450.

(f) All the debts at the start of the year were subsequently paid but O'Foole thinks that £60 of the year-end debts should be written off.

(g) It is agreed that all the unidentified payments are in fact drawings.

(h) Your fees will be £165.

The first task is to prepare the opening balance sheet and hence determine the owner's equity at 1 January 19X5.

Balance Sheet as at 1 January 19X5

	£	£
Assets		
Shop		6,000
Fixtures and fittings		800
Inventory		2,400
Debtors		300
Prepaid expenses (320 + 350)		670
Cash in hand		20
		10,190
less:		
Liabilities		
Loan	6,000	
Interest on loan	300	
Creditors	1,100	
Accrued expenses	30	
Bank overdraft	200	7,630
Capital account at 1 January 19X5		£2,560

A summary of the cash (bank) account is given in the question so there is little point in repeating it; however, we need to prepare an account showing payments and receipts made in cash.

	£		£
Opening balance	20	Wages	260
		Suppliers	300
Cash received from		Sundry expenses	420
customers		Drawings	1,872
(balancing figure)	15,362	Amounts banked	12,500
		Closing balance	30
	£15,382		£15,382

We have assumed that all receipts from customers were in the form of cash but had some of the customers paid O'Foole by cheque it would not have made any difference to the final results.

In a practical case the next stage would be to set up a ledger by using the balances shown in the opening balance sheet and then make the necessary postings from the bank and cash accounts. However, we shall restrict ourselves to the provision of the necessary workings.

Trade debtors

	£		£
Opening balance b/d	300	Cash	15,362
		Bad debts	60
Sales*	15,512	Closing balance c/d	390
	£15,812		£15,812

Trade creditors

	£		£
Bank	7,200	Opening balance b/d	1,100
Cash	300	Purchases*	7,720
Closing balance c/d	1,320		
	£8,820		£8,820

Wages

	£		£
Bank	1,800	Opening balance b/d	30
Cash	260	Wages*	2,070
Closing balance c/d	40		
	£2,100		£2,100

Rates

	£		£
Opening balance b/d	350	Rates*	1,500
Bank	1,600	Closing balance c/d	450
	£1,950		£1,950

Insurance

	£		£
Opening balance b/d	320	Insurance*	720
Bank	800	Closing balance c/d	400
	£1,120		£1,120

* Balancing figures

Loan interest

	£		£
Closing balance c/d	900	Opening balance b/d	300
		Interest*	600
	£900		£900

Fixtures and fittings

	£		£
Opening balance b/d	800	Depreciation*	150
Bank	200	Closing balance c/d	850
	£1,000		£1,000

DONAGHADEE GENERAL TRADING COMPANY
(Prop. S. O'Foole)

Trading and Profit and Loss Account

Year ended 31 December 19X5

		£	£
Sales			15,512
less			
	Inventory 1 January 19X5	2,400	
	Purchases	7,720	
		10,120	
less	Inventory 31 December 19X5	3,200	6,920
Gross profit			8,592
less	Wages	2,070	
	Rates	1,500	
	Accountant's fees	165	
	Insurance	720	
	Loan interest	600	
	Bad debts	60	
	Sundry expenses	420	
	Depreciation of fixtures and fittings	150	5,685
Net profit			£2,907

Balance Sheet as at 31 December 19X5

	£	£	£
Fixed Assets			
Premises at cost			6,000
Fixtures and fittings at valuation			850
			6,850

	£	£	£
Fixed assets c/f			6,850
Current assets			
Inventory at cost		3,200	
Trade debtors		390	
Prepaid expenses (450 + 400)		850	
Cash in hand		30	
		4,470	
less Current liabilities			
Trade creditors	1,320		
Accrued expenses (40 + 900 + 165)	1,105		
Bank overdraft	700	3,125	1,345
			£8,195
O'Foole's capital account			
Balance 1 January 19X5			2,560
add Profit for the year			2,907
			5,467
less Drawings (1,400 + 1,872)			3,272
			2,195
Loan account			6,000
			£8,195

THE ACCOUNTS OF CLUBS, SOCIETIES AND ASSOCIATIONS

In this section we shall discuss the problems of accounting for entities which are (a) not incorporated under the Companies Act and (b) whose objectives are to provide services to their members or the pursuit of one or a number of activities rather than the earning of profit. Such entities may be, and often are, very small in both membership and wealth. However, they can also be very large like the Automobile Association which in 1974 had over 5,000,000 members and net assets with a book value of over £20,000,000.

So long as subscriptions are charged, there will be a need for some financial records, the minimum possible being a cash book and a petty cash book. Clubs which rely on this minimum package often confine their annual accounts to a *receipts and payments account*. The account is simply a summary of the cash received and paid for a period. This form of report is adequate for many clubs but has important deficiencies when used by clubs which have substantial assets (in addition to cash) and liabilities. The arguments in favour of accrual accounting apply to clubs as well as to profit-making entities, and most large clubs do produce financial statements based on accrual accounting.

In fact the only differences between the accrual accounting statements produced by clubs and by profit-making entities are terminological. The main differences between the terms used are given below:

Profit-making entity	*Club*
(e.g. a sole trader)	
Profit and loss account	Income and expenditure account
Profit for the year	Excess (or surplus) of income over expenditure for the year
Loss for the year	Excess (or surplus) of expenditure over income for the year
Capital account	Accumulated (or general) fund

The balance sheet continues to be described as a balance sheet.

Actually some profit-making entities also describe their profit and loss accounts as income and expenditure accounts. This is usually done by such concerns as professional businesses (doctors, solicitors, etc.) and property companies which, it is argued, do not trade in the normal way. The justification does not stand up to rigorous, or even casual examination, and there does not appear to be any logical justification for the practice. However, there seems to be little harm in it.

Occasionally you might encounter a cross between a receipts and payments account and an income and expenditure account, called a receipts and expenditure account. As can be construed from the title revenue is not recognized until the cash is actually received, while the accruals concept is applied to expenses. The profit concept produced by this asymmetric application of accounting conventions is the most conservative possible basis of profit determination. This approach is rare and its use is generally restricted to professional businesses.

Many clubs produce income and expenditure accounts and balance sheets but rely on an incomplete records system which is why, as in this book, the two topics are often dealt with together.

There are a number of topics which, although they are not necessarily unique to the accounts of clubs, have special relevance to them.

Presentation

We believe that the undue use of technical terms cannot be justified in any form of financial report, and especially not in the case of clubs. For not only is it likely that the 'average' club member has even less financial knowledge than the 'average' shareholder and less access to financial advisers, but it is also probable that he will take a more active part in running the club than shareholders take in running the companies in which they hold shares.

Another point is that clubs generally do not trade, or if they do, trading only forms a part of their activities. So the standard division of the overall profit and loss account into manufacturing, trading and profit and loss sections is inappropriate. Generally clubs obtain income from a number of different sources, and so care should be taken to ensure that the income and expenditure account is something more than a mere listing of income and expenditure. A good general rule is to bring together income and expenditure that can be identified as relating to the same activity. Say, for example, a tennis club runs a tournament the expenses of which were covered, in part, by entry fees, then the expense of the tournament could be shown as follows:

	£	£
Expenses of Easter Tournament	150	
less Entry fees	20	130

If the entry fees were judged to be insignificant then only the net expense would be shown.

Many clubs have bars, or, to put it another way, we are informed that there are a number of clubs which do not have bars. It is customary to show on the face of (or as a note attached to) the income and expenditure account the trading and profit and loss account for the bar. If it appears as a note the residual profit or loss must appear as an item in the income and expenditure account.

The accounts of the London Welsh Rugby Football Club are shown on pages 64–65. Clearly considerable thought has gone into their design and we would, at this stage, draw our readers' attention to the distinctions that have been made between:

(a) Revenue-earning activities against which it is not possible or desirable to set off related expenditure;
(b) Profits which have been earned from a number of ventures; and
(c) General expenses.

Special Funds

Clubs may receive donations or other forms of income which are tied to a specific purpose, for example, a political association may have a special election fund or it may wish to make a transfer from its general funds to the special fund.

The simplest way of dealing with this requires no more than a reclassification of the accumulated (or general) fund. Thus if a donation is received the entry is:

	Debit	*Credit*
Cash	£105	
Election fund		£105

or, if a transfer is made from the accumulated fund:

	Debit	*Credit*
Accumulated fund	£1,200	
Election fund		£1,200

Having established the fund, any expenditure which relates to it is not charged against the income and expenditure account but, instead, may be shown on the face of the balance sheet, as a deduction from the special fund. This is illustrated below:

UTOPIAN BRANCH OF THE HYPOTHETICAL PARTY

Balance Sheet as at 31st December 19X4

	£	£
Accumulated fund		
Balance 1 January 19X4		12,000
add Excess of income over expenditure		
for the year	5,000	
less Transfer to the election fund	2,000	3,000
		15,000
Election fund		
Balance at 1 January 19X4		3,000
add Donations	1,800	
Transfer from accumulated fund	2,000	3,800
		6,800
less Election expenses		1,580	5,220
		£20,220
Sundry assets *less* Liabilities		£20,220

The book-keeping entries shown above will not automatically lead to cash, or other liquid assets, being available for the devoted Hypothetrician may well have contributed cash of £105 as a contribution towards election expenses but the rather less devoted committee may have put the cash towards paying for the extension to the bar. The election fund exists but the assets representing it may be liquid only in the sense of being drinkable. In order to ensure that cash is available the club must take additional steps; for example, it can open a special bank account and ensure that the balance on that account is equal to the balance on the fund account.

An alternative is to separate the fund completely from the remaining activities, and this will require the preparation of a separate income and expenditure account and balance sheet. This alternative has to be adopted when the fund, although associated with the activities of the club, is set up under a legal agreement such as a trust fund.

The method adopted by the London Welsh R.F.C. is a sensible, if unusual, approach. The reader will note that the balance sheet shows how much of the accumulated fund has been sunk. The first three items in this section are fixed assets whilst the last two items appear to represent funds

LONDON WELSH RUGBY FOOTBALL CLUB

INCOME & EXPENDITURE ACCOUNT – SEASON 1975/76

1974/75	WE HAVE EARNED FROM	£	£
9534	Subscriptions	12521	
1006	Donations	1081	
3693	Gates and Car Parks	8211	
580	Hire of Ground and Broadcasts	250	
1032	Programme Sales	1475	
700	Programme Adverts	829	
994	Guarantees & R.F.U. K.O. Comp. 1975/76 ...	4036	
1791	Bank and Building Society Interest	2196	
710	R.F.U. Knock-Out Competition 1974/75	262	
	PROFITS ON		
5993	Bar	6385	
824	Sweepstake	1530	
139	Shop	188	
145	International Tickets	196	
251	Entertainments	592	
			39752
26852			
	WE HAVE SPENT ON		
5507	Travelling	8465	
1920	Club Entertainment	1873	
1295	Printing and Stationery	1499	
1188	Printing of Programmes	1266	
1111	Postage and Telephone	1728	
102	Subscriptions and Donations	78	
3490	Ground Equipment and Improvements	1061	
229	Laundry	253	
1602	Kit and Medical Supplies	1834	
110	Corporation Tax	1287	
170	Insurances	288	
95	Television	129	
358	Schoolboys	448	
353	Mini Rugby	543	
357	Sundries	679	
73	Hire of Grounds	—	
543	Provision for U.S. Tour	1000	
1008	Cost of Catering	999	
	OLD DEER PARK		
8050	Monthly Payments	9450	
2436	Percentage of Subs, Bar, Gates	3973	
			36853
29997			
£3145	(*Deficit*) Surplus for Season		£2899

Figure 3.2

LONDON WELSH RUGBY FOOTBALL CLUB

BALANCE SHEET AS AT 30th April, 1976

WE HAVE ACCUMULATED	£	£
Balance as at 1st May, 1975		42465
Add Sale of Permanent Seats	12	
Surplus for the Season	2899	
	2911	
Less New Stand Extension—Depreciation	1000	
		1911
		44376

OF WHICH WE HAVE SUNK
AT THE OLD DEER PARK

In the Stand	7302		
Less Depreciation to date	7301		
New Extension	7840	1	
Less Depreciation to date	5000		
		2840	
Bar Equipment	462		
Less Depreciation to date	343		
		119	
Reconstruction Fund		16797	
John Dawes—Lions Room		9502	
			29259

LEAVING WITH US	£15117

REPRESENTED BY:

Total realisable resources made up as follows:		
Stocks at Cost	5265	
Sundry Debtors	2887	
Cash at bank, on Deposit and in Hand	31607	
	39759	
Less Amount owing to Creditors	24642	
		£15117

Note: – The Club has guaranteed Loans of £2400 in respect of the New Pavilion.

We have examined the above Balance Sheet and attached Income and Expenditure Account and certify that they are in accordance with the books, records, and information and explanations furnished to us.

Signed J. ARTHUR JONES
Chartered Accountant } Hon. Auditors
G. V. OWEN

Figure 3.2

which have been set aside for specific purposes. The underlying idea is good, for it is indeed helpful to see the assets which are available for the specific purpose. However, the use of the term 'fund' is misleading, since a fund is usually taken to be a source of assets rather than the asset itself.

Outstanding Subscriptions

It is not uncommon, indeed it is more than likely, that a person resigning from a club does not bother to send the secretary a formal letter of resignation. The resigning member just does not bother to pay the next subscription. Because of this practice, many clubs only take credit for subscriptions received in cash and ignore outstanding subscriptions even if they use accrual accounting for all other items.

Life Subscriptions and Entry Fees

The problem with these items is that they cover more than one year. Strictly, the best way of dealing with them is to estimate the life expectancy of the member and to credit the amounts to the income and expenditure account over that period. This is rarely, if ever, done, and life subscriptions and entry fees may either be credited to the income and expenditure account in the period in which the member joins, or credited to that account over an arbitrary time period, or credited direct to the accumulated fund.

We shall conclude this section by presenting an example illustrating the conversion of a receipts and payments account into an income and expenditure account.

Example 3.3

The receipts and payments account of the Chelsea Croquet and Wrestling Club for the year ended 31 December 19X4 is as follows:

Receipts	£	Payments	£
Opening balance	800	Rent of croquet lawn	1,200
Subscriptions	4,000	Rates of clubhouse	800
Bar sales	18,200	Bar purchases	14,000
Entrance fees	800	Wages of part-time barman	1,800
Donation	3,000	Coaching fees for school-children's croquet course	700
Gate money from wrestling tournaments	1,200	Hire of extra seating for wrestling tournament	380
Sales of programmes at tournaments	10	Other wrestling tournament expenses	200
Closing balance	2,450	Hoops, clubs and mallets	180
		Extension to clubhouse	8,000
		Sundry clubhouse expenses	3,200
	£30,460		£30,460

1. An analysis of subscriptions reveals the following:

	Croquet Members	Wrestling Members	Total
	£	£	£
Received in 19X3 for 19X4	£120	£60	£180
Received in 19X4 for 19X3	80	1,200	
for 19X4	1,480	1,000	
for 19X5	220	20	
	£1,780	£2,220	£4,000

The club does not wish to take credit for outstanding subscriptions.

2. Entrance fees are to be credited direct to the accumulated fund.

3. The donation of £3,000 was to establish the programme of croquet-coaching courses for schoolchildren.

4. The club owns its own clubhouse which cost £14,000. Hoops, clubs and mallets are to be charged against the income and expenditure account in the period in which they are acquired. The club's wrestling section constructed a ring at a total cost of £800 in 19X2 and it is thought that this will last for 5 years.

5. Sundry assets and liabilities at the start and end of the year were:

	1 January 19X4	31 December 19X4
	£	£
Bar stocks	2,010	1,870
Creditors – bar purchases	1,840	1,950
– hire of extra seats for wrestling tournaments	—	80
Prepaid rates	200	250
Sundry clubhouse expenses owing	70	90
Cash in hand	520	450

6. We are asked to prepare an income and expenditure account and a balance sheet and are further instructed that the income and expenditure account should distinguish, as far as is possible, between the activities of the two sections.

We use the same procedures as with incomplete records and start by preparing the opening balance sheet.

CHELSEA CROQUET AND WRESTLING CLUB
Balance Sheet as at 1 January 19X4

	£	£
Assets		
Club house		14,000
Ring (£800 – 320)		480
Bar stocks		2,010
Prepaid rates		200
Balance at bank and cash in hand		800
c/f		17,490

	£	£
Assets c/f		17,490
less Liabilities		
Subscriptions received in advance	180	
Creditors for bar purchases	1,840	
Sundry clubhouse expenses	70	2,090
Accumulated fund at 1 January 19X4		£15,400

CHELSEA CROQUET AND WRESTLING CLUB
Income and Expenditure Account
Year ended 31 December 19X4

	£	£	£
Croquet section			
Subscriptions (120 + 1,780 − 220)		1,680	
less			
Rent of croquet lawn	1,200		
Hoops, clubs and mallets	180	1,380	300
Wrestling section			
Subscriptions (60 + 2,220 − 20)		2,260	
Tournament gate money	1,200		
less expenses (380 + 200 + 80 − 10)	650	550	
		2,810	
less			
Depreciation of ring		160	2,650
			2,950
Bar profits (see below)			2,150
			5,100
less			
Rates of club house			
(200 + 800 − 250)		750	
Sundry clubhouse expenses			
(90 + 3,200 − 70)		3,220	3,970
Excess of income over expenditure for the year			£1,130

Bar Account

	£	£
Sales		18,200
less Opening stock	2,010	
Purchases (1,950 + 14,000 − 1,840)	14,110	
	16,120	
less Closing stock	1,870	14,250
Gross profit		3,950
less Barman's wages		1,800
Profit		£2,150

Balance Sheet as at 31 December 19X4

	Cost	Accumulated depreciation	Net book value
Fixed assets			
Clubhouse	22,000	—	22,000
Wrestling ring	800	480	320
	£22,800	£480	22,320
Current assets			
Bar stocks		1,870	
Prepaid rates		250	
Cash in hand		450	
		2,570	
less Current liabilities			
Creditors (1,950 + 80 + 90)	2,120		
Subscriptions received in advance	240		
Bank overdraft (2,450 + 450)	2,900	5,260	(2,690)
			£19,630
Accumulated fund			
Balance 1 January 19X4		15,400	
add Excess of income over expenditure			
for the year		1,130	
Entrance fees		800	17,330
Coaching fund			
Donations		3,000	
less coaching expenses		700	2,300
			£19,630

EXERCISES

3.1 'The objectives of a golf club are very different from those of a grocer, yet the only differences between their financial accounts are terminological.'
Comment.

3.2 Wren received a legacy of £20,000 on 1st January 1973 and on that date purchased a small retail business. The completion statement from the solicitor revealed the following:

	£
Freehold shop property	10,000
Goodwill	2,000
Stock in trade	1,600
Trade debtors	400
Shop fixtures	2,600
Rates in advance to 31st March 1973	100
	£16,700

The legacy was used to discharge the amount due on completion and the balance was paid into a newly opened business bank account.

Wren had not kept proper records of his business transactions but was able to supply the following information:

1. A summary of the cash till rolls showed his shop takings for the year to be £25,505; this includes all cash received from debtors including those at 1 January 1973.

2. The takings had been paid periodically into bank after payment of the following cash expenses:

	£
Wrapping materials	525
Staff wages and national insurance	3,423
Purchases for resale	165
Petrol and oil	236

3. Personal cash drawings were estimated at £20 per week and goods taken for own use at £2 per week.

4. A summary of the bank statements showed:

	£		£
Legacy – residual balance	3,300	Purchases for resale	14,863
Sale of fixtures (cost £200)	130	Motor expenses	728
Loan at 10 per cent p.a. Robin	2,000	Delivery van (cost – 1 April 1973)	1,200
Cash banked	19,900	General expenses	625
		Loan interest (6 months to 30th September)	100
		Private cheques	1,329
		Electricity	228
		Rates (year to 31 March 1974)	500
		Balance per statement on 31 December 1973	5,757
	£25,330		£25,330

A cheque drawn on 28 December 1973 of £125 for goods purchased was presented at the bank on 4 January 1974.

5. During the year bad debts of £223 arose and were irrecoverable. The trade debtors on 31 December 1973 amounted to £637 of which £100 is doubtful and for which provision should be made.

6. On 31 December 1973 there were

	£
Stock in trade	2,360
Stock of wrapping materials	53
Trade creditors – purchases	358
Electricity accrued	50

Accountancy fees accrued	100
Cash float in till	180

7. The difference arising on the cash statement was discussed with Wren but remained unexplained and was dealt with in an appropriate manner.

8. Depreciation is to be provided at the rate of 10 per cent per annum on the fixtures and 20 per cent per annum on the van.

You are required to prepare in vertical form:
(a) Trading and profit and loss account for the year ended 31 December 1973, and
(b) Balance sheet as on that date.
(The Institute of Chartered Accountants in England and Wales, Foundation Examination, October, 1974)

3.3 Oliver, who owns a retail shop which is managed by Sykes, finds Sykes stealing from the shop till and dismisses him on 30 September, 1975, the accounting year end. Oliver then supplies the following information:

1.

	30 September 1974	30 September 1975
	£	£
Stock	8,250	10,375
Creditors – goods for resale	16,900	22,123
Trade debtors	1,260	1,870
Cash float in till	200	Nil

2. During the year to 30 September 1975, takings of £60,134 had been banked; the following items were paid from takings before they were banked:

	£
Oliver – Drawings	8,000
Sykes – Salary	4,000
Purchases for resale	1,365
Petty cash expenses	275
Wages	£50 per week

3. During the year to 30 September 1975, cheque payments to suppliers (all goods for resale) amounted to £55,537.

4. Oliver's gross profit margin for the year is estimated at 40 per cent on cost.

You are required to:
(a) compute the estimated amount of cash stolen by Sykes during the year to 30 September 1975, and
(b) discuss three factors which could account for the estimate in (a) being overstated.

(The Institute of Chartered Accountants in England and Wales, Foundation Examination, October 1975)

3.4 The treasurer of the Moor Bowling Club disappeared on 31st March 1983, taking with him the majority of the books and records of the club. The club's year end is 31st March. At the request of the club's committee you are asked to examine the financial implications of the treasurer's disappearance. From discussions with the committee you learn that certain information relating to receipts and payments is recorded in the club's minute book. In addition you obtain duplicate bank statements, returned cheques and paying in slips. Having examined these together with the accounts for the year ended 31st March 1982 you assemble the following information:

1. The balance sheet as on 31st March 1982 showed the following:

	£	£
Fixed assets		2,000
Stock	1,002	
Debtors – overdue subscriptions (6 members at £30)	180	
Balance at bank	247	
Cash in hand	115	
	1,544	
Creditors	550	
		994
		2,994
Accumulated fund		994
Brewery loan		2,000
		2,994

Creditors comprise:	
Amount due to brewery for supplies	426
Greenkeeper ⎱ amounts due for quarter	76
Steward ⎰ to 31st March 1982	48
	550

2. The following summaries of the minute book provided by the secretary appear relevant:

(i)   **11th June 1982.** The accounts for the year ended 31st March 1982 were presented and approved. It was reported that one of the overdue subscriptions had been paid. The membership of the other five overdue members was deemed to lapse from 1st April 1982. Payments to the greenkeeper and the steward totalling £124, which had been provided in the accounts, were approved. The subscription for the year ended 31st March 1983 was fixed at £32 per member. There were 100 members (following the lapses referred to above). Bar sales totalled £2,900 in April and May and showed a gross profit of 32% of sales.

(ii)   **11th September 1982.** There had been 94 entries for the annual competition. The entry fee was £2 per entrant. The prizes, two dozen bottles of sherry, were taken from the bar stock. The cost to the bar was £3 per bottle. The greenkeeper's and steward's quarterly payments totalling £124 had been paid for the quarter to 30th June. 65 subscriptions had been received to date. Bar sales totalled £2,940 in June, July and August and showed a gross profit of 28% of sales.

(iii) **12th December 1982.** Bar sales totalled £3,100 in September, October and November and showed a gross profit of 33% of sales. The greenkeeper had resigned on 1st October and been paid up to date. The steward had been paid, in cash, £48 for the quarter ended 30th September 1982.

(iv)   **11th March 1983.** Bar sales totalled £3,400 in December, January and February and showed a gross profit of 31% of sales. Two members had resigned without their subscriptions being received. All other subscriptions had been received.

3. Summarised copy bank statements for the year ended 31st March 1983 show the following:

	£	£
Opening balance	247	
Receipts – cash and cheques	12,336	
Payments		9,404
Closing balance		3,179
	12,583	12,583

The cheque payments comprise:

	£
Greenkeeper and steward (quarter ended 31st March 1982) ..	124
Part repayment of brewery loan (including interest of £200) ..	1,200
Brewery for supplies	5,722
Lawnmower	244
Improvements to green and pavilion	1,214
Repairs	900
	9,404

4. The secretary informs you that certain payments for wines and spirits from a local supermarket had been made from cash takings.

5. Four new members had joined in March 1983 and had paid their subscriptions of £32 each for the year ended 31st March 1984 direct to the secretary. Following the disappearance of the treasurer, the secretary had paid the steward's two outstanding quarterly fees from this cash and had banked the balance in April 1983.

6. As on 31st March 1983 all fixed assets are to be revalued at £4,000. Depreciation is to be ignored.

7. The records for bar takings in March could not be located. In view of a rise in bar prices on 1st March 1983 you estimate the gross profit would have been 34% on sales. The supermarket confirmed that there were no purchases by the club during March 1983. As on 28th February 1983, £450 was due to the brewery for supplies. Stock at cost as on 28th February 1983 was £920 and as on 31st March 1983 £875. The brewery confirmed that supplies of £728 were delivered to the club in March 1983. The balance due to the brewery for supplies of £1,178 as on 31st March 1983 was paid in April.

You are required to prepare an income and expenditure account for the year ended 31st March 1983, identifying the amount of the treasurer's defalcations, and a balance sheet as on that date.

(The Institute of Chartered Accountants in England and Wales, Accounting Techniques, May 1983.)

3.5 Bob Dean has been in business for some years as a grocer. He has hitherto prepared his own accounts, but he has experienced increasing difficulties with his Inspector of Taxes. You have been recommended to him as a competent accountant and he telephoned you in December 19X8 to ask you to prepare his accounts for the year ended 30 November 19X8. You were rather busy and did not have enough time to visit Dean; so you asked him to send you certain records. He, accordingly, sent you the following letter:

Dear Mr. Land,

Thank you very much for agreeing to prepare my accounts for the year to 30 November 19X8. I am afraid that I can't find a copy of the accounts I prepared for last year, but I hope that the following information will be sufficient.

I own a small 'lock-up' shop the freehold of which I purchased six years ago for £10,000. My only other assets are a van I use to deliver goods and my car which I never use for business purposes. The van cost me £2,300 on 1 December 19X6. I usually keep my vans for four years and I expect that I will be able to get £700 when I trade it in.

I purchase all my goods on credit and I have a small number of credit customers. I had some trouble keeping track of my credit purchases and sales some years ago and I now keep pretty good records of these transactions. I enclose all the invoices, etc. As you can see, I owed my suppliers

£1,826 on 30 November 19X7 and £1,725 on 30 November 19X8. My credit customers owed me £287 on 30 November 19X7 and £324 on 30 November 19X8 but I fear that I won't be able to collect £56 of the £324.

I always count the stock myself and I reckon that my stock on 30 November 19X7 was £562 and on 30 November 19X8, £2,843. I was ill at the end of last November and I didn't get to counting the stock until the Christmas holiday; so I had to adjust my stock take for sales and purchases since the year end. I am afraid I cannot send you detailed stock sheets because I can't find them.

As I told you I work full-time in the shop myself but old age is creeping up on me and I've employed an assistant since 1 June 19X8. I pay her £200 per month out of the takings. I also pay for my petrol out of the takings, and this came to £232 for the year. Otherwise I pay all my takings into the bank although I do keep a float. It used to be £30 but I increased it to £50 three or four months ago.

I enclose my bank statements for both my current and deposit accounts and on the former, I have made sufficient notes for you to identify the nature of the payments.

I hope that you'll be able to keep your fees down. My costs are going up all the time. My insurance premium for both the van and the shop went up by 40 per cent. In fact the only thing that did not go up was the cost of the van licence.

Yours sincerely
B. Dean

A summary of the information obtained from Dean's current account bank statements is given below:

	£	£
Balance 1 December 19X7		467
add		
Sundry bankings of cash takings	18,992	
Sundry cheques received from credit customers	5,255	24,247
		24,714
less		
Sundry cheques		
To suppliers of goods	18,834	
Cash drawings	1,200	
Sundry expenses	118	
Other payments		
19X8		
Jan 10 Electricity (quarter ended 31 December X7)	30	
Mar 3 Insurance, car (year ended 28 February X9)	46	
Mar 5 Insurance, shop (year ended 31 March X9)	42	

		£	£
Apr 20	Electricity (quarter ended 31 March X8)	32	
May 29	Licence for van (year ended 31 May X9)	40	
May 31	Insurance, van (year ended 31 May X9)	84	
Jul 5	Repairs, van	58	
Jul 17	Electricity (quarter ended 30 June X8)	28	
Aug 1	Transfer to Deposit Account	4,000	
Oct 8	Electricity (quarter ended 30 September X8)	36	24,548

Balance 30 November 19X8   £166

The deposit account statement shows that the account was opened with the transfer of £4,000 from the current account on 1 August 19X8 and that no other items were recorded in the period 1 August–30 November.

Your experience of businesses of a similar nature to Dean's suggests that they usually earn a gross profit of between 25 and 28 per cent. You estimate that your fee will be £45.

Required:

(a) Prepare, on the basis of the above information, Dean's trading and profit and loss account for the year ended 30 November 19X8 and his balance sheet as at that date.
(b) Draw up a list of questions to put to Dean when you meet him.

4 | *Partnership Accounts*

The general nature of partnerships was outlined in Chapter 1 and we shall now deal with the question of partnership accounts. For a detailed review of the law relating to partnerships readers are referred to a legal text but we must put our feet gingerly into legal waters if we are to carry out our task. The most important piece of legislation affecting partnerships is the Partnership Act, 1890. This comparatively old act is short (only 50 sections) and lucid – there are not many modern acts which can be so described!

The Partnership Act defines a partnership as the relationship which subsists between persons carrying on a business in common with a view to profit – a succinct definition, but one which requires careful interpretation. For example, neither the sharing of profit, e.g. by an employee, nor the joint ownership of property will of themselves automatically give rise to the creation of a partnership. The main test is whether the partners agree to act together and, in particular, agree to act as each others' agents in the context of the business of the partnership. A partner is liable for the acts of all the other partners so long as they are, apparently, acting in the ordinary course of business; so the decision whether a partnership exists or not can be one of considerable importance.

There is one exception, i.e. the comparatively rare *Limited Partnerships* (Limited Partnerships Act, 1907). In such partnerships one or more of the partners may be limited partners who are only liable up to the limit of their registered capital. Such partners may not take an active part in the management of the partnership and limited partnerships must register certain details with the Registrar of Companies. These include the registered capitals of the limited partners. Note that the term 'limited' applies to one or more of the partners; the partnership itself cannot be limited, and there must be at least one general partner who will be personally liable for the debts of the partnership.

There is a limit, generally twenty, in the number of partners allowed by law, but under the provisions of the Companies Act 1967 certain types of partnerships are permitted to have an unlimited number of partners. The favoured classes are solicitors, accountants qualified to audit limited companies (essentially chartered and certified accountants) and members of stock exchanges.

One reason why there can be some doubt about whether a partnership exists or not is that it is possible for a partnership to exist in the absence of a written agreement between the partners. However, sensible partners will enter into a partnership agreement which should include the following points:

1. The name and nature of the business of the partnership.

2. The term of the partnership, which may be for a fixed or an indefinite period. The latter type are called partnerships at will.

3. The amount of the capital to be contributed by each partner.

4. The manner in which the profit of the partnership should be shared.

5. Whether interest should be charged on partners' drawings. The extent of drawings to be allowed.

6. Provisions for the preparation and audit of financial statements.

7. The way in which the business should be run, e.g. what types of decision can be arrived at by a majority decision and which require unanimity; management responsibilities.

8. Provision for the admission of new partners and the withdrawal by death or otherwise, of partners.

The Partnership Act of 1890 contains certain provisions which come into force in the absence of a partnership agreement. These will be discussed later.

Capital, Current and Drawings Accounts

One obvious difference between the accounts of a sole trader and a partnership is that in the latter case it is necessary to divide the owners' equity between the partners. However, very many partnerships go further and divide the owner's equity of each partner between capital and current accounts.

The capital account represents the amounts which the partners agree that they will retain in the partnership and is sometimes called *fixed capital*. The capital is usually the amount which the partners introduced at the birth of the partnership or, in the case of a partner joining an existing partnership, the amount contributed on admission. Of course the amount of the fixed capital can be varied by agreement between the partners.

The current accounts represent the balance of the partners' equity and, in general, represent each partner's accumulated share of profits less any amounts withdrawn to date.

In order to reflect the distinction separate ledger accounts, i.e. capital and current accounts, are maintained in the ledger for each partner. In addition, this distinction also appears in the balance sheet.

Partners usually withdraw cash from the partnership at regular intervals, and in order not to clutter the current account with too much detail a drawings account is often opened for each partner. At the end of each year the balances on the drawings accounts are transferred to the current accounts. In order to discourage excessive drawings and to achieve equity between partners, it is sometimes, though rarely, agreed that interest should be charged on drawings. The interest is usually calculated on the amount of each slice of drawings from the date of drawing to the end of the year. Any such interest is credited to the profit and loss appropriation account (see below) and debited to the partner's current account. A better way of dealing with this problem is to have a formal agreement about the amounts and timings of the drawings.

The Appropriation of Profit

In the case of a sole trader all the profit goes to one person, the owner, but, of course, this is not so in partnerships – thus partnership accounts must include an additional statement showing how the profit or loss for the year is divided between the partners. This statement is usually called the profit and loss appropriation account.

Unless the partnership is to operate without an agreement the partners will have to agree on the way in which profits, and losses, should be shared between them, i.e. they must fix the *profit-sharing ratio*. This ratio will depend on a number of factors (not least of which is the negotiating powers of the partners) which may include the following: the amounts of capital introduced by the partners, the amount of time each partner devotes to the business and the skill and experience of the partners. However, many partnership agreements take specific account of these factors and use a more complex approach, basing the apportionment of profit on the following three considerations.

Interest on capital (and possibly on current accounts)
Salaries
Share of balance.

Of the above, only the third is essential.

Interest on Capital
In order to compensate the partners who have contributed the larger capital stakes, partners can be credited with the interest on their capital. The rate is usually fixed in the partnership agreement and therefore often does not reflect the changes in the market rate of interest which have occurred since the establishment of the partnership.

The partners may also agree to give interest on the credit balances, or an average of the credit balances over the year, appearing on their individual current accounts. This will be especially relevant when the balances are large and when they differ substantially between partners.

Salaries

Some or all the partners may be credited with a fixed sum known as their salaries. These amounts are not included in the profit and loss account as a charge against profits, but are shown in the appropriation account since they are a component of the profit-sharing agreement.

The introduction of a salary component in the profit-sharing arrangement can be a sensible way of rewarding partners who provide more valuable services to the partnership either through the amount of time they spend on its affairs or because of the particular skills they can contribute. This approach is preferred to the alternative of giving such partners a greater share of profits, because a greater share in profits also means a greater share in losses.

A common use of the salary alternative is to compensate junior partners (often called salaried partners) who receive only a small share of their earnings by way of interest on capital and profit sharing. Such partners often have very little effective say in the management of the partnership, and their position is not all that different from employees save for the important exception that they are personally liable for the debts of the partnership.

Partners will be credited with their salaries, and with interest on capital and current accounts, even if the partnership makes a loss or a profit which is not large enough to cover salaries and interest. In such cases, the existence of the salary and interest provision means that a loss will have to be apportioned between the partners in their profit- (and loss-) sharing ratio. Whatever basis is selected, each partner's share of profit (or loss) is credited (or debited) to his current account.

Example 4.1

A, B and C are in partnership and their partnership agreement includes the following provisions:

1. Interest at 5 per cent per annum is to be allowed on capital accounts and charged on drawings. No interest to be allowed on current account balances.

2. B is to receive a salary of £4,000 per annum and C is to receive £8,000 per annum.

3. The profit-sharing ratio is:

    A 50 per cent,   B 40 per cent and   C 10 per cent

The summarized trial balance of the partnership as at 31 December 19X4 was as follows:

	Debit			Credit
	£			£
Drawings accounts A	8,000	Capital accounts	A	10,000
B	6,000		B	9,000
C	4,000		C	1,000
Sundry assets *less*		Current accounts	A	3,000
Liabilities	27,750		B	1,000
			C	2,000
		Profit for 19X4		19,750
	£45,750			£45,750

A and B made their drawings in two equal instalments on 30 June and 31 December 19X4 while C drew £1,000 at the end of each quarter.

Profit and Loss Appropriation Account
Year ended 31st December 19X4

	£	£	£
Net profit for the year			19,750
add interest on drawings			
A		100	
B		75	
C		75	250
			20,000
Interest on capital			
A		500	
B		450	
C		50	1,000
Salaries			
B		4,000	
C		8,000	12,000
Share of balance			
A (50 per cent)		3,500	
B (40 per cent)		2,800	
C (10 per cent)		700	7,000	£20,000

The share of the balance is found by first of all working out what the balance is, i.e. £7,000. This is then divided in the profit-sharing ratio.

The interest on drawings can be found as follows:

A	5 per cent p.a. on £4,000 for 6 months		£100
B	5 per cent p.a. on £3,000 for 6 months		£75
C	5 per cent p.a. on £1,000 for 9 months	37.5	
	5 per cent p.a. on £1,000 for 6 months	25.0	
	5 per cent p.a. on £1,000 for 3 months	12.5	£75

Current Accounts

	A	B	C		A	B	C
	£	£	£		£	£	£
Drawings accounts	8,000	6,000	4,000	Balances b/d	3,000	1,000	2,000
Profit and loss appropriation account				Profit and loss appropriation account			
Interest on drawings	100	75	75	Interest on capital	500	450	50
				Salaries		4,000	8,000
				Share of balance	3,500	2,800	700
Closing balances c/d		2,175	6,675	Closing balance c/d	1,100		
	£8,100	£8,250	£10,750		£8,100	£8,250	£10,750
Balance b/d	1,100			Balances b/d		2,175	6,675

Note that A's drawings exceed the opening balance on his current account and his share of the year's profit. Although this may be in contravention of the partnership agreement, it does happen from time to time, one reason being that the drawings are made during the year before the final profit is known. Depending on the attitude of his partners and the terms of the agreement, A may have to take remedial action, e.g. contribute sufficient cash to clear the debit balance.

In practice each current account will have a separate page in the ledger, although the above format, *columnar form*, is a useful one, especially in an examination. Indeed examiners like it so much that they often tell a candidate that they must prepare capital and current accounts in columnar form.

A, B AND C
Balance Sheet as at 31 December 19X4

Partners' equity		£	£	£
		Capital accounts	*Current accounts*	
	A	10,000	(1,100)	8,900
	B	9,000	2,175	11,175
	C	1,000	6,675	7,675
		£20,000	£7,750	£27,750

represented by

Sundry assets *less* Liabilities   £27,750

The layout of the partners' equity section of the partnership balance sheet can take various forms. The format used above is a good one in that it shows each partner's total share as well as the total of the fixed capital of the partnership. A common alternative format is:

	£	£
Capital accounts		
A	10,000	
B	9,000	
C	1,000	20,000
Current accounts		
A	(1,100)	
B	2,175	
C	6,675	7,750
		£27,750

It is customary in the case of sole traders to show, on the face of the balance sheet, a reconciliation between the owners' equity at the start of the year and the owners' closing equity. To do this in the case of a partnership would result in a very cluttered balance sheet. It is therefore a good idea to produce, as part of the partnership's financial accounts, a statement providing such a reconciliation. The statement will, of course, be simply a summary of the partners' current accounts.

Partners' Current Accounts

	£ Total	£ A	£ B	£ C
Balances 1 January 19X4	6,000	3,000	1,000	2,000
add				
Interest on capital	1,000	500	450	50
Salaries	12,000	—	4,000	8,000
Share of balance	7,000	3,500	2,800	700
	26,000	7,000	8,250	10,750
less				
Drawings	18,000	8,000	6,000	4,000
Interest on drawings	250 18,250	100 8,100	75 6,075	75 4,075
Balances 31 December 19X4	£7,750	£(1,100)	£2,175	£6,675

Example 4.2

In order to illustrate the position where there is a loss or a profit which is too small to cover interest on capital and salaries, we shall use the information provided in Example 4.1 except that we will assume that the profit for the year is £9,750. The profit and loss appropriation account would then be:

	£	£	£
Net profit for the year			9,750
add Interest on drawings			
A		100	
B		75	
C		75	250
			10,000
Interest on capital			
A	500		
B	450		
C	50	1,000	
Salaries			
B	4,000		
C	8,000	12,000	
Share of loss			
A (50 per cent)	1,500		
B (40 per cent)	1,200		
C (10 per cent)	300	£(3,000)	£10,000

Note that the interest and salaries are calculated according to the partnership agreement. The deficit resulting after this is then divided in the profit- (and loss-) sharing ratio.

Partners' Loan Accounts

Partners can make advances to the partnership over and above their capital contributions. In such cases the amount of the loan would be credited to a separate loan account and kept apart from their capital and current accounts. Partners' loans are treated in very much the same way as loans from outsiders. Loan interest is, therefore, shown in the profit and loss account as a charge against profit and is not debited to the appropriation account. On the dissolution of the partnership the loan would be paid before partners' capital but would rank after the amounts due to outsiders (See page 99).

Lack of a Partnership Agreement

If there is no partnership agreement, Sections 24 and 25 of the Partnership Act 1890 are applied. It must be noted that the agreement need not be in writing and the existence and terms of an agreement can be implied from the actions of the partners, e.g. by accepting a set of accounts which include a given profit-sharing basis. The provisions of the Act that are relevant to the apportionment of profit are:

(a) Profits and losses are to be shared equally
(b) No interest to be allowed on capital
(c) No interest to be charged on drawings
(d) No salaries
(e) Interest at 5 per cent to be allowed on partners' loan accounts.

The Peculiar Problems of Partnerships

By the nature of partnerships there are a number of events which call for special treatment, i.e.

The admission of a partner,
A change in the profit-sharing ratio,
The retirement or death of a partner.

Now if the partners agree that the value of the partnership is equal to the book value of the assets less liabilities, i.e. that there are no 'unrecorded assets', the entries necessary to deal with these events are very simple. However, conventional historical cost accounting does not attempt to disclose the value of the firm and so, in practice, the entries can become a little complex. To this complexity can be added the problems caused by the number of available methods which exist.

It may be helpful, however, if we first showed how the above events would be treated if there were no unrecorded assets. Suppose A, B and C are in partnership sharing profit and losses in the ratio of 40 per cent, 40 per cent and 20 per cent and that their summary balance sheet as at 31 December 19X6 is:

	Capital account	Current account	
	£	£	£
A	10,000	4,000	14,000
B	8,000	5,000	13,000
C	2,000	3,000	5,000
	£20,000	£12,000	£32,000
Sundry assets *less* liabilities			£32,000

Now suppose that a new partner, D, is admitted to the partnership on 31 December 19X6 and that the new profit-sharing ratio is A 40 per cent, B 40 per cent, C 10 per cent, D 10 per cent. D is to introduce capital of £4,000 which he does by paying that amount into the partnership bank account. The only entry required is the crediting of D's capital account and the debiting of the partnership's bank account with £4,000. Now the value of the firm increases from £32,000 to £36,000 but since the value of the owners' equities of the old partners remain the same at £14,000, £13,000 and £5,000 respectively no further entry is required. It is of course true that there will now be a new profit-sharing ratio, but that only affects the apportionment of future profits, and we must assume that the partners have been rational in that the new profit-sharing ratio reflects the respective values of the contribution of the partners to the future activities of the partnership.

Now let us relax our convenient assumption and suppose that the partners believe that the value of the partnership at 31 December 19X6 is £40,000 not £32,000. At some time, perhaps at the dissolution of the partnership, the extra unrecorded value will be converted into tangible assets and will either be included in future profits or in the profit on realization of the assets of the partnership. Of course, the partnership may not make £40,000 on realization, but this would be deemed to have been due to losses made after 31 December 19X6. Now if no action is taken in regard to this difference on the admission of the new partner, D will be 'given' a share – 10 per cent (his share in profits) of the unrecorded asset. The methods that are adopted to prevent this happening are discussed below (in the section headed 'goodwill'). Exactly the same arguments can be applied if there is a change in the profit-sharing ratio of the old partners. If, at the date of the change, they agree that there are no incorrectly valued assets there is no problem, and no entry is required.

If our assumption holds, the retirement or death of a partner produces no accounting problems. Suppose A dies, then his estate is entitled to his share of the partnership, £14,000 and the only, but often considerable, problem is how the partnership can pay the £14,000 without harming the business.

Goodwill

There are two factors that can give rise to the existence of the incorrectly valued assets referred to above. One is that there may be a difference between the current value of an individual asset and the amount at which it is shown in the accounts. If agreement can be reached about the current value of the asset this factor produces few accounting problems. The second factor, termed *goodwill*, is the one which usually produces the greatest problems.

Goodwill can usefully be illustrated numerically as follows: X is in the process of selling his business to Y. Y considers all the assets of the business and, after deducting the liabilities, arrives at a valuation of the assets less liabilities of £100,000. However, X wants £120,000 for the business and Y happily agrees to this price for he believes that the business has some goodwill.

Goodwill is then:

	£
The value of the business	120,000
less The sum of the values of the individual assets *less* Liabilities	100,000
Goodwill	£20,000

In other words, goodwill is the difference between the value of the business as a whole and the value of the sum of the parts. The idea behind goodwill is that the particular bundle of assets comprising the business will, in the future, generate larger profits than could be obtained if an exactly similar bundle of assets was newly brought together to carry out the same business.

There are a large number of factors which can give rise to goodwill. They include the reputation of the business with customers and suppliers, its location, its efficient and stable workforce, etc. If goodwill has been purchased, as in the above example, it will appear as an asset in the balance sheet of the purchasing firm until it is written off against owners' equity. However, by its nature, goodwill is subject to considerable fluctuations. A smile by a salesman may, marginally, increase it while the rude response to a complaint may, marginally, reduce it. A change in parking regulations could destroy or increase manyfold the goodwill of a small shop. Because of the difficulties involved in valuing the asset of goodwill objectively, other than at the time of purchase, no attempt is made to record changes in purchased goodwill, and non-purchased goodwill is generally not recognized as an asset, but see page 91 for an exception. In fact, many firms go further and write off purchased goodwill, either immediately or over an arbitrary time period, to owners' equity.

So far we have assumed that the values can be agreed on without difficulty, but of course this is not usually true. Reasonable estimates can often be made of the values of individual assets by professional valuers and others without too much difficulty (but often at considerable expense). Such valuations are usually done on the basis of comparison. The valuer notes the amounts at which similar assets have been traded recently and adjusts this figure to take account of any different features of the asset being valued and of any market changes. So it is comparatively easy to value a two-year-old Ford Escort that has done 20,000 miles because there are plenty of other such Escorts around; but each business tends to be very different from all other businesses and so the valuation of a specific business is a far more difficult task.

In Chapter 10, we shall discuss the problems of valuation in far more detail and when doing so draw on modern thinking on the question which is based, with varying degrees of success, on some logical framework. At this stage we will introduce the reader to some traditional, crude, rules of thumb which are used to estimate the goodwill figure, and hence the value of a business.

Valuation of Goodwill

If the partnership agreement does not contain any provision about the way in which goodwill is to be evaluated, the matter will be one of negotiation. In order to avoid the heat that would be generated by such discussions, partnership agreements might specify a mechanical formula which can be easily applied. The following are some of the methods that may be found.

Average Profit

Goodwill = x times the average profit of the last y years. Both x and y

need to be specified. Sometimes a weighted average is used, weighted so as
to give a greater importance to the profits of more recent years.

Example 4.3

The partnership agreement of P, Q and R provides that goodwill should be taken as
being equal to 2 years' (x) purchase of the weighted average profit of the last 3 years (y).
The weightings are 3 for the most recent year, 2 for the second and 1 for the third year.
    Profits for the last three years are:

19X5	£10,000		19X6	£4,000	19X7	£1,000
			£		£	
	1	x	10,000		10,000	
	2	x	4,000		8,000	
	3	x	1,000		3,000	
	—					
	6				£21,000	
	=					

Weighted average $= \dfrac{£21,000}{6} = £3,500$

Goodwill $= 2 \times £3,500 = £7,000$

This method, of course, has no logical basis and can produce some very
strange results. Suppose that the net tangible assets of P, Q and R are
£500,000, and remember that the whole idea of goodwill is that the partnership is worth more than that. The best profit made in the last three years was
£10,000 i.e. 2 per cent on £500,000; so it seems that unless the period of
19X5–X7 is exceptional, the bundle of assets making up P, Q and R is not
generating greater profits than would be expected from assets with a value of
£500,000.

Indeed they would get a greater profit if they wound up the partnership
and invested in a building society. This looks to be a case where there may be
'badwill' rather than goodwill, since it is possible that if the same bundle of
assets were brought together to form a new firm a larger profit could be
achieved.

Another drawback of this method is that it uses past results, while
goodwill, like any other asset, is concerned with future prospects. The
method is thus based on the assumption that the results of past periods can
be used to say something about future results. The second method also relies
on this assumption.

Average Revenue

With this method, average revenue is substituted for average profits
and goodwill is calculated by multiplying the average revenue (i.e. sales) of
an agreed period by a specified number. This method is often used by professional firms such as accountants (who should know better). All the arguments marshalled against the 'average profit' method can also be applied
here, with the additional point that this method can produce a figure for
goodwill even if the business has not seen a profit in years.

Future Profits

We shall show in Chapter 10 that the more sensible approach to valuing a business is not to rely on some 'magic formula' but to:

(a) Estimate the future cash flows that will be generated by the firm.
(b) Value that stream of cash flows, which gives the value of the business.
(c) Goodwill is then the difference between the value of the business derived from (b) and the value of the assets less liabilities.

A variant of this approach, which substitutes profit for cash, is sometimes encountered.

Example 4.4

The profits of A, B and C are expected to be £29,000 per year. A fair charge for the services provided by the partners to the partnership is £14,000. Considering the type of the business it is considered that a return of 15 per cent should be obtained from an investment of this nature. The partnership has tangible net assets of £80,000.

	£
Estimated annual profits	29,000
less Charge for the services of the partners	14,000
Return	£15,000

Then if V is the value of the partnership, V x required rate of return = £15,000. This assumes that the return will remain constant at £15,000 p.a. for ever, but other assumptions can be incorporated

$$V = \frac{£15,000}{0.15} = £100,000$$

	£
Value of the partnership	100,000
less Value of tangible net assets	80,000
Goodwill	£20,000

Whilst this is a more sensible and logical approach, it does require subjective forecasts of both the near-term and the long-term future. These forecasts can, of course, easily be the subject of considerable disagreement.

Super Profits

This method is similar to the above and under certain assumptions will produce the same figure for goodwill. Here a charge for the capital employed in the business as well as for the services of the partners is deducted from the expected annual profit and the remaining profit is called the annual *super profits*. Goodwill is then calculated as some multiple of the super profits. Some of the more common variations on this theme will be shown in the following example.

Example 4.5

The facts are as in Example 4.4.

	£	£
Estimated annual profit		29,000
less Charge for interest on capital employed, 15 per cent of £80,000	12,000	
Charge for partners' services	14,000	26,000
'Super profits'		£3,000

Assuming a return of 15 per cent (the same rate of return required on the tangible assets) the goodwill figure is, as before:

$$\frac{3.000}{0.15} = \text{£}20,000$$

However, and this is where the super profits method differs from the previous method, the super profits may be considered to be more risky than the normal return, and so the required rate of return on goodwill is considered to be greater than the required rate of return on the tangible assets. If the rate of return on super profits is increased to 20 per cent, then

$$\text{Goodwill} = \frac{\text{£}3,000}{0.20} = \text{£}15,000$$

In general:

$$\text{Goodwill} = \frac{\text{Annual super profits}}{i}$$

where i is the required rate of return.

Yet other variants are based on the view that super profits only last for a limited period; so goodwill is sometimes values as x years' purchase of the annual super profits.

We should emphasize that none of the above methods is totally satisfactory but we have presented them because they are found in practice.

We will now return to the particular problems of partnerships, outlined on pages 85 ff, where we explained that the treatment of changes in the composition of the partnership or in the profit-sharing ratio would be straightforward if the value of the business was equal to the book value of the assets less liabilities. We have now shown that, in general, this will not be the case because of the existence of goodwill and because of possible differences between the current and book values of individual assets. We shall now examine some of the methods that are employed to deal with goodwill and differences in asset valuations, when there is a change in the partnership arrangements.

Treatment of Goodwill on the Admission of a New Partner

There are at least three ways of dealing with this, They are:

   A. Recognize the asset of goodwill in the books of the existing partnership. See Example 4.6A.

   B. Do not recognize the goodwill. The new partner to pay the cash required to buy his share of goodwill into the partnership. See Example 4.6B.

   C. As B except that the new partner pays the original partners for goodwill and they withdraw their shares of the cash from the partnership. See Example 4.6C.

Example 4.6

The following facts will be common to Examples 4.6A–C. A and B are in partnership sharing profit and losses in the ratio A 75 per cent; B 25 per cent. On 31 December 19X5 they admit a new partner N and it is agreed that the new profit-sharing ratio shall be A 50 per cent, B 40 per cent and N 10 per cent. N is to introduce cash of £2,600. A and B's summarized balance sheet as at 31 December 19X5 is as follows:

Capital accounts	£	Sundry assets *less* Liabilities	£
A	12,000		22,000
B	10,000		
	£22,000		£22,000

Goodwill is agreed to be £6,000 and is not included in the above assets figure. (For simplicity we have assumed that A and B have zero balances on their current accounts as at 31 December 19X5.)

Example 4.6A

Goodwill is to be recognized as an asset in the books. Note that this is an example where 'non-purchased' goodwill is recorded as an asset.
   The steps are:

	Journal entries	£	£
(a) Recognize the asset of goodwill crediting the capital accounts of the existing partners in their original profit-sharing ratio	Goodwill A Capital a/c B Capital a/c	6,000	4,500 1,500
(b) N introduces capital in the form of cash	Cash N Capital a/c	2,600	2,600

Capital accounts

	A £	B £	N £		A £	B £	N £
				Balances b/d	12,000	10,000	
Balances c/d	16,500	11,500	2,600	Goodwill a/c	4,500	1,500	
				Cash			2,600
	£16,500	£11,500	£2,600		£16,500	£11,500	£2,600
				Balances b/d	16,500	11,500	2,600

Balance sheet after adjustments.

Capital accounts	£		£
A	16,500	Goodwill	6,000
B	11,500	Cash	2,600
N	2,600	Sundry assets	
		less Liabilities	22,000
	£30,600		£30,600

Example 4.6B (Where there is to be no account for goodwill)

Probably the easiest way of proceeding here is to open a goodwill account temporarily. The steps are then:

Journal entries

		£	£
(a) Recognize the asset, crediting the capital accounts of the existing partners in their original profit-sharing ratio. (A 75 per cent, B 25 per cent)	Goodwill A Capital a/c B Capital a/c	6,000	4,500 1,500
(b) N pays in cash to cover his share of goodwill, 10 per cent of £6,000, and his capital.	Cash N Capital a/c	2,600	2,600
(c) The Goodwill Account is closed, and the required debit to the partners' capital accounts uses the new profit-sharing ratio. (A 50 per cent, B 40 per cent, N 10 per cent)	A Capital a/c B Capital a/c N Capital a/c Goodwill	3,000 2,400 600	6,000

Note that steps (a) and (c) could be combined to give the following journal entry.

	Debit £	Credit £
B Capital a/c	900	
N Capital a/c	600	
A Capital a/c		1,500

One way of arriving at those figures is:

	Total	A	B	N
	£	£	£	£
Goodwill in old profit-sharing ratio	6,000	4,500	1,500	
Goodwill in new profit-sharing ratio	6,000	3,000	2,400	600
Difference (+ credit, − debit)		+£1,500	−£900	−£600

A perceptive reader may wonder why B's capital account is debited when A's is credited. The reason is that the new arrangements made on the admission of N have resulted in a change in the profit-sharing proportions between A and B.

Under the old arrangements A and B shared profits in the ratio of 75:25 or 3:1 while the profit-sharing ratio under the new arrangements is 50:40 or 1·25:1. Thus B's share of the profit has increased in comparison to A's, and it is necessary for B to 'pay' A for his increased share of the undisclosed goodwill.

Capital accounts

	A	B	N			A	B	N
	£	£	£			£	£	£
					Balances b/d	12,000	10,000	
Goodwill	3,000	2,400	600		Goodwill	4,500	1,500	
Balances c/d	13,500	9,100	2,000		Cash			2,600
	£16,500	£11,500	£2,600			£16,500	£11,500	£2,600
					Balances b/d	13,500	9,100	2,000

Balance sheet after adjustments:

Capital accounts	£		£
A	13,500	Cash	2,600
B	9,100	Sundry assets	
N	2,000	*less* Liabilities	22,000
	£24,600		£24,600

If N does not have sufficient cash to pay for his share of goodwill the necessary amounts could be paid over an agreed period of time by transfers from N's current accounts, i.e. out of his share of the profits. A similar arrangement could be used to enable a new partner to build up his capital contribution.

Example 4.6C (Where the new partner is to pay the original partners)

The only entry that will have any effect on the accounts of the partnership will be the one recording the capital contribution by N of £2,000. It makes no difference whether the payments for goodwill are effected through the books of the partnership or made outside the partnership. The balance sheet after the admission of N is:

Capital accounts	£		£
A	12,000	Cash	2,000
B	10,000	Sundry assets	
N	2,000	*less* Liabilities	22,000
	£24,000		£24,000

The method shown on page 94 can be used to work out who should pay what and to whom. It shows that not only has N to pay all his £600 to A but that B also has to pay A £900 because of the increase in B's profit share. If the profit-sharing ratio between A and B had remained unchanged, N's payment of £600 would be divided between A and B in their old profit-sharing ratio. For suppose that the new profit-sharing ratio is:

A 67·5 per cent B 22·5% N 10 per cent, i.e. maintaining the 3:1 ratio between A and B.

Then

	Total £	A £	B £	N £
Goodwill in old profit-sharing ratio	6,000	4,500	1,500	—
Goodwill in new profit-sharing ratio	6,000	4,050	1,350	600
Difference (+ credit, − debit)		+£450	+£150	−£600

Thus 75 per cent of £600 = £450 is paid by N to A and 25 per cent of £600 = £150 is paid to B.

Change in the Profit-sharing Ratio

We have already dealt with this as part of Example 4.6 where the introduction of a new partner was accompanied by a change in the profit-sharing ratio between the old partners. However, in order to focus on the points at issue we will introduce an example where there are no other factors to cloud the change in the profit-sharing ratio. The normal method is to make a transfer between the partners' capital account along the lines of Example 4.6B.

Example 4.7

The facts are as in Example 4.6, except that as at 31 December 19X5 there is a change in the profit-sharing ratio, no new partner being admitted.

The old profit-sharing ratio was A 75 per cent, B 25 per cent and the new profit-sharing ratio is to be A 50 per cent, B 50 per cent.

	Total £	A £	B £
Goodwill in old profit-sharing ratio	6,000	4,500	1,500
Goodwill in new profit-sharing ratio	6,000	3,000	3,000
Difference (+ credit, − debit)		+£1,500	−£1,500

Since B will receive a greater share of profit in the future he will be credited, when the goodwill is changed into profit, with part of the goodwill that 'belongs' to A. Hence B must recompense A and this is done by increasing A's capital or current account (as agreed by the partners) by £1,500 at the expense of B's capital or current account. The required journal entry is:

B Capital account	£1,500
A Capital account	£1,500

We have used the short-cut method here. Exactly the same result would have been achieved if we had temporarily opened a goodwill account as shown in Example 4.6B. Alternatively, B could pay A £1,500 in which case no adjustment would be required in the books of the partnership.

Undervalued Assets other than Goodwill

In the above we have confined our discussion to goodwill but exactly the same principles would apply if it were agreed that there was a significant difference between the current and book values of any of the tangible assets at the date of the change in the partnership arrangements. It is likely that the method outlined in Example 4.6A would be followed, i.e. the asset would be revalued and the new value of the asset would be retained in the books. This point will be illustrated in Example 4.8.

The Death or Retirement of a Partner

The basic point is that all assets should be revalued so that the outgoing partner can be credited with his share of the unrecorded assets. It may be that there are some unrecorded capital losses in which case the outgoing partner's capital account would have to be debited. Since the latter case is far less common we shall not spend any time on it, other than to say that the technique used is exactly the same as the 'unrecorded assets' case. We assume that accounts have been prepared at the date of the partner's departure. We shall deal later with the problems that arise when this does not happen.

Example 4.8

A, B and C are in partnership sharing profits and losses in the ratio 2:1:1. C died on 31 December 19X5 and the partnership's balance sheet as at that date was

	Capital accounts	Current accounts			
	£	£	£		£
A	10,000	3,000	13,000	Freehold land	14,000
B	12,000	5,000	17,000	Sundry assets	
C	8,000	2,000	10,000	*less* Liabilities	26,000
	£30,000	£10,000	£40,000		£40,000

It was agreed between A and B and C's representative that the freehold land should be revalued at £18,000 and, by using the method outlined in the partnership agreement, goodwill at 31 December 19X5 is valued at £6,000. A and B agree that, in future, they will share profits and losses equally and that they wish to show the enhanced value of the land in the books; however, they do not wish to open a goodwill account.

The capital accounts will then become:

	A £	B £	C £		A £	B £	C £
Goodwill	3,000	3,000		Balances	10,000	12,000	8,000
				Freehold land	2,000	1,000	1,000
Balances c/d	12,000	11,500	12,500	Goodwill	3,000	1,500	1,500
				Current account			2,000
	£15,000	£14,500	£12,500		£15,000	£14,500	£12,500
				Balances b/d	12,000	11,500	12,500

Note that, as before, goodwill has been written off against the remaining partners' capital accounts in their new profit-sharing ratio. There is no longer any point in distinguishing between C's capital and current accounts and the balance on his current account has therefore been transferred to his capital account.

The balance sheet now appears as follows:

	Capital accounts £	Current accounts £	£		£
A	12,000	3,000	15,000	Freehold land	18,000
B	11,500	5,000	16,500		
	£23,500	£8,000	31,500	Sundry assets	
				less Liabilities	26,000
C's account			12,500		
			£44,000		£44,000

So far so easy, but having worked out the outgoing partner's share of the firm the obligation must now be discharged. The partnership agreement may specify how this is done; alternatively the matter might be negotiated when the partner leaves. Otherwise our old friend, the Partnership Act 1890, has a few things to say on the matter.

We shall describe below some of the many available alternatives and we shall conclude this section by outlining the appropriate sections of the Act.

(a) Immediate Payment

This is obviously the simplest alternative from the point of view of the book-keeper, but it is likely to be the most difficult from the point of view of the financial management of the firm.

The outgoing partner's account will be debited, the appropriate asset account credited with the amount due, and the matter is over. The appropriate asset account is usually, but not always, the cash account. The parties may agree that the outgoing partner can take over, at an agreed valuation, some of the assets of the partnership, e.g. a car which the outgoing partner had used.

(b) Payment by Instalments

The book-keeping is almost as simple. The balance on the outgoing partner's capital account is transferred to a loan account. It then becomes a loan to the partnership and will be treated in the same way as any other loan.

Sometimes it is agreed that the rate of interest should be based on the profit or that the old partner should continue to receive a share in the profits. Such an agreement, so long as it is properly executed in writing, will not mean that the old partner retains his status as a partner with all the burdens of the rank. However, with this sort of arrangement, he would become a deferred creditor in the event of the bankruptcy of the firm.

(c) Discharge by the Payment of an Annuity

An annuity is a fixed sum which is paid at regular intervals. It might be agreed that the old partners should discharge their liability by paying an annuity to the outgoing partner or some specified persons until the death of the annuitant (i.e. the recipient of the annuity) or the last survivor if there is more than one.

The balance on the outgoing partner's capital account is transferred to the credit of an account, the *annuity suspense account*. Each year that account is credited with an amount representing interest, at an agreed rate, on the declining balance of the account, the debit being to the profit and loss account. The payments are debited to the annuity suspense account. The purpose of the interest charge is to recognize the fact that the partnership has had the benefit of the funds available as a result of the delay in the discharge of the liability.

The annuity is like a loan with an added gamble. If the annuitant dies early, the suspense account will have a credit balance representing the amount that will not now have to be paid, while if the annuitant lingers on, a greater sum will have to be paid than if a loan account had been established at the same rate of interest.

If, at the date of death of the annuitant, there is a credit balance on the annuity suspense account it is transferred to the remaining partners' capital or current accounts in accordance with the *old* profit-sharing ratio. The original ratio is used because the gain does not arise as a result of the activities since the change. By contrast, the annuity interest debited to the profit and loss account is charged in the *existing* profit-sharing ratio since the partnership is currently receiving the benefit from the use of the funds. Similarly, if a new partner had been admitted after the date of departure, he would not be credited with a share of the balance. If the annuitant insists in outliving the account and is still alive and kicking when the annuity suspense account runs out, then all future payments will be debited to the old partners' capital, or current accounts, according to the old profit-sharing ratio.

Example 4.8A

Following on from Example 4.8, it is agreed that C's widow should be paid an annuity of £2,000 per year, payable in advance on 1 January of each year. A and B agree that 10 per cent is an appropriate rate of interest. Mrs C died on 31 December 19X8. The annuity suspense account then appears as follows:

Annuity suspense account

19X6		£	19X6		£
1 Jan	Cash	2,000	1 Jan	C Capital a/c	12,500
31 Dec	Balance c/d	11,550	31 Dec	Profit and loss interest	
				(10 per cent of £10,500)	1,050
		£13,550			£13,550
19X7			19X7		
1 Jan	Cash	2,000	1 Jan	Balance c/d	11,550
31 Dec	Balance c/d	10,505	31 Dec	Profit and loss, interest	955
		£12,505			£12,505
19X8			19X8		
1 Jan	Cash	2,000	1 Jan	Balance b/d	10,505
31 Dec	Capital a/c		31 Dec	Profit and loss, interest	850
	A $(\frac{2}{3})$	6,237			
	B $(\frac{1}{3})$	3,118			
		£11,355			£11,355

(d) Use of Life Policies

One way of ensuring that some cash is available on the death or retirement of a partner is to take out an assurance policy on the lives of the partners. The premiums are paid by the partnership and the partners are the beneficiaries under the policy. The policy may be 'whole life', i.e. the benefit is payable on the death of the assured person or an endowment policy maturing at the expected date of retirement.

The Partnership Act 1890

Man's ingenuity is such that many other ways of dealing with the departure of a partner have been devised, but man's stubbornness is such that, on occasions, no agreement can be made. One of the functions of the Partnership Act 1890 is to provide against this eventuality.

Basically a departing partner is entitled to the repayment of his capital (this includes the balance on his current account) due to him after the adjustment for any unrecorded assets, i.e. taking account of the current valuation of assets, including goodwill, and liabilities. If the amount is not settled immediately, the departing partner or his representative is entitled to either interest at 5 per cent per annum or such share of the profits as the court may determine to be attributable to the use of his share of the partnership assets. The latter calculation is a difficult one; a sensible way to proceed would be to deduct from the profit a reasonable charge for the services of the remaining partners and to apportion the balance on the basis of the 'revalued' capitals.

Absence of Accounts at the Date of Change in Partnership Arrangements

It is obviously sensible to produce a balance sheet as at the date of change and a profit and loss account covering the period from the date of the last balance sheet to the date of change. However, there will be circumstances when this is not done, for example, the partners may agree to make a retrospective change in the profit-sharing ratio.

The basic principle is that the profit for the year should be apportioned between the periods before and after the date of change. There are no laid-down rules as to how this should be done, and the method employed will depend on the circumstances. An example of this type of situation is provided in an appendix to the chapter.

Dissolution of Partnerships

We have, implicitly, assumed above that the retirement of a partner did not lead to the dissolution of the partnership.* We shall now consider this question and shall first outline the basic method before looking at a few complications.

The assets have to be sold and the liabilities paid. The difference between the net proceeds and the net book value of the assets less liabilities is termed the 'profit or loss on realization' and is credited or debited to the partners in their profit-sharing ratio. The balances on the partners' current accounts are transferred to their capital accounts.

If, after this, all the capital accounts are in credit, the total of the capital accounts will equal the cash available, and the final step in the dissolution will be the distribution of the cash to the partners according to the balance on their accounts. If any of the capital accounts end up with a debit balance, the partner or partners concerned will have to pay in sufficient cash to clear the deficit. The method is then as before. In order to help achieve the above a *realization account* is opened and the balances of the various asset accounts are debited to it (so closing the asset accounts). The proceeds from the sale of the assets are credited to the realization account so that the balance on that account is the profit or loss on realization of the assets.

If there is any 'profit' on paying off liabilities, because of cash discounts, for example, the gain will be credited to the realization account, while any loss, which could occur if a provision is found to be inadequate, is debited to the account.

Dissolution and the Partnership Act 1890

Section 44 of the Act provides that the order in which the assets of the firm must be applied are

First: In paying outsiders
Second: In paying, proportionally to each partner, amounts advanced over and above their capital
Third: In paying the amounts due in respect of the partners' capital and current accounts.

---

* Technically a partnership is dissolved when a new partner is admitted or when an existing partner leaves the firm. However, this technicality is usually ignored when the business of the partnership is to continue.

Example 4.9

X, Y and Z were in partnership sharing profits and losses in the ratio 5:4:1. They decided to dissolve the partnership on 31 December 19X3, and the balance sheet as at that date was:

	Capital accounts £	Current accounts £	£	Fixed assets	£	£
X	6,000	2,000	8,000	Land	6,000	
Y	4,000	1,000	5,000	Motor vehicles	3,000	9,000
Z	1,000	(4,000)	(3,000)	Current assets		
	£11,000	£(1,000)	10,000	Inventory	2,000	
				Debtors	3,000	
Partners advance, X			4,000	Cash	2,000	7,000
Current liability						
Creditors			2,000			
			£16,000			£16,000

We shall describe below the steps that have to be taken to dissolve the partnership and show the necessary journal entries.

Required journal entries

	Debit	Credit	£
(a) Transfer of the balance on the current accounts to the capital accounts.	X Current a/c Y Current a/c Z Capital a/c	X Capital a/c Y Capital a/c Z Current a/c	2,000 1,000 4,000
(b) Transfer the balances from the asset accounts, other than cash, to the realization account.	Realization a/c	{ Land Motor vehicles Inventory Debtors	6,000 3,000 2,000 3,000
(c) The land is sold for £8,000.	Cash	Realization a/c	8,000
(d) It is agreed that X and Y should take over the vehicles, at their net book values.	X Capital a/c } Y Capital a/c	Realization a/c	2,000 1,000
(e) Inventory and debtors are sold *en bloc* for £4,000	Cash	Realization a/c	4,000
(f) X, Y and Z agree, in return for £800, to recommend their customers to take their future business to PL Ltd.	Cash	Realization a/c	800
(g) The creditors are settled, after taking cash discounts, for £1,800	Creditors Creditors	Cash Realization a/c	1,800 200
(h) X's advance is repaid.	X's Advance a/c	Cash	4,000

Required journal entries

	Debit	Credit	£
(i) The profit on realization is transferred to the partners' capital accounts in their profit-sharing ratio.	Realization a/c	⎧ X Capital a/c (50 per cent)	1,000
		⎨ Y Capital a/c (40 per cent)	800
		⎩ Z Capital a/c (10 per cent)	200
(j) Z pays in £2,800 to clear the debit balance on his capital account.	Cash	Z Capital a/c	2,800
(k) The remaining cash is paid to the partners on the basis of their capital account balances.	X Capital a/c	Cash	7,000
	Y Capital a/c	Cash	4,800

Capital accounts

	X £	Y £	Z £		X £	Y £	Z £
Current a/c (a)			4,000	Balances	6,000	4,000	1,000
Realization a/c (d)	2,000	1,000		Current a/c (a)	2,000	1,000	
				Realization a/c (i)	1,000	800	200
				Cash (j)			2,800
	2,000	1,000	4,000		9,000	5,800	4,000
Cash (k)	7,000	4,800					
	£9,000	£5,800	£4,000		£9,000	£5,800	£4,000

Realization accounts

		£			£
Land	(b)	6,000	Cash	(c)	8,000
Motor vehicles	(b)	3,000	X Capital a/c	(d)	2,000
Inventory	(b)	2,000	Y Capital a/c	(d)	1,000
Debtors	(b)	3,000	Cash	(e)	4,000
			Cash	(f)	800
			Creditors	(g)	200
		14,000			16,000
Profit on realization	(i)				
X Capital a/c (50 per cent)		1,000			
Y Capital a/c (40 per cent)		800			
Z Capital a/c (10 per cent)		200			
		£16,000			£16,000

Cash account

Balance		2,000	Creditors	(g)	1,800
Realization a/c	(c)	8,000	X's Advance a/c	(h)	4,000
Realization a/c	(e)	4,000			
Realization a/c	(f)	800			
Z Capital a/c	(j)	2,800			
		17,600			5,800
			Balance distributed to		
			the partners	(k)	
			X Capital a/c		7,000
			Y Capital a/c		4,800
		£17,600			£17,600

Non-cash Proceeds

Part or all of the proceeds of the sale of the assets may not have been for cash. Typically, some or all the assets may be sold to a limited company in exchange for shares. There are then two problems, the partners must agree on the value of the shares and how the shares should be divided between them.

So far as the book-keeping is concerned, an account will be opened to record the non-cash items. Then, if we assume that the non-cash element is shares, the entries relating to the account are:

Debit	Shares account	} with the agreed
Credit	Realization account	value of the shares.

and

Debit	Capital accounts	} with the value of the shares
Credit	Shares account	distributed to the partners.

The Rule in Garner v Murray

In Example 4.9, Z, the partner with a debit balance on his capital account, was able to find sufficient cash to make good the deficiency. But what would happen if he did not have sufficient resources? X and Y would have to stand the loss, but how should the loss be divided between them?

Until the leading case of Garner *v* Murray (1904) it was generally agreed that the loss should be apportioned between the remaining partners in their profit-sharing ratios. However, the decision in the Garner *v* Murray case changed accountant's thinking on the subject. The usual interpretation of the decision is that, subject to any agreement to the contrary, the deficiency should be borne in the ratios of the partners' last agreed capitals, i.e. the balances shown in the capital accounts on the most recent balance sheet. However, the controversy about the decision has continued ever since, and it has been suggested that the usual interpretation is an over-simplification.*

* Gibson, C. J., 'Partner's liability', *Accountancy*, September 1970

We do not wish to enter the controversy here and would refer interested readers to Gibson's article. The trouble arises when there are insufficient assets to repay a partner's advance account in full; otherwise the usual interpretation of the rule is acceptable. Since this did not occur in Example 4.9 we can use that example to illustrate the conventional interpretation of the Garner *v* Murray rule, that is that a partner's deficiency should be shared between the other partners, using the capital ratios.

Example 4.9A

Suppose that, in Example 4.9, Z could only contribute £800, so leaving a deficiency on his capital account of £2,000. Then, since the balances on the capital accounts of the remaining partners were X £6,000 and Y £4,000, the deficiency is divided between X and Y in the ratio of 6:4.

Capital accounts

	X £	Y £	Z £		X £	Y £	Z £
Current a/c (a)			4,000	Balances	6,000	4,000	1,000
Realization a/c (d)	2,000	1,000		Current a/cs (a)	2,000	1,000	
Z's capital a/c	1,200	800		Realization a/c (i)	1,000	800	200
				Cash			800
				X & Y capital a/cs			2,000
	3,200	1,800	4,000		9,000	5,800	4,000
Cash	5,800	4,000					
	£9,000	£5,800	£4,000		£9,000	£5,800	£4,000

We would repeat that the rule in Garner *v* Murray only applies if the partnership agreement does not provide against the eventuality of a partner's failing to make good any deficiency.

Piecemeal Realization and Interim Distributions

So far it must have looked as if a magic wand had been waved over our dissolutions, for they have happened instantaneously. However, in practice a dissolution will last for some months, or even years, and the partners may not wish, or may not be able, to wait until the dissolution is completed before getting their hands on the money. Thus, it is common for partners to withdraw cash as the assets are realized. However, there is an inherent danger in this practice, because if the partners take out too much, too early, and losses are incurred on the realization of the remaining assets, there may not be enough cash to pay the creditors. But even if there is enough left to pay the creditors, there is the further danger that too hasty a distribution of cash could mean that a partner would have to repay some of the cash already received – a dangerous position for a number of reasons, not the least of which is that he might have spent the money.

The safest way to proceed is take the extreme conservative position and assume that all the remaining assets will prove valueless. Thus, so far as creditors are concerned, no cash should be distributed to the partners until all the creditors have been paid. Similarly, partners' advances should be repaid before there is any repayment of capital. These precautions will not generally present any difficulties because the creditors' position can, usually, be quickly sorted out. Any delay in a dissolution is usually caused by the sale of assets, in particular the desire to obtain the best price for them.

After the creditors and any partners' loan accounts have been paid, the interim distributions can be made. When doing so, it is assumed that the remaining assets (except cash) will prove to be valueless and the resulting notional loss on realization – the total book value of the assets less the cash realized to date – is debited to the partners' capital accounts in the profit-and loss-sharing ratio. If any of the capital accounts are then in debit (after transferring any balances on current and drawings accounts) the debit balances can be apportioned between the other partners by using the Garner *v* Murray rule. This process is continued until no debit balances remain. At this stage the total of the credit balances on the partners' capital accounts will equal the cash available and the distribution may be made in accordance with those balances.

This calculation will be performed outside the books of the partnership and the only entries in the books will be the credits to cash and the debits to the capital accounts representing the cash distributed.

JOINT VENTURES

This title is applied to partnerships which are formed for a specific operation. Typically the partners will also be in business on their own account but agree to come together for a special purpose; hence joint ventures are of comparatively short duration. The partners may come together again for other projects but in such cases, unless a permanent partnership is established, they will be treated as separate joint ventures. Joint ventures are now rare but are still found from time to time; for example, they are used to exploit North Sea oil resources.

There are, basically, two ways of dealing with the accounts of joint ventures.

One method is to keep a separate set of books, and in this case the accounting treatment will not differ from the standard method of dealing with partnerships described earlier in this chapter. In practice it is often found that the partners in the joint enterprise provide services for it, e.g. the provision of office accommodation, and will therefore charge the joint venture for this service. In their own books they will debit the investment in joint venture account and credit the appropriate expense accounts. In the books of the joint venture, the expenses will be treated as an introduction of capital; so the partner's capital account will be credited with the amount of the expense, and the debit will be made to the expense accounts.

Sometimes no separate bank account will be opened for the joint venture, all receipts and payments being dealt with in the partners' own bank accounts. In such a case, the partners' joint venture capital account will be credited with payments made and debited with cash received on behalf of the venture. There is little point in distinguishing between capital and current accounts unless the participants agree that a charge for capital should be included in the appropriation of profit calculations.

In the alternative method a separate set of books is not opened. Instead the transactions undertaken by each partner on behalf of the joint venture will be recorded in the books of his own business. Each partner will open a joint venture account in his books, and debit expenses and credit revenue to it in respect of his participation.

In order to determine the profit and the final settlement between the partners, the information recorded in the joint venture accounts must be brought together. The steps are as follows.

1. A statement, which is not part of the books of any of the partners, is prepared combining the details included in the various joint venture accounts. This statement is usually called a *memorandum joint venture account*,* and is the profit and loss account of the joint venture.

2. The profit, or loss, of the joint venture can then be found and its apportionment (based on the agreement between the partners) can be calculated.

3. Each partner will debit his own joint venture account and credit his general profit and loss account with his share of profit.

4. The final cash settlement is made between the partners. Partners with credit balances on their joint venture accounts, after dealing with their share of profit or loss, will pay those partners whose accounts are in debit.

The above four steps will be illustrated in the following example.

---

* As a general rule 'memorandum' refers to statements which do not form part of the double-entry system.

Example 4.10

(a) After the completion of the joint venture but before the preparation of the memorandum joint venture account, the books of the two constituent partners A and B might read
as follows.

A's Books	B's Books

Joint venture with B account	*Joint venture with A account*
Balance *a*			Balance *b*

So A has incurred more of the joint venture expenses than he has received in receipts
and vice versa for B.

(b) The profit on the joint venture is then $b - a$ and we will assume that this is shared
between A and B in the ratio 3:1.

(c) Each partner will then debit his joint venture account and credit his general profit
and loss account with his share of the profit. Their joint venture accounts will then be:

A's Books	B's Books

Joint venture with B account	*Joint venture with A account*
Opening balance a			Opening balance b
Profit and loss		Profit and loss	
a/c $\frac{3}{4}(b-a)$		a/c $\frac{1}{4}(b-a)$	
Closing balance		Closing balance	
$= a + \frac{3}{4}(b-a)$		$= b - \frac{1}{4}(b-a)$	
$= \frac{1}{4}(a + 3b)$ debit		$= \frac{1}{4}(a + 3b)$ credit	

(d) The payment by B to A of $£\frac{1}{4}(a + 3b)$ will settle the position between them and close
the two joint venture accounts.

For those of our readers who do not find algebra to their taste we will present
a further, numerical, example.

Example 4.11

Jim Graves is a wine merchant trading in a country town. He wishes to participate in a
London wine auction but feels that it would be safer if he did so in collaboration with a
London merchant who could provide office and storage facilities as well as additional
customers. Accordingly, he enters into an agreement with Fred La Tour. Graves and La
Tour agree to share profit and losses equally.
   The transactions of the joint venture are:

1. On 2 January La Tour purchased wine at a cost of £11,000; on the same date
   Graves gave La Tour a cheque for £3,000 towards the payment.

2. Each partner sent details of the purchase to his own customers drawing their
   attention to the special prices offered. The costs of the mailing, paid on 10
   January, were: paid by La Tour £800, paid by Graves £500.

3. The carriage charges paid by the partners on 1 March were: La Tour £200,
   Graves £1,400.

4. Sales made by the partners were La Tour, £8,000, Graves £4,000. The cash was banked on 3 March. The special offer did not prove to be as successful as had been hoped and it was decided that the venture should be terminated on 1 April. It was agreed that La Tour should take over the unsold wine and that £2,800 would be a reasonable estimate of its value.

5. Since a high proportion of the sales were made in La Tour's shop it was agreed that La Tour should charge the joint venture with £800 for selling expenses in addition to storage charges of £300.

6. The final settlement between the partners was made on 16 April. The various accounts will then appear as follows:

Graves' Books

Joint venture with La Tour account

		£			£
Jan 2	Bank (La Tour)	3,000	Mar 3	Bank (Sales)	4,000
Jan 10	Bank (Mailing)	500	Apr 1	Profit and loss a/c	
Mar 1	Bank (Carriage)	1,400		(Share of loss)	100
		4,900			4,100
			Apr 16	Bank (La Tour)	800
		£4,900			£4,900

La Tour's Books

Joint venture with Graves account

		£			£
Jan 2	Bank (Purchases)	11,000	Jan 2	Bank (Graves)	3,000
Jan 10	Bank (Mailing)	800	Mar 3	Bank (Sales)	8,000
Mar 1	Bank (Carriage)	200	Apr 1	Inventory (unsold wine)	2,800
Apr 1	Selling expenses a/c	800	Apr 1	Profit and loss a/c	
Apr 1	Storage charges a/c	300		(Share of loss)	100
		£13,100			13,900
Apr 16	Bank (Graves)	800			
		£13,900			£13,900

Memorandum Joint Venture Account

	£	£		£	£
Purchases		11,000	Sales G.	4,000	
			LT.	8,000	12,000
Mailing G.	500		Wine taken		
LT.	800	1,300	over by LT.		2,800
Carriage G.	1,400				
LT.	200	1,600	Loss		
			G. ($\frac{1}{2}$)	100	
Shop Expenses (LT)		800	LT. ($\frac{1}{2}$)	100	200
Storage Charges (LT)		300			
		£15,000			£15,000

APPENDIX: *An extended example of partnership accounts*

The following appendix consists of a fairly detailed example of a change in the composition of a partnership with the added complication that financial statements had not been prepared at the date of change.

The following trial balance was extracted from the books of Plug, a partnership, as at 31 December 19X5.

	Debit £	Credit £
Balance at bank	2,120	
Capital accounts P		20,000
Q		4,000
R		5,000
Creditors		18,000
Current accounts P		1,000
Q		2,000
R		1,000
Debtors	25,000	
Drawings P	6,000	
Q	6,000	
R	2,000	
Fixtures and fittings, at cost	4,000	
Accumulated depreciation		3,000
Motor vehicles, at cost	16,000	
Accumulated depreciation		9,000
Purchases	242,000	
Rates	7,000	
Rent	8,000	
Salaries	10,000	
Sales		300,000
Selling expenses	4,500	
Inventory, 1 Jan 19X5	22,000	
Sundry expenses	5,500	
Wages	4,680	
Payment made by N for goodwill		1,800
	£364,800	£364,800

1. You are also told that:
   (a) As at 31 December 19X5

Prepaid expenses	Rates	£1,000
	Sundry expenses	£500

Accrued expenses	Wages	£600
	Rent	£2,000
Inventory, at cost		£24,000

(b) Depreciation is to be provided at the following rates:

Fixtures and fittings,	10 per cent on cost
Motor vehicles,	20 per cent on cost.

2. Up to 30 June 19X5 P, Q and R were the three partners, and their partnership agreement provided that profit and losses should be divided in the ratio of 5:3:2 after charging 5 per cent interest on capital and a salary to Q of £4,000.

3. On 30 June 19X5 R retired from the partnership. It was agreed that goodwill should be valued at £18,000 at that date but otherwise the book value of the assets less liabilities was a reasonable estimate of their current values. On his departure from the partnership R took with him a car (cost £6,000, accumulated depreciation at 1 January 19X5, £4,000) and certain office furniture (cost £1,000, accumulated depreciation, 1 January 19X5, £600). P and Q agreed that the furniture should be a retirement gift from the partnership and that the necessary adjustment should be made through their current accounts. It was also agreed that R should be paid interest, at 10 per cent per annum, on the amount due to him from the date of his retirement.

4. On 30 June 19X5, N, who had been employed as a manager was admitted to the partnership. It was agreed that, after charging interest on capital at 10 per cent per annum and crediting Q and N with salaries of £6,000 and £12,000 per year respectively, that the balance should be divided as between P, Q and N in the ratio 6:3:1.

5. It was agreed that N should introduce sufficient cash into the partnership to pay for his share of goodwill; this he did on 30 June 19X5. N's capital contribution is to be £4,000 and this is to be built up by transfers from his current account as at 31 December of each year. The amount of the transfer to be the lower of £1,000 or 50 per cent of his share of the 'balance of profit'.

6. The partners do not wish to open an account for goodwill and all the necessary adjustments are to be made through the capital accounts.

7. Sales were at a constant rate throughout the year except that the sales for October, November and December were each twice the sales of the other months.

8. The only salary earner was N and the charge of £10,000 represents the total amount paid to him during the year in 12 equal monthly instalments.

9. The number of wage earners had remained constant during the year but all wage earners received a 20 per cent increase in pay on 1 July 19X5.

Required

(a) The partnership's trading and profit and loss accounts for the year ended 31 December 19X5 and for the periods 1 January 19X5 to 30 June 19X5 and 1 July 19X5 to 31 December 19X5 and the appropriation accounts for the two periods.
(b) The balance sheet as at 31 December 19X5.
(c) The partners' capital and current accounts and R's loan account.

PLUG
Trading and Profit and Loss Accounts
Year ended 31 December 19X5

		Year		*1 January–30 June*		*1 July–31 December*	
		£	£	£	£	£	£
Sales			300,000				
less	Opening Inventory	22,000					
	Purchases	242,000					
		264,000					
less	Closing inventory	24,000	240,000				
	Gross profit		60,000		24,000		36,000
less	Salaries	5,000		5,000		—	
	Wages	5,280		2,400		2,880	
	Selling expenses	4,500		1,800		2,700	
	Rent	10,000		5,000		5,000	
	Rates	6,000		3,000		3,000	
	Sundry expenses	5,000		2,500		2,500	
	Loan interest	314		—		314	
	Depreciation						
	Motor vehicles	2,600		1,600		1,000	
	Fixtures and fittings	350		200		150	
			39,044		21,500		17,544
	Net profit		£20,956		£2,500		£18,456

Appropriation Accounts
1 January–30 June 19X5

	£	£	£
Net profit			2,500
less Interest on capital			
P 2½ per cent of £20,000	500		
Q 2½ per cent of £4,000	100		
R 2½ per cent of £5,000	125	725	

	£	£	£
Salary Q		2,000	
		2,725	
Share of loss			
P 50 per cent	112		
Q 30 per cent	68		
R 20 per cent	45	(225)	£2,500

1 July–31 December 19X5

	£	£	£
Net profit			18,456
less Interest on capital			
P 5 per cent of £18,200	910		
Q 5 per cent of £4,000	200	1,110	
Salaries			
Q	3,000		
N	6,000	9,000	
Share or profit			
P 60 per cent	5,007		
Q 30 per cent	2,504		
N 10 per cent	835	8,346	£18,456

Balance Sheet as at 31 December 19X5

Fixed assets	Cost	Accumulated depreciation	Net book value
	£	£	£
Motor vehicles	10,000	7,000	3,000
Fixtures and fittings	3,000	2,700	300
	£13,000	£9,700	3,300
Current assets			
Inventory, at cost		24,000	
Debtors		25,000	
Prepaid expenses (1,000 + 500)		1,500	
Balance at bank		2,120	
		52,620	
less Current liabilities			
Creditors	18,000		
Accrued expenses			
(2,000 + 600)	2,600	20,600	32,020
			£35,320

Capital accounts

Debit side

		P £	Q £	R £	N £
Jun 30	Current account			920	
30	Loan account			7,680	
30	Goodwill	10,800	5,400		1,800
30	Balances c/d	18,200	4,000		
		£29,000	£9,400	£8,600	£1,800
Dec 31	Balances c/d	18,200	4,000		418
		£18,200	£4,000		£418

Credit side

		P £	Q £	R £	N £
Jan 1	Opening balances	20,000	4,000	5,000	
Jun 30	Goodwill	9,000	5,400	3,600	
30	Cash				1,800
		£29,000	£9,400	£8,600	£1,800
Jul 1	Balances b/d	18,200	4,000		
Dec 31	Current account				418
		£18,200	£4,000		£418
Jan 1	Balances b/d	18,200	4,000		418

Current accounts

Debit side

		P £	Q £	R £	N £
Jun 30	Drawings			2,000	
30	Share of loss	112	68	45	
30	Fixtures and fittings	219	131		
Dec 31	Drawings	6,000	6,000		
31	Salaries account				5,000
31	Capital account				418
31	Balances c/d	1,086	3,605		1,417
		£7,417	£9,804	£2,045	£6,835

Credit side

		P £	Q £	R £	N £
Jan 1	Opening balances	1,000	1,000	1,000	
Jun 30	Interest on capital	500	100	125	
30	Salary		2,000		
30	Capital account			920	
Dec 31	Interest on capital	910	200		
31	Salaries		3,000		6,000
31	Share of profit	5,007	2,504		835
		£7,417	£9,804	£2,045	£6,835
Jan 1	Balances b/d	1,086	3,605		1,417

	Capital Accounts	*Current Accounts*	
P	18,200	1,086	19,286
Q	4,000	3,605	7,605
N	418	1,417	1,835
	£22,618	£6,108	28,726

Loan account – R   6,594

£35,320

R Loan Account

		£			£
Jun 30	Motor vehicles	1,400	Jun 30	Capital a/c	7,680
Dec 31	Balance c/d	6,594	Dec 31	Interest, 5 per cent on £6,280	314
		£7,994			£7,994
			Jan 1	Balance b/d	6,594

1. The first step is to apportion the revenue and expenses between the two time periods so that the profit for the first period can be found. Note that the profit for the second half of the year cannot be found until the partnership's indebtedness to R and, hence, the loan interest payable is calculated.

   1.1 *Gross Profit.* We will assume that the gross profit percentage has remained constant over the year and, as we are not given any indication to the contrary, this seems to be a sensible assumption. Thus the gross profit will be apportioned on the basis of sales. If average monthly sales in the first half-year are x, the sales in the first half-year will be $6x$, and in the second half-year $9x$ (sales of the last 3 months being twice the previous monthly average). Then gross profit for the first half-year = $6x/15x$ of £60,000 = £24,000 and £36,000 for the second half-year.

   1.2 *Salaries.* Since N was a partner for the second half-year, the payments made to him called salaries are in fact drawings. Thus the £5,000 paid in the second half-year have been debited to his current account.

   1.3 *Wages.* Let x be the amount paid in the first half-year. Then, since all workers received an increase of 20 per cent on 1 July, the total expense for the year which is £4,680 + £600 = £5,280 is equal to x + $120/100x = 2 \cdot 2x$

$$i.e. \ 2 \cdot 2x = £5,280$$
$$x = £2,400$$

and the wages for the second half-year = £2,880.

1.4 *Selling expenses.*   These have been apportioned on the same basis as sales.

i.e.	first half-year	6/15 of £4,500 = £1,800
	second half-year	9/15 of £4,500 = £2,700.

1.5 *Rent, Rates and Sundry Expenses.*   These have been apportioned on the basis of time.

1.6 *Depreciation*

	Cost		*Accumulated depreciation*
	£	£	£
Motor vehicles			
Balance 1 January	16,000		9,000
Depreciation charge first half-year, 10 per cent of £16,000			1,600
			10,600
Taken over R	(6,000)	$\left\{ \begin{array}{l} (4,000) \\ (600) \end{array} \right.$	(4,600)
	10,000		6,000
Depreciation charge second half-year, 10 per cent of £10,000			1,000
Balance 31 December	£10,000		£7,000
Fixtures and fittings			
Balance 1 January	4,000		3,000
Depreciation charge first half-year, 5 per cent of £4,000			200
			3,200
Given to R	(1,000)	$\left\{ \begin{array}{l} (600) \\ (50 \cdot) \end{array} \right.$	(650)
	3,000		2,550
Depreciation charge second half-year, 5 per cent of £3,000			150
	£3,000		£2,700

1.7 *N's Capital Contribution* (Note 5, Page 111). The transfer from N's current account is 50 per cent of his share of the profit, after interest and salaries (50 per cent of £835). This is lower than £1,000.

2. The entries relating to the departure of R now have to be made.

2.1 *Goodwill*. £18,000, the agreed value of the goodwill has been credited to the capital accounts of the original partners in the old profit-sharing ratio and debited to the capital accounts of the remaining, and new, partners in the new profit-sharing ratio.

2.2 *R's Take-over of the Motor Vehicle*. The net book value as at 30 June X5 is debited to R's loan account. Note that the accumulated depreciation at 30 June 19X5 is £4,000 plus the depreciation charge for the first half-year, (£600). See working 1.6.

2.3 *Gift to R of the Office Furniture*. Since this transfer is to be a gift, the net book value cannot be debited to R's loan account but instead is debited to P and Q in the ratio of 5:3. The complete journal entry being:

	Debit £	Credit £
Fixtures and fittings		
– accumulated depreciation	650	
P current account	219	
Q current account	131	
Fixtures and fittings, at cost		1,000

2.4 The balances on R's current and capital accounts are transferred to his loan account.

EXERCISES

4.1 'Goodwill is clearly seen to be significant when partners change their partnership arrangements yet the asset is often not included in a partnership balance sheet.'
Comment.

4.2 Tom, Dick and Harry have agreed to form a partnership to operate as motor vehicle dealers.

Tom is an experienced businessman with a wide range of other interests, but he has no experience of the motor trade. He will contribute about 70 per cent of the capital of the partnership and will devote about one day a week to the business of the partnership.

Dick, who will contribute about 30 per cent of the capital, has for a number of years been the manager of a successful firm of motor vehicle dealers. He will work full-time for the partnership.

Harry is a young salesman. He claims that he will be able to retain the business of a number of large organizations when he moves from his present employers to join the partnership. His capital contribution will be nominal, but he will devote all his time to the partnership.

Discuss the factors that Tom, Dick and Harry might take into account when settling the profit-sharing arrangements.

4.3 Hawes and Peters are partners, sharing profits and losses in the ratio 3:2. The following is the trial balance in the partnership books at 31 December, 1975:

		£	£
Capital account at 1 January 1975	– Hawes		16,400
	– Peters		13,200
Drawings	– Hawes	3,600	
	– Peters	2,400	
Provision for doubtful debts			480
Purchases		101,640	
Sales			131,860
Vans at cost		11,600	
Fittings at cost		2,400	
Provision for depreciation	– vans		5,920
	– fittings		1,140
Stock 1 January 1975		17,360	
Petty cash		40	
Office expenses		6,400	
Vehicle expenses		3,960	
Motor car at cost (1 January 1975)		1,600	
Debtors and creditors		12,200	4,200
Bank			540
Wages		7,360	
Insurance		620	
Discounts allowed		2,560	
		£173,740	£173,740

The following additional information is available:

   (i)   Stock at 31 December 1975 was valued at £26,380.
  (ii)   Depreciation is to be provided at 10 per cent per annum, on the written down value of the fittings and at 20 per cent per annum on the written down value of the vans and car. Hawes is to bear personally £400 of the vehicle expenses and one half of the depreciation charge on the car.
 (iii)   No rent has been paid on the business premises during the year because of a dispute with the landlord. The rental agreement provides for a rent of £928 per year.
  (iv)   The partners are entitled to interest on capital at 10 per cent per annum.

(v) Bad debts of £200 are to be written off, and the provision for doubtful debts to be adjusted to $2\frac{1}{2}$ per cent of the remaining debtors.
(vi) Insurance, £70, has been paid in advance of 31 December 1975.
(vii) Wages, £370, were owing at 31 December 1975.
(viii) An item of £70 for bank charges appears in the bank statement but has not yet been entered into the partnership bank account.

Required:
Prepare the Trading, Profit and Loss Account for the year ended 31 December 1975 and a Balance Sheet as at that date. (Ignore Taxation)

(The Association of Certified Accountants, Foundation Examination – Part A, Accounting I, June 1976)

4.4 Yew, May and Holly have been in partnership for a number of years sharing profits in the ratio 6:5:3. Work in progress was not brought into the accounts.

The balance sheet of the partnership as on 31 March 1976 showed the following position:

	£		£	£
Capital accounts:		Fixed assets		22,400
Yew	25,000	Goodwill		12,950
May	18,000	Current assets		
Holly	8,700	Debtors	73,500	
		Balance at bank	10,450	
Sundry creditors	67,600			83,950
	£119,300			£119,300

On 31 March 1976 Yew retired from the partnership and it was agreed to admit Oak as a partner on the following terms:

1. Goodwill in the old partnership was to be revalued to two years purchase of the average profits over the last three years. The profits of the last three years have been £12,400, £13,600, and £14,005. Goodwill was to be written off in the new partnership.

2. Yew to take his car out of the partnership assets at an agreed value of £1,000. The car had been included in the accounts as on 31 March 1976 at a written down value of £594.

3. Although work in progress had not been and will not be included in the partnership accounts the new partners were to credit Yew with his share based on an estimate that work in progress was equivalent to 20 per cent of the debtors.

4. The new partnership of May, Holly and Oak were to share profits in the ratio 5:3:2. The initial capital to be £25,000 subscribed in the profit-sharing ratios.

5. May, Holly and Oak were each to pay to Yew the sum of £5,000 out of their personal resources in part repayment of his share of the partnership.

6. Yew to lend to Oak any amount required to make up his capital in the firm from the monies due to him, and any further balance due to Yew was to be left in the new partnership as a loan, bearing interest at 9 per cent per annum. Any adjustments required to be the capital accounts of May and Holly were to be paid into or withdrawn from the partnership bank account.

You are required to prepare:

(a) the capital accounts, in columnar form, of the partners reflecting the adjustments required on the change in partnership, and
(b) a balance sheet on completion.

(The Institute of Chartered Accountants in England and Wales, Professional Examination 1, Financial Accounting I, May, 1976)

4.5 Bull and Bear have been partners for some years with the following profit-sharing arrangements:

Interest on capital accounts, 5 per cent.
Salaries, Bull – £2,000, Bear – £4,000
Share of balance, Bull – $\frac{2}{3}$, Bear – $\frac{1}{3}$.
The profit has been about £23,000 for the last few years. Their balance sheet as at 31 December 19X2 was as follows:

	Capital accounts	Current accounts	
	£	£	£
Bull	30,000	5,000	35,000
Bear	10,000	15,000	25,000
	£40,000	£20,000	£60,000

Sundry assets *less* Liabilities   £60,000

Bull proposes that Stag, who is at present a manager employed by the partnership at a salary of £8,000 per annum, be admitted as a partner from 1 January 19X3 and that the new profit-sharing arrangements should be:

Interest on capital accounts, 12 per cent
Salaries, Bull – £2,000, Bear – £2,000, Stag – £5,000
Share of balance, Bull 40 per cent, Bear 40 per cent, Stag, 20 per cent.

If Stag's total share of the profit falls below £7,000, the deficiency should be made up equally by the other two partners, Stag should introduce capital of £2,000.

Goodwill should be calculated by using the 'super profit' method and the following estimates:

1. A fair charge for the management services provided by Bull and Bear is £12,000 per annum.

2. That a rate of return of 12 per cent per annum on the tangible assets can be expected.

3. That the required rate of return on the 'super profits' is 16 per cent per annum.

Goodwill should not be recorded on the books and the necessary payments for goodwill should be made outside the partnership.

Required:

(a) A statement showing the required payments for goodwill.
(b) The profit and loss appropriation account for 19X3 based on the assumption that the profit will be the same as in 19X2.
(c) A report comparing the present positions of each of the three parties with that which would exist if the proposed changes were implemented.

4.6 P, Q, R and S were in partnership, sharing profits and losses in the ratio 4:3:2:1. They decided to dissolve the partnership on 31 December 19X3 at which date the balance sheet of the partnership was as follows:

	£	£		£
Capital accounts			Goodwill	2,000
P	6,000		Land and	
Q	3,000		buildings	11,000
R	6,000		Inventory	2,000
S	2,000	17,000	Debtors	4,000
Creditors		3,000	Balance at bank	1,000
		£20,000		£20,000

The assets were realized as follows:

		£
Jan 5	Inventory	1,800
8	Debtors (part)	1,600
Feb 2	Goodwill	600
2	Land and buildings (part)	2,200
Mar 1	Debtors (balance)	2,000
1	Land and buildings (balance)	12,000

The partners decided that, as soon as the creditors were paid, any cash received should be immediately distributed to the partners.

All the creditors were paid on 11 January, after deducting cash discounts of £200. On 1 March it was decided that the remaining debts were irrecoverable and that the dissolution should be considered as being completed.

Required
Prepare a schedule setting out the payments that could be made to the partners subject to the proviso that there should be no possibility that any of the partners would be called upon to repay any cash. Realization expenses should be ignored.

(At each distribution, assume that the remaining assets will be valueless and, if necessary, apply the Garner *v* Murray rule).

4.7 Bryn and Dai are in partnership as general traders. They do not have an office and operate from a room in Bryn's house. Bryn charges the partnership £600 per year for the use of the room and both partners charge 70 per cent of their telephone bills and 90 per cent of their car expenses to the partnership. Bryn and Dai have not got a partnership agreement and their profit or loss sharing arrangements are governed by the appropriate provisions of the Partnership Act, 1890.

The balance sheet of the partnership as at 31 December 19X8 was as follows:

Balance Sheet as at 31 December 19X8

	Capital accounts	*Current accounts*	
	£	£	£
Bryn	1,000	(532)	468
Dai	1,000	(215)	785
	£2,000	£(747)	1,253
Partner's loan account – Bryn			2,000
			£3,253

Fixed assets		
Fixtures and fittings at cost	600	
less Accumulated depreciation	200	400

Current assets	
Trade debtors	2,420
Balance at bank	1,276
	3,696

Less Current liabilities
   Trade creditors   843   2,853

                                             £3,253

Early in 19X9 Bryn and Dai received an offer which they judged to be too good to refuse, but it involved a heavy cash outlay. Bryn and Dai did not have enough cash or an agreeable bank manager so they approached Jeremy with a proposal that they should establish a joint venture to take advantage of the opportunity. Jeremy agreed and the venture was established on the following terms:

(a) Jeremy would provide £4,000 and receive interest at 15 per cent per annum on this amount.
(b) Each party would receive a commission of 10 per cent of the selling price on the sales made by themselves.
(c) Bryn and Dai would charge the joint venture with £200 for administration expenses.
(d) Profits or losses should be shared:
    Jeremy 30 per cent, Bryn and Dai 70 per cent.

During 19X9 Bryn and Dai made the following sales and purchases:

		£
Sales	– joint venture	3,500
	– on their own account	20,234
Purchases	– joint venture	4,600
	– on their own account	11,304

A summary of Bryn and Dai's cash book for 19X9 is as follows:

	£		£
Opening balance	1,276	Suppliers	15,824
Jeremy	4,000	Sundry expenses	
Customers	22,561	– for joint venture	264
		– for partnership	4,321
		Drawings – Bryn	3,729
Closing balance	252	– Dai	3,951
	£28,089		£28,089

The above payments do not include any payments to the partners other than drawings.

The partners received Jeremy's cheque on 1 March 19X9.

It was agreed that the joint venture should be terminated on 31 December 19X9. Goods costing £400 purchased for the venture were unsold and Bryn and Dai took them over at cost. The partners had no other goods in stock at the year end.

Jeremy's sales of joint venture goods amounted to £2,800 and he incurred sundry expenses of £216 on behalf of the venture.

Bryn and Dai's telephone and car expenses for 19X9 were:

	Bryn	Dai
	£	£
Telephone	120	80
Car	360	420

Depreciation on the partnership's fixtures and fittings should be provided at 10 per cent on cost.

Required:

(a) The joint venture account in the books of Bryn and Dai.
(b) The memorandum joint venture account.
(c) Bryn and Dai's current accounts for the year ended 31 December 19X9.
(d) Bryn and Dai's trading and profit and loss account for the year ended 31 December 19X9 and their balance sheet as at that date.

Appendix to Section A

This appendix deals with examination technique and can be safely ignored by those fortunate readers who do not have to concern themselves with such horrors as examinations.

In the first volume we introduced readers to the 'worksheet' approach to the preparation of financial statements – a method that closely approximates to the methods that are used in the real world. However, unfortunately and surprisingly, the examinations of the professional accounting bodies (and of the academic bodies, come to that) do not usually test candidates in the use of worksheets. Instead, mainly because of the severe time constraints experienced at such times, candidates are forced to use certain artificial methods when answering questions that call for the preparation of financial statements from a trial balance and a list of adjustments. This seems to be an appropriate point for us to introduce readers to this problem and suggest techniques which may be of help in examinations. We would emphasize that each student should develop his own approach – practice is essential – and that the methods shown in the following example should be viewed in this light.

Probably the quickest way of doing the standard examination question is to make maximum use of the question paper by using the trial balance, provided as part of the question, as the basis of a worksheet. There are, however, two great difficulties. Some examination bodies use such small paper sizes and print that it would require a practised miniaturist to insert figures on the face of the question. A more general and significant difficulty is that all examiners require that 'full workings should be submitted' and all sensible candidates want to ensure that examiners get them. Now, since it is not the practice in the United Kingdom to return the question papers with the examination scripts, a candidate who does most of his workings on the question paper is putting himself at a considerable disadvantage. The answer, as usual, is to compromise; so candidates who make use of the question paper should also include sufficient workings with their scripts. But what is sufficient?

                                         Foundation in Accounting

Credit is given in examinations for using the correct method even if there has been, say, an arithmetical error in working out the answer. Thus examiners want to see how the figures in the answer have been found, so that, if there is an error, they can judge its importance and decide whether they can give any credit for using the correct method. So the answer to the above question is that the workings should be such as to demonstrate that the correct method has been used.

Now all this should be so obvious as not to be worth saying, but we are continually surprised by the number of examination candidates who fail to do themselves justice because they omit to submit their workings. It is particularly galling to have to fail a marginal candidate when one suspects that he did use the right methods but just failed to show them. Remember that examiners, in general, prefer to pass people.

The following trial balance as at 31 December 19X4 was taken from the ledger of L and M. L and M partners who share profit and losses in the ratio of 2:1 after charging salaries of £4,000 to L and £3,000 to M.

	Debit £	Credit £
Balance at bank	1,200	
Capital accounts		
L		10,000
M		8,000
Current accounts		
L		3,000
M		2,000
Drawings accounts		
L	3,500	
M	2,800	
Electricity	3,000	
Freehold land	18,700	
Insurance	800	
Purchases	83,000	
Purchase ledger control account	500	6,500
Rates	5,000	
Sales		126,000
Sales ledger control account	10,000	
Inventory, 1 Jan 19X4	5,000	
Sundry expenses	1,000	
Sundry fixed assets, at cost	16,000	
Accumulated depreciation at 1 Jan 19X4		12,000
Wages	17,000	
	£167,500	£167,500

The following information is relevant:

1. Depreciation for the year on the sundry fixed assets is to be provided at 20 per cent on the reducing balance (adjustment (a) on the following trial balance). No depreciation is to be provided on the freehold land.

2. At 31 December 19X4 £400 was owed for electricity (b) and wages due amounted to £900 (c).

3. At 31 December 19X4 rates had been prepaid in the amount of £700 (d) and the insurance prepaid was £300 (e).

4. Inventory, at cost, at 31 December 19X4 was £7,000 (f).

Required:
L and M's trading, profit and loss, and profit and loss appropriation accounts for the year ended on 31 December 19X4 and their balance sheet as at that date.

The first thing to do, even if you are short of time, is to read the question carefully. Some people like to glance through the question first to get some idea about the scope before reading it properly the second time.

The second step is to carry out the necessary adjustments. The adjustments can be done on the face of the trial balance as shown below, and as each adjustment is done the relevant paragraph of the additional information can be ticked. Note that it will probably be necessary to add captions below the original trial balance totals as shown below. Some people find it helpful to mark each item on the trial balance to indicate whether it is a trading account (T), a profit and loss account (P) or a balance sheet (B) item.

If the above is done, the trial balance section of the question paper will appear as follows:

		Debit £	*Credit* £
B	Balance at bank	1,200	
B	Capital accounts		
	L		10,000
	M		8,000
B	Current accounts		
	L		3,000
	M		2,000
B	Drawings accounts		
	L	3,500	
	M	2,800	
	c/f	7,500	23,000

		Debit £	Credit £
	b/f	7,500	23,000
P	Electricity	{ +400 *(b)* 3,000	
B	Freehold land	18,700	
P	Insurance	{ −300 *(e)* 800	
T	Purchases	83,000	
B	Purchase ledger control account	{ −500 *(g)* 500	6,500
P	Rates	{ −700 *(d)* 5,000	
T	Sales		126,000
B	Sales ledger control account	{ +500 *(g)* 10,000	
B + T	Inventory, 1 Jan 19X4	{ +7,000 *(f)* 5,000	+7,000 *(f)*
P	Sundry expenses	1,000	
B	Sundry fixed assets, at cost	16,000	
B	Accumulated depreciation at 1 Jan 19X4		{ +800 *(a)* 12,000
P	Wages	{ +900 *(c)* 17,000	
		£167,500	£167,500
P	Depreciation expenses 20 per cent of £4,000	800 *(a)*	
B	Accrued expenses		{ 400 *(b)* 900 *(c)*
B	Prepaid expenses	{ 700 *(d)* 300 *(e)*	

Most of the above adjustments should be self-evident but we would draw our readers' attention to our treatment of the debit balances on the purchase ledger. These debit balances should not, for balance sheet purposes, be deducted from the credit balances on the purchase ledger but, instead, should be added to the debit balances on the sales ledger. This is an example of an adjustment which the examiner does not thrust into the face of the candidate but leaves him to see that it is needed. Another popular example of this is to have a line in the trial balance at 31 December saying, for instance, loan interest to 30 June so that if the loan was still outstanding after 30 June, the candidate has to recognize that loan interest has to be accrued.

We will now present the answer, and indicate the amount of working which a candidate would be advised to show.

L and M
Trading, Profit and Loss, and Profit and Loss Appropriation Accounts for the Year Ended 31 December 19X4

	£	£	£
Sales			126,000
less Inventory, 1 Jan 19X4		5,000	
Purchases		83,000	
		88,000	
less Inventory, 31 Dec 19X4		7,000	81,000
Gross profit			45,000
less Wages (£17,000 + £900)		17,900	
Electricity (£3,000 + £400)		3,400	
Insurance (£800 − £300)		500	
Rates (£5,000 − £700)		4,300	
Depreciation 20 per cent of (£16,000−£12,000)		800	
Sundry expenses		1,000	27,900
Net profit			17,100
Salaries			
L	4,000		
M	3,000	7,000	
Share of balance			
L ($\frac{2}{3}$)	6,733		
M ($\frac{1}{3}$)	3,367	10,100	£17,100

Balance Sheet as at 31 December 19X4

	Cost	Accumulated depreciation	Net book value
	£	£	£
Fixed assets			
Freehold land	18,700	—	18,700
Sundries	16,000	12,800	3,200
	£34,700	£12,800	£21,900
Current assets			
Inventory		7,000	
Trade debtors (£10,000 + £500)		10,500	
Prepaid expenses (£700 + £300)		1,000	
Balance at Bank		1,200	
c/f		19,700	21,900

	£	£	£
b/f		19,700	21,900
less Current liabilities			
Trade creditors	6,500		
Accrued expenses (£400 + £900)	1,300	7,800	11,900
			£33,800

	Capital accounts £	*Current accounts* £	
L	10,000	10,233	20,233
M	8,000	5,567	13,567
	£18,000	15,800	£33,800

Workings
Current accounts

	L £	M £		L £	M £
Drawings	3,500	2,800	Opening balances	3,000	2,000
Closing balances	10,233	5,567	Salaries	4,000	3,000
			Share of profit	6,733	3,367
	£13,733	£8,367		£13,733	£8,367

Some might argue that we have shown too much by way of workings on the face of the profit and loss account and balance sheet, and that it would be better to use more notes, e.g. to show the prepaid expenses as follows:

	£
Rates	700
Insurance	300
	£1,000

We agree that our treatment does not result in a pretty set of financial statements, and that candidates using it may lose some marks for presentation. However, our method is a quick and convenient way of showing the workings. The current accounts are a very important step in this type of question and we have therefore dealt with them fully in our workings. The share of profit in our example was not exactly divisible by three. This often happens and candidates should not be unduly alarmed if they find this occurring in their solutions. In fact we would go further and say that candidates should not necessarily be too upset if their balance sheet does not balance for, generally, few marks are lost for arithmetical errors. The worst thing to do is to spend valuable time looking for the reason for the difference. If your balance sheet does not balance and you do not feel that you have made an error of principle, move on and then, only if you have time at the end of the examination, go back to check your arithmetic.

The last step that you should take if you want to be proficient at this type of question is the most important one. Practice.

SECTION B

5 | *Limited Companies—1*

In Chapter 1 we introduced readers to limited companies, traced their historical development and described how they differ from partnerships and sole traders. In this chapter we shall deal with the question of accounting for limited companies.

The first thing to stress is that the basic features of a limited company balance sheet and profit and loss account are the same as those of any other form of entity. In the balance sheet the treatment of assets and liabilities is basically the same but, of course, the particular nature of limited companies calls for changes in the owners' equity section. Similarly, in the profit and loss account the principal differences are found in the appropriation account – that part of the profit and loss account which shows how the profit or loss for the period has been divided. However, one important difference which must concern us is the legal requirement that limited companies must publish their accounts. The relevant legislation specifies certain information which must be included in the published financial statements of a limited company.

We will start by considering the special nature of limited companies and deal with the problems of the form and content of the published accounts in Chapter 7.

The main statutes concerning limited companies are the Companies Acts 1948, 1967, 1976, 1980 and 1981. These Acts are also concerned with other sorts of companies – unlimited companies and companies limited by guarantee. Such companies are comparatively rare, and we will use this convenient excuse to ignore them (under the Companies Act 1980, no new companies limited by guarantee having a share capital can be formed). We shall confine our attention to the normal type of limited company, *companies limited by shares*, which is usually what is meant when people talk of 'limited companies'.

Although this is not a legal textbook it is necessary for us to introduce the reader to some company law.

Formation of Limited Companies

A limited company is formed by a minimum of two people registering the company by lodging certain documents with the Registrar of Companies and by the payment of the necessary fees. Of these documents the most important are the Memorandum and Articles of Association.

The Memorandum is concerned with the relationship between the company and the outside world. It must contain five clauses which are:

1. The name of the company.

   The name of a public company must end with the words 'public limited company' or the abbreviation 'p.l.c.' while the names of private companies must end with 'limited' or 'ltd'. Companies registered in Wales may choose to use the Welsh language in which case the names must end with 'cwmni cyfyngedig cyhoeddus' or 'c.c.c.' for public companies or 'cyfyngedig' or 'cyf' for private companies. However, in order not to mislead the English, a Welsh public company which exercises the right to use the Welsh language must state in English the fact that it is a public limited company in all official publications, including its note-papers and in notices which must be conspicuously displayed in every place where it carries on its business.

   The difference between a public and private company is explained on page 135.

2. The country of domicile, England, Wales or Scotland, depending on the country in which the registered office is situated. English and Welsh companies deal with the Registrar of Companies situated in Cardiff, while Scottish companies deal with his counterpart, also called the Registrar of Companies, in Edinburgh.

3. The objects of the company.

   The objects clause is very important because of the concept of *ultra vires*. A limited company only has the capacity to engage in activities that are covered by its objects clause and it has no legal right to act beyond them. Any action not allowed by the objects clause is *ultra vires* (beyond the powers granted to the Company). Any contracts made by a company in connection with an activity that is *ultra vires* are void, and this seriously affects the position of other parties to the contract.* To counter the difficulties caused by this concept, most objects clauses cover a wide range of activities.

4. A statement that the liability of members is limited.

---

* The *ultra vires* doctrine is the subject of the first directive of the EEC (see page 000) which prohibits the application of the doctrine to contracts entered into, in good faith, by a third party. This directive has been accepted by the United Kingdom government and, hence, it overrides British law.

5. The amount of the share capital, (known as the authorized share capital) divided into shares of a fixed amount. It should be noted that the company does not have to issue the whole of its authorized share capital, but that this amount represents the maximum amount that can be issued without the need to change the memorandum and, in certain cases, pay additional fees.

The contents of the memorandum can be changed with varying degrees of difficulty except that, for some reason, no change can be made in the country of domicile.

The Articles of Association are the rules which govern the internal relationships of the company. They deal with such matters as the voting rights of shareholders, and the powers and duties of directors. The Companies Act, 1948, contains a schedule which is a model set of articles known as Table A. The persons forming the limited company need not actually register articles of their own. If they do not do so the articles contained in Table A will apply to that company.

Once the Registrar of Companies has received the memorandum, articles, the other necessary documents and, of course, the required fees, he can issue the necessary certificates and the company is born.

The Nature of Shares and Limited Liability

The memorandum must specify the share capital of the limited company and this must be divided into shares of fixed amount. We will now discuss the meaning of this provision.

Let us consider a company with an authorized share capital of £1,000 divided into 2,000 shares of 50 pence each. Fifty pence is the *nominal* or *par* value of each share. This means little more than that the ownership of the company is potentially divisible into 2,000 parts or shares. As mentioned above, a company does not have to issue all its authorized shares; thus the number of shares issued may range from two (since the minimum number of members of a limited company is two) to 2,000.

The reader may well be wondering why we have not, so far, mentioned the monetary values; the answer is that, in general, they do not mean very much. A company issues (or sells) shares in exchange for cash or some other consideration. It need not issue its shares at the nominal value, in our example, 50 pence. The company can always issue them for more than 50 pence, i.e. at a premium. So, for example, had our company issued 1,000 shares there is no reason to suppose that the amount of capital subscribed by its owners was £500. In all probability it would have been more, since it is common practice to issue shares at a premium but rare to issue them at a discount*.

Shares may be *partly paid*. This means that the shareholders can be called upon to pay the necessary amounts to make them fully paid. In

---

* Under the Companies Act 1980 firms cannot now issue shares at a discount. Prior to the Act firms could under certain restricted circumstances, issue shares at a discount.

practice, however, virtually all shares are fully paid – other than during the course of their issue (see page 140) and in such cases the shareholders will have no additional liability. (Note that the phrase 'limited liability' refers to the shareholders rather than to the company which is always fully liable for its debts.) So if a company goes into liquidation and is unable to pay off all its debts its creditors cannot, if the shares are fully paid, look to the owners for recompense out of their private assets. This is, of course, one of the principal differences between limited companies and partnerships and sole traders.

Private and Public Companies

The Companies Act 1980 distinguishes two types of limited companies – public and private. A public company is one which:

(a) in its memorandum states that it is to be a public company
(b) has a minimum allotted share capital of £50,000, of which at least one-quarter of the nominal value of the allotted shares and the whole of any premium is paid up. A public company cannot do business until the Registrar of Companies certifies that the company has complied with the capital requirements.

A private company is a company which is not a public company. The only significant restriction imposed on private companies is that it is an offence to offer its shares or debentures to the public. The Companies Act 1980 specifies certain requirements for changing from private status to public, and vice versa.

Listed and Unlisted Companies

This distinction does not come from the law but depends on whether the shares of a company are traded on the Stock Exchange, i.e. are listed. Because of the restriction on the offering of its shares and debentures to the public, private companies cannot be listed companies. Consequently all listed companies must be public companies. However, the converse does not hold, and only a minority of public companies are listed.

The Stock Exchange has certain rules about the information that must be included in the accounts of companies whose shares are listed and we will deal with these in Chapter 7.

One may also see in published accounts a statement that the company is, or is not, a *close* company. This distinction flows from tax law and need not concern us here.

Dividends

Dividends are the means by which the company distributes profits to the shareholders. The rules governing the payment of dividends will be found in the company's articles. The following brief description is based on the provisions of Table A but even if the company has registered its own articles they will usually follow the same lines.

Article 115 of Table A states 'The directors may from time to time pay to the members such interim dividends as appear to the directors to be justified by the profits of the company'. The wording is interesting in that it suggests that the directors are paying the interim dividends out of their own pockets. The important thing is that the directors have the power to make interim distributions. Some companies, especially those listed on the Stock Exchange, pay one interim divided per year. The final dividend is declared by the company, that is by the members at the company's Annual General Meeting, but the amount is decided by the directors. Article 114 of Table A states 'The company in general meeting may declare dividends, but no dividend shall exceed the amount recommended by the directors'. Thus the members can reduce the proposed amount of the final dividend but cannot increase it.

The fact that the final dividend is declared at a general meeting (usually the annual meeting) is the reason why most published sets of accounts contain the phrase 'proposed dividend', the accounts being sent to members prior to the meeting.

Dividends are sometimes expressed as a percentage of the nominal value of the shares. This is, in many ways, an unfortunate practice since the nominal value of the share is not a meaningful figure. This is especially so when a company has been established for some time and the current value of the shares is far in excess of the nominal value. Thus a dividend, which offers only a modest return based on the current value of the share, may, when expressed as a percentage of the nominal value, appear to be very large. This can, and does, give rise to confusion. A more sensible practice, which is now adopted by many companies, is to express the dividend as so many pence per share.

Different Types of Share Capital

A company can have more than one type of share. They differ in their voting rights, in the priority in the payment of dividends, and in the return of capital on the liquidation of the company. Essentially, the types differ in the trade-off they offer between risk and return. The safer the return, the smaller the maximum amount of the dividend.

The voting, rights, etc., attaching to the various classes of share vary from company to company, and depend mainly on the contents of the articles.

In descending order of safety the different types of shares may be classified as follows:

Preference
Ordinary
Deferred.

Preference Shares

The shares are described as, say, 10 per cent £1 preference shares, the £1 being the nominal value and 10 per cent (of £1) being the maximum dividend payable on the shares. The preference shareholders have first priority in the dividend stakes, but they are not guaranteed a dividend. However, if the preference shareholders do not receive the maximum dividend, no other class of shareholder can receive a dividend. Usually the preference shareholders also receive priority when the company is wound up, but this has to be provided for in the company's articles or memorandum.

Example 5.1

The following is the balance sheet of Fell Limited just before liquidation.

	£		£
8 per cent Preference shares of £1 each	10,000	Sundry assets	50,000
Ordinary shares of £1 each	20,000		
	30,000		
Undistributed profits	8,000		
	38,000		
Sundry creditors	12,000		
	£50,000		£50,000

(a) Assume that the assets only realize £24,000. Then the creditors will be paid, leaving £12,000 for the shareholders. Assuming that they receive preference in a winding up, the preference shareholders will get their capital of £10,000 repaid in full leaving only £2,000 to be divided between the unfortunate ordinary shareholders.

(b) Now assume that the assets realized £48,000. Both classes of shareholders will have their capital returned. The position is:

	£	£
From the disposal of the assets		48,000
less Repayment of creditors	12,000	
Return of capital		
Preference shareholders	10,000	
Ordinary shareholders	20,000	42,000
Surplus		£ 6,000

Usually the whole of the surplus of £6,000 would go to the ordinary shareholders. However, the articles on the terms of the issue of the shares might allow the preference shareholders to receive a part of the surplus.

Preference shares are usually *cumulative*, that is, unpaid preference dividends from prior years must be paid before the other shareholders can be paid a dividend. With *non-cumulative* preference shares, each year is taken on its own and the non-payment (or passing) of a preference dividend in one year would have no effect on subsequent years. Preference shares are assumed to be cumulative unless the contrary is stated.

Participating preference shares are a rare breed. They enable their holders to receive, in certain circumstances, an additional dividend in excess of the stated return; this could happen when the dividend paid to the ordinary shareholders exceeds a specified amount.

A company can issue two or more classes of preference shares such that they are ranked in order of priority for the payment of dividend and repayment of capital.

Preference shares usually do not have any voting rights, but they sometimes gain such if their dividends fall into arrears.

Ordinary Shares

While a company need not have preference shares it must have ordinary shares. Ordinary shareholders are not entitled to a fixed dividend but are entitled to all the profits after the payment of any preference dividends. However, in practice, companies generally do not pay out the whole of their profits by way of dividends.

If profits are low, the preference shareholders may get their dividend, while the ordinary shareholders get nothing, but, if the profits are high, the preference shareholders would receive no more than the agreed dividend while the ordinary shareholders could be rewarded for the extra risks they carry. On liquidation the ordinary shareholders come last but they are usually entitled to the whole of any surplus on liquidation.

The ordinary shareholders are the effective owners of the company and they usually have voting rights which are in proportion to the number of shares held. Some companies have non-voting ordinary shares which are often called A ordinary shares. This device allows the original owners of the company to issue ordinary shares while retaining control of the company through their ownership of the original, voting shares.

The use of non-voting shares has been much attacked in recent years and it is possible that future company legislation will abolish them.

Ordinary shares are sometimes divided into preferred and deferred ordinary shares, the former having most of the characteristics of preference shares.

If shares are simply described as 'shares' without the adornment of any qualification they are ordinary shares.

Deferred Shares

Much of what was said above about ordinary shares changes if the company has deferred shares; however, this type of share is rare nowadays. Deferred shares rank after ordinary shares which means that some limit has to be put on the dividend paid to ordinary shareholders.

Deferred shares are sometimes called founders' or management shares, and as suggested by the alternative title they were commonly issued to the founders of the company. They can carry substantial voting rights and are another way by which the founders can retain control of the company.

Redeemable Shares

Shares may be *redeemable*, in which case the company, according to the terms under which they were issued, can repay the shareholders thus cancelling the shares. Prior to the Companies Act 1981 only preference shares could be redeemable but now all types of shares can be issued as redeemable shares. We shall discuss later, in the section on capital redemption reserves, the steps that have to be taken when shares are redeemed.

Stock

A company can convert the fully paid shares into stock, e.g. a share capital consisting of 5,000 ordinary shares of £1 each can be converted into £5,000 stock. It makes very little difference. Theoretically there is the difference that shares can only be transferred from one person to another in whole units while stock can be transferred in fractional amounts, e.g. £17·13. However, most companies will only allow transfers of stock to be made in pound units. There were certain technical advantages in converting shares into stock before the passage of the Companies Act, 1948, which is why the reader will find that many companies have capital stock, though it is doubtful whether any company would now bother to convert shares into stock.

Shares of No Par Value

As has been explained above, the nominal value of shares serve no real purpose and, indeed, can be misleading. It is possible to have shares of no par value, and these are found in the United States. Unfortunately, although it has been suggested that they be introduced in the United Kingdom the suggestions have not been put into effect, and so the shares of British companies must have a par or nominal value. Future company legislation may change this.

The Balance Sheets of Limited Companies

It will be useful at this stage to consider the owners' equity section of the balance sheet of a limited company. A simple version is outlined in Example 5.2.

Example 5.2

	£	£
Share capital:		
Authorized		
10,000 (11 per cent) £1 Preference shares	10,000	
400,000 Ordinary shares of 25 pence	100,000	
	£110,000	
Issued and fully paid		
4,000 (11 per cent) £1 Preference shares		4,000
200,000 Ordinary shares of 25 pence		50,000
		54,000
Share premium account		12,000
Retained earnings		86,000
		£152,000

Notes
1.   The Companies Acts require that the amount of the authorized share capital be shown.
2.   The share premium account represents the difference between the sums received from the issue of shares and their nominal value and, under the terms of the Companies Acts, must be shown separately on the balance sheet. The share premium account will be discussed in more detail later.
3.   Retained earnings is the difference between the total profits made by the company from its formation less the dividends it has paid. Other phrases that may be found to describe the same thing are unappropriated profits or profit and loss account.

Accounting for the Issue of Shares

Shares can be issued in return for assets other than cash but in this section we shall concentrate on the problem of accounting for an issue made for cash.

To begin at the end: the aim is to increase the asset account and increase the share capital account and, if appropriate, the share premium. If a company issued 100,000 £1 ordinary shares at £1·20 each, the transaction could be recorded by the following journal entry:

| | *Debit* | *Credit* |
	£	£
Cash	120,000	
£1 Ordinary shares		100,000
Share premium account		20,000

However, life is not that simple, and the issue of shares usually calls for somewhat more complex treatment. To understand the book-keeping involved, it is necessary for the reader to know something about the way in which shares are issued. We will confine our explanation to one fairly usual approach. There are a number of variations, but we shall not deal with these now.

1. A general invitation is issued to the public, inviting them to apply for shares at a stated price. Since, in the past, many investors have been misled by issues made by unscrupulous characters, this activity is now subject to a number of legal constraints. One is that the invitation must be accompanied by a statement, known as a *prospectus*, which must give certain specified information about the financial affairs of the company. This is an important document, details of which will have to be mastered by any student of accounting; but we shall, at this stage, pass it by.

2. The potential shareholders may only be required to pay a part of the issue price when they apply for the shares. But, often, the whole amount must be paid on application.

3. If the number of shares applied for exceeds the number on offer, i.e. the issue is oversubscribed, the company will have to decide how the shares should be rationed out. There is no standard method; some

companies do not like having a large number of shareholders with only small holdings, on the grounds of expense. Other companies like to have many shareholders of this type because there is less chance of larger groups coming together and changing the control of the company. As an example, a company which favoured the second approach might decide to satisfy all applications for less than 100 shares and let everyone else have, say, 60 per cent of the number of shares applied for.

4. At this stage the shares are said to be *allotted*. Excess application monies are either repaid or may be kept by the company and set off against the next payment due. The Companies Act 1980 provides that a public limited company cannot allot shares until at least one quarter of the nominal value and the whole of any premium relating to each share has been paid up.

5. The successful shareholders are then asked for the next payment which is the amount due on allotment.

6. There may be additional instalments called *calls*, typically one or two. The whole process may be completed in a couple of months, but it may last for a year or two. In any balance sheet produced during this period the shares would be described as being partly paid.

In order to account for the share issue it is customary to open an application and allotments account and the necessary number of calls accounts.

In the following example, we shall give an illustration of a case in which the share price is payable in instalments. If the terms of the issue were that the whole of the issue price was payable on application the method would be simpler but based on the same principles.

Example 5.3

X Limited decides to issue 200,000 £1 ordinary shares at £1·20 each. The terms of the issue are 30 pence on application, 45 pence (including the premium) on allotment, 20 pence to be called one month after allotment, with the final call of 25 pence being made four months after allotment.

| Date | Transactions | Required journal entries | | |
		Debit	Credit	£
29 May	Applications were received for 300,000 shares	Cash	Applications and allotment	90,000
1 Jun	The shares were allotted so that every applicant received two thirds of the number of shares applied for Excess application monies were held against the amount due on allotment.	Applications and allotment	Ordinary share capital Share premium	110,000 40,000

Date	Transactions	Required journal entries		
		Debit	Credit	£
3 Jun	The cash due on allotment was received.	Cash	Application and allotment	60,000
1 Jul	The first call is made.	First call	Ordinary share capital	40,000
3 Jul	The cash is received.	Cash	First call	40,000
1 Oct	The second call is made.	Second call	Ordinary share capital	50,000
3 Oct	The cash is received.	Cash	Second call	50,000

Ledger Accounts
Application and allotment

		£			£
1 Jun	Ordinary share capital	110,000	29 May	Cash	90,000
1 Jun	Share premium	40,000	3 Jun	Cash	60,000
		£150,000			£150,000

First call

		£			£
1 Jul	Ordinary share capital	40,000	3 Jul	Cash	40,000
		£40,000			£40,000

Second call

		£			£
1 Oct	Ordinary share capital	50,000	3 Oct	Cash	50,000
		£50,000			£50,000

Ordinary share capital

		£
1 Jun	Application and allotment	110,000
1 Jul	First call	40,000
1 Oct	Second call	50,000
		200,000

Share premium

		£
1 Jun	Application and allotment	40,000

Note how in the example the ordinary share capital account and the share premium accounts are built up at the dates the shares are allotted and the calls made.

It might be thought that the use of the call accounts would make the process cumbersome without adding anything useful. However, they do serve a useful purpose since they make it easier to deal with the problem caused by those who fail to pay the required amounts on the due dates.

Suppose someone who was originally allotted 10,000 shares fails to pay the second call, the ordinary share capital would still show a balance of £200,000 but there would be a debit balance of £2,500 on the second call account, representing the sums unpaid on that call. This procedure is preferable to the alternative of showing a balance of £197,500 on the ordinary share capital account, since this would not reflect the fact that the call had been made.

The existence of call accounts also makes it easier to record the generosity of a shareholder who pays calls in advance; the prepayment can be credited to the appropriate call account.

Calls in arrear and advance are presented in the balance sheet as shown below.

	£	£
Issued share capital		
200,000 Ordinary shares of £1 each		
75 pence called	150,000	
less Calls in arrear	12,000	
	138,000	
add Calls in advance	600	138,600
Share premium account		40,000

Forfeited Shares

The articles usually give the directors the right to make forfeit the shares of a shareholder who fails to pay the amounts required. The defaulter would not be refunded the amounts which he has already paid. The nominal value of the shares would be transferred to the credit of a *forfeited shares account*, as would the debit balance on the call accounts and no adjustment would be made to the share premium account. The balance on the forfeited shares account would be shown on the balance sheet after the issued share capital.

Forfeited shares can be reissued, the minimum price being the amount unpaid by the defaulter. If a greater sum is received the excess is credited to the share premium account.

Example 5.4

The facts are as in Example 5.3, except that the second call is not paid on 10,000 shares. The shares are made forfeit on 1 December and are reissued, at 60 pence per share, on 1

March of the following year. The ledger accounts, in which the balances have been brought down as at 31 December (the year end) are as follows.

Second call

		£			£
1 Oct	Ordinary share capital	50,000	3 Oct	Cash	47,500
			1 Dec	Forfeited shares	2,500
		£50,000			£50,000

Ordinary share capital

		£			£
1 Dec	Forfeited shares	10,000	1 Jun	Application and allotment	110,000
31 Dec	Balance c/d	190,000	1 Jul	First call	40,000
			1 Oct	Second call	50,000
		£200,000			£200,000
			1 Jan	Balance c/d	190,000
			1 Mar	Forfeited shares	10,000

Forfeited shares

		£			£
1 Dec	Second call	2,500	1 Dec	Ordinary share capital	10,000
31 Dec	Balance c/d	7,500			
		£10,000			£10,000
1 Mar	Ordinary share capital	10,000	1 Jan	Balance b/d	7,500
1 Mar	Share premium	3,500	1 Mar	Cash	6,000
		£13,500			£13,500

Share premium

		£			£
31 Dec	Balance c/d	40,000	1 Jun	Application and allotment	40,000
		£40,000			£30,000
			1 Jan	Balance b/d	40,000
			1 Mar	Forfeited shares	3,500

Convertible Loan Stocks

These have the characteristics of both long-term loans and ordinary shares and they have become an increasingly popular method of raising finance since the early 1960s. They are issued in the same manner as loan stocks and a fixed rate of interest is paid on them. However, the loan stock can be converted on certain dates into a specified number of ordinary shares, at the convertible loan stock owner's option.

Suppose that in 1970 A Limited issued £1,000 worth of convertible loan stock on the following terms (written into the trust deed*):

1. The interest rate is 10 per cent paid annually.

2. The loan stock can be converted at the rate of 200 ordinary 25p shares for £100 of loan stock, in 1977.

3. If the owner wants to convert, he must do so in July of the particular year (this keeps the administrative expenses lower).

A Limited will debit convertible loan stock account with £1,000 and this will appear as a separate heading in the balance sheet. If, say, £500 worth of loan stock is converted into 1,000 ordinary shares in 1977 then the following journal entry will be required:

	£	£
Convertible loan stock account	500	
Ordinary share capital account		250
Share premium account		250

Convertible stocks are usually listed in the stock market (if the ordinary shares are also listed) and their values are largely related to the price of the corresponding ordinary shares. Readers who are interested in the valuation of convertible loan stocks and their use in company financing should consult a financial management text such as Van Horne's *Financial Management and Policy* or Samuels and Wilkes, *Management of Company Finance*.

Longer-term Liabilities

By longer-term liabilities we mean those liabilities that are not due for repayment within a year of the balance sheet date – non-current liabilities. These liabilities are often called *loan capital* since they are capital in the sense that they are a source of assets. However, they must be distinguished from share capital. The suppliers of the loan capital are not members of the company and do not share in its ownership. They are rewarded by the payment of *interest* while shareholders receive dividends. If the creditors are not paid their interest at the due date they can take action which could lead to the liquidation of the company. Such powers should be contrasted with the position of, say, preference shareholders who can only curse, or possibly vote out the directors, if they do not receive their dividends.

Limited companies usually obtain their longer-term liabilities by the issue of *debenture stock*. The *debenture* itself is simply a written acknowledgement of a debt; generally, it contains provisions concerning the rate of

*A trust deed is a document which states the terms on which the issue of the stock is made.

interest, the dates of payment of the interest and repayment of the loan. The stock part of the title comes from the fact that the debt is arranged in such a way that the rights attaching to it can be easily transferred in fractions from one person to another. For example, suppose Y Limited issues £80,000 of debenture stock of which A acquires £2,000. A can sell the whole or part of his stock to someone else. Debentures* may be listed on the Stock Exchange and the price is usually quoted by jobbers for £100 nominal value of debenture stock.

Debentures are issued in a similar way to shares and the accounting treatment follows the method we described above for the issue of shares.

Debentures are usually secured either as a *fixed charge*, which means that it is secured against a specific asset or assets, or as a *floating charge*, i.e. secured against the general assets of the business. A debenture which is not secured is called a *naked debenture*.

Since the population of debenture holders may be large and constantly changing, it would be difficult, if not impossible, for the debenture holders as a body to exercise their rights in the event of a default. It is therefore usual to appoint trustees (often a bank) to act on their behalf. If the debenture carries a fixed charge, the trustees can, on default, seize the asset, sell it, repay the debenture holders and hand back any surplus cash to the company. If the debenture is floating, the trustees can appoint a receiver, or receiver and manager, who disposes of enough of the company's assets to repay the debenture holders. However, in the latter case the receiver would first have to settle the, so-called, preferential creditors who include employees and the Inland Revenue.

The Burdens Imposed on Limited Liability Companies

As explained in Chapter 1, limited liability companies are the entities through which most of the economic activities of the non-government sector are conducted, and as a result the law takes a much greater interest in the affairs of limited companies than it does in the activities of sole traders and partnerships. The reasons for this were discussed in Chapter 1 but they can be summarized as stewardship and the need to protect and give information to creditors and investors. The burdens imposed on limited liability companies are basically:

1. A public company can only reduce its capital with the permission of the court. A private limited company can reduce its subscribed capital following procedures laid down in the Companies Act, 1981 which affords protection for the interests of preference shareholders and creditors.

2. A company must publish its accounts (although smaller companies are only required to publish a summarized balance sheet).

We shall deal with these separately.

*Strictly we should say debenture stock but most people abbreviate the phrase.

Restrictions on the reduction of subscribed capital

The sources of the owners' equity of a limited company are subscribed capital, the earnings that have not been withdrawn and unrealised surpluses on the revaluation of fixed assets.

Prior to the passing of the Companies Act, 1981 a basic tenet of British Company Law was that a company could only reduce its subscribed capital with the permission of the Court. This remains the position so far as public companies are concerned but private companies are now able, under certain restricted conditions, to reduce their capital.

The purpose of the rule is the protection of creditors and preference shareholders. The main security for loans is the cash flow that will be generated by the assets of the business. For if these prove to be sufficient, loans can be repaid. But, if they are not, the creditors could call for the liquidation of the company, and when the assets are realized the creditors would be repaid in preference to the shareholders, thus providing the creditors with a second line of defence. Thus the higher the proportion of subscribed share capital in the total sources of finance, the safer is the creditor. We will illustrate this in Example 5.5.

Example 5.5

Suppose, for simplicity, that FM Limited, a public company, has only one form of asset which, at the moment, produces a return of 10 per cent per annum.

FM Limited's balance sheet is as follows:

	£		£
Issued share capital	120,000	Sundry assets	300,000
Retained earnings	80,000		
	200,000		
8 per cent Unsecured debentures	100,000		
	£300,000		£300,000

and the expected annual profit and loss account is:

	£
Return on assets	30,000
less Debenture interest	8,000
	£22,000

The debenture holders can feel reasonably safe.

(a)   The return on the assets would have to fall by £22,000, that is by 73 per cent, before it will be insufficient to cover the debenture interest and

(b)   If the company were wound up the debenture holders would be repaid in full even if the assets realized only $33\frac{1}{3}$ per cent of their book value.

However, the position of the debenture holders is not as safe as all that, for the company could sell off enough of its assets to pay the maximum dividend of £80,000 the balance of retained earnings. We will assume that the assets are sold at their book value. The balance sheet and profit and loss account would then be:

	£		£
Issued share capital	120,000	Sundry assets	220,000
8 per cent Unsecured debentures	100,000		
	£220,000		£220,000

	£
Return on assets (10 per cent of £220,000)	22,000
less Debenture interest	8,000
Profit	£14,000

But even if the maximum dividend were paid the debenture holders would be fairly safe. By using the same reasoning as above, the return could fall by 64 per cent and the assets would only need to fetch 45 per cent of their book value.

Now suppose that there was no law saying that a company cannot reduce its subscribed capital. Say, the company purchased and cancelled 80 per cent of its shares, then, again assuming that sufficient assets are realized at their book value, the balance sheet and profit and loss account could appear as follows:

	£		£
Issued share capital	24,000	Sundry assets	124,000
8 per cent Unsecured debentures	100,000		
	£124,000		£124,000

	£
Return on assets	12,400
less Debenture interest	8,000
Profit	£4,400

The debenture holders are now in a much more exposed position. If the return fell by as little as £4,400, (35 per cent) and if the assets could not be disposed of for 81 per cent or more of their book value, the debenture holders would be in trouble.

This rule is an important one from the point of view of company law but it is not, in practice, very successful in protecting creditors, for many companies do go into liquidation without being able to repay their creditors in full. In terms of the above analysis, the reasons for the failure of this form of protection is firstly that subscribed capital often forms only a small part of the sources of funds; indeed many companies have an issued share capital of only a few hundred pounds. Secondly when companies do go bust they often do so in a big way, with the result that the assets only realize a small fraction of their book value.

A further important reason for the failure of the safeguard is that it is not possible to legislate against a company making losses. So a balance sheet with features such as the following represents a possible and legal position:

	£
Share capital	200,000
Accumulated losses	(150,000)
	50,000
Debentures	100,000
	£150,000
Sundry assets *less* Liabilities	£150,000

The Companies Act, 1980 does provide some protection for those concerned with public companies in that Section 34 requires that directors of a public company must convene an extraordinary general meeting of the company if they become aware that the net assets are one half or less of the amount of the called up share capital. The meeting is for the purpose of considering what measures can and ought to be taken and will clearly act as a warning to creditors and potential creditors.

An important consequence of the restriction on the reduction of subscribed capital is that dividends can only be paid out of profits.

Profits Available for Dividend

Since dividends can only be paid out of profits, the question of what constitutes profit has to be considered. Until the Companies Act 1980, the definition of profits available for dividend was based on a number of leading legal cases and this produced some unsatisfactory and doubtful results. Section 39 of the Companies Act 1980 defined profits available for distribution as "its accumulated, realised profits, so far as previously not utilised by distribution or capitalisation, less its accumulated realised losses, so far as not previously written off". This definition precludes a company from paying dividends out of current profits without making good losses of previous years. Prior to the passing of the 1980 Act, a dividend could be paid without making good accumulated losses – this follows the decision in *Ammonia Soda Co. Ltd.* v *Chamberlain* (1918). The available profits also have to be realized and thus dividends cannot be paid out of unrealized profits arising on fixed asset revaluations (dividends can, however, be paid out of realized capital profits). In addition to complying with Section 39 of the Companies Act 1980, a public company must not make a dividend distribution if this would reduce its net assets below the aggregate of its called up share capital and undistributable reserves (Section 40, Companies Act 1980). This effectively means that, for public companies only, any excess of unrealized losses over unrealized profits on the revaluation of fixed assets reduces the amount available for distribution. Undistributable reserves are made up of the share premium account, the capital redemption reserve fund, unrealized profits (less unrealized losses unless previously written off), and any other reserve which the company is prohibited from distributing by statute or by its memorandum or articles.

If a company (public or private) wishes to pay an interim dividend which exceeds the amount available based on its last audited annual financial statements it must prepare interim accounts which indicate that sufficient profits are available to justify the dividend. In the case of public companies the interim accounts must be delivered to the Registrar of Companies (Section 43, Companies Act 1980).

While a company can pay a dividend based on realized capital profits, it is important to distinguish between capital profits and trading profits.

If a chain of fish and chip shops sells its fried potatoes for more than they cost to produce, it has earned a trading profit which will be reflected in the profit and loss account. If it makes a profit by selling one of the shops, the profit is termed a capital profit and this will be shown separately in the profit and loss account.

In general, capital profits are those earned on the disposal of fixed assets, but note that we are referring to the profit that comes from selling an asset for more than it cost. We do not mean the writing back to the profit and loss account of excess depreciation charges, even though this is often called a profit on the sale of fixed assets.

The distinction between the two sorts of profit is an important one, because if a company is to survive it needs to be able to make a profit on its normal trading activities. The user of the accounts must be made aware of the distinction if he is to get a clear idea of what went on during the year under review, and the distinction also helps the user to make predictions of future results. For normal trading activities will always go on but capital activities must, by definition, be isolated (if they are not isolated the purchase and sale of 'fixed assets' may be considered part of the normal activities of the company).

We should emphasize that we have been discussing the maximum dividend payable subject to legal constraints. Generally this is not a binding constraint since most companies would not wish to pay the maximum dividend as they would prefer to use part of the cash available for investment. Thus, for the vast majority of companies the problem of determining the maximum dividend is not a matter of great practical importance. The situation may change if in the future, company legislation relates the maximum dividend to profits derived from current cost accounts. As will be explained in Section C the current cost profits of many companies are much lower than their historical cost profits and hence if dividends are related to current cost profits the question of determining the maximum dividend may become a more important issue.

Reserves

A distinction can be made between statutory and non-statutory reserves. Statutory reserves are those which are created by force of law (the Companies Acts, 1948, 1980 and 1981) and result from the restrictions placed on the reduction of subscribed capital.

Statutory Reserves

The Share Premium Account

As we have already explained, the share premium account represents the excess of the sums received from the issue of shares over their nominal value. The source of this reserve is the capital subscribed by the owners, while the source of all the other reserves are gains made by the company.

The issue of shares at a premium is useful because it enables the company to issue shares of a type that is already in existence without harming the position of the existing shareholders. Suppose that A1 Limited has the following balance sheet:

	£	£
Share capital		
Authorised		
100,000 £1 Ordinary shares	£100,000	
Issued and fully paid		
60,000 £1 Ordinary shares		60,000
Reserves		
Retained earnings		20,000
		£80,000
Sundry assets *less* Liabilities		£80,000

Suppose that the market price of A1's shares is £1·50 giving the company a total market value of £90,000, and that A1 wishes to raise £30,000 from the issue of shares.

If the shares were issued at their nominal value of £1, 30,000 shares would have to be issued and the total market value would increase by £30,000 to £120,000. This would give a share value of £1·33 (£120,000 ÷ 90,000). So the new shareholders would gain at the expense of the old ones.

To avoid this, 20,000 shares would be issued at a premium of 50 pence per share and the balance sheet would appear as follows:

	£	£
Share capital		
Authorized		
100,000 £1 Ordinary shares	£100,000	
Issued and fully paid		
80,000 £1 Ordinary shares		80,000

	£	£

Reserves

Share premium account	10,000	
Retained earnings	20,000	30,000
		£110,000

| Sundry assets *less* Liabilities | | £110,000 |

The value of the company would be, as before, £120,000, but since ownership of the company is represented by 80,000 shares the value per share would be £1·50 which would be fair from the point of view of both old and new shareholders.

The share premium account cannot be used as the basis of a dividend because to do so would result in the reduction of subscribed capital. It can, however, be used for a limited number of purposes (Section 56, Companies Act, 1948), i.e.

1. In paying up unissued shares of the company to be issued to the members as fully paid bonus shares (We shall discuss bonus shares a little later).
2. To write off preliminary expenses and the expenses of, or discount allowed on, any issue of shares or debentures of the company. Preliminary expenses are the expenses incurred in the flotation of the company and include such items as legal costs, stamp duties and the cost of printing the various documents.
3. To provide for the premium payable on the redemption of redeemable preference shares or debentures. A premium in this context is where the amounts repaid exceed the nominal value of the securities redeemed, e.g. if a debenture is redeemed at a premium of 10 per cent the holder of £100 of debentures will be repaid £110.

The Companies Act 1981 (Sections 34–39) provides relief from the need to create a share premium account in certain limited circumstances associated with cases where shares are issued in order to acquire another company or as part of the reconstruction of a group of companies (see Chapter 8).

Capital Redemption Reserve

Before 1929 companies could not purchase their own shares. This lack of freedom produced a degree of inflexibility so, in 1929, the law was changed to allow the issue of redeemable preference shares. When the shares are issued the terms of the redemption must be stated, i.e. whether the shares will be redeemed at par or at a (usually small) premium and whether the shares will be redeemed on a stated date or between two stated dates or at any date selected at the company's option. The introduction of this type of share allowed a new or expanding company to raise a substantial amount of cash by the issue of shares but to replace a part of that share capital by retained earnings or borrowings at an appropriate time.

The Companies Act 1981 considerably extended the ability of companies to change their capital structure. Both public and private companies can now issue redeemable shares of all types, including ordinary shares, (Section 45 (1)) and all companies were given the right to purchase their own shares, which need not be redeemable shares, (Section 46 (1)). In either case the company's articles must include a specific provision authorising the action. One important overriding restriction must be noted. To ensure that a company is not left without any shareholders at all, companies cannot issue all their shares as redeemable shares nor can they purchase shares if as a result there would be no shareholders holding shares other than redeemable shares.

Despite these freedoms, public companies are not permitted to reduce their subscribed share capital (other than with the sanction of the Court as part of a scheme for the reconstruction of the company). We will discuss later the steps that have to be taken by a public company in order to ensure that its subscribed capital is not reduced. Private companies have the same rights as public companies in this respect but they can also, in certain circumstances, reduce their capital by purchasing shares 'out of capital'. This topic will be dealt with later.

The Distinction between the Redemption and Purchase of Shares

Only shares which are described as being redeemable can be redeemed and the price that will be paid to the shareholders will be specified when the shares are issued. This will normally be equal to or only a little more than the nominal value. In contrast, all types of shares (including redeemable shares) can be purchased and the price paid will not be specified in advance but will depend on circumstances prevailing at the date of purchase; in the case of listed companies the price will often be the current market price.

Many provisions of the Act apply equally to the redemption and purchase of shares and in order to avoid the continual use of the phrase 'redemption or purchase' we will use the word 'acquisition' when describing provisions which apply to both types of transaction.

Acquisition of its own Shares by Public Companies

A public company must not, without the sanction of the Court, reduce its subscribed capital; thus when a public company acquires its own shares it must do one, or a combination of two things:
1. It can issue shares to replace the nominal value of the shares acquired.
2. Transfer an amount, equal to the nominal value of the shares redeemed, from retained earnings, or any reserve available for dividends, to the credit of an account called the *capital redemption reserve*. This amount is now 'frozen' or capitalized, that is, it is no longer available for dividend. If this alternative is adopted, the shares are said to be redeemed or purchased out of earnings.

If the second alternative is used, subscribed share capital is maintained as the total of the issued share capital (plus any share premium) and the capital redemption reserve following the acquisition will be equal to the share capital (plus any share premium) before the acquisition.

The capital redemption reserve is not available for the payment of a dividend and can only be used to issue bonus shares (Companies Act, 1981 Section 54).

If the shares are redeemed or purchased at a premium, i.e. at a price in excess of their nominal value, the premium must be paid out of the distributable profits of the company unless the shares acquired were originally issued at a premium. In this case the premium payable on acquisition can be paid out of the issue of new shares up to an amount equal to the lower of:

(i)   The premiums received by the company on the issue of the shares subsequently acquired.

(ii) The current balance on the share premium account which can include any premiums received on the issue of the new shares (i.e. the shares issued to support the purchase or redemption).

In other words the increase in the value of the shares during the period they were in issue must, in general, be paid out of the distributable profits of the company. Note that the Act does not require the creation of a capital redemption reserve because the payment represents a distribution of profits to the owners of the acquired shares and is not a reduction in the subscribed capital. However, the amount of the premium which is paid from the issue of shares must be deducted from the share premium account.

The above procedures are illustrated in example 5.6.

Example 5.6

The following is a summary of XYZ Limited's balance sheet as at 31 December 19X9:

	£		£
400 £1 ordinary shares	400	Sundry assets less	
Share Premium Account	200	liabilities	1,600
	600		
Retained Earnings	1,000		
	£1,600		£1,600

Note that all the shares were issued for £1.50 each i.e. at a premium of 50 pence per share.

Assume that the company purchased 100 of its shares for £2.50 each on 31 December 19X9.

Purchase out of Earnings
    There are two stages in the process. The actual purchase will be effected by opening a 'purchase of shares' account to which will be credited the nominal value of the shares purchased and the appropriate transfer from retained earnings. The cash payment will be debited to the 'purchase of shares' account.

In summary the required journal entries are:

	£	£
Ordinary Share Capital Account	100	
Retained Earnings	150	
Purchase of Shares Account		250
Purchase of Shares Account	250	
Cash		250

£100, being equal to the nominal value of the shares purchased, must be transferred from retained earnings to the capital redemption reserve account i.e.

	£	£
Retained Earnings	100	
Capital Redemption Reserve		100

The balance sheet after the purchase would then appear as follows:

	£		£
300 £1 Ordinary Shares	300	Sundry assets	
Share Premium Account	200	*less* liabilities	
Capital Redemption Reserve	100	£(1,600 − 250)	1,350
	600		
Retained Earnings			
£(1,000 − 250)	750		
	£1,350		£1,350

Note that of the total of subscribed capital plus reserves not available for distribution, £600, is maintained.

Purchase out of the Proceeds of an Issue of New Shares

In the above context we will consider two cases, one where the premium on redemption is paid entirely out of earnings and one where maximum use is made of the provisions of Section 45(6) of the Companies Act 1981 whereby part of the premium on acquisition is paid out of the proceeds of the issue.

Premium paid out of earnings

If the need to create a capital redemption reserve is to be avoided, the Act requires that the proceeds of the issue equal the nominal value of the shares acquired (Section 53(2)). If we assume that shares can be issued at the same price, £2.50, as is paid for the shares which are purchased then only 40 shares need be issued to raise £100. In this case the premium on the issued shares will be £1.50 per share.

The journal entry required to record the purchase of the shares is the same as shown in the earlier part of the example.

The following additional entry is required:

	£	£
Cash	100	
Ordinary Share Capital Account		40
Share Premium Account		60

being the issue of 40 £1 Ordinary Shares at a premium of £1.50 per share.

The summarised balance sheet will then be as follows:

340 £1 Ordinary Shares	340	Sundry assets	
Share Premium Account		less liabilities	
£(200 + 60)	260	£(1,600 − 250 + 100)	1,450
	600		
Retained Earnings			
£(1,000 − 150)	850		
	£1,450		£1,450

Premium paid out of the issue of new shares

The total premium received on the issue of the shares subsequently purchased was £50 (100 × £0.50) and since the current balance on the share premium account is greater than £50, the Act allows £50 of the premium payable on the purchase to be paid out of the proceeds of the issue of shares. Thus if the company wishes, for example, to make the minimum reduction in the reserves available for dividends it would issue 60 shares to raise £150. In which case the required journal entries will be as follows:

	£	£
Ordinary Share Capital Account	100	
Retained Earnings	150	
Purchase of Shares Account		250
Purchase of Shares Account	250	
Cash		250

being the purchase of 100 £1 Ordinary Shares at £2.50 per share.

Cash	150	
Ordinary Share Capital Account		60
Share Premium Account		90

being the issue of 60 £1 Ordinary Shares at £2.50 per share.

Share Premium Account	50	
Retained Earnings		50

being that element of the premium on purchase which is financed from the issue of new shares.

The summarised balance sheet reflecting the above adjustments is as follows:

	£		£
Ordinary Share Capital	360	Sundry assets	
Share Premium Account		less liabilities	
£(200 + 90 − 50)	240	£(1,600 − 250 + 150)	1,500
	600		
Retained Earnings			
£(1,000 − 150 + 50)	900		
	£1,500		£1,500

Note that we have considered the extreme cases in this example. If the company had, for example, issued only 30 shares at £2.50 then it would be necessary to transfer

£25, the difference between the nominal value of the shares acquired (£100) and the total proceeds of the fresh issue (£75), to the capital redemption reserve.

Redemption and Purchase of own shares by Private Companies out of Capital

Private companies have the same rights to acquire their own shares as public companies but they have the additional power to acquire shares out of capital (Companies Act 1981, Section 54).

The Act stipulates that the maximum payment (known as the *permissible capital payment*) that may be made out of capital is the amount which added to any available profits of the company and the proceeds of any fresh issue made for the purposes of the purchase or redemption of its own shares is equal to the cost of the acquisition (including any premium). In other words a payment out of capital is only possible when all the distributable reserves of the company have been extinguished.

If the permissible capital payment (plus the proceeds of any issue of shares made for the purposes of acquisition) is less than the nominal value of the shares acquired, the difference must be credited to the capital redemption reserve. If, on the other hand, the permissible capital payment (plus any proceeds from a fresh issue of shares) is greater than the nominal value of the shares acquired, the differences must be debited either to a non-distributable reserve (share premium account, capital redemption reserve account or a revaluation reserve representing unrealised profits on fixed assets) or to the issued share capital.

Example 5.7

Assume that the balance sheet of Handel Limited, a private company, as at 31 December 19X5 can be summarised as follows:

	£		£
Share Capital		Sundry assets	
100 £1 shares	100	less liabilities	310
Share Premium	200		
	300		
Retained Earnings	10		
	£310		£310

(i)   Let us suppose that the company purchases 50 shares for £4 each. The permissible capital payment is then:

Cost of the purchase	200
Less:	
Distributable Reserves	10
Permissible capital payment	£190

The difference between the permissible capital payment (£190) and the nominal value of the shares acquired (£50) is £140 and we will assume that this amount is to be debited to the share premium account.

The balance sheet following the purchase is then as given below:

	Balance sheet before purchase £	Adjustments £	Balance sheet after purchase £
Share capital	100	− 50	50
Share Premium	200	− 140	60
	300		110
Retained Earnings	10	− 10	—
	£310	−£200	£110
Sundry assets less liabilities	£310	−£200	£110

(ii) Let us suppose that the above purchase was supported by the issue of 20 shares at £4 each.

The permissible capital payment is then:

	£	£
Cost of purchase		200
Less:		
Distributable Reserves	10	
Proceeds of new issue	80	90
Permissible capital payment		£110

The permissible capital payment (£110) plus the proceeds of the issue (£80) equals £190. The difference between £190 and the nominal value of the shares acquired (£50) is £140 and this amount must be debited to the issued capital or the non-distributable reserves. This is the same figure as emerged in the first part of the example as the proceeds of the issue are deducted to arrive at the permissible capital payment but the same amount is added to the permissible capital payment to arrive at the amount to be debited to the capital or non-distributable reserves.

The balance sheet reflecting the change is shown below:

	Balance sheet before purchase £	Adjustments £	Balance sheet after purchase £
Share Capital	100	− 50 + 20	70
Share Premium	200	− 140 + 60	120
	300		190
Retained Earnings	10	− 10	—
	£310	−£120	£190
Sundry assets less liabilities	310	− 200 + 80	190
	£310	−£120	£190

(iii) In order to illustrate the situation where the permissible capital payment is greater than the nominal value of the shares acquired we will assume that the 50 shares were purchased for 50 pence each.

The permissible capital payment is then:

	£
Cost of the purchase	25
Less:	
Distributable Reserves	10
Permissible capital payment	£15

Since the permissible capital payment is less than the nominal value of the shares acquired the difference £35 (£50–£15) must be transferred to a capital redemption reserve.

The balance sheet reflecting the change is shown below:

	Balance sheet before purchase £	Adjustments £	Balance sheet after purchase £
Share Capital	100	– 50	50
Share Premium	200		200
Capital Redemption Reserve	—	+ 35	35
	300		285
Retained Earnings	10	– 10	—
	£310	–£25	£285
Sundry assets less liabilities	£310	–£25	£285

Protection afforded to Shareholders on the Purchase by a Company of its own Shares other than out of Capital (Companies Act 1981, Sections 46 to 49)

The Act distinguishes between two types of transactions, *market purchases* where the purchase is made in the normal way on a recognised stock exchange and other types of purchases which are described as *off-market purchases*. In general only public companies whose shares are listed on a recognised stock exchange can make market purchases.

The difference between the two types of transaction is important with regard to the rights and interests of the shareholders. In the case of a market purchase the shares acquired will already be on the market in the hands of jobbers and if an excessively high price is paid all the remaining shareholders will suffer proportionally depending on the size of their holdings. In contrast an element of selectivity will exist in the case of off-market purchases in that the shares of identifiable shareholders will be acquired. Thus, if an excessively high price is paid, the owners of the shares purchased (who may include the directors) will gain at the expense of the remaining shareholders. Thus the Act imposes more onerous conditions on off-market purchases than are applied to market purchases.

Off-Market Purchases

In the case of an off-market purchase the terms of the proposed contract must be approved in advance by a special resolution.* The holders of the shares which are proposed to be purchased may not vote in respect of the shares which are the subject of the resolution.

In the case of a public company the authority for a proposed contract must specify a date on which the authority is to expire.

If a company makes an off-market purchase contract certain details of the purchase must be lodged with the Registrar of Companies where they will be available for public inspection.

Market Purchases

A market purchase cannot be made unless it has first been authorised by the company at a General Meeting. In this case only a simple majority is required. The authority must:

(a) specify the maximum number of shares which can be acquired;
(b) determine both the maximum and minimum prices which may be paid for these shares. The authority may refer to specific sums or may provide a formula for calculating the price which does not depend on any person's discretion or opinion;
(c) specify the date on which the authority is to expire which must not be more than eighteen months after the date on which the resolution was passed.

Protection afforded to Shareholders and Creditors in the case of Payments out of Capital (Companies Act 1981, Sections 55 to 58)

Only private companies are allowed to reduce their subscribed capital by paying more for the shares acquired than is represented by the profits available for distribution. Since this freedom means that the protection which is available to creditors and holders of preference share capital is eroded, the Act imposes very stringent conditions on private companies which reduce their capital. At this stage it is not necessary to recapitulate the relevant provisions of the Act in detail but the main features are summarised below:

1. *Agreement by Shareholders*
   The action must be approved by a special resolution of the company. The holders of the shares which are the subject of the resolution may not participate in the vote in respect of those shares; they may, however, participate in respect of any other shares which they hold.

---

* A special resolution requires that 21 days' notice of the proposal be given and has to receive a majority of at least 75% of the vote.

2. *The Directors must make a 'Statutory Declaration'*
   The statutory declaration is a statement made by the directors that in their opinion:
   (a) the company should, in the period immediately following the payment out of capital, be able to pay its debts, and
   (b) that in the year following the payment the company will be able to carry on its business as a going concern and will be able to pay its debts as they fall due.
   A report of the auditors addressed to the directors must be attached to the statutory declaration. The auditors are required to state that they are not aware of anything which indicates that the opinion expressed by the directors is unreasonable in all the circumstances.

3. *Publicity*
   Within a week of the passing of the special resolution the facts of the resolution must be advertised in the *Gazette* (an official publication), and a national newspaper. As an alternative to the advertisement in a national newspaper notice of the resolution may be given in writing to all the creditors.
   A copy of the statutory declaration and auditors report must be filed with the Registrar of Companies while copies of the documents must be made available at the company's registered office for five weeks for inspection by shareholders and creditors.

4. *Right of appeal to the Court*
   Any creditor and any member (other than those who voted in favour of the resolution) may, within five weeks of the date of the special resolution, ask the Court to cancel the resolution. The Court can adjourn the proceedings to see whether an arrangement can be made which would satisfy the dissentient shareholders or creditors. The Court has the power to cancel or confirm the resolution and if it confirms the resolution it may alter it in respect of such features which are specified in the Act.

5. *Liability of past shareholders and directors where the company is unable to pay its debts.*
   If a company is wound up within a year of the date of a payment out of capital and is unable to pay all its debts, a liability attaches to the former shareholders who received payment and to the directors who signed the statutory declaration. The former shareholders are liable to repay the sum received out of capital while its directors are jointly and severally liable with each of the former shareholders.

The advantages of allowing companies to purchase their own shares

Before returning to the treatment of reserves it might be helpful if we briefly discussed the advantages of allowing companies freedom to purchase their own shares. Readers who wish to study this question in more depth should refer to the Government Discussion Document ("Green Paper")

"The Purchase by a Company of its Own Shares"* This paper was published in 1980 and presages the 1981 Act in respect of the right to purchase shares. A large part of the paper is taken up by a section written by Professor L. C. B. Gower (the Department of Trade's Research Adviser on Company Law) which very clearly set out the options available to the Government and the advantages that had been claimed for the adoption of a more liberal policy with regard to the purchase by companies of their own shares.

The major factors which led the Government to amend the law are summarised in the introduction to the Green Paper (which was the section written by the Department of Trade) which states:

'The Government attaches particular importance to the principal economic arguments in favour of a relaxation of the present law. For private companies, a change should make investment and participation in such companies more attractive, by providing shareholders with a further means of disposing of their shares and by permitting the remaining members to maintain control and ownership of the business. Different considerations apply to companies whose shares are dealt in on a market. Public companies with surplus cash resources could find it useful to be able to buy their own shares and thus return surplus resources to shareholders, thereby removing the pressure on such companies to employ those surplus resources in uneconomic ways, and enabling shareholders to deploy the resources to better effect.'**

It should be noted that the changes made in respect of private companies have given such entities certain advantages which had previously only been available to unincorporated partnerships. A partnership can 'buy out' any of the partners but before the 1981 Act a shareholder could only dispose of his shares by selling them to somebody else. However, the Articles of private companies almost always give the directors the absolute right to refuse the registration of new shareholders. Thus, the sale had to be to someone acceptable to the directors. In practice this often meant that the sale had to be to existing shareholders as directors did not wish to see a share in the ownership of the company being taken by an outsider. The result was that the marketability of the shares was much reduced and the price obtained by an outgoing shareholder was often low compared with the value of the company as a whole.

The Government obviously hopes that the rights granted to private companies will encourage investment in private companies because potential shareholders will believe that it will be easier for them to dispose of their holdings at a reasonable price.

Taxation considerations are also relevant and it must be noted that existing taxation legislation does not encourage the increased flexibility in company organisation which it is hoped will be brought about by the changes

* HMSO, Cmnd 7944
** 'The purchase of a company of its own shares' Cmnd 7944, p. 1.

in the Companies Act, 1981. However, a review of tax legislation was promised in the Green Paper and it is likely there will be changes in tax legislation in the future.

Unrealized Profits

Accumulated unrealized profits (less unrealized losses) arising on the revaluation of fixed assets are not available for distribution by a company to its members. Hence, unrealized profits (or surpluses) should not be credited to the profit and loss account but instead credited to a revaluation reserve account. Unrealized losses should, however, be debited to the profit and loss account as extraordinary items (see Chapter 7) except to the extent that they are reductions in unrealized profits which had previously been credited to the revaluation reserve account.

Non-statutory Reserves

Some reserves have restrictions placed upon their use because of agreements made by the company. An example of this is sinking fund accounts created for the redemption of debentures. We shall discuss these later.

The remaining reserves are those which are created by the directors by transfers from retained earnings. The reserves may have a specific title such as 'fixed asset replacement reserve' or may be simply described as a 'general reserve'. These reserves are simply subdivisions of retained earnings and have only an informational effect, the message being that although, legally, the earnings could be distributed the directors consider that dividends should be restricted because of the need to retain funds in the company. However, directors can unmake any reserves of that kind that they create; so their establishment does not prevent dividends being paid if the directors change their mind.

The fact that such a reserve has been given a specific title does not, necessarily, imply that the company has sufficient liquid resources to, say, replace fixed assets.

In rare circumstances a reserve might be represented by specifically earmarked assets, usually investments outside the business. These reserves are usually called *reserve funds*. The capital redemption reserve is not a fund and should not be described as such but, following the usual practice, we have called it a fund because it was so named in the Companies Act, 1948.

Capitalization Issues (Bonus or Scrip Issues)*

It is possible for the directors to ensure that a part of retained earnings, or other reserve, can never be used as the basis of a dividend by the capitalization of a part of that reserve. This is done by making a *capitalization issue*. Such an issue consists of issuing all shareholders with additional shares in proportion to the original holdings. At the end of the exercise more shares

---

* The term 'bonus issue' has now gone out of popular use, except for people who set examinations (the term is used in the 1948 Companies Act). The reason for this is that it is a misnomer – 'bonus issues' do not create any tangible benefits for shareholders.

are in issue but the proportion of the shares held by each shareholder, which is the important point, remains the same.

It should be noted that the capitalization issue has had no effect on the assets of the company, nor has it had any effect on the way ownership of the company is divided between the shareholders. The only real change is that slightly more protection is, in theory, given to creditors.

In theory, therefore, a capitalization issue should have no effect on the total market value of the shares. Thus, if the market price per share before a one for one capitalization issue is £2 the market price should fall to £1 per share after the issue. However, in practice the total value of the shares usually increases; in the example used above the market price per share after the issue would be greater than £1. The reason for this is the market's expectation that the total dividends payable in the future will increase following the issue since companies rarely reduce the dividend payable per share in proportion to the increased number of shares. Thus it is the expectation of increased dividends and not the capitalization issue itself which leads to the increase in the total market value of the shares.

Some firms have offered their shareholders the option of receiving additional shares in lieu of dividends. In such cases, a shareholder who opts to take the shares will increase his holding in the company compared to those shareholders who choose to receive the cash dividends.

We have introduced a fair number of points in the last few pages and we will now present an example in order to illustrate some of them. The example is even more artificial than usual.

Example 5.8

The owners' equity section of A2 Limited's balance sheet as at 31 December 19X1 was as follows:

Share capital

	Authorized	Issued and fully paid
	£	£
Redeemable 10 per cent Preference shares	10,000	10,000
£1 Ordinary shares	100,000	30,000
	£110,000	
		40,000

Reserves		
Share premium account	8,000	
Reserve for replacement of fixed assets	6,000	
General reserve	3,000	
Retained earnings	13,000	30,000
		£70,000

(a)   Profit for 19X2 before dividends, £35,000
(b)   Ordinary dividends for 19X2:
       Interim, paid 1 September 19X2, 5 per cent
       Final, 10 per cent
(c)   The preference shares were redeemed on 1 January 19X2 at a premium of 5 per cent. The redemption was supported by an issue of 6,000 ordinary shares at par.

(d)   4,000 ordinary shares were issued at £1·10 per share on 1 October 19X2.
(e)   On 31 December 19X2 £2,000 was transferred from the retained earnings to the reserve for the replacement of fixed assets. The balance on the general reserve account was transferred back to the retained earnings account.
(f)   A capitalization issue was made on 1 January 19X3 so as to increase the number of ordinary shares issued to 60,000. The issue is to be made out of the share premium account and the capital redemption reserve fund with any balance being issued out of retained earnings.

Journal Entries
  The following are summary journal entries; the full entries for the issue of shares have been shown before.

19X2		£	£
1 Jan	10 per cent Redeemable preference shares	10,000	
	Share premium account	500	
	Cash		10,500
	The payment to the preference shareholders, with the premium on redemption being written off against the share premium account		
	Cash	6,000	
	£1 Ordinary shares		6,000
	The issue of 6,000 ordinary shares at par		
	Retained earnings	4,000	
	Capital redemption reserve fund		4,000
	The creation of the necessary capital redemption reserve fund		
1 Sep	Retained earnings	1,800	
	Cash		1,800
	The payment of the ordinary dividend of 5 per cent on 36,000 ordinary shares		
1 Oct	Cash	4,400	
	£1 Ordinary shares		4,000
	Share premium account		400
	Being the issue of 4,000 ordinary shares		
31 Dec	Sundry accounts	35,000	
	Retained earnings		35,000
	The closure of the revenue and expense accounts and the transfer of the profit for the year to retained earnings		
	Retained earnings	2,000	
	Reserve for replacement of fixed assets		2,000
	General reserve	3,000	
	Retained earnings		3,000
	The transfers to and from the reserves		
	Retained earnings	4,000	
	Dividends payable		4,000
	The proposed dividend of 10 per cent on 40,000 ordinary shares		
19X3			
1 Jan	Share premium account	7,900	
	Capital redemption reserve fund	4,000	
	Retained earnings	8,100	
	£1 Ordinary shares		20,000
	The 1 for 2 capitalization issue		

The appropriation section of A2 Limited's profit and loss account for the year ended 31 December 19X2 is as follows:

	£	£	£
Profit for the year *less* Appropriation			35,000
Dividends on ordinary shares			
Paid, interim dividend of 5 per cent	1,800		
Proposed, final dividend of 10 per cent	4,000	5,800	
Transfers to reserves			
Capital redemption reserve fund	4,000		
Reserve for the replacement of fixed assets	2,000		
	6,000		
less Transfer from the general reserve account	3,000	3,000	8,800
			26,200
Retained earnings 1 Jan 19X2			13,000
Retained earnings 31 Dec 19X2			£39,200

The owners' equity section of the balance sheet at 31 December 19X2 and 1 January 19X3 (just after the capitalization issue) are:

	31 Dec X2		*1 Jan X3*	
	£	£	£	£
Share capital				
£1 Ordinary shares		40,000		60,000
Reserves				
Share premium account	7,900		—	
Capital redemption reserve fund	4,000		—	
Reserve for the replacement of fixed assets	8,000		8,000	
Retained earnings	39,200	59,100	31,100	39,100
		£99,100		£99,100

The Redemption of Debentures

Debenture holders are creditors not shareholders and so the law does not require companies to create a non-distributable reserve on the redemption of debentures. Even so, unless the cash used for the redemption is raised by the issue of shares or a fresh issue of debentures, it is often argued that the company should make a transfer from retained earnings to the general reserve account of an amount equal to the nominal value of the debentures redeemed. The logic for this transfer is that the debentures represented a long-term source of capital which has now been replaced by a source provided by the owners (retained earnings) and that it would be undesirable for a dividend to be paid out of this source, since that would reduce the capital invested in the business. We should emphasize that a general reserve still, in law, remains available for dividend but its creation is simply a notice of the directors' intention to place some restrictions on the payment of dividends.

Sinking Funds

Debentures often constitute a significant proportion of the capital sources of a company and the redemption of debentures may well require a good deal of cash. Unless the company is able, and wishes, to raise an alternative source of long-term capital, the liquidity problem may well be considerable at the date of the redemption for it is unlikely that a company would, in the normal course of events, have large cash balances available. Indeed it is not, in general, sensible for a company to keep a large balance in the bank, for the purpose of a business is to employ assets and transform resources in order to earn profits (hopefully, it should be able to earn a greater return on assets employed in the business than it would earn on a bank deposit account).

Thus if it is to ensure that sufficient cash is available at the due date of redemption the company may have to make special arrangements. It is not enough to restrict the payment of dividends, for although an increase in retained earnings means that assets less liabilities will be increased, there is no guarantee that a sufficient cash balance will be included in the assets. Additional steps have to be taken, and so some companies save up the necessary cash. They often do this by investing sufficient amounts, outside the company, in liquid assets so that the cash invested plus the interest earned will be enough to repay the debenture holders. This may be done entirely at the company's volition or this procedure may be required by the terms of the agreement under which the debentures were issued.

As we said before, it is likely that the company will obtain a lesser return on those assets than the assets employed in the business, but some companies feel that the associated decrease in risk makes up for the diminished return.

The difference between this approach and the creation of a reserve is that, in this case, assets are specifically earmarked for the particular purpose. The assets still belong to the company, but in order to make the special nature of the assets clear to the users of the accounts a part of owners' equity, of an amount equal to the assets involved, is segregated and is known as a fund. When the assets and the associated fund are built up year by year the fund is known as a *sinking fund*.

Sinking funds are also used for purposes other than the redemption of debentures. In general they are used when a company wants to ensure that a given amount of cash will be available at a given date. One might be used, for example, to help replace an asset, such as a lease, the date of expiration of which is known with certainty.

The Basic Method

Given that it is agreed to use a sinking fund, the steps are:

1. Decide on the amount of the annual investment in sinking fund assets. If the investment is of a type which carries a fixed rate of interest and which will produce a known amount on realization then the annual sum necessary to achieve a specified amount at a future date can be calculated exactly. Otherwise the amount of the annual

investment will have to be estimated.

2. On the purchase of the sinking fund investments (£A)

SF investment

Debit sinking fund investment   A
Credit cash

and

SF account

Debit retained earnings   A
Credit sinking fund account

3. On the receipt of interest on sinking fund investments (£B) which is reinvested

SF investment	*SF account*
$A + B$	$A + B$

Debit sinking fund investment
Credit sinking fund account

Note that at all times the balance on the sinking fund investment account is equal, but opposite, to the balance on the sinking fund account.

4. On the redemption of the debentures (it is assumed that the realization of the sinking fund investments exactly produces the required amount).

	Debit	*Credit*
Sale of sinking fund investment	Cash	Sinking fund investment
Repayment of debenture stock	Debenture stock	Cash
Close the balance on the sinking fund account	Sinking fund account	General reserve

The balance of the sinking fund account is usually transferred to a general reserve to indicate that the source of finance previously provided by the debenture holders will, in the future, be provided by the shareholders.

If the sinking fund had been used to help in the replacement of an asset the same basic method would be used, the only difference being that there would be no point in closing the sinking fund account by transfer to a general reserve; the transfer would be to retained earnings.

Redemption by Purchasing in the Open Market

A company has the right to purchase its own debentures on the open market and, so long as it has the cash, it would do so when the market price falls below the present value* of the remaining interest payments and the amount due on redemption. If a sinking fund is used, the purchase of the shares would be financed by the sale of sinking fund investments. Any profit or loss on the sale of sinking fund investments will be credited or debited to the sinking fund account. If the debentures are purchased for less than their nominal value, the difference is credited to a reserve account. If purchased for more than the nominal value the premium is debited to that reserve account or, if one does not exist, to the share premium account, and if that does not exist, to retained earnings.

Statutory Books

One of the most important obligations placed by law on a limited company is the requirement that it should disclose certain information about itself. The best-known example of this is the need to publish the annual accounts, but there are other ways in which this requirement is manifested.

The Companies Acts require limited companies to keep certain books, called statutory books, some of which have to be made available for inspection by certain groups.

The books are:

1. *Register of Members.* This records the names of the shareholders and the number of shares (or amount of stock) held by them and, indeed, the transfer of ownership of shares is not completed until the change is recorded in the register of members. Clearly it is important that existing and potential shareholders should be able to find who shares in the ownership of the company; so the law requires the company to make the register available for inspection for at least two hours of each business day. Members can inspect the register without charge but members of the public can be charged a fee which is not to exceed five pence. But an inspection of this register may not produce useful results because of the existence of nominee holdings; the shares need not be registered in the names of their beneficial owners but can be registered instead in the name of a person, or more usually a company, which holds the shares on behalf of the actual owner.

2. *Register of Substantial Shareholdings in Public Companies* In order to avoid the possibility that people could use nominee holdings to build up large shareholdings without others being aware of it, the Companies Act 1981 requires that anyone whose holding of voting shares in a public company exceeds a prescribed proportion must notify the fact in writing to the company. They must also inform the company of any changes. The prescribed proportion is specified by the Secretary of State for Trade by Statutory Instrument and is currently 10%. Public companies must keep a register to record the information.

* See Chapter 10.

3. *Register of Debenture Holders.* This is similar to the register of members.

4. *Register of Charges.* A charge exists when a loan is secured. As we explained above, when discussing debentures, the charge may be fixed or floating. The register of charges must include, in connection with all charges given by a company to its creditors, a short description of the assets charged, the amount of the charge, and the names of the persons entitled to the charge. This information is particularly useful to creditors and potential creditors, in order to help them assess the risks involved in lending to the company.

5. *A Register of Directors and Secretaries.*

6. *A Register of Directors' Interests in Shares and Debentures of the Company* (including those held by a director's spouse and children). Directors have the advantage of knowing about the affairs of the company and could make use of this information to indulge in what is known as 'insider trading'. For example they could sell their shares just before the announcement of bad news, such as a reduction of profit, pushes down the market price of the shares. This register helps curb the temptation of directors to engage in such activities, since the dates of their purchases and sales of shares and debentures are recorded therein.

7. *Directors' Service Contracts.* A service contract is one in which the company agrees to employ the director for a certain number of years. When one reads of directors being paid large sums for compensation for loss of office it usually means that they have been removed during the currency of a service contract. In reality the two parties to service contracts are the directors as individuals, and the directors on behalf of the company, and the concept of stewardship requires that members should be made aware of how generous the directors have been to the directors. Copies of the service contract must be made available for inspection by members.

8. *Minute books.* Minute books must be kept for meetings of directors and for general meetings of shareholders.

9. *Books of Account.* The legal details relating to these were discussed on page 57.

Of the above, the books of account and the minute books of the directors' meetings are private, while the right to inspect the minute book of the general meetings is restricted to members. The rest can be inspected by members of the public as well as members, the conditions being similar to those applying to the register of members.

The Annual Return

All companies are required to submit a return to the appropriate Registrar of Companies each calendar year showing certain specified information. Although most of the information in the annual return will be found in the statutory books, it is obviously convenient for those interested in the affairs of a number of companies to find the information in one place and not have to make a tour of the various registered offices. However, although the Companies Act provides for penalties to be paid if the annual return is not submitted in due time, the penalties are rarely enforced and many companies are somewhat tardy in filing their returns.

The Act requires copies of certain documents to be annexed to the annual return; these are:

1. The balance sheet and profit and loss account of the company,
2. The directors' report, and
3. The auditors' report.

"Small companies" (see Chapter 7) are not required to file their profit and loss account and directors' report.

The contents of the above documents are of great interest to us and will be the subject of Chapter 7.

Any member of the public can go to the Registrar of Companies and, on payment of a modest fee call for the file on any limited company in which he will find the annual returns and the annexed documents, and it is in this way that the accounts of a company are made available to the public.

EXERCISES

5.1 Discuss the extent to which company legislation in the United Kingdom seeks to protect the interests of creditors.

5.2 'The important sections of a balance sheet of a limited company are those dealing with the assets and liabilities. The information contained in the owners' equity is largely irrelevant'.

Discuss.

5.3 A shareholder in a quoted company is concerned because she receives such small dividends. She has looked at the last annual report and seen that there is a large bank balance. In addition the balance sheet shows the following items which she believes could be used to increase the dividend.

1. a large 'share premium account'
2. substantial 'unappropriated profits'
3. a large 'reserve for general contingencies'
4. a large 'provision for depreciation'
5. a substantial 'provision for deferred taxation'

You are required to prepare a brief explanation of the nature of these items suitable for this shareholder, indicating which of the items, if any, are relevant to her problem.

(The Institute of Chartered Accountants in England and Wales, Professional Examination II (Financial Accounting II) July 1975.)
(*Note:* deferred taxation is introduced in Chapter 6.)

5.4 The following balances appeared in the accounting records of Cleveland Ltd, a wholesale grocer, on 1st January 1982:

	£
Stock	33,274
Trade debtors	91,400
Trade creditors	63,275
Accrued expenses – wages	1,720
Prepayment – rates	860
Plant and machinery – cost	134,270
accumulated depreciation	45,822
Ordinary share capital – shares of £1 each, fully paid ...	60,000
Retained profits	22,729
Share premium	20,500
Freehold land – cost	82,000
10% Preference share capital – shares of £1 each fully paid	120,000
Provision for doubtful debts	914
Proposed dividend – ordinary shares	12,400

The books balanced when the figure for balance at bank was entered.
    The following information is available at the accounting year end on 31st December 1982 and relates to activity during the year:

	£
(1) Credit sales	453,272
Cash sales	128,949
Purchases on credit	427,854
Bad debts written off	6,221
Discounts allowed	8,572
Discounts received from suppliers	4,727
Sales allowances to customers	5,824
Goods returned to suppliers	4,728

(2) Monies received from credit sales amounted to £426,305; it is considered prudent to increase the doubtful debt provision at 31st December 1982 to 2% of trade debtors.

(3) An unsecured loan of £50,000 was received on 1st October 1982; interest of 12% per annum was payable annually in arrear.

(4) On 15th November 1982 £30,000 was received from the sale of freehold land which cost £21,000 in 1979; the remaining land was revalued at £85,000.

(5) Machinery which cost £25,000 on 1st October 1976 was sold on 1st October 1982 for £8,000. Depreciation has been and is provided from

the date of purchase and to the date of sale at the rate of 10% per annum on the straight-line basis.

(6) The following payments have been made:

	£
Trade creditors	349,044
Salaries and wages	82,853
Selling and distribution expenses	40,997
Establishment expenses – rent, rates, heating and lighting	15,621
General administration expenses	8,725
Dividends – Preference	12,000
Ordinary – final (1981)	12,400
interim	7,500
Directors' salaries	25,000
Plant and machinery (1st October 1982)	80,000

(7) All money transactions passed through the bank account.

(8) Stock costing £21,000 was destroyed by fire on 27th December 1982. The company has full insurance cover and has submitted a claim.

On 31st December 1982 account had to be taken of:

(1) stock costing £82,758 which included some slow-moving items which were sold in January 1983 for £7,260 at a loss of £2,500,

(2) rates prepaid £970,

(3) a claim for damages by a customer; legal advice indicates a likely settlement between £4,000 and £5,000,

(4) wages accrued £1,950, and

(5) the recommendations of the directors regarding:
    (i) the transfer of £6,000 to plant replacement reserve, and
    (ii) a proposed final dividend of 10p per share.

You are required to:
(a) prepare Trading, Profit and Loss and Appropriation Account for the year to 31st December 1982 and Balance Sheet as on that date, and
(b) comment on any features you consider significant in the accounts you have prepared.

(The Institute of Chartered Accountants in England and Wales, Foundation Examination, May 1983.)

5.5 The following is the summarized balance sheet of Duff Limited as at 31 December 19X3.

	£	£
Share Capital		
12 per cent £1 Preference shares		100,000
£1 Ordinary shares		500,000
		600,000
Reserves		
Share premium account	60,000	
Reserve for the replacement of fixed assets	40,000	
Debenture redemption sinking fund	30,000	
Retained earnings	220,000	350,000
		950,000
15 per cent Debentures		100,000
		£1,050,000
Debenture redemption sinking fund investments		30,000
Sundry assets *less* Liabilities		1,020,000
		£1,050,000

The following transactions took place during the year ended 31 December 19X4.

(a) The preference shares were redeemed out of profits on 1 January 19X4 at a premium of 5 per cent. The premium on redemption was written off against the share premium account.

(b) 30,000 ordinary shares were issued for £1·30 each during March and April 19X4 on the following terms:

   (i) 60 pence on application,
  (ii) 40 pence on allotment (including the premium),
 (iii) the balance to be called one month after allotment.

Applications were received for 40,000 shares. Of the excess cash, £2,500 was returned and the balance was retained against the amount due on allotment. The shares were allotted on 1 Apr and the cash due on allotment was received. The call was made on 1 May but call money in respect of 2,000 shares was not received. The shares were declared forfeit on 1 Jun and reissued for £1·10 each on 10 Jun.

(c) Debenture interest was paid on 30 Jun and 31 Dec.

(d) Debentures with a nominal value of £10,000 were redeemed for £11,000 on 1 Jul. The purchase was financed by the sale of debenture redemption sinking fund investments (the investments were sold for their net book value). The premium on redemption was charged to the share premium account.

(e) Interest on the debenture redemption sinking fund investments for the year amounted to £3,200.
(f) Duff Limited's profit for the year before debenture interest, dividends and appropriations was £150,000.
(g) On 31 Dec the following transfers from retained earnings were made. To the reserve for the replacement of fixed assets £5,000; to the debenture redemption sinking fund £8,000.
(h) An interim dividend of 3 pence per share was paid on 1 Oct and a final dividend of 5 pence per share is proposed.

Required:
1. Full journal entries recording the above transactions.
2. Duff Limited's summarized balance sheet as at 31 December 19X4.

5.6 Herman, Lisa and Pauline are in partnership as the Bacchus Off Licence, sharing profits in the ratio 5:4:3. Accounts had been made up annually to 31st March. However, in view of the growth of the business they agreed to incorporate the business as a limited company (Bacchus Ltd) with effect from 1st October 1982. New books of account not having been opened for the company, all transactions have been recorded in the existing partnership books. The trial balance as on 31st March 1983 (which does not incorporate the adjustments arising from the information below) together with the closing balances as on 31st March 1982 are as follows:

	31st March 1983		31st March 1982	
	£	£	£	£
Capital accounts – Herman		50,000		50,000
Lisa ...		40,000		40,000
Pauline		30,000		30,000
Drawings – Herman	17,240			
Lisa	14,960			
Pauline	15,920			
Interest free loan from Herman advanced 28th February 1983 ...		12,000		
Shop premises	124,204		120,204	
Creditors		135,249		17,395
Debtors	9,464		9,170	
Shop fittings	16,409		11,407	
Purchases	474,205			
Sales		727,911		
Wages	43,464			
Stock 31st March 1982 ...	44,692		44,692	
Bank balance	203,878			48,078
Sundry expenses	30,724			
	995,160	995,160	185,473	185.473

The terms of the agreement for incorporation provide the following:

(1) Sales, gross profit, depreciation, wages and sundry expenses are deemed to have accrued evenly over the twelve month period ended 31st March 1983.

(2) The purchase consideration, which was to be allocated in profit sharing ratio, by the new limited company was £200,000 of which £108,000 was in shares and the balance on loan accounts.

(3) The vendors were to retain the bank balance and to be responsible for the collection of debtors and payment of creditors as on 30th September 1982. The balance due from the vendors was to be treated as additional drawings.

(4) Herman, Lisa and Pauline were each to receive directors' emoluments from Bacchus Ltd of £15,000 for the six months ended 31st March 1983. Their drawings had been made in equal monthly instalments, and in the period from 1st October 1982 to 31st March 1983 are to be treated as payments on account of directors' emoluments.

(5) Depreciation is to be provided on a straight line basis both for the partnership and the new company at the following rates:—
Shop fittings ...   .   10% per annum
Shop premises   ...   ...   2% per annum
Additions to fixed assets had been acquired and paid for as on 1st April 1982.

(6) As on 30th September 1982 the following information is provided:
Debtors ...   .   £10,207   (all received by 31st March 1983)
Creditors   ...   ...   £15,294   (all paid by 31st March 1983)
Stock £49,247

(7) Stock as on 31st March 1983 was £50,704.

You are required to prepare:
(a) the bank account for the six months ended 30th September 1982.
(b) the partnership realisation accounts together with the partners' capital accounts, to reflect the dissolution of the partnership as on 30th September 1982, and
(c) a trading and profit and loss account of Bacchus Ltd for the six months ended 31st March 1983 and a balance sheet as on that date.

(The Institute of Chartered Accountants in England and Wales, Accounting Techniques, May 1983.)

6 | *Taxation in Accounts*

Whole books, indeed entire encyclopaedias, have been written on the subject of taxation and even they do not cover every point. Thus, a single chapter on the subject can have only very limited aims and we should immediately spell out the main objective of this chapter. It is to give the reader sufficient background information to understand the treatment of taxation in the accounts of limited companies. We shall touch on the impact of taxation on sole traders and partnerships but, because taxation is not usually included in the accounts of such entities, we shall devote far less attention to these topics. We should add a very strong warning that our treatment of taxation must, perforce, be compressed and simplified and the contents of this chapter should not be used as a guide to taxation law and practice.

INCOME TAX

Individuals are subject to income tax on their income from all sources, e.g. salaries and wages, profit and dividends. We do not intend to deal with the mechanics of the collection of income tax at this stage* but simply concern ourselves with the main principles.

The taxpayer's income from all sources is added and from this total a number of deductions are made representing tax reliefs and allowances. These are based on such factors as the taxpayer's marital status, his allowable expenses in employment and so on. Income tax is levied on the result of this sum and the rates of tax are applied to the successive bands of income. In 1983/84 the rates were:

* The effect of the PAYE system on firms' accounting records was outlined in Volume 1.

Income band	*Income tax rate*
£	
0 – 14,600	30 per cent
14,601 – 17,200	40 per cent
17,201 – 21,800	50 per cent
21,801 – 28,900	55 per cent
over 28,900	60 per cent

If a taxpayer has investment income of more than £7,100 he would have to pay an additional rate of tax of 15% known as the *investment income surcharge* on the excess of the investment income over £7,100.

The lowest rate of income tax, 30 per cent, is known as the *basic rate*, while the maximum rate applied to any taxpayer is known as his *marginal rate*.

We will now present a simple example of an income tax computation:

Example 6.1

	£	£
Salary		25,000
Interest received (gross)		5,000
		30,000
Less:		
Allowances and reliefs		
Personal (married rate)	2,795	
Expenses in employment (allowable)	225	3,020
Income tax payable on		£26,980
Total tax payable:		
Up to £14,600 at 30 per cent		4,380
On next £ 2,600 at 40 per cent		1,040
On next £ 4,600 at 50 per cent		2,300
On next £ 5,180 at 55 per cent		2,849
£26,980		£10,569

Income Tax on the Profits of Partnerships and Sole Traders

The profits of partnerships and sole traders are subject to income tax. Normally income tax is calculated on the preceding year basis. This means that the profit that enters into the income tax computation of a given income tax year is the profit of the last completed accounting year. Income tax years run from 6 April to 5 April; so the profit for the accounting year ended on, say 30th September 1983 is treated as income for the next complete tax year, which is 1984/85 (6 April 1984 to 5 April 1985). Income tax on business profits is payable in two equal instalments, on 1 January of the income tax year and the following 1 July. Income tax on the profits for the year ended 30 September 1983 is thus payable on 1 January 1985 and 1 July 1985.

Normally the profit disclosed by the accounts is adjusted for income tax purposes. The principles behind these adjustments are the same for income tax and corporation tax, and we shall deal with this matter in the section of this chapter devoted to corporation tax.

It is not the practice in the United Kingdom to show the tax charge and the liability for any taxation due in the accounts of sole traders and partnerships. The reason for this is that the income tax depends on the personal circumstances of the owner and is not solely a function of the affairs of the business. However, it could be argued that this omission does result in certain grave deficiencies in the accounts. Although the payment of tax is a personal, and not a business matter, those sole traders and partners who do not have significant assets other than their businesses can only discharge their taxation liabilities by making drawings from their businesses. Thus in many cases taxation is in effect a charge on the business which is not disclosed in the accounts.

VALUE ADDED TAX (VAT)

VAT is a tax on consumers which is collected by trading and manufacturing companies, partnerships and sole traders. However in certain circumstances a business may itself bear VAT.

We shall first discuss the main principles. A business acquires inputs, e.g. buys raw materials, pays expenses. Some of the inputs are subject to VAT and the suppliers of the inputs will charge the business for the VAT. Suppose that, in a three-month period, A Limited acquires VATable inputs which cost £2,000 on which the VAT is, at a rate of 15 per cent, £300. The suppliers of the inputs will be accountable to the Customs and Excise, the government department responsible for the scheme, for the £300.

Let us also suppose that, in the same three-month period, A Limited sells goods to final consumers with a total invoiced value of £10,000 on which the VAT is £1,500. A Limited will have to pay the Customs and Excise the difference between the VAT charged and the VAT paid, i.e. £1,500 – £300 = £1,200. Note that A Limited does not itself suffer VAT, it simply acts as the collecting agent.

The final consumers who have to pay the VAT of £1,500 are the individuals who are going to consume the product for their own gratification and not use it in their own businesses.

As might be expected there are one or two exceptions and complications.

Some activities are *zero rated*, and these include food and publishing. Traders in such businesses do not charge their customers with VAT but are able to claim VAT paid on their inputs. Other businesses are *exempt*, e.g. banks and insurance companies. It may be thought that it must be advantageous to be exempt from a tax scheme, but that is not the case here. Exempt businesses, like zero-rated businesses, pay VAT on inputs and do not invoice their customers for VAT, but in contrast they cannot reclaim the VAT that they have paid.

Traders with an annual turnover of less than £18,000 in 1983/84 can choose whether or not to register as VAT traders. If it is decided not to register, the business will be in the same position as an exempt one.

The treatment of VAT in the books of businesses (other than exempt ones) is straightforward in principle. A VAT account is opened and the VAT incurred on inputs is debited to the account, while VAT charged to customers is credited to the account. The balance on the VAT account is, then, the amount due to, or from, the Customs and Excise. Settlement of VAT is made at three-monthly intervals; so the asset or liability represented by this account at the year end is a current item and will be shown as such in the balance sheet.

Firms which carry on exempt, as well as non-exempt activities, will have to divide the VAT paid on inputs between the two activities. This is normally done on the basis of the ratio between the monetary values of the firm's output of exempt and non-exempt items. For example, suppose C Limited's sales of exempt items for a period were £100,000 and its sales of non-exempt items £200,000. Then only two-thirds of the VAT on the inputs can be set off against the VAT collected and C Limited will have to bear one-third of the VAT itself. The VAT borne by the business is usually debited to the expense or fixed asset accounts to which the associated inputs have been debited.

In addition to the above, there are certain inputs on which the associated VAT cannot be set off against the VAT collected whatever the nature of the business. These inputs include those relating to business entertaining and the purchase of motor cars other than for resale. These 'non-deductible' VAT payments are charged to the appropriate expense and fixed asset account and not to the VAT account.

Accounting for Value-added Tax: Statement of Standard Accounting Practice 5 (Issued April 1974)

This statement is concerned with the treatment of VAT in the profit and loss account and balance sheet. The standard is as follows:

'(i) Turnover shown in the profit and loss account should exclude VAT on taxable outputs. If it is desired to show also the gross turnover, the VAT relevant to that turnover should be shown as a deduction in arriving at the turnover exclusive of VAT, and

(ii) irrecoverable VAT allocatable to fixed assets and to other items disclosed separately in published accounts should be included in their cost where practicable and material.'

VAT affects all types of business entities but the last tax which we shall discuss only applies to companies.

CORPORATION TAX

A limited company is subject to corporation tax on both its trading profit and its realized capital gains. At the time of writing the rates of taxation relevant to companies are:

Corporation tax   52 per cent

Small companies rate	
(up to £100,000 taxable profits)	38 per cent
Basic rate of income tax	30 per cent
Advance corporation tax rate	3/7

However, in order to simplify the examples, a corporation tax rate of 50% will generally be used in this section.

The Adjustment of the Profit Disclosed by the Profit and Loss Account

The trading profit on which the tax is charged is based on, but is generally not the same as, the accounting profit. The main reasons for the adjustments are:

(a) Some items which are properly chargeable in the profit and loss account are not allowed by the tax legislation as a charge against tax. These include, entertaining (other than of overseas customers) and certain donations.

(b) Dividends which a company receives from another United Kingdom company are called *franked investment income* (FII). A company does not have to pay corporation tax on FII because the dividend paying company will already have paid corporation tax on the profits out of which the dividend has been paid.

(c) There may be timing differences. One of the most important examples of this is depreciation. Whatever depreciation pattern is used by the company in its accounts, the company must use, for taxation purposes, a depreciation pattern sanctioned by the taxation statutes. The allowances given in place of depreciation are known as capital allowances. Another example of a timing difference would be the use by a company of a stock valuation method which is not approved by the Inland Revenue. For tax purposes, the profit would have to be recomputed using an acceptable method.

The first step in the corporation tax computation is the adjustment of profit and an example of this is given in Example 6.2.

Example 6.2

PAPER LIMITED
Profit and Loss Account
Year ended 31 December 19X8

	£	£
Sales		23,000
less Cost of goods sold	12,000	
Overheads (including a donation to the X Party of £1,000)	4,000	
Depreciation	3,000	19,000
Profit on trading activities		4,000
Dividend received (FII)		2,000
Profit before taxation		£6,000

Adjustment of Profit

	£	£
Profit per accounts		6,000
add Depreciation	3,000	
Political donations	1,000	4,000
		10,000
less Franked investment income	2,000	
Capital allowances (say)	5,000	7,000
Profit subject to corporation tax		£3,000

Capital Gains

Whether a profit is considered a trading profit or a capital gain depends on the normal trading activities of the company. Thus a profit on the sale of a building would be considered as a trading profit, if made by a property company, and a capital gain, if made by a manufacturing company. However, if the manufacturing company starts to make a habit of buying and selling factories the Inland Revenue would seek to have the resulting profits treated as trading profits.

The law relating to the taxation of capital gains is complicated and we do not wish to deal with this topic in any detail. But the following points should be noted at this stage.

In the case of an asset purchased after 5 April 1965 (the date on which the taxation of capital gains was introduced) the chargeable gain (or capital loss) is based on the difference between the selling price and cost. (There are numerous exceptions and exemptions.) In a period of inflation a significant part of any gain on the disposal of an asset which has been held over a long period is caused by the inflation itself and does not result in an increase in the real wealth of the taxpayer.* The government allows taxpayers a crude form of relief to counter this problem by taxing capital gains at a lower rate than profits, i.e. 30 per cent compared to 52 per cent. Formally a fraction of the chargeable gain is taxed at the 'normal' rate of corporation tax; with the normal rate of 52 per cent the fraction is 30/52.

Rate of Corporation Tax

A *financial year* for corporation tax purposes is a year ending on 31 March and is referred to by the date at the start of the year – the financial year 1974 is the year 1 April 1974 to 31 March 1975.

If a company's accounting period covers more than one financial year and if the corporation tax rate is changed the accounting profit is apportioned, on a time basis, between the two financial years. For example, assume that Howe Limited's adjusted profit for the year ended 31 December 19X8 is £80,000 and that the corporation tax rate for the financial year 19X7

* For gains after April 1982, a form of inflation adjustment is allowed for Capital Gains Tax.

is 55 per cent and, for 19X8, 50 per cent. The corporation tax payable for the year ended 31 December 19X8 is:

$\frac{1}{4}$ of £80,000 @ 55 per cent + $\frac{3}{4}$ of £80,000 @ 50 per cent = £41,000

The rate of corporation tax is not fixed until the end of the financial year; for example, the rate for the financial year 19X6 is announced in the 19X7 budget statement which is usually made in March or April. Thus companies generally do not know the rate of tax which will apply to a part of their profit when preparing their annual accounts. The latest known corporation tax rate will usually be taken, and if there is a change in the rate, an adjustment will have to be made in the following year's accounts.

There is a special rate of corporation tax for companies which have low profits. The rate is known as the *small companies rate*. The rate for the financial year 1983 is 38 per cent and to qualify the company's profit (defined as adjusted trading profit plus chargeable gains and franked investment income) must be less than £100,000. If a company's profit is between £100,000 and £500,000 it is eligible for *tapering relief*. Profits £500,000 are subject to the rigour of the full rate. The formulae used to calculate the amount of the tapering relief is a complex one which need not concern us now.

Date on which Tax is Payable

A company which was subject to income tax, i.e. existed prior to the 1965 Finance Act, and which has not subsequently changed its accounting period is still subject to the income tax law concerning the time lag between the end of the accounting period and the date on which any corporation tax is payable. The income tax rule for companies was that tax was payable on the 1st January of the first complete year (6 April–5 April) following the end of the accounting year. This rule is similar to the one which applies to individuals, except that individuals pay their tax on business profits in two equal instalments, on 1 January and the following 1 July.

The position relating to companies is illustrated below:

Accounting year end	Next complete tax year	Tax payable
30 Sep 82	1983/84	1 Jan 84
6 Apr 82	1983/84	1 Jan 84
5 Apr 82	1982/83	1 Jan 83

For other companies, corporation tax is due nine months after the end of the accounting period or one month after the issue of the assessment (a statement issued by the Inland Revenue showing the amount of tax payable), whichever is the later.

The above rules refer to the mainstream payment and not the advance corporation tax payments. We shall deal with the distinction between the two in a later section.

Corporation tax payable within twelve months of the balance sheet date should be shown in the balance sheet under current liabilities, and be described as 'taxation currently payable' or by a similar phrase. Tax payable more than twelve months after the balance sheet date may be aggregated with taxation currently payable under current liabilities or may be shown separately in the balance sheet described as, for example, 'future taxation payable 1 January 19X8'.

Capital Allowances

Capital allowances are the reliefs given by income tax law in place of the depreciation charged in the company's accounts. Originally the purpose of this adjustment to the accounting profit was to prevent companies delaying the payment of tax by the use of high rates of depreciation.

The objective has now been completely reversed, for capital allowances are now used as part of the government's battery of investment incentives as it is believed that the ability to obtain substantial tax relief in the year of acquisition encourages investment. Until quite recently companies were able to set off 100 per cent of the cost of plant and machinery against tax in the year of acquisition. It should be noted that the term 'plant and machinery' in this context covers a wide range of physical assets including fixtures and fittings, office equipment and commercial vehicles. Industrial buildings are subject to a different system whereby only a proportion of the cost can be charged against tax in the year of acquisition while annual allowances are available over the life of the asset.

When an item of plant and machinery is sold the proceeds of sale is added to the profits subject to corporation tax in the year of disposal.* Thus over the life of the asset the same total amount (cost less proceeds of sale) is allowed against tax as is charged in the accounts as depreciation. However, relief against tax and the depreciation charges occur in different time periods and hence capital allowances give rise to timing differences. We will return to this topic in the section on 'Deferred Taxation'.

Losses

Trading losses and losses on capital transactions are dealt with in different ways.

The most common ways of dealing with trading losses include the following:

(a) The company can reclaim any corporation tax paid in respect of the preceding accounting period (in certain circumstances the taxation paid for the last three years can be reclaimed).

(b) A company which is a member of a group can, in certain circum-

---

* If the company still owns plant and machinery purchased prior to March 1972, the date of introduction of the present system, of capital allowances, different procedures apply but the same principle holds.

stances, transfer its trading losses to other members of the group who would then be able to set off the loss transferred against their own taxable profits of the same accounting period. This is known as *group relief*.

(c) The loss can be carried forward and set against future profits of the same trade.

Capital losses can only be relieved against capital profits of the same or future accounting periods.

It should be noted that a company may report a healthy accounting profit but yet have a loss for the purposes of taxation. This is due to the differences between the accounting and the taxable profits which we discussed earlier; in particular, a profitable company which has spent a significant sum on the acquisition of fixed assets may well, because of capital allowances, have a loss for tax purposes.

Advance Corporation Tax

When a company pays a dividend it must also pay a proportion of that dividend to the Inland Revenue and this is known as the Advance Corporation Tax (ACT) payment.

So far as the dividend paying company is concerned, ACT is exactly that. It is a payment in advance, and it will be deducted from the corporation tax payment due in respect of the period in which the dividend is paid. Hence it does not increase the total charge for corporation tax but simply brings forward the date of payment of part of that charge. For example, suppose that a company has a profit, adjusted for corporation tax, of £60,000 for the year ended 31 December 19X2. If the company did not pay any dividends in that year it would pay corporation tax of £30,000 on the due date (30 September 19X3 or 1 January 19X4 depending on whether the income tax rules still apply). Now suppose that the company paid a dividend of £14,000 during 19X2. In that case it would have to pay ACT of 3/7 of £14,000 = £6,000* but since this is an advance payment of corporation tax the amount that would otherwise be payable on the due date (30 September 19X3 or 1 January 19X4) would be reduced by £6,000 to £24,000. The reduced payment on the due date is termed the *mainstream corporation tax*. Thus, in general the total payment for the year is the sum of the ACT and the mainstream payment.

The shareholders do not only get a dividend, they also receive a *tax credit* which is equal to the ACT on their share of the total dividend, i.e. 3/7 of the cash received. Suppose a shareholder receives a net dividend of £70, then a tax credit of £30 will be associated with the payment. The shareholder is considered to have received a dividend of £100 from which income tax, at the basic rate of 30 per cent, has been deducted. So if a shareholder is only subject to income tax at the basic rate he will have no more tax to pay. However, if the shareholder is subject to tax at a higher rate he will be taxed on £100 but will be able to set off the tax credit of £30 against his final liability. If

* ACT is payable 14 days after the end of the quarter in which the dividend was paid

the taxpayer is not liable to income tax he will be able to reclaim the £30 from the Inland Revenue.

We have, so far, assumed that the dividend paying company did not itself receive any dividends. We will now consider the two effects of the receipt of a dividend from a United Kingdom limited company, i.e. a dividend which was paid out of profits which were subject to corporation tax (franked investment income).

Although the dividend will not be subject to corporation tax, the 'tax credit' associated with the dividend is not, so far as a profit-making company is concerned, recoverable. The recommended practice is to show in the profit and loss account the dividend received as being the cash received plus the tax credit, while showing the tax credit as 'tax attributable to franked investment income' as part of the tax charge. The position of companies with an adjusted loss for corporation tax is more complex and is outside the scope of this book.

The receipt of a dividend will, however, affect the ACT payable by the recipient company. It is able to set off the ACT that was paid on dividends received during an accounting period against ACT due on its own distribution within the same period.

Suppose a company received FII of £30,000, i.e. cash of £21,000 and a tax credit of £9,000. If, in the same accounting period, it pays a dividend of £35,000 to its shareholders the ACT payment will be 3/7 of (£35,000 − £21,000) = £6,000.

It is possible to have a surplus of FII and this will generally occur when the taxpaying company has an excess of dividends received over dividends paid over a year.

Suppose that in the above example the company had only paid a dividend of £14,000 then no ACT would be payable since the dividends received exceeded the dividends paid. There would however be a surplus FII of £7,000 (£21,000 − £14,000). This surplus is carried forward and will reduce the ACT that would otherwise be payable in the future. As before, the situation is more complex if the company is making tax losses.

Example 6.3

	Year 1	Year 2	Year 3
Profits subject to corporation tax	£400,000	£200,000	£600,000
FII (net)	14,000	42,000	21,000
Dividends paid (net)	35,000	7,000	70,000

Year 1
Dividends paid exceed dividends received (FII). Hence ACT will be payable which will amount to 3/7 (£35,000 − £14,000) = £9,000.

	£
The total corporation tax payable for the year is 50 per cent of £400,000	200,000
less ACT	9,000
Mainstream corporation tax	£191,000

Year 2

In Year 2 less was paid in dividends than was received, hence no ACT is payable and the mainstream corporation tax payment is 50 per cent of £200,000 = £100,000.

There is however a surplus of FII of £35,000 (£42,000 – £7,000) which is carried forward.

Year 3

In order to calculate the ACT payable in Year 3 the net dividends received plus the surplus FII brought forward from Year 2 have to be subtracted from the net dividend paid. Hence:

ACT = 3/7 (£70,000 – £21,000 – £35,000) = £6,000

	£
Total corporation tax payable for the year 50 per cent of £600,000	300,000
Less ACT	6,000
Mainstream corporation tax	£294,000

Surplus Advance Corporation Tax

Surplus ACT arises when the taxation charge for a year is not large enough for the whole of the ACT to be set off against it. It will obviously arise when a company pays a dividend in a year for which it has a taxable loss. However, it can also exist when the company has a taxable profit, for there is a limit to the amount of the ACT that can be set off against the mainstream payment. The maximum ACT is that amount which, when added to the associated dividend, would equal the profit subject to corporation tax. With an ACT rate of 3/7 this means that the mainstream payment cannot be reduced to less than 20 per cent of the taxable profit.

Profit subject to corporation tax	£ 50,000
Dividends paid (net)	£140,000
ACT paid	£ 60,000

Let x be the amount of the associated dividend
$$\text{Then: } x + 3x/7 = £50,000$$
$$x = £35,000$$

The maximum ACT set off is £15,000 (3/7 of £35,000) and the surplus ACT is £45,000 (£60,000 – £15,000).

Surplus ACT cannot be repaid in cash but it can be set off against the mainstream payments of the last two years, subject to the above restriction. Additionally, a parent company may surrender its current year's surplus ACT to a subsidiary company but not vice versa. Otherwise surplus ACT can be carried forward to be set off against future mainstream payments. If it is considered that the ACT cannot be recovered in the near future it will be written off as a charge to the profit and loss account, where it will be described as irrecoverable ACT. This does not affect its existence and, if the surplus ACT is eventually used, it will have to be written back to the profit and loss account.

In recent years many companies, especially manufacturing companies, have because of the availability of 100% first year capital allowances and stock relief (see page 189), reported healthy profits in their financial accounts, out of which dividends are paid, while having adjusted losses for corporation tax purposes. In such circumstances there is no mainstream corporation tax payment from which the ACT can be deducted and in many cases a substantial ACT surplus exists which will reduce the corporation tax payments that would fall to be made in the future. In the meantime it is fair to say that the amount of corporation tax actually paid by such companies depends not on their profits but on the size of their dividends.

Note the difference between surplus FII and surplus ACT. The existence of surplus FII will not reduce the total of any corporation tax that would otherwise be payable in the future but will mean that its payment will be deferred. Surplus FII will, until it is used up, obviate the need to pay ACT but this simply means that there will be a corresponding increase in the mainstream tax payments. Surplus ACT, on the other hand, serves to reduce the total of future tax payments since its existence means that a deduction can be made from the next mainstream tax payment.

ACT on proposed dividends

It is important to remember that it is the date of payment of the dividend that determines the mainstream tax payment from which the associated ACT will be deducted. This point does cause certain complications so far as proposed dividends are concerned. Let us suppose that A Limited has proposed a final dividend of £70,000 from the year ended 30 June 19X2 and let us also assume that the mainstream corporation tax is payable nine months after the year end.

The balance sheet as at 30 June 19X2 will include a current liability of £70,000 for the proposed dividend which will be paid on, say, the 1 August 19X2.

However, an additional current liability must be recognized for, assuming that the company has no FII, the payment of the dividend will trigger a payment of ACT of £30,000 and this must also be included as a current liability in the balance sheet.

The ACT will be set off against the mainstream tax payment for the year in which the dividend is paid, i.e. the year ended 30 June 19X3, and the mainstream payment for that year is due for payment on 31 March 19X4. Now the tax liability for the year ended 30 June 19X3 is not included in the balance sheet as at 30 June 19X2, so there is no liability from which the ACT on the proposed dividend can be deducted. The ACT on the proposed dividend will at best be recovered by deduction from a payment which is due 21 months after 30 June 19X2 and hence the ACT must be regarded as being a deferred asset. Thus, the proposed dividend of £70,000 will give rise to a current liability of £30,000 (the ACT payable following the payment of a dividend) and a deferred asset of £30,000 (the ACT which can be recovered from the mainstream payment on 31 March 19X4). Since the liability is a current liability and the asset is a deferred asset it would not be correct to set one off against the other and exclude them from the balance sheet. Instead both the current liability and the deferred asset must both be included in the balance sheet as at 30 June 19X2.

We have thus far assumed that the ACT on the proposed dividend is recoverable. The ACT will obviously be recoverable if the company makes sufficient taxable profits in the year in which the dividend is actually paid. The ACT will also, for the reasons given on page 198, be recoverable if there is a sufficient balance on a deferred taxation account. If neither of the conditions holds the ACT would be regarded as irrecoverable and in that case the ACT would be written off to the profit and loss account.

The entries consequent on the proposal of a dividend may be summarized as follows:

ACT deemed to be recoverable

Debit P & L Account Proposed Dividend	£70,000
Debit Balance Sheet Deferred Asset (ACT)	£30,000
Credit Balance Sheet, Current Liability, Dividends payable	£70,000
Credit Balance Sheet, Current Liability Corporation Tax Payable (ACT)	£30,000

ACT deemed to be irrecoverable

Debit P & L Account, Proposed Dividend	£70,000
Debit P & L Account, Irrecoverable ACT	£30,000

Credits as above.

Stock Relief

One of the most important problems resulting from a high rate of inflation is that profits tend to be overstated since, in the historical cost system, the cost of goods sold is based on the original, and not the current, costs. As these 'inflationary' profits were subject to tax, many companies ran into liquidity difficulties since their after-tax cash flows were not sufficient for them fully to replenish their inventories. The Chancellor, in his November 1974 Budget, introduced a crude form of relief to counter this problem. The form of relief was the placing of an upper limit on the amount of any increase in the book value of the inventory to be included in the taxable profits. The relief has, with modifications, been granted in each subsequent year.

The principle behind Stock Relief can be illustrated by the following simple example. Suppose that a company starts a year with an opening stock of 100 units which cost £10 each, purchased goods costing £10,000 during the year which were sold for the same amount and finished the year with a stock of 100 units. However, as prices increased over the year the cost of the closing stock was £15 per unit. The historical cost profit and loss account for the year would then be as follows:

	£	£
Sales		10,000
Opening Stock (100 x £10)	1,000	
Purchases	10,000	
	11,000	
Less: Closing Stock (100 x £15)	1,500	9,500
Profit		£ 500

The only reason why the company's profit and loss account discloses a profit is the difference between the book values of the opening and closing stock. The company did not generate any cash during the year as the receipts from sales were exactly matched by the cost of purchases and hence the only way in which the company could pay tax on its profit would be by borrowing or by releasing cash by reducing its stock. This example illustrates one of the major limitations of historical cost accounting a subject which will be discussed in greater detail in Section C.

The example also demonstrates the problem faced by many companies in the mid seventies in that a significant proportion of reported profits was due to the so called 'stock profits'. However, if the difference between the book values of opening and closing stock is simply due to price increases (as in the above example) the amount represents the sum that has to be reinvested if the company is to continue to hold the same physical quantity of stock.

The original form of stock relief limited the amount of stock profit subject to tax but did so in a crude way insofar that no regard was paid to whether the differences in the book values of stock was due to price or volume changes. Thus, to take the above example, the same relief would have been given even if prices had remained constant and the closing stock had consisted of 150 units at £10 each i.e., if the company had actually made a profit of £500 which was invested in additional stock. Under certain circumstances, for example, when there was a fall in the book value of stock, stock relief granted in the past could be reclaimed or 'clawed back'. Thus with the original form of stock relief consideration had to be given as to whether it had to be included as part of a company's deferred taxation computations.

A revised simplified system of Stock Relief was introduced by the Finance Act 1981. The main features of the revised relief are:

(a) Relief is given on the value of the opening stock (but the first £2,000 is disregarded).
(b) The relief is calculated by applying an "all-stocks" price index published by the Treasury, which is intended to disclose price movements of stock values in general. Thus, the same index is applied to all companies irrespective of the industries in which they operate.

To illustrate the above let us assume that a company's opening stock at 1 January 1984 is £102,000 and that the "all-stocks" index increased by 10%

over the year ended 31 December 1984. Thus the stock relief available in respect of the company's tax liability for the year ended 31 December 1984 is:

$$10\% \times \pounds(102,000 - 2,000) = \pounds10,000$$

If stock values fall no relief can be claimed but, unlike the previous system, there is now no 'clawback' of past relief.

Deferred Taxation

As we have already noted there may be, in any one year, a considerable difference between the accounting and taxable profits. Some of the difference might be caused by, say, expenses which are not allowable against taxation but, generally, the greater part of the difference will be caused by timing differences. A timing difference occurs when either an expense is allowed for tax or a profit is made subject to tax in a different year from the one in which the expense or profit is recognized in the accounts. An example of a timing difference affecting expenses is capital allowances.

The essence of a timing difference is the belief that it will be reversed. Thus if a company receives an allowance against tax in advance of the year in which the expense is charged in the accounts, the company will have to 'pay' for this in that no allowance will be granted in the year in which the expense is recognized.

For simplicity we shall first concentrate on timing differences caused by capital allowances.

As has been outlined earlier, capital allowances are usually given at a faster rate than the rate at which depreciation is charged. If a company spent about the same amount on plant and machinery each year, this would not produce any significant difficulties, but consider the cases of companies which purchase plant on an irregular basis. The tax charge in years in which the assets are new will be low as compared with the profit, while the tax charge will be high, relative to profits, in years in which the majority of assets are old.

A simplified example might help. Suppose we have a company which has only one fixed asset, costing £100, which lasts for two years and has a zero scrap value. Further suppose that the profit before depreciation and tax is £120 per year. The company purchased the asset in 19X1 and the profit and loss accounts for 19X1 and 19X2 are as follows:

	19X1	19X2
	£	£
Profit before depreciation and tax	120	120
less Depreciation	50	50
Profit before tax	70	70
less Corporation tax	10	60
Profit after tax	£ 60	£ 10

The corporation tax computations being:	*19X1*	*19X2*
	£	£
Profit before tax	70	70
add Depreciation	50	50
	120	120
less Capital allowances		
(say 100 per cent allowed in 1st year)	100	—
Profit subject to corporation tax	£ 20	£120
Corporation tax payable at, say 50 per cent	£ 10	£ 60

It can be seen that although the company has had a constant pre-tax profit the profits after taxation have varied considerably. Such variations could make it difficult for the reader of a company's accounts to be able to make a judgement concerning the company's position.

In order to avoid such distortions it is possible to adopt a procedure whereby the tax charge shown in the profit and loss account is the tax that would have been charged if the capital allowances and depreciation followed the same time pattern. This process is known as accounting for deferred taxation (in the USA the process is called 'comprehensive tax allocation').

It must be emphasized that the adoption of this procedure does not affect the corporation tax payable to the Inland Revenue. In years in which the tax charge is greater than the tax payable the difference is credited to the deferred taxation account which is shown in the balance sheet. In years in which the reverse holds the deferred taxation account is reduced; the corresponding credit being made to the taxation section of the profit and loss account.

To return to the above example, assume that the firm uses this approach. The profit and loss accounts for 19X1 and 19X2 would then be as follows:

	19X1				*19X2*	
	£					£
Profit before taxation	70					70
less Taxation						
Corporation tax						
payable on the results						
of the year	10				60	
add Transfer to the			*less* Transfer from the			
deferred taxation			deferred taxation			
account	25	35	account	25	35	
Profit after taxation		£ 35				£ 35

On the balance sheet as at the end of 19X1 there will be a credit balance on the deferred taxation account of £25.

There are two ways of dealing with deferred taxation – the *deferral* and *liability* methods – which differ in the way in which they treat changes in the corporation tax rate.

In the case of the deferral method, the balance on the deferred taxation account is the tax on the difference between depreciation charged and capital allowances received, using the tax rate which prevailed on the date on which the original timing difference occurred. And it is this tax rate which is applied when the timing difference is reversed. A change in the corporation tax rate does not affect the balance on the deferred taxation account.

In contrast, the liability method uses the current tax rate. The required balance on the deferred taxation account at, say, 31 December 19X5, will be the tax at the rate prevailing on that date, on the difference between the depreciation charged and capital allowances received. When the timing differences are reversed, the appropriate tax rate is that prevailing at the date of reversal. Thus, when there is a change in the corporation tax rate, an adjustment has to be made to the deferred taxation account which will increase or decrease the tax charge in the year in which the rate is changed.

The differences between the two methods can be summarized by saying that the deferral method concentrates on the differences between the tax that was paid and the tax that should have been paid (if there had been no difference between capital allowances and depreciation), while the liability method considers the difference between the allowances against tax that were granted and those which should have been given.

The two methods are illustrated in the following example.

Example 6.4

Asset A was purchased for £800 in the year ended 31 December 19X4 when the tax rate was 50 per cent. The asset attracted a 100 per cent first-year allowance, but it is to be depreciated at 25 per cent on a straight-line basis. The corporation tax rate increased to 60 per cent in the year ended 31 December 19X6.

Liability Method
19X4
The asset was purchased in 19X4 which means that the originating timing difference occurs in this year.

	£
Allowance given for tax	
Capital Allowances 100 per cent of £800	800
Depreciation charged in the accounts	
25 per cent of £800	200
Originating timing difference	£600

The Corporation Tax rate for 19X4 was 50 per cent and hence the corporation tax actually payable for 19X4 was £300 (50 per cent of £600) less than it would have been had capital allowances been equal to depreciation.

Thus £300 is debited to the profit and loss account and credited to the deferred taxation account.

19X5
'The timing difference reverses in this year since there are no capital allowances avail-

able in respect of the asset. Hence:

	£
Capital Allowances	0
Depreciation	200
Reversal of timing difference	£200

Thus the corporation tax payable for 19X5 was £100 (50 per cent of £200) more than it would have been had there been no difference between capital allowances and depreciation. In order to reflect this £100 is credited to the tax section of the profit and loss account (so that the tax charge is £100 less than the tax payable). The corresponding debit is to the deferred taxation account.

In practice an alternative approach is used to arrive at the required transfer between the deferred taxation account and the profit and loss account. The alternative method, which will be described below, is more convenient in practice because it only requires a knowledge of the difference between the net book value of the asset in the company's books (cost less accumulated depreciation) and the asset written down value for tax purposes (cost less capital allowances received to date). The method also makes it easier to deal with changes in the rate of corporation tax.

The argument is that the balance on the deferred taxation account should be the product of the current corporation tax rate and the difference between the capital allowances received to date and the depreciation charged to date. The difference between the asset's net book value (NBV) and written down value (WDV) is equivalent to the difference between depreciation and capital allowances, since

NBV   = cost − depreciation charged
WDV   = cost − capital allowances received
NBV−WDV = capital allowances − depreciation charged.

We will now apply the alternative approach to 19X5.

	£
NBV of asset, £800 − 50 per cent of £800	400
WDV	0
Difference	£400
Required balance on the deferred taxation accounts	
as at 31 December 19X5 credit of 50 per cent of £400	200
Balance at 1 January 19X5, credit	300
Difference	£100

Thus £100 is debited to the deferred taxation account and credited to the tax section of the profit and loss account.

19X6
There was a change in the corporation tax rate in this year. In order to isolate the effect of the change it is convenient to restate the existing balance in terms of the new tax rate.

	£	
Existing balance, 50 per cent of £400	200	credit
Restated balance, 60 per cent of £400	240	credit
Difference	£40	credit

Thus the deferred taxation account is credited with £40 and the profit and loss debited with £40. This additional debit to the profit and loss account reflects the fact that the company has 'lost £40' in the sense that capital allowances were obtained in a period when they were less valuable because of the lower tax rate.

We will now consider the effect of the reversal of the timing differences in 19X6.

	£
NBV of asset at 31 December 19X6	
£800 − 75 per cent of £800	200
WDV of asset at 31 December 19X6	0
Difference	£200

Therefore

	£
Required closing balance on the Deferred Taxation Account	
at 31 December 19X6 60 per cent of £200	120
Existing balance (restated as above)	240
Difference	£120

Hence the reversal of the timing difference results in the deferred taxation account being debited and the profit and loss account credited with £120.

19X7

By 31 December 19X7 the asset is fully written off in the financial accounts and hence no balance is required on the deferred taxation account. Thus £120 (the balance at 31 December 19X6) is debited to the deferred taxation account and credited to the profit and loss account.

The deferred taxation account will appear as follows:

Deferred taxation account

		£				£
31 Dec X4 Balance	c/d	300	31 Dec X4			
			Profit and loss account			300
		£300				£300
31 Dec X5			1 Jan X5 Balance	b/d		300
Profit and loss account		100				
Balance	c/d	200				
		£300				£300
31 Dec X6			1 Jan X6 Balance	b/d		200
Profit and loss account		120	31 Dec X6			
Balance	c/d	120	Profit and loss account			40
		£240				£240
31 Dec X7			1 Jan X7 Balance	b/d		120
Profit and loss account		120				
		£120				£120

Deferral Method

With this method account is taken of the tax resulting from the timing differences and the reversing entries are based on the tax rate applicable at the time of occurrence of the originating timing difference. Hence a change in the rate of tax has no effect on the balance of the deferred taxation account.

19X4

	£
Originating Timing Difference	
Tax on capital allowances 50 per cent of £800	400
Tax on depreciation 50 per cent of £200	100
Difference	£300

Thus (as with the liability method) £300 is credited to the deferred taxation account and debited to the profit and loss account.

19X5

	£
Tax on depreciation 50 per cent of £200	100
Tax on capital allowances	0
	£100

In 19X5 the timing difference reverses and hence £100 is debited to the deferred taxation account and credited to the profit and loss account.

19X6 and 19X7
The adjustments for 19X6 and 19X7 would be the same as in 19X5 despite the change in the tax rate which occurred in 19X6.

The deferral method can be said to better satisfy the matching convention because the reversals depend only on circumstances which existed at the time the original timing difference took place and are not affected by changes in the tax rate. However, the liability method is simpler to use because all that is required to determine the required balance on the deferred taxation account is knowledge of the difference between the capital allowances received to date and the depreciation charged to date. When using the deferral method the accountant has to keep track of the individual assets or, at least, of groups of assets acquired at the same tax rate. The liability method is the most commonly found method because it is easier to use.

Asset Revaluation
When a company revalues an asset the surplus is credited to a capital reserve. However, if the asset were sold at the new valuation there might well be corporation tax payable as a result of a capital gain. If this is the case the potential tax charge can be shown in the accounts in two ways:

(a) By way of a note to the accounts, or
(b) By crediting the estimated tax liability (on the assumption that the asset was sold at the new valuation) to the deferred tax account and crediting only the net surplus to capital reserve.

First attempts at standardization
The ASC issued SSAP11, Accounting for Deferred Taxation in August 1975. The standard specified that deferred taxation should be

accounted for on *all* material timing differences using either the deferral or the liability method. Although the vast majority of major British companies accounted for deferred taxation even before the issue of SSAP11* many industrialists and others were highly critical of the requirement of SSAP11 that companies should account for all timing differences. It was argued that many companies' expenditure in money terms on fixed assets increased year by year and hence the reversal of the timing differences would be offset by new originating timing differences. It was also argued that it was unlikely that stock relief would be clawed back by the Inland Revenue and hence it was not necessary to treat stock relief as a timing difference. The consequence of accounting for deferred taxation on all purchases of fixed assets and stock relief, it was suggested, would result in a substantial understatement of the after tax profit of many companies and would be accompanied by the building up of substantial (and, so it was argued, unnecessary) balances on the deferred taxation account.

As a result of the criticism SSAP11 was withdrawn before it came into effect and was eventually replaced by SSAP15.

Accounting for Deferred Taxation: Statement of Standard Accounting Practice 15 (Issued October 1978)

The main feature of SSAP15 is the requirement that deferred taxation should be accounted on all originating timing differences except where the tax effects of the timing differences can be demonstrated with reasonable probability to continue in the future.

The phrase 'reasonable probability' is by no means precise but the statement does provide some further guidance in that it states:

"It will be reasonable to assume that timing differences will not reverse and tax liabilities will therefore not crystallise if, but only if, the company is a going concern and:

(a) directors are able to foresee on reasonable evidence that no liability is likely to arise as a result of reversal of timing differences for some considerable period (at least three years) ahead; and

(b) there is no indication that after this period the situation is likely to change so as to crystallise the liabilities"**

Where the above criteria are not fully satisfied, the standard permits companies to provide for part of the full potential deferred taxation. The partial amount which is not dealt with through the deferred taxation account must be based on 'substantiated calculations and assumptions' which should be explained in the financial statements. If either no account or only a partial account is taken of timing differences the total potential amount of deferred tax for all timing differences must be disclosed by way of a note to the accounts. The note should distinguish between the various principal

---

* 280 of the 300 companies surveyed by the ICAEW in the year to 30 June 1975 maintained deferred taxation accounts.
** SSAP15, paragraph 28

categories of deferred tax* and show for each category the amount that has been provided for in the accounts.

It can be seen that the main difference between SSAP11 and SSAP15 is that the latter relegates all or part of the potential deferred tax to the notes to the accounts.

SSAP15 does not specify whether companies should use the liability or deferral method. However, it does state that adjustments to the balance on deferred taxation account resulting from a change in the rate of taxation (which only occurs with the liability method) should be separately disclosed as part of the tax charge for the period. The other main disclosure requirements are:

Profit and Loss Account

Deferred taxation dealt with in the profit and loss account should be shown separately as a component of the total tax charge or credit either on the face of the profit and loss account or by way of note.

Balance Sheet

Deferred taxation balances should be shown separately in the balance sheet and described as 'deferred taxation'. The standard specifies that the balances should not be shown as part of shareholders' funds. A note to the financial statements should indicate the nature and amount of the major elements comprising the balance on the deferred taxation account and describe the method of calculation adopted.

Recoverable ACT and the Deferred Taxation Account

As was mentioned on page 189 ACT on proposed dividends can be regarded as being recoverable if it is covered by a suitable balance on the deferred taxation account. The part of the deferred taxation account which can be used for this purpose is that part which relates to revenue items (i.e. capital allowances and stock appreciation relief).

The rationale for deducting ACT on proposed dividends from the deferred taxation account can best be understood if we think of the deferred tax account as representing a potential liability. If the company makes taxable profits in the future, that liability will crystallize and the asset of ACT will be realized by deduction from the corporation tax due. If the company does not make any taxable profits, then the ACT asset will not be realized but, at the same time, the deferred tax account will not become a liability.

The way in which corporation tax and associated items should be presented in the financial accounts is regulated by SSAP8.

* In addition to the three categories discussed in the text, capital allowances, stock appreciation relief and the revaluation of assets, the standard refers to two other categories: short term timing differences arising from the use of the receipts and payments basis for taxation purposes associated with the accruals basis in the financial accounts and surpluses on the disposal of fixed assets which are subject to rollover relief.

The Treatment of Taxation under the Imputation System* in the Accounts of Companies Statement of Standard Accounting Practice 8 (Issued August 1974)

The standard can be summarized as follows:

(a) *Dividends received from United Kingdom companies (FII)*
These should be included in the profit and loss account as the amount of cash received (or receivable) plus the tax credit.

(b) *The taxation section in the profit and loss account*
This should show:
  (i)   The total amount of United Kingdom corporation tax specifying total corporation tax on the income of the year before setting off any recoverable advance corporation tax (where such tax includes transfers to and from the deferred taxation account these should be separately disclosed if material).
  (ii) Tax attributable to FII.
  (iii) Irrecoverable ACT.
  (iv) The total overseas taxation.

(c) *Dividends paid and payable*
The amounts shown in the profit and loss account and balance sheet should not include the associated ACT (i.e. the actual cash paid or payable to the shareholders should be disclosed).

(d) *ACT on proposed dividends*
ACT on proposed dividends (whether recoverable or irrecoverable) should be included in the balance sheet as a current tax liability. If the ACT is considered recoverable (see below) it should be deducted from the deferred taxation account (but only if that account is due to capital allowances or stock relief). If a suitable deferred taxation account does not exist, recoverable ACT should be shown as a deferred asset.

Recoverable ACT is the amount paid or payable on outgoing dividend paid and proposed which can be:

(i)   set off against a corporation tax liability on the profits of the period under review or of previous periods.
(ii) expected to be recoverable taking into account expected profits and dividends – normally those of the next accounting period only, or
(iii) properly set off against a credit balance on deferred tax account.

As we explained, in the earlier section on advance corporation tax, irrecoverable ACT should be written off as a charge to the profit and loss account.

---

* The term imputation system is used to describe the present basis of corporation tax which was introduced in 1973. An alternative system of corporation tax was used before that date.

A number of the above points are illustrated in the following example.

Example 6.7

The rates of tax assumed are, corporation tax 50 per cent and ACT 3/7.
    The following are summaries of the draft accounts of Wine Limited for the year ending 30 June 19X6. They are complete except for the entries relating to the proposed dividend and the corporation tax charge for the year.

Profit and Loss Account
Year ended 30 June 19X6

	£
Profit from trading	240,000
Dividend received (net)	7,000
	247,000
less Interim dividend paid	21,000
	226,000
Retained earnings 1 July 19X5	100,000
Retained earnings 30 June 19X6	£326,000

Balance Sheet as at 30 June 19X6

	£	£		£	£
Share capital		200,000	Fixed assets		500,000
Retained earnings		326,000	Current assets		308,000
		526,000	ACT paid on		
			interim dividend (b)		6,000
Deferred taxation					
account		80,000			
Current liabilities					
Taxation currently					
payable					
(a)	65,000				
Sundries	143,000	208,000			
		£814,000			£814,000

Notes to the above:

(a) Corporation tax payable, on 1 January 19X7, based on the profits for the year ended 30 June 19X5.
(b) 3/7 of (Dividend paid − FII)

$$= 3/7 \text{ of } (£21,000 - £7,000) = £6,000$$

The relevant information is as follows:

(i) The 19X6 profit, adjusted for corporation tax, is £200,000.
(ii) A transfer of £20,000 to the deferred taxation account is required.
(iii) A final dividend of £35,000 (net) is proposed.

WINE LIMITED
Profit and Loss Account
Year ended 30 June 19X6

	£	£
Profit from trading		240,000
Dividend received		10,000
Profits before taxation		250,000
Taxation		
Corporation tax based on the profits for the year, at 50 per cent (after making a transfer of £20,000 to the deferred taxation account)	120,000	
Tax attributable to United Kingdom dividends received	3,000	123,000
Profit after taxation		127,000
less Dividends		
Interim, paid	21,000	
Final, proposed	35,000	56,000
		71,000
Retained earnings 1 July 19X5		100,000
Retained earnings 30 June 19X6		£171,000

Balance Sheet as at 30 June 19X6

Notes	£	£	£
Fixed assets			500,000
Current assets		308,000	
less Current liabilities			
Sundries	143,000		
1. Taxation currently payable	80,000		
Proposed dividend	35,000	258,000	50,000
			£550,000
Share capital			200,000
Retained earnings			171,000
			371,000
2. Deferred taxation account			85,000
3. Future taxation, payable 1 January 19X8			94,000
			£550,000

Notes	£
1. From draft accounts	65,000
ACT on proposed dividend (3/7 of £35,000)	15,000
	£80,000
2. Original balance	80,000
add Transfer from profit and loss account	20,000
	100,000
less ACT on proposed dividend	15,000
	£85,000

3. Corporation tax payable on the profits for the year   100,000
   less ACT paid during the year   6,000

                                                      £94,000

Investment Incentives and Government Grants

Over the years governments have employed a number of different measures in an attempt to influence the business policies of companies. For a number of years investment was encouraged by allowing companies to claim 100 per cent first-year allowances. In the more distant past – the mid 1960s – cash grants were used to achieve the same purpose.

At the moment there are a number of different varieties of grants and other forms of inducements available to companies, most of which apply to companies operating in the development areas. These are areas of the country which the government has decided need extra help because of their high rates of unemployment. In an attempt to reduce the level of unemployment, the government provides a range of inducements to companies to move to these areas or, if already there, expand their operations. The inducements take a number of forms including rent free factories, loans at low rates of interest, cash grants towards the purchase of certain assets and contributions towards workers' wages.

towards the purchase of certain assets and contributions towards workers' wages.

The Accounting Treatment of Government Grants: SSAP4 (Issued April 1974)

The treatment of government grants is the subject of SSAP4.

Those grants relating to revenue expenditure do not give rise to any accounting problems because such grants should, clearly, be credited to the profit and loss account for the period to which the expenditure relates. The accounting treatment of grants relating to the purchase of fixed assets is not as obvious.

The alternatives may be summarized as follows:

(a) Credit the whole of the grant to the profit and loss account in the period in which it is received.
(b) Treat the grant as a source of funds and credit the grant to a non-distributable reserve.
(c) Credit the grant to the profit and loss account over the useful life of the asset. This can be done either by:
   (i) reducing the cost of acquisition of the fixed asset which will result in a lower depreciation charge, or
   (ii) treating the grant as a deferred credit and transferring the credit to the profit and loss account over the life of the asset.

The third method (c) is selected in the Standard because it more closely adheres to the matching convention.

If method (c)(ii) is selected, the amount of the deferred credit should, if material, be shown separately in the balance sheet. It should not be shown as part of the shareholders' funds.

EXERCISES

6.1 Discuss the arguments for and against the use of deferred taxation accounts.

6.2 In this question, assume that the corporation tax rate is, and has been, 50 per cent, the basic rate of income tax is 30 per cent, and the ACT rate 3/7.

a. The following is a summary of the profit and loss accounts of Bug Limited (an old-established United Kingdom company) for the year ended 31 December 19X5.

		£(000)
Sales		800
less: Cost of sales	300	
Depreciation	100	
Other overheads		
(including an amount disallowable		
for tax – £20,000)	200	600
		200
less: Dividend paid		70
		£130

The capital allowances for 19X5 are £80,000. A deferred taxation account is not maintained.

Required:
(a) The corporation tax charge that should be shown in the profit and loss account for the year ended 31 December 19X5.
(b) When will it be paid and how much will be paid on that date?

b. The following is a section of Stone Limited's profit and loss account for the year ended 30 June 19X5 and a summary of the balance as at that date. Stone Limited is an old-established United Kingdom Company.

Profit and Loss Account
Year ended 30 June 19X5

	£
Profit before taxation	100,000
less Corporation tax at 50 per cent	60,000
	40,000
Retained earnings 1 July 19X4	30,000
	£70,000

Balance Sheet as at 30 June 19X5

Fixed assets			210,000
Current assets		80,000	
less Current liabilities			
Taxation	10,000		
Others	50,000	60,000	20,000
			£230,000
Share capital, 100,000 £1 shares			100,000
Retained earnings			70,000
Corporation tax payable			£170,000
1 January 19X7			60,000
			£230,000

It is now proposed to pay a dividend of 7 pence per share.

Required:
(a) Redraft the above statements to incorporate the proposed dividend.
(b) Mr X pays income tax at the basic rate while Mr Y's total income is such that he is not liable to pay income tax. They both own 200 shares in Stone Limited. How much cash will they receive as a result of the payment of the proposed dividend?

c. Bank Limited was established in 1969. Its accounting year end is 30 September. Its profits subject to corporation tax, dividends received (all FII) and dividends paid for a three-year period are given below:

	Year ended 30 September		
	19X3	*19X4*	*19X5*
	£	£	£
Profits subject to corporation tax	60,000	80,000	70,000
Dividends received, net of ACT	7,000	—	14,000
Interim dividends paid in year, net of ACT	3,500	—	3,500
Proposed dividends (paid in the following year) net of ACT	14,000	7,000	10,500

There was no proposed dividend outstanding at 30 September 19X2.

Required:
The amounts and dates of the mainstream corporation tax payments in respect of the three years.

6.3 Ace Limited started trading on 1 January 19X2. In the year ended 31

December 19X2 it purchased plant and machinery costing £200,000 and freehold land (which does not attract capital allowances) costing £300,000. Plant and machinery is depreciated at 20 per cent on the reducing balance basis. A 100% first year allowance was granted on the purchase of plant.

The Corporation Tax rate for the period 1 January 19X2 to 31 March 19X4 was 50 per cent and was increased to 60 per cent on 1 April 19X4.

On 31 December 19X3 Ace Limited revalued its freehold buildings at £380,000 and this valuation is to be reflected in the books. If the land had been sold for £380,000 on 31 December 19X3 the tax payable on the gain would have been £24,000.

Ace Limited's pre tax accounting profits for the years 19X2 to 19X4 are shown below; depreciation is the only item for which adjustment has to be made in the tax computations.

Year	19X2	19X3	19X4
Profit (£)	400,000	450,000	500,000

Required:
The taxation section of Ace Limited's profit and loss account for each of the years 19X2 to 19X4 and, where appropriate, the deferred taxation account for the period, on the following alternative assumptions:

(a) That a deferred taxation account is not maintained.
(b) That all timing differences are dealt with through the deferred taxation account using the liability method.
(c) That any timing differences are dealt with through the deferred taxation account using the deferral method.

6.4 Thug Limited, an old established company, had agreed tax losses of £60,000 at 31 December 19X4.
You are given the following information (all figures £000).

		19X5	*19X6*	*19X7*
(a)	Profit per accounts	40	100	120
	Entertaining expenses			
	(not allowed against tax)	6	12	8
	Depreciation		10	10
	Dividends paid (net)			7
	ACT paid			3
	Dividends proposed (net) as at			
	the end of the year			14

(b) The fixed assets acquired in 19X6 cost £50,000 and a 100 per cent first-year allowance was granted.
(c) The corporation tax rate has been 50 per cent and ACT has been 3/7 of net dividends for the relevant period.
(d) A deferred taxation account was established in 19X6.

Required:

Show the necessary extracts from the profit and loss accounts for the years ended 31 December 19X6 and 31 December 19X7 and the balance sheets as at those dates relating to dividends, taxation (including ACT) and deferred taxation.

6.5 The following is a summary of the trial balance of Grind Limited as at 31 December 19X5.

	£	£
Net trading profit		100,000
Dividends received (net of tax) on 10 September 19X5		28,000
Freehold land, at cost	100,000	
Other fixed assets, at net book value	1,040,000	
Current assets	810,000	
Current liabilities		430,000
Share capital		1,000,000
Deferred tax account		100,000
Retained earnings as at 1 January 19X5		300,000
Corporation tax payable for the year ended 31 December 19X4		30,000
Interim dividend (net of tax) paid on 20 September 19X5	35,000	
ACT paid	3,000	
	£1,988,000	£1,988,000

1. A final dividend of £14,000 (net of ACT) is proposed.

2. Included in the charges against net trading profit were items disallowable for tax amounting to £10,000.

3. The depreciation charge for 19X5 was £30,000. During the year 'other fixed assets' costing £20,000 were acquired, all of which attracted 100 per cent first year allowances.

4. All timing differences are dealt with through the deferred taxation account.

5. The deferred tax account balance shown above is due solely to capital allowances and the corporation tax rate was 50 per cent for the whole of the period over which the account was built up.

6. The directors wish to revalue the land at £150,000. The estimated capital gains tax that would be payable if the land were sold for that amount is £10,000.

7.   The ACT rate is 3/7 and the corporation tax rate 50 per cent.

Required:

The firm's income statement for the year ended 31 December 19X5 and the balance sheet as at that date.
(Assume that the firm is an old-established one.)

7 | Limited Companies — 2: Annual Accounts

Each year every limited company has to prepare final accounts which must be laid before the company at a general meeting and circulated before the meeting to members and debenture holders. Companies must also file their accounts with the Registrar of Companies, along with their annual returns; 'small' and 'middle sized' companies (see page 235) are only required to file abridged accounts although they must present full accounts to their members and debenture holders.

What information should be included in the accounts and on what bases should they be prepared? The main sources of authority and guidance are:

The Law
The Stock Exchange (listed companies only)
Professional accounting bodies.

We shall take each one in turn.

THE LAW

Historically, a feature of British Company Law was the flexibility afforded to companies. The relevant company legislation specified certain minimum information which had to be disclosed but did not specify to any significant extent the way in which the accounts should be presented nor the bases on which they should be prepared.

The Companies Act, 1981, represented a radical departure from the traditional British approach. One of the main objectives of the 1981 Act was the incorporation of the provisions of the EEC Fourth Directive into British law and hence the Act contains numerous features of the very different and far more prescriptive approach adopted by certain Western European countries, notably France and Germany. Hence the 1981 Act specifies a number of different formats for the profit and loss account and balance sheet and companies must in general present their accounts in accordance with one or other of the formats included in the Act. In addition the Act restricts the choice of accounting methods that can be employed in the preparation of the accounts. The latter change did not, however, have a substantial effect on financial accounting practice insofar that the methods specified in the Act are in general those which were in use in the UK. In many instances the Act gave legislative effect to the provision of the various Statements of Standard Accounting Practice which had been issued by the Accounting Standards Committee.

The present state of company legislation is confusing because there are now four major Companies Acts – 1948, 1967, 1976 and 1981 – which affect the annual accounts of limited companies. The position is made even more confusing in that some of the provisions of the 1981 Act were enacted by amending the corresponding sections of the 1948 Act. It is hoped that a consolidating Act will be introduced whereby all the legislation relating to company accounts will be incorporated into one Act.

It is Section 1 of the Companies Act 1976 which lays upon the directors of the companies the obligation to prepare annual accounts, while the provisions relating to the content of accounts are in general to be found in the 1948 Act (as amended by the 1981 Act), the 1967 Act and the 1981 Act itself.

Section 149 of the Companies Act 1948 amongst other things provided that published accounts must show a 'true and fair' view while the information which had to be included in the accounts was, in the main, specified in Schedule 8 of that Act. Both the Section and the Schedule were amended by the 1981 Act; Section 149 being replaced by Section 1 of the Companies Act 1981 while the old Schedule 8 was replaced by Schedule 1 of the 1981 Act. The original portions of the 1948 Act were renumbered Section 149A and Schedule 8A.

The first part of Section 1 of the Companies Act 1981 states

(1) The accounts of a company prepared under section 1 of the Companies Act 1976 shall comply with the requirements of Schedule 8* to this Act (so far as applicable) with respect to the form and content of the balance sheet and profit and loss account and any additional information to be provided by way of notes to the accounts.

(2) Every balance sheet of a company so prepared shall give a true and fair view of the state of affairs of the company as at the end of its financial year, and every profit and loss account of a company so prepared shall give a true and fair view of the profit or loss of the company for the financial year.

* This is in fact Schedule 1 of the Companies Act, 1981 which as explained above replaces the original Schedule 8 of the 1948 Act. We must apologise for labouring these complex points about the changes in the numbering of parts of the 1948 Act but it is important for readers to be aware that they should not rely on the copies of the original version of the 1948 Act and that, in particular, references to Schedule 8 of the 1948 Act now actually refer to Schedule 1 of the 1981 Act.

True and Fair

The words 'true and fair' must be approached with caution, for the phrase does not mean correct or accurate in the same sense that there is only one correct set of accounts which describes a given set of activities. The words 'true and fair' are generally interpreted as meaning that the accounts have to be drawn up in accordance with generally accepted accounting principles, that they have been prepared as objectively as possible (free from bias), that reasonable estimates have been made of those items which, by their nature, have to be estimated and that all material facts have been disclosed. It would, perhaps, have been better if the Act had used 'honest' in place of 'true' since the phrase 'honest and fair' would give the layman a better idea of what is intended.

The 1981 Act makes it clear that the need for accounts to show a true and fair view overrides the requirements of the Eighth Schedule to the 1948 Act (First Schedule to the 1981 Act) and all the other requirements of the Companies Acts 1948 to 1981 so far as the matters to be included in the company's accounts are concerned (Section 1 Companies Act, 1981). Thus the accounts must include such information which is required for a true and fair view to be shown even if there is no specific requirement for the disclosure of that particular item of information in any of the Companies Acts. Further, if, due to the special circumstances facing a company, adherence to any of the provisions of the Companies Acts relating to the accounts means that either or both the balance sheet and profit and loss account would not give a true and fair view, the directors of the company must depart from that requirement but if they do so, they must provide particulars of the departure, its justification and its effect on the accounts.

The Formats

The 1981 Companies Act includes two different formats for the balance sheet and four for the profit and loss account. The directors must select formats for the balance sheet and profit and loss account which must be rigidly applied, thus the items must be shown in the order and under the headings and sub-headings given in the adopted format. Once the profit and loss and balance sheet formats are selected the same ones must be used each year unless it is the opinion of the directors that there are special reasons for a change, in which case the reasons for the change must be explained in a note to the accounts in the year in which the change is first adopted.

Items in the format are preceded by letters, roman numbers or arabic numbers. Companies are not required to include these letters or numbers in their accounts but the distinction between them is important in that companies are allowed to combine items which are assigned arabic numbers if either:

(a) the individual amounts are not material in assessing the state of affairs or profit or loss of the company for that year, or

(b) the combination facilitates that assessment.

Corresponding amounts for the preceding financial year must be given but where the previous year's item is not comparable with the amount shown for the current year the former amount must be adjusted and the particulars and reasons for the adjustment stated.

The Balance Sheet Formats

Format 1 for the balance sheet is reproduced in Figure 7.1. It will be noted that the structure of Format 1 is such that the total of the net assets is shown as being equal to the capital and reserves which is in fact the way most UK companies present their published balance sheet. We will not reproduce the alternative Format 2 which can be found in the Act. In that format the total of the assets is shown as being equal to the total of the capital and reserves plus liabilities.

We have reproduced the whole of Format 1 for completeness, but readers need not concern themselves with all the items at this stage. In some cases the items will only very rarely be met in practice, while other items refer to matters such as group companies which will be introduced later in the book. We have therefore shown in bold type those items upon which we suggest readers should concentrate at this time but obviously no such distinction is made in the Act.

Figure 7.1(a)

BALANCE SHEET FORMAT

Format I

A. **Called up share capital not paid** (*1*)

B. **Fixed assets**
  I **Intangible assets**
    1. **Development costs**
    2. **Concessions, patents, licences, trade marks and similar rights and assets** (*2*)
    3. **Goodwill** (*3*)
    4. **Payments on account.**

  II **Tangible assets**
    1. **Land and buildings**
    2. **Plant and machinery**
    3. **Fixtures, fittings, tools and equipment**
    4. **Payments on account and assets in course of construction**

  III **Investments**
    1. Shares in group companies
    2. Loans to group companies
    3. Shares in related companies
    4. Loans to related companies
    5. **Other investments other than loans**
    6. **Other loans**
    7. **Own shares** (*4*)

C. Current assets
  I **Stocks**
   1. **Raw materials and consumables**
   2. **Work in progress**
   3. **Finished goods and goods for resale**
   4. **Payments on account**

  II **Debtors (5)**
   1. **Trade debtors**
   2. Amounts owed by group companies
   3. Amounts owed by related companies
   4. **Other debtors**
   5. **Called up share capital not paid (1)**
   6. **Prepayments and accrued income (6)**

  III **Investments**
   1. Shares in group companies
   2. Own shares (4)
   3. **Other investments**

  IV **Cash at bank and in hand**

D. Prepayments and accrued income (6)

E. Creditors: amounts falling due within one year
   1. **Debenture loans (7)**
   2. **Bank loans and overdrafts**
   3. **Payments received on account (8)**
   4. **Trade creditors**
   5. **Bills of exchange payable**
   6. Amounts owed to group companies
   7. Amounts owed to related companies
   8. **Other creditors including taxation and social security (9)**
   9. **Accruals and deferred income (10)**

F. Net current assets (liabilities) (11)

G. Total assets less current liabilities

H. Creditors: amounts falling due after more than one year
   1. **Debenture loans (7)**
   2. **Bank loans and overdrafts**
   3. **Payments received on account (8)**
   4. **Trade creditors**
   5. **Bills of exchange payable**
   6. Amounts owed to group companies
   7. Amounts owed to related companies
   8. **Other creditors including taxation and social security (9)**
   9. **Accruals and deferred income (10).**

I. Provisions for liabilities and charges
   1. **Pensions and similar obligations**
   2. **Taxation, including deferred taxation**
   3. **Other provisions**

J. Accruals and deferred income (10)

K. Capital and reserves
  I **Called up share capital (12)**
  II **Share premium account**
  III **Revaluation reserve**

IV **Other reserves**
    1. Capital redemption reserve
    2. Reserve for own shares
    3. Reserves provided for by the articles of association
    4. Other reserves

V **Profit and loss account.**

NOTES TO BALANCE SHEET FORMAT 1

1. *Called up share capital not paid.*

   These may be shown either in position A or C.II.5.

2. *Concessions, patents, licences, trade marks and similar rights and assets.*

   These can only be included if the assets were acquired for valuable consideration or were created by the company itself.

3. *Goodwill.*

   Only goodwill acquired for a valuable consideration can be included.

5. *Debtors.*

   The amount falling due after more than one year must be shown separately for each item included under debtors.

6. *Prepayments and accrued income.*

   These may be shown either in positions C.II.6 or D.

7. *Debenture loans.*

   The amount of any convertible loans shall be shown separately.

8. *Payments received on account.*

   These should be shown separately (at E3 or H3 depending on their terms) unless they are shown as deductions from stock.

9. *Other creditors including taxation and social security.*

   The amount for creditors in respect of taxation and social security (at E8 or H8) must be shown separately from the amount for other creditors.

10. *Accruals and deferred income.*

    These items may either be shown at position J or at E9 and H9.

11. *Net current assets (liabilities).*

    This is C + D − E. The Act emphasises that 'prepayments and accrued income' must be included in net current assets irrespective of the option selected (see note 6).

Profit and Loss Account Formats

The four profit and loss account formats are shown in figure 7.2. All the items are preceded by an arabic number hence they can be combined if the amounts are not material. However, certain key figures must be disclosed as the Act specifically states that:

"Every profit and loss account of a company shall show the amount of the company's profit or loss on ordinary activities before taxation" and

"Every profit and loss account of a company shall show separately as additional items –

(a) any amount set aside or prepared to be set aside to, or withdrawn or proposed to be withdrawn from, reserves; and

(b) the aggregate amount of any dividends paid and proposed."*

Figure 7.2
PROFIT AND LOSS ACCOUNT FORMATS

Format 1

1. Turnover
2. Cost of sales (*14*)
3. Gross profit or loss
4. Distribution costs (*14*)
5. Administrative expenses (*14*)
6. Other operating income
7. Income from shares in group companies
8. Income from shares in related companies
9. Income from other fixed asset investments (*15*)
10. Other interest receivable and similar income (*15*)
11. Amounts written off investments
12. Interest payable and similar charges (*16*)
13. Tax on profit or loss on ordinary activities
14. Profit or loss on ordinary activities after taxation
15. Extraordinary income
16. Extraordinary charges
17. Extraordinary profit or loss
18. Tax on extraordinary profit or loss
19. Other taxes not shown under the above items
20. Profit or loss for the financial year

Format 2

1. Turnover
2. Change in stocks of finished goods and in work progress
3. Own work capitalised
4. Other operating income
5. (*a*) Raw materials and consumables
    (*b*) Other external charges
6. Staff costs:
    (*a*) wages and salaries
    (*b*) social security costs
    (*c*) other pension costs
7. (*a*) Depreciation and other amounts written off tangible and intangible fixed assets
    (*b*) Exceptional amounts written off current assets
8. Other operating charges
9. Income from shares in group companies
10. Income from shares in related companies
11. Income from other fixed asset investments (*15*)

* Paragraphs 6 and 7 of the 1st schedule of the 1981 Companies Act.

12. Other interest receivable and similar income (*15*)
13. Amounts written off investments
14. Interest payable and similar charges (*16*)
15. Tax on profit or loss on ordinary activities
16. Profit or loss on ordinary activities after taxation
17. Extraordinary income
18. Extraordinary charges
19. Extraordinary profit or loss
20. Tax on extraordinary profit or loss
21. Other taxes not shown under the above items
22. Profit or loss for the financial year

Format 3

A. Charges
  1. Cost of sales (*14*)
  2. Distribution costs (*14*)
  3. Administrative expenses (*14*)
  4. Amounts written off investments
  5. Interest payable and similar charges (*16*)
  6. Tax on profit or loss on ordinary activities
  7. Profit or loss on ordinary activities after taxation
  8. Extraordinary charges
  9. Tax on extraordinary profit or loss
  10. Other taxes not shown under the above items
  11. Profit or loss for the financial year

B. Income
  1. Turnover
  2. Other operating income
  3. Income from shares in group companies
  4. Income from shares in related companies
  5. Income from other fixed asset investments (*15*)
  6. Other interest receivable and similar income (*15*)
  7. Profit or loss on ordinary activities after taxation
  8. Extraordinary income
  9. Profit or loss for the financial year

Format 4

A. Charges
  1. Reduction in stocks of finished goods and in work in progress
  2. (*a*) Raw materials and consumables
     (*b*) Other external charges
  3. Staff costs:
     (*a*) wages and salaries
     (*b*) social security costs
     (*c*) other pension costs
  4. (*a*) Depreciation and other amounts written off tangible and intangible fixed assets
     (*b*) Exceptional amounts written off current assets
  5. Other operating charges
  6. Amounts written off investments
  7. Interest payable and similar charges (*16*)
  8. Tax on profit or loss on ordinary activities
  9. Profit or loss on ordinary activities after taxation
  10. Extraordinary charges
  11. Tax on extraordinary profit or loss
  12. Other taxes not shown under the above items
  13. Profit or loss for the financial year

B. Income
1. Turnover
2. Increase in stocks of finished goods and in work in progress
3. Own work capitalised
4. Other operating income
5. Income from shares in group companies
6. Income from shares in related companies
7. Income from other fixed asset investments *(15)*
8. Other interest receivable and similar income *(15)*
9. Profit or loss on ordinary activities after taxation
10. Extraordinary income
11. Profit or loss for the financial year

NOTES ON THE PROFIT AND LOSS ACCOUNT FORMATS

(14) Cost of sales: distribution costs: administrative expenses
(Format 1, items 2, 4 and 5 and Format 3, items A.1, 2 and 3.)

These items shall be stated after taking into account any necessary provisions for depreciation or diminution in value of assets.

(15) Income from other fixed asset investments: other interest receivable and similar income
(Format 1, items 9 and 10: Format 2, items 11 and 12: Format 3, items B.5 and 6: Format 4, items B.7 and 8.)

Income and interest derived from group companies shall be shown separately from income and interest derived from other sources.

(16) Interest payable and similar charges
(Format 1, item 12: Format 2, item 14: Format 3, item A.5: Format 4, item A.7.)

The amount payable to group companies shall be shown separately.

(17) Formats 1 and 3

The amount of any provisions for depreciation and diminution in value of tangible and intangible fixed assets falling to be shown under items 7(*a*) and A.4(*a*) respectively in Formats 2 and 4 shall be disclosed in a note to the accounts in any case where the profit and loss account is prepared by reference to Format 1 or Format 3.

The differences between the Profit and Loss Account Formats

The four formats allow companies to use either the horizontal approach (in the sense that income and expenditure are both shown in aggregate) or the vertical approach (i.e. expenditure is deducted from income). In addition companies may either classify items by function or by type. If items are classified by function the total cost of sales is shown which will include the cost of raw materials and those elements of other expenses, such as labour and depreciation, which comprise the cost of goods sold. In contrast if expenditure is classified by type then, for example, the total labour cost (staff costs) is shown but is not analysed as between production, distribution and administration.

In terms of the above the four formats can be categorized as follows:

	Expenditure classified by	
	Function	*Type*
Vertical	Format 1	Format 2
Horizontal	Format 3	Format 4

If either Format 1 or 3 is selected the total depreciation charge will have to be split between the cost of sales, distribution and administrative expenses, which means that companies will have to allocate their fixed costs to the different activities. Since under these formats the separate elements for depreciation need not be shown the Act requires that the total depreciation charge be shown in a note to the accounts.

The decision of whether to adopt the horizontal or vertical approach is not very important in that it is merely a matter of presentation. The choice between the function and type of expense style of classification is much more significant in that different information has to be disclosed. If the functional classification is adopted the user of the account will gain an insight into the way in which the business operates in that he will be able to ascertain the cost of sales (and hence the gross profit), distribution costs and administrative expenses. If the profit and loss account shows the type of expenditure then the user will be able to discover the total expenditure on wages and salaries, raw materials and consumables and other services. However, much of this information will have to be disclosed even if a functional format is used as in this case the total depreciation charge together with details of staff costs will have to be shown in notes to the accounts. Hence, the adoption of a functional format means that more information is available to the users of accounts.

Accounting Principles and Rules

Part II of the Schedule 1 of the Companies Act 1981 lays down certain principles and rules which have to be applied to company accounts prepared for publication (or circulation to shareholders and debenture holders in the cases of small and medium sized companies).

As was stated earlier the relevant company legislation in the United Kingdom prior to the Companies Act 1981 did not contain any provision as to the principles underlying the preparation of annual accounts (other than to declare that the accounts must show a 'true and fair' view) but rather concentrated on the specification of the matters which had to be disclosed in the accounts. The accounting principles and rules contained in the 1981 Act therefore represent a departure from the traditional approach. As will be seen the rules and principles specify in the broadest terms the way in which the accounts should be prepared, for example the rules include the requirement that fixed assets with a limited life should be depreciated over that life but no particular method of depreciation is specified.

Accounting Principles

These are as follows:
1. The company shall be presumed to be carrying on business as a going concern.

2. Accounting policies shall be applied consistently from one financial year to the next.

3. The amount of any item shall be determined on a prudent basis, and in particular
    a) only profits realized at the balance sheet date shall be included in the profit and loss account; and
    b) all liabilities and losses which have arisen or are likely to arise in respect of the financial year to which the accounts relate or a previous financial year shall be taken into account, including those which only become apparent between the balance sheet date and the date on which it is signed on behalf of the board of directors in pursuance of section 155 of this Act.

4. All income and charges relating to the financial year to which the accounts relate shall be taken into account, without regard to the date of receipt or payment.

5. In determining the aggregate amount of any item the amount of each individual asset or liability that fails to be taken into account shall be determined separately.*

The principles follow closely the accounting concepts introduced in SSAP2 (see page 239) viz going concern, accruals, prudence and consistancy.

If in the opinion of the directors there are special reasons for departing from any of the principles, if, for example, there is reason to suppose that the company will soon be wound up and cannot be presumed as being a 'going concern', they may do so but particulars of the departure, the reasons for it and its effect, must be stated in a note to the accounts.

The Accounting Rules

The Act specifies two sets of accounting rules. One set, the historical cost accounting rules, is based on the historical cost convention. The second set which is called the 'Alternative Accounting Rules' is based on current cost accounting principles. The inclusion of the two alternatives means that companies can so far as the law is concerned prepare accounts under either

* Paragraphs 10-14 of Schedule 1, Companies'Act 1981 (or Schedule 8, Companies Act 1948)

the historical cost or current cost conventions*.

Companies can also use a mixture of the two sets of rules. They can, for example, value land and buildings for the purposes of the accounts by reference to the 'alternative accounting rules', i.e. at market value, while using the historical cost accounting rules for all the other items in the accounts. This facility did not represent a departure from existing practice in the United Kingdom as companies already had the power to revalue assets even within the context of what were otherwise historical cost accounts.

Historical Cost Accounting Rules

The following is a precis of the relevent sections of Schedule 1, Companies Act 1981. In order to highlight the basic points some simplifications have had to be made.

A   *Fixed Assets*

A1   *Definition*
An asset is a fixed asset if it is intended for use on a continuing basis in the company's activities.

A2   *To be shown at cost*
Subject to any provision for depreciation the amount to be included in respect of any fixed asset shall be its purchase price or production cost.

A3   *Depreciation*
In the case of a fixed asset which has a limited useful life depreciation shall be provided over the asset's useful economic life.

A4   *Other Diminutions in Value*
(i)   Investments (included in BIII of either of the balance sheet formats). Where such an investment has fallen in value, the balance sheet value of the asset may (not shall) be written down. The provision for the fall in value shall be disclosed in a note to the account unless included in the profit and loss account.
(ii)   Other fixed assets. A provision for the diminution in value shall (not may) be made if the fall in value is expected to be permanent. This applies whether the fixed asset has a limited useful life or not.
Note that the fact that a fixed asset's net realisable value is less than its balance sheet value does not of itself constitute evidence of a permanent diminution of value. The test is whether, given the way in which the fixed asset will be used,

---

* In order to comply with SSAP 16, Current Cost Accounting, companies must publish information based on both approaches. See Chapter 12.

the company will be able to recover the cost of the fixed asset over its expected life. Any provision for diminution must be shown in a note.to the accounts unless it is included in the profit and loss account.

A5   *Development Costs*
The Act states that notwithstanding the fact that there is an item for development costs in the balance sheet formats, an amount can only be shown in respect of development costs in special circumstances. The question of what are the appropriate special circumstances are not explored in the Act but it is presumed that it is the intention that development costs should only be capitalised when the criteria specified in SSAP 13, Accounting for Research and Development (see page 246). If an amount representing capitalized development costs is included in the balance sheet the following information must be given by way of a note to the accounts:
(i)   the period over which the capitalized development costs are being or will be, written off, and
(ii)   the reasons for capitalizing the development costs.

A6   *Goodwill*
If goodwill is treated as an asset it must be written off over a period not exceeding its useful economic life. The period over which the goodwill is to be written off and the reasons for selecting the period must be stated in a note to the accounts. We will discuss the topic of goodwill in greater depth in Chapter 8.

B   *Current Assets*

B1   *Definition*
All assets other than fixed assets (see page 219).

B2   *Net realizable value below cost.*
If the net realizable value of any current asset is lower than its purchase price or production cost it must be shown in the balance sheet at its net realizable value.

C   *Miscellaneous Provisions*
C1   *'Base Stock' method permitted*
Tangible fixed assets and the stock of raw materials and consumables can be included in the balance sheet at a fixed quantity or value so long as:
(i)   the total value of such items is not material in assessing the company's state of affairs, and
(ii)   the quantity, value and composition of the item so treated are not subject to material variations.

C2 *Determination of Purchase Price or Production Cost*
   (i) The purchase price of an asset is the actual price paid plus any costs of acquisition.
   (ii) The production cost of an asset is determined by adding to the purchase price of raw materials and consumables those overheads which are directly attributable to the production of the asset. In addition a company *may* add a reasonable proportion of indirect overheads relating to production but only to the extent that they relate to the period of production. A company can also, if it wishes, include in the cost of production of the asset to the extent that it accrues in respect of the period of production. The amount of any interest included must be disclosed in a note to the accounts.
   (iii) In the case of current assets distribution costs may not be included in production costs.

D *Valuation of Stock and Fungible Assets*
   D1 *Definition*
   Assets are *fungible* if the assets in a class are substantially indistinguishable one from another.

   D2 *Permitted Methods*
   Stock and fungible items can be valued by reference to one of the following methods:
   (i) First In First Out (FIFO)
   (ii) Last In First Out (LIFO)
   (iii) Weighted average price
   (iv) Any other method similar to one of the above.

   D3 *Difference between Historical Cost and Replacement Cost*
   The difference between the balance sheet value of any items whose value is based on one of the methods specified in D2 and their replacement cost must be disclosed in a note to the accounts.

The Alternative Accounting Rules

We will for completeness include a brief summary of these rules at this stage although readers will be better able to appreciate the significance and impact of the alternative rules after they have studied section C 'Current Value Accounting'.

The rules allow companies to value fixed assets (other than goodwill) at either market value or at their current cost. The market value need not be based on a valuation made at the balance sheet date but can relate to an earlier valuation. The Act does not define current cost but, in practice, this may be taken to refer to the 'value to the business' of assets as defined in SSAP 16 'Current Cost Accounting' (see chapter 12).

In addition the alternative accounting rules enable companies to value stock at current cost.

If any fixed assets are included in the accounts at market value or current cost then:

(a) depreciation must be provided on that amount rather than on the asset's purchase price or production cost, and

(b) the basis of the valuation must be described, and

(c) the comparable amounts based on the application of the historical cost accounting rules must be stated in notes to the accounts i.e., the cost of the asset, the depreciation charge for the year and the aggregate depreciation to date.

Any adjustments to the value of assets shall be dealt with in the *revaluation reserve account*. Thus, if market value or current cost exceeds the purchase price or production cost the difference is credited to the revaluation reserve account while if there is a fall in the market value or current cost of the asset the revaluation reserve account is debited.

Note that the revaluation reserve account cannot have a debit balance. Thus an account can be debited to the account only if the amount in question was previously credited to the account.

Notes to the Accounts (Disclosure Requirements)

The various Company Acts specify items which must be disclosed by way of a note to the accounts if not otherwise shown. Currently many of the disclosure requirements are contained in Part 3 of the First Schedule of the Companies Act 1981 but there are, however, certain requirements of earlier Acts which still have legislative force. In some cases, principally those relating to threshold levels for disclosure, amendments – have been made by subsequent Statutory Instruments (denoted by SI).

Our summary of the disclosure requirements is provided on pages 222 to 233. The summaries of the disclosure requirements are shown in **BOLD ITALIC** type while our comments are shown in normal type. References are to the First Schedule of the Companies Act, 1981, unless otherwise stated.

1. Disclosure of Accounting Policies (36)
The accounting policies adopted by the company must be stated.

Accounting policies may be simply defined as the methods used by companies in preparing accounts. The selection of an accounting policy is only relevant where there are a number of possible methods (or bases) as there are with regard to such issues as the treatment of stock and depreciation. A fuller discussion of the nature of accounting policies is provided later (page 239) in the section on SSAP2 'Disclosure of Accounting Policies'.

2. Share Capital and Debentures (38 to 41)

2.1 **The following information shall be given with respect to the company's share capital –**

2.1.1   *the authorised share capital; and*

2.1.2   *where shares of more than one class have been allotted, the number and aggregate nominal value of shares of each class allotted.*

2.2   *If any part of the allotted share capital consists of redeemable shares, the following information shall be given –*

2.2.1   *the earliest and latest dates on which the company has power to redeem those shares;*

2.2.2   *whether those shares must be redeemed in any event or are liable to be redeemed at the opinion of the company; and*

2.2.3   *whether any (and, if so, what) premium is payable on redemption.*

2.3   *If the company has allotted any shares or issued debentures during the financial year, the following information shall be given –*

2.3.1   *the reason for making the allotment;*

2.3.2   *the classes of shares allotted or debentures issued, and*

2.3.3   *as respects each class of shares or debenture the number allotted or issued, their aggregate nominal value, and the consideration received by the company.*

In addition, if any person (for example holders of convertible loan stocks) has the right to be allotted shares in the future, details of the right must be provided.

3. Fixed Assets (42 to 44)

3.1   *In respect of each class of fixed asset shown in the balance sheet the following amounts, as at both the beginning and end of the financial year, must be shown:*

3.1.1   *the purchase price or production cost*

3.1.2   *the cumulative provision for depreciation.*

If the alternative accounting rules have been applied the appropriate current costs will replace the purchase price or production cost in 3.1.

3.1   **Details must be provided if:**

    3.2.1   **the effect on the balance sheet of assets acquired or disposed of during the period and of any revisions in the value of any assets which are based on the alternative accounting rules.**

    3.2.2   **the depreciation charge for the year for each class of fixed asset.**

3.3   **In the case of any fixed assets (other than listed investments) whose balance sheet values are based on the alternative accounting rules the following information must be provided:**

    3.3.1   **the years (so far as they are known) in which the assets were valued and the values so determined, and**

    3.3.2   **in the case of assets which have been valued during the year, the basis of valuation and the names or qualifications of the persons responsible for the valuation.**

3.4   **In the case of land and building a note shall state the amounts which are ascribable to land of a freehold tenure and to a leasehold tenure. The latter figure must be analysed as between land held on a long lease or a short lease. A long lease is one which has not less than fifty years to run at the balance sheet date.**

4. Investments (45)

4.1   **The Act requires in respect of items described in the balance sheet as investments (whether classified as fixed or current assets) that the following must be stated;**

    4.1.1   **the amount attributable to listed investments**

    4.1.2   **the amount of the above which is attributable to investments which are listed on a recognised stock exchange and the amount of other listed investments.**

4.2   **There also needs to be shown the aggregate market value of the listed investments if this amount is different from the balance sheet value as well as both the market value and stock exchange value of any investment of which the former value is, for the purposes of the accounts, taken as being higher than the latter.**

The above provisions obviously help the user of accounts gain an impression about the current value and marketability of a company's investments. The distinction drawn between the investment's market value and stock exchange price may be thought to be illogical in that the stock exchange price is a market value. However, it must be recognized that the stock exchange price is that at which small parcels of shares (relative to the total shares issued) are traded. A company may hold a large parcel of shares which alternatively might fetch a higher price if sold en block because they would help the purchaser gain control of a company or they might realize a lower price because the sale of a large quantity of shares might depress the stock exchange price.

5. Reserves and Provisions (46)

5.1 **Where any amount is transferred –**

5.1.1 **to or from any reserves, or**

5.1.2 **to any provisions for liabilities and charges, or**

5.1.3 **from any provisions for liabilities and charges otherwise than for the purpose for which the provision was established the following information must be shown.**

5.1.4 **the amount of the reserves or provisions as at the date of the beginning of the financial year and as at the balance sheet date respectively;**

5.1.5 **any amounts transferred to or from the reserves or provisions during that year; and**

5.1.6 **the source and application respectively of any amounts so transferred.**

A provision for liabilities and charges (as distinct from the provision for depreciation) is defined in paragraph 87 of the First Schedule of the 1981 Act as 'any amount retained as reasonably necessary for the purpose of providing for any liability or loss which is either likely to be incurred, or certain to be incurred but uncertain as to amount or as to the date on which it will arise'.

The element of judgement involved in establishing a provision for liabilities or charges is a justification for the requirement that detailed information relating to such items should be disclosed.

5.2 **Particulars shall be given of each provision included in the item "other provisions" in the company's balance sheet in any case where the amount of that provision is material.**

6. Provisions for Taxation (47)

The amount of any provisions for taxation other than deferred taxation shall be stated.

7. Details of Indebtedness (48)

7.1   *In respect of each item shown under creditors in the balance sheet the aggregate amount of any amounts which are repayable more than five years after the balance sheet date must be given; separate totals must be given for debts which are and are not repayable by instalments.*

A debt, repayable by instalments, is included in the above so long as at least one of the instalments is due more than five years after the balance sheet date.

7.2   *In respect of any item covered by the above the terms of the repayments and the rate of interest payable on the debt must be stated. However, if the number of debts is such that the statement would, in the opinion of the directors, be of excessive length it is sufficient to give a general indication of the repayment terms and the rates of interest.*

7.3   *In respect of each item shown under "creditors" in the company's balance sheet there shall be stated –*

7.3.1   *the aggregate amount of any debts included under that item in respect of which any security has been given; and*
7.3.2   *an indication of the nature of the securities so given.*

8. Dividends in Arrears (49)

If any fixed cumulative dividends on the company's shares are in arrear, there shall be stated –

8.1   *the amount of the arrears; and*

8.2   *the period for which the dividends or, if there is more than one class, each class of them are in arrear.*

9. Guarantees made by the Company (50(1) and 50(2))

9.1   *Particulars shall be given of any charge on the assets of the company to secure the liabilities of any other person, including, where practicable, the amount secured.*

9.2   *The following information shall be given with respect to any other contingent liability not provided for –*

9.2.1   *the amount or estimated amount of that liability;*

9.2.2   *its legal nature; and*

9.2.3   *whether any valuable security has been provided by the company in connection with that liability and if so, what.*

10. Proposed Capital Expenditure (50(3))
There shall be stated, where practicable –

10.1 *the aggregate amount or estimated amount of contracts for capital expenditure, so far as not provided for; and*

10.2 *the aggregate amount or estimated amount of capital expenditure authorised by the directors which has not been contracted for.*

11. Pension Commitments (50(4))
Particulars shall be given for –

11.1 *any pension commitments included under any provision shown in the company's balance sheet; and*

11.2 *any such commitments for which no provision has been made;*

And where any such commitment relates wholly or partly to pensions payable to past directors of the company separate particulars shall be given of that commitment so far as it relates to such pensions.

12. Other Financial Commitments (50(5))
Particulars shall be given of any other financial commitments which –

12.1 *have not been provided for; and*

12.2 *are relevant to assessing the company's state of affairs.*

13. Proposed Dividends (51(3))
The total amount of the dividends recommended for distribution must be stated.

Note to the Profit and Loss Accounts

14. Turnover (55)

14.1 *If in the course of the financial year the company has carried on business of two or more classes that, in the opinion of the directors, differ substantially from each other, there shall be stated in respect of each class (describing it) –*

14.1.1 *the amount of the turnover attributable to that class; and*

14.1.2 *the amount of the profit or loss of the company before taxation which is in the opinion of the directors attributable to that class.*

14.2 *If in the course of the financial year the company has supplied markets that, in the opinion of the directors, differ substantially from each other, the amount of the turnover attributable to each such market shall also be stated.*

In this paragraph "market" means a market delimited by geographical bounds.

14.3 *Where in the opinion of the directors the disclosure of any information relating to turnover would be seriously prejudicial to the interests of the company, that information need not be disclosed, but the fact that any such information has not been disclosed must be stated.*

15. Directors' Remuneration (1948 Act, Section 196, 1967 Act, Sections 6 and 7).
For all companies the aggregate of the following must be shown

15.1 *directors' emoluments, distinguishing between amounts paid for services as a director and other emoluments;*

15.2 *directors' or past directors' pensions but excluding amounts paid out of a pension fund which is substantially maintained by contributions paid into it;*

15.3 *compensation to directors or past directors for loss of office;*

15.4 *in addition, if the aggregate directors' emoluments exceed £40,000 (SI, 1979)*

    15.4.1 *the total emoluments of any person who was chairman of the company during the year;*

    15.4.2 *the total emolument of the highest paid director unless he was chairman;*

    15.4.3 *the numbers of directors whose emoluments fall in successive brackets of £5,000 (SI, 1979)*

    15.4.4 *the number of directors who have waived (given up) their rights to receive emoluments and the total emoluments waived.*

The above is fairly detailed and the Act is even more complex because of the provisions relating to payments made by subsidiary companies.

The following points may help the reader understand the above:

(i)   Emoluments include taxable expense allowances, benefits in kind, and contributions made to pension schemes. The distinction between payments made for services as director and other services is not always clear. Consider a person working full time for the company as a manager. Then his salary might be considered as 'other emoluments' while any directors' fees would be treated as payments made for services as a director.

(ii) In deciding whether the emoluments exceed £15,000, contributions to pension schemes are included but such contributions are ignored for the purposes of the detailed analysis. A practical reason for this is that it may not be possible to apportion between the different directors the total contribution made to the fund.

A similar inconsistency applies to emoluments paid to directors who work wholly or mainly outside the United Kingdom. Their emoluments count in deciding whether the total is greater than £40,000 but are ignored (including any part paid for the services in the United Kingdom) for the purposes of the analysis required under heading 15.4.

The reason for this disclosure requirement is self-evident and is rooted in the stewardship concept. However, the item is rarely of great importance in helping to predict future outcomes.

16. Particulars of Staff (56)
There must be stated:

16.1 **the average number of persons employed by the company in the financial year divided, where applicable, between different 'categories'.**

It is left to the directors to decide, having regard to the way in which the company's affairs are organized, the categories over which the staff numbers should be analysed. One obvious approach would be to show the numbers of salaried and wage earning staff. A possibly more informative approach would be to disclose the number of employees engaged directly in production and those not so engaged.

16.2 **If they are not shown in the profit and loss account the following amounts must be disclosed in the notes:**

16.2.1 **wages and salaries paid or payable in respect of the financial year**

16.2.2 **social security costs incurred by the company on behalf of its employees.**

16.2.3 **other pension costs so incurred.**

17. Employees earning more than £20,000 per year (Section 8 Companies Act, 1967) (SI, 1979)

The number of employees earning more than £20,000 in brackets of £5,000 must be shown.

Employees who work wholly or mainly outside the United Kingdom are exempt from this provision.

The information may be disclosed in the following way.

The number of employees (other than directors and employees working wholly or mainly outside the United Kingdom) whose total emoluments fall in the given ranges were:

Between £20,001 and £25,000	2
Between £25,001 and £30,000	1
Between £40,001 and £45,000	1

A similar form of presentation may be used to show directors' emoluments, only in that case the first band is 'less than £5,000'.

The reason for this disclosure requirement, which appeared for the first time in the 1967 Act, is not obvious. One motive may have been the wish to prevent people, who can exercise effective control by reason of their shareholdings, from circumventing the requirement to disclose their remuneration by not becoming directors. The salaries of senior employees and directors are often considered to be of great 'news value' by financial journalists.

18. Interest (53(2))

The charge for interest in respect of each of the following must be stated:

18.1 **bank loans and overdrafts and other loans made to the company which are:**

18.1.1 **repayable otherwise than by instalments where the repayments are due within a period of five years following the end of the financial year, or**

18.1.2 **if repayable by instalments where the last instalment falls due for the repayment before the end of the five year period, and**

18.2 **loans of any other kind made to the company.**

The above provision does not apply to interest on loans from group companies (see Chapter 8) but otherwise applies to all loans whether made on the security of debentures or not. Subject to the forgoing the total interest charge must be analysed between two categories; interest on short and medium term liabilities (less than five years) and interest on longer term liabilities. A loan repayable by instalments is treated as a long term loan if at least one instalment is not due for payment within the five year period.

There are two main reasons why interest should be disclosed.

Some companies are financed mainly through owners' equity, while other companies make considerable use of loan finance. Companies in the first category will, all other things being equal, pay more in dividends and less in interest than the second type of company. The disclosure of interest expense makes it easier to compare the results of companies which differ in this way.

The second reason is that knowledge of the amount of the interest expense can help in assessing the risk associated with the company, for, if a company cannot pay the interest due, the creditors can force it into liquidation or take other unpleasant action. Clearly a company with a high interest charge relative to profits is in a vulnerable position.*

19. Redemption of share capital and loans (53(3))
There must be shown the amounts respectively set aside for:

19.1 *redemption of share capital, and*

19.2 *redemption of loans.*

20. Income from listed investments (53(4))
There must be shown the amount of income from listed investments.

In order to comply with any of the profit and loss account formats the total income from investments treated as fixed assets must be shown in addition to the total income from other sources.

21. Rental income (53(5))
The total amount of rent from land must be shown. The amount must be shown after the deduction of ground rent, rates and other outgoings.

The above need only be shown if rent received in respect of land forms a substantial part of the company's revenue for the financial year. The Act does not define 'substantial'.

22. Hire of Plant and Machinery (53(6))
There must be shown the total charge to the profit and loss account in respect of the hire of machinery.

Reference has already been made to the need to show the total depreciation charge for the financial year (see page 216).

It is reasonable that companies should be required to disclose the charge for depreciation because the expense is, in general, substantial and because it is one whose amount depends on the exercise of judgement. Hire charges are similar to depreciation, in that they can both be viewed as being the expense of using a fixed asset. It is then reasonable to require that this item also be disclosed, so as to enable users of accounts to make better comparisons of results of companies that hire assets with the results of companies

* See Chapter 13

which own their assets. Hire purchase payments are not treated as hire charges for this purpose although, legally, they are such. Instead the interest element in the hire purchase instalments will be shown under interest expense.

There is no need to show hire charges for land and buildings, i.e. rent.

23. Auditors' Remuneration (53(7))
The remuneration of the auditors (including expenses) must be shown

The reason why this expense should be disclosed rather than fees paid for other professional services, e.g. the company's solicitor, flows from the special relationship that exists between the auditors and the shareholders, i.e. the auditors are appointed by the company in general meeting, and they report to the shareholders.

24. Taxation (54)

24.1 **The basis on which the charge for United Kingdom corporation tax and United Kingdom income tax is computed shall be stated.**

24.2 **Particulars shall be given of any special circumstances which affect liability in respect of taxation of profits income or capital gains for the financial year or liability in respect of taxation of profits, income or capital gains for succeeding financial years.**

24.3 **The following amounts shall be stated –**

24.3.1 **the amount of the charge for United Kingdom corporation tax;**

24.3.2 **if that amount would have been greater but for relief from double taxation, the amount which it would have been but for such relief;**

24.3.3 **the amount of the charge for United Kingdom income tax; and**

24.3.4 **the amount of the charge for taxation imposed outside the United Kingdom of profits, income and (so far as charged to revenue) capital gains.**

24.4 **The above amounts must be given, if appropriate, in respect of the two places in the profit and loss account where taxation appears viz 'tax on profit or loss on ordinary activities' and 'tax on extraordinary profit or loss'.**

The distinction between ordinary and extraordinary activities will be discussed on page 241. The effect of the requirement summarized in paragraph 24.4 is that the taxation consequences of extraordinary items needs to be identified and disclosed.

25. Items relating to preceding years (57(11))

Where any amount relating to any preceding financial year is included in any item in the profit and loss account the effect shall be stated.

26. Extraordinary and Exceptional Items (57(2) and 57(3))

26.1 *Particulars shall be given of any extraordinary income or charges arising in the financial year.*

26.2. *The effect shall be stated of any transactions that are exceptional by virtue of size or incidence though they fall within the ordinary activities of the company.*

General Matters

27. Foreign Currencies

Where sums originally denominated in foreign currencies have been brought into account under any items shown in the balance sheet or profit and loss account, the basis on which those sums have been translated into sterling shall be stated.

28. Comparative Figures

With certain limited exceptions in respect of every item stated in a note to the accounts the corresponding amount for the financial year immediately preceding that to which the accounts relate shall also be stated and where the corresponding amount is not comparable, it shall be adjusted and particulars of the adjustment and the reasons for it shall be given.

The Directors' Report

A directors' report must be attached to every balance sheet laid before the company and, with the exception of "small companies", filed with the Registrar of Companies. Prior to the Companies Act 1981 there was no statutory requirement for the report to be audited but auditors are now required to consider whether the information given in the directors' report is consistent with the audited balance sheet and profit and loss account. (Section 15, Companies Act, 1981)

As before our summary of the disclosure requirements, shown on pages 233 to 235, is shown in italic type.

1. *The directors must report on the development of the company (Section 157(1), CA 1948 as amended by Section 13(1) CA 1981).*

The directors are required to provide "a fair review of the development of the business of the company and its subsidiaries during the financial year ending with the balance sheet date and of their position at the end of it. As might be expected auditors will, from time to time, have some difficulty in interpreting the meaning of fairness in relation to this section when deciding whether the review is in fact consistent with the information disclosed by the profit and loss account and balance sheet.

2.   *The recommended dividend and the amount which the directors propose to transfer to reserves must be stated* (Section 157(1), CA 1948).

3.   *The names of all persons who were directors during the year must be disclosed* (Section 16(1), CA 1967).

4.   *The principal activities of the company and its subsidiaries must be described* (Section 16(1), CA 1967).

5.   *Any significant changes in the fixed assets of the company or its subsidiaries must be described* (Section 16(1)(a), CA 1967).

6.   *If, in the opinion of the directors, the difference between the market value of land held as fixed assets and its book value is significant, the members' attention should be drawn to the difference, which should be quantified as precisely as possible* (Section 16(1)(a), CA 1967).

For the purposes of the above provision, land includes any building which may be situated thereon.

This provision was an early recognition of the need to disclose information about the current value of assets. Land and building being the item for which, for most companies, the difference between historic cost and market value is the most significant.

7.   *The extent of all directors' interests in the shares or debentures of the company or its subsidiaries as at the balance sheet date must be disclosed, together with corresponding details for the beginning of the financial year or at the date of appointment of a director, if later* (Section 16(1)(e), CA 1967).

The above information can, if the directors so decide, be provided by way of a note to the accounts instead of being included in the directors' report.

8.   *Particulars of any important event affecting the company or any of its subsidiaries which have occurred since the end of the year must be provided.* (Section 16(1)(f) CA 1967 as amended by Section 13(3) CA 1981).

9. ***An indication of the likely future developments in the business of the company and of its subsidiaries must be given*** (Section 16(1)(f) CA 1967 as amended by Section 13(3) CA 1981).

10. ***An indication of the activities (if any) of the company and its subsidiaries in the field of research and development must be included.*** (Section 16(1)(f) CA 1967 as amended by Section 13(3) CA 1981).

11. ***If the total of political and charitable donations made during the year exceeds £50 the separate totals of each must be disclosed. If any individual political contribution exceeds £50 the amount and the name of the recipient must be given.*** (Section 19, CA 1967).

We would repeat that we have only provided a summary of the major disclosure requirements and have not attempted to deal with every point or every exception. We would also point out that certain classes of companies are exempt from a number of provisions. The classes are banking and discount, insurance and shipping companies.

Accounting Exemptions available to 'Small' and 'Medium Sized' Companies

Prior to the Companies Act, 1967, certain smaller limited companies ('exempt private companies') were not required to file copies of their accounts with the Registrar of Companies i.e. they do not have to 'publish' their accounts although the accounts had to be circulated to shareholders. Following the withdrawal of the concession there were very few differences between the legal requirements imposed on small and large companies in respect of both the publication of accounts and the information which had to be included in them. The result was what many regarded as being an unhappy compromise in that company legislation required too much of smaller companies but too little from larger companies. This problem was addressed in the Companies Act, 1981 in that, following the developments in the EEC's Fourth Directive, companies were divided into three classes – small, medium and large companies. Unfortunately, the concessions afforded to small and medium size companies relate only to the publication of accounts in that they are not required to file their full accounts with the Registrar. All companies must, however, prepare for their shareholders, full accounts which comply with the disclosure provisions of the 1981 and earlier Companies Acts. Thus, small and medium sized companies wishing to take advantage of the so called accounting exemptions have, in effect, to prepare two sets of accounts. It can also be argued that many small companies have to waste time and money in preparing full accounts which are unnecessarily detailed.

Criteria for Small and Medium Sized Companies

A company is not entitled to take advantage of the accounting exemptions whatever its size if the company is a public company or a banking company, an insurance company or a shipping company or if it is a member of a group of companies one of the other members of which is ineligible.

The numerical criteria used to categorize companies are specified in Section 8 of the 1981 Act. A company qualifies as a small or medium sized company for a particular year if both in respect of that year and the financial year immediately preceding it the company satisfies at least two of the qualifying conditions specified below.

Small Companies

The qualifying conditions are:

(i)   Turnover not exceeding £1,400,000.

(ii)   Balance sheet total (essentially total assets) not exceeding £700,000.

(iii)   Average number of employees not exceeding 50.

Medium Sized Companies

The qualifying conditions are:

(i)   Turnover not exceeding £5,750,000.

(ii)   Balance sheet total not exceeding £2,800,000.

(iii)   Average number of employees not exceeding 250.

Exemptions for Small Companies

Small companies are only required to file a modified balance sheet with the Registrar of Companies; they are not required to file a profit and loss account or directors' report. The modified balance sheet is an abbreviated form of the selected balance sheet format showing only the information assigned either letters or Roman numbers in the formats. There are, however, two exceptions. It is necessary to split the debtors' and creditors' figures between the amounts due within a year and those which run for a longer period.

Small companies are not required to publish all the notes to the accounts specified in the Act. The only notes which they must publish are those relating to:

(i)   The company's accounting policies.

(ii) The company's share capital.

(iii) Particulars of allotments of shares during the financial year.

(iv) Particulars of the company's indebtedness in respect of the debts which are repayable more than five years from the balance sheet date.

(v)   Details of securities given in respect of any debts.

(vi) The basis used for translating foreign currency amounts into sterling.

(vii) Corresponding amounts in respect of the previous financial year.

Exemptions for medium sized companies

The exemptions available to medium sized companies are much more modest than those which apply to small companies. Medium sized companies must file their full balance sheets and directors' reports. They can, however, file a modified version of the profit and loss account whereby the account starts with the "gross profit or loss" i.e. medium sized companies need not disclose in their modified profit and loss account their turnover or cost of sales. In addition, medium sized companies need not provide analyses of turnover and profit in the notes to the accounts.

The exemptions available to small and medium sized companies in the preparation of the modified accounts are summarized in Figure 7.3. Readers are reminded that the modifications apply to the accounts filed with the Registrar of Companies. All limited companies are required to circulate full accounts to their shareholders.

Figure 7.3

Features of Modified Accounts

	Small Companies	Medium Size Companies
Profit and Loss Account	Not required	Can start with 'gross profit or loss'
Balance Sheet	Only main headings (i.e. those assigned letters or Roman numerals required)	No modifications
Directors' report	Not required	No modifications
Notes to the accounts	Selected items only (see above)	Analyses of turnover and profit not required

Signatures of the Directors

All balance sheets must be signed on behalf of the Board of Directors by two directors, or, if there is only one director, by that director (Section 155, Companies Act, 1948). In the case of modified accounts the balance sheet must include a statement by the directors, immediately above their signatures, that they have relied on the exemptions for individual accounts and that they have done so on the grounds that the company is entitled to the benefit of those exemptions as a small or (as the case may be) a medium sized company (Section 7(3), Companies Act, 1981).

Special considerations apply to the auditor of companies which take advantage of the exemptions. These will be discussed on page 254.

STOCK EXCHANGE REGULATIONS

Companies must satisfy certain conditions if they wish to have their shares traded on the Stock Exchange. Of these, the most relevant to the subject of this chapter are:

1. That the company must publish an interim report stating amongst other matters, the profit after tax for the first six months of the accounting year and any interim dividend payable.

2. That the directors' report should contain or be accompanied by:

   (a) A geographical analysis of turnover and contribution to trading results of any trading operations carried on outside the United Kingdom, and

   (b) A statement by the directors of the reason for adopting an alternative basis of accounting in any case where the auditors have stated that the accounts are not drawn up in accordance with the standard accounting practices approved by the accountancy bodies.

   (c) A statement of the principle countries in which each subsidiary operates.

   (d) An explanation of material differences between the results reported in the accounts and those made in a published forecast.

   (e) Particulars of each company in which an investment of over 20 per cent of the equity is held.

   (f) A statement showing the amounts of bank loans and overdrafts and of other borrowings repayable within various periods of up to five years or more.

(g) A statement of interest capitalized in the year and an indication of the amount and treatment of any related tax relief.

(h) A statement of the interests of each director in the share capital.

(i) A statement of substantial interests in the share capital of the company held by persons other than directors.

(j) The position of the company as to 'close company' status and, where applicable, investment trust status.

(k) Details of contracts in which directors are materially interested.

(l) A statement of waivers of emoluments by directors.

(m) A statement of waivers of dividends by shareholders.

(n) A statement of the unexpired period of any service contract of any director proposed for re-election.

It should be noted that the above legal and Stock Exchange regulations relate to minimum disclosure requirements. Companies can of course reveal considerably more detail of their activities – few companies do so to any significant extent.

STATEMENTS OF STANDARD ACCOUNTING PRACTICE

We have already introduced the Accounting Standards Committee (ASC) in Chapter 1 and discussed its manner of operating through the issue of Statements of Standard Accounting Practice (SSAP) by the various professional accounting bodies associated with the Committee. We shall, at this stage, summarize some of the standards that are relevant to the aims and content of this book.

SSAP 2: Disclosure of Accounting Policies (issued November 1971)

The following important definitions are given in the standard:

Fundamental accounting concepts – the broad basic assumptions which underlie the periodic financial accounts of business enterprises.

Accounting bases – those methods which have been developed for expressing or applying fundamental accounting concepts to financial transactions and items.

Accounting policies – the specific accounting bases judged by business enterprises to be the most appropriate to their circumstances and adopted by them for the purpose of preparing their financial accounts.

The statement identified four fundamental concepts which are 'regarded as having general acceptability', but notes that their relative importance will vary depending on the circumstances of the particular case.

The four fundamental concepts are:

(a) *going concern* concept – the enterprise will continue in operational existence for the foreseeable future.

(b) *accruals* concept – revenue and costs are accrued (recognized as they are earned or incurred, not as money is received or paid), matched with one another so far as the relationship can be established or justifiably assumed and dealt with in the profit and loss account of the period to which they relate. However, when the accruals concept is inconsistent with the prudence concept the latter prevails.

(c) *consistency* – there is consistency of accounting treatment of like items within each accounting period and from one period to the next.

(d) *prudence* – revenue and profits are not anticipated, but are recognized by inclusion in the profit and loss account only when realized in the form either of cash or of other assets, the ultimate cash realization of which can be assessed with reasonable certainty. Provision is made for all known liabilities (expenses and losses) whether the amount of these is known with certainty or is a best estimate.

The Standard

1. If accounts are prepared on the basis of assumptions which differ materially from any of the above four fundamental accounting concepts the fact and the reason for the deviation should be explained. In the absence of a clear statement to the contrary, there is a presumption that the four fundamental accounting concepts have been observed.

2. The accounting policies followed for dealing with items which are judged material or critical in determining the profit or loss for the year and in stating the financial position should be disclosed by way of notes to the accounts. The explanations should be clear, fair, and as brief as possible.

The relationship between concepts, bases and policies, can be explained in the following way. In general, a number of different methods of dealing with a given transaction or event have been developed, all of which rely on the assumptions described as the fundamental accounting concepts. The various methods are referred to as the accounting bases. For example, the accounting bases available for dealing with the depreciation of fixed assets include the straight-line, reducing balance and sum of the years' digits methods. The method selected by a company from the available bases is that company's accounting policy for the particular transaction.

The Statement should not be seen as an attempt to construct a theory of accounting and, indeed, the ASC itself disavows any such claim. It does attempt to describe current practice and emphasizes that the fundamental accounting concepts are working assumptions that have general acceptance at the present time.

The definitions are useful in an area where the words principles, concepts, rules, etc., have been used with much abandon but with little agreement as to their meaning and the differences between them.

The second part of the Statement is important in that an explanation of the accounting policies helps users to understand more easily the significance of items included in the accounts and to make comparisons between the results of companies which use different policies.

SSAP 6: Extraordinary Items and Prior Year Adjustments (issued April 1974, Revised April 1975)

This standard was introduced to bring consistency to the treatment of transactions that were outside the normal trading activities of the company. The differentiation of profit and losses from normal trading operations and those which were not so is considered to be important in forecasting future events.

It is best to start by looking at a couple of definitions included in the Standard.

(a) *Extraordinary items* – those items which derive from events or transactions which are outside the ordinary activities of the business and which are both material and not expected to recur frequently or regularly. They do not include items which, though exceptional on account of size and incidence (and which therefore may require separate disclosure), derive from the ordinary activities of the business.

(b) *Prior year adjustments* – these are material adjustments applicable to prior years arising from changes in accounting policies and from the correction of fundamental errors. They do not include the normal recurring corrections of accounting estimates made in prior years.

The Standard itself is as follows:

1.   The profit and loss account for the year should show a profit or loss after extraordinary items, and reflect all profits and losses recog-

nized in the accounts for the year, other than prior year adjustments and unrealized surpluses on revaluation of fixed assets,
which should be credited direct to reserves.

2. Items of abnormal size and incidence which are derived from the
   ordinary activities of the business should be included in arriving at
   the profit for the year before taxation and extraordinary items,
   and their nature and size disclosed.

3. Extraordinary items (net of attributable taxation) should be
   shown separately in the profit and loss account after the results
   derived from ordinary activities, and their nature and size should
   be disclosed.

4. Prior year adjustments (net of attributable taxation) should be
   accounted for by restating the profits of prior years, i.e. the opening balance on retained profits should be restated.

Examples of extraordinary items include profits and losses arising
from (a) the closure of a significant part of the business and (b) the sale of an
investment not acquired for the purposes of resale. Losses arising from providing against a loss on a contract or from the making of abnormal write-offs
against debtors and inventory do not constitute extraordinary items because
they derive from the ordinary activities of the business.

Prior year items are of two kinds: those due to changes made in
accounting policies, e.g. switching from one method of stock evaluation to
another, and those due to the correction of fundamental errors made when
preparing past accounts. The latter have to be really substantial in that the
accounts would have been withdrawn, had the error been discovered in
time, on the grounds that they did not give a true and fair view. An example
of this, hopefully rare, item would be the discovery that substantial assets
which had been included in the last balance sheet had, by that date, been
destroyed, with the loss not being covered by insurance.

One reason for the issue of this Statement was concern about the practice of reserve accounting or, to follow American terminology, the use of the
dirty surplus method. In reserve accounting, companies charge and credit
extraordinary and prior year items direct to reserves rather than pass them
through the profit and loss account. The justification for the practice is that
the inclusion of such items in the profit and loss account distorts it and makes
it less useful as a predictor of future results. The ASC is of the view that all
profits and losses should be reflected in the profit and loss account and a
number of reasons can be advanced to support their position.

Two of the main ones are as follows:

(a) The decision as to what should, or should not, be excluded from the
    profit and loss account must be a subjective one. It had been noted that
    some companies were more prone to exclude debits rather than
    credits.

(b) Although, by definition, extraordinary items occur infrequently, most large companies will have in most years, some item which could be classified as 'extraordinary', and to exclude them from the profit and loss account would result in a distorted view of profit.

The method suggested by the ASC seems to retain the advantages claimed for reserve accounting without suffering from its defects.

SSAP 9: Stock and Work in Progress* (issued May 1975)

There are numerous methods of valuing and accounting for stock and work in progress, and the Standard was released in order to bring some consistency to this area.

The standard may be summarized as follows:

1. The amount at which stocks and work in progress, other than long-term contract work in progress, is stated should be the total of the lower of cost and net realizable value of the separate items of stock and work in progress or of groups of similar items.

2. Long-term contract work in progress should be stated at cost plus any attributable profit, less any foreseeable losses and progress payments received and receivable. If, however, anticipated losses on individual contracts exceed costs incurred to date less progress payments, such excesses should be shown separately as provisions.

3. The accounting policies used in calculating cost, net realizable value, attributable profit and foreseeable losses should be stated.

4. Stocks and work in progress should be subclassified in balance sheets in a manner which is appropriate to the business.

5. In connection with long-term contracts the following should be stated in the balance sheet:

   (a) The amount of work in progress at cost plus attributable profit, less foreseeable losses.

   (b) Cash received and receivable as progress payments.

SSAP 12: Accounting for Depreciation (issued January 1978)

The standard is:

1. Provision for depreciation of fixed assets having a finite useful life should be made by allocating the cost (or revalued amount) less

---

* Chapter 2 described accounting for stock and work in progress (See pages 26–35).

estimated residual values of the assets as fairly as possible to the periods expected to benefit from their use.

2. Where there is a revision of the estimated useful life of an asset, the unamortized cost should be charged over the revised remaining useful life.

3. However, if at any time the unamortized cost of an asset is seen to be irrecoverable in full, it should be written down immediately to the estimated recoverable amount which should be charged over the remaining useful life.

4. Where there is a charge from one method of depreciation to another, the unamortized cost of the assets should be written off over the remaining useful life on the new basis commencing with the period in which the change is made. The effect should be disclosed in the year of change, if material.

5. Where assets are revalued in the financial statements, the provision for depreciation should be based on the revalued amount and current estimate of remaining useful life, with disclosure in the year of change, of the effect of the revaluation, if material.

6. The following should be disclosed in the financial statements for each major class of depreciable asset:

(a) the depreciation methods used;

(b) the useful lives or the depreciation rates used;

(c) total depreciation allocated for the period;

(d) the gross amount of depreciable assets and the related accumulated depreciation.

We shall now provide an example illustrating the effect of some of the above proposals.

Example 7.1

The following show the cost of fixed assets and accumulated depreciation at the start of 1978.

	Cost £	Accumulated depreciation £	Net book value £
Freehold land and buildings	100,000	—	100,000
Asset A	12,000	8,000	4,000
Asset B	80,000	42,000	38,000
	£192,000	£50,000	£142,000

No fixed assets were purchased or sold during 1978.

In preparing the accounts for 1978 the following factors have to be taken into account:

(a) The freehold land and buildings were purchased on 1 January 1968. No depreciation has been provided in the past, but following SSAP 12 it is now considered necessary. It is estimated that of the total cost of £100,000, £40,000 related to the land and £60,000 to the building. The building has an estimated life of 40 years.

(b) When asset A was purchased on 1 January 1970 it was expected that the asset would have a useful life of twelve years and a zero scrap value. The straight-line method of depreciation was selected, i.e., the depreciation charge was £1,000 per year. At the end of 1978 it was decided that the asset would last for only another year.

(c) The product made on asset B is no longer competitive. It is worth retaining the asset, which has a very low net realizable value, but its current value to the company at the start of 1978 was only about £20,000. The asset will last until the end of 1981.

Freehold Land and Buildings

If we assume that the buildings are to be written off on a straight-line basis the depreciation charge for 1978 is £1,500. If this amount had been charged since 1968 the accumulated depreciation at 31 December 1977 would have been £15,000. Since this arises from a change in accounting policies, it is a prior year item and should, following SSAP 6, be deducted from the opening balance of retained earnings in the following way:

Retained earnings at the start of the year:

	£	£
As stated	300,000	
Less Prior year item (note (d))	15,000	285,000

Note (d) should describe the reason for the change and should say what the profit for 1977 (the preceding year) would have been had the buildings been depreciated in that year.

Asset A

Following SSAP 12 the depreciation charge for 1978 should be £2,000, i.e. £4,000/2, since it is now thought that the asset will last for two years from 1 January 1978. The ASC rejected the alternative of making a prior year adjustment to bring the accumulated depreciation up to the amount that would have been charged if it had been realized, from the date of purchase, that the asset would last for only ten years.

Asset B

The difference between the net book value and the value at the start of 1978 £18,000, has to be written off in 1978, but it is not an extraordinary item since it is not an event which is outside the normal activities of the company. However, because of its size the amount should be stated in the accounts, and an explanation given. The 'normal' depreciation charge for 1978, using the straight-line method is £5,000.

Freehold land does not normally depreciate and hence there is no requirement to provide for depreciation. Buildings do, however, depreciate and SSAP 12 requires firms to charge depreciation. Where fixed assets are sold for amounts greater or less than book values, the profit or loss, if material, should be disclosed separately in the accounts. Any profits or losses arising on the disposal of fixed assets when the whole or a substantial part of the business is discontinued should be dealt with as extraordinary items.

Property and investment companies objected strongly to SSAP 12 on the grounds that it did not show a true and fair view of their profits, and because it may unfairly restrict dividend distributions. While substantial gains can be made on holding property assets, these are not reflected in the profit and loss account and yet the depreciation charge will be increased because of revaluations. This assymetric treatment of depreciation and property revaluations led to the ASC issuing a new standard to take account of what are termed investment properties (see page 251).

SSAP 13: Accounting for Research and Development (issued January 1978)

The accounting treatment of research and development is of great interest not only because of the fascinating nature of many of the actual projects, but also because of the accounting issues involved.

The problem of accounting for research and development highlights the conflict between accruals and prudence in a sharper way than most other areas of accounting debate.

Following the accruals concept, accountants seek to match the expenses with the related revenue but, following the prudence concept, expenditure is written off in the period in which it is incurred unless its relationship to the revenue of a future period can be established with reasonable certainty.

The ASC distinguishes three types of research and development expenditure:

(a) *pure (or basic) research:* original investigation undertaken in order to gain new scientific or technical knowledge and understanding: basic research is not primarily directed towards any specific practical aim or application;

(b) *applied research:* original investigation undertaken in order to gain new scientific or technical knowledge, and directed towards a specific practical aim or objective:

(c) *development:* the use of scientific or technical knowledge in order to produce new or substantially improved materials, devices, products, processes, systems or services prior to the commencement of commercial production.

SSAP 13 states that expenditure on pure and applied research should be written off in the year of expenditure. Development expenditure should also be written off in the year of expenditure, except in certain circumstances.

The standard is:

1. The cost of fixed assets acquired or constructed in order to provide facilities for research and development activities over a number of accounting periods should be capitalized and written off over their useful life.

2. Expenditure on pure and applied research (other than that referred to in (1) above) should be written off in the year of expenditure.

3. Development expenditure should be written off in the year of expenditure except in the following circumstances, when it may be deferred to future periods:

   (a) there is a clearly defined project, and

   (b) the related expenditure is separately identifiable, and

   (c) the outcome of such a project has been assessed with reasonable certainty as to –

   (i) its technical feasibility, and
   (ii) its ultimate commercial viability considered in the light of factors such as likely market conditions (including competing products), public opinion, consumer and environmental legislation, and

   (d) if further development costs are to be incurred on the same project, the aggregate of such costs together with related production, selling and administration costs are reasonably expected to be more than covered by related future revenues, and

   (e) adequate resources exist, or are reasonably expected to be available, to enable the project to be completed and to provide any consequential increases in working capital.

4. In the foregoing circumstances development expenditure may be deferred to the extent that its recovery can reasonably be regarded as assured.

5. The criteria for determining whether development expenditure may be deferred should be applied consistently.

6. If development costs are deferred to future periods, their amortization should commence with the commercial production of the product or process, and should be allocated on a systematic basis to each accounting period, by reference to either the sale or use of

the product or process or the period over which the product or process is expected to be sold or used.

7. Deferred development expenditure should be reviewed at the end of each accounting period and where the circumstances which have justified the deferral of the expenditure (see (3) above) no longer apply, or are considered doubtful, the expenditure, to the extent to which it is considered to be irrecoverable, should be written off immediately.

8. Development expenditure once written off should not be reinstated, even though the uncertainties which had led to its being written off no longer apply.

9. Movements on deferred development expenditure and the amount carried forward at the beginning and the end of the period should be disclosed.

10. Deferred development expenditure should be separately disclosed and should not be included in current assets.

11. The accounting policy followed should be clearly explained.

The ASC considered the case for a fuller disclosure of research and development activities, e.g. a description of the nature, status and costs of individual research and development projects, whether written off or not. They concluded, however, that to call for such detailed disclosure would raise considerable problems of definition and hence they proposed that disclosure should be limited to the movements of unamortized development expenditure during the year. We believe the narrower scope of disclosure is unfortunate because a detailed description of research and development can be of great significance in judging the future prospects of a company.

SSAP 17: Accounting for Post Balance Sheet events (issued September 1980)

There is inevitably a delay between the end of an accounting period and the date of publication of the financial statements. The objective of SSAP 17 is to ensure that users of accounts are supplied with information about significant events which occurred in part of that period. The standard is only concerned with *post balance sheet events* which are defined as events which occur between the balance sheet date and the date on which the financial statements are approved by the Board of Directors. However, reference is made in the explanatory section of the standard to events which occur after the date on which the financial statements are approved by the Directors and it is suggested that Directors should consider the publication of details relating to such events so that the users of financial statements are not misled.

The standard distinguishes between *adjusting* and *non-adjusting* post balance sheet events.

Adjusting events are defined as those which provide additional evidence of conditions existing at the balance sheet date and which will hence call for the revision of the amounts at which items are stated in the financial statements. Examples of adjusting events are the insolvency of a debtor, the receipt of information about tax rates and the agreement of an insurance claim. Further examples of adjusting (and non-adjusting) events are provided in an appendix to SSAP 17.

Non-adjusting events are events which concern conditions which did not exist at the balance sheet date. These events should be disclosed as a note to the financial statements but will not require a change in the accounts themselves, examples of non-adjusting events are the issue of shares and debentures, the purchase and sale of fixed assets and strikes or other labour disputes.

The standard itself may be summarized as follows:

1. Financial statements should be prepared on the basis of conditions existing at the balance sheet date.

2. A material post balance sheet event requires changes in the amounts to be included in financial statements where:

   (a) it is an adjusting event; or

   (b) it indicates that application of the going concern concept to the whole or a material part of the company is not appropriate.

3. A material post balance sheet event should be disclosed where:

   (a) it is a non-adjusting event of such materiality that its non-disclosure would affect the ability of the users of financial statements to reach a proper understanding of the financial position; or

   (b) it is the reversal or maturity after the year end of a transaction entered into before the year end, the substance of which was primarily to alter the appearance of the company's balance sheet (often known as window dressing).

4. In respect of each post balance sheet event which is required to be disclosed under (3) above, the following information should be stated by way of notes in financial statements:

   (a) the nature of the event; and

   (b) an estimate of the financial effect, or a statement that it is not practicable to make such an estimate.

5.   The estimate of the financial effect should be disclosed before taking account of taxation, and the taxation implications should be explained where necessary for a proper understanding of the financial position.

6.   The date on which the financial statements are approved by the Board of Directors should be disclosed in the financial statements.

SSAP 18: Accounting for Contingencies (issued September 1980)

A contingency is defined by the ASC as a condition which exists at the balance sheet date, where the outcome will be confirmed only on the occurrence or non-occurrence of one or more uncertain future events. A contingent gain or loss is a gain or loss dependent on a contingency.

The Standard itself is as follows:

1.   In addition to amounts accrued under the fundamental concept of prudence in SSAP 2 'Disclosure of accounting policies,' a material contingent loss should be accrued in financial statements where it is probable that a future event will confirm a loss which can be estimated with reasonable accuracy at the date on which the financial statements are approved by the board of directors.

2.   A material contingent loss not accrued under (1) above should be disclosed except where the possibility of loss is remote.

3.   Contingent gains should not be accrued in financial statements. A material contingent gain should be disclosed in financial statements only if it is probable that the gain will be realized.

4.   In respect of each contingency which is required to be disclosed under paragraphs 2 and 3 above, the following information should be stated by way of notes in financial statements:

  (a) the nature of the contingency; and

  (b) the uncertainties which are expected to affect the ultimate outcome; and

  (c) a prudent estimate of the financial effect, made at the date on which the financial statements are approved by the board of directors; or a statement that it is not practicable to make such an estimate.

5.   Where there is disclosure of an estimate of the financial effect of a contingency, the amount disclosed should be the potential finan-

cial effect. In the case of a contingent loss, this should be reduced by:

(a) any amounts accrued; and

(b) the amounts of any components where the possibility of loss is remote.

The net amount only need be disclosed.

6. The estimate of the financial effect should be disclosed before taking account of taxation, and the taxation implications of a contingency crystallizing should be explained where necessary for a proper understanding of the financial position.

7. Where both the nature of, and the uncertainties which affect, a contingency in respect of an individual transaction are common to a large number of similar transactions, the financial effect of the contingency need not be individually estimated but may be based on the group of similar transactions. In these circumstances the separate contingencies need not be individually disclosed.

SSAP 19: Accounting for Investment Properties (issued November 1981)

Under the general accounting requirements of SSAP 12 'Accounting for Depreciation,' fixed assets are subject to annual depreciation charges to reflect on a systematic basis the consumption, wearing out and use of the asset in the course of the business of an enterprise. Under those general requirements it is accepted that an increase in the value of such a fixed asset does not remove the necessity to charge depreciation to reflect on a systematic basis the consumption of the asset. However, for the reasons given on page 245, property companies objected strongly to SSAP 12 and the ASC have accepted their argument and are now of the opinion that a different accounting treatment is required for a fixed asset which is held as a disposable investment and not for consumption in the business operations of an enterprise. In such a case the current value of the investment, and changes in that current value, are of prime importance rather than a calculation of systematic annual depreciation. Consequently, for the proper appreciation of the financial position, a different accounting treatment is considered appropriate for fixed assets held as disposable investments, and this is the subject of SSAP 19.

SSAP 19 requires a system of current value accounting for properties which are fixed assets but nevertheless held as disposable investments (called in the Standard 'investment properties').

An investment property is a disposable investment interest in land and buildings, on which construction work and development have been completed and which is held for its investment potential; any rental income being negotiated at arm's length. Thus if the property is occupied it must be occupied by someone other than the owners. Specifically, the standard excludes from the definition of investment properties, properties which are owned and occupied by a company for its own purpose as well as properties let to and occupied by another company in the same group of companies as the owner.

The most important point in the standard is that investment properties should not be subject to periodic charges for depreciation on the basis set out in SSAP 12 with the exception of properties held on a lease 'which should be depreciated on the basis set out in SSAP 12 at least over the period when the unexpired term is 20 years or less'.* Thus companies must depreciate leasehold investment properties for the last 20 years of the lease but may do so over a longer period.

In order for the accounts to show a realistic position investment properties must be included in the balance sheet at their 'open market value' and not cost. Open market value is not defined in the standard but an obvious basis is the estimated net realizable value of the property. The standard does not specifically require annual revaluations but these would be required to fulfil the spirit of the standard unless there was evidence that the change in value over the year was immaterial.

The names of the persons making the valuation or particulars of their qualifications should be disclosed together with the bases of valuation used by them. If a person making a valuation is an employee or officer of the company or group which owns the property this fact should be disclosed.

Changes in the value of an investment property should not be taken to the profit and loss account but should be disclosed as a movement in an investment property revaluation reserve, unless the total of the investment property revaluation reserve is insufficient to cover a deficit, in which case the amount by which the deficit exceeds the amount in the investment property revaluation reserve should be charged in the profit and loss account. These requirements should be read in conjunction with, and do not override, paragraph 10 of SSAP 6 'Extraordinary items and prior year adjustments'. (See page 241)

The book values of the investment properties and investment property revaluation reserve should be displayed prominently in the financial statements.

The other SSAPs that have been issued up to December 1983, and have not been withdrawn, are:

SSAP 1:   Accounting for the results of associated companies (see Chapter 8).
SSAP 3:   Earnings per share (see Chapter 13).
SSAP 4:   The accounting treatment of government grants (see Chapter 6).
SSAP 5:   Accounting for value-added tax (see Chapter 6).

* SSAP 19, paragraph 10

SSAP 8:	The treatment of taxation under the imputation system in the accounts of companies (see Chapter 6).
SSAP 10:	Statements of source and application of funds (see Chapter 9).
SSAP 14:	Group Accounts (see Chapter 8).
SSAP 15:	Accounting for deferred taxation (see Chapter 6).
SSAP 16:	Current Cost Accounting (see Chapter 12).
SSAP 20:	Foreign Currency Translation.

THE AUDITOR

We have explained that limited companies must publish a good deal of information about their activities, but this will be of little use if potential users do not have enough confidence in its reliability to use it. This is one reason why all limited companies must have professionally qualified auditors. The other main reason comes from the stewardship concept, since the annual accounts are the means by which the directors report to the shareholders on what they have done with the resources that the shareholders have committed to their care.

An auditor of a limited company must be a member of one of the three Institutes of Chartered Accountants,* or of the Association of Certified Accountants, or be specially authorized by the Department of Trade.

The auditor's statutory responsibilities include the following:

1. He must report to the members on the accounts submitted to them, saying whether or not in his opinion the balance sheet gives a true and fair view of the state of the company's affairs at the balance sheet date, whether the profit and loss account gives a true and fair view of the profit or loss for the period covered by the accounts and whether the accounts comply with the Companies Acts.

2. In preparing his report he must also carry out such investigations as to enable him to form an opinion whether:

   (a) proper books have been kept, and
   (b) the balance sheet and profit and loss account agree with the books of account.

The auditor need not mention 2(a) and 2(b) in his report unless he cannot come to the opinion that the provisions have been satisfied.

Note the emphasis on the word opinion – the auditor is not required to state that they do give a true and fair view. It is thus misleading to talk about the auditor 'certifying' the accounts since this implies a greater degree of certainty than can be expected to exist. Another common error is to talk

---

* Of England and Wales, Ireland and Scotland.

about the auditor's 'preparing the accounts' or 'changing the accounts'. The accounts are the responsibility of the directors and the auditor's job is simply to report on them.

If the auditor is satisfied he makes an *unqualified* or *clean* audit report. Otherwise the auditor must give a qualified audit report. The qualification may be that he cannot give an opinion because, for example, of inaccuracies in the underlying records. The qualification may be a total one such as 'in our opinion the balance sheet does not give a true and fair view of the state of the company's affairs as at 31 December 1975, and the profit and loss account does not give a true and fair view of the profit for the year ended on that date because the accounts have been prepared on the basis of the going concern convention, the application of which is, in our opinion, not appropriate in the circumstances facing the company'. On the other hand, the qualification may only refer to a single item, for example, 'in our opinion the balance sheet gives a true and fair view . . . except that we believe that an inadequate provision has been made against doubtful debts'.

There is nothing to stop auditors agreeing with the directors that they should go beyond their statutory duties and report on supplementary statements provided with the accounts.

Auditors are charged by their professional bodies with the duty of ensuring that standards of accounting practice are adhered to or, if they are not, that the reasons for any variation are explained. Auditors who fail to do this may be subject to disciplinary action by the professional bodies of which they are members.

The Auditor and Small and Medium Sized Companies

The auditor has additional duties in respect of small and medium sized companies. If modified accounts are filed with the Registrar the auditor must report to the directors that in the auditors' opinion the requirements for exemption have been satisfied. The modified accounts must be accompanied by a special report from the auditors stating that in their opinion the requirements for exemption have been satisfied and reproducing the complete text of the audit report on the full accounts.

EXERCISES

7.1 To what extent should accounting practices be determined by legislation (such as the Companies Acts, etc.), by the Stock Exchange or by the professional accounting institutions?

7.2 Safewrap Ltd, a trading company, has an authorized share capital of £1,000,000 divided into ordinary shares of 20p each.

Draft management accounts extracted from the books of the company as on 31st July 1983, showed the following position:

Profit and Loss Account

	Packing materials division £'000	Printing division £'000	Plastic hardware division £'000
Sales	2,720	2,060	2,120
Less cost of sales	1,865	1,372	1,496
	855	688	624
Deduct:			
Warehouse and drivers' wages	222	142	110
Office salaries	104	86	62
Motor van expenses	22	26	14
Warehouse overhead	31	18	24
Office overhead	16	17	21
Directors' salaries	18	15	12
Bad debts	4	2	3
Sales commissions	125	92	106
Audit fee	6	7	7
Depreciation:			
motor vans	42	28	30
fixtures and fittings	6	9	5
buildings	15	16	9
Bank — loan interest	20	20	20
— overdraft interest	15	15	15
	646	493	438
Net profit for year	209	195	186

Balance Sheet

	£'000	£'000		£'000	£'000
Share capital:			Fixed assets:		
Issued ordinary shares ...		1,000	Freehold land		1,200
Revenue reserves:			Buildings, at cost	2,000	
Balance as on 31st July,			*Less* depreciation	200	
1982	829				1,800
Net profit for year	590		Fixtures & fittings, at cost	496	
		1,419	*Less* depreciation	416	
		2,419			80
Trade creditors	3,249		Motor vans, at cost ...	692	
Bank loan	522		*Less* depreciation	392	
Bank overdraft	410				300
		4,181			3,380
			Current assets:		
			Stocks, at cost	2,120	
			Debtors	1,100	
					3,220
		6,600			6,600

You are also given the following additional information:

1.   Each of the three divisions of the business has a director in charge and there is a non-executive chairman. The interests of the directors in the shares of the company which have remained unchanged throughout the year are as follows:

		Shares
P. Matthews—packing materials ...		60,000
B. Good—printing		65,000
G. Gnome—plastic hardware ...		135,000
L. Ordnose—chairman		1,240,000

In addition, B. Good and his wife are interested in a further 1,000,000 shares under a family settlement.

Mr. G. Gnome was appointed a director on 1st August, 1982. The remaining directors have been in office for many years.

2.   Provision is to be made for directors' fees of £6,000 for each director.

3.   Depreciation on buildings is provided on a straight line basis over fifty years. Fixtures and fittings and motor vans are depreciated on a reducing balance basis.

4.   The bank loan is repayable on 1st August 1995, and is secured by a mortgage on the freehold land and buildings.

5.   Provision is made for corporation tax based on the results of the year (calculated at 52%) estimated at £303,000, and payable on 1st May 1984.

6.   The company employs, on average, 113 people in the packing materials division, 79 in printing and 60 in plastic hardware. It is company policy to try to achieve a level of employment of disabled persons of at least 5%. In the year ended 31st July 1983 a donation of £1,000 had been made to the Disabled Persons Charitable Trust.

7.   The directors recommend the payment of an ordinary dividend of 5p per share. The related advance corporation tax is considered to be recoverable.

You are required to prepare the company's financial statements and the directors' report for the year ended 31st July 1983, in accordance with generally accepted accounting principles and in a form suitable for presentation to members.

NOTES:

The information given may be taken as if it included all that is necessary to satisfy the requirements of the Companies Acts, 1948 to 1981.

Ignore the requirement to prepare a statement of source and application of funds. Corresponding figures are not required.

Institute of Chartered Accountants in England and Wales, Financial Accounting I, Nov. 1983.

7.3 Sellby Ltd, a trading company, employing 15 people, has an authorized share capital of £200,000 divided into 100,000 8% preference shares of £1 each and 1,000,000 ordinary shares of 10p each. A trial balance extracted from the books of the company as on 30th April 1983 showed the following position:

	£'000	£'000
Preference share capital		100
Ordinary share capital (fully paid)		50
Profit and loss account, as on 30th April 1982		15
Corporation tax		12
Creditors		154
Debtors	324	
Sales (all in United Kingdom)		1,250
Purchases	880	
Stocks, as on 30th April 1982	75	
Distribution expenses	129	
Administrative expenses	139	
Audit fees	2	
Fixtures and fittings	10	
Motor vans	27	
Directors' remuneration	39	
Preference dividend paid	4	
Interim ordinary dividend paid	3	
Advance corporation tax	3	
Bank medium term loan		50
Bank loan interest	6	
Hire purchase balances not yet due		20
Hire purchase interest paid	4	
Bank balance	6	
	1,651	1,651

The following information is also relevant:

1. Directors' remuneration consists of managing director's salary £12,000, chairman's salary £15,000 and fees paid equally to all four directors of £3,000 each.

2. Fixtures and fittings had originally cost £20,000 and motor vans had cost £36,000. Depreciation is to be provided on cost at 20% and 25% respectively.

3. Stocks as on 30th April 1983 amounted to £80,000.

4. Provision is to be made for corporation tax based on the results of the year (calculated at 38%) estimated at £17,000, payable on 1st January 1985.

5.   The bank medium term loan was granted on 1st May 1980 for a fixed
      term of 10 years.

6.   The hire purchase agreements were for 3 years with effect from 1st
      May 1982.

7.   The directors recommend payment of the second half-year's dividend
      on the preference shares and a final ordinary dividend of 2p per share.
      The related advance corporation tax is considered to be recoverable.

8.   The directors have decided that the financial statements shall be
      prepared in accordance with the appropriate Companies Act 1981
      formats.

You are required to prepare:

(a) the company's financial statements for the year ended 30th April 1983 in
     accordance with generally accepted accounting principles and in a form
     suitable for presentation to members, and
(b) the modified accounts which the company can present to the Registrar
     of Companies.

The information given may be taken as if it included all that is necessary to
satisfy the requirements of the Companies Acts 1948 to 1981.

Note: Ignore the requirements to disclose accounting policies and to prepare
a statement of source and application of funds.

Institute of Chartered Accountants in England and Wales, Financial Accounting, 1 November
1983

7.4 The directors of Trunfair Ltd, a trading company, are due to approve
the company's financial statements for the year ended 31st July 1983.

Since the financial statements were originally prepared the following
material information has become available:

1.   On 1st September 1983 a major design fault was found in a new
      product and it was withdrawn from the market. Stocks of the product
      have been returned to Trunfair Ltd's supplier for a full refund. The
      company had committed itself to an advertising schedule for this new
      product involving total expenditure of £300,000, to be written off
      evenly over three years. £150,000 had been spent in the first year to
      31st July 1983.

2.   On 15th September 1983 torrential rain caused flooding at the
      company's riverside warehouse resulting in an uninsured stock loss
      totalling £200,000.

3.   Bills receivable of £120,000 had been discounted at the bank on 15th

July 1983. The bills were dishonoured on presentation at the maturity date on 16th September 1983.

You are required to advise the directors on the effect the above information should have on the financial statements for the year ended 31st July 1983, giving your reasons.

Institute of Chartered Accountants in England and Wales, Financial Accounting I, May 1983.

7.5 Fenn Limited owns one large machine which was, at the start of 19X3, three years old. Fenn's other fixed assets are insignificant and may be ignored for the purposes of the question. When the machine was purchased in 19X0 it was estimated that it would have an operating life of 12,500 hours. Under normal conditions the machine would be used for about 2,500 hours per year and it was, accordingly, decided that its cost less anticipated scrap value should be written off in equal instalments over five years. The machine cost £22,000 and its anticipated scrap value was £2,000. Thus at 31 December 19X2 the accumulated depreciation was £12,000.

Assume that each of the following events and reassessments was made in January 19X3. State how each would, if at all, affect the treatment of the machinery in the accounts for 19X3. Treat each part of the question as being independent of the others.

(a) Double shift work was introduced for the whole of 19X3 and the machine was operated for 5,000 hours.

(b) Owing to a change in the demand for the product, the machine was taken out of regular service on 1 January 19X3. The machine was not sold but retained for use at times of peak demand. If the machine had not been available, certain work would have to have been sent to subcontractors. The net cost of this work would have been £2,000 in 19X3. It is expected that the machine would be used on this basis (for the same number of hours per year) until the end of 19X5, and would have a scrap value of £1,000 at that time.

(c) It is now expected that the machine's scrap value will be £3,000.

(d) A spanner was left in the machine in January 19X3. This necessitated major repairs costing £6,000. As a result of this work the remaining life of the machine was increased by 2,500 hours.

(e) The price of the product manufactured by the machine has risen substantially, thus increasing the profit (before depreciation) applicable to the product from £6,000 to £8,000 per annum.

(f) As (e) except that the price has fallen and the profit (before depreciation) is now £2,200 per annum.

260

Foundation in Accounting

(g) A technical reappraisal suggests that the expected effective life of the machine as at the start of 19X3 is 10,000 hours.

7.6 The following were included in the balances extracted from the books of Unfortunate Limited as at 31 December 19X5.

		£
(a)	Bad debts expense	24,000
(b)	Research and development expense	242,000
(c)	Cash embezzled by a former director	1,500,000
(d)	Additional provision for damages and costs in respect of a case brought against the company for an infringement of a patent	18,000
(e)	Inventory	268,000
(f)	Profit on sale of an office block	206,000

Further details are provided below:

1. The bad debts expense has been about £3,000 per annum for some years. The increase in the expense for this year was due to debiting the account with £20,000 paid in advance to a supplier of goods who went into liquidation before discharging his obligation to Unfortunate Limited.

2. An analysis of the research and development account disclosed the following:

	£
Cost of construction of laboratory equipment which has an estimated life of five years	30,000
Development of project AQ 43	120,000
General research	92,000
	£242,000

Project AQ 43 has already proved successful. 10,000 units of the associated product were sold in 19X5 and future sales are estimated at 20,000 units in 19X6 and 10,000 in 19X7.

3. The embezzlement occurred in 19X4 but it was not discovered until 19X5.

4. The case started in 19X5. Unfortunate Limited has accepted that it did infringe the patent and the only matter outstanding is the amount of the damages and costs. A provision of £20,000 was made at 31 December 19X4 but this is now considered to be inadequate.

5. An analysis of the inventory account disclosed the following:

Raw Materials

	Cost	Net realizable value	
	£	£	£
Category A	28,000	26,000	
Category B	45,000	52,000	
	£73,000	£78,000	

Total, at the lower of cost and net realizable value	73,000
Work in progress, at cost (net realizable value £60,000)	47,000
Finished goods, at net realizable value (cost £96,000)	85,000
	205,000

Long-term contracts

		Contract		
	A	B	C	
Cost	30,000	50,000	20,000	
add Attributable profit (loss)	12,000	(5,000)	(6,000)	
	42,000	45,000	14,000	
less Cash received	16,000	22,000	—	
Total	£26,000	£23,000	£14,000	63,000
				268,000

The following are not reflected in the above

(i) It is expected that the eventual total loss on Contract C will amount to £25,000.

(ii) A progress payment of £10,000 in respect of Contract A which was invoiced in December 19X5 was received in January 19X6.

6. The office block had previously housed Unfortunate Limited's head office.

Required:

State how each of the above should be reflected in Unfortunate Limited's published accounts for 19X5. Your answers should include references to appropriate Statements of Standard Accounting Practice and Exposure Drafts.

8 | *Consolidated Accounts*

INTRODUCTION

A significant feature of modern business practice in the United Kingdom is that the vast majority of the larger limited companies are members of groups of companies. For example, of the 300 major British companies surveyed by the Institute of Chartered Accountants in England and Wales in 1975 no less than 295 were members of a group.

A group exists when one company – the *parent* or *holding* company – owns another company – the *subsidiary* company. The parent need not own all the shares of the subsidiary. The test is whether the investing company can control the other company. We will discuss later on pages 274–5 what exactly constitutes control for the purposes of deciding whether a holding/subsidiary company relationship exists.

The Nature of the Problem

In order to illustrate why the existence of a group of companies requires special accounting treatment we will introduce the following example.

Suppose that on 1 January Year 1, two companies, H Limited and A Limited, started business and that, except for one factor, they were identical. The only difference is that A Limited carries on the trade itself while H Limited forms a subsidiary company, S Limited, to conduct the business. The only function of H Limited is to receive dividends from its subsidiary which are then paid to its shareholders. We will ignore taxation and assume that no expenses are incurred by H Limited. Let us assume that H Limited and A Limited each started with a capital of £10,000, that the trading profits are £1,000 per year, and that dividends of £200 are paid each year.

The three balance sheets as at 1 January Year 1 were:

H Limited
Share capital   £10,000   Shares in S Ltd   £10,000

S Limited
Share capital   £10,000   Sundry assets   £10,000

A Limited
Share capital   £10,000   Sundry assets   £10,000

The various profit and loss accounts for, say, year 8 are:

	H Ltd £	S Ltd £	A Ltd £
Profit from trading	—	1,000	1,000
Dividends received	200	—	—
	200	1,000	1,000
less			
Dividends paid	200	200	200
	—	800	800
Retained earnings, Start of Year 8	—	5,600	5,600
End of Year 8	£ —	£6,400	£6,400

The balance sheets as at the end of Year 8 are:

	H Ltd	S Ltd	A Ltd
Sundry assets	—	16,400	16,400
Shares in S Limited, at cost	10,000	—	—
	£10,000	£16,400	£16,400
Share capital	10,000	10,000	10,000
Retained earnings	—	6,400	6,400
	£10,000	£16,400	£16,400

· Now suppose that the shareholders of H Limited were presented only with the balance sheet and profit and loss account of that company. It is clear that they would receive an extremely misleading and incomplete description of the state and results of their investment. They would be given no indication of the profits earned by the business they, albeit indirectly, own. They would receive no information about how the funds which have not been distributed have been used. The information supplied to the shareholders of

H Limited should be contrasted with that provided to the shareholders of A Limited.

It can be seen that, if no special steps were taken, the directors of companies could avoid the disclosure requirements of the Companies Act by creating a subsidiary company to conduct the business. One way of solving the problem is to ensure that the shareholders of H Limited are supplied with the accounts of S Limited. This approach is practicable in a simple case such as the one illustrated, but it would not be very helpful in cases where there are numerous subsidiaries.

Consolidated Accounts

In general, a more useful approach is to produce a balance sheet and profit and loss account which cover the activities of the group as a whole. These accounts are known as consolidated accounts. This is a reasonable approach, for it recognizes the fact that a group of companies represents an economic entity, i.e. a bundle of assets subject to common ownership.

There are, in practice, many complexities associated with the preparation of consolidated accounts, and so, in this chapter we shall concentrate on the basic principles which are, as we hope we shall be able to demonstrate, relatively straightforward.

There are two main bases for the preparation of consolidated accounts. The one that is almost universally employed in the United Kingdom is known as the *purchase* or *acquisition* method. The alternative, which is used to a greater extent in the United States is called the *pooling* or *merger* method. We shall first discuss the purchase method.

PURCHASE METHOD OF CONSOLIDATION

Wholly-owned Subsidiaries

It will be best if we start with a simple example. Suppose that on 1 January 19X2 H Limited purchased all the shares of S Limited for £17,000. The balance sheets as at that date were as follows:

	H Ltd *£000*	*S Ltd* *£000*
Sundry assets	35	21
10,000 shares in S Limited	17	—
	£52	£21
Share capital, £1 shares	30	10
Retained earnings	10	4
	40	14
Sundry liabilities	12	7
	£52	£21

Note that H Limited paid £17,000 for S Limited and has, as a result, acquired assets less liabilities with a net book value of £14,000. We will assume that there is no difference between the current (at the date of acquisition) and net book values of the asset and liabilities. It is not surprising to find a difference between the price paid for the business as a whole and the net book value of the assets less liabilities because of the existence of goodwill which we discussed on pages 86 and 87. We will deal with the situation where there is a difference between the book and current values on page 269.

The excess of the cost of the shares over the net book value of the assets less liabilities acquired is known by various terms of which the following are, perhaps, the most common.

Excess of the cost of shares in the subsidiary over the book value of the net assets of the subsidiary company as at the date of acquisition.
Goodwill
Goodwill on consolidation
Cost of control
Premium arising on consolidation

Of the above terms the first is the best because it is an accurate description of the item. However, it is a cumbersome description and we shall, therefore, use the shorter term 'goodwill on consolidation'.

We stated earlier that the objective of a consolidated balance sheet is to describe the state of the group as a whole. In our example, therefore, it should show total tangible assets of £56,000 (£35,000 + £21,000) and total liabilities of £19,000 (£12,000 + £7,000). In addition, it must also recognize the existence of the additional asset of goodwill on consolidation.

The consolidated balance sheet can be prepared by replacing the cost of shares in the subsidiary shown in the holding company's balance sheet by the assets acquired plus the goodwill on consolidation less the liabilities taken over, i.e.

	H Ltd's Balance Sheet £000			*Consolidated Balance Sheet £000*
			Debit	
Sundry assets	35		£K21	56
Shares in subsidiary	17			
		Goodwill on consolidation	Debit £K3	3
	£52			£59
Share capital	30			30
Retained earnings	10			10
	40		Credit	40
Sundry liabilities	12		£K7	19
	£52			£59

In practice it is usually easier to calculate goodwill on consolidation in an, apparently, different way. To do this we note that the fundamental accounting identity* is

$$A = L + E$$

or

$$A - L = E$$

i.e. at any time the owners' equity (share capital and reserves) equals assets less liabilities.

Now goodwill on consolidation (G) = cost of shares in subsidiary (C) less net book value of assets less liabilities acquired $(A_s - L_s)$

i.e. $$G = C - (A_s - L_s)$$

Substituting $E_s = A_s - L_s$ where E_s is the owners' equity of the subsidiary company we obtain

$$G = C - E_s$$

i.e. goodwill on consolidation is the excess of the cost of shares in the subsidiary over the owners' equity of the subsidiary as at the date of acquisition.

It should be noted that this method is a convenient way of calculating goodwill on consolidation because it only requires knowledge of the owners' equity at the date of acquisition but that the meaning of goodwill on consolidation is as stated above – the difference between the cost of shares and the net book values of the assets less liabilities of the subsidiary as at the date of acquisition.

There are numerous ways of showing the workings underlying the preparation of consolidated accounts. We will use a consolidated worksheet of the following form:

Consolidated Balance Sheet Worksheet
All figures £000

	H Ltd	S Ltd	Sub-total	Adjustments Debit	Adjustments Credit	Consolidated Balance Sheet
Sundry assets	35	21	56			56
Shares in S Ltd	17	—	17		17	—
Goodwill on consolidation				3		3
	£52	£21	£73			£59
Share capital	30	10	40	10		30
Retained earnings	10	4	14	4		10
	40	14	54			40
Sundry liabilities	12	7	19			19
	£52	£21	£73	£17	£17	£59

* See Chapter 3 of Volume 1.

The adjustment displayed above is:

Cost of shares (£K17) minus owners' equity of the subsidiary at the date of acquisition (£K10 + £K4) = goodwill on consolidation (£K3).

Now let us suppose that the profits made by the two companies in 19X2 were H Limited £5,000, and S Limited £2,000, but that no dividends were paid. For simplicity, we will assume that the profits resulted in increases in sundry assets, i.e. the sundry liabilities remain unchanged.

The balance sheets of the two companies at 31 December 19X2 are shown on the following consolidated worksheet:

Consolidated Balance Sheet Worksheet at 31 December 19X2
All figures £000

	H Ltd	S Ltd	Sub-total	Adjustments Debit	Credit	Consolidated Balance Sheet
Sundry assets	40	23	63			63
Shares in S Ltd	17	—	17		17	—
Goodwill on consolidation				3		3
	£57	£23	£80			£66
Share capital	30	10	40	10		30
Retained earnings	15	6	21	4		17
	45	16	61			47
Sundry liabilities	12	7	19			19
	£57	£23	£80	£17	£17	£66

Note that the consolidation adjustment at 31 December 19X2 is the same as the one which applied at 1 January 19X2, the date of acquisition. This is because the adjustment relates to circumstances that applied at the date of acquisition and, as long as the goodwill is not written off (see page 270) the adjustment will remain constant for all future consolidated balance sheets.

The consolidated balance sheet of H Limited and its subsidiary company as at 31 December 19X2 is shown on the following page together with a commentary describing its various components.

The treatment of owners' equity in the consolidated balance sheet deserves special mention. The share capital shown in the consolidated balance sheet is the share capital of the holding company. This reflects the fact that the share capital of the holding company represents the funds that have been supplied to the group through the subscription of share capital by the ultimate owners. The share capital of the subsidiary company is an intra-group item in that it is owned by the holding company. The item does not represent funds subscribed by the owners of H, and hence it would be incorrect to include the share capital of the subsidiary as part of the share capital of the group.

H LIMITED
AND ITS SUBSIDIARY

Consolidated Balance Sheet
as at 31 December 19X2

£000

Sundry assets	63	The total assets of the companies comprising the group
Goodwill on consolidation	3	The difference between the cost of shares in the subsidiary company and the net book value of the subsidiary's assets less liabilities as at the date of acquisition.
	£66	
Share capital	30	The share capital of the holding company.
Retained earnings	17	The retained earnings of the holding company plus the change in retained earnings in the subsidiary between the date of acquisition and the balance sheet date.
	47	
Sundry liabilities	19	The total of the liabilities of the companies comprising the group
	£66	

When the holding company purchased the subsidiary company it simply acquired a bundle of assets and took over certain liabilities. It did not acquire any retained earnings.* Hence it would be wrong to show the retained earnings at acquisition as part of the retained earnings of the group. However, the increase in retained earnings since acquisition is another matter. This represents profits which have been earned by the group and thus should be included in the retained earnings of the group.

The above discussion has been couched in terms of retained earnings. However, exactly the same principles apply to any other form of reserve. The reserves at acquisition are not added to the reserves of the group but are 'eliminated' in the goodwill adjustment. Changes in the reserves since acquisition, on the other hand, are reflected in the consolidated balance sheet.

*Note that this interpretation only relates to the 'purchase' method. An alternative view is taken when the 'pooling' method is employed, see page 297.

The reason for the form of the goodwill adjustment used above can now be seen. The issued share capital of the subsidiary and its reserves as at the date of acquisition are eliminated by setting them off against the cost of the investment in the subsidiary with the difference being goodwill on consolidation.

The creation of a holding/subsidiary company relation has no effect on the balance sheet of the subsidiary company* and has only a minor effect on the balance sheet of the holding company. The general principle is that the transfer of shares between shareholders is an event that is not recorded in the accounting records and financial statements of the company concerned, and this principle holds even if the transfer results in the company becoming a subsidiary of another. So far as the holding company's balance sheet is concerned, the only difference between the treatment of an asset representing shares in a subsidiary company with that representing the ownership of shares in other companies is that the former is described as such, on the face of the holding company's balance sheet. The asset of shares in subsidiary companies, will be shown in the balance sheet at cost or valuation and will not be directly influenced by the net book value of the subsidiary's assets less liabilities for we are still using the historical cost basis of accounting.

The Nature of Goodwill on Consolidation

Goodwill is a word which frequently occurs in accounting and it is a word which often causes confusion. One reason for this is that it has at least two meanings. Goodwill is used to describe the total difference between the price paid for a company or a business and the net book value of the assets less liabilities acquired. Now it may often be possible to assign part, or all, of the total difference to a particular asset or assets. If this can be done, any remaining balance of goodwill is due to those tangible factors which, as we described on pages 86–7 of Chapter 4, may make the value of the business as a whole greater than the sum of the values of the parts. These intangible factors are often referred to as the goodwill of the business, and hence we have the terminological problem that goodwill may be used to describe both the total difference and one of the elements which make up that difference.

In practice a considerable proportion of the goodwill on consolidation may be caused by differences between the current values of particular assets and their net book values. When this occurs, the holding company is faced with three options. It can do nothing, i.e. make no adjustment, and treat the whole of the difference as goodwill on consolidation. It can, through its control over the subsidiary, arrange for the assets concerned to be revalued, as at the date of acquisition, in the books of the subsidiary company. If this second alternative were selected, the goodwill on consolidation would be reduced, or possibly eliminated altogether. Finally, it might not require the subsidiary to make the revaluation in its books but, instead, treat the revaluation as a consolidation adjustment. The selection of the third alternative will lead to the same consolidated accounts as would be produced by using the second approach.

*The assets of the subsidiary may, however, be revalued as at the date of acquisition.

The first approach does not appear to have much merit in so far as it is not as informative as the two other alternatives. The third approach appears to be somewhat illogical in that if the difference is significant enough to be reported to the shareholders of the holding company in the consolidated accounts, it should also be reflected in the accounts of the subsidiary company. However, there may be some point in adopting this approach when the subsidiary is not one which is 'wholly owned'. Following the issue of SSAP 14 (Group Accounts) in September 1978 companies are now required to adopt either the second or third approach.

Goodwill – What Should We Do with It?

Given that goodwill on consolidation has been created, we must consider what can be done with it. There are, once again, three alternatives. One is to do nothing, i.e. the goodwill on consolidation will appear on every future consolidated balance sheet at the same amount. This approach was used in our earlier example. The second alternative is to write off the goodwill against the reserves of the group in instalments over an arbitrarily selected number of years. The third alternative is to write off the whole of the goodwill against the reserves of the group at the date of acquisition.

Prior to the passage of the Companies Act 1981 there were wide variations in the method of dealing with goodwill on consolidation. Many companies retained goodwill at cost whilst many others wrote it off against reserves immediately on acquisition. Some companies adopted a compromise position whereby goodwill was not written off but was shown in all future consolidated balance sheets as a deduction from share capital and reserves of the group – when goodwill was treated in this way it was called a 'dangling debit'. It was difficult to justify such a variety in practice in that it could not, in general, be argued that the difference in treatment was due to the differing circumstances faced by individual companies. Very few British companies wrote off goodwill by instalments – the method which is favoured in the United States. The position in the UK has now changed following the implementation of the Fourth Directive of the EEC by the 1981 Companies Act. The directive requires companies to write off goodwill over a maximum period of five years but it does grant member countries the right to permit companies within their jurisdiction to write off goodwill over a longer period so long as that period does not exceed the useful economic life of the asset 1* the 1981 Act allows British companies to write off goodwill over this longer period.

In order to examine the question whether the item on consolidation adds anything to the informational content of a consolidated balance sheet we should put ourselves in the place of a user of accounts who notes that the consolidated balance sheet shows an amount of, say, £1m under this heading. What can he infer from the existence of this item? He will be able to tell

* The Act also prohibits the carrying of goodwill as an asset unless it was acquired for valuable consideration.

that the holding company, at some time in the past, acquired one or more subsidiaries for sums exceeding the net book value of the assets less liabilities acquired. In general, he will not know how many subsidiaries are involved, when they were acquired or, more importantly, whether the circumstances which gave rise to the existence of the item still prevail. He will also note that the existence of the item is to a large measure fortuitous in that its existence depends on whether the holding company had, at some stage, acquired a company which had already traded or had, instead, built the business up itself. Thus, one might find two identical groups of companies with exactly the same 'real' assets and liabilities and the same prospects but yet one might show a sizeable asset of goodwill on consolidation while the other group might have none. In the light of these observations the authors are led to the view that little in the way of useful information is provided by the inclusion of goodwill in consolidated balance sheets. However, it must be admitted that many British groups do not share this view. They might well argue that, on acquisition, the group did purchase an asset, albeit of an intangible nature, and that the purchase should be recorded. The argument against writing it off is that so long as the subsidiary continues to operate effectively (at least as well as it did before acquisition) there is *prima facie* evidence that the 'value' of the goodwill on consolidation is being maintained if not increased. Our counter argument is on the grounds of consistency. If one used this argument for purchased goodwill, why should it not also be applied to non-purchased goodwill, i.e. the goodwill built up by the holding company and by the subsidiaries since they became part of the group?

The Accounting Standards Committee addressed the issue of the treatment of goodwill in ED30 (Accounting for Goodwill). The various methods of dealing with goodwill are discussed in the Exposure Draft which rejects the idea that goodwill on consolidation should be retained as an asset indefinitely. The ASC believes that the value of purchased goodwill is bound to decline with the passage of time even though it might be replaced to a greater or lesser extent by nonpurchased (or internally generated) goodwill. But as internally generated goodwill is not reflected in the Balance Sheet it would be inconsistent to retain purchased goodwill on the grounds that it is being replaced by nonpurchased goodwill.

Having finally decided that goodwill should be written off, the ASC could not be as categoric on the issue of whether it should be written off immediately or over a period. The ASC could not identify any theoretical reason which would assist in the choice between the two alternatives.

The main arguments in favour of an immediate writeoff have been given above. The main argument in favour of writing goodwill off over a period relates to the accruals (or matching) convention. The purchase of a business involving goodwill implies that the purchaser expects to earn *super profits* (see page 89, Chapter 4) and hence it is argued that the cost of buying those super profits – goodwill – should be matched with the profits as they are earned. Hence if the proposals of the Exposure Draft are implemented companies would be permitted to either:

(a) amortize goodwill (or write it off) through the profit and loss account over its estimated useful economic life – which should not exceed 20 years. (Note that the write off should be charged to the profit and loss account as an expense in arriving at the profit or loss on normal operations i.e. the write off is not an extraordinary item nor should it be charged directly to reserves), or

(b) write it off immediately directly against reserves representing realized profits.

Capital Reserve on Consolidation or Negative Goodwill

We have so far assumed that the price paid for the shares in the subsidiary company by the holding company exceeded the net book value of the assets less liabilities of the subsidiary as at the date of acquisition. We will now consider what happens when this is not the case and the price paid is less than the net book value of the assets less liabilities.

Mechanically, there is no change in the procedure used to prepare the consolidated balance sheet. That is, the price paid by the holding company (a debit) is compared with the share capital and reserves of the subsidiary at the date of acquisition (a credit). The only change is that the outcome of the working is a credit balance which may be called negative goodwill, *capital reserve on consolidation*, or discount on acquisition.

In order to illustrate the emergence of a capital reserve on consolidation we will return to our earlier example (see page 264) except that we will now assume that H Limited paid £12,000 for all the shares in S Limited which had, at the date of acquisition, assets of £21,000 and liabilities of £7,000. We will also increase H Limited's sundry assets by £5,000 to compensate for the reduction in the cost of the shares. The consolidated balance sheet at the date of acquisition is then:

	H Limited's Balance Sheet £000		Consolidated Balance Sheet £000
Sundry assets	40	Debit £K21	61
Shares in subsidiary	12		
	£52		£61
Share capital	30		30
Retained earnings	10		10
Capital reserve on consolidation		Credit £K2.	2
	40		42
Sundry liabilities	12	Credit £K7	19
	£52		£61

As has been mentioned SSAP 14 requires that for the purposes of the consolidated accounts the assets of the subsidiary should be valued on the basis of the 'fair value to the acquiring company'*. No specific reference is made of liabilities but it must be assumed, on the grounds of consistancy, that the intention is that the same principle should apply to liabilities. Therefore if part of the reason why the price paid for the company is less than the net book value of the assets less liabilities can be assigned to specific assets or liabilities the 'fair value' of the asset or liability should be used for consolidation purposes and hence the capital reserve on consolidation would be partially or wholly eliminated.

However, the reason for the difference referred to above may simply reflect the fact that the company whose shares have been acquired has been badly managed and that the 'fair value' of the assets less liabilities may be equal to, or even greater, than their net book value at the date of acquisition.

In that case the capital reserve on consolidation will not be eliminated; indeed it may even be greater than the difference between the cost of the shares and the net book value of the asset less liabilities if, say, the assets are revalued upwards.

A capital reserve on consolidation is a special case of a capital reserve arising from the revaluation of assets. A capital reserve on revaluation occurs when the assets are included in the books of the company at an amount which is in excess of cost. This description applies equally to a capital reserve on consolidation. To take the above example, £12,000 was paid for assets less liabilities which had a net book value (which we will assume is equal to this fair value) of £14,000. A capital reserve on consolidation will arise if it is decided that the assets less liabilities will continue to be shown at £14,000.

There is no question of the capital reserve on consolidation having any effect on the reserves available for the payment of dividends. The reserve appears in the consolidated, not the holding company's, balance sheet, and it is the free reserves of the holding company that are of relevance when deciding the maximum dividend that can legally be paid to the shareholders of the holding company.

Exposure Draft 30 recognizes two different forms of what it calls negative goodwill. One arises when the purchase of the relevant business is made at a bargain price because, for example, the seller had to raise cash quickly by selling his business as a forced sale. The second occurs when the acquiring company believes that the newly purchased subsidiary will continue to make losses for some time or that there may be other costs which are associated with the purchase.

The first set of circumstances is obviously closer to the above simple example. In such a case the ED30 proposals are that the negative goodwill should be treated as an unrealized reserve.

As time passes the surplus will become realized as the assets originally acquired for a bargain price are used up either through their sale or through the process of depreciation. The ED therefore proposes that over a period of

---

*SSAP 14, paragraph 29.

time related to that in which the assets are consumed, transfers are made from unrealized to realized reserves.*

In the second set of circumstances where losses or other costs are anticipated, ED30 proposes that the credit balance – being the difference between the cost of the investment and the fair value of the assets less liabilities – should be regarded as a provision and included as such in the consolidated balance sheet. The provision should then be released to the profit and loss account (or written back) over the period in which it is thought that the losses will occur.

It will be appreciated that it will be difficult to estimate precisely the periods over which unrealized reserves will be translated into realized reserves or the provision is released to the profit and loss account. The ED30 proposals are that each investment should be considered in its own right and that the practice adopted by some companies of setting off negative goodwill against positive goodwill should stop.

THE DEFINITION OF A SUBSIDIARY COMPANY

We have so far dealt only with wholly owned subsidiaries, but a holding/subsidiary company relationship can exist even if the holding company does not own all the shares in the subsidiary. If this is the case, the subsidiary is known as a *partly owned subsidiary*. The legal criteria which are applied to establish whether a company is a subsidiary of another is provided in Section 154 of the Companies Act, 1948. The appropriate provisions can be summarized as follows:

Company S is a subsidiary of company H if and only if:
either
  (a) H owns more than 50 per cent of the nominal value of the equity share capital of S, *or*
  (b) H is a member of S *and* controls the composition of its board of directors, *or*
  (c) S is a subsidiary of another company which is itself a subsidiary of H.
      Equity share capital is defined in the same section of the Act as follows:

'issued share capital excluding any part thereof which, neither as respects dividends nor as respects capital carries any right to participate beyond a specified amount in a distribution'.

Equity shares are normally, but not always, one and the same thing as ordinary shares. For simplicity, we shall assume in the rest of this chapter that the normal relationship exists.

It should be noted that a company can, potentially, be a subsidiary of two companies – one which owns more than 50 per cent of its equity shares

---

*As was pointed out earlier the distinction between realized and unrealized reserves is of no significance in the case of a consolidated balance sheet. The distinction is relevant, however, in the instance of a company which acquires an incorporated business in that only realized reserves are available for distribution.

and one which, being a shareholder, controls the composition of its board of directors – but this is unlikely to occur in practice.

The fact that the holding/subsidiary relationship does not have to be direct means that the holding company can effectively own only a small proportion of the shares in the subsidiary but yet control it. For example,

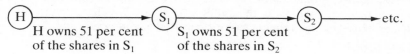

In the above, H Limited only owns some 26 per cent of the shares in S_2 Limited but S_2 Limited is a subsidiary of H Limited because it is a subsidiary of S_1 Limited. This sort of structure, which is found in the real world, enables the holding company to control a greater bundle of assets than it owns. The above is a simple example of the type of structure used for this purpose. In practice far more complex structures will be found.

PARTLY OWNED SUBSIDIARIES

Consolidated Balance Sheets

The basic principle is that the consolidated balance sheet should show the total assets and total liabilities of the group. Thus, for example, the total fixed assets shown on the consolidated balance sheet will be the same whether H owns 100 per cent or 51 per cent of the shares in S. In the case of a partly owned subsidiary the total pool of assets less liabilities has been partly financed by the 'other shareholders' in the subsidiary company, and this source must be shown on the face of the consolidated balance sheet where it is usually described as a *minority interest*.

We shall, as before, introduce this topic by means of a simple example. The balance sheets of H Limited and S Limited as at 31 December 19X2, the date on which H acquired its shares in S, are shown below:

	H Ltd £000	S Ltd £000
Sundry assets less liabilities	75	50
8,000 shares in S Limited	42	—
	£117	£50
Share capital		
£1 Ordinary shares	70	10
Retained earnings	47	40
	£117	£50

Note that H owns 80 per cent of the shares in S.

H Limited paid £42,000 for 80 per cent of the assets less liabilities of S Limited. The goodwill on consolidation is then £42,000 less 80 per cent of £50,000 = £2,000. Of the total assets less liabilities of the subsidiary 20 per cent had been obtained from funds supplied by the outside shareholders in the subsidiary and this 'source of assets', amounting to £10,000, will appear on the consolidated balance sheet described as 'minority interest'.

The 'conversion' of the holding company's balance sheet into the consolidated balance sheet can be illustrated as follows.

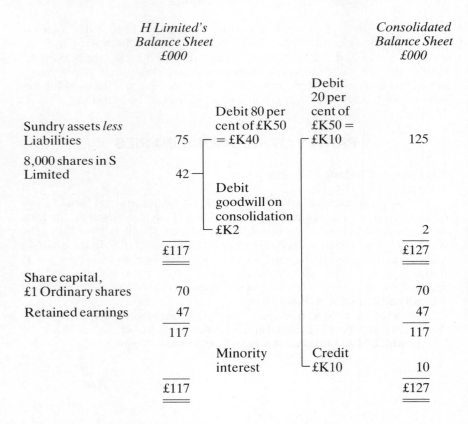

	H Limited's Balance Sheet £000			*Consolidated Balance Sheet £000*
			Debit 20 per cent of £K50 =	
		Debit 80 per cent of £K50	£K10	
Sundry assets *less* Liabilities	75	= £K40		125
8,000 shares in S Limited	42			
		Debit goodwill on consolidation £K2		2
	£117			£127
Share capital, £1 Ordinary shares	70			70
Retained earnings	47			47
	117			117
		Minority interest	Credit £K10	10
	£117			£127

In order to illustrate the use of a consolidated worksheet in the case of a partly owned subsidiary we will now assume that the profits made by the two companies in 19X3 were:

H Limited £12,000 and S Limited £5,000 and that neither company paid any dividends in the year.

The balance sheets of the two companies at 31 December 19X3 are shown below:

Consolidated Balance Sheet Worksheet
All figures £000

	H Ltd	S Ltd	Sub-totals	Adjustments Debit	Adjustments Credit	Consolidated Balance Sheet
Sundry assets less liabilities	87	55	142			142
8,000 shares in S Ltd	42	—	42		(a) 42	
Goodwill on consolidation				(a) 2		2
	£129	£55	£184			£144
Share capital, £1 shares	70	10	80	(a) 8 (b) 2		70
Retained earnings	59	45	104	(a) 32 (b) 9		63
	129	55	184			133
Minority interest					(b) 11	11
	£129	£55	£184	£53	£53	£144

The two adjustments displayed on the worksheet can be explained as follows:

	Debit £000	Credit £000
(a) The 'goodwill' adjustment		
Goodwill on consolidation	2	
Share capital of subsidiary 80 per cent of £10,000	8	
Retained earnings of subsidiary 80 per cent of retained earnings at acquisition, i.e. 80 per cent of £40,000	32	
Shares in subsidiary		42
(b) The 'minority interest' adjustment		
Share capital of subsidiary 20 per cent of £10,000	2	
Retained earnings of subsidiary 20 per cent of *current* retained earnings, i.e. 20 per cent of £45,000	9	
Minority interest		11

We should emphasize, as we did earlier, that the above form of adjustment is simply a convenient way of producing the consolidated balance sheet. The meaning of the terms goodwill on consolidation and minority interest is still best expressed in terms of the assets and liabilities of the subsidiary, i.e.

Goodwill on consolidation
  = Cost of shares in the subsidiary minus holding company's share of the share capital and reserves of the subsidiary as at the date of acquisition.
  = Cost of shares in the subsidiary minus holding company's share in the net book value of the assets less liabilities of the subsidiary as at the date of acquisition.

Minority interest
  = Outside shareholders' interest in the share capital and reserves of the subsidiary at the *balance sheet date*
  = Outside shareholders' interest in the assets less liabilities of the subsidiary at the *balance sheet date*.

The consolidated balance sheet as at 31 December 19X3 together with our commentary is shown below:

H LIMITED AND ITS SUBSIDIARY

Consolidated Balance Sheet
as at 31 December 19X3

£000

Sundry assets *less* Liabilities	142	The total of the assets less liabilities of the companies comprising the group.
Goodwill on consolidation	2	The difference between the cost of shares in the subsidiary and the holding company's share of the net book value of the subsidiary's assets less liabilities as at the date of acquisition.
	£144	
Share capital	70	The share capital of the holding company.
Retained earnings	63	The retained earnings (or in general, the reserves) of the holding company plus the holding company's share in the change in the retained earnings of the subsidiary company since acquisition.
	133	Total interest of the shareholders of the holding company.

£000

Minority interest | 11 | The outside shareholders' share of the book value of the assets less liabilities of the subsidiary company as at the balance sheet date.

£144

The reserves of the subsidiary often produce problems for students. It should be noted that the reserves are divided into three parts as illustrated below:

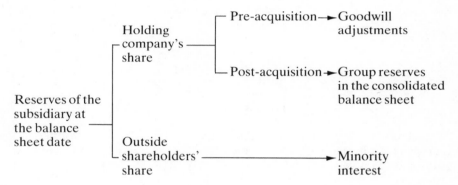

The Consolidated Profit and Loss Account

Two basic objectives can be seen underlying the construction of consolidated accounts. One is based on the view that a group of companies essentially consists of a set of assets less liabilities subject to common control – they are *economic entities* – and thus the consolidated accounts should show the state of the group as a whole as well as the results of the group for the period under review. This view of the function of consolidated accounts has been termed the *entity concept*. The other view is that the consolidated accounts are, mainly, prepared for the shareholders of the holding company. Thus it is argued that the consolidated accounts should concentrate on reporting the state and results of the group from the point of view of the shareholders of the holding company. This approach has been called the *proprietary concept.** In the context of consolidated accounts the two approaches do not always conflict, but there are one or two areas – e.g. unrealized profit on inter-company sales, see page 285 – where the two

*The difference between the entity and proprietary concepts emerges in a number of different areas in accounting. In particular, it plays an important part in the controversy surrounding the introduction of current value accounting, see Chapter 12.

approaches arrive at different destinations.

On the whole, the standard form of consolidated profit and loss account satisfies both objectives. The basic structure is shown below:

Totals for all the companies comprising the group	Sales	x	Entity concept
	less Expenses	x	
	Profit of the group before taxation	x	
	less Taxation	x	
	Profit of the group after taxation	x	
	less Minority interest share in the profits for the year	x	Change from entity to proprietary
Transfers made by holding company and its share of subsidiary company transfers	Profit after taxation attributable to the shareholders of the holding company	x	Proprietary concept
	less Transfers to reserves	x	
		x	
Dividends paid, and proposed, to the shareholders of the holding company	*less* Dividends	x	
		x	
Holding company's retained earnings and its share of the post-acquisition retained earnings of the subsidiary	*add* Opening retained earnings	x	
	Closing retained earnings	£x	

The first section of the consolidated profit and loss account shows the total revenue, expenses and taxation charges of all the companies in the group. Thus the user of the accounts is provided with some indication of how successful the managers of the holding company have been in operating the total assets under their control. It should be noted that the amount of the profit of the group after taxation is independent of the existence and extent of the minority interests in the subsidiaries.

The minority interest's share in the profit of the group is deducted after group profit after tax. If a subsidiary company only has ordinary shares in issue the minority interest's share in its profits will be x per cent (x being the proportion of the ordinary shares held by the outside shareholders) of the subsidiary's profit after tax. Note that this figure is independent of the size of any dividends paid by the subsidiary companies – the figure represents the minority interest's share of the profits for the year and not their share of the distributed profit.

The third section of the account satisfies the proprietary concept in that it starts with that part of the group's profit for the year attributable to the shareholders of the holding company and then shows the transfers to reserves and dividends which are attributable to these shareholders.

We will now illustrate the construction of a consolidated profit and loss account by continuing the saga which we left on page 279.

The profit and loss accounts of H Limited and S Limited for the year ended 31 December 19X4 and their balance sheets as at that date are shown below:

Profit and Loss Accounts

	H Ltd £000	S Ltd £000
Sales	180	160
less Expenses	130	100
	50	60
add Dividends received from S Ltd	16	—
Profit before tax	66	60
less Taxation*	25	30
	41	30
less Dividends paid	15	20
	26	10
Retained earnings 1 January 19X4	59	45
Retained earnings 31 December 19X4	£85	£55

Balance Sheets

	H Ltd £000	S Ltd £000
Sundry assets *less* Liabilities	113	65
8,000 shares in S Limited	42	—
	£155	£65

*A holding company is not normally subject to tax on dividends received from a subsidiary company.

	H Ltd £000	S Ltd £000
Share capital, £1 shares	70	10
Retained earnings	85	55
	£155	£65

Note
1. There was no inter-company trading during the year.
2. On 31 December 19X2, the date on which H purchased its holding of shares in S, the remained earnings of S Limited amounted to £40,000.

We present below a consolidated profit and loss account working sheet. Note that for convenience we have changed the position of the dividend received from S Limited in H's profit and loss account. In the work-sheet it is shown following the trading profit after taxation.

Consolidated Profit and Loss Account Worksheet
All figures £000

	H Ltd	S Ltd	Sub-totals	Adjustments Debit	Adjustments Credit	Consolidated Profit and Loss Account
Sales	180	160	340			340
less Expenses	130	100	230			230
	50	60	110			110
less Taxation	25	30	55			55
Trading profit after tax	25	30	55			55
Minority interest				(a)(i) 6		6
						49
Dividends received from S	16	—	16	(b) 16		—
	41	30	71			49
					(b) 16	
less Dividends paid	15	20	35		(a)(ii) 4	15
	26	10	36			34
Opening retained earnings	59	45	104	(c) 32 (a)(iii) 9		63
	£85	£55	£140	63	20	£97
Adjustments carried to the consolidated balance sheet				(a)(ii) 4	(a)(i) 6 (a)(iii) 9 (c) 32	
				£67	£67	

It will be as well if we explain the above adjustments.

The outside shareholders' share in the profits for the year of the subsidiary (adjustment (a)(i)) is 20 per cent of S Limited's profit after tax, i.e. 20 per cent of £30,000 = £6,000. This figure is 'debited' to the consolidated profit and loss account and 'credited' to the minority interest shown on the face of the balance sheet.

The subsidiary paid a dividend of £20,000. Eighty per cent of this was paid to the holding company and the balance (£4,000) to the minority interest shareholders. The £16,000 paid to the holding company cancels out the £16,000 shown as being the dividend received from the subsidiary (adjustment (b)). The balance of the dividend is 'debited' to the minority interest figure in the consolidated balance sheet (adjustment (a)(ii)).

In order to see what has happened we need to consider adjustments (a)(i) and (a)(ii) together. The outside shareholders' share in the profits for the year was £6,000 and they have been paid dividends of £4,000. Thus, their share of the reserves of the subsidiary has increased by £2,000 and this is the net amount (£6,000 − £4,000) which is 'credited' to the minority interest shown on the consolidated balance sheet, i.e. the minority interest as at 31 December 19X4 will be £2,000 larger than the corresponding figure at 31 December 19X3.

The two adjustments ((a)(iii) and (c)) made to opening retained earnings have already been introduced in the context of the consolidated balance sheet. Adjustment (a)(iii) shows the minority interest share in the retained earnings of the subsidiary as at the beginning of the year – 20 per cent of £45,000 = £9,000, while adjustment (c) deals with the holding company's share of the retained earnings of the subsidiary as at the date of acquisition – part of the 'goodwill adjustment'.

The adjustments described as being carried to the consolidated balance sheet are those items which are shown on the following consolidated balance sheet worksheet as being debited or credited to retained earnings.

Consolidated Balance Sheet Worksheet

All figures £000

	H Ltd	S Ltd	Sub-totals	Adjustments Debit	Adjustments Credit	Consolidated Balance Sheet
Sundry assets *less* Liabilities	113	65	178			178
8,000 shares in S Ltd	42	—	42		(c) 42	
Goodwill on consolidation				(c) 2		2
	£155	£65	£220			£180
Share capital £1 shares	70	10	80	{ (c) 8 (a″) 2 }		70
Retained earnings	85	55	140	{ (a′) 11* (c) 32 }		97
	155	65	220			167
Minority interest					(a) 13	13
	£155	£65	£220	£55	£55	£180

*Adjustment (a′) can be reconciled with adjustments (a)(i), (a)(ii) and (a)(iii) on the consolidated profit and loss account work sheet as follows:

		£000
Outside shareholders' share in:		
Opening retained earnings	(a)(iii)	9
Profit for the year	(a)(i)	6
		15
less Dividends paid in year	(a)(ii)	4
		£11

The necessary figures for the preparation of the consolidated accounts are provided in the final pair of columns in the worksheets. We shall not, at this stage, use space in presenting the accounts for we shall illustrate their layout on page 294 at the end of a more detailed example.

There are in practice a number of technical problems associated with the preparation of consolidated accounts: for example, the payment, by a subsidiary, of dividends out of pre-acquisition dividends, the problems which arise if the companies in the group do not have a common year-end and a long list of et ceteras. The aim of this chapter is to concentrate on basic ideas and so will avoid many of these issues; but there are a few topics which we should now cover.

Inter-company Balances and Trading

As long as all the companies in the group share the same year end the treatment of inter-company balances should present few difficulties, as they will normally cancel out. However, there may be instances where this will not happen because, for example, goods are in transit between two companies. Assume that just before the year end subsidiary S_1 sent goods invoiced at £10,000 to subsidiary S_2. S_1 will have debited the invoiced value of the goods to S_2's account but, if they had not arrived by the year end, S_2 may not have credited S_1's account in its books. Thus when preparing consolidated accounts the accountant must check to see whether the inter-company balances agree. If they do not, he must find the reason for the difference and make a suitable adjustment in the consolidation workings. In this example he would probably debit inventory and credit S_2's account in the books of S_1.

Similar remarks to the above can be made about certain aspects of inter-company trading. Suppose that S_2 has in issue £60,000 debentures and that 70 per cent are held by its fellow subsidiary S_1. Then 70 per cent of the debenture interest paid by S_2 will cancel with the debenture interest received by S_1 and the debenture interest expense charged in the consolidated profit and loss account will consist only of the balance paid to the 'outside' debenture holders. Similarly only 30 per cent of the debentures will appear on the consolidated balance sheet as a liability of the group.

Somewhat different considerations apply to inter-company sales and purchases. Let us suppose that S_1 sells goods in a partly finished condition to

S_2 which completes them and then sells them to the eventual customers. The transaction between S_1 and S_2 will be shown as a sale in the accounts of S_1 and as a purchase in the accounts of S_2. When the goods are finally sold it will also be shown as a sale by S_2. Hence it could be argued that if no adjustment were made the consolidated profit and loss account would show an inflated figure, because of double counting, for sales and purchases. Thus an adjustment should be made when preparing the consolidated profit and loss account. The sales figure should be debited and the purchases (or cost of goods sold expense) credited with the invoiced value of the goods sold by one member of the group to another. It should be noted that the adjustment will have no effect on the profit of the group.

Unrealized Profits on Inter-company Sales

A slightly more complicated position arises if some of the goods sold by one member of the group to another remain unsold at the year end.

Suppose that the holding company (H) sold goods which cost £20,000 to a subsidiary S_1 for £24,000, and that the goods remain unsold at the year end. Let us also suppose that H owns 70 per cent of S_1.

The goods will be included in the year-end inventory of S_1 at £24,000, and unless an adjustment is made, this will result in the inventory being included in the consolidated balance sheet at a figure in excess of cost to the group, and, accordingly, some unrealized profit will be included in the profit of the group. One might argue that if the transaction were at arm's length, i.e. as between two independent parties, no adjustment would be required. However, this view is generally considered to be contrary to the tenets of historical cost accounting and so, unless the amount concerned is insignificant, an adjustment is normally made. One question is whether the whole of the £4,000 should be considered as unrealized. Some accountants argue, following the entity concept, that, from the point of view of the group, none of the goods have been sold and that the whole of the £4,000 is unrealized. On the other hand, following the proprietary concept, other accountants would argue that since 30 per cent of the subsidiary is owned by outside interests, 30 per cent of the profit has been earned and that any adjustment for unrealized profit should be based on 70 per cent of £4,000 = £2,800.

There is little in the way of general agreement between accountants on this issue and the British professional bodies have offered little in the way of guidance. It does seem that the balance of opinion is shifting away from the view that only a proportion of the difference between historical cost and invoiced value should be treated as unrealized.* But even if it were agreed that the whole of the difference should be treated as being unrealized profit, there remains the question of what should be done when the profit has been made by a partly owned subsidiary. Suppose that S_1 had sold the goods to H. Should 30 per cent of the unrealized profit be charged against minority interest or should the whole of the charge be made against the profits of the

Group Accounts, R. M. Wilkins, Institute of Chartered Accountants in England and Wales, (2nd Edition), 1979.

group? Both approaches have their advocates, but there is some evidence that most groups now charge the whole of the adjustment against group profits.* We shall use this method in the example that follows on page 287.

Preference Shares in Subsidiary Companies

We have so far assumed that the subsidiary companies have only one class of share, but we should now consider the effect of preference shares on the determination of minority interest. In the straightforward case where preference dividends are paid up to date, the minority interest share in profit for the year will be the amount of preference dividend payable in the year. Complications arise when a subsidiary has cumulative preference shares and has failed to pay a dividend. In such a case it seems best to show the maximum dividend payable as part of the minority interest's share of profits, on the grounds that no dividend can be paid to the ordinary shareholders, including the holding company, until the arrears have been cleared.

In the balance sheet, the minority interest is made up of the nominal value of the preference shares plus any arrears of cumulative dividends.

If the holding company owns any of the preference shares a standard 'goodwill adjustment' is made, i.e. the cost of the shares is compared with their nominal value and the difference is added to or subtracted from the goodwill on consolidation.

More on Minority Interest

The minority interest figure which appears on the consolidated balance sheet represents a source of funds. It does not represent a creditor and, more importantly, it cannot become a debtor. If a subsidiary has accumulated losses of such an extent that they exceed its share capital and other reserves, the minority interest calculation will result in a debit balance. However, this is not an asset in that the minority interest shareholders cannot (so long as the shares are fully paid) be called upon to contribute further funds. In these circumstances the group might well decide not to include the subsidiary in the consolidated accounts (see page 296) but if it does decide to 'consolidate' the subsidiary the debit balance on minority interest would be written off against the reserves of the group.

If one of the partly owned subsidiaries has, at the year end, proposed dividends, there is a question of the treatment of that part of the proposed dividends which are payable to the outside shareholders. So far as the group is concerned, these dividends are current liabilities and they should, if material, be shown as such in the consolidated balance sheet. However, many groups include the amount in the balance sheet minority interest figure and this approach may, or may not, be combined with a note stating the amount of the proposed dividends included in minority interest.

*Wilkins, *op. cit.*

We shall now present a reasonably detailed example which includes many of the points that we have introduced above. Two points should be made about the example. In order to avoid unnecessary detail, it includes only one subsidiary, but the existence of other subsidiaries would not give rise to any additional principles. We have also compressed a good deal of the details which do not require consolidation adjustments. Thus the example does not, as perhaps it should, indicate that the vast majority of the items appearing in the consolidated accounts are derived by simply adding together the items found in the accounts of the individual companies.

Example 8.1

The profit and loss accounts of H Limited and its subsidiary S Limited for the year ended 31 December 19X8 together with their balance sheet as at that date are given below:

| | Profit and Loss Accounts | | | |
| | H Limited | | S Limited | |
	£000	£000	£000	£000
Sales		800		400
less Opening stock	100		48	
Purchases	570		272	
	670		320	
less Closing stock	120	550	40	280
Gross profit		250		120
less Sundry expenses	130		54	
Debenture interest	—	130	12	66
		120		54
add Debenture interest received	3			
Dividends received and receivable	20	23		—
Profit before tax		143		54
less Taxation on the profits				
for the year		65		20
Profit after tax		78		34
less Dividends paid:				
Preference shares	—		2	
Ordinary shares	14		—	
Dividends proposed:				
Preference shares	—		2	
Ordinary shares	26	40	20	24
		38		10
Retained earnings at 1 January 19X8		113		20
Retained earnings at 31 December 19X8		£151		£30

| | Balance Sheets | | | |
| | H Limited | | S Limited | |
	£000	£000	£000	£000
Fixed assets, net book value		275		200
Shares in subsidiary, at cost				
£20,000 10 per cent £1				
Preference shares		19		
90,000 £1 Ordinary shares		175		
c/f		469		200

	H Limited		S Limited	
	£000	£000	£000	£000
b/f		469		200
£20,000 15 per cent Debenture stock of S Limited		20		
Current assets				
Stock	120		40	
Cash	10		3	
Sundries	148	278	85	128
Current account with H Limited		—		32
		£767		£360
Issued share capital				
£40,000 10 per cent £1 Preference shares		—		40
£1 Ordinary shares		300		100
		300		140
Reserves				
Share premium account		160		20
Retained earnings		151		30
		611		190
15 per cent Debentures		—		80
Current liabilities				
Proposed dividends	26		22	
Sundries	119	145	68	90
Current account with S Limited		11		—
		£767		£360

Notes

(a)   H Limited acquired its holding of shares in S Limited some years ago. S Limited's reserves as at the date of acquisition were

Share premium	£20,000
Retained earnings	£40,000

(b)   The difference between the balances on the current accounts is explained as follows:

	£000	£000
Balance per S Limited's accounts		32
less Cash sent by H to S but not received by the latter until January 19X9	2	
H has debited its share of S's proposed dividends to the current account		
Preference dividends	1	
Ordinary dividends	18	21
Balance per H Limited's account		£11

(c)   S Limited sells goods to the holding company. An analysis of the transactions is
given below:

	Cost £000	Invoiced Value £000
In H Limited's stock at 1 January 19X8	18	24
Sold to H Limited during the year	96	128
In H Limited's stock at 31 December 19X8	30	40

The policy of the group is to treat the whole of the difference between cost and
invoiced value as unrealized profit and to charge the entire provision against group
reserves.

We will start with the consolidated balance sheet worksheet:

Consolidated Balance Sheet Worksheet

	H Ltd £000	S Ltd £000	Sub-totals £000	Adjustments Debit £000	Adjustments Credit £000	Consolidated Balance Sheet £000
Fixed assets, net book value,	275	200	475			475
Shares in S Ltd 20,000 Preference shares	19		19		B1 19	—
90,000 Ordinary shares	175		175		B2 175	—
Debentures in S Ltd	20		20		A4 20	—
Stock	120	40	160			160
Cash	10	3	13	A1 2		15
Sundry current assets	148	85	233		A1 2	233
Current account, H Ltd	—	32	32		A3 30	—
Goodwill on consolidation			—	B2 31	B1 1	30
	£767	£360	£1,127			£913
£1 Preference shares	—	40	40	B1 20 / C1 20		—
£1 Ordinary shares	300	100	400	B2 90 / C2 10		300
Share premium account	160	20	180	B2 18 / C2 2		160
Retained earnings	151	30	181	B2 36 / C2 3 / D1 10		132
15 per cent Debentures	—	80	80	A4 20		60
Proposed dividends	26	22	48	A2 19		29
Sundry current liabilities	119	68	187			187
Current account, S Ltd	11		11	A3 30	A2 19	—
Minority interest					C1 20 / C2 15	35
Provision for unrealized profit					D1 10	10
	£767	£360	£1,127	£311	£311	£913

We will now explain the above adjustments in journal form.

The 'A adjustments' deal with the clearing of the inter-company balances.

		Debit £000	Credit £000
A1	Cash	2	
	H Ltd current account in the books of S		2
A2	Proposed dividends	19	
	S Ltd current account in the books of H		19
A3	S Ltd current account in the books of H	30	
	H Ltd current account in the books of S		30
A4	15 per cent Debentures (S Ltd's books)	20	
	Debentures in S Ltd		20

The 'B adjustments' deal with goodwill, B1 relates to the preference shares and B2 to the ordinary shares

		Debit	Credit
B1	S Ltd £1 Preference shares	20	
	Cost of preference shares		19
	Goodwill on consolidation		1
B2	S Ltd ordinary shares (90 per cent of £K100)	90	
	Share premium account (90 per cent of £K20)	18	
	Retained earnings (90 per cent of £K40)	36	
	Goodwill on consolidation	31	
	Cost of ordinary shares		175

The 'C adjustments' deal with the minority interest, C1 for preference shareholders and C2 for ordinary shareholders.

		Debit	Credit
C1	S Ltd's £1 Preference shares	20	
	Minority interest		20
C2	S Ltd's £1 Ordinary shares	10	
	Share premium account (10 per cent of £K20)	2	
	Retained earnings (10 per cent of £K30)	3	
	Minority interest		15

The last adjustment provides for the unrealized profit on closing stock. The whole of the unrealized profit is charged against group retained earnings and no part of it has been charged against minority interest.

		Debit	Credit
D1	Retained earnings	10	
	Provision against unrealized profit		10

Consolidated Profit and Loss Account Worksheet

	H Ltd	S Ltd	Sub-totals	Adjustments Debit	Adjustments Credit	Consolidated Profit and Loss Account
( ) credits	£000	£000	£000	£000	£000	£000
Sales	(800)	(400)	(1,200)	A5 128		(1,072)
Cost of goods sold expense	550	280	830		A5 96	702
Sundry expenses	130	54	184			184
Debenture interest expense	—	12	12		A6 3	9
Profit before tax	(120)	(54)	(174)			(177)
c/f	(120)	(54)	(174)	128	131	(177)

( ) credits	H Ltd	S Ltd	Sub-totals	Adjustments Debit	Adjustments Credit	Consolidated Profit and Loss Account
	£000	£000	£000	£000	£000	£000
b/f	(120)	(54)	(174)	128	131	(177)
Taxation	65	20	85			85
Profit after tax	(55)	(34)	(89)			(92)
Minority interest share				C3 2 ⎫ C4 3 ⎭		5
						(87)
Debenture interest received	(3)	/	(3)	A6 3		—
Dividends received and receivable	(20)		(20)	A7 20		—
	(78)	(34)	(112)			(87)
Provision against unrealized profit expense				D3 4		4
						(83)
Dividends Paid:						
Preference	—	2	2		⎰ A7 1 ⎱ ⎱ C5 1 ⎰	—
Ordinary	14	—	14			14
Dividends proposed:						
Preference	—	2	2		⎰ A7 1 ⎱ ⎱ C5 1 ⎰	—
Ordinary	26	20	46		⎰ A7 18 ⎱ ⎱ C6 2 ⎰	26
	(38)	(10)	(48)			(43)
Retained earnings 1 Jan X8	(113)	(20)	(133)	⎰ B2 36 ⎱ C7 2 D2 6		(89)
	£(151)	£(30)	£(181)	204	155	£(132)
Adjustments carried to the consolidated balance sheet				C5 2 C6 2	B2 36 C3 2 C4 3 C7 2 D2 6 D3 4	
				£208	£208	

In the above we have lettered the groups of adjustments in the same way as in the consolidated balance sheet worksheet.

A   *Elimination of Inter-company Balances and Trading*

A5   The sales made by S to H are eliminated because they represent intra-group trans-
       actions. Hence:

	Debit £000	Credit £000
Sales	128	
Cost of goods sold expense		128

A6   The debenture interest received by H from the debentures in S is set off against
       the total interest paid by S.
A7   The setting off of the dividends paid and proposed by S to H.

B   *Goodwill adjustments*
B2   The opening retained earnings are debited with the holding company's share of
       S's retained earnings at acquisition, i.e. 90 per cent of £40,000 = £36,000, the
       credit is part of the overall goodwill adjustment (B2 on the consolidated balance
       sheet worksheet). Note that S's retained earnings have decreased since acquisi-
       tion. All this means is that H's share of the change in S's retained earnings since
       acquisition are deducted from group profit.

C   *Minority Interest Adjustment*
C3   The share of profits for the year attributable to the 'outside' preference share-
       holders is the amount of the dividends due to them, i.e. 50 per cent of £4,000 =
       £2,000. The share of profits attributable to the 'outside' ordinary shareholders is
       10 per cent of the total profit attributable to ordinary shareholders, i.e.

	£000
S Limited's profit for the year	34
less Profit attributable to preference shareholders (including dividend payable to H Limited).	4
Profit attributable to ordinary shareholders	£30

Minority interest in the above 10 per cent of £30,000	= £3,000
Total minority interest share in profit = £3,000 + £2,000	= £5,000

C4   See C3
C5   The dividends paid and proposed to outside preference
       shareholders are debited to 'balance sheet' minority interest.
C6   As C5 but for outside ordinary shareholders.
C7   The minority interest (only applicable to ordinary shareholders)
       share of opening retained earnings = 10 per cent of £20,000   = £2,000

It might be useful if we summarized the position concerning minority interest.

	Minority Interest in		
	Preference Shares £000	Ordinary Shares £000	Total £000
Nominal value of shares	20	10	
Share of share premium account	—	2	
Share in opening retained earnings (C7)	—	2	
Share in profit for the year (C3 and C4)	2	3	
	22	17	39
less			
Dividends paid and proposed (C5 and C6)	2	2	4
	£20	£15	£35

D   *Unrealized Profit Adjustments*
D2   The unrealized profit at the start of the year was £24,000 − £18,000 = £6,000 and in

the consolidated workings of the previous year, a provision for unrealized profit account would have been established with a balance of £6,000 which would have been built up by charges made against group profits, i.e. the opening retained earnings must also be reduced by £6,000. Thus:

	Debit £000	Credit £000
Opening retained earnings	6	
Provision against unrealized profit (a balance sheet adjustment).		6

D3 The unrealized profit at the year end is £10,000 and since the existing balance (see above) is £6,000, the difference is made up by charging £4,000 against group profits for the year, i.e.

	Debit £000	Credit £000
Provision against unrealized profit expense	4	
Provision against unrealized profit (a balance sheet adjustment)		4

Note that the sum of the adjustments D2 and D3 make up the adjustment D1 shown on the consolidated balance sheet worksheet.

We would point out that there are methods other than the above which can be used to bring about the desired end.

The consolidated accounts are given below:

H LIMITED AND ITS SUBSIDIARY

Consolidated Profit and Loss Account
Year ended 31 December 19X8

	£000	£000
Sales		1,072
less		
Cost of goods sold	702	
Sundry expenses	184	
Debenture interest	9	
Increase in provision for unrealized profit	4	899
Profit of the group before taxation		173
less Taxation		85
Profit of the group after taxation		88
less Minority interest share in the profits of the subsidiary company		5
Profit for the year attributable to the shareholders of the holding company		83
less Dividends:		
Paid	14	
Proposed	26	40
		43
Retained earnings as at 1 January 19X8		89
Retained earnings as at 31 December 19X8		£132

Consolidated Balance Sheet as at 31 December 19X8

	£000	£000	£000
Fixed assets, net book value			475
Excess of cost of shares in the subsidiaries over the book value of its net assets as at the date of acquisition			30
Current assets			
Inventory	160		
less Provision against unrealized profit	10	150	
Sundry current assets		233	
Cash		15	
		398	
less Current liabilities			
Proposed dividends payable to:			
Shareholders in the holding company	26		
Shareholders in the subsidiary company	3		
	29		
Sundry current liabilities	187	216	182
			£687
Issued share capital			
Ordinary shares of £1 each			300
Reserves			
Share premium account		160	
Retained earnings		132	292
			592
Minority interest			35
15 per cent Debentures			60
			£687

Note

If the proposals of ED30 are implemented the excess cost of shares in the subsidiary over the book value of its net assets as at the date of acquisition (goodwill on consolidation) of £30,000 would either have to have been written off immediately on acquisition against realised reserves or charged to the consolidated profit and loss account over a specified period of years. In the latter case the original goodwill on consolidation of £30,000 would have already been reduced and, assuming that the goodwill is being written off over 5 years, the additional consolidation adjustment required in 1988 would be:

	Debit £000	Credit £000
Consolidated P & L account	6	
Goodwill		6

CONSOLIDATED ACCOUNTS – LEGAL PROVISIONS

The basic legal provisions are found in Sections 150 and 151 of the Companies Act 1948, and the following is a summary of the main provisions.

Where, at the end of a financial year, a company has subsidiaries, accounts or statements (group accounts) dealing with the state of affairs and profit and loss of the company and the subsidiaries shall be laid before the company in general meeting, together with the company's own balance sheet and profit and loss account.

The Act suggests that two balance sheets and two profit and loss accounts be presented, one of each for the holding company and the group. However, the directors of the holding company are given a considerable degree of latitude, for the group accounts may be prepared in any other form if they believe that the adopted form will disclose the same or equivalent information and will be readily appreciated by members of the holding company. In particular, the group accounts may be wholly or partly incorporated in the holding company's own balance sheet and profit and loss account. The normal, almost universal, practice is to take advantage of part of this provision and present two balance sheets and one profit and loss account, the latter incorporating the results of both the group and the holding company.

If only one profit and loss account is to be presented, the Act requires that the account should show how much of the consolidated profit or loss for the year is dealt with in the accounts of the holding company. Thus, the basic form of consolidated profit and loss account which we introduced earlier will be suitable as long as the account shows how much of the profit is included in the holding company's accounts and, consequently, how much has been dealt with in the accounts of the subsidiary companies. In practice, a similar analysis is often provided showing the treatment of closing retained earnings.

An example of a form of combined profit and loss account, starting with the profit before taxation, suitable for publication which uses the figures from Example 8.1, is provided below:

H LIMITED
Consolidated Profit and Loss Account
for the Year Ended 31 December 19X8

	£000	£000
Profit before taxation (Note 1)		173
less		
Taxation		
United Kingdom corporation tax (x per cent)		
based on the profit for the year		85
Profit after taxation		88
less		
Minority interest share in the profits of the		
subsidiary company		5
Profit for the year attributable to the shareholders		
of the holding company dealt with in the holding		
company's accounts	54	
Retained by the subsidiary	29	
c/f		83

	£000	£000
b/f	—	83
less		
Dividends (Note 2)		40
Retained earnings for the year		43
Retained earnings at 1 January 19X8		89
Retained earnings at 31 December 19X8 dealt with in the accounts of the		
Holding company	141*	
Subsidiary company	(9*)	£132

*See the consolidated profit and loss account worksheet on page 291.

Balance per H Limited's profit and loss account		151
less Provision for the unrealized profit on inventory		10
		£141

Balance per S Limited's profit and loss account		30
less Minority interest share (10 per cent)	3	
H Limited's share as at the date of acquisition	36	39
		£(9)

Notes 1 and 2 would show the information specified by the Companies Acts. In general, the disclosure requirement for 'combined' profit and loss accounts is that the appropriate revenue and expense item should be shown in aggregate; for example, the total depreciation charge of all the companies making up the group must be shown. There are one or two exceptions, the most important of which relates to the remuneration of directors and employees earning more than £30,000 per year. Basically, the Act only requires the publication of details relating to directors and employees of the holding company, but the total remuneration paid by all the companies in the group to those individuals must be shown.

It is not always necessary to publish group accounts, for they are not required where the holding company is, at the end of the financial year, itself the wholly owned subsidiary of another limited company in the United Kingdom.

The Acts also allow a group to exclude one or more subsidiaries from the consolidated accounts. This can be done when, in the opinion of the directors of the holding company:

(i) the inclusion of the subsidiary company would be impracticable, or would be of no real value in view of the insignificant amounts involved, or would involve expense or delay out of proportion to the value to the members of the holding company;

(ii) the inclusion of the subsidiary company would be misleading, or harmful to the business of the holding company or any of its subsidiaries; or

   (iii) the business of the holding company and that of a subsidiary are
so different that they cannot reasonably be treated as a single
undertaking.

The permission of the Department of Trade is required if (ii) or (iii) above is
the reason for non-consolidation.

If a subsidiary is excluded, a statement must be annexed to the consolidated accounts which, along with other matters, must include details of the
holding company's share in the profit or loss of the excluded subsidiary.

Purchase Consideration Other than Cash

The purchase consideration used by the holding company to purchase
the shares in a subsidiary from the former shareholders can take various
forms. The company will often use cash for relatively small acquisitions, but
in large acquisitions the purchase consideration will normally consist of the
issue of shares and/or debentures in the holding company which might, or
might not, be accompanied by a cash element. If any part of the purchase
consideration is satisfied by the issue of shares, debentures, etc., the
problem of valuation has to be considered. For firms whose shares are
actively traded on the Stock Exchange the current market price is generally
used. If the shares are not quoted or if there is little activity in the quoted
shares then the value will have to be estimated.

In many ways the value placed on the shares issued is not all that
significant. The *number* of shares issued is a quite different matter; this is
highly significant because on that will depend the relative rights of the existing and new shareholders in the holding company. The value placed on the
issue has no effect on the tangible assets and liabilities of any of the companies involved in the acquisition. It will have an effect on the share
premium account of the holding company and the goodwill on consolidation
appearing on the consolidated balance sheet. The higher the value, the
greater the share premium account and the goodwill on consolidation.

MERGER OR POOLING OF INTEREST

We have so far concentrated on describing the normal British method of
consolidation – the purchase (or acquisition) method – but it should be noted
that the method of preparation of consolidated accounts is not set out in any
statute. The Companies Act, 1948 says little more than:

> 'The group accounts laid before a company shall give a true and fair
> view of the state of affairs and profit and loss of the company and the sub-
> sidiaries dealt with thereby as a whole, so far as concerns members of the
> holding company' (Section 152(1), Companies Act, 1948).

An alternative method of preparing consolidated accounts – known as
the *merger* (in the United Kingdom) or *pooling of interest*, or just *pooling* (in

the United States) – has been used by a few British companies in recent years and has been extensively used in the United States. The method was used, for example, when British Motor Holdings merged with Leyland to form British Leyland in 1968.

The difference between the two methods can be seen from their names. The purchase (or acquisition) method is based on the notion that one company purchased, or took over, another company, and the group balance sheet is viewed as a restatement of the holding company's balance sheet, with the asset of cost of shares in subsidiaries being replaced by the underlying assets and liabilities.

The merger, or pooling of interest, method is said to be appropriate when two companies merge on a more or less equal basis, and when the purchase consideration consists of an issue of shares. The importance of the latter point is that the merger method is based on the assumption that, broadly, the same body of shareholders exists after the combination as before it, and that all that has happened is that the shareholders have now pooled their interests so that they now share an interest in the total pool of assets. In such circumstances it is argued that it is of no importance whether A Limited issues its shares to the shareholders of B Limited, or vice versa, or, indeed, whether a third company is formed and issues its shares to the shareholders of both companies. What matters is the way in which the shares of the holding company are distributed between the shareholders of the two original companies, and not whether A Limited or B Limited or a third company becomes the holding company. Under the purchase method, it does matter which company becomes the holding company, for on that decision will depend the goodwill on consolidation and the retained earnings of the group.

We shall first introduce the basic principles of the merger method and then return to a comparison of the two methods.

The basic principle of the merger method is 'make as few adjustments as possible'. The idea is that since two companies have been brought together in such a way that the same people will own the same businesses, the consolidated balance sheet should, so far as possible, simply be the sum of the individual balance sheets. In particular, the reserves of the 'acquired company' as at the date of the merger will be included in the reserves of the group. The only items on the two balance sheets that have to be eliminated on consolidation are the cost of shares shown in the 'holding' company balance sheet and the nominal value of the shares of the 'subsidiary' company. On consolidation these two are compared, and if the first exceeds the second the resulting debit is charged against the reserves of the group; if the second is larger than the first, the credit balance is treated as a capital reserve on the consolidated balance sheet.

Since the basic principle of the merger approach is that the transaction is simply an exchange of shares, no attempt is made to value, for the purposes of the accounts, the shares issued by the 'acquiring' company. They will be shown on that company's balance sheet as being issued at their nominal value, and hence the adjustment on consolidation reduces to a comparison of the nominal value of the shares issued with the nominal value of the shares of the company 'acquired'. Thus the decision whether the merger or acquisition method will be used on consolidation will have an effect on the balance sheet of the holding company. If the acquisition method is used, an attempt will be made to value the shares issued (generally at a premium) and the asset, cost of shares in subsidiary, will be shown at this estimated value. On the other hand, if the merger method is employed, the shares issued by the holding company will be treated as being issued at par (no share premium account) and the asset, cost of shares in subsidiary, will, consequently, appear in the holding company's balance sheet at a lower figure. Hence, it could be argued that one of the drawbacks of the merger method is that the treatment of the shares in the subsidiary in the accounts of the holding company is totally unrealistic.

It should be noted that an important consequence of the merger method is that goodwill on consolidation cannot possibly arise.

The following example shows the difference between the merger and acquisition methods:

Example 8.2

The balance sheets of the two companies just before the combination are shown below:

	A £000	B £000
Sundry assets *less* Liabilities	£280	£100
Share capital, £1 shares	100	60
Retained earnings	180	40
	£280	£100

For the purposes of the combination, A Limited is valued at £K300 and B Limited, £K150. Thus, the shareholders of A Limited should have twice as many shares in the holding company as the shareholders of B Limited. So if the combination is to be effected by A Limited issuing shares, it will issue 50,000 shares to the shareholders of B, whilst if B Limited is to be the holding company it will have to issue 120,000 of its shares to the shareholders of A Limited. Note that these ratios are based on the values placed on the two companies for the purpose of the combination and will be independent of the accounting method used to record the consolidation.

Let us assume that A Limited is to be the holding company and that the merger method is to be used. The balance sheet of A Limited just after the issue of shares is shown on the following consolidated balance sheet worksheet:

Consolidated Balance Sheet Worksheet (All figures £000)

	A	B	Sub-total	Adjustments Debit	Credit	Consolidated Balance Sheet
Sundry assets *less* Liabilities	280	100	380			380
Cost of shares in B Limited	50	—	50		50	
	£330	£100	£430			£380
Share capital	150	60	210	60		150
Retained earnings	180	40	220			220
Capital reserve on consolidation					10	10
	£330	£100	£430	£60	£60	£380

We will now assume that the acquisition method had been used. In this case, the shares issued by A Limited would be valued at £K150 and, of this, £K100 would appear as the share premium.

Consolidated Balance Sheet Worksheet (All figures £000)

	A	B	Sub-total	Adjustments Debit	Credit	Consolidated Balance Sheet
Sundry assets *less* Liabilities	280	100	380			380
Cost of shares in B Limited	150		150		150	
Goodwill on consolidation				50		50
	£430	£100	£530			£430
Share capital	150	60	210	60		150
Share premium	100		100			100
Retained earnings	180	40	220	40		180
	£430	£100	£530	£150	£150	£430

It has been argued that the fact that the merger method cannot give rise to the recognition of any goodwill on consolidation is one of the reasons why it has proved popular in the United States. For in the United States it is mandatory, when using the acquisition basis, to write off goodwill on consolidation as a charge against profits over a given number of years. Thus the use of the acquisition method (in circumstances which yield goodwill on consolidation) as compared to the merger method will result in the group reporting lower profits in the future until the goodwill is fully written off. Now it is true that, if the amount and nature of the write-off of goodwill is disclosed, there is no reason why the users of the accounts should be 'misled' by the item. However, it appears that a number of groups believe that shareholders and others pay considerable attention to the final profit figure but pay less (if any) attention to the way that figure is made up. Thus, it is likely that some American groups use the merger method in order to avoid the reduction in group profits that would have resulted from the writing off of goodwill.

The Consolidated Profit and Loss Account

A consolidated profit and loss account based on the merger method will differ from one based on the acquisition method in only two respects. Firstly, since with the merger method there can be no goodwill on consolidation, amortization of goodwill will not be found in the consolidated profit and loss account. The second difference occurs in a year during which a new subsidiary is added to the group. Under the acquisition method, only that portion of the subsidiary's profits which were earned since the date of acquisition will be included in the group profit for the year. However, under the merger method, the whole of the profit of the new subsidiary will be included in the profits of the group. It has been suggested that this difference is one of the factors which gave rise to certain 'abuses' of the merger method by some groups in the United States. A number of groups have been accused of obtaining, or maintaining, a reputation for earning increasing profits over the years by 'buying profits', i.e. by purchasing profitable companies towards the end of the holding company's accounting year, and including the whole of the profit of the subsidiary, including the proportion earned before acquisition, in the group profit for the year.

To some extent the possibility of misleading users of accounts is reduced if comparative figures are shown which disclose the total profit of the companies involved in the merger in the preceeding year.

Criteria for the Merger Method

The position regarding the treatment of goodwill and precombination profits of companies adopting the merger method was thrown into doubt by the tax case of *Shearer v Bercain* (1980). Here, the High Court ruled that merger accounting was not consistent with Section 56 of the Companies Act, 1948 and that such cases should be treated in a similar manner to the acquisition method. Hence a share premium account should be opened, if the purchase consideration was in excess of the net assets acquired, and precombination profits of the subsidiary would not be available for distribution. The decision in *Shearer v Bercain* threw into doubt the legality of dividend distributions made by holding companies who had used the merger method.

In consideration of the decision in *Shearer v Bercain*, Sections 36–41 of the Companies Act 1981 set out to provide relief from the requirements of Section 56 of the 1948 Act. For the relief to be available the company issuing the shares must have secured at least 90% of the equity of the other company or companies. Section 38 of the 1981 Act provides that where a new holding company acquires other companies as subsidiaries on an exchange of shares basis, the precombination profits of the subsidiary remain distributable. Retrospective relief is granted to companies who have adopted merger accounting, but who had not raised a share premium account.

One of the earliest exposure drafts* issued by the ASC was on the subject of acquisitions and mergers. The exposure draft included a set of criteria which would have to be satisfied if the combination was to be treated as a merger. In particular, it was proposed that the maximum allowed difference in size should be a ratio of three to one, i.e. the shareholders of the largest company involved in the combination could not have more than three times the voting rights in the amalgamated company than the shareholders of any other company.

It was also proposed that the directors of the holding company should not be allowed any latitude in deciding whether to treat a combination as an acquisition or a merger. If the combination satisfied the conditions for a merger it would have to be treated as such, otherwise it would have to be treated as an acquisition. Thus, the adoption of the proposals contained in the exposure draft would have resulted in the far more extensive use of the

*ED3 Accounting for Acquisitions and Mergers issued in January 1971.

merger method than had hitherto been seen in the United Kingdom and it has not yet been followed by the issue of a Statement of Standard Accounting Practice.

This was a controversial exposure draft particularly as doubts were expressed about its legal implications; doubts which were eventually confirmed by the *Shearer v Bercain* judgment.

ED3 was allowed to remain in suspense for a number of years but, following the passage of the Companies Act 1981, the ASC felt able to return to the subject and in October 1982 replaced ED3 by ED31 (Accounting for Acquisitions and Mergers). In one important respect ED31 followed the same line as its predecessor in proposing that no latitude should be allowed in the choice between merger and acquisition accounting. Business combinations which came within the definition of mergers should be treated as such while other combinations would have to be treated as acquisitions. A major difference between the two Exposure Drafts is the rejection in ED31 of the need for the combining companies to be of more or less the same size. This was rejected both on the grounds that any limit was bound to be arbitrary but also because the ASC were now of the view that the notion that one of the companies should not dominate the other was not relevant. The key element in the revised proposal was that to qualify as a merger the terms of the combination should be such as to ensure that the same body of shareholders continued to have an interest in the enlarged enterprise and that no material resources should leave the group, i.e. that the purchase consideration should be in the form of shares and not (except for a small margin of up to 10%) cash.

Group Accounts – Statement of Standard Accounting Practice 14
(issued September 1978)

This Standard is mainly concerned with matters such as the circumstances in which subsidiaries can be excluded from the group accounts and the information which should be disclosed in such cases. In many ways the objective of the Standard is to achieve a greater consistency in the interpretation of the relevant company legislation.

SSAP14 does not deal with the problems of goodwill on consolidation nor does it make a contribution to the merger versus acquisition methods debate. The feature of the Standard which has the greatest influence on accounting practice is the requirement that a subsidiary's assets, other than goodwill, should be stated at their fair values as at the date of acquisition.

ASSOCIATED COMPANIES

The arguments which were advanced, on pages 263–4, about the desirability of preparing consolidated accounts can be extended to those situations where one company owns a substantial share (but not a controlling interest) of another company and can exercise significant influence over the conduct of that company. Following the terminology used in SSAP 1 (see below) we will refer to the company which owns the shares as the *investing company* and the company whose shares are held as the *associated company*.

Readers will remember that the Companies Act only require the publication of consolidated accounts where the investing company owns more than 50 per cent of the equity shares or can control the composition of the board of directors of the (subsidiary) company. Thus, the provisions do not apply to those situations where, for example, two companies each own 50 per cent of the shares of a third company, or where a few companies together join to undertake a joint venture and establish a limited company to carry on the business. In these circumstances the jointly owned company may not be a subsidiary of any of the investing companies, but all the investing companies may share in its control. These, and similar arrangements are akin to a partnership between limited companies.

Such arrangements have existed for many years, but they became increasingly popular in the 1960s, and they resulted in a considerable variation in accounting practice. Some companies treated their investment in an associated company in the same way as an investment in any other company, that is, the investment was shown at cost and the income recognized as arising from the investment was confined to dividends receivable during the period. Other companies took the view that this approach did not adequately reflect the state of the company's investment, and therefore adopted the alternative approach of reporting as income their share of the profits of the associated companies. Accordingly they showed each such investment at cost plus their share in the change in retained earnings of the associated company since acquisition.

This matter was the subject of SSAP 1, *Accounting for the results of Associated Companies*, which was issued in January, 1971. The ASC took the view that the second approach, which is known as the equity method of accounting, was preferable and based this conclusion on the reasoning that '. . . the investing company actively participates in the commercial and policy decisions of its associated companies; it thus has a measure of direct responsibility for the return on its investment and should account for its stewardship . . .'.

As part of the ongoing review of accounting standards, the ASC revised SSAP1 in 1982. In the (revised) SSAP1 an associated company was defined as follows:

An *associated company* is a company not being a subsidiary of the investing group or company in which:
(a) the interest of the investing group or company is effectively that of a partner in a joint venture or consortium and the investing group or company is in a position to exercise a significant influence over the company in which the investment is made; or
(b) the interest of the investing group or company is for the long term and is substantial and, having regard to the disposition of the other shareholdings, the investing group or company is in a position to exercise a significant influence over the company in which the investment is made.

Significant influence over a company essentially involves participation in the financial and operating policy decisions of that company (including dividend policy) but not necessarily control of those policies. Representation on the board of directors is indicative of such participation, but will neither necessarily give conclusive evidence of it nor be the only method by which the investing company may participate in policy decisions.

Where the interest of the investing group or company is not effectively that of a partner or joint venture or consortium but amounts to 20% of the equity voting rights of a company, it should be presumed that the investing group or company has the ability to exercise significant influence over that company unless it can be clearly demonstrated otherwise. For example, there may exist one or more other large shareholdings which prevent the exercise of such influence.

Where the interest of the investing group or company is not effectively that of a partner in a joint venture or consortium and amounts to less than 20% of the equity voting rights of a company it should be presumed that the investing group or company does not have the ability to exercise significant influence unless it can clearly demonstrate otherwise. Unless there are exceptional circumstances, this demonstration should include a statement from the company in which the investment is made that it accepts that the investing group or company is in a position to exercise significant influence over it.

The actual standard may be summarized as follows:

1. In the investing company's own accounts the investment in the associated company should be shown at cost or valuation, and the income recognized from the investment should be the dividends received and receivable for the period.

2. In the consolidated balance sheet the investing group's interest in the associated company is shown as the total of:

   (a) its share in the net assets of the associated company (other than any goodwill which might be included in the associated company's balance sheet)

   (b) its share of any goodwill shown in the associated company's balance sheet.

   (c) any goodwill (positive or negative) arising from the investing company's acquisition of the shares of the associated company to the extent that it has not been written off.

Item (a) must be disclosed separately but (b) and (c) may be shown as one amount. In other words the amount to be included in the consolidated balance sheet is the investing group's share in the net assets of the associated company at the balance sheet date plus (or minus) any goodwill yet to be written off. *

3. The consolidated profit and loss account should show separately the investing group's share in:

(a) the pre-tax profit or loss of the associated company
(b) the tax borne by the associated company, and
(c) the aggregate net profit (or loss) retained by the associated company.

It should be noted that the SSAP does not require the investing group's share in the turnover of associated companies or its share of the various profit and loss account items, which need to be disclosed in the published profit and loss account, to be shown or included in the overall consolidated figures.

4. The investing group's share of the post acquisition accumulated reserves of associated companies and any movements therein should be disclosed in the consolidated financial statements.

5. If the investing company does not have to publish consolidated accounts, its own accounts should be suitably modified so as to show, by way of note, the required information.

We will conclude by presenting a simple example illustrating how the results of an associated company are incorporated in a set of consolidated accounts. The example will also show the differences in the consolidated accounts which would result if the company in question is not regarded as an associated company.

Example 8.3

The following are the summarized balance sheet of H, S and A as at 31 December 19X4 and the summarized profit and loss accounts are for the year ended on that date.

	H £	S £	A £
Balance Sheets			
£1 Ordinary shares	20,000	20,000	40,000
Retained earnings	100,000	40,000	200,000
	£120,000	£60,000	£240,000
20,000 shares in S, at cost	20,000	—	—
10,000 shares in A, at cost	10,000	—	—
Sundry assets/*less* Liabilities	90,000	60,000	240,000
	£120,000	£60,000	£240,000

*It must be remembered that the revision of SSAP1 predates any implementation of ED30 which might require the writing off of positive and negative goodwill.

Profit and Loss Accounts	H £	S £	A £
Profit before tax	60,000*	20,000	280,000
less Corporation tax	24,000	10,000	160,000
	36,000	10,000	120,000
less Dividends, paid	—	—	10,000
	36,000	10,000	110,000
Retained earnings 1 January 19X4	64,000	30,000	90,000
Retained earnings 31 December 19X4	£100,000	£40,000	£200,000

*Profit before taxation for H Limited is stated after crediting dividends of £2,500 received from A Limited (H owns 25 per cent of A's shares).

H purchased its shares in S at the date of formation of that company and its shares in A when A had retained earnings of £20,000.

(a) We will first assume that A Limited is not an associated company of H Limited, i.e. although it owns a substantial proportion of the shares of A it is not in a position to exercise a significant influence over the policy-making of A Limited. In this case the consolidated accounts would appear as follows:

H LIMITED AND ITS SUBSIDIARY COMPANY

Consolidated Balance Sheet as at 31 December 19X4

	£		£
£1 Ordinary shares	20,000	Shares in A, at cost	10,000
Retained earnings	140,000	Sundry assets *less* Liabilities	150,000
	£160,000		£160,000

Consolidated Profit and Loss Account
for the Year ended 31 December 19X4

	£
Operating profit	77,500
Dividend from A	2,500
	80,000
less Corporation tax	34,000
Profit after tax	46,000
Retained earnings, 1 January 19X4	94,000
Retained earnings, 31 December 19X4	£140,000

Note
The only consolidation adjustment required in respect of S Limited is the setting off of the cost of the investment with the nominal value of the shares acquired (which are both £20,000).

(b) We will now assume that A Limited should be treated as an associated company. The consolidated balance sheet worksheet might appear as follows:

Consolidated Balance Sheet Worksheet
All figures £000

	H Ltd	S Ltd	Sub-totals	Adjustments Debit	Credit	Consolidated Balance Sheet
Share capital	20	20	40	(a) 20		20
Realized Reserve					(b) 5	5
Retained Earnings	100	40	140		(b) 45	185
	£120	£60	£180			£210
Shares in:						
S Ltd	20		20		(a) 20	
A Ltd	10		10		(b) 10	
H Ltd interest in A Ltd				(b) 60		60
Sundry assets less liabilities	90	60	150			150
	£120	£60	£180	£80	£80	£210

Adjustment (a) represents the consolidation adjustment for S Ltd.

Adjustment (b) can be explained as follows:

An inspection of A Limited's balance sheet at 31 December 19X4 shows that H's interest in A is £60,000 (25% of £240,000).

H's share in the increase of A's post acquisition reserves is 25% of £(200,000–20,000) = £45,000. When this is added to the cost of the investment we obtain £55,000 which is less than £60,000. The difference is due to the fact that there was negative goodwill (or surplus on acquisition) in respect of H Limited's purchase of its interest in the shares of A.

	£
Nominal Values of shares acquired	10,000
H's share of A's reserves at acquisition	5,000
	£15,000
less	
Cost of shares	10,000
Surplus	£5,000

It has been assumed that the £5,000 surplus is in respect of assets which have been consumed and hence the amount has been credited to a realized reserve. Adjustment (b) is thus built up as follows:

	£
Cost of investment	10,000
H's share in A's post acquisition reserves	45,000
Realized reserve	5,000
H's interest in A	£60,000

The consolidated balance sheet would then appear as follows:

H LIMITED AND ITS SUBSIDIARY COMPANY
(incorporating an Associated Company)

Consolidated Balance Sheet as at 31 December 19X4

£1 Ordinary shares	20,000	Sundry assets	
Realized Reserve	5,000	less liabilities	150,000
Retained Earnings	185,000	Interest in an	
		Associated Company	60,000
	£210,000		£210,000

EXERCISES

8.1 Carl Limited acquired its first subsidiary (Dry Limited) in 19X2 and consolidated accounts were prepared for that year by using the acquisition method. The subsidiary is partly owned; Carl Limited owns 80 per cent of the ordinary shares but none of the preference shares of Dry Limited. The managing director of Carl Limited is familiar with the nature of accounting statements but knows nothing about consolidated accounts.

Prepare a report for the managing director which:

1. Explains the nature and function of consolidated accounts;
2. Explains those terms which appear in consolidated accounts but not in the accounts of an individual company; and
3. Outlines the various ways of treating 'goodwill on consolidation' and discusses the advantages and disadvantages of each alternative.

8.2 The following balance sheets are all as at 31 December 19X3. In each case prepare the consolidated balance sheet as at that date.

(a)	*H Ltd*	*S Ltd*
Fixed assets	15,000	8,000
5,000 shares in S Limited	8,000	
Current assets	10,000	6,000
	£33,000	£14,000

	H Ltd	S Ltd
Ordinary shares of £1 each	20,000	5,000
Retained earnings	8,000	7,000
	28,000	12,000
Current liabilities	5,000	2,000
	£33,000	£14,000

H Limited acquired the shares in S Limited on 31 December 19X1 when S Limited had retained earnings of £1,000.

(b) As part (a) except that S Limited's retained earnings as at 31 December 19X1 were £6,000.

(c)

	H Ltd	S Ltd
	£	£
Sundry assets *less* Liabilities	18,000	14,000
8,000 shares in S Limited	12,000	—
	£30,000	£14,000
Ordinary shares of £1 each	20,000	10,000
Retained earnings	10,000	4,000
	£30,000	£14,000

When H acquired its shares in S Limited that company had retained earnings of £8,000.

(d)

	Fair Ltd	Bad Ltd	Good Ltd
	£	£	£
Sundry assets *less* Liabilities	40,000	(2,000)	£16,000
15,000 Shares in Bad Limited	4,000		
8,000 Shares in Good Limited	12,000		
	£56,000	£(2,000)	£16,000
Ordinary shares of £1 each	20,000	20,000	10,000
Share premium account	5,000	3,000	2,000
Retained earnings	31,000	(25,000)	4,000
	£56,000	£(2,000)	£16,000

Balances at dates of acquisition

	Bad Ltd	Good Ltd
	£	£
Share premium	3,000	2,000
Retained earnings	16,000 (Debit)	1,000 (Credit)

8.3 The following summarized trial balances are as at 31 December 19X2. In each part prepare the consolidated profit and loss account for the year ended 31 December 19X2 and the consolidated balance sheet as at that date.

(a)

	H Ltd £000	S Ltd £000
Share capital, £1 shares	10	5
Retained earnings, 1 January 19X2	40	16
Sales	70	50
Dividends received	4	—
	£124	£71
5,000 shares in S Limited	8	—
Sundry assets *less* Liabilities	56	25
Cost of goods sold	40	30
Sundry expenses	18	12
Dividends paid	2	4
	£124	£71

H acquired its holding in S some years ago when S had retained earnings of £2,000.

(b)

	H Ltd £000	S Ltd £000
Share capital, £1 shares	40·0	10·0
Retained earnings, 1 January 19X2	30·0	24·0
Sales	80·0	60·0
Dividend received	1·6	—
	£151·6	£94·0
8,000 shares in S Ltd	34·0	
Sundry assets *less* Liabilities	47·6	40·0
Cost of goods sold	50·0	40·0
Sundry expenses	16·0	12·0
Dividends paid	4.0	2.0
	£151·6	£94·0

H acquired its holding in S some years ago when S had retained earnings of £20,000.

During 19X2 H sold S goods, which had cost H £16,000, at a mark-up of 50 per cent on cost. One quarter of the goods were included in S Ltd's inventory at the year end.

8.4 The following are the summarized balance sheets of Pride Limited, Fall Limited and Decline Limited as at 31 December 19X6 and the summarized profit and loss accounts for the year ended on that date.

Balance Sheets

	Pride £	*Fall* £	*Decline* £
£1 Ordinary Shares	100,000	20,000	10,000
£1 5 per cent Redeemable preference shares	—	10,000	—
Profit and Loss Account	40,000	22,000	5,000
	£140,000	£52,000	£15,000
15,000 Ordinary shares in Fall Limited	20,000	—	—
4,000 Ordinary shares in Decline Limited	6,000	—	—
Sundry assets *less* Liabilities	74,000	41,500	10,000
Balance at bank	50,000	15,000	8,000
	150,000	56,500	18,000
less Proposed dividends	10,000	4,500	3,000
	£140,000	£52,000	£15,000

Profit and Loss Accounts

		Pride £		*Fall* £		*Decline* £
Profit before tax		50,000		30,000		8,000
less Corporation tax		20,000		10,400		3,000
		30,000		19,600		5,000
less Dividends						
Paid: ordinary shares	5,000		2,000			
Proposed: Preference shares	—		500		—	
Ordinary shares	10,000	15,000	4,000	6,500	3,000	3,000
		15,000		13,100		2,000
Balance b/f		25,000		8,900		3,000
Balance c/f		£40,000		£22,000		£5,000

1. Pride Limited purchased its shares in Fall and Decline on 31 December 19X2 when the balances (both credit) on the profit and loss accounts were

    Fall £2,000   Decline   £1,000

2. Pride Limited has not provided in its 19X6 accounts for the dividends receivable.

Required:

Prepare the consolidated balance sheet of Pride Limited and its subsidiary company as at 31 December 19X6 assuming that

      (i) Decline Limited is not an associated company of Pride Limited
and
      (ii) It is an associated company.

8.5 The following are the balance sheets of H Limited and S Limited as at 31 December 19X2.

	H Ltd £000	S Ltd £000
Assets	£1,000	£600
Liabilities	300	200
Share capital, £1 shares	100	50
Retained earnings	600	350
	£1,000	£600

On 1 January 19X3 H Limited purchased the whole of the share capital of S Limited issuing, as the purchase consideration, 80,000 £1 shares. On that date H Limited's shares had a market value of £6 each.

      Earnings for 19X3 were:

H Limited	£100,000
S Limited	£ 50,000

Assume that the liabilities remain unchanged and that no dividends were paid.

Required:

H Limited's balance sheet and the consolidated balance sheet as at 31 December 19X3 on the alternative assumptions that:

(a) The purchase method is used;
(b) The pooling method is used.

(Assume that any goodwill is to be written off over 10 years.)

8.6 Grab Ltd, Hand Ltd, and Tight Ltd have issued share capital in ordinary shares of £1 each of £500,000, £250,000 and £200,000 respectively.

The summarized profit and loss accounts of the companies for the year ended 30th June 1983 showed the following:

	Grab Ltd £	Hand Ltd £	Tight Ltd £
Turnover	3,070,400	1,260,000	890,604
Deduct:			
Cost of sales	2,454,360	940,000	801,900
Gross profit	616,040	320,000	88,704
Deduct:			
Distribution costs	162,170	70,890	29,604
Administration expenses	156,890	71,860	16,296
Debenture interest (gross)		22,000	
	319,060	164,750	45,900
	296,980	155,250	42,804
Interim dividend received	24,000		
Proposed dividend receivable	46,000		
	366,980	155,250	42,804
Less:			
Provision for corporation tax	156,640	82,280	20,592
	210,340	72,970	22,212
Appropriations:			
Interim dividends paid	50,000	30,000	
Proposed dividends	125,000	35,000	20,000
	175,000	65,000	20,000
	35,340	7,970	2,212
Balance brought forward on 1st July 1982 .	115,670	47,860	14,800
	151,010	55,830	17,012

You also obtain the following information:
(1) Grab Ltd acquired 200,000 shares in Hand Ltd on 1st July 1980 when there had been a balance on profit and loss account of £40,000.
(2) On 1st October 1982 Grab Ltd acquired 180,000 shares in Tight Ltd whose profits accrue evenly throughout the year.
(3) Grab Ltd buys goods for resale from Hand Ltd which yield a profit to Hand Ltd of 25% on selling price. On 30th June 1983 Grab Ltd held in stock goods purchased from Hand Ltd for £20,000. On 30th June 1982 the amount of stock so held had been £28,000 and during the year ended 30th June 1983, sales made by Hand Ltd to Grab Ltd had totalled £220,000.

(4) Hand Ltd buys goods for resale from Tight Ltd on a regular basis at £20,000 per month. Tight Ltd achieves a profit on selling price of 10%. Stock of goods purchased from Tight Ltd and still held on 30th June 1983, amounted to £40,000 at cost to Hand Ltd. Stock of goods purchased from Tight Ltd held at 30th June 1982 had been £35,000.

You are required to prepare a consolidated profit and loss account of Grab Ltd and its subsidiaries for the year ended 30th June 1983 together with consolidation schedules.

NOTE: Ignore advance corporation tax.

The Institute of Chartered Accountants in England and Wales, Financial Accounting I, November 1983.

8.7 The following accounts are the Consolidated Balance Sheet and Parent Company Balance Sheet for Alpha Ltd as at 30 June 1982.

		Consolidated Balance Sheet		*Parent Company*
		£		£
Ordinary shares		140,000		140,000
Capital Reserve		92,400		92,400
Profit and Loss Account		79,884		35,280
Minority Interest		12,320		
		324,604		267,680
Fixed Assets				
Freehold Premises		127,400		84,000
Plant and Machinery		62,720		50,400
Goodwill		85,680		—
Investment in subsidiary (50,400 shares)				151,200
Current Assets				
Stock	121,604		71,120	
Debtors	70,420		46,760	
Dividend Receivable	—		5,040	
Cash at Bank	24,360		—	
	216,384		122,920	
Current Liabilities				
Creditors	128,660		69,720	
Corporation Tax	27,160		20,720	
Bank Overdraft	—		39,200	
Proposed Dividend	11,760		11,200	
	167,580		140,840	

Working Capital	48,804	(17,920)
	£324,604	£267,680

Notes:
  (i) There is only one subsidiary company called Beta Ltd.
 (ii) There are no capital reserves in the subsidiary.
(iii) Alpha produced stock for sale to the subsidiary at a cost of £3,360 in May 1982. The stock was invoiced to the subsidiary at £4,200 and is still on hand at the subsidiary's warehouse on 30 June 1982. The invoice had not been settled on 30 June 1982.
 (iv) The Profit and Loss of the subsidiary had a credit balance of £16,800 at the date of acquisition.
  (v) There is a right of set-off between overdrafts and bank balances.

Required:
(a) Prepare the Balance Sheet as at 30 June 1982 of the subsidiary company from the information given above.
(b) Briefly discuss the main reasons for the publication of consolidated accounts.

The Association of Certified Accountants, Advanced Accounting Practice, June 1982.

9 | Funds Flow Statements and Cash Budgeting

INTRODUCTION

In the long run, a profit will result in an increase in the company's cash balance but, as Keynes observed 'in the long run, we are all dead'. In our context the quotation could be amended to read 'in the long run, unless the management is careful, the company may be liquidated'. In the short run, the making of a profit will not necessarily result in an increased cash balance.

This observation leads us to two questions. The first relates to the importance of the distinction between cash and profit. The second is concerned with the usefulness of the information provided by the balance sheet and profit and loss account in the problem of deciding whether the company has, or will be able to generate, sufficient cash to finance its operations.

The first question is easily answered – the distinction is vital. Cash is the very life-blood of a company for, although it can make losses and survive, its demise would be instantaneous should it run out of cash.

The balance sheet does give some information about the cash position of the company, for it discloses its cash balance as well as those assets which will be converted into cash in the near future (current assets) and those liabilities which are due for payment either immediately or in the near future (current liabilities). However, the balance sheet only provides a static picture showing the position at a point in time and does not show how the company has financed its activities during the period under review. The profit and loss account is a dynamic statement in that it explains the reasons for changes, but the change explained is that of the retained profit of the company and the account gives no information about changes in the company's liquidity.

The importance of the distinction between cash and profit and the scant attention paid to this by the profit and loss account has resulted in the development of *sources and applications of funds statements*. Such state-

316

ments do not, generally, provide information that is not found in the balance sheet and profit and loss account. However, they reclassify this information so as to show the way in which the company financed its activities in the period covered by the statements.

Before discussing the statements in any detail we should first deal with the reasons why there is a difference between a company's profit or loss for a period and the change in its cash balance.

Profit, Cash and Working Capital

Figure 9.1 illustrates what may be termed the working capital cycle.

Figure 9.1.

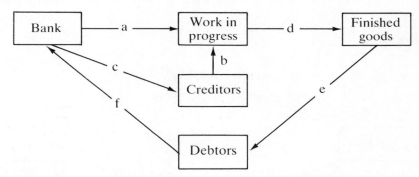

The assets constituting work in progress are either purchased for cash (flow a) or on credit (flow b). Creditors have to be paid (flow c). Work in progress is converted to finished goods (flow d) which, when sold, gives rise to debtors (flow e). Finally, the debtors pay and we return to cash (flow f).

A somewhat simplified version of the above will be sufficient for the purposes of our explanation and this is illustrated in Figure 9.2.

Figure 9.2.

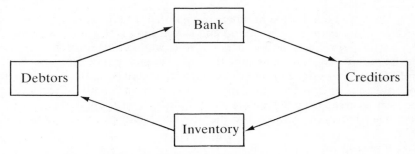

The flows comprising the above cycle are:

1. Bank   – Creditors, cash paid to creditors

2. Creditors – Inventory, goods purchased on credit

3. Inventory – Debtors, goods sold on credit

4. Debtors – Bank,   cash paid by debtors

The difference between the short and long run for a given company depends on the speed of the cycle. At one extreme, in the case of, say, a barrow boy who buys and sells for cash, the cycle may be completed in a day, and profit and cash movement will be in step. The other extreme may be illustrated by a whisky distillery whose cycle would last for some years because of the length of the inventory stage, caused by the need to mature the product. There will then be a considerable difference between cash flows and profit. In particular, the cash flow out will precede the profit by a number of years, while the time-lag between the recognition of profit and the receipt of cash will be less, and depend on the credit period allowed to debtors.

Figure 9.3.

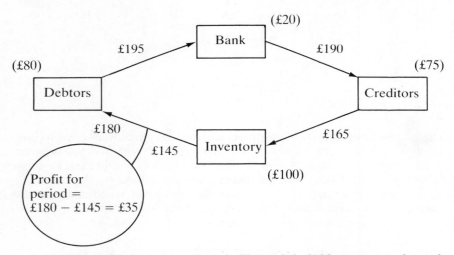

We have added some numbers in Figure 9.3. £190 represents the cash paid to creditors during the period and so on. £145 is the outflow of inventory for the period, i.e. the cost of goods sold, while £180 represents the sales for the period. Thus, if we assume that there are no depreciating assets, the profit for the period is £35. We can see that the increase in the bank balance does not equal the profit, for the increase depends on the difference between the cash received from customers and the cash paid to suppliers.

The figures in brackets are the opening balances for the period and thus:

Opening working capital

= Bank + Inventory + Debtors –Creditors

= £20 + £100 + £80 – £75

= £125.

The closing balances on the various components of working capital are:

Bank balance = £ 20 + £195 − £190 = £ 25
Creditors   = £ 75 + £165 − £190 = £ 50
Inventory   = £100 + £165 − £145 = £120
Debtors   = £ 80 + £180 − £195 = £ 65

and the closing working capital is given by:

Closing working capital

= Bank + Inventory + Debtors − Creditors
= £25 + £120 + £65 − £50
= £160.

Although we can see that the profit for the period did not result in an equal increase in the bank balance, it is evident that, with our assumptions, the profit of £35 did result in an increase in working capital of that amount.

	£
Closing working capital	160
less Opening working capital	125
Increase	£ 35

Now, let us assume that the company has depreciating assets and that the depreciation charge for the period is £10. The profit is thus reduced from £35 to £25 but there is no corresponding change in the increase of working capital. This is understandable because depreciation represents the reduction of a fixed asset and fixed assets do not form part of the working capital.

We can now see that a statement explaining the difference between the profit and the increase in the bank balance can be presented in the following two steps:

1. An explanation of the difference between profit and the increase in working capital due to items charged or credited in the profit and loss account which do not involve changes in working capital, e.g. depreciation.

2. An explanation of the change in the composition of working capital.

So far as the second point is concerned, it can be seen that for a given level of profit, and all other things being equal, the greater the increase in the other current assets, i.e. inventory and debtors, the smaller the increase in the bank balance. For example, suppose that in Figure 9.3, the flow from debtors to cash was £180 instead of £195. The closing debtors figure would be £15 more and the closing bank balance would be £15 less, while the total of working capital would remain unchanged. Similarly, for a given level of profit and with other factors being held constant the greater the increase in current liabilities the greater the increase in the bank balance.

The position is summarized in Table 9.1.

Table 9.1

Change, all other things being equal.	For a given level of profit the bank balance will be:
Current assets other than cash, increase	Smaller
decrease	Larger
Current liabilities, increase	Larger
decrease	Smaller

We are now able to present a simple example of a flow of funds statement – funds representing working capital.

Example 9.1

The following are the balance sheets of Hart Limited as at 1 January 19X4 and 31 March 19X4.

The figures assumed are consistent with those used in Figure 9.3.

	1 January 19X4		31 March 19X4	
	£	£	£	£
Fixed assets, net book value		500		490
Current assets				
Inventory	100		120	
Debtors	80		65	
Balance at bank	20		25	
	200		210	
less Current liabilities				
Creditors	75	125	50	160
		£625		£650
Share capital		400		400
Retained earnings		225		250
		£625		£650

We assume:

(i) That no fixed assets have been purchased or sold during the period, i.e. that the reduction in their net book value is solely due to the depreciation expense, £10, for the period.

(ii)   That no dividends have been paid and that the profit for the period is £25, i.e. the increase in retained earnings.

(iii) That the only item charged, or credited, in the profit and loss account not involving a change in working capital is the depreciation expense of £10.

The statement of the sources and applications of funds based on the above is as follows:

HART LIMITED

Statement of the Sources and Applications of Funds
For the Period 1 January — 31 March 19X4

	£	£
Sources of funds		
Profit for the period		25
add Adjustments for items not involving changes in funds (depreciation)		10
Funds generated from operations		35
Increase/decrease in working capital		
Increase in inventory	20	
Decrease in debtors	(15)	
Decrease in creditors	25	
	30	
Increase in bank balance	5	
		£35

In the above we have used the term *funds* to describe working capital. We shall show later that there are other definitions of funds and that the use of the alternative definitions of funds will give rise to different forms of funds statements.

Sources and Applications of Funds Other than from Operations

So far we have only considered changes in funds due to the manufacturing and trading activities of the company, i.e. due to its operations. In our example, the operations resulted in an increase in funds. An activity which results in an increase in funds is called a *source* of funds. However, its operations could have led to a decrease in funds – an activity which results in a decrease of funds is called an *application* of funds.

In reality there are many other sources and applications of funds, and these may be summarized as follows:

Sources

1.   The proceeds from the issue of shares
2.   Increases in longer-term loans, including debentures
3.   Sales of fixed assets.

Applications

1.   Redemption of redeemable preference shares
2.   Decreases in longer-term liabilities, including debentures
3.   Purchases of fixed assets
4.   Dividends
5.   Taxation (but see below).

Dividends and taxation are sometimes treated as deductions from the source of funds from operations rather than as applications in their own right. In our view, dividends should be shown as applications, since the decision as to the amount of the dividend is under the control of the company. On the other hand, we believe that taxation is better shown as a deduction from the source from operations, since the payment of tax is not at the discretion of the company. However, it appears that the usual practice is to treat tax as an application and we will, having made our protest, show it as such in the examples of this chapter.

The Format of Funds Statements

One basic form of sources and applications of funds statement is:

PARK LIMITED

Statement of Sources and Applications of Funds
Year ended 31 December 19X8

	£	£	£
1. *Sources – From operations*			
Profit before tax			*x*
Adjustment for items not involving			
the movement of funds: Depreciation			*x*
Total generated from operations			*x*
Funds from other sources			
Issue of shares for cash		*x*	
Sale of motor vehicles		*x*	
			x
			x
2. *Applications of funds*			
Dividends		*x*	
Taxation		*x*	
Purchase of plant and machinery		*x*	
			x
			x

3. *Increase or decrease in working capital*

Increase in inventory	x
Decrease in debtors	$.(x)$
Increase in creditors	(x)
	x

Movement in net liquid funds

Increase (decrease) in			
Cash balances	(x)		
Short-term investments	x	x	$£x$

The items in brackets are negative figures.

The sources of funds are presented first, and it is the custom to start with the funds from operations. The section starts with the profit before tax (thus showing the link between the statement and the profit and loss account) to which is added, or subtracted, any items charged, or credited, in the profit and loss account which do not involve a movement of funds.

Some accountants present this section in the following manner:

Sources from operations	£
Profit before tax	120
add Depreciation	90
	210

This is a misleading form of presentation because it implies that depreciation is a source of funds. Depreciation is not a source of funds; doubling the depreciation charge will not affect the funds generated during the period.

The funds from 'other sources' are added to the funds generated from operations to give the total of the sources of funds.

We have assumed that one of the 'other sources' is an issue of shares. One sometimes finds this item shown as follows:

	£
Increase in share capital	100
Increase in share premium	30
	130

This is another misleading form of presentation because it suggests that the increase in the share premium account is a source of funds, but movements on reserves do not increase or decrease funds. The source of funds, of £130 in this case, is the issue of shares and the source should be shown as such. However, it is sensible to show, by way of note, that the shares were issued at a premium, so that the user may reconcile the item with the figures in the balance sheet.

The two points we have made about the form of presentation are not mere pedantry. We believe that communication with non-accountants is a very important part of the accountant's task, and he should not make his job more difficult by using forms of presentation which could, so easily, give rise to misunderstanding.

The second part of the statement shows the way funds have been applied, or used, and the difference between the sources and applications represents the increase or decrease in working capital (funds) for the period.

The last part of the statement reconciles the change in working capital with the change in the cash and bank balance. It is usual to include 'short-term investments' as part of the cash and bank position so long as these investments are capable of being immediately realized.

Sale of Fixed Assets

The sales of fixed assets sometimes give rise to difficulty. The source of funds resulting from the disposal of fixed assets is the proceeds from sale, which increases net working capital either in the form of cash or debtors, and not the net book value of the asset sold.

'Profit on the sale of fixed assets' is the writing back, to the credit of the profit and loss account, of an excess depreciation charge, i.e. 'negative depreciation' and this does not involve a movement in working capital. This is, therefore, one of the items included in the adjustment to the pre-tax profits. The loss on sale of fixed assets is an additional depreciation charge and is treated in the same way as depreciation.

Preparation of Sources and Applications Statements

The statements are usually produced from the opening and closing balance sheets and the linking profit and loss account. Usually some additional information is required, especially concerning the sale and purchase of fixed assets. However, if the additional information were not provided it would still be possible to prepare the sources and applications statement, but the statement could then only include the net increase in fixed assets. This point reinforces the observation, made earlier, that a sources and applications of funds statement is no more than a reclassification of the information provided in the profit and loss account for the period and the opening and closing balance sheets.

It is possible to use a systematic approach for the preparation of the sources and applications statements which involves the interplay of debits and credits such that, if the debts and credit are properly juggled, the sources and applications statement is automatically produced. However, we believe that a more informal method is, in all but very complex examples, better suited to this task, and this approach can be summarized as follows:

1.   Examine the profit and loss account and note any charges or

credits not involving the movement of funds.

2. Prepare a schedule showing the differences between the opening and closing balance sheets and consider this list, identifying the various sources and applications.

This method is illustrated in Example 9.2.

Example 9.2

The following are summaries of the balance sheet of Prince Limited at 1 January 19X2 and 31 December 19X2 and its profit and loss account for 19X2.

			Change	
	31 Dec X2	*1 Jan X2*	*+*	*−*
	£000	*£000*	*£000*	*£000*
Fixed assets, net book value				
Freehold properties	18,200	15,200	3,000	
Plant and machinery	108,400	103,100	5,300	
Motor vehicles	5,300	4,800	500	
	131,900	123,100		
Current assets				
Inventory	28,200	26,500	1,700	
Debtors and prepayments	17,200	19,400		2,200
Cash and short-term deposits		1,720		1,720
	45,400	47,620		
Current liabilities				
Creditors and accrued expenses	19,100	22,800	3,700	
Taxation currently payable	11,200	9,800		1,400
Proposed dividend	1,200	1,000		200
Overdraft	800	—		800
	32,300	33,600		
Net current assets	13,100	14,020		
Net assets	£145,000	£137,120		
Ordinary share capital	50,000	43,000		7,000
Share premium account	24,000	20,000		4,000
General reserve	43,000	40,000		3,000
Retained earnings	3,500	3,120		380
	120,500	106,120		
Debentures	14,000	22,000	8,000	
Deferred taxation	10,500	9,000		1,500
	£145,000	£137,120		
			£22,200	£22,200

In the above schedule of changes + represents increases in debit balances and − represents increases in credit balances.

Profit and Loss Account
Year ended 31 December 19X2

	£000	£000
Profit before taxation		11,080
less Corporation tax (including a transfer of		
£1,500,000 to the deferred taxation account)		5,700
Profit after taxation		5,380
less Dividends		
Paid	800	
Proposed	1,200	2,000
		3,380
less Transfer to the general reserve		3,000
		380
add Retained earnings 1 January 19X2		3,120
		£3,500

Note: ACT will be ignored in this example

Profit before taxation is stated after charging:

	£000
Depreciation: Plant and machinery	12,420
Motor vehicles	1,220
Loss on sale of plant and machinery	240
and after crediting:	
Profit on sale of motor vehicles	50

The plant sold during the year had cost £2,800,000 and had a net book value, at the date of sale, of £600,000. Similar details for the vehicles sold were, cost, £600,000 and, net book value, £120,000.

We will first show the workings.

1. Sources of Funds from Operations

This is a straightforward working which simply involves the adding back of those expenses which do not involve the movement of funds and the subtraction of the corresponding credits, i.e.

	£000
Profit before tax	11,080
add	
Depreciation and loss on	
sale of fixed assets	13,880
	24,960
less	
Profit on sale of fixed assets	50
Funds from operations	£24,910

2. Taxation

A part of the total tax charge of £5,700,000 does not represent an application of funds – the transfer to the deferred taxation account of £1,500,000. The balance, £4,200,000, does represent a reduction in funds, as we have defined that term, since the liability for taxation has been shown as a current liability. Thus the application of funds relating to taxation will be shown as £4,200,000. There are some problems, however, for non-accountants will be confused if they see a tax charge of £5,700,000 in the profit and loss account and an application in the funds statement of £4,200,000, and it could be argued that the funds statement omits a significant event. We shall return to this point later.

3. Dividends

The payment of the interim dividend of £800,000 was an application of funds in that the payment reduced cash while the proposed dividend is, similarly, treated as an application, since the proposal gave rise to a current liability and, hence, reduced working capital.

We shall now move to the schedule of changes in the balance sheet items.

4. Freehold Properties

It does not appear that there have been any sales of freehold properties and, since the company does not depreciate this asset, it seems that the increase in the balance for this item represents the purchase of freehold property. The application of funds for this item is:

Purchase of freehold properties £3,000,000.

5. Plant and Machinery

The position here is a little more complex. The difference between the opening and closing balances can be explained as follows:

Closing net book value
= Opening net book value + Cost of new assets
   − Net book value of assets sold − Depreciation charge for the year.

There is only one unknown in this equation, the cost of new assets, and this can easily be found by substitution.

$$108,400,000 = 103,100,000 + x - 600,000 - 12,420,000$$
$$x = £18,320,000$$

The application of funds resulting from the purchase of plant and machinery is £18,320,000.

Since we know the net book value of the plant and machinery sold and the 'loss on sale' we can calculate the proceeds of sale:

	£000
Net book value	600
less Loss on sale	240
	£360

The source of funds resulting from the sale of plant and machinery is £360,000.

6. Motor Vehicles

We can use the same method that we used for plant and machinery.

	£000	£000	£000
Closing net book value			5,300
less Opening net book value		4,800	
less Net book value of assets sold	120		
Depreciation charge	1,220	1,340	3,460
Cost of vehicles acquired during the year			£1,840

	£000
Net book value of assets sold	120
add Profit on sale	50
Proceeds	£170

Application. Purchase of motor vehicles £1,840,000.
Source, Sale of motor vehicles £170,000.

7. Current Assets and Liabilities

(a)   The changes on the individual balances will appear in the section of the statement explaining the difference between the changes in working capital and the changes in the cash balance.

(b)   The total change in the cash position is a decrease of £1,720,000 + £800,000 = £2,520,000.

8. Share Capital and Share Premium

It appears that the source of funds resulting from the issue of shares is £7,000,000 + £4,000,000 = £11,000,000.

9. General Reserve

The transfer to general reserve simply represents a retitling of a portion of owners' equity and has no effect on funds.

10. Retained Earnings

We have already dealt with the funds generated by operations.

11. Debentures

Debentures with a nominal value of £8,000,000 have been redeemed and, since it does not appear that there was a loss or gain on redemption, we assume that they were redeemed at their nominal value.
Application. Redemption of debentures £8,000,000.

12. Deferred Taxation

As has already been explained, this change does not involve the movement of funds.
We have completed the workings and the funds statement can now be prepared.

PRINCE LIMITED

Statement of Sources and Applications of Funds
Year ended 31 December 19X2

	£000	£000	£000
Sources of Funds			
From operations			
Profit before tax			11,080
Adjustments for items not			
involving the movement			
of funds:			

Depreciation	13,880	
less Profit on sale	50	13,830
Total generated from operations		24,910

Funds from other sources
Issue of shares for cash (issued at a premium of £4,000,000)		11,000
Sale of fixed assets,		
Plant and machinery	360	
Motor vehicles	170	530
		36,440

Applications of Funds
Dividends		2,000	
Taxation		4,200	
Repayment of debentures		8,000	
Purchase of fixed assets:			
Freehold property	3,000		
Plant and machinery	18,320		
Motor vehicles	1,840	23,160	37,360
Decrease in working capital			920

Increase or decrease in working capital

	Decrease	Increase
Increase in inventory		1,700
Decrease in debtors and prepayments	2,200	
Decrease in creditors and accrued expenses		3,700
Increase in taxation currently payable	1,400	
Increase in proposed dividend	200	
	5,400	3,800
		1,600
Decrease in cash and short-term investments	2,520	£920

Uses and Limitations of Funds Statements

We have, at last, presented an extended example of a funds statement and we should now consider the uses and limitations of such statements.

A funds statement highlights the way in which the company has financed its activities. In our example we can see that the main sources of funds were from operations (internally generated) and from the issue of shares (externally generated). It also demonstrates that the funds generated from operations were considerably larger than the reported profit for the period because of the depreciation expense. We can also see how the funds have been applied. In the above example it can be seen that a fairly modest proportion of the funds raised was applied to dividends, and that tax took its bite of the rest. The largest portion was spent on the acquisition of fixed assets, while a significant proportion was used to repay debentures. The funds applied in the year marginally exceeded the sources, with the result that working capital at the end of the year was slightly less than the corresponding amount as at the start of the year.

The above analysis of Prince Limited's financial policies was quickly and easily prepared from the funds statement. A user who had only been given the profit and loss account and balance sheets could have produced the same analysis, but it would have taken him considerably longer. This is, of course, one of the prime purposes of a funds statement, i.e. the provision, in an easily assimilated form, of significant information about the way in which the operations of the company were financed.

The provision of a funds statement helps to answer a number of questions. Some examples of these questions are:

1. What proportions of the funds obtained were internally and externally generated?

2. Why did the bank balance decrease even though the company made a profit?

3. How were the purchases of fixed assets financed?

4. How did the company manage to pay a dividend given that it made a loss?

These are interesting questions but there is little point in asking, or answering them, unless they provide some information about the company's future. The real purpose of a historical statement of sources and applications of funds is to provide users with information about the company's financing over a past period that will help them in making judgements about the company's future prospects.

Let us take an over-dramatic example; suppose a funds statement revealed that a significant proportion of a company's fixed assets has had to be sold in order to finance the payment of the dividends. It is clear that this is a procedure which could not be continued over the long run and that, unless a change in the company's circumstances can be foreseen, its dividend-paying ability must be suspect.

When it comes to the making of judgements about a company's future prospects all the available evidence, as well as judgement and intuition, must be used. Thus the historical funds statement must be used in conjunction with other information. A detailed treatment of this area goes beyond the limits of this text, but some of the relevant points will be discussed later in this chapter and in Chapter 13.

One of the features of the standard form of a funds statement that we have presented so far is that there is a considerable difference between the first two sections of the statement and the third. The first two sections, those dealing with the sources and applications of funds, include all the relevant information about the period under review, e.g. the total amount applied to the purchase of fixed assets for a year will be shown, as will the total amount obtained from the issue of debentures. The third section, which shows the change in the composition of working capital is, on the whole, based on the comparison of the position at two dates, the beginning and end of the period.

The statement can give no indication about any problems caused by the existence of seasonal peaks. Thus on a comparison of the year-ends, a company's cash position may appear perfectly satisfactory but the company may need to have a considerably higher cash balance at some time during the year. A funds statement will not reveal how the necessary increase was achieved. A month by month, or even week by week, cash budget would have to be produced if this information is to be provided. We shall deal with the question of cash budgets later in this chapter but we should say that an outsider, who has to rely on a company's published accounts (including the funds statement), would have to make many heroic assumptions if he were to attempt to prepare a detailed cash budget.

A further problem is that the third section of the funds statement may be significantly affected by, say, delaying the payment of creditors for a couple of days or by ensuring that a substantial quantity of purchases are made in the first few days of the following period rather than in the last few days of the period under review. This is illustrated in Example 9.3.

Example 9.3

The working capital of Ice Limited at 1 January 19X6 and 31 December 19X6 are given below. The year end position is based on the assumption that the company is pursuing its 'normal' policies in respect of the level of stock holding and the length of credit taken on purchases.

	1 Jan X6 £	31 Dec X6 £
Inventory	360,000	366,000
Debtors	240,000	244,000
Bank	100,000	120,000
	700,000	730,000
less Creditors	140,000	142,000
Working capital	£560,000	£588,000

The third section of a funds statement would then appear as follows:

	Decrease £	Increase £	£
Increase in working capital			28,000
Increase in inventory		6,000	
Increase in debtors		4,000	
Increase in creditors	2,000		
		10,000	
		2,000	
		8,000	
Increase in bank balance		20,000	£28,000

Now let us assume that Ice Limited delays the payment of £80,000 to creditors by a few days and asks its suppliers to deliver goods, costing £60,000, in the first few days of 19X7 instead of at the end of 19X6.

The working capital at 31 December 19X6 would then be:

		£
Inventory		306,000
Debtors		244,000
Bank		200,000
		750,000
less Creditors		162,000
		£588,000

and the relevant section of a funds statement would appear as follows:

	Increase	*Decrease*	
	£	£	£
Increase in working capital			28,000
Decrease in inventory		54,000	
Increase in debtors	4,000		
Increase in creditors		22,000	
		76,000	
		4,000	
		72,000	
Increase in bank balance		100,000	£28,000

The use of a funds statement that disclosed the position shown in the second case would not know whether the changes in the composition of working capital were the result of a permanent change in policy or circumstances or were caused by temporary fluctuations of the sort assumed in the example.

Statements of Sources and Applications of Funds: SSAP 10 (Issued July 1975)

In the United States it had, for some years, been common practice to present a funds statement along with the published profit and loss account and balance sheet. In contrast, few British companies followed this practice, but the position changed as a result of the issue of SSAP 10.

In the explanatory notes the statement points out that the funds statement is not a replacement for the profit and loss account and balance sheet and that its contents are a selection, reclassification and summarization of information contained in those two statements. The funds statement should be produced in such a way as to show how its figures reconcile with the information provided in the profit and loss account and balance sheet.

The objective of a funds statement is seen as being the disclosure of the way in which the operations of the company have been financed and the way in which its financial resources have been used. The format selected for the statement should be designed so as to achieve this objective.

The statement should show the movement of *net liquid funds* which are defined, in the statement, as 'cash at bank and in hand and cash equivalents (e.g. investments held as current assets) less bank overdrafts and other borrowings repayable within one year of the accounting date'.

The actual standard is as follows:

1. The standard applies to all financial accounts intended to give a true and fair view of the financial position and profit or loss other than those of enterprises with a turnover of less than £25,000 per annum.

2. Audited financial statements, other than enterprises with a turnover of less than £25,000 per annum, should include a statement of sources and applications of funds both for the period under review and for the corresponding previous period.

3. The statement should show the profit or loss for the period together with the adjustments required for items which did not use (or provide) funds in the period. The following other sources and applications of funds should, where material, also be shown.

    (a) dividends paid;

    (b) acquisitions and disposals of fixed and other non-current assets;

    (c) funds raised by increasing, or expended in repaying or redeeming, medium or long-term loans or the issued capital of the company;

    (d) increase or decrease in working capital subdivided into its components, and movements in net liquid funds.

4. Where the accounts are those of a group, the statement should be framed so as to reflect the operations of the group.

It can be seen in paragraph 3(a) that the standard calls for the disclosure of the dividends *paid* in the period. This is different from the way we have treated dividends so far, in that the application of funds was based on the dividends *declared* for the period.

This means that the basis of the definition of funds must also be changed, for funds will now have to be defined as working capital ignoring dividends payable. This point is not brought out in the actual standard, or in the introductory commentary, since funds are not defined in the statement. The statement has an Appendix* which includes a number of examples of funds statements and, in these examples, tax is treated in the same way as dividends, i.e. the applications figure is the taxation paid in the period. Thus the funds concept used is working capital excluding taxation and dividends payable. The difference between the two approaches is illustrated in Example 9.4.

*The appendix is not part of the standard.

Example 9.4

White Limited's summarized profit and loss account for the year ended 31 December 19X3 is:

	£	£
Profit for the year before tax		1,000
less Corporation tax based on the profit for the year		450
Profit after tax		550
less Dividends		
Paid	60	
Proposed	100	160
		390
Retained earnings 1 January 19X3		500
Retained earnings 31 December 19X3		£890

The depreciation charge for the year was £100. White Limited's balance sheets as at 31 December 19X2 and 19X3 are:

	31 Dec X2			31 Dec X3		
	£	£	£	£	£	£
Fixed assets, net book value			1,200			1,450
Current assets						
Sundries		1,020			1,200	
Cash		80			140	
		1,100			1,340	
less Current liabilities						
Sundries	100			110		
Proposed dividend	80			100		
Taxation	790	970	130	860	1,070	270
			£1,330			£1,720
Share capital			830			830
Retained earnings			500			890
			£1,330			£1,720

ACT is ignored in this example
The dividends paid in 19X3 were £80 + £160 − £100 = £140
and the taxation paid £790 + £450 − £860 = £380

We present below two funds statements. In (a) the method advocated in SSAP 10 is used, i.e. the taxation and dividends applications are based on the actual payments while in (b) the applications are the amounts charged in the profit and loss account. For convenience, we shall describe (a) as the *cash method* and (b) the *accrual method*.

Statement of Sources and Applications of Funds
Year ended 31 December 19X3

	(a)		(b)	
	Cash Method		Accrual Method	
	£	£	£	£
Sources				
Funds generated from operations		1,100		1,100

Applications

Purchases of fixed assets	350		350	
Taxation	380		450	
Dividends	140	870	160	960
Increase in funds		230		140
Increase in sundry current assets	180		180	
Increase in sundry current liabilities	(10)		(10)	
Increase in proposed dividends	—		(20)	
Increase in taxation payable	—		(70)	
	170		80	
Increase in cash	60	£230	60	£140

In our view it is unfortunate that the Accounting Standards Committee adopted their method. Their treatment of dividends is not consistent with the treatment of other liabilities. Proposed dividends are generally paid within a few months of the end of the year, and thus the proposal of the dividend does give rise to a liability which may well be due for payment before other liabilities which are treated as deductions from funds in the preparation of a funds statement.

Imagine a company which did not propose a dividend for 19X2, did not pay an interim dividend in 19X3 but proposed a final dividend for 19X3. The funds statement for 19X3 would not show any application of funds arising from dividends. We suggest that such a statement would be misleading.

An argument in favour of the Accounting Standard Committee's method, but one which is not made in the statement, is that the tax and dividends figures both represent the total flows for the period. They are thus unlike the remaining items in the third section of the funds statement, which are based on the differences between the balances at the start and end of the year.

Taxation in Funds Statements

The corporation tax charge for many companies is, to the extent that it has not been discharged by an advance corporation tax payment, not payable within twelve months of the balance sheet date. Thus they may have at a year end, two mainstream liabilities of which one is payable within a year – the liability in respect of the previous year.

In accordance with the provisions of the Companies Act, 1981 that creditors must be analysed between amounts due within one year and after one year the two liabilities have to be shown separately.

The requirement does not create problems with the ASC method since the tax application is the actual payment. This is a further advantage of their method. However, if the funds statement is based on the strict working capital definition of funds the separate treatment of the two liabilities does produce a minor difficulty. The tax application is the amount by which funds are decreased, i.e. the sum that was previously treated as a future (non-current) liability and which has now become a current liability.

This is an instance of a general problem, which applies to both the ASC method and the alternative approach, which exists when a long-term liability, or asset, becomes a current liability or asset. For example, a loan repayable on 30 June 19X4 would not be included as a current liability in a balance sheet drawn up as at 31 December 19X2, but would be so regarded in the balance sheet of 31 December 19X3. This change in classification will give rise to an application of funds in the funds statement for 19X3. This item could be described in the following way:

Application.   Reduction in funds due to the recognition as a
                                  current liability of an outstanding loan which is
                                  now repayable within one year.

Other Definitions of Funds

We started this chapter by defining funds as working capital. We then presented a modification of this definition, and showed that funds could be considered as being working capital, ignoring the liabilities for tax and proposed dividends. A number of other bases have been suggested, i.e.:

All financial resources,
Working capital, excluding inventory, i.e. net monetary assets,
Cash.

All Financial Resources
Some important events do not result in a change in working capital and, hence, will not appear in a funds statement if funds are defined as working capital or some modified form of working capital.

An example is the issue of shares in exchange for fixed assets. This is clearly a significant transaction but, since the issue of shares does not result in an increase in working capital, and as the acquisition of the fixed assets does not lead to a decrease in working capital, it will not be reflected in a funds statement of the type so far described.

There are a number of ways of dealing with this:

1.   Assume that the shares were issued for cash and the fixed assets were acquired for cash. A note should be appended to the funds statement explaining the nature of the assumption. This is probably the best alternative.

2.   Describe the transaction in a note to the funds statement.

3.   Change the definition of funds to incorporate 'all financial resources'.

The third method has not been the subject of much discussion in the

United Kingdom but it has received some attention in the United States. The rationale for this third method is the wish that a funds statement should disclose the financial aspects of all significant transactions. We suggest, however, that the first method can do this without departing from the concept that funds should provide a measure of liquidity.

Net Monetary Assets

Working capital is usually taken as a measure of liquidity, comprising as it does cash plus those assets which will be converted into cash in the 'near future' less those liabilities which are repayable either immediately or in the 'near future'. In most cases, the critical period for the purpose of the foregoing is one year from the balance sheet date but a longer period is appropriate if the operating cycle (see Figure 9.1) is longer than twelve months. In particular, for some companies, a number of years might have to elapse before its inventory is converted into cash, even though inventory is included as a current asset. In such cases it would be misleading if inventory were treated as a liquid asset for the purposes of a funds statement. Thus, it can be argued that funds should, in these instances, be defined as working capital excluding inventory, i.e. net monetary assets.

In terms of the funds statements that we have presented so far, the only change, if funds were defined as net monetary assets, would be in the position of the inventory adjustment. The increase or decrease of the inventory would not appear in the third section of the funds statement but would, instead, be shown as an application of funds (if there was an increase in inventory) or as a source of funds (if a decrease in the inventory).

Cash

We have argued that funds should provide a measure of the liquidity of a company. An obvious extension of this idea is to define funds as cash.

Confusingly there are two different forms of statement which may be described as cash flow statements. One form is nothing more than a different way of presenting a funds statement of the type we described before. The second form consists, essentially, of a summary of the company's cash book for the period. In other words the statement would be the company's receipts and payments account for the period (see Chapter 3).

Another cause of confusion is that the phrase 'cash flow for the period' is, sometimes, misleadingly used to describe the increase in working capital from operations, usually profit plus depreciation.

The first version of the cash flow statement simply rejects the need to separate the third section of the sources and applications statement from the first two. All sources are lumped together whether they represent the issue of shares or, say, a decrease in inventory.

By using the figures in Example 9.2, a cash flow statement of the first type might, in a summarized form, appear as follows:

Cash Flow Statement
Year ended 31 December 19X2

	£	£
Sources		
From operations: Profit before tax	11,080	
Adjustment for items not involving the movement of funds	13,830	24,910
Issue of shares		11,000
Sale of fixed assets		530
Decrease in debtors		2,200
		38,640
Applications		
Dividends	1,800*	
Taxation	2,800*	
Repayment of debentures	8,000	
Purchase of fixed assets	23,160	
Increase in inventory	1,700	
Decrease in creditors	3,700	41,160
Decrease in cash		£2,520

*Amounts paid in the year.

In our view there is little, if anything, to commend in the above form of statement. It gives no more information than was provided in Example 9.2. It actually provides less, in that it does not differentiate between flows and the changes in balances.

The second form of cash flow statement is, we believe, much more useful and informative. In fact it has been suggested that this type of statement should replace the conventional accounts and form the basis of an alternative basis of accounting called cash flow accounting.

CASH FLOW ACCOUNTING

In its most extreme form, the argument is that the published profit and loss account and balance sheet should be replaced by a statement showing the cash flows in and out for the period under review, together with similar information for the past few years and a projection of the cash flows for the next few years. A less extreme view is that such information should be published as a supplementary statement to the profit and loss account and balance sheet. In our discussion we shall concentrate on the more moderate position.

So far as historical cash flow statements are concerned, one of the arguments in favour of their publication is similar to one we discussed in the context of funds flow statements. This is that cash is a key resource and that conventional accounts do not give it sufficient emphasis.

Another argument is that historical cash flow statements are totally objective and do not depend on the valuation of uncompleted events or on the accounting policies selected. For example, the cash paid for inventory is shown as a cash flow out in the period in which the payment is made, and the problem of deciding on a method of inventory valuation disappears. This contrasts with funds statements which are a reclassification of the conventional accounts which are based on accrual accounting. Thus funds statements will depend, for example, on the method employed to evaluate inventory.

The question whether projected cash flow statements should be published is a much more contentious issue, and may be viewed as a conflict between relevance and reliability. Clearly the information is highly relevant. In fact if those interested in the affairs of a company could be provided with an accurate projection of future cash flows they would, so far as decision-making is concerned, require no other accounting information. For example, the potential investor would know the cash flows that would be applied to the payment of dividends while the potential creditor could assure himself that sufficient cash would be available to cover the payment of interest and the repayment of the loan.

The problem is, of course, that although the information would be highly relevant, it would also be highly unreliable. The advocates of the publication of projected cash flow statements contend that the advantage of relevance would outweigh the disadvantage of unreliability. They also point out that, over time, users could make their own judgement about a company's ability to forecast future cash flows by observing its past success in forecasting.

The discussion of the conflict between relevance and reliability will not go far beyond an exchange of assertions until much more is known about the information needs of users of accounting statements. It can be said, however, that it is unlikely that advocates of publication will be able to convince the business community or, perhaps more importantly, legislators of the strength of their case in the near future, if ever.

A detailed discussion of cash accounting goes beyond the scope of this book, but the following is presented in order to give the reader a flavour of the approach and because it highlights the deficiencies of the first type of cash flow statement.

Figure 9.4 (page 341) illustrates the main cash flow summary. The notes A to F refer to supplementary statements which would show how the summary figures are made up.

The description of the various causes of cash flows are, except for discretionary items, self-evident. By discretionary items we mean those cash flows which are not actually required in order for the company to achieve its planned output and sales in the short run. The discretionary cash flows are incurred in order to maintain the long-term strength of the company and might include fundamental research or prestige advertising, i.e. advertising whose purpose is to keep the name of the company before the public rather than maintaining sales in the short run.

Two sets of figures are provided for past periods – F is the forecast and A the actual cash flows. Presenting the information in that way helps users come to an opinion about the forecasting skill of management.

CASH BUDGETS

Earlier in this chapter we indicated that funds statements do not indicate the extent of seasonal peaks and, of course, the same point can be made about cash flow statements. Thus, even if a projected funds statement were available it might not disclose that the company might, say, run out of cash part way through the year. For although, on an annual basis, the company's liquidity position appears healthy it may be that it cannot easily weather its seasonal peaks.

In order to consider the effect of seasonal differences, it would be necessary to produce a detailed cash budget. The budget may be on a day-by-day basis or be weekly, monthly or quarterly depending on the circumstances. A cash budget is an internal management tool and is not directly concerned with reporting on cash and funds movements as are the statements discussed earlier in this chapter. We are, however, presenting the topic at this stage, because it has such strong links with the rest of the chapter and because it emphasizes the factors that have to be considered when examining cash changes.

In the following description of the method of preparing cash budgets we will assume that a monthly budget is to be presented for a trading company.

The following items will need to be considered:

1. The sales for each month, the proportion of the sales that will be on credit and the average credit period taken by customers must be estimated.

2. The company's inventory holding policy which will, with the above projection, yield estimates of the purchases required for each month. The proportion of purchases made on credit and the average credit period will also have to be estimated.

3. The monthly totals of overhead expenses and the extent to which they are paid in advance or in arrear must be estimated.

4. The timing of other cash flows, e.g. purchases and sales of fixed assets, taxation and dividends must be estimated.

Example 9.5 demonstrates the preparation of a monthly cash budget.

Figure 9.4

Cash Flow Statement, Year ended 30 June 1985

Cash flows due to:	Note	1981 F A	1982 F A	1983 F A	1984 F A	1985 F A	Total F A
(1) Cash and bank balances at the start of the year							
(2) Manufacturing/trading operations	A						
(3) Purchases/sales of fixed assets	B						
(4) Discretionary items	C						
(5) Financial transactions – capital	D						
(6) Taxation	E						
(7) Distributable cash flow							
(8) Interest and dividends	F						
(9) Cash and bank balances at the end of the year							

Forecasts

1986	1987	1988	Total

Example 9.5

Nan Limited's balance sheet as at 1 January 19X6 is as follows:

	£	£	£
Fixed assets, at cost		18,000	
less Accumulated depreciation		8,000	10,000
Current assets			
Inventory, at cost		16,000	
Debtors		11,000	
Prepaid rates		500	
Balance at bank		1,000	
		28,500	10,000
less Current liabilities			
Creditors	15,000		
Rent payable	1,000		
Proposed dividend	900	16,900	11,600
			£21,600
Share capital			12,000
Retained earnings			9,600
			£21,600

1. Sales for the eight months to August 19X6 are expected to be:

	£
January	20,000
February	20,000
March	30,000
April	40,000
May	50,000
June	30,000
July	30,000
August	20,000

It is also estimated that:

1.1 60 per cent of sales will be on credit.

1.2 80 per cent of debtors will pay in the month following the sale, 10 per cent in the second month and 5 per cent in the third month.

1.3 5 per cent of the debtors will have to be written off as bad debts.

2. The average mark-up will be $33\frac{1}{3}$ per cent.

3. In early January it was decided to change the company's inventory holding policy. In future Nan Limited will ensure that its inventory at the end of each month will be sufficient to cover the sales of the following month plus 20 per cent of the goods required for the sales of the next month. Suppliers will allow one month's credit.

4. Wages will amount to £1,800 per month, except in April and May when overtime

will increase the figure to £1,950 per month. All wages are paid in the month in which they are incurred.

5. Rates of £2,600 for the year ended 31 March 19X7 will have to be paid in April 19X6.

6. Rent is £1,000 per month and is paid in arrears, every three months: February, May, etc.

7. Fixed assets costing £2,000 will be purchased at the end of March. A deposit of £1,000 will have to be paid in that month with the balance being paid in May. Depreciation is provided at 20 per cent per annum on cost on all fixed assets.

8. Overheads, other than those referred to above, will amount to £600 per month. They are all paid in the month in which they are incurred.

9. The proposed dividend will be paid in February.

10. All the creditors outstanding at 1 January 19X6 will be paid in January while, of the debtors outstanding at that date, 80 per cent will be received in January and the balance will be collected in February.

We will show how the cash budget for the period 1 January 19X6 to 30th June 19X6 can be prepared. We will also show the budgeted trading and profit and loss account for the six months to 30 June 19X6 and the budgeted balance sheet as at that date.

Taxation will be ignored in this example.

We will start by preparing a schedule showing the cash received from credit customers:

Month (n)	Credit Sales	Cash received from				Total
		Debtors at 1 Jan 19X6	Sales of month (n − 1) (80 per cent)	(n − 2) (10 per cent)	(n − 3) (5 per cent)	
	£	£	£	£	£	£
January	12,000	8,800	—	—	—	8,800
February	12,000	2,200	9,600	—	—	11,800
March	18,000	—	9,600	1,200	—	10,800
April	24,000	—	14,400	1,200	600	16,200
May	30,000	—	19,200	1,800	600	21,600
June	18,000	—	24,000	2,400	900	27,300
						£96,500
Debtors at 30 June 19X6						
July			14,400	3,000	1,200	18,600
August				1,800	1,500	3,300
September					900	900
						£22,800

If the average mark-up is $33\frac{1}{3}$ per cent the gross profit ratio is 25 per cent.

For if g = gross profit ratio, s = sales and c = cost of goods sold, then

$$s - g = c$$

and $s - \frac{1}{3}c = c$

$$s = \frac{4}{3}c$$

$$c = \frac{3}{4}s$$

The following schedule shows the cash that it is expected will be paid to the suppliers of goods.

1 Month (n)	2 Cost of goods sold, 75 per cent of sales	3 Opening Inventory	4 Closing Inventory (n + 1) + 20 per cent (n + 2)	5 Purchases 2 − 3 + 4	6 Payment made in month
	£	£	£	£	
January	75 per cent of 20,000 = 15,000	16,000	15,000 + 20 per cent of 22,500 = 19,500	18,500	Feb.
Feb	75 per cent of 20,000 = 15,000	19,500	22,500 + 20 per cent of 30,000 = 28,500	24,000	March
March	75 per cent of 30,000 = 22,500	28,500	30,000 + 20 per cent of 37,500 = 37,500	31,500	April
April	75 per cent of 40,000 = 30,000	37,500	37,500 + 20 per cent of 22,500 = 42,000	34,500	May
May	75 per cent of 50,000 = 37,500	42,000	22,500 + 20 per cent of 22,500 = 27,000	22,500	June
June	75 per cent of 30,000 = 22,500	27,000	22,500 + 20 per cent of 15,000 = 25,500	21,000	July
July	75 per cent of 30,000 = 22,500				
August	75 per cent of 20,000 = 15,000				
				£152,000	

We are now in a position to prepare the cash budget. Note its form. This is a very convenient way of presenting such statements.

	January	February	March	April	May	June	Total
	£	£	£	£	£	£	£
Receipts							
Opening balance	1,000	400					1,000
Cash sales	8,000	8,000	12,000	16,000	20,000	12,000	76,000
Credit customers	8,800	11,800	10,800	16,200	21,600	27,300	96,500
	17,800	20,200	22,800	32,200	41,600	39,300	173,500
Closing balance (overdraft)		4,600	9,200	13,650	13,100		
	£17,800	£24,800	£32,000	£45,850	£54,700	£39,300	£173,500

	January	February	March	April	May	June	Total
	£	£	£	£	£	£	£
Payments							
Opening balance (overdraft)			4,600	9,200	13,650	13,100	
Suppliers	15,000	18,500	24,000	31,500	34,500	22,500	146,000
Wages	1,800	1,800	1,800	1,950	1,950	1,800	11,100
Rent		3,000			3,000		6,000
Rates				2,600			2,600
Overheads	600	600	600	600	600	600	3,600
Dividends		900					900
Fixed assets			1,000		1,000		2,000
	17,400	24,800	32,000	45,850	54,700	38,000	172,200
Closing balance	400					1,300	1,300
	£17,800	£24,800	£32,000	£45,850	£54,700	£39,300	£173,500

NAN LIMITED

Budgeted Trading and Profit and Loss Account
1 January—30 June 19X6

	£	£
Sales		190,000
less Opening inventory	16,000	
Purchases	152,000	
	168,000	
less Closing inventory	25,500	142,500
Gross profit (25%)		47,500
less		
Wages	11,100	
Rent	6,000	
Rates (500 + 2,600 − 1,950)	1,150	
Overheads	3,600	
Bad debts (5 per cent of credit sales)	5,700	
Depreciation	1,900	29,450
Net profit		18,050
Retained earnings 1 January 19X6		9,600
Retained earnings 30 June 19X6		£27,650

Budgeted Balance Sheet as at 30 June 19X6

	£	£	£
Fixed assets, at cost		20,000	
less Accumulated depreciation		9,900	10,100
Current assets			
Inventory at cost		25,500	
Debtors		22,800	
Prepaid rates		1,950	
Balance at bank		1,300	
		51,550	

less			
Current liabilities			
Creditors	21,000		
Rent payable	1,000	22,000	29,550
			£39,650
Share capital			12,000
Retained earnings			27,650
			£39,650

Interest payable on the bank overdraft has been omitted from the above budgeted financial statement.

Note that the budgeted financial statements disclose a profit and an increase in the balance at bank. Neither these statements, nor any funds statements based on them, disclose that the company would have to carry a substantial overdraft for some time during the period if it is to carry out its plans.

EXERCISES

9.1 Sources and applications of funds statements.

What are they?   How useful are they?   What are their limitations?

9.2 The balance sheets of Miss Phoebe, a spinner by trade, as on 31 December were as follows:

	1975		1974	
	£	£	£	£
Capital account				
Balance at beginning of year	20,000		12,000	
Net profit for the year	12,000		11,000	
Surplus on revaluation of land	7,000		—	
	39,000		23,000	
less: Withdrawals	5,000		3,000	
		34,000		20,000
Loan – W. Shadbolt		12,000		20,000
Trade creditors		10,000		9,000
Bank overdraft		1,600		—
		£57,600		£49,000
Freehold land (as revalued)		27,000		20,000
Spinning machines				
Cost	1,500		1,000	
Accumulated depreciation	900		600	
		600		400
Property at Tower Green		—		2,000
Stock		12,000		8,000
Trade debtors		18,000		12,000
Balance at bank		—		6,600
		£57,600		£49,000

The only fixed asset disposed of during the year was the property at Tower Green which realized £5,000; the surplus on disposal is included in the net profit for the year.

The turnover (all on credit) had increased from £60,000 in 1974 to £75,000 in 1975.

Miss Phoebe is rather perturbed as her bank manager, for the first time, has asked to see her although she told him over the telephone that her turnover, capital and profits had never been higher. She now turns to you for advice so that her visit to the bank may not be too traumatic.

You are required:

(a) to prepare a statement which explains in a meaningful way the reasons for the change in the balance at bank during the year, and

(b) to outline and discuss any points which you anticipate the bank manager may raise on examination of the accounts.

(The Institute of Chartered Accountants in England and Wales, Foundation Examination, April 1976)

9.3 On 31st December 1980, the accounts of Compare Ltd showed the following:

Balance Sheet

	1980 £'000	1980 £'000	1979 £'000	1979 £'000
Assets employed:				
Fixed assets		1,800		750
Goodwill		110		150
Current assets				
Stocks	982		696	
Debtors	708		583	
Quoted investments – short term ...	342		250	
Cash	26		23	
		2,058		1,552
		3,968		2,452
Deduct Current liabilities				
Creditors	813		553	
Bank overdraft	362		148	
		1,175		701
		2,793		1,751
Financed by:				
Share capital		1,500		1,500
Reserves		293		251
Loan stock		1,000		—
		2,793		1,751

Profit and Loss Account

	1980		1979	
	£'000	£'000	£'000	£'000
Trading profit for year before taxation ...		460		418
after charging:				
Directors' remuneration	26		22	
Depreciation	350		250	
Audit fees	9		7	
Corporation tax on profit for year		218		194
		242		224
Appropriations:				
Goodwill written off	40		45	
Dividend	160		150	
		200		195
Retained profit of year		42		29
Balance brought forward		251		222
Balance carried forward		293		251

You also obtain the following information:

(1)   £1,000,000 12% unsecured loan stock 1995 was issued at par on 1st July 1980.

(2)	Creditors	£'000	£'000
	Trade creditors and accrued expenses	435	209
	Taxation	218	194
	Dividends	160	150
		813	553

(3)	Additions to fixed assets	1,400	260

You are required to prepare the statement of source and application of funds of Compare Ltd for the year ended 31st December 1980, so far as the information given allows.

Corresponding figures are not required.

(The Institute of Chartered Accountants in England and Wales, Financial Accounting 1, May 1981)

9.4 Adsum Ltd was formed on 1st January 1980 to carry on the trade of wholesaler of a standard type of calculator. On that date 400,000 ordinary shares of 25p each were issued at 40p each and were fully paid up in cash. In addition, 40,000 20% preference shares of £1 each were issued at par and fully paid in full consideration for the acquisition of leasehold premises, the lease of which expires on 31st December 1999; the preference dividend is payable on 31st December.

The company is interested in negotiating a bank overdraft and the bank manager has asked for an estimate of its financial requirements for the six months to 30th June 1980. The company has given you the following information:

(1)   Expected sales of calculators – January   1,000
                                       February–April 2,000 per month
                                       May–August   3,000 per month

(2)   The expected selling price is £50 per calculator and the estimated gross profit percentage on sales is 20%.

(3)   Stocks at the end of each month are planned to be sufficient to cover the following two months' sales; adequate supplies are to be purchased in January to meet this requirement.

(4)   If purchases in any month are settled by the end of the following month, a 2% discount is received.

(5)   All sales are on credit and debtors are expected to take an average of two months' credit; it is considered prudent to provide 3% for bad and doubtful debts.

(6)   Motor vehicles costing £50,000 were purchased on 1st January fully utilizing the proceeds of a 15% Debenture issued at par, interest payable annually in arrear; the vehicles are expected to realize 25% of their cost price when replaced at the end of two years. It is planned to redeem the Debenture out of retained profits at the end of 5 years.

(7)   It is anticipated that equity shareholders will expect a dividend return of 15% per annum on their capital investment.

(8)   Wages and other trading expenses payable in cash are expected to amount to £10,000 per month.
(Ignore any bank interest arising on the overdraft.)

You are required to prepare:
(a)   a cash budget for each of the months to June 1980, indicating the month-end overdraft requirement,
(b)   a budgeted Trading, Profit and Loss and Appropriation Account for the six months to 30th June 1980, and
(c)   a budgeted Balance Sheet as on 30th June 1980.

(The Institute of Chartered Accountants in England and Wales, Foundation Examination, November 1980.)

9.5 Given the information that follows, prepare a cash budget for the

Downtown Department Store for the first six months of 1977.

(a)   Sales are 80 per cent for credit and 20 per cent for cash.

(b)   In terms of credit sales, 60 per cent are collected in the month after the sale, 30 per cent in the second month and 10 per cent in the third month. There are no bad debts.

(c)   Sales are estimated as:

October 1976	£300,000
November 1976	£400,000
December 1976	£500,000
January 1977	£250,000
February 1977	£200,000
March 1977	£200,000
April 1977	£300,000
May 1977	£250,000
June 1977	£200,000
July 1977	£300,000

(d)   The store has a gross margin of 20 per cent and pays for each month's anticipated sales in the preceding month.

(e)   Wages and salaries paid are:

1977	£
January	30,000
February	40,000
March	50,000
April	50,000
May	40,000
June	35,000

(f)   Rent is £2,000 per month

(g)   A quarterly payment of debenture interest is made in March and June. There are £600,000 (6 per cent per annum) debentures in issue.

(h)   Monthly depreciation expense amounts to £20,000.

(i)   A payment for capital equipment of £30,000 is due in June.

(j)   In April the store has to pay its annual tax bill for the year 1976. As yet there has been no formal assessment of tax, and so the payment has to be estimated. The published pre-tax profit for 1976 (after depreciation) is £200,000. Depreciation was £100,000 and capital allowances £200,000. The tax rate is 60 per cent.

(k)   the opening cash balance was £50,000.

9.6 On 1st January 1981 Faust acquired the goodwill of a wholesale fancy goods business for the sum of £10,000 and paid £3,500 premium for a lease of warehouse premises at a rent of £1,000 per annum. The lease is to expire on 31st December 1985. The finance for the goodwill, the premium on the lease and the first year's rent payment was transferred from Faust's building society account into the business bank account. He has asked you to assist him in projections of the trading position over the first six months of the business.

Faust provides you with the following additional information:
(1)   A gross profit of 20% on gross sales before discount can be achieved and maintained.
(2)   Sales before discount, and purchases are budgeted as follows:

	Gross sales before discounts £	Goods purchased £
January	12,000	36,800
February	16,000	16,000
March	18,000	19,200
April	20,000	24,000
May	24,000	25,600
June	30,000	16,000

(3)   60% of sales will be on credit terms. The remainder will be for cash. Credit terms are settlement at the end of the month after sale. A 5% settlement discount is available for debts settled on those terms.

Faust anticipates that 20% of his credit customers will not take advantage of these terms and will settle one month later.

(4)   Purchases will be made from two suppliers in equal proportions. One supplier requires payment in the month of delivery; the second requires payment in the month following delivery.

(5)   Rates totalling £960 will be payable on 30th June 1981 for the year ended 31st March 1982. Rates of £240 for the three months to 31st March 1981 were paid privately by Faust.

(6)   Wages will be £300 per month.

(7)   An electricity bill will be paid in April estimated at £250 to cover the first three months supplies.

(8)   Postages will be £50 per month.

(9)   A van will be purchased for £2,400 on 1st April 1981 which is to be
       written off over four years. 3 months' depreciation is to be provided.

You are required to prepare:
(a)   a monthly cash flow forecast for the six months period ending on 30th
       June 1981.
(b)   a forecast trading account for the six months period ending on 30th
       June 1981, and
(c)   a budgeted balance sheet as on 30th June 1981.

(The Institute of Chartered Accountants in England and Wales, Accounting Techniques, May
1981.)

SECTION C

10 | *Current Value Accounting*

For a number of years accounting academics have been conscious of the failings of the historical cost model but they have been, and still are, far from agreement on what to put in its place. In contrast, most practitioners appeared to be satisfied with the basic method and felt that the major problem of the historical cost model was that it allowed the use of so many alternative accounting methods, LIFO/FIFO, etc. Thus, the main activity of a number of professional bodies, so far as accounting principles were concerned, consisted of attempts to adjudicate between the various alternative methods and to obtain a greater degree of uniformity in accounting practice.

There was, and is, an alternative view that such activities are inherently unwise because the vastly different circumstances affecting different businesses justify the application of different accounting methods.

Adherents of both schools of thought tend to share one view, which is often implied by their arguments even if not explicitly stated. That is: if only we could select the 'right' accounting methods (which may or may not depend on the circumstances of the particular business) then the correct profit would result.

We argue that there is no one correct basis of accounting and, hence, no one correct measurement of profit. For as we shall show later in this section of the book, for some purposes it is relevant to value assets on the basis of the price that would be obtained if the assets were sold, while for other purposes it would be more helpful to base their values on the price the business would currently have to pay to acquire them. Given this point, we should consider whether the historical cost basis of accountancy – which we will refer to in the following pages as the traditional model – is of relevance for any purpose.

Clearly the traditional model has severe shortcomings when used to satisfy some objectives which accounting might be expected to serve. This will be illustrated in the following examples.

Example 10.1

A Limited and B Limited are both property companies. They each own the freeholds of a number of office blocks, which are rented to various organizations. Their other assets and liabilities are insignificant and can be ignored for the purposes of the argument.

	A Limited	B Limited
Assets, at book value employed during 1975	£1,000,000	£2,000,000
Profit for 1975	£200,000	£150,000
Profit, as a percentage of assets employed	20 per cent	$7\frac{1}{2}$ per cent

On the basis of the above information, which has been obtained from the financial statements of the two companies, it appears that A Limited is the more profitable company. However, suppose you discover that both companies base their balance sheets on historical cost and that A Limited's premises were purchased in 1920 and B Limited's were acquired in 1960. The picture now changes.

It should be clear to most readers that the cost of the premises, £1,000,000 in 1920, is irrelevant so far as judging the profitability of the company is concerned. The current value of A Limited's assets will be far greater than £1,000,000 and, in all probability, its annual profit, expressed as a percentage of the current value of its assets, will be less than $7\frac{1}{2}$ per cent. The same remarks can be applied to B Limited, but with less force because of the shorter time period involved. It is quite likely that B Limited's profit, expressed as a percentage of the current value of its assets is higher than A Limited's.

Let us make the simplifying, but not unreasonable assumption, that the success of a company should be measured in terms of the rate of return that it earns on the current value of its assets. If the assumption is accepted, it is clear that the information disclosed by the historical cost financial statements is of little help in the making of judgements about the success of a business. The information disclosed does not help the user to judge the success of the business in absolute terms or help him compare the performance of a number of businesses even where they are engaged in similar activities.

Thus, it appears that, to the extent that one of the objectives of accounting is the provision of information that helps users judge the success or otherwise of the company, the historical cost method fails.

Example 10.2

Suppose John bought 100 widgets for £20 on 1 January 19X4 and sold them for £35 on 30 September 19X4.

Ignoring overheads, the historical cost accounting profit on this transaction is £15. But is that, necessarily, the increase in John's wealth? Let us suppose that prices have, on average, increased by 25 per cent in the period 1 January 19X4 to 30 September 19X4. This means that to be as well off at 30 September as he was on 1 January John would need to have cash of £20 plus 25 per cent of £20, i.e. £25. It could thus be argued that £10 (£35 − £25) provides a better measurement of John's increase in wealth than £15.

Let us further suppose that John intends to continue as a trader in widgets and that it would cost him £30 at 30 September 19X4 to replace the widgets sold on that date. (John, being a trader in widgets, can be assumed to be in a position to buy widgets for less than his selling price.)

It could be argued that John's profit is only £5. People taking this view would justify the statement by comparing John's position at 1 January and 30 September as follows:

Assets at 30 September	100 widgets	£5 cash
Assets at 1 January	100 widgets	
Profit for the period = increase in assets =	—	£5 cash

On the basis of the assumption that John intends to continue to trade in widgets the proponents of the £5 position argue that it would not matter whether John has purchased a fresh supply of 100 widgets or not. If he had done so by the 30 September he would have to put aside £30 to pay for them.

The £5 argument is that the profit should be based on the difference between revenue and the current cost of earning the revenue (in this case the current cost of the widgets). Those who take this position say that if a trader assumes that the historical cost profit (£15) is a safe guide to what he can consume and the tax authorities consider that this profit figure is a reasonable basis on which to levy tax, then the business would only be able to carry on its activities at a reduced scale if at all.

For example, say that John decides that he can, with prudence, consume 10 per cent of his pre-tax profit and that the tax man will take 50 per cent of the profit, John will then be left with £26 cash.

Sale of widgets		35
less Consumption 10 per cent of £15	1.5	
Tax 50 per cent of £15	7.5	9
Leaving cash of		£26

So now John would only be able to buy 87 widgets ($\frac{26}{30} \times 100$) and will have to trade at a lower volume unless he can obtain additional capital.

This example highlights the defects of historical cost accounting in providing information that is useful in the consumption decision, and it also casts doubt on its use as the basis for taxation.

A common feature in the above examples, is lack of comparability. Historical cost accounting makes it difficult, if not impossible, to compare the results of different companies, or, indeed, to compare the results of the same company over time. There is also the problem, illustrated in Example 10.2, of comparing revenue with expenses when these are expressed in pounds which are not equivalent units.

We selected some of the more obvious points for our case against historical cost accounting. Indeed they are so obvious and can have such a distorting effect on a company's financial statements, that the basic method has, in some cases, been modified to deal with them. For example, in the United Kingdom many companies from time to time, revalue assets such as land and buildings. In addition, as we outlined in Chapter 7, the Companies Acts force companies to disclose certain details about land held as fixed assets. Thus, the users will be provided with some information about the current value of land even if it is not revalued for the purposes of the accounts.

The practice of revaluing assets has not been followed in all countries, and it is not done in the United States for example. Revaluation involves a departure from the basic historical cost method, and the need to have such 'exceptions' casts some doubt on the validity of the basic method.

The defects of the historical cost model are such that it is likely that for most, if not all, purposes an accounting system or systems based on current values will be more helpful. The phrase 'current value' is helpful but vague, and we must now be more precise about what we mean by it.

We will start by considering individual assets and the possible approaches to their valuation.

THE NATURE AND VALUATION OF ASSETS

In order to value an asset it is necessary to consider the nature of an asset. Practically every writer on accounting has provided his own definition; we will not add to the confusion but quote one which appears to be one of the more reasonable:

> 'Assets represent expected future economic benefits, rights to which have been acquired by the enterprise as a result of some current or past transaction'.*

The benefits referred to are economic benefits. Basically, this means benefits that can be expressed in money terms. Thus an asset should be valued in terms of the cash that will flow to the owner as a result of his ownership of the asset. The asset might itself add to future cash receipts, e.g. inventory held for resale, or reduce future cash payments, e.g. prepaid rates. This practical, but possibly Philistine point, means that assets that delight the eye but not the pocket are valueless for our purpose.

Let us now consider three possible bases for the valuation of an asset.

1. Net Realizable Value

The net realizable value is the estimate of the amount that the owner would receive from the immediate sale of the asset less the anticipated costs that would have to be incurred in selling it.

2. Replacement Cost

This is the estimated amount that would have to be paid in order to replace the asset.

3. Value in Use or Economic Value

This is the estimated present value to the owner, of the cash flows that would be generated if he did not sell the asset but instead retained it for his own use. We will discuss the meaning of 'present value' below.

There is no commonly agreed name for this basis of valuation, as is the case with replacement cost and net realizable value. The Sandilands' committee used the phrase 'economic value' (their inverted commas) and we will accordingly use the latter description.

---

* Robert T. Sprouse and Maurice Moonitz, *A Tentative Set of Broad Accounting Principles for Business Enterprises*, Accounting Research Study No. 3, American Institute of Certified Public Accountants, 1962.

MARKET VALUES

Both net realizable value and replacement cost are market values; that is, they are based on the prices at which the assets are traded.

In cases where the asset is only one of many identical, or virtually identical, assets which are constantly being bought and sold the net realizable values and the replacement costs can usually be easily, and objectively, determined from published price lists, etc. In such circumstances the difference between an asset's net realizable value and replacement cost will, often, be comparatively small and depend upon the level of expenses and profit taken by traders in the particular asset.

Where the asset is unique, or at least one that is not commonly traded, the estimation of the market values will not be as easy or as objective. Consider a machine tool specially designed for a particular company. In determining its replacement cost one should ignore the design costs, for this work has already been done. If records are available of the number of labour hours and the physical amount of raw material and components that were used in the manufacture of the machine, reference to current wage rates and component costs will enable the current replacement cost to be estimated. If the asset is not of a type that is commonly traded, the difference between the replacement cost and the net realizable value is likely to be more significant. In particular, if the asset is one which was especially made for its owner, its net realizable value may be very low – the scrap value of the materials – or even negative if there are costs associated with its disposal.

Despite what we have written above, we admit that the estimation of replacement costs and net realizable values is not as easy a job as some accounting reformers seem to believe, and that the practical implementation of a system based on current values requires a good deal of thought and research.

'ECONOMIC VALUE'

The concept of 'economic value' is a little more difficult to grasp than the two bases we discussed above. One major problem is, that if the asset is retained for use, the cash flows will accrue over time and the valuation of the stream of cash flows must take account of the timings, as well as the magnitudes, of the cash flows.

Suppose that we are attempting to value an asset which will generate the following stream of net cash flows:

Now	Exactly 1 year later	Exactly 2 years later
£10	£20	£30

Obviously to value the stream of cash flows, and hence the 'economic value' of the asset, at £60 would be to ignore the fact that the owner has to wait for one, or two, years for a major proportion of the cash.

The stream of cash flows can be valued by calculating its *present value*. The concept of present value is an extremely important one which plays a significant role in investment appraisal, e.g. in such questions as whether to invest in the shares of a given company or whether to purchase a particular asset.

The present value of £*A* which is to be received in *n* years time at a discount rate of *r*, expressed as a decimal (e.g. an 8 per cent rate is written as 0·08) is:

$$£\frac{A}{(1+r)^n}$$

The derivation of this formula is shown in the appendix to this chapter.

Thus, taking the above example, the present value of the stream of cash flows, assuming a discount rate of 0·10 (10 per cent) is:

$$£10 + \frac{£20}{(1·1)} + \frac{£30}{(1·1)^2} = £53.$$

The question of the selection of the appropriate discount rate is a complex one but it can be said to depend on three factors:

1. The cost of funds. This will be the average cost of funds raised by the owner. In the case of a limited company it will be the average cost of the various sources of funds, share capital, retained earnings, loan capital, etc.

2. The opportunity cost of funds. This is the rate of return that is forgone if the owner invests his funds in the investment under review. For example, suppose that the owner of the above asset would, had he not purchased it, have put his money in a bank deposit account which pays interest at a rate of 0·06 (6 per cent) per annum, then 0·06 is the opportunity cost.

3. The owner's rate of time preference. A rate of time preference expresses an individual's impatience for money. To take a simple example, suppose that Mr X is indifferent between receiving £100 now and £108 in one year's time. His rate of time preference, *r*, is that rate of discount that equates the present value of £108 receivable in one year's time with £100 receivable now, i.e.

$$£100 = \frac{£108}{(1+r)}$$

$$1 + r = 1·08$$

$$r = 0·08$$

The more impatient the individual, the higher his rate of time preference. Suppose Mr Y would prefer to receive £100 now rather than receive

£108 in a year's time and that he would need to have £117 in one year's time to just compensate him for the delay, then his rate of time preference is:

$$£100 = \frac{£117}{(1 + r)}$$

$$1 + r = 1{\cdot}17$$

$$r = 0{\cdot}17$$

In general, the appropriate rate of discount is the highest of factors (a), (b) or (c).

The above has been only a very brief introduction to a complex and important subject, but it is sufficient for our present purpose. This is to show that the estimated 'economic value' of the asset depends on estimates of the future cash flows and the selected discount rate and that the discount rate itself depends on the particular circumstances facing the person on whose behalf the asset is being valued.

It is clear that 'economic value' is far more subjective than replacement cost and net realizable value, for the magnitudes and timings of the cash flows must be estimated without the help of manufacturers' price lists and the like. In addition, replacement cost and net realizable value do not involve the selection of a discount rate which not only has to be estimated but which also depends on the opportunities and preferences of particular individuals.

DEPRIVAL VALUE

Each of the above three methods is relevant to decision-making. Given that an asset is owned, the owner will compare its 'economic value' with its net realizable value in order to decide whether to sell the asset immediately or to retain it. If the decision is whether to acquire (or replace) an asset, the decision-maker will compare the replacement cost with the higher of the asset's net realizable value and 'economic value' to see whether the acquisition (or replacement) would be worth while. Given the relevance of the three methods of valuation, cases can be made for using each of them as the basis for current value accounting, and we will discuss the various arguments later. However, much current opinion is that current value accounting should be based on a combination of the three methods known as *deprival value*.

Deprival value is based on the simple, but powerful, idea that the value of an asset to its owner is the loss he would suffer if he were deprived of it. The idea was first suggested, in 1937, by J. C. Bonbright, who wrote:

'The value of a property to its owner is identical in amount with the adverse value of the entire loss, direct and indirect, that the owner might expect to suffer if he were to be deprived of the property'.*

* J. C. Bonbright, *The Valuation of Property*, Michie, Charlottesville, Va., 1965.

It can be seen from the above definition that the deprival value of an asset cannot be greater than its replacement cost, for, if the owner were deprived of his asset, his maximum loss would be the cost of replacing it.

We should also take into consideration any loss the owner would suffer as a result of any delay that there might be in replacing the asset and we could extend our definition of replacement cost to include such losses. However, this would mean that a considerable degree of subjectivity might well be added to the, reasonably objective, market-based replacement cost. The estimate of any losses due to delay will depend on such subjective factors as, for example, the estimate of the number of customers who would take their business elsewhere rather than waiting. Very often this additional, indirect, loss is ignored and the replacement cost is taken to be the direct cost of replacing the asset. There are, however, circumstances where the indirect loss would be so significant that the extended definition of replacement cost would have to be employed.

Replacement cost is the appropriate measure of an asset's deprival value in those circumstances where the owner would, if deprived of the asset, find it worth replacing. For, subject to the observation made above, if the owner lost his asset he could restore his original position by replacing the asset and his loss would be the cost of replacement.

It should be noted that a rational owner (and this analysis assumes that we are dealing with rational owners) would only feel it worth replacing the asset if its replacement cost were less than the benefits he would gain by its replacement, i.e. the higher of its net realizable value and 'economic value'.

Let us now consider an asset that the owner would not wish to replace. We must ask what the owner intends doing with the asset. He will either:

Sell it immediately,
i.e. its net realizable value is greater than its 'economic value'
or
Keep it,
i.e. its 'economic value' is greater than its net realizable value.

Since the owner would not replace the asset, it is clear that the best return obtainable from the ownership of the asset, the higher of the net realizable value and the 'economic value' is less than the replacement cost. In this case the deprival value is not the replacement cost but the higher of the net realizable value and 'economic value'.

Putting the two cases together, we can obtain the following rule for finding the deprival value of an asset.

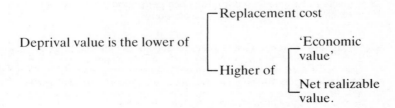

Deprival value is the lower of
- Replacement cost
- Higher of
  - 'Economic value'
  - Net realizable value.

We move up to replacement cost when the asset would be worth replacing, and down the diagram if the owner does not believe replacement worth while.

Fixed assets often present special problems. It may be that use cannot be made of the market to determine replacement cost because assets of the type being values are no longer being traded. There is also the problem of attempting to find the replacement cost of a partly used asset. It may, in certain circumstances, be helpful to think in terms of the 'units of service' that the asset is capable of providing.

X Limited owns a five-year-old lorry that has a capacity of 5 tons. It is believed that the lorry will be able to operate for another 100,000 miles. Such lorries are no longer produced, and the firm would, if deprived of the lorry, replace it by one with a capacity of 10 tons. The replacement cost of a new 10-ton lorry is £16,000, but this is not the relevant figure since we are seeking to value a used lorry. The cost of a secondhand 10-ton lorry with a life of 50,000 miles is £4,000, and this can be taken as the deprival value of the lorry. The approach is to accept that a lorry that can carry 10 tons for 50,000 miles, i.e. 500,000 ton miles, is equivalent to a lorry that can carry 5 tons for 100,000 miles, since it is considered that a ton mile is the appropriate unit of service in these circumstances.

We will now present an example showing how the deprival value of assets can be determined by using that, most useful of illustrations, a barrow-boy.

Example 10.3

Sid is a barrow-boy who, currently, owns the following business assets.

1. One barrow. The replacement cost of a barrow in the same condition as Sid's is £80 and its net realizable value is £45. If deprived of his barrow, Sid would replace it.

2. One set of scales. Sid purchased the scales from an even sharper businessman than himself and they are far more intricate and accurate than Sid, or the Trading Standards Inspectorate, require. It would cost Sid £50 to purchase a secondhand set of scales of equivalent condition to his own, but he would only get £30 if he sold his existing set. Sid would not replace these scales if they were lost, but given that he has them he will keep them.

3. A quantity of cabbages which cost him 12 pence per pound and which he expects to be able to sell for 16 pence per pound. He believes that he can replace the cabbages for 13 pence per pound.

4. A quantity of oranges which he purchased under special conditions (something to do with 'the back of a lorry') for 4 pence each and which he will be able to sell for 8 pence each. Sid does not normally have access to oranges on wholesale terms and any future supplies would cost him 9 pence each. Since the local supermarket is able to sell oranges for 8½ pence, Sid will not replace the oranges when they are sold.

The deprival value of Sid's assets are shown below:

RC – replacement cost, NRV – net realizable value
and EV – 'economic value'

Asset	Basis	Deprival Value Amount	Note
Barrow	RC	£80	1
Scales	EV	£30 > (?) > £50	2
Cabbages	RC	13 pence per pound	1
Oranges	NRV	8 pence each	3

Notes

1. He would replace these assets; thus their replacement costs are lower than the higher of their 'economic value' and net realizable value.

2. He would not replace this asset if it were lost thus he believes that its 'economic value' is less than its replacement cost (£50). On the other hand he is retaining it for use; so he must believe that its 'economic value' is greater than its net realizable value (£30). In a simple case such as this the 'economic value' would probably be taken to be the current cost of purchasing a set of scales appropriate to his needs, taking into account the age of Sid's present machine. In other circumstances, the estimate will be more subjective but, at least, the 'economic value' will be bounded by two market values, since 'economic value' is the deprival value only when it is greater than the net realizable value and less than replacement cost.

3. Since there is not much of a demand for old oranges, it is likely that Sid will get more from selling them now than from keeping them, i.e. the net realizable value is greater than the 'economic value', but as the net realizable value is less than the replacement cost the former gives us the oranges' deprival value.

VALUATION OF LIABILITIES

Although a considerable amount of thought has been given to the valuation of assets, hardly any attention has been paid to the valuation of liabilities. Basically the question is whether account should be taken of the dates on which liabilities fall due for payment. For example, suppose that A Limited owes both Mr P and Mr Q £1,000 each but that Mr P's loan is due for immediate repayment, while Mr Q does not have to be repaid for another three years. Both loans will appear on A Limited's balance sheet at £1,000 but it is clear that they do not have both the same value, or rather, cause A Limited the same amount of pain. If A Limited's Fairy Godmother appeared and said that, with a wave of her magic calculating machine, she could extinguish one of the loans, there is no doubt that A Limited would select Mr P's loan for removal.

We have already seen how present values can deal with the problem of the timing of cash flows, and that concept can be used to value liabilities; that is, they could be shown on balance sheets at their present values. Mr P's loan would still appear as £1,000 but Mr Q's loan would then be shown by using a discount rate of 0·09, at $\dfrac{£1,000}{(1·09)^3} = £772.$

Having introduced the question of the valuation of liabilities we will leave it, for this problem is still some way from resolution and the first phase of accounting reform is, as we shall see, concerned only with the valuation of the assets. However, it is important to realize that it can be argued that it is illogical to include assets at their current value without dealing with liabilities in the same way. Henceforth, we shall assume that liabilities are included on the balance sheet at their nominal, or face, values.

BALANCE SHEETS AND CURRENT VALUES

We will now move on from the problem of valuing individual assets and consider current value balance sheets. If we wanted to produce a balance sheet that disclosed the valuation of the business as a whole, the present value approach offers an ideal towards which we could aim.

A business consists of a bundle of assets (less liabilities) which will generate a stream of cash flows. If we could estimate those cash flows and select the appropriate discount rate we could find the present value of the cash flows and this would give us both the value of the business, and a very simple balance sheet:

Present value of future cash flows   £20

Owners' equity   £20

We have already indicated that there are, to say the least, a few practical problems that prevent the implementation of the above approach. Therefore we are forced to adopt an asset by asset approach, i.e. the current value balance sheet will not attempt to disclose the current value of the business as a whole but rather show the current value of the individual assets.

This means that the use of current value balance sheets will not eliminate the problem of goodwill that we introduced in Chapter 4. In terms of the above analysis, goodwill is the difference between the present value of the future cash flows and the sum of the current values of the assets less the liabilities.

As we have seen there are a number of different bases for the valuation of assets. A balance sheet based exclusively on net realizable values of the assets would disclose significant information. It would provide a measure of the company's flexibility, i.e. the ease with which the company could switch from its present business to a more profitable one by selling all, or a major portion, of its assets. More importantly, it would provide an indication of the risks involved in investing in, or lending to, the company. If the business proved to be totally unprofitable, the company could, at least, sell its assets and thus provide some return to the creditors and, possibly, the owners.

A balance sheet based purely on replacement cost is likely to be less useful. It would show how much would have to be spent to aquire the same bundle of assets as the company at present owns. However, as we have seen, it would probably not be worth while replacing all the assets, and so a total reliance on replacement cost would not be all that helpful. This brings us to deprival value which can be considered as being a modified form of replacement cost accounting, for the deprival value of most assets will be their replacement costs.

It has been argued that, since a number of different bases of valuation are useful, the balance sheet should show them all. This so-called multi-columnar balance sheet could have columns for, say, net realizable value, deprival value and, to satisfy the traditionalists, historical cost. An advantage of this approach is that the presentation of, in effect, three balance sheets means that, at least three different profit figures would be disclosed. This would emphasize the point that there is no *one* correct profit figure or, correspondingly, *one* correct basis of valuation. However, this view is a minority one, for the more generally accepted counter argument is that the presentation of a number of balance sheets and associated profit and loss accounts would confuse the users of the accounts.

As will be shown in Chapter 12 the variant of current value accounting which has been introduced in the United Kingdom – which is called current cost accounting – uses a basis of asset valuation called 'value to the business', which is closely akin to deprival value.

GAINS AND CURRENT VALUE ACCOUNTING

We will now examine the nature of profit and loss accounts that may be associated with current value balance sheets. We shall assume, for the purposes of this section, that there is no change in the general price level. That is, we shall concentrate on changes in relative prices.

We will assume that the owners of the company have not introduced any additional capital during the period under review or made any drawings, i.e. no dividends have been paid. With this assumption, we can obtain the total gain for the period by comparing the assets less liabilities at the end of the period with the assets less liabilities at the start of the period. It should be noted that each different basis of valuation will generate a different gain.

We have used the word 'gain' rather than 'profit', because, as we shall see later, there is considerable controversy about what part of the total gain may be regarded as profit.

Example 10.4

It might be helpful if we presented a simple numerical illustration. We will use the deprival value basis and assume that, in this case, the deprival value will be the replacement cost of the assets. Suppose that on 1 January 19X2 James started business with £1,000 and on 2 January purchased 100 widgets at £10 each. Sixty of the widgets were sold on 1 September 19X2 for £18, at which date their replacement cost was £12 each. At 31 December 19X2 the replacement cost per widget had increased to £15.

Let us first compare James' closing and opening current value balance sheets.

Balance Sheet as at 31 December 19X2

	£	£
Stock of widgets, 40 @ £15	600	
Cash (60 × £18)	1,080	
c/f	1,680	1,680

		£	£
b/f			1,680
Share capital		1,000	
Reserves		680	
		£1,680	

Balance Sheet as at 1 January 19X2

Cash	£1,000	1,000
Share capital	£1,000	
Total gain for 19X2		£680

Our task is to analyse the total gain of £680.

It will be helpful if we first consider that part of the gain that resulted from the widgets that were sold.

Widgets costing £600 (60 × £10) were sold for £1,080 – a gain of £480 and this is, of course, the profit that would be disclosed by traditional historical cost accounting.

However, this profit is the result of two activities, i.e. the holding of the widgets in a period in which their replacement cost increased from £10 to £12 and their sale at a price which exceeded their replacement cost at the date of sale. These are both significant activities which should be reported on, and they depend on different factors. The *holding gain* reflects James' skill (or luck) in buying the widgets before a price rise while the profit deemed to be earned at the time of the sale, the *operating gain*, reflects James' position in the market, i.e. his ability to sell widgets for more than their current cost to himself, and his efficiency as a salesman.

We can now analyse the gain of £480 as follows:

	£	£
Operating gain		
Sale of widgets		1,080
less Current value of the widgets as at the date of sale (60 × £12)		720
Operating gain		360
Holding gain		
Increase in the current value of the widgets sold during the period they were held.		
Current value at the date of sale	720	
less Current value (historical cost) at date of purchase (60 × £10)	600	120
		£480

Both of the above gains are *realized*, i.e. they arise from assets which have been sold.

If we now consider the remainder of the total gain for the year we can see that it is due to the increase in the current value of the unsold widgets. This is also a holding gain but because the assets have not yet been sold, or otherwise used up, it is termed an *unrealized holding gain*.

The unrealized holding gain in this case is:

	£
Current value of widgets at the end of the year 40 × £15	600
less Current value (historical cost) of widgets at the date of purchase, 40 × £10	400
	£200

The position is illustrated in the following diagram which highlights the point that holding gains result from an activity which covers a period of time while the operating gain arises instantaneously.

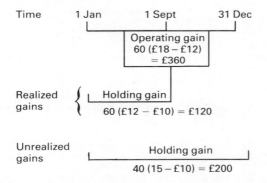

A statement of James's total gains for 19X2 can be presented as follows:

JAMES
Statement of Total Gains for 19X2

	£
Sales	1,080
less Current value of widgets at the date of sale	720
Operating gain	360
Holding gains	
Realized 60 (£12 – £10)	120
Realized gains	480
Unrealized 40 (£15 – £10)	200
Total gain	£680

The above illustration shows the way that the current value principle is extended to the profit and loss account. Expenses are defined as the amount of assets that are used up in the earning of revenue. In current value accounting assets are shown in the balance sheet at their current values so it is reasonable to show, in the profit and loss account, expenses as the current values of the assets used up as at the dates they are consumed.

In addition to operating and holding gains, one might also identify another type of gain – these have been called *extraordinary gains*. These result from any difference between the amount realized from the sale of an asset which does not form part of the company's normal output (e.g. fixed assets and investments) and their deprival value as at the date of disposal. A gain of this description is, of course, a realized gain.

The various gains are illustrated in Figure 10.1.

Figure 10.1

For convenience we summarize below definitions of the various gains.

Operating Gain

An operating gain is the difference between revenue and the deprival value of the inputs used up by the company in earning the revenue as at the dates they are used.

Extraordinary Gain

An extraordinary gain is the difference between the amount realized from the disposal of assets which do not form part of the company's normal output and their deprival value at the date of disposal.

Holding Gains

A holding gain is the difference between the original cost of the asset and either its deprival value at the date the asset is used (realized holding gains) or its deprival value at the balance sheet date (unrealized holding gains).

GAINS AND PROFITS

We should now consider which of the various components of the total gain should be considered as being the profit for the period, that is, which parts of the total gain should be regarded as being available for distribution. There is also the question of determining the profit on which a company should be taxed but we shall, at this stage, concentrate on the accounting, rather than the taxation, aspect of the question.

There are basically three views as to which components may be regarded as profit.

1. Profit = Operating and Extraordinary Gains

The argument in favour of this view is that if the company is to continue in the same business at the same level of activity the existence of holding gains does not benefit the company. If the replacement cost of the assets has increased during the holding period the company has not gained, for it will have to replace the assets at the higher price. Thus, it can be argued that holding gains represent the amount that must be set aside in order for the company to replenish its assets.

2. Profit = All Gains

The argument in favour of this view is that the first approach mixes up two things – the recognition of profit and the investment plans of the company, i.e. that there is a distinction between profit and liquidity and the need to invest. The adherents of the second approach believe that the total gain should be regarded as profit, since it represents an estimate of the increase in the value of the business over a period. (It can only be an estimate for the reason set out on page 364). The fact that some of the profit has not yet been turned into cash (the unrealized holding gain) is not seen as a reason for saying that it is not part of profit. Nor is it believed that the need to invest additional cash in the replacement of assets at the higher price should affect the recognition of profit. Instead it is said that the position facing a company is more realistically reported by stating that the profit is £x but the dividends may be restricted because of the company's liquidity position and its need for cash in the future. The cash needs depend on the company's plans for investment which may, or may not, involve staying in the same business. To recognize only the operating and extraordinary gains as profit hides the fact that the decision to stay in the same business has already been made.

3. Profit = All Gains except Unrealized Holding Gains

This view is broadly in line with the above but places more stress on the need to consider the liquidity of the company. The argument is that, since the unrealized holding gain has not yet been converted into cash or debtors, it should not be treated as profit. This approach brings us back to our old friend the historical cost profit.

Distinction between Holding and Operating Gains

To say that both operating and holding gains should be treated as profit is not to suggest that the distinction between them is not very important. Indeed, much of the case against traditional historical cost accounting could be made in terms of the way it neglects the difference and presents a figure of profit which mixes up realized holding and operating gains.

As we have already stated, the two gains are the result of two different activities and success in one may outweigh, or at least partly compensate, failure in the other activity. For example, a manufacturing company may only show a profit for the year because it was fortunate in purchasing its raw materials just before a sharp increase in their price, since (because of its inefficiency as a manufacturer and/or seller of its products) its selling price was less than the current cost of the inputs used in the manufacturing process. That is, large holding gains may have offset operating losses. The disclosure of this information might well help the user of the accounts form expectations about the future performance of the company. The user may believe that it is unlikely that the company would be able to take advantage of price increases in this way again, and that it will not be able to improve the efficiency of its manufacturing and selling processes. He would, in such circumstances, presumably predict a fairly bleak future.

APPENDIX: PRESENT VALUES

Assume a sum of £A is invested at r (expressed as a decimal) rate of interest compounded annually.

Then after one year we have

$$£A + £Ar = £A(1 + r)$$

and after two years

$$£A(1 + r) + r£A(1 + r) = £A(1 + r)^2$$

and, so on; thus after n years we have

$$£A(1 + r)^n$$

Therefore, it can be said that the receipt of £A now is equivalent to the receipt of:

$$£A(1 + r)^n \text{ after } n \text{ years.}$$

Similarly we could say that under the above conditions that we are indifferent to:

$$\frac{£A}{(1 + r)^n} \text{ now}$$

and

$$£A \text{ after } n \text{ years}$$

$$\frac{£A}{(1 + r)^n}$$ is termed the *present value* of £A

receivable after n years (r being the appropriate rate of interest).

Example

The present value of £100 receivable after 3 years at 12 per cent is

$$\frac{£100}{(1 \cdot 12)^3} = £100 \times 0 \cdot 712 = £71 \cdot 2.$$

Check

Suppose we start with	£	71·20
Interest for year 1		8·52
We start year 2 with		79·72
Interest for year 2		9·57
We start year 3 with		89·29
Interest for year 3		10·71
After 3 years we have	£	100·00

Present value tables exist which give the values of $\dfrac{1}{(1 + r)^n}$ for various values

of r and n.

An extract from a present value table is given below:

Present Value of £1

Periods (n)					*Discount Rates* (r)						
	4%	6%	8%	9%	10%	11%	12%	13%	14%	16%	18%
1	0·962	0·943	0·926	0·917	0·909	0·901	0·893	0·885	0·877	0·862	0·848
2	0·925	0·890	0·857	0·842	0·826	0·812	0·797	0·783	0·770	0·743	0·718
3	0·889	0·840	0·794	0·772	0·751	0·731	0·712	0·693	0·675	0·641	0·609
4	0·855	0·792	0·735	0·708	0·683	0·659	0·636	0·613	0·592	0·552	0·516
5	0·822	0·747	0·681	0·650	0·621	0·594	0·567	0·543	0·519	0·476	0·437
6	0·790	0·705	0·630	0·596	0·564	0·535	0·507	0·480	0·456	0·410	0·370
7	0·760	0·665	0·584	0·547	0·513	0·482	0·452	0·425	0·400	0·354	0·314
8	0·731	0·627	0·540	0·502	0·466	0·434	0·404	0·376	0·351	0·305	0·266
9	0·703	0·592	0·500	0·460	0·424	0·391	0·361	0·333	0·308	0·263	0·226
10	0·676	0·558	0·463	0·422	0·386	0·352	0·322	0·295	0·270	0·227	0·191
15	0·555	0·417	0·315	0·274	0·239	0·209	0·183	0·160	0·140	0·108	0·084
20	0·456	0·312	0·214	0·178	0·149	0·124	0·104	0·087	0·073	0·051	0·036
30	0·308	0·174	0·099	0·075	0·057	0·044	0·033	0·026	0·020	0·012	0·007
50	0·141	0·054	0·021	0·013	0·008	0·005	0·004	0·002	0·001	0·001	0·000

EXERCISES

10.1 'All gains are profits and all profits are gains'. Discuss.

10.2 What is meant by the statement that the use of historical cost accounting means that the accounts produced lack comparability? Discuss the problems caused by a lack of comparability to users of accounts.

10.3 (a) Find the present values (PV) of the following cash streams which are generated by various assets, assuming a discount rate of (i) 10 per cent and (ii) 16 per cent.

End of Year (£)

Asset	1	2	3	4	5
A	+200	+300	+200	+100	+100
B	+200	+200	+200	+200	+200
C	+180	+160	+140	+100	+50
D	+240	+300	+140	+60	-100

(b) What are the deprival values of the above assets under both assumptions, given that the assets' replacement costs (RC) and net realizable values (NRV) are as given below?

Asset	RC £	NRV £
A	800	700
B	600	400
C	100	480
D	540	520

10.4 On 1 January 19X4, Stan started a business selling pleasure boats and small yachts. His starting capital was £1,000,000. On 2 January he bought 10 boats for £50,000 each and on 10 July he bought a further 15 boats for £60,000 each. He made the following sales (the figures in brackets are the replacement costs at those dates).

January 30	2 boats @ £70,000 each	(£50,000)
February 25	1 boat @ £55,000	(£55,000)
February 28	2 boats @ £60,000 each	(£55,000)
March 30	3 boats @ £65,000 each	(£60,000)
April 30	1 boat @ £70,000	(£65,000)
June 30	1 boat @ £70,000	(£75,000)
August 10	4 boats @ £80,000 each	(£60,000)
September 20	5 boats @ £90,000 each	(£70,000)
October 10	3 boats @ £100,000 each	(£80,000)

The replacement cost of the boats at 31 December 19X4 was £90,000 each.

(a) Compute a statement of Stan's total gain for 19X4.

(b) Which elements of the total gain might be regarded as the profit for the year? Outline the arguments that can be advanced for and against the various alternatives.

11 | *Accounting for Changes in the General Price Level*

Over the years a large number of accounting academics and others have argued for a major change in the basic method of accounting. Two main schools of thought can be identified. One set of reformers calls for the adoption of what has come to be termed current purchasing power (CPP) accounting. In this method the historical cost basis is maintained, but the various pounds in the accounts are converted to pounds of current purchasing power. This reform may be described as the ultimate in modifying the traditional approach. The other set of reformers calls for the total abandonment of historical cost accounting and for its replacement by a system based on current values. The second school can be divided into those who believe that the reformed system should also include adjustments for changes in the general purchasing power of money and those who feel that such adjustments do not have a place in the new world of accounting.

For many years practising accountants have resisted these proposals. The general attitude was a mixture of self-satisfaction, based on the view that there was little wrong with the existing methods, and a more reasonable belief that the proposals would mean that accounting statements would stray too far from the desired level of objectivity. The dam burst in the late 1960s and early 1970s. This was evidenced, so far as the United Kingdom is concerned, by the issue, by the ASC of *Exposure Draft 8: Accounting for Changes in the Purchasing Power of Money* in January 1973. The proposed standard was that certain classes of limited companies should publish supplementary accounting statements based on the CPP approach. This proposal was confirmed by the issue of *Provisional Statement of Standard Accounting Practice 7*, in May 1974.

However, the government did not appear to be satisfied with this approach for, having seen the way the professional accounting bodies were moving, it established a committee of enquiry into inflation accounting in January 1974, i.e. after the appearance of the exposure draft but before the issue of the PSSAP 7. The committee, a majority of whose members were

374

non-accountants, was under the chairmanship of Mr (now Sir) Francis Sandilands. The committee's report, usually referred to as the 'Sandilands Report' was issued in September 1975 and came down in favour of a system of accounting based on current values without any adjustment for changes in general purchasing power. The government, even though there had been a change in administration, accepted the report, and a group called the "Inflation Accounting Steering Group" (IASG) was established and charged with the task of preparing an initial standard accounting practice based on the Sandilands proposals. The IASG produced Exposure Draft 18, Current Cost Accounting, in November 1976 but this was not acceptable to the accounting profession and was withdrawn. It was replaced by Exposure Draft 24 in April 1979 and the proposals of this ED were accepted and led to the publication Statement of Standard Accounting Practice 16 in March 1980.

SSAP 16 will form the subject of Chapter 12 but at this stage we will concentrate on CPP accounting. While the acceptance of current cost accounting by the British accountancy profession resulted in the withdrawal of PSSAP 7 it is still important that accountants should be aware of the basic principles of current purchasing power accounting.

CURRENT PURCHASING POWER ACCOUNTING

Money is not, of itself, of much value. Its nutritional and calorific value is small and, as a form of clothing, it would not long withstand cold and rain. A miser gets a kick from contemplating and counting his money but even that pleasure probably stems from the power the possession of the money affords him. Money is valuable because it enables its possessor to obtain goods and services, i.e. the power to command resources.

Conventional accounting treats money as a stable commodity and hence pounds of 1970 are added to and subtracted from pounds of 1920, and the result, according to the advocates of CPP accounting, is a nonsense.

The argument in favour of CPP accounting is outlined below.

The value of money depends on what it can buy. Thus one should not, for example, say that the profit on a transaction is the difference between the number of pound notes that were paid for the asset with the number of pound notes that were received when the asset was sold. Instead, we should compare the purchasing power that was given up when the asset was acquired with the purchasing power that was gained as a result of the sale of the asset.

Before proceeding further, we should consider how we can measure changes in the general purchasing power of money.

MEASURING CHANGES
IN THE GENERAL PURCHASING POWER OF MONEY

The prices of some goods and services increase by more than other prices; indeed some prices actually fall. The problem is, therefore, to find the average change in prices. This is not a straightforward exercise, for among other factors it must be recognized that some price changes are more important than others.

Assume that we have an economy in which there are only two products, bread and beer and suppose that, last year, the price of bread increased by 20 per cent while the price of beer increased by 30 per cent. What is the average price increase? It is 25 per cent only from the point of view of those who consider bread and beer to be equally important. Those who believe that bread is more important than beer would feel that the average price increase was between 20 and 25 per cent. Similarly, those who attached greater importance to the price of beer would say that the average price increase was between 25 and 30 per cent.

If a statistician were asked to work out the average price increase for the above economy he would try to find out the 'average' view of people as to the relative importance of bread and beer. Suppose that he felt that there was evidence that the average view was that bread is twice as important as beer. He could then work out a weighted average, giving bread a weight of 2 and beer a weight of 1, as follows:

	Price increase	Weight	Price increase × weight %
Bread	20 per cent	2	40
Beer	30 per cent	1	30
		3	70

Average price increase $= \frac{70}{3} = 23\frac{1}{3}$ per cent.

Note that this could be said to be a 'double average'. The product of the basic calculation is an average but the weights that were included in the calculation depended on the average view of the relative importance of the two products. This means that the answer of $23\frac{1}{3}$ per cent is only really applicable for people who consider bread as being twice as important as beer and that different people would consider that prices had, on average, increased by different amounts, depending on their consumption patterns.

If we now leave our simple two-product economy for the real world we meet another difficulty. The technical content of goods and services may have improved over time. A nine-inch television set may have cost about £60 in 1952 and would, if it were a black and white set, cost about the same today. Does this mean that there has been no change in the price of television sets? Probably not, for anyone who remembers the flickering, bulky set of the 1950s is aware that the modern version is very much better. It would be more reasonable to say that the price of television sets has fallen. A second example can be taken from the services field. The cost of medical treatment, as measured by the price charged by a doctor for an hour of his time, has increased manyfold since, say, 1930. But, taking into account the increased knowledge possessed by the present-day medical profession, it could be argued that at least part of the increase is due to an increase in the quality of the product.

Figure 11.1

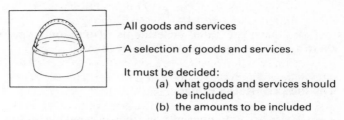

All goods and services

A selection of goods and services.

It must be decided:
  (a) what goods and services should be included
  (b) the amounts to be included

Some of the problems facing a person attempting to measure the average change in prices are illustrated in Figure 11.1. He must select a sample of goods and services and decide how much of each good and service should be included in his calculation, i.e. he must decide on the relative weights. Given that he has selected his basket of goods and services he can then measure the average price change, but even then, he must try to hold constant the technical quality of goods and services.

Index Numbers

For a detailed treatment of the topic of index numbers readers are recommended to a basic statistics textbook. However, for the benefit of those who have not yet had the pleasure of studying such a treasury of delight we should, at this stage, introduce the topic, for price level changes are usually expressed by way of index numbers.

The basic notion can best be introduced by means of a simple example. Suppose that a series of numbers, say the annual sales, in units, of a company, is as follows:

19X1	19X2	19X3	19X4	19X5
20,000	22,000	18,000	24,000	28,000

A base year has to be selected and the sales for that year are expressed as 100, i.e. the index number for the base year is 100. Suppose we take 19X1 as the base year (but we need not have selected the first year of the series as the base year).

Sales for the other years are then expressed in terms of the base year, e.g. the index number for 19X2 is:

$$\frac{22,000}{20,000} \times 100 = 110$$

In general the formula is:

$$\text{Index for year } n = \frac{\text{Quantity for year } n}{\text{Quantity for base year}} \times 100$$

The series of index numbers in this case is:

19X1	19X2	19X3	19X4	19X5
100	110	90	120	140

We have presented an example of only one type of index number; there are many variations on the basic theme.

The Index of Retail Prices

There are a number of price indices available in the United Kingdom which serve to estimate changes in the average, or general, level of prices. Some indices include all goods and services in the economy while others – consumer price indices – only seek to measure changes in average prices in so far as they affect the goods and services purchased by individuals for consumption, thus, the price of bread would be included while the price of machine tools would not.

Perhaps the most commonly quoted general consumer price index in the United Kingdom is the index of retail prices (RPI) which is often referred to as the Cost of Living Index.

The RPI is based on a sample of goods and services used by individuals. The weights used in its calculation are based on the consumption patterns, obtained on a sample basis, of those households whose heads are in the 'middle income' range – pensioners, students and the well-off are excluded. The index is produced monthly and is published in the *Monthly Digest of Statistics* about three weeks after the end of the appropriate month.

The ASC selected the RPI as the most suitable index for the preparation of CPP accounts on the grounds that CPP accounts should show the results of the company in terms of the purchasing power of its ultimate owners (people), and that that was most appropriately done by means of a consumer price index.

Conversion to Pounds of Current Purchasing Power

The task is to convert expenditure and receipts made or received in pounds of 'past purchasing power' into pounds of current purchasing power. To do this, a general price index is used in the following way. Say £18 was spent in 19X2 when the index was 132 and that the index is now 158. We need to know how much money the consumer would now require in order to purchase a similar bundle of goods and services as he could have purchased for £18 in 19X2.

Assume that the base year for index number series is 19X0, i.e. the index for 19X0 is 100.

In order to purchase a similar bundle of goods and services that could be bought for £100 in 19X0 the consumer would have needed £132 in 19X2 and £158 now.

£132 (in 19X2) is equivalent to £158 (now)

Thus £18 (in 19X2) is equivalent to $\frac{158}{132} \times$ £18 (now) = £21.5 (now)

In general:

$$\text{Converted amount (£)} = \text{Actual amount (£)} \times \frac{\text{Current index number}}{\text{Index number at date of transaction}}$$

The basic approach is straightforward and is little different from the process of converting foreign currencies into pounds sterling.

The following examples show how the method can be applied to sales and fixed assets.

Example 11.1

Sales for 19X5 in actual pounds are:

	£
First quarter	18,000
Second quarter	23,000
Third quarter	19,000
Fourth quarter	26,000

Assume that the sales all took place half way through the appropriate quarter. Assume that the year end (current) index is 160 and the indexes half way through the four quarters are, 143, 152, 148 and 156.

The sales figure in the CPP profit and loss account for 19X5 is £91,559, and is computed as follows:

Quarter	Actual £	Conversion factor	CPP £
1	18,000	160/143	20,140
2	23,000	160/152	24,211
3	19,000	160/148	20,541
4	26,000	160/156	26,667
			£91,559

Example 11.2

A fixed asset was purchased in 19X2, when the index was 123, for £120,000. The index at the end of 19X5 is 160. The asset is being written off over 10 years on a straight-line basis, i.e. £12,000 per year will be shown as the depreciation expense in the historical cost profit and loss account.

The depreciation charge in the CPP profit and loss account for 19X5 is $12,000 \times \frac{160}{123} = £15,610$

As at the end of 19X5, 40 per cent of the asset has been written off and the entries in the historical cost balance sheet as at 31 December 19X5 in respect of the fixed assets, are as follows:

	Cost	Accumulated depreciation	Net book value
Fixed asset	£120,000	£48,000	£72,000

These three figures are in 'pounds of 19X2' and have to be converted into '19X5 year-end pounds'. The asset will, therefore, appear in the CPP balance sheet as follows:

Cost of fixed asset	£
$120,000 \times \frac{160}{123}$	156,098
less Accumulated Depreciation	
$48,000 \times \frac{160}{123}$	62,439
Net book value	£93,659

Note that the denominator in the above calculations is the index at the date of acquisition of the fixed asset.

CPP Accounts and Current Values

We have already explained that CPP accounts are based on historical cost. They do not attempt to incorporate current values, other than to the extent that they already impinge on the traditional method. For example, the 'lower of cost or market value'* (COMA) is still applied.

Suppose that a company's closing stock had a historical cost of £1,000 and that it was, on average, purchased when a suitable general price index was 120 while the year-end index number is 132.

The converted closing stock figure is then

$$£1,000 \times \frac{132}{120} = £1,100$$

But suppose that the net realizable value of the stock at the year end was only £1,060. Then the COMA rule would be applied and the CPP closing stock figure would be written down to £1,060.

Note that this does not involve the application of a new principle. However, there will be circumstances, such as the above, where the COMA rule will have to be applied when preparing the CPP accounts, even though it was not invoked when drawing up the conventional accounts.

Losses and Gains on Holding Monetary Assets and Liabilities

There is one class of asset and liability where to ignore current values would produce absurd results. We refer to monetary assets and liabilities. These are those assets and liabilities that are fixed by contract or otherwise in terms of numbers of pounds, regardless of changes in the purchasing power of money.

Cash, debtors and creditors are obvious examples of monetary items, but we shall discuss the composition of net monetary assets (monetary assets less monetary liabilities) in more detail later.

Suppose that Claude started a business on 1 January 19X2 (index 100) by putting £120 into a bank account but engaged in no other transactions

---

*See Chapter 7 of Volume 1.

during the year ended 31 December 19X2 (Year-end index 140). Clearly it would be incorrect to convert his closing bank balance and say that it was £120 × 140/100 = £168, for if Claude went to his bank on 31 December 19X2 and closed his account he would only be given 120 pound notes.

What has happened is that he has lost purchasing power by holding, in a period of rising prices, an asset which is fixed in money terms. His loss, measured in year-end pounds, being £168 − £120 = £48. That is, in order to command the same power over resources at 31 December 19X2 as he could at 1 January 19X2, Claude would have to have £168 (but he only has £120).

If Claude had started his business by borrowing money (or by purchasing goods on credit) he would have gained in purchasing power because he would repay the loan with less valuable pounds than the pounds he obtained from the creditor when the loan was established.

When converting a traditional profit and loss account and balance sheet into a set of CPP accounts, the balance sheet values for the monetary assets and liabilities will remain the same. However, an additional item will appear in the CPP profit and loss account, and this is the loss or gain on the company's net monetary asset position.

The following examples illustrate the calculation of the loss or gain in different circumstances.

Example 11.3

11.3.1   X borrowed £100 on 1 January 19X5 when the index was 116. He used the money to purchase physical, i.e. non-monetary, assets. There were no other transactions in 19X5.

       X's gain on owing money, expressed in year-end pounds, given that the index at 31 December 19X5 is 143, can be found as follows:

	£
Purchasing power (in year-end pounds) obtained on the receipt of the loan:	
£100 × $\frac{143}{116}$	123
Purchasing power that would have to be sacrificed if the loan were repaid at the year end	100
Gain, in year-end pounds	£ 23

(Note that X will probably have to pay interest on the loan and this has not been included in the analysis)

11.3.2   Y started business by introducing cash of £250 on 1 January 19X5 and did nothing else that year. Index numbers are as in 11.3.1. Then his loss on holding net monetary assets in the year can be calculated as follows:

	£
Purchasing power of £250 at 1 January 19X5 expressed in year-end pounds	
£250 × $\frac{143}{116}$	308
Actual purchasing power in year-end pounds	250
Loss, in year-end pounds	£ 58

11.3.3   The facts are as in 11.3.1, except that X repaid
          the loan on 30 June 19X5 when the index was 131.   £

          Purchasing power (in pounds of 30 June 19X5)
             obtained on the receipt of the loan:
                £100 × $\frac{131}{116}$ 113

          Purchasing power given on 30 June 19X5   100
          Gain, in 30 June 19X5 pounds   £ 13

          Gain in 31 December 19X5 pounds
             = £13 × $\frac{143}{131}$ =   £ 14

In general if ML = monetary liability

Gain (year-end pounds)

$$= \left\{ ML \times \frac{\text{Index when liability was repaid}}{\text{Index when liability was created}} - ML \right\} \times \frac{\text{Index at year end}}{\substack{\text{Index when} \\ \text{liability was} \\ \text{repaid}}}$$

Where the liability is outstanding at the year end, we take the index at the year end as being the index when the liability is repaid.

The above equation then becomes:

Gain (year-end pounds)

$$= ML \times \frac{\text{Index at year end}}{\text{Index when liability was created}} - ML$$

Similar expressions giving the loss on holding a monetary asset (MA), can be obtained by replacing ML by − MA in the above.

Of course the net monetary positions of companies are constantly changing, and the best way of dealing with this is to treat each increase in net monetary assets as a monetary asset outstanding at the year end and each decrease as a liability outstanding at the year end.

To show that this method gives the same answer we will return to Example 11.3.3 and rework it using the alternative method.

                                                                            Year-end
                                                                            pounds

1 January   The creation of the liability, all
             other things being equal, reduces
             net monetary assets.

     c/f   Gain, £100 × $\frac{143}{116}$ − £100   23 *b/f* 23

30 June   The repayment of the loan, all
other things being equal, increases
net monetary assets.

$$\text{Loss, } £100 \times \tfrac{143}{131} - £100 \qquad\qquad 9$$

Net gain expressed in year-end pounds   £14

By using the above approach a company's loss or gain on its net monetary position can conveniently be calculated as follows:

1.   Identify the timings of all increases and decreases in net monetary assets and convert the increases and decreases to year-end pounds by using the formula

$$\text{Actual amount} \times \frac{\text{Year-end index}}{\text{Index at date of increase or decrease}}$$

The opening balance is treated as an increase if opening monetary assets exceed the monetary liabilities and vice versa.

2.   Find the net total of the converted increases and decreases.

3.   Compare the total of the converted net monetary assets with the actual total.

4.   If actual net monetary assets exceed converted net monetary assets, the company has gained in purchasing power during the period and vice versa.

Note that the above requires us to identify the dates of the transactions that change the net total of monetary assets. We need not consider those transactions which simply result in a change in the composition of net monetary assets. For example, if a company purchases goods on credit, the transaction immediately produces a reduction in net monetary assets by virtue of the increase in creditors. The subsequent payment reduces cash and creditors but does not affect the total.
Example 11.4 shows a convenient way of applying the above method.

Example 11.4

Index numbers:	1 January 19X5	116
	30 June 19X5	131
	31 December 19X5	143

P Limited started 19X5 with cash of £100 but with no other monetary assets or liabilities.
The relevant transactions for 19X5 were:

30 June	Purchased goods for £320
	Sold goods for £400
	Paid sundry expenses of £140
31 December	Sold goods for £80.

Note that it does not matter whether the sales and purchases were for cash or credit. A sale for cash increases cash, a sale on credit increases debtors but both are monetary assets. The payment of cash by a debtor does not change the total of the net monetary assets, only its composition.

Date	Trans-action	Actual (£) Increases	Actual (£) Decreases	Conversion factor	Converted (£) Increases	Converted (£) Decreases
1 Jan	Opening balance	100		143/116	123	
30 June	Purchases		320 ⎫			
	Sales	400	⎬	143/131		65
	Expenses		140 ⎭			
31 Dec	Sales	80		143/143	80	
		580	460		203	65
	Net	£120			£138	

Gain = £120 − £138 = − £18 (a loss)

A company's net monetary assets are essentially made up of its net working capital, except stock, and its longer-term liabilities. The longer-term liabilities will include tax payable as well as debentures and other forms of loan capital.

The factors that give rise to a loss on a company's short and long-term monetary position are different. The short-term position depends on the company's policy and needs in relation to its investment in working capital. The longer-term position depends on the extent to which the company has decided to make use of loan capital as a long-term form of finance. Thus, when preparing CPP accounts, it is usual to report separately on gains (or losses) on the company's short-term (working capital except stock) and long-term position.

The rights of preference shareholders are usually fixed in money terms. This is so if they are entitled to a constant dividend and to a fixed sum payable on the liquidation of the company. In such a case preference shares would be included in the long-term net monetary assets.

Equity Share Capital and Reserves

These are not monetary items and will be restated in terms of current purchasing power. Indeed this is the key to the concept of CPP profit, for such a profit is only made if the purchasing power represented by the owners' equity at the year end is greater than the purchasing power, expressed in year-end pounds, of the owners' equity at the start of the year, after adjusting for capital introduced and withdrawn.

We will now introduce a simple example of a set of CPP accounts.

Example 11.5

ZR Limited started business on 1 January 19X4 with a share capital of £700, and immediately purchased plant, with a life of 4 years, for £200 and stock for £400. Half the goods were sold in 19X4 for £330; the remainder were sold for £350 in 19X5. In 19X5 further purchases were made for £910 and all these goods were on hand at the year end.
  Sundry operating expenses were: 19X4 £33, and 19X5 £98.
  A suitable general price index moved as follows:

	19X4	19X5
1 January	100	120
30 June	110	140
31 December	120	160

  In order to prepare the CPP accounts we must find out on what dates the transactions took place; we shall assume that all transactions took place half way through the appropriate year unless it is otherwise stated.

19X4	Historical cost accounts £	£	Factor	CPP £	Accounts £
Profit and Loss Account			120/110		360
Sales		330	120/100	480	
less Purchases	400		120/100	240	
less: closing stock	200				
	——			240	
	200		120/100	60	
Depreciation	50		120/110	36	336
Sundry expenses	33	283		——	——
	——	——			24
Trading profit		47			
Loss on short-term net					47
monetary position		—			——
			(loss)		£23
Profit for year		£47			
Balance Sheet					
Fixed assets (NBV)		150	120/100		180
Stock		200	120/100		240
Cash + debtors − creditors		397			397
		£747			£817
Share capital		700	120/100		840
Retained earnings		47			(23)
		£747			£817

Workings
Loss/gain on net monetary position

Date	Trans-action	Actual (£) Increase	Decrease	Conversion factor	Converted (£) Increase	Decrease
1 Jan	Capital introduced	700		120/100	840	
1 Jan	Purchase of plant		200	120/100		240
1 Jan	Purchases		400	120/100		480
30 Jun	Sales	330		120/110	360	
30 Jun	Expenses		33	120/110		36
		£1,030	£633		£1,200	£756

| | Net | £397 | | | £444 | |

Gain = £397 − £444 = − £47.

19X5	Historical cost accounts £	£	Factor	CPP accounts £	£
Profit and Loss Account					
Sales		350	160/140		400
less Opening stock	200		160/100	320	
Purchases	910		160/140	1,040	
	1,110			1,360	
less Closing stock	910		160/140	1,040	
	200			320	
Depreciation	50		160/100	80	
Sundry expenses	98	348	160/140	112	512
Trading profit		2	(loss)		(112)
Loss on short-term monetary position		—			38
		2			(150)
Opening retained earnings		47	(23 × 160/120)[+]		(31)
Closing retained earnings		£49			£(181)
Balance Sheet		£			£
Fixed assets (NBV)		100	160/100		160
Stock		910	160/140		1,040
		£ 1,010			£1,200
Share capital		700	160/100		1,120
Retained earnings		49			(181)
		749			939
Creditors − Debtors − bank		261			261
		£ 1,010			£1,200

Workings
Loss/gain on net monetary position

Date	Transaction	Actual (£) Increase	Actual (£) Decrease	Factor	Converted (£) Increase	Converted (£) Decrease
1 Jan	Opening balance	397		160/120	529	
30 Jun	Sales	350		160/140	400	
30 Jun	Purchases		910	160/140		1,040
30 Jun	Expenses		98	160/140		112
		£747	£1,008		£929	£1,152
	Net		£261			£223

Gain $= -$ £261 $- (-$£223$) = -$ £38
+ Retained earnings at 1 January 19X5, in pounds of 1 January 19X5, were £23.
So retained earnings at 1 January 19X5, in pounds of 31 December 19X5

$$= £23 \times \tfrac{160}{120} = £31.$$

DIFFERENCES BETWEEN HISTORICAL COST AND CPP PROFITS

At this stage, it will be useful if we outline the reasons for the differences between the profit disclosed by the traditional accounts and the CPP profit. We have already discussed one of the causes, the loss or gain on net monetary assets. There are two others.

Time Lag between the Acquisition and Use of an Input

Practically all businesses have to acquire assets which are used up in the earning of revenue. Goods have to be bought if they are to be sold while, in general, fixed assets have to be acquired which will be used up over a period of years.

In the profit and loss account the 'using-up' of the assets are the expenses which are matched with the associated revenue. As the assets have to be acquired before they are used, the expenses will, in times of rising prices, represent 'more valuable' pounds than the matched pounds of revenue. Thus, in the process of converting the traditional accounts into CPP accounts the pounds of expenses will be subject to a greater upward adjustment than the pounds of revenue.

Example 11.6 concentrates on this point.

Example 11.6

A firm starts business, when the general price index (GPI) is 100, with a share capital of £100 and immediately purchases, for that amount, an input to its resource transformation process. It holds the input while the GPI increases to 120 and then uses up to four-fifths of the input to achieve sales of £150. The GPI at the year end is also 120. There are no other expenses.

	Historical cost		CPP
Profit and Loss Account	£		£
Sales	150		150
less Expenses	80	(80 × 120/100)	96
Profit	£70		£54
Balance Sheet			
Cash	150		150
Asset, being unused input	20	(20 × 120/100)	24
	£170		£174
Share capital	100	(100 × 120/100)	120
Retained earnings	70		54
	£170		£174

N.B. The input could either be inventory or fixed assets – the same principle applies.

When prices are rising the time-lag effect means that, all other things being equal, the CPP profit will be less than the historical cost profit or, the CPP loss will be greater than the historical cost loss. The greater the time lag, the greater will be the difference. Thus, the effect will be greater in the case of companies which own a considerable quantity of fixed assets and those which hold stocks for a lengthy period.

Restatement of Mid-year Pounds in Terms of Year-end Pounds

If one thinks of the activity of a business as consisting of a series of different transactions, it is clear that the profit for a year is made up of a series of profits expressed in pounds of different dates. These are all converted to year-end pounds, and this adjustment will, in times of rising prices, make the CPP profit greater than the historical cost profit since a mid-year £1 is converted to £(1 + *x* per cent) when expressed in year-end pounds.

The three factors which cause the differences between CPP and historical cost profits are illustrated in Example 11.7.

Example 11.7

The facts are as in Example 11.6 except that the accounts are prepared when the index is 160.

	Historical cost		CPP
Profit and Loss Account	£		£
Sales	150	(150 × 160/120)	200
less Expenses	80	(80 × 160/100)	128
	70		72
less Loss on short-term monetary position	—		50
Profit	£70		£22

Balance Sheet			
Cash	150		150
Asset (being unused input)	20	(20 × 160/100)	32
	£170		£182
Share capital	100	(100 × 160/100)	160
Retained earnings	70		22
	£170		£182

Workings
Loss on short-term monetary position

Transaction	Actual (£)		Factor	Converted (£)	
	Increase	Decrease		Increase	Decrease
Introduction of capital	100		160/100	160	
Purchase of assets		100	160/100		160
Sales	150		160/120	200	
	£250	£100		£360	£160
Net	£150			£200	

Gain = £150 − £200 = − £50

The time-lag effect can be calculated as follows:
Historical cost of asset used is £80.
Historical cost, restated in pounds of the date the asset was used (see Example 11.6) = £80 × 120/100 = £96.
Difference = £96 − £80 = £16. This will serve to reduce the historical cost profit.
From the above, the profit expressed in pounds of the date when the goods were sold was:

	£
Sales	150
less Expenses	96
Profit	£ 54

Converting this profit to year-end pounds we get £54 × $\frac{160}{120}$ = £72. The difference of £18 (£72 − £54) increases the historical cost profit.

Reconciliation of CPP and Historical Cost Profits

	£	£
Historical cost profit		70
add		
The effect of restating the profit in year-end pounds		18
		88
less		
Loss on short-term monetary position	50	
The effect of the time lag between the acquisition and use of inputs	16	66
CPP profit		£22

It can be seen from the above that it is not possible to estimate the CPP profit by making a casual inspection of the traditional accounts and saying (given that the rate of inflation is 20 per cent per annum) that 'the historical cost profit is £10m so the CPP profit is about £8m, i.e. 20 per cent less'.

The difference between the CPP and historical profit depends on the interplay of the three factors. We shall consider each factor separately and assume that the general price level is increasing.

(a)   The CPP profit may be less or more than the historical cost profit depending on whether the company has made a loss or gain on its net monetary position.

(b)   The time-lag effect means that the CPP profit will be less than the historical cost profit.

(c)   The restatement factor means that, if the company has made a profit on the traditional basis, the CPP profit will be larger, while if the traditional accounts disclose a loss, the CPP loss will be greater.

Of the three factors, the first two are, generally, the more important. Thus, it is not surprising to discover that companies which have few depreciating assets and which make considerable use of debt as a source of finance (for example property companies), have a larger CPP profit than an historical cost profit. On the other hand, companies with significant fixed assets and which do not make much use of debt, such as engineering companies, have, in general, far lower CPP profits than historical cost profits.

Current purchasing power accounting is not a new technique. It was first described in English in a book published in 1936 by an American, Professor Henry Sweeney. The book was entitled *Stabilized Accounting*, this being an alternative name for CPP accounting. The method described by Sweeney was not new in 1936 but was based on work done in Germany during the period of hyper-inflation in the 1920s.

The technique burst upon the British business scene in the 1970s with the publication of PSSAP 7. But it seems that it was more a shooting star than a permanent feature of the accounting heaven. There are now comparatively few people who would say that CPP accounting is, itself, the ideal vehicle for accounting reform.

The reader may feel, having read the above, that he has wasted his time mastering CPP accounting. This is not so, for as we explained at the start of this chapter, there is considerable dispute whether the reformed system should, even if based on current value accounting, include adjustments for changes in general purchasing power. If this view is taken, then the reformed system will have to include many of the features of the CPP method. This debate is likely to continue for some considerable time.

This is an appropriate note on which to conclude this chapter and move on to Chapter 12 and the current cost accounting.

EXERCISES

11.1 Discuss the problems involved in measuring changes in the general purchasing power of money.

11.2 In each of the following pairs the two companies are identical except for the stated difference. In 19X5 each company reported the same historical cost profit as the company with which it is paired.

For each pair of companies compare the current purchasing power (CPP) profits for 19X5 assuming that the general price index increased over the period.

  (i) Company A: Has a small equity base and makes extensive use of long-term debt as a source of finance.

        Company B: Has a larger equity base and makes very little use of long-term debt.

 (ii) Company C: Owns all the plant and machinery used in the business.

        Company D: Rents most of the plant and machinery.

(iii) Company E: Pays its trade creditors promptly and also is very efficient in collecting debts.

        Company F: Pays and collects more slowly.

(iv) Company G: Depreciates the plant and machinery on a straight-line basis over 12 years.

        Company H: Depreciates the plant and machinery on a straight line basis over 8 years.

(v) Company I: Does not carry a large inventory but prefers to purchase goods on a day-to-day basis.

Company J: Keeps about 6 month's inventory on hand.

11.3 Con Limited started business as management consultants on 1 January 19X4. Its historical cost balance sheet as at 31 December 19X4 was:

	£		£
Share capital (subscribed 1 January 19X4)	8,800	Fixed assets (purchased 1 January 19X4)	8,000
Retained earnings	600	*less* Accumulated depreciation	800
	9,400		7,200
Overdraft	800	Debtors for fees	3,000
	£10,200		£10,200

During the year ended 31 December 19X5 Con Limited sent out invoices amounting to £30,000 and received £28,000 from debtors. It paid wages and sundry expenses amounting to £24,000 during the year. Fixed assets are depreciated at 10 per cent on the reducing balance.

A suitable general price index moved as follows:

	1 Jan X4	1 Jan X5	30 Jun X5	31 Dec X5
Index	80	100	120	140

Work in progress and taxation may be ignored, and there were no creditors or debtors (other than fees) at 31 December 19X5.

Assume that the transactions took place evenly over the year.

Prepare CPP accounts for 19X5.

11.4 Money Limited's historical cost balance sheet as at 31 December 19X4 was as follows:

	£	£	£
Fixed assets, net book value			2,350
Current assets			
Inventory		400	
Debtors for goods		300	
Cash		160	
c/f		860	2,350

	£	£	£
b/f		860	2,350
less Current liabilities			
Creditors for goods	250		
Proposed dividends	100		
Taxation	60	410	450
			£2,800

	£
Share capital	1,000
Retained earnings	800
	1,800
10 per cent debentures	1,000
	£2,800

Sales for 19X5 were £6,000, purchases £2,400 and sundry expenses £800.

If x is the sales and y the purchases of quarter 1, the sales and purchases for the other quarters are:

	Q2	Q3	Q4
Sales	x	$2x$	$2x$
Purchases	y	$2y$	$2y$

All suppliers are paid in the quarter following that in which the purchases are made. Fifty per cent of cash due from customers is received in the quarter in which the sales are made and the remainder is collected in the following quarter.

Sundry expenses were incurred evenly over the year and were paid as they were incurred.

Debenture interest was paid in quarters 2 and 4. The proposed dividend was paid in quarter 1, and the tax in quarter 3. The corporation tax charge for 19X5 was £80 and a dividend of £120 is proposed for the year.

A suitable general price index at 1 January 19X5 was 90 and at 31 December 19X5, 125. The average indices for the four quarters of 19X5 were:

	Q1	Q2	Q3	Q4
	100	110	115	120

Required:

Money Limited's gain or loss on its holding of net monetary items for 19X5.

11.5 The following are the income statement for the year ended 31 December 19X2 and the balance sheet as at 31 December 19X1 and 31 December 19X2 of Impossible Limited, based on historic cost.

	£	£
Profit and Loss Account		
Sales		1,200
less Opening inventory	100	
Purchases	800	
	900	
less Closing inventory	100	800
		400
less Expenses	150	
Depreciation	100	250
		150
add Dividend received		30
		180
less Proposed dividend		60
		120
Retained earnings at 1 January 19X2		100
Retained earnings at 31 December 19X2		£220

Balance Sheets

	31 December 19X2			31 December 19X1		
	£	£	£	£	£	£
Fixed assets, cost		800			500	
less Accumulated depreciation		300	500		200	300
Investment, at cost			100			100
Current assets						
Inventory		100			100	
Accounts receivable		140			150	
Cash		60			130	
		300			380	
less Current liabilities						
Accounts payable	120			100		
Proposed dividend	60	180	120	80	180	200
			£720			£600
Share capital			500			500
Retained earnings			220			100
			£720			£600

1. The following is an analysis of the fixed assets at 31 December 19X2.

Date of purchase	Cost	Depreciation charged to 31 December 19X1	Depreciation charge for 19X2	Index at date of purchase
1 January 19X0	£500	£200	£60	100
1 January 19X2	£300	—	£40	120
	£800	£200	£100	

£300

2. Inventory is valued on the FIFO basis and the average age of the units in inventory is three months.

3. The investment was acquired and the share capital subscribed on 1 January 19X0 (index 100).

4. A suitable general price index at various dates were:

	1 Oct X1	31 Dec X1	Average for 19X2	1 Oct X2	31 Dec X2
Index	110	120	140	150	160

5. Ignore taxation.

Prepare Impossible Limited's profit and loss account for the year ended 31 December 19X2 and its balance sheet as at that date, both expressed in pounds of 31 December 19X2.

12 | *Current Cost Accounting*

In March 1980 the Accounting Standards Committee issued SSAP 16, 'Current Cost Accounting', and at the same time published 'Guidance Notes on SSAP 16'. The Guidance Notes do not form part of SSAP 16 but they do cover a range of practical matters with the intention that the notes should help entities comply with the provisions of SSAP 16.

Scope of SSAP 16

The standard applies to all companies which have any class of share or loan listed on the stock exchange as well as to other larger entities. In order for an entity to be excluded on the grounds of size it must satisfy at least two of the following three criteria:

(a)   a turnover of less than £5,000,000 per annum

(b)   a balance sheet total (net book value of fixed assets plus investments plus current assets) compiled on the historical cost basis at the start of the relevant accounting period of less than £2,500,000.

(c)   an average number of UK employees of less than 250.

In addition certain types of business, including insurance companies, property investment and unit trusts are not required to apply the provisions of SSAP 16. The same exemption is granted to entities whose primary financial objective is not the earning of profit, for example, trade unions and charities.

The annual financial statements of entities which have to comply with SSAP 16 must include current cost accounts produced in accordance with the provision of the standard together with historical cost accounts or historical cost information. Thus, entities can either produce both current cost and historical cost accounts or simply the current cost accounts together with adequate historical cost information; the information should be sufficient as to enable a user of the accounts to ascertain the historical cost profit for the period. As we pointed out in Chapter 7 the requirements of the Companies Act, 1948 regarding the principles underlying the preparation of the accounts of limited companies are couched in very general terms and hence the omission of historical cost accounts would not constitute a breach of the Act.

THE MAIN PRINCIPLES OF CURRENT COST ACCOUNTING

We will first outline the main principles of current cost accounting (CCA) and will then provide a highly simplified example before proceeding to discuss the provisions of SSAP 16 in greater detail.

The Unit of Account

Current cost accounts are expressed in terms of the monetary unit (the pound). No adjustment is made for changes in general purchasing power. This follows from the recommendations of the Sandilands Committee who rejected both the CPP approval and the integration of CPP and current value accounting. This point will be discussed in a little more detail later in the Chapter (see pages 449 to 451). However, as will be described, SSAP 16 specifies a number of voluntary statements which companies can publish along with current cost accounts if they so decide and one of these is a statement of the change in shareholders' equity interest after allowing for the change in the general purchasing power of money.

The CCA Balance Sheet

In a CCA balance sheet assets should be recorded as their 'value to the business'. At this stage it is sufficient to state that the value to the business basis of valuation is very similar to the deprival value concept which we introduced in Chapter 10. In general, it will be fixed assets and stock which will be disclosed at different figures in a current cost balance sheet as compared with a historical balance sheet. The deprival value of monetary assets such as cash and debtors is equal to their face (or nominal) value and will therefore appear at the same values in balance sheets prepared under both conventions.

It can be argued that deferred monetary assets represent an exception to this rule as a strict application of the deprival value approach to the valuation of a debt which will not be repaid for, say, three years would value the asset at the present value of the future cash flow rather than the nominal value of the debt. While this argument is correct in principle the general view is that its implementation would cause considerable difficulties, especially the selection of the appropriate discount rate, and thus all monetary assets are recorded at their nominal values. Similarly, all liabilities including long term liabilities, are shown at their nominal values in the current cost balance sheet.

The current cost balance sheet includes a *current cost reserve account* to which all (realized and unrealized) holding gains are credited and holding losses are debited. In SSAP 16 holding gains and losses are referred to as *revaluation surpluses* and *deficits* and we shall henceforth adopt this terminology. As will be shown later the current cost reserve account is also used for other purposes.

THE CURRENT COST PROFIT AND LOSS ACCOUNT

A striking feature of the current cost profit and loss account is that it discloses two profit figures the *current cost operating profit* and the *current cost profit attributable to shareholders*. We shall deal with each of these in turn.

Current Cost Operating Profit

In Chapter 10 we defined an operating gain as the difference between the revenue for the period and the deprival value of the assets used up by the company in earning revenue measured at the dates of consumption. As we will show the current cost operating profit is a development of the operating gain concept. The difference between the two is that a monetary working capital adjustment is made when calculating the current cost operating profit.

The definition of current cost operating profit, together with two other important definitions, are given in paragraphs 38–40 of SSAP 16. These are reproduced below in reverse order:

Current cost operating profit is the surplus arising from the ordinary activities of the business in the period after allowing for the impact of price changes on the funds needed to continue the existing business and maintain its operating capability, whether financed by share capital or borrowing. It is calculated before interest on net borrowing and taxation (paragraph 40)

The *operating capability* of the business is the amount of goods and services which the business is able to supply with its existing resources in the relevant period. These resources are represented in accounting terms by the net operating assets at current cost (paragraph 39)

Net operating assets comprise the fixed assets (including trade investments), stock and monetary working capital dealt with in an historical cost balance sheet (paragraph 38)

Let us now examine the above definitions in some detail.

The current cost operating profit is the surplus on the 'ordinary activities' of the business; thus extraordinary items are not included in its computation.

It is the surplus 'after allowing for the impact of price changes on the funds needed to continue the existing business and maintain its operating capability'. The idea here is that a current cost operating profit is only achieved if (assuming that no capital is introduced or withdrawn) at the end of the period the company has sufficient funds to continue in existence and is able to maintain its operating capability (the latter will usually be the more stringent condition).

The concept here is a clear one, a company has only earned a surplus if it is at least as 'well off' at the end of the period as it was at the start. While the concept is clear its practical implementation is not because of the difficulties associated with the question of the measurement of welloffness. SSAP 16 deals with the problem by measuring welloffness in terms of a business' 'operating capability' but this is itself a vague concept and as can be seen above it is necessary to provide three further links in the argument before one arrives at a procedure which is capable of implementation in the context of an accounting system.

The first link is the statement that 'operating capability' is taken to be the goods and services which the business is able to supply in the relevant period. It will be instructive to consider what this would mean in the case of a very simple company trading in only one type of product. It might be that A Limited had sufficient funds at the start of 19X2 to produce and sell 100 widgets per month.*

Then it might be argued that A Limited's surplus for 19X2 is the difference between the funds available at the conclusion of 19X2 and the funds required to support the production and sale of 100 units per month at the prices prevailing at 31st December 19X2. It is obvious that such an approach based on the direct measurement of the quantity of goods and services supplied by the business will not work in the case of businesses which supply a wide range of goods and services which in any event change over time.

The ASC was thus forced to make a second step by moving from the measurement of output to the measurement of resources. Thus 'the operating capability of the business is the amount of goods and services which the business is able to supply with its *existing resources*'. While the point is not made clearly in the definition it is obvious from the rest of SSAP 16 that the business' resources are to be regarded as a proxy for the output which the business is able to sustain.

We have now reached the third link in the argument because paragraphs 38 and 39 state that resources may be regarded as comprising the fixed assets, stock, and monetary working capital** of a business.

*The meaning of 'relevant period' in the definition of operating capability is not altogether clear. Does it mean the accounting period or, and this seems more likely, does it cover the period of the working capital cycle (see Chapter 9)? However, since this definition is only a step towards the final outcome, this lack of clarity is not of great practical importance.

**Monetary working capital is discussed on page 430 but at this stage it can be stated that it usually consists of debtors and creditors and, possibly, cash and balances at banks and over-drafts.

The final section of the definition of current cost operating profit states that the surplus must be calculated regardless of the extent to which the resources (as defined) have been financed by borrowings. It must be pointed out that in this context 'borrowings' exclude current liabilities, the amount of which will have an impact on the calculation of current cost operating profit. As will be explained later the level of a business' long term borrowings will affect the current cost profit attributable to shareholders.

Following the above discussion and bearing in mind the various caveats it is possible to simplify and compress the definition of current cost operating profit as follows:

Current cost operating profit is the surplus for the period after allowing for the impact on price changes on the firms' fixed assets, stock and monetary working capital.

The Three Current Cost Operating Adjustments

In order to derive the current cost operating profit from the profit before interest and taxation three adjustments (known as the *current cost operating adjustments*) have to be made. These are:

1. The cost of sales adjustment (COSA). This is the difference between the cost of goods sold expense based on current cost (i.e. value to the business) and historical cost. (The COSA is the realized holding gain on stock).

2. The Depreciation Adjustment. This is the difference between the current cost and historical cost depreciation expense for the period. This is the realized holding gain on fixed assets.

3. The Monetary Working Capital Adjustment. This is (in times of rising prices) the additional sum which the business needs to invest in monetary working capital in order to maintain it in 'real terms', i.e. so that it can sustain the same level of activity. To take a simple example, assume that a company buys and sells on the following credit terms, debtors are allowed two months while creditors allow one month. Let us also assume that the company sells 100 units per month. The goods originally cost the company £20 each and were sold at a markup of 50%, i.e. for £30 each. If other items are ignored the company's investment in monetary working capital was:

Debtors 2 (month) × 100 × £30	£6,000
Less Creditors 1 (month) × 100 × £20	£2,000
Monetary Working Capital	£4,000

Now let us suppose that the cost of the goods to the company increase by 20% and that the company can pass the increase on to its customers, i.e. the markup of 50% is maintained. Then after the changes have worked their way through the system the company's investment in monetary working capital is:

Debtors 2 × 100 × £36	£7,200
Less Creditors 1 × 100 × £24	£2,400
Monetary Working Capital	£4,800

Thus it can be seen that, if it is the case that given the circumstances faced by the company the original credit terms have to be maintained, then it will have to invest an additional £800 in monetary working capital; in the simple example £800 is the monetary working capital adjustment.

We will now present a highly simplified example to show the impact of the three current cost operating adjustments. We must emphasize that the purpose of the example is to illustrate the basic principles involved and that the methods used to derive the three adjustments may not be suitable for use in practice, or in more complex artificial examples.

Example 12.1

A Limited's balance sheet at 1st January 19X5 is given below. All prices have remained constant since the formation of A Limited and here the balance sheet satisfies both the historical cost and current cost conventions:

	£		£
Share capital	1,200	Fixed Assets, cost	1,600
Reserves	1,800		
	3,000		
Long term loan		Stock	2,000
(interest free)	1,000		
		Debtors	1,000
		less Creditors	600
		Monetary Working	
		Capital	400
	£4,000		£4,000

Notes
1. The fixed assets were purchased on 1st January 19X5 and have an estimated life of 4 years. The assets are depreciated on a straight line basis; a zero scrap value is assumed.

2. All transactions took place on 30th June 19X5. In the period 1st January 19X5 to 30th June 19X5 the replacement cost* of the fixed assets increased by 30% and the replacement cost of stock increased by 20%.

---

*In this example it is assumed that the value to the business of assets is in all cases equal to their replacement costs.

3.   On 30th June 19X5, A Limited:

    (i) Collected all the debts outstanding at the start of the year, £1,000, and paid all the opening creditors, £600.

    (ii) Sold all the opening stock for £3,250 and purchased the same physical volume of stock for £2,400. £2,050 of sales and £1,680 of the purchases were for cash, thus closing debtors are £1,200 and the closing creditors are £720. Note that with these assumptions the relationship between stock, debtors and creditors shown in the opening balance sheet has been maintained in that they have all increased by 20%.

    (iii) Paid overheads of £100.

4.   A Limited's closing cash balance is then:

	£	£
Received from debtors		1,000
Cash sales		2,050
		3,050
Less Paid to creditors	600	
Cash purchases	1,680	
Overheads	100	2,380
		£ 670

It will be assumed (see page 430) that cash does not form part of monetary working capital.

A Limited's historical cost accounts for 19X5 are given below:

Historical Cost Profit and Loss Account
Year ended 31st December 19X5

	£	£
Sales		3,250
Less Opening stock	2,000	
Purchases	2,400	
	4,400	
Less Closing stock	2,400	
Cost of goods sold		2,000
Gross Profit		1,250
Less Overheads	100	
Depreciation	400	500
Net Profit		£ 750

Historical Cost Balance Sheet
as at 31st December 19X5

	£		£
Share capital	1,200	Fixed Assets	
Reserves at 1st Jan X5	1,800	net book value	1,200
Profit for 19X5	750	Stock, cost	2,400
	3,750	Debtors	1,200
Long term loan		*less* Creditors	720
(interest free)	1,000	Monetary Working	
		Capital	480
		Bank	670
	£4,750		£4,750

We will now calculate the three current cost operating adjustments.

1. *Cost of Sales*

We have assumed that all the opening stock was sold on 30th June 19X5. The replacement cost of the goods on that date was £2,400. Thus, the Realized Holding Gain on the stock was £400 (£2,400 − £2,000) while the operating gain was £850 (£3,250 (sales proceeds) − £2,400).

Thus, £2,400 is the cost of goods sold expense in the current cost profit and loss account.

The purpose of the current cost operating adjustment is to explain the differences between the historical cost profit (before interest, extraordinary items and taxation) and the current cost operating profit. The cost of goods sold expense in the historical cost profit account is £2,000. The cost of sales adjustment is £2,400 − £2,000 = £400.

2. *The Depreciation Adjustment*

The fixed asset is being written off over 4 years on a straight line basis assuming a zero scrap value. In other words it is assumed that 25% of the asset is used up each year. On the 30th June 19X5, the date on which it is assumed that all transactions took place, the replacement cost of the fixed assets was £2,080 i.e. 30% greater than the historical cost.

The depreciation charge in the current cost profit and loss account is then $\frac{£2,080}{4}$ = £520. Since the depreciation charge in the historical cost profit and loss account is £400 the depreciation adjustment is £120.

3. *Monetary Working Capital Adjustment (MWCA)*

In this simple example we assumed that the trade debtors and creditors both increased in proportion to the increase in the cost of the company's trading stock i.e. by 20%.

The opening balance on monetary working capital was £400 and hence in this example the MWCA is 0.20 × £400 = £80.

We can now find the current cost operating profit:

	£	£
Historical cost profit before taxation and interest		750
Less Current Cost Operating adjustments		
Cost of Sales Adjustment	400	
Depreciation Adjustment	120	
Monetary Working Capital Adjustment	80	600
Current Cost Operating Profit		£150

We will complete the accounts in example 12.2 after a discussion of the current cost profit attributable to shareholders.

Current Cost Profit Attributable to Shareholders

The current cost profit attributable to shareholders is defined as:

'the surplus for the period after allowing for the impact of price changes on the funds needed to maintain their (the shareholders') proportion of the operating capability. It is calculated after interest, taxation and extraordinary items'.*

In order to derive the current cost profit attributable to shareholders from the current cost operating profit the following adjustments are made:

(i)   The gearing adjustment (see below) which is normally in times of rising prices a credit adjustment.

(ii) Interest payable and receivable

(iii) Extraordinary items

(iv) Taxation

The Gearing Adjustment

In deriving the cost operating profit we confined our attention to the net operating assets of the business. We were interested in the amounts that had to be set aside to take account of the impact of the price increases on the stock, fixed assets and monetary working capital. The result is that the current cost operating profit is the maximum amount that could be paid out by way of dividends (or taxation) while allowing the company to replace its operating assets. Note that in example 12.1 the closing bank balance was £670. If a dividend equal to the current cost operating profit of £150 had been paid the bank balance would have been reduced to £520 and this is the amount required to replace the fixed asset used up during the year**. We need only consider the fixed assets in this context because the company has already purchased the replacement stock at the new higher price and has already increased its investment in monetary working capital.

The replacement cost of the fixed asset at the date on which one quarter of it was consumed (i.e. depreciation of 25% was recognized) was £2,080 and 25% of £2,080 is £520, which is equal to bank balance which would remain after the payment of a dividend of £150.

The current cost operating profit can therefore be regarded as the maximum that could be paid by way of interest on loans, dividends and taxation which would allow the company to maintain the net operating assets. However, this does not take account of the fact that most companies finance their assets through a mixture of owners' equity and long term loans of one form or another. It can therefore be argued that to say that the dividend should not exceed the company's current cost operating profit is unduly

---

*SSAP 16, paragraph 41

** Note that in more complex examples the existence of backlog depreciation (see page 414) could lead to a different result.

restrictive from the point of view of the shareholders as it might be expected that part of the additional investment required to cope with increased prices will be provided by the long term creditors.

SSAP 16 therefore requires an adjustment to be made to the current cost operating profit which takes account of the fact that a proportion of the additional funds required to cope with the increase in prices is attributable to the long term creditors. The adjustment is known as the *gearing adjustment* and is effected by crediting (in times of rising prices) the current cost profit and loss account with a proportion of the total of the three current cost operating adjustments. The proportion depends on the relationship between the long term funds provided by the shareholders and creditors. This relationship is known as the company's *gearing*. Gearing can be defined in a number of different ways but for the purposes of calculating the gearing adjustment gearing is defined in the following form:

$$\frac{\text{Long Term Creditors}^*}{\text{Long Term Creditors plus Shareholders' Interest}}$$

Thus if one third of the long term finance is deemed to be provided by creditors a credit of one third of the total of the current cost operating adjustments is made to the current cost profit and loss account. The corresponding debit is made to the current cost reserve account.

It can be said that the current cost operating profit is a profit measure viewed from the point of view of the business while the purpose of the current cost profit attributable to shareholders is to show the position from the standpoint of the shareholders (both ordinary and preference). The latter profit shows the surplus after allowing for the impact of price increases on the funds needed to maintain the shareholders' proportion of the operating capability; this can be regarded as the maximum dividend that could be paid to shareholders without reducing their interest in the net operating assets of the business.

In addition to the gearing adjustment other adjustments are made to the current cost operating profit to arrive at the current cost profit attributable to shareholders. Since the current cost operating profit is calculated without regard to the way in which the assets are financed it is not appropriate to include other interest payable or receivable in the computation of that aspect of profit but interest payable will reduce the maximum dividend that can be paid to shareholders while the maximum dividend will be increased by the amount of any interest received. The maximum size of the dividend is obviously reduced by the amount of taxation borne by the company and hence the current cost profit attributable to shareholders is stated after taxation. By definition the current cost operating profit only relates to 'ordinary activities' but no such limitation is included in the definition of the current cost profit attributable to shareholders and thus extra-

---

*For the purposes of current cost accounting some adjustment might have to be made to long term creditors to arrive at what is called net borrowing which is used to calculate the gearing adjustment (see page 435).

ordinary items are included in the adjustments which are made to the current cost operating profit to arrive at the current cost profit attributable to shareholders.

As we have now introduced the basic principles underlying the current cost profit attributable to shareholders we can now conclude in example 12.2 the accounts which we started to prepare in example 12.1. Example 12.2 will also include the format of a current cost profit and loss account as illustrated in an appendix to SSAP 16. At the conclusion of example 12.2 we will return to our discussion of the current cost profit attributable to shareholders and suggest that the definition provided in SSAP 16 is capable of improvement.

Example 12.2

This example continues the illustration which was started in example 12.1.

In concluding that example we calculated the three current cost operating adjustments and the current cost operating profit.

We must now deal with the 'other side' of the entries relating to the current cost operating adjustments. The cost of sales and monetary working capital adjustments are credited to the current cost reserve account and the depreciation adjustment is credited to the Fixed Assets – Accumulated Depreciation Account.

Before proceeding to calculate the gearing adjustment we will prepare an interim current cost balance sheet. As we shall see later it is necessary to prepare the balance sheet in order to calculate the gearing adjustment. The current cost profit and loss account only deals with realized revaluation surpluses which will be debited to the appropriate asset account (fixed assets, stock) and credited to the revaluation reserve account. In this simple example there is no unrealized revaluation surplus on stock as it has been assumed that the cost of stock has not increased from the date of purchase. There is, however, an unrealized surplus arising from the increase in the replacement cost of fixed assets. The value to the business of the fixed assets at 1 January 19X5 was £1,600 and, ignoring depreciation, this increased by 30% to £2,080 by 31 December 19X5. The total revaluation surplus is £480 and of this a quarter is considered to be realized; i.e. the £120 depreciation adjustment, and the balance is unrealized. In order to show the complete picture £480 has to be credited to the current cost reserve account and debited to Fixed Assets – Cost Account. The phrase 'Fixed Asset – Cost Account' is not appropriate to the current cost accounting model and hence it is replaced by 'Fixed Assets – Gross Replacement Cost Account'.

We are now in a position to prepare the current cost balance sheet at 31 December 19X5 before the gearing adjustment:

	Historical Cost Balance Sheet as at 31 Dec 19X5	Changes	Current Cost Balance Sheet as at 31 Dec 19X5 before the Gearing Adjustment
	£	£	£
Fixed Assets			
Cost/Gross Replacement Cost	1,600	(a) 480	2,080
Accumulated Depreciation	(400)	(b) (120)	(520)
Stock	2,400		2,400
Debtors	1,200		£ 1,200
Bank	670		670
	£5,470		£5,830

Share Capital	1,200		1,200
Reserves at 1 Jan X5	1,800		1,800
Profit for 19X5	750	{ (b) (120) { (c) (400) { (d) (80)	150
Current Cost Reserve		{ (a) 480 { (c) 400 { (d) 80	960
Shareholders' interest	3,750		4,110
Long Term Loan	1,000		1,000
Creditors	720		720
	£5,470		£5,830

Gearing Adjustment

The gearing adjustment is the product of the gearing proportion and the sum of the current cost operating adjustments. The latter figure is known, £600 (see example 12.1) and the difficulty is to calculate the gearing proportion, i.e. the relationship between net borrowing (in this case the long term loan) and shareholders' interest. If we inspect the opening balance sheet (see page 401) it can be seen that the relevant proportion is:

$$\frac{\text{Net Borrowing}}{\text{Net Borrowing} + \text{Shareholders' Interest}}$$

$$= \frac{£1,000}{£3,000 + £1,000} = 0.25$$

Now it can be argued that if outsiders were prepared to finance 25% of the company's net operating assets on 1 January 19X5 then, in the absence of evidence to the contrary, it might be argued that they would be prepared to maintain this level of gearing by lending additional sums to match the increase in the shareholders' interest. If this argument was accepted the gearing proportion would be 0.25.

However, SSAP 16 specifies that the proportion should in general be based on the average values of net borrowing and shareholders' interest and we will therefore adopt this approach and use the averages of the values disclosed by the opening and closing balance sheets.

		1 Jan X5 £	31 Dec X5 £	Average £
Net borrowing	(L)	1,000	1,000	1,000
Shareholders' Interest	(S)	3,000	4,110	3,555

The gearing proportion is:

$$\frac{L}{L+S} = \frac{1,000}{4,555} = 0.22$$

Note that the figures are taken from the current cost accounts and that the shareholders' interest at 31 December 19X5 can be found even though the gearing adjustment is unknown. The recognition of the gearing adjustment does not change the total of shareholders' interest but simply alters its composition; the balance on the profit and loss account, will, usually, be increased with a corresponding decrease in the current cost reserve.

The total of the current cost operating adjustments is £600 (debit) and as the gearing proportion is 0.22 the gearing adjustment is 0.22 × £600 = £132. Thus £132 will be credited to the current cost profit and loss account and debited to the current cost reserve account.

Current Cost Accounts

We are now in a position to present A Limited's current cost accounts. We will follow the format illustrated in the appendix to SSAP 16 but will not, in this introductory example, display all the notes to the accounts which are specified and suggested in the standard.

A Limited
Current Cost Profit and Loss Account
Year ended 31 December 19X5

		£
Turnover		£3,250
Profit before interest and taxation on the historical cost basis		750
Less Current cost operating adjustments (Note 1)		600
Current Cost Operating Profit		150
Less		
Gearing adjustment	(132)	
Interest payable less receivable	—	(132)
Current cost profit before taxation		282
Less Taxation		—
Current Cost Profit Attributable to Shareholders		282
Dividends		—
Retained current cost profit for the year		£ 282

Statement of retained profits/reserves

	£
Retained current cost profit of the year	282
Movements on current cost reserve (Note 2)	828
Movements on other reserves	—
	1,110
Retained reserves at the beginning of the year	1,800
Retained reserves at the end of the year	£2,910

Current Cost Balance Sheet as at 31st December 19X5

	£	£
Fixed Assets		
Gross Replacement Cost		2,080
Accumulated Depreciation		520
Net Replacement Cost		1,560
Current Assets less Liabilities		
Stock	2,400	
Net monetary assets (£1,200 − £720)	480	
Balance at Bank	670	3,550
		£5,110

Financed by:

		£
Share Capital and Reserves		
Share Capital		1,200
Current Cost Reserve		828
Other Reserves and Retained Profits		2,082
Shareholders' interest		4,110
Long Term Loan		1,000
		£5,110

Notes

1. *Current Cost Operating Adjustments*

	£
Cost of Sales	400
Monetary Working Capital	80
Depreciation	120
	£600

2. *Current Cost Reserve*

	£	£	£
Balance at 1st January 19X5			Nil
Revaluation surpluses reflecting price changes:			
Fixed Assets	480		
Stock	400	880	
Monetary working capital adjustment		80	
Gearing adjustment		(132)	828
			£828
of which – realized			468
unrealized			360
			£828

In this case the only unrealised surplus is in respect of the fixed assets and is the difference between the net replacement cost as disclosed in the current cost balance sheet (£1,560) and the net book value of the fixed assets as shown in the historical cost balance sheet (£1,200). The balance of the current cost reserve account is made up of realised surpluses.

Current Cost Attributable to Shareholders and the Gearing Adjustment

Now we have presented a complete, albeit simple, example of a set of current cost accounts we can re-examine the interpretation that can be placed on the current cost profit attributable to shareholders. Let us assume that A Limited – the subject of examples 12.1 and 12.2 – paid a dividend of £282 which would be equal to the current cost profit attributable to shareholders. The bank balance would fall to £388 and hence the remaining balance would not be sufficient to replace the 25% of the fixed asset used up in the course of the year, i.e. £520 (see page 404).

The shortfall is due to the gearing adjustment which represents the impact of price increases on that proportion of the assets financed by net borrowing. Thus, it can be seen that unless the suppliers of net borrowings actually do increase their loans, the payment of a dividend equal to the current cost profit attributable to shareholders will lead to a potential decrease in the operating capability of the business. It could be argued that it is unfortunate that the definition of current cost profit attributable to shareholders does not refer to the potential erosion of the operating capability of the business.

We have now completed our introduction to current cost accounting in which we have attempted to provide an overview of the complete system and we will now discuss the main elements of current cost accounting in a little more detail. It must be emphasized that it will not be possible to cover all aspects exhaustively in the space available but we will indicate those areas where further reading will be required.

Value to the business

The value to the business approach to asset valuation which is a key element of current cost accounting is very similar to the Deprival Value basis which we introduced in Chapter 10 but there are some slight differences the practical importance of which relate to those circumstances where the value to the business is not given by an asset's replacement cost. The definition of value to the business provided in SSAP 16 is as follows:

"Value to the business is:

(a) net current replacement cost:

 or, if a permanent diminution to below net current replacement cost has been recognized,

(b) recoverable amount"*

where the recoverable amount is defined as "the greater of the net realizable value of and asset, and, where applicable, the amount recoverable from its further use"**

The phrase net current replacement cost is the CCA equivalent of historical cost's net book value. As we shall show (see page 411), fixed assets are normally valued by the application of a conventional depreciation method to the replacement cost of an unused asset, i.e. the asset's gross current replacement cost.

An asset's value to the business will not be based on replacement cost when there has been a 'permanent diminution' before replacement cost. SSAP 16 does not discuss the circumstances where a permanent diminution has been recognized but some help is provided in the Guidance Notes in the

---

*SSAP 16, para 42
**SSAP 16, para 43

case of fixed assets*.

Two situations are described. The asset may be one which is withdrawn from use and is to be sold or scrapped. In this case the recoverable amount is the current realizable amount net of realization expenses. It will be noted that in these circumstances the asset would normally be reclassified as a current asset. The second case is where the asset continues in use for a period and in these circumstances the asset would be valued by reference to the estimated cash flows arising from future use and its ultimate disposal. The Guidance Notes emphasize that in most circumstances it would not be necessary to discount the future cash flows. No justification is provided from this departure from a strict application of the principles of deprival value but it is likely that the change was made in order to avoid the difficulties associated with the selection of an appropriate discount rate. In any event, it will usually be difficult to associate cash flows with a particular asset and it is clear that the identification and valuation of fixed assets which continue in use but which are to be valued at a figure less than their net current replacement cost will usually be a highly subjective process.

The treatment of stock and work in process is usually much clearer. The value to the business of stock and work in process will be the lower of current replacement and net realizable value.

Fixed Assets

While no distinction between different classes of fixed assets is made in SSAP 16, the Guidance Notes distinguish between plant and machinery (defined as physical assets other than land and buildings), land and buildings and wasting and intangible assets.

Plant and Machinery

We will first deal with the more common situation where the value to the business of a fixed asset is based on its replacement cost.

The general rule is that the value to the business of an existing asset is the net current cost of a replacement asset which has a similar useful output or service capacity.** Note that the emphasis is placed on what the asset can do rather than the asset itself. However, in most cases the value to the business of fixed assets is found by 'revaluing' the existing asset in terms of its current replacement cost. We shall concentrate on the more common situation but we shall briefly discuss other cases later in this section.

The net current replacement cost of plant and machinery is based on its gross replacement cost (usually the replacement cost of a new asset) and the proportion of the asset which is deemed to remain at the date of valuation. In other words the introduction of current cost accounting did not mean that the problems associated with depreciation were avoided. It is still necessary

*Guidance Notes to SSAP 16, paragraph 29

**Guidance Notes to SSAP 16, paragraph 10

to estimate the life of an asset, its scrap value and to decide on the way in which the asset is to be written off or depreciated. SSAP 16 is silent on the question of how the gross replacement cost of a fixed asset should be determined but the topic is dealt with at some length in the Guidance Notes, where it is suggested (paragraph 17) that the most convenient method of calculating the gross current replacement cost of a fixed asset is normally through the application of relevant price indices to the existing gross book values. A business can use indices produced and published by Government Agencies* or generally recognized privately produced indices. Alternatively the indices can be prepared by the business itself on the basis of its own purchasing experience. It can be seen that the ASC is not prescriptive about the way in which the data requirements for current cost accounting should be satisfied and that companies are allowed a considerable amount of lattitude. This approach does enable more realistic figures to be produced, in the sense that the figures can reflect more closely the circumstances surrounding the particular business, but it does mean a potential loss of objectivity and comparability. Objectivity might be lost in those cases where a company relies on its own experience for it will obviously be difficult for an outsider to check the figures. The considerable degree of lattitude allowed does generally lead to a loss of comparability, in that given a range of alternatives exists different businesses may select different alternatives. For example, two businesses may have similar holdings of fixed assets but one may choose to use an officially produced index while the other may use an internally produced index.

Another problem is the extent to which a company's holding of plant and machinery are disaggregated for the purposes of the application of index numbers. A separate series of index numbers would normally be applied to the main sub-categories of plant and machinery; vehicles, furniture and fittings and machinery. However, a company which is engaged in a number of different industries might decide to use different index numbers for assets used in each of the different trades.

While the use of different index numbers will produce different results for the gross current replacement cost of fixed assets, the differences will be reduced over time as the underlying causes of price increases, including the costs of raw materials and labour, will effect all series of index numbers. Thus, companies should, having selected their indices, continue to use the same indices in succeeding periods. This remark, as should all other similar statements about the consistent use of accounting methods, must be qualified by the observation that methods should be changed if it is believed that they no longer produce realistic results.

The problems caused by the lattitude allowed by the ASC should not be exaggerated since the variations in the values of fixed assets disclosed in current cost balance sheets will normally be far less than those which are found in historical cost balance sheets as in the historical cost system the values will usually depend on the dates on which the assets were acquired.

---

*HM Stationery Office publishes 'Price Index Numbers for Current Cost Accounting' and 'Current Cost Accounting – Guide to price indices for Overseas Countries'.

Cases where the use of index numbers will not be appropriate

It may be found that there is no suitable price index for a particular asset. Even where apparently suitable indices are available the directors may believe that their use may not yield realistic current replacement costs. This may occur because there have been substantial technological changes or because the original cost of the assets (to which the index would be applied) was affected by special circumstances which are unlikely to be repeated and for which allowance cannot accurately be made. In such cases the gross current replacement cost of the asset should be based on expert opinion or other evidence of its current cost.

One aspect of the general problem is discussed in some detail in appendix (i) of the Guidance Notes which is entitled 'Modern equivalent asset'. This appendix deals with those situations where there is a substantial difference between the asset whose value is being sought and its modern equivalent in respect of one or more of three features, operating costs, life, or output. It is suggested in the appendix that the problem might be reduced by the use of broadly based price indices which because they cover a greater range of assets will be less affected by the improvements in the particular type of asset. However, in extreme cases where major assets are involved it may be necessary to make specific calculations which take account of changes in service potential.

Suppose that X Ltd. purchased a machine for £120,000 on 1st January 19X4 when an appropriate price index was 120. The machine had an estimated life of ten years. Let us assume that on 31st December 19X9 the value of the price index increased to 160. However, the modern machines have lower operating costs; we will assume that the operating costs of the modern machines are some £6,000 per year less than those of the old machines and the cost of the new machines are £180,000 each*. Should the gross current replacement cost be £180,000 or £160,000 (i.e. £120,000 × 160/120) or some other figure? In this case it is likely that the best estimate will be obtained by adjusting the identified cost of replacement to take account of the differences between the features of the old and new machines. In this case the only difference is the lower operating costs and the present value of the savings could be calculated. If a discount rate of 16% is used the present value of £6,000 per year for ten years is £29,000 and on this basis the gross current replacement cost of the asset is £151,000 (£180,000 − £29,000).

It must be emphasized that calculations of the above type are only required in the case of substantial assets. In the vast majority of cases the gross current replacement cost will be found by the application of a suitable price index.

The difference between the gross current replacement cost at the balance sheet date and the equivalent value at the start of the year (or historical cost if the asset was purchased during the year) is credited (or debited if prices fall) to the current cost reserve account.

---

*Note that the current price of the new machine is not the same as the value that would be derived from the application of the price index. The reason for this is that an index is an average figure based on the movements of the prices of a number of items.

Depreciation of Plant and Machinery

The principle of current cost accounting requires that the depreciation expense for the year should be the 'value to the business' of the assets consumed during the year. Strict adherence to the principle requires that the depreciation expense be based on the asset's average value for the year (assuming that transactions take place evenly over the year) but the Guidance Notes suggest that in practice the value may be based on either the fixed asset's average value for the year or its value at the end of the year.

Backlog Depreciation

In a current cost accounting balance sheet plant and machinery will be shown at net current replacement cost, i.e. gross current replacement cost less accumulated depreciation. As with historical cost accounting the accumulated depreciation can be regarded as the proportion of the asset which is deemed to have been consumed or used up at the balance sheet date. There is however, an additional problem in current cost accounting because the accumulated depreciation will not be equal to the sum of the depreciation charges made in the profit and loss account. The difference between the required balance on accumulated depreciation and the sum of the depreciation charges is known as *backlog depreciation*. There are two elements in backlog depreciation. Current year backlog depreciation will arise when depreciation is based on the average value for the year and not the year end value.

Suppose that an asset was purchased for £5,000 on 1st January 19X3 when the index was 100. The asset is to be written off on a straight line basis over five years with a zero scrap value. Let us assume that the index on 31st December 19X3 was 130.

The gross current replacement cost at 31st December 19X3 is £6,500 (£5,000 × 130/100) and the current cost accounting depreciation charge for 19X3 based on average values is:

$$0.20 \text{ of } \tfrac{1}{2} £(5,000 + 6,500) = £1,150$$

But at 31st December 19X3 20% of the asset has been used up and hence the required balance on accumulated depreciation at that date is 0.20 of £6,500 = £1,300 and the asset will appear on the current cost balance sheet at 31st December 19X3 as follows:

	£
	£
Gross current replacement cost	6,500
Less: Accumulated Depreciation	1,300
Net current replacement cost	£5,200

The difference between the required balance on the accumulated depreciation account £1,300 and the depreciation charge for the year £1,150 is the current year backlog of £150. This figure is debited to the current cost reserve account and hence the net credit to the current cost reserve account in respect of the asset is:

	£
Increase in gross current replacement cost £6,500 − £5,000	1,500
Less: Backlog depreciation	150
	£1,350

The second element of backlog depreciation, prior year backlog, will arise in years other than the one in which the asset is purchased. Prior year backlog is caused by the revaluation of that part of the asset which has already been used up. Let us suppose that the price index applicable to the asset referred to above increased to 150 by 31st December 19X4. The increase in the gross replacement cost of the asset in 19X4 is £1,000 (i.e. £6,500 × 150/130 − £6,500). But 20% of the asset had been used up by 1st January 19X4 and hence 20% of the increase in the gross current replacement cost is regarded as the prior year element of backlog depreciation.

The following extended example shows the impact of both elements of backlog depreciation.

Machine X was purchased for £10,000 on 1 January 19X4 and it was expected that it would last for four years. We will assume that estimates of the asset's gross replacement cost will be based on a price index. Since the asset is expected to last for four years it might be helpful if we visualized the asset as consisting of four blocks each of which will be used up in each of the four years.

Assume that the index was 100 on 1 January 19X4 and 110 on 31 December 19X4.

The position at the end of 19X4 may be illustrated as follows:

Block 1	Block 2	Block 3	Block 4
	£2,750	£2,750	£2,750	£2,750

Depreciation
charge £2,625

 Backlog depreciation

The asset is revalued — the gross replacement cost at 31 December 19X4 is £11,000 (£10,000 × $\frac{110}{100}$) and each of the blocks is £2,750.

The depreciation charge for 19X4 based on average values is $\frac{£\frac{1}{2}(10,000 + 11,000)}{4}$ = £2,625. But at the end of the year one of the blocks has been used up i.e. the backlog depreciation is £125 (£2,750 − £2,625).

The net revaluation surplus is then the difference between the gross replacement cost of the asset and its cost less backlog depreciation, i.e. £11,000 − £10,000 − £125 = £875. The net current replacement cost at the year end is £11,000 − (£2,625 + £125) = £8,250.

19X5

Assume that there is no change in the estimated life of the asset and that the year-end index is 115.

The gross replacement cost of the asset is increased to £11,500 (£11,000 × $\frac{115}{110}$) and each of the blocks is now £2,875 (25 per cent of £11,500).

$$\text{Depreciation charge for 19X5} = \frac{£\frac{1}{2}(11,000 + 11,500)}{4} = £2,812.$$

Diagramatically the position is:

Block 1   Block 2   Block 3   Block 4
used up in   used up in
19X4   19X5

       2,875   2,875   2,875   2,875

  Written off in   Depreciation
       19X4   charge
      £2,750   £2,812

Backlog depreciation

Backlog depreciation for 19X5 is made up of two components (as will be the case for all years other than the one in which an asset is purchased). The first £125 is due to the increase in the valuation of the block that was consumed in 19X4. The block is now valued at £2,875 but only £2,750 was written off. The second part is a consequence of calculating depreciation on the average value of the asset. The second component is £63 (£2,875 − £2,812). The total backlog depreciation is thus £188 (£125 + £63).

The above discussion may be summarized as follows:

	£	£
Gross current replacement cost 31st December 19X5		11,500
Net current replacement cost 31st December 19X5 (50 per cent of £11,500)		5,750
Accumulated depreciation required at 31st December 19X5		5,750
Less:		
Accumulated depreciation 1st January 19X5	2,750	
Depreciation charge for 19X5	2,812	5,562
Backlog depreciation		£ 188

The net revaluation surplus for 19X5 is given by: £

Increase in gross current replacement cost
£11,500 − £11,000 500

Less: Backlog depreciation 188

Net revaluation surplus £312

19X6

We will once again assume that there is no change in the estimated life of the asset. We will assume that the price index declines in 19X6 and it should be noted that exactly the same principles apply.

Let the year end index be 111.

Gross current replacement cost at
31st December 19X6 $= £11,500 \times \frac{111}{115} = £11,100$

The depreciation charge for 19X6 is then

$$\frac{£\frac{1}{2}(11,500 + £11,100)}{4} = £2,825$$

The backlog depreciation for 19X6 can then be calculated as follows:

	£	£
Gross current replacement cost at 31 December 19X6 $£11,500 \times \frac{111}{115}$		11,100
Net current replacement cost at 31 December 19X6 (25 per cent of £11,100)		2,775
Accumulated depreciation required at 31 December 19X6		8,325
less Accumulated depreciation 31 December 19X5	5,750	
Depreciation charge for 19X6	2,825	8,575
Backlog depreciation		£(250)

The total net deficit on revaluation is given by:

	£
Decrease in gross current replacement cost 11,500 − 11,100	400
less Backlog depreciation	250
Net revaluation deficit	£150

The net revaluation deficit will be debited to the current cost reserve account.

We should point out the effect on the funds required for the replacement of the asset of not charging backlog depreciation to the profit and loss account. If the whole of the current cost profits are paid out as dividends, insufficient assets will be retained, whether in a liquid form or not, to replace the asset. In order to illustrate this point we will suppose that the recently mentioned machine X was the company's sole asset and that its balance sheet as at the date of acquisition of the machine was:

Share capital	£10,000
Machine	£10,000

We will also assume that in each year the whole of the current cost profit was distributed and that the machine was sold, for its net current replacement cost of £2,775 on 1 January 19X7. The company's balance sheet, just after the sale would be:

	£
Share capital	10,000
Current cost reserve	1,037
	£11,037
Sundry assets *less* Liabilities	£11,037

The balance of the current cost reserve account at 1 January 19X7 is:

	£
19X4 Increase	875
19X5 Increase	312
	1,187
less	
19X6 Decrease	150
	£1,037

The sources of the company's assets less liabilities at 1st January 19X7 were:

	£
Sale of machine	2,775
Funds not distributed being equal to the sum of the depreciation charges (£2,625 + £2,812 + £2,825)	8,262
	£11,037

£11,100 would be required to replace the machine on 1st January 19X7. The difference of £63 between this and the £11,037 available is the cumulative total of backlog depreciation that has accrued over the life of the machine (i.e. £125 + £188 − £250 = £63).

Backlog depreciation is debited to the current cost reserve account and not the current cost profit and loss account because of the principle that the current cost profit should be based on the difference between the revenue for the period and the 'value to the business' of the assets used up in period.

Land and Buildings

SSAP 16 makes no distinction between different types of fixed assets but the Guidance Notes suggest that different ways of applying the same basic principles should be adopted in certain cases. One example is land and buildings. The Guidance Notes draw a distinction between specialized and non-specialized buildings. Specialized buildings are those which are by their nature rarely sold except as part of the business in which they are used e.g. oil refineries. Clearly such buildings are essentially large chunks of machinery and it is suggested that specialized buildings should be treated in the same way as the generality of plant and machinery. Thus their value to the business will normally be found by reference to the gross current replacement cost of the asset as adjusted by the recognition of depreciation. The land, associated with specialized buildings should, however, be treated in the same way as non-specialized buildings.

A different approach is advocated for all land and for non-specialized buildings because the value to the business of such assets will normally be found by an expert valuation in their present condition.

The value to the business of plant and machinery can also be based on expert opinion but there are two differences between the use of expert opinion in the case of plant and machinery and land and buildings. In the case of plant and machinery expert opinion will only be used in the minority of instances and valuations made will be of the gross current replacement cost. In contrast land and non-specialised buildings will always be based on expert opinion and in these cases it will be the net current replacement cost. A consequence of the second of the two differences is that a current cost balance sheet will disclose only the net current replacement cost of land and non-specialized buildings (i.e. the 'gross value' and accumulated depreciation are not shown).

Land and non-specialized buildings which are to be retained by the business should be valued by reference to the estimated cost of purchasing the property on the open market. The value may be increased by virtue of expenditure on adaption but adaption costs should be valued in the same way as plant and machinery. Land and non-specialized buildings which are surplus to the present and future needs of the business should be valued at their net realizable value; the open market value less the costs of disposal.

Valuation should be made by professionally qualified and experienced valuers but need not be made annually, however, it is expected that no more than five years should elapse between valuations.

Depreciation of non-specialized buildings

SSAP 12 (Accounting for depreciation) applies to current cost accounting and hence depreciation must be provided on buildings. The difficulty is to distinguish in a year in which a revaluation is made between changes due to price movements which are credited, or debited, to the current cost reserve account and changes due to the reduction in service potential which are charged to the current cost profit and loss account as the depreciation expense.

Let us assume that the value to the business of a non-specialized building at 1st January 19X1 is £800,000 and that the building's estimated life measured from that date was 21 years. Suppose that the building was revalued at 31st December 19X1 at £900,000 but that no change was made in the estimate of the life of the asset (20 years from 31st December 19X1).

The depreciation charge for 19X1 can be regarded as being equal to £900,000 divided by the remaining life of the building, 20 years, i.e. £45,000. The value before the depreciation charge is £900,000 + £45,000 = £945,000 and as the value to the business of the building at the beginning of the year was £800,000, the transfer to the current cost reserve is £945,000 − £800,000 = £145,000. The adjustments can be summarized as follows:

Debit, Land and Buildings	£100,000
Debit, Profit and Loss Account	
(the depreciation expense)	45,000
Credit, Current Cost Reserve	145,000

If the building is not revalued in 19X2 the depreciation expense for 19X2 would, given that depreciation is being provided on a straight line basis, be the same as the 19X1 figure. In general, if straight line depreciation is used (which is of course usually adopted for such assets), the depreciation expense for a year in which the asset is not revalued is found by dividing the value of the asset at the beginning of the year by its life measured from the same date.

Wasting and Intangible Assets

Wasting assets are those fixed assets such as mines which could not be renewed in their present location. If they are included in a balance sheet they should be included at their value to the business using the best estimate of current costs.

Intangible assets such as patents and copyrights present particular problems. The Guidance Notes suggest that they should if possible be shown at their value to the business but if this is not practicable they should be included in the current cost balance sheet at their historical cost.

Investments

Investments which are treated as current assets are included in the current cost balance sheet at cost unless, as with historical cost accounting, part of the cost has been written off.

Other investments (other than those in associated companies) should be shown at the directors' valuation. If the investments are listed and there is a material difference between the directors' estimate and the mid market price, the basis of the valuation and the reasons for the difference should be stated by way of a note to the accounts.

An investment in an associated company should be shown in the balance sheet of the investing company or in the group balance sheet at the appropriate proportion of the associated company's net assets valued by reference to current cost accounting principles plus, if applicable, any goodwill arising on acquisition.

Goodwill on Consolidation

SSAP 14 requires that the net assets of a subsidiary should be revalued at the date of acquisition. Hence, the difference between the cost of the investment and the book value of the assets less liabilities at the date of acquisition will only relate to intangible assets which means that the goodwill on consolidation in the group's current cost balance sheet will be the same as the corresponding figure in the historical cost balance sheet. If the goodwill on consolidation had been established before the introduction of SSAP 14 it is possible that the subsidiary's assets were not revalued at the date of acquisition. In such a case goodwill consolidation will include an element due to the difference between the current costs and book values of the subsidiary's assets at the date of acquisition i.e. the unrealized surpluses. When preparing the consolidated current cost balance sheet an adjustment has to be made to remove this portion of the goodwill on consolidation and this is effected by crediting goodwill and debiting the current cost reserve account with an estimate of the unrealized surplus on the subsidiary's assets at the date of acquisition.

Readers who wish to know more of the problems associated with the preparation of group current cost accounts should refer to Part IV of the guidance notes to SSAP 16.

Disposal of Fixed Assets

When an asset is sold the difference between the net current replacement cost at the date of sale and the equivalent value at the last balance sheet date should be taken to the current cost reserve. If there is a difference on disposal, it is charged or credited to the current cost profit and loss account.

Entries following the recognition of a permanent diminution to below net current replacement cost

The general rule is that only changes due to price movements should be credited or debited to the current cost reserve account. Changes in net book value due to changes in service potential are dealt with in the profit and loss account. The recognition of a permanent diminution to below net current replacement cost is regarded as a decision which is based on a change in service potential of an asset and hence the difference between the asset's net current replacement cost and its recoverable amount (i.e. the greater of its net realizable value and the amount recoverable from further use) is charged to the profit and loss account. If the asset is retained the amounts recoverable from future use will be written off to the profit and loss account. However, the Guidance Notes propose that if there are subsequent changes in the price level the remaining recoverable amount should be adjusted through the current cost reserve account.

Stock

A distinction has to be made between stock which is and which is not subject to the cost of sales adjustment (COSA). The distinction is not clear cut but it can be said that stock subject to the COSA is that part of a business stock which will be replaced by identical or broadly similar items. In contrast, stock not subject to the COSA will consist of those items whose replacement costs cannot be determined and those items of stock which are not to be replaced by the purchase of identical or broadly similar items.

The cost of goods sold expense in the current cost profit and loss account relating to stock subject to the COSA is based on the stock's value to the business at the date of consumption while the closing stock is included in the closing balance sheet at its value to the business at the balance sheet date. Stock *not* subject to the COSA is treated differently and is included in both the current cost profit and loss account and balance sheet at historical cost. However, the impact of price changes on stock not subject to the COSA is reflected in the accounts in so far that such stock is treated as part of the business' monetary working capital and hence affects the monetary working capital adjustment. We will return to the topic of stock not subject to COSA after dealing with the monetary working capital adjustment.

Stock subject to the Cost of Sales Adjustment

The value to the business of stock is the lower of its current replacement cost and its net realizable value (the latter being the recoverable amount of stock). The comparison of current replacement cost and net realizable value should ideally be made separately for each item. Where this is impracticable the comparison should be made of groups of similar items. A comparison of the total replacement cost of stock and work in progress with its total net realizable value is rejected on the grounds that it could result in the overstatement of the value to the business of the stock and work in progress. For example:

	Replacement cost	Net realizable value
Item A	£10	£12
Item B	14	8
	£24	£20

The value to the business of stock is £18 (£10 + £8) and not £20.

No single method is prescribed for determining the current replacement cost of stock. The Guidance Notes simply suggest that the methods should be appropriate to the circumstances of the business. In many instances the use of suitable price indices is found to be the most convenient method. The current replacement cost of work in progress and finished goods can be obtained by calculating the current replacement costs of the various inputs (raw materials, labour and overheads) which have been used to bring the stock and work in progress to its present condition.

Cost of Goods Sold Expense

The principle of current cost accounting requires that the cost of goods sold expense should be based on the 'value to the business' of the goods sold. This will normally be their replacement cost as at the dates of sale. In order to strictly apply this principle, companies would have to know these current replacement costs.

Suppose that a company sells goods which have an historical cost of £30 and that it can be shown that it would cost the company £38 to replace them at the date of sale. The entry dealing with the cost of goods sold expense would then appear as follows:

	Debit £	Credit £
Cost of goods sold expense	38	
Stock		30
Current Cost Reserve Account		8

The Averaging Method

When stock and work in progress includes a large number of different items it will usually be impractical to determine the value to the business of each unit as it is sold. In practice a commonly used method which is based on the use of price indices is the averaging method which is the subject of Appendix (iii) of the Guidance Notes.

Underlying the averaging method is the assumption that the cost of purchases* made during a period is an acceptable approximation to the current replacement cost (RC) of goods at the dates of sale.

Suppose that Anne Limited's purchases and sales for March 19X9 are as follows:

	2 March	5 March	18 March	25 March
Purchases	5 units @ £10		10 units @ £13	
Sales		8 units		12 units

*For simplicity we will only refer to purchases but similar principles are applicable to manufacturing companies.

The CCA cost of goods sold is:

$$8 \text{ units} \times \text{RC at 5 March} + 12 \text{ units} \times \text{RC at 25 March}$$

If the averaging method is used, and the calculations are on a monthly basis, the cost of goods sold expense will be:

20 units × £12 (average cost of purchases in March, i.e. £180 ÷ 15)

It is argued that the approximation is acceptable when stock volumes are reasonably constant or have changed at a fairly steady rate. Conversely, the approximation would not be acceptable if, say, purchases were made infrequently in large quantities, with sales taking place more evenly during the intervening periods.

The objective of the averaging method is to find a *cost of sales adjustment* such that:

Historical cost of goods sold + cost of sales adjustment = number of units sold × average cost of purchases.

Suppose that we are presented with the following information:

	£
Book values, based on FIFO of:	
Opening stock	400
Closing stock	2,000
Average cost per unit of:	
Opening stock	4
Purchases made during the year	6
Closing stock	10

The increase in the book value of the stock is £1,600 some of it due to increase in physical volume and some to increased prices. We first need to see how much of the increase is due to the change in the physical volume. This can be done by thinking in terms of equivalent units (total book value divided by the average cost per unit).

Opening stock

$$\text{Number of equivalent units} = \frac{\text{Book value}}{\text{Average cost}} = \frac{£400}{£4} = 100$$

Closing stock

$$\text{Number of equivalent units} = \frac{\text{Book value}}{\text{Average cost}} = \frac{£2,000}{£10} = 200$$

These are equivalent and not actual units, because there will be a number of different types of goods in stock, and all we have been told is the average cost of units.

For the purposes of our explanation we will assume that the purchases for the year amounted to £7,200, but note that the figure has been assumed simply to aid in the exposition; it is not required in the calculation of the cost of sales adjustments.

If the purchases were £7,200, then, at an average cost of £6, the number of equivalent units purchased during the year $= \dfrac{£7,200}{£6} = 1,200.$

Thus, the position may be summarized as follows:

	Equivalent units	Average cost £	Total £
Opening stock	100	4	400
Purchases	1,200	6	7,200
	1,300		7,600
less Closing stock	200	10	2,000
	1,100		£5,600

We can see that 1,100 equivalent units were sold during the year and the FIFO historical cost of goods sold expense is £5,600.

The required amount for this expense in the current cost accounts is:

Number of units sold × average purchase price = 1,100 × £6 = £6,600

The required cost of sales adjustment is, therefore:

£6,600 − £5,600 = £1,000.

Let us now see how the cost of sales adjustment can be calculated without the use of the purchases figure.

It will be useful if we could see why the traditional FIFO expense does not equal £6,600. The reasons are highlighted in the following statement which breaks down the cost of goods sold for the year into two components:

(a) Items included in opening stock, and
(b) Items purchased during the year.

		Cost of goods sold based on			
		FIFO		Average cost of purchases	
		£		£	
(a)	Opening stock 100 × £4	400	100 × £6	600	
(b)	Purchases *less* Closing stock 1,200 × £6 less 200 × £10	5,200	1,000 × £6	6,000	
		£5,600		£6,600	

(a) With FIFO, the units in the opening stock are charged at the average cost of the opening stock while we want them to be charged at the average cost of the purchases made during the year under review.

   It can be seen that the required adjustment in this example, is:

$$100(£6 - £4) = £200$$

or, in general,
number of equivalent units in opening stock multiplied by the difference between the average cost of purchases and the average cost of units constituting opening stock.

(b) The reason for this part of the difference is that the last 200 equivalent units purchased during the year have a higher average cost than the purchases for the year as a whole. The required adjustment in this example is:

$$200\,(£10 - £6) = £800$$

or, in general,
number of equivalent units in closing stock multiplied by the difference between the average cost of the closing stock and the average cost of purchases.

The verbal explanations are getting rather long; so it might be helpful if we resorted to some algebra.

Let S_1 be the book value of the opening stock and S_3 the book value of the closing stock. Let P_1 = average cost of opening stock, P_2 = average cost of purchases and P_3 = average cost of closing stock.

The cost of sales adjustment is then

$$\frac{S_1}{P_1}\,(P_2 - P_1) + \frac{S_3}{P_3}\,(P_3 - P_2)$$

Substituting the figures we have used above, we obtain

$$\frac{£400}{£4}\,(£6 - £4) + \frac{£2,000}{£10}\,(£10 - £6) = 100 \times £2 + 200 \times £4 = £1,000$$

The above formula is presented in a slightly different way in the Guidance Notes* but they are both based on the same principles.

*The formula given in the Guidance Notes is, using the above notation,

$$\text{COSA} = (S_3 - S_1) - P_2 \left(\frac{S_3}{P_3} - \frac{S_1}{P_1} \right)$$

which can be transformed into the formula given in the text, i.e.

$$\text{COSA} = S_3 - P_2 \times \frac{S_3}{P_3} - S_1 + S_1 \times \frac{P_2}{P_1}$$

$$= \frac{S_1}{P_1}(P_2 - P_1) + \frac{S_3}{P_3}(P_3 - P_2)$$

The COSA can be calculated for the year as a whole if it can be assumed that either the volume of stock remained reasonably constant over the year or that any change in volume occurred at a fairly even rate. If neither of these assumptions hold the COSA must be calculated for shorter periods over which the assumptions are applicable. Thus, if the volume of stock fluctuates wildly over the year it may be necessary to calculate the COSA at monthly or even shorter intervals. As will be seen the COSA is related to the monetary working capital adjustment and the two calculations must be made in respect of the same time periods.

The implementation of the provisions concerning stock and the cost of sales adjustment is illustrated in Example 12.3.

Example 12.3

Bill Limited uses a FIFO basis of stock valuation and does not own any fixed assets. Its historical cost balance sheets as at 31st December 19X1, 19X2 and 19X3 are summarized below:

Balance sheets	31 Dec X1	31 Dec X2	31 Dec X3
	£	£	£
Stocks	190	180	260
Bank	310	340	350
	£500	£520	£610

	31 Dec X1	31 Dec X2	31 Dec X3
	£	£	£
Share capital	400	400	400
Retained earnings	100	120	210
	£500	£520	£610

It is assumed that the balance at bank does not form part of the business monetary working capital (see page 430).

The company's profit and loss accounts for the years ended 31 December 19X2 and 19X3 are:

	19X2	19X3
	£	£
Sales	1,000	1,400
less Cost of goods sold	700	1,000
	300	400
less Expenses	280	310
	20	90
Opening retained earnings	100	120
Closing retained earnings	£120	£210

The company has produced its own stock price index. The average period for which stock is held is two months, i.e. the average age of stock is one month.

The relevant index numbers are as follows:

30 November 19X1	120
Average for 19X2	140
30 November 19X2	148
31 December 19X2	150
Average for 19X3	155
30 November 19X3	160
31 December 19X3	164

The cost of sales adjustment will be calculated as follows:

$$\text{Cost of sales adjustment} = \frac{S_1}{P_1}(P_2 - P_1) + \frac{S_3}{P_3}(P_3 - P_2)$$

where

S_1 = book value of opening stock

S_3 = book value of closing stock

P_1 = average price of opening stock (stock price index at the date of purchase of opening stock)

P_2 = average price for the year (average stock price index)

P_3 = average price of closing stock (stock price index at the date of purchase of closing stock)

$$19X2 \text{ Cost of sales adjustment} = \frac{£190}{120}(140 - 120) + \frac{£180}{148}(148 - 140)$$

$$= £31 \cdot 7 + £9 \cdot 7 = £41 \cdot 4$$

$$19X3 \text{ Cost of sales adjustment} = \frac{£180}{148}(155 - 148) + \frac{£260}{160}(160 - 155)$$

$$= £8 \cdot 5 + £8 \cdot 1 = £16 \cdot 6$$

The above represents the realized holding gains. We must also calculate the unrealized revaluation surplus, i.e. the difference between the cost of the stock and its value to the business at the balance sheet date.

31 December 19X2   £

Value to the business

Historical cost $\times \dfrac{150}{148}$ 182·4

less Historical cost   180·0

Unrealized revaluation surplus   £   2·4

31 December 19X3   £

Value to the business

Historical cost $\times \dfrac{164}{160}$ 266·5

less Historical cost   260·0

Unrealized revaluation surplus   £   6·5

The net surpluses on revaluation are then:

19X2		£
Realized revaluation surplus (cost of sales adjustment)		41·4
Unrealized revaluation surplus		2·4
Total net surplus		£43·8

19X3	£	£
Realized revaluation surplus (cost of sales adjustment)	16·6	
less Unrealized revaluation surplus at 31 December 19X2	2·4	14·2
Unrealized revaluation surplus at 31 December 19X3		6·5
Total net surplus		£20·7

It is assumed that the opening stock of 19X3 was sold during the year. The unrealized revaluation surplus on opening stock is thus part of the gain realized in 19X3 and it has been deducted from the cost of sales adjustment when calculating the total net surplus for the year. No such adjustment was required in 19X2 because that was the year in which current cost accounting was introduced and no unrealized revaluation surpluses were recognized on the opening stock for that year.

The current cost accounting profit and loss accounts for the years ended 31 December 19X2 and 19X3 are:

	19X2		19X3	
	£	£	£	£
Sales		1,000·0		1,400·0
less Historical cost of goods sold	700·0		1,000·0	
Cost of sales adjustment	41·4	741·4	16·6	1,016·6
Gross profit		258·6		383·4
less Expenses		280·0		310·0
Current cost operating profit for the year (loss in 19X2)		£(21·4)		£73·4

The current cost balance sheets are given below:

	31 December 19X2		31 December 19X3	
	£	£	£	£
Stock		182·4		266·5
Bank		340·0		350·0
		£522·4		£616·5
Share capital		400·0		400·0
Current Cost Reserve				
Balance 1 January	—		43·8	
Transfer for the year	43·8	43·8	20·7	64·5
Retained Earnings				
Balance 1 January	100·0		78·6	
Increase/Decrease	(21·4)	78·6	73·4	152·0
		£522·4		£616·5

In this example all revaluation surpluses have been positive but the same principles would be applied had any of the gains been negative.

Monetary Working Capital Adjustment

We will now return to the third of the current cost operating adjustments, the Monetary Working Capital Adjustment (MWCA). This adjustment was introduced on page 400 where we pointed out that its purpose is to indicate the additional amounts which a business needs to invest in its monetary working capital to cope with increases* in the prices of the goods and services which give rise to the need for a business to invest in monetary working capital.

SSAP 16 defines monetary working capital as the aggregate of

"(a) trade debtors, prepayments and trade bills receivable, plus,

 (b) stock not subject to a cost of sales adjustment, less

 (c) trade creditors, accruals and trade bills payable,

insofar as they arise from the day to day operating activities of the business as distinct from transactions of a capital nature"**

Note that dividends payable do not form part of monetary working capital; dividends payable are included with shareholders' interest (see page 435).

The standard recognises that a business' bank balances and overdrafts may fluctuate with the levels of stock or the three elements of monetary working capital. Thus, a firm engaged in a seasonal business will find that at certain periods of the year its balance at bank will be high (or overdraft low) but that the balance will be reduced as stocks are built up and then converted into debtors before the cycle of "cash to cash" is completed. If the price of the raw materials and other costs of production increase in the period in which the bank balance is high the firm will only be able to buy or manufacture a lesser quantity of stock unless additional working capital is obtained. Thus, that part of bank balances or overdrafts arising from fluctuations in the volume of stock or in the elements of monetary working capital as defined above plus any cash floats required to support the day to day operation of the business should be included in monetary working capital if to do so would have a material effect on the current cost operating profit.

The treatment of bank balances and overdrafts in current cost accounting is not wholly satisfactory because of the subjective judgements that are involved in deciding the extent to which, if at all, bank balances and overdrafts should be included in monetary working capital. To have excluded the

---

*We will assume that prices are increasing but the same principles will apply is prices fall. In such a case the MWCA will be credited to the current cost profit and loss account and debited to the current cost reserve account.

**SSAP 16, paragraph 44

possibility of including bank balances and overdrafts in monetary working capital would have been undesirable in that the impact of price increases on businesses which have significant fluctuations in the level of bank balances would not have been fully reflected in their current cost accounts, but the solution to the problem adopted in SSAP 16 will mean that inter-firm comparisons will be hindered in certain instances.

Calculation of the MWCA

The principles underlying the calculation of the MWCA are exactly the same as those which apply to the COSA and in the vast majority of instances the averaging method is found to be the most convenient approach. Thus, appropriate series of index numbers will have to be selected for the different elements of monetary working capital. The COSA and MWCA are closely related because, all other things being equal, an increase in stock will be associated with a decrease in monetary working capital and vice versa. Thus, the COSA and MWCA should be calculated for the same time periods.

In principle separate series of index numbers should be used for each element of monetary working capital but for reasons which will be given below one series may be used for all elements which may, in appropriate cases, be the same as is used to calculate the COSA. Indeed, SSAP 16 allows companies to combine the MWCA and COSA as one adjustment in suitable circumstances.

The index for debtors should be based on the price movements of those goods and services which comprise the cost of goods sold on credit. In very many cases this will be the same as the index used for the stock of finished goods; a different index might however be appropriate if certain goods are sold mostly on credit while other items are usually sold for cash. Strictly, the adjustment should be made on the basis of the debtors figure less the profit element but the Guidance Notes suggest that the total debtors figure can be used if to do so provides a fair approximation.

The creditors' index should be based on those items which are financed by creditors. However, even though the absolute index figures for debtors and creditors may be different the Guidance Notes suggest that a single index can be used if the percentage changes in the debtors' and creditors' indices for the period are similar.

Consideration needs to be paid to the average ages of the debtors and creditors, for example if the company's year end is 31st December and the average age of debtors is two months the appropriate index number is that which relates to the 31st October. However, this sophistication is only necessary when it produces a materially different figure for the MWCA than that based on the year end values of the index numbers.

In those cases where cash, bank balances and overdrafts are included in the monetary working capital the index should be based on price changes relating to those items which are acquired by the business.

Negative Monetary Working Capital

If a business' monetary working capital is negative (i.e. the liabilities exceed the assets) only the difference between the negative balance and the stock subject to the COSA is included in the calculation of the MWCA while the excess of the negative monetary working capital over the stock subject to the COSA is included in net borrowings (see page 435). This procedure is based on the assumption that the negative monetary working capital is the source of finance for stock subject to the COSA and that only the excess (as defined above) is to be regarded as a source of finance for other assets.

Stock not subject to the COSA

The basic principle underlying the treatment of stock *subject to* the COSA is the assumption that stock sold will be replaced by identical or similar items so that a current net replacement cost of the stock which is consumed can be found. There are, however, numerous instances where this assumption does not hold. For example, a "general trader" may not confine his attention to a particular line or lines of goods and may be prepared to take advantage of whatever opportunities become available. He may use the cash generated from the sale of, say, government surplus trousers to purchase, say, jigsaw puzzles. In such a case it would not be appropriate to charge the current cost profit and loss with the net replacement cost of government surplus trousers (even if the figure could be determined).

The impact of inflation (i.e. general price increases) must, however, be taken into account for if it is not the operating capability of the business will be reduced in real terms.

In those cases where it would be impossible or inappropriate to calculate the COSA (i.e. to charge the current cost profit and loss account with the 'value to the business' of the stock at the dates of sale) the impact of price increases is recognized by including the stock as part of monetary working capital. Thus as adjustment will be made which reflects the additional amounts that have to be invested in the business to deal with impact of increased prices. As the adjustment is incorporated in the MWCA it means that it will be based on the levels of stock not subject to the COSA and the appropriate price indices. The stock levels which will be included in the calculation will, at the minimum, be those which existed at the beginning and end of the year but stock levels at other dates might be included if the MWCA is calculated for periods of less than a year.

The Guidance Notes suggest that the index which should be applied to the stock and subject to the COSA in the MWCA calculation should be based on price changes 'most appropriate to the stock in question and the general nature of the business.* If a suitable price index is not available a general price index should be used. In fact, the only effect on the current cost operating profit (and hence on the current cost profit attributable to shareholders) of the decision on whether or not part of the stock of the business should or should not be made subject to the COSA arises from the use of the different, more broadly based, price index which will be used in the latter case.

---

*Guidance Notes to SSAP 16, paragraph 102

There is though a difference in the way in which the two different types of stock are treated in the current cost balance sheet. Stock subject to the COSA is of course included at 'value to the business' but stock not subject to historical cost. In other words, in the latter case no attempt is made to estimate the unrealised revaluation surplus.

The more difficult matters relating to stock, including the question of what stock should be treated as part of monetary working capital is dealt with in paragraphs 76 to 87 of the Guidance Notes to SSAP 16. In general, it can be said that stock will be included in monetary working capital, i.e. will not be subject to the COSA, when the stock will not be replaced or when, perhaps because the stock will only be replaced after a delay as is the case with seasonal agricultural products, the future replacement cost cannot be estimated with reasonable accuracy. Two specific examples can usefully be mentioned at this stage:

1. *Contract Work in Progress*

    The Guidance Notes suggest that contracts can for the purposes of CCA be divided into two groups, those of a broadly repetitive nature and unique contracts. (In practice, it is far from obvious that such a clear cut distinction can be made). Contracts of a broadly repetitive nature are treated in exactly the same way as the generality of stock and work in progress and a COSA is calculated based on the price movements of the inputs used in the contract. Unique contracts present difficulties as, by definition, they will not be repeated. The Guidance Notes suggest that a COSA should, if practicable, be calculated on based indices appropriate to the business; otherwise unique contracts should be treated as a monetary asset and be subject to the MWCA and not the COSA.

2. *Dealing Stock*

    Dealing stock describes stock which is purchased by a business because of a belief that its price will increase and that a profit will be gained by resale in the market in which they were purchased. This means that at the date of sale the replacement cost of the goods will be the same or very close to their selling price. Note the difference between the foregoing position and that of a retailer who expects to be able to sell goods for more than the current cost of replacing them. The rationale for the transaction involving dealing stock was the anticipation that a profit would be earned from a price increase but the inclusion of a COSA in the current cost profit and loss account would eliminate all or most of the profit. Thus, dealing stock is included in monetary working capital and hence is subject to the MWCA.

The Gearing Adjustment

We have already introduced the gearing adjustment (see page 404) and discussed how it might be regarded as that proportion of the additional funds required to be invested in the business to cope with the impact of price increases which would be provided by creditors on the assumption that the level of gearing is maintained. There is an alternative way of interpreting the gearing adjustment which is retrospective in nature in that it is argued that the adjustment reflects what has taken place rather than what may take place. The ASC has adopted this alternative view* which may be summarized as follows:

(i) Fixed assets and working capital are commonly financed in part by borrowings.

(ii) The borrowings are (almost always) fixed in monetary terms thus the liability remains constant even though prices increase.

(iii) However, if prices increase the value of the assets partially financed by the borrowings will increase and the difference between the new value of the assets and the loan (less interest payable on the borrowings) accrues to the shareholders.

(iv) The gain is realised as the assets are used or sold in the ordinary course of business.

The above argument is used to justify the inclusion of the gearing adjustment in the current cost profit and loss account which is equal to:

The sum of the current cost operating adjustments multiplied by the gearing proportion which is the ratio of long term (or net) borrowings to the sum of long term borrowings and shareholders' interest.

Many people feel that the ASC's argument is not wholly convincing (it was for this reason that we did not use it earlier) for a number of reasons. It is not clear that the gearing adjustment does provide a measure of the realized element of the gain which accrues to debtors in a period of inflation** depending as it does on the three current cost operating adjustments and that a better reflection of the gain to the shareholders would be found by directly measuring the 'real fall' in the value of the liabilities; in other words the distinction between the realized and unrealized elements of the gain is artificial and unhelpful. Some would go so far as to argue that the fall in the real value of the liabilities should be measured by reference to a general price index and therefore suggest that the CPP gain on the long-term monetary position of the business is a better reflection of the gain and that this figure should be included in a modified version of current cost accounts.

---

*See paragraphs 18 and 19 of SSAP 16 and paragraphs 106 to 108 of the Guidance Notes

**It should be pointed out that the interest charged on a loan will include an element which the market believes to be reasonable compensation for anticipated inflation and, strictly, the debtor only gains if actual inflation exceeds the inflation compensation element of the interest charge

Now we have stated our reservations we will now provide further details about the SSAP 16 version of the gearing adjustment.

The gearing proportion is the ratio of net borrowing (as defined below) to the total of net borrowing and shareholders' interest* (including proposed dividends) as disclosed in the current cost balance sheets. Average values of net borrowings and shareholders' interest are required in the computation of the gearing proportion and the averages are usually the simple arithmetic averages of the appropriate figures in the opening and closing balance sheets. More intricate calculations are required if there have been substantial changes in the financing or asset structures of the business during the year.

Net borrowing is defined as follows:

"Net borrowing is the excess of:

(a) the aggregate of all liabilities and provisions fixed in monetary terms (including convertible debentures and deferred tax but excluding proposed dividends) other than those included within monetary working capital and other than those which are, in substance, equity capital, over

(b) the aggregate of all current assets other than those subject to a cost of sales adjustment and those included within monetary working capital**

Note that bank balances which are not included in monetary working capital will be included in paragraph (b) of the above definition and hence it may be found that net borrowing is negative i.e. the total of (b) exceeds the total of (a). In such an instance SSAP 16 specifies that a gearing adjustment should not be made. This is a further example of the problems associated with the ASC's definition of the gearing adjustment as the gain in holding long term liabilities in a period of rising prices is not reflected in the accounts on the grounds that the whole of the liabilities is used to finance non-operating assets, i.e. those assets included in the definition of net borrowings. SSAP 16 also does not allow a business to make any adjustment to reflect the impact of price changes on the non-operating assets which although logical in terms of the definition of current cost profit attributable to shareholders does mean that a possibly important consequence of price changes on a business is not reflected in the accounts. For example, it is likely that negative net borrowing will exist in a period in which a business holds a large bank balance in contemplation of a major acquisition of some sort. If prices increase during this period the business will suffer a loss in that its ability to make the acquisition will be impaired but this loss will not be reflected in the current cost accounts.

---

*Note that shareholders' interest and net borrowing equals net operating assets so an alternative definition of the gearing proportion is the ratio of net borrowing to net operating assets

**SSAP 16, paragraph 45

This possible shortcoming in current cost accounting is an indication of the fact that the CCA model as outlined in SSAP 16 must be regarded as an interim stage in the development of a comprehensive method*.

We are now in a position to present a more detailed example of the preparation of a set of current cost accounts.

Example 12.4

Taxation will be ignored in this example.

Tan Limited owns a small chain of retail shops which specialize in the sale of high fidelity widgets. It also owns a small fleet of delivery vans as well as a number of cars for the use of the directors.

Its current cost and historical cost balance sheets as at 31 December Year 9 are given below:

TAN LIMITED

Balance Sheets as at 31 December Year 9

	Current Cost			Historical Cost		
	£000	£000	£000	£000	£000	£000
Fixed Assets	Gross Current RC	Acc Dep	Net Current RC	Cost	Acc Dep	Net Book Value
Freehold land	50·0	—	50·0	30·0	—	30·0
Fixtures and fittings	100·0	24·0	76·0	80·0	19·0	61·0
Motor vehicles	18·0	4·5	13·5	16·0	4·0	12·0
	£168·0	£28·5	139·5			
Freehold buildings			160·0	100·0	28·0	72·0
			299·5	£226·0	£51·0	175·0
Current Assets						
Stock		92·9			90·0	
Trade debtors and prepayments		30·0			30·0	
		122·9			120·0	
Current Liabilities						
Trade Creditors and Accrued Expenses	50·0			50·0		
Dividends Payable	10·0			10·0		
Overdraft	27·0	87·0	35·9	27·0	87·0	33·0
			£335·4			£208·0
Share Capital						
Ordinary Shares of £1 each			50·0			50·0
Current Cost Reserve			187·4			
Retained Earnings			38·0			98·0
			275·4			148·0
10% Debentures			60·0			60·0
			£335·4			£208·0

*Other factors which support this view is the fact that the ASC allowed certain types of businesses, e.g. insurance and property companies, to be exempt from the provisions of SSAP 16

Tan Limited's *historical cost* profit and loss account for year 10 is given below:

		£000	£000
Sales			500
Less:	Opening stock	90	
	Purchases	340	
		430	
Less:	Closing stock	110	320
Less:			180
	Wages and sundry expenses	132	
	Debenture Interest	6	
	Depreciation		
	Buildings	4	
	Fixtures and fittings	8	
	Motor vehicles	5	155
Profit for the year			25
Less: Dividends			6
			19
Opening retained earnings			98
Closing retained earnings			£117

Tan Limited's historical cost balance sheet as at the end of year 10 is given below:

	£000	*£000*	*£000*
		Accumulated	
	Cost	*Depreciation*	*Net*
Freehold land	30·0	—	30·0
Fixtures and Fittings	80·0	27·0	53·0
Motor Vehicles	20·0	9·0	11·0
Freehold Buildings	100·0	32·0	68·0
	£230·0	£68·0	162·0
Current Assets			
Stock		110·0	
Trade Debtors and Prepayments		40·0	
		150·0	
Current Liabilities			
Trade Creditors and Accruals	66·0		
Dividends Payable	6·0		
Overdraft	13·0	85·0	65·0
			£227·0
Share Capital			
Ordinary Shares of £1 each			50·0
Retained Earnings			117·0
			167·0
10% Debentures			60·0
			£227·0

We will state the necessary assumptions regarding dates of purchase of assets and the movements of prices in the course of the example but it will be helpful if we discussed the composition of the balance of the current cost reserve account as at the end of year 9. The balance is made up of a number of elements viz the unrealized surplus and other adjustments. The unrealized surpluses consist of the sum of the differences between the values of stock and fixed assets as shown in the current cost and historical cost balance sheets, i.e.

Stock	£K(92·9 − 90·0)	2,900
Fixed Assets	£K(299·5 − 175·0)	£124,500
Unrealized revaluation surpluses as at end of 9		£127,400

The remainder of the balance on the current cost reserve account, £60,000, is the sum of the current cost operating adjustments (other than the depreciation adjustment) charged to the current cost profit and loss accounts since the introduction of current cost accounting by Tan Limited less (assuming that they have all been credits) the sum of the gearing adjustments for the same period. Had current cost accounting been introduced for the first time in year 10 the current cost balance sheet would have been prepared at the end of year 9 but in this case the balance on the current cost reserve account would have consisted solely of the unrealized revaluation surpluses at that date (£127,400) and the balance of retained earnings would be shown to be £98,000.

We will for convenience set out the workings required in the following sections:

A   Cost of sales adjustment and stock
B   Monetary working capital adjustment
C   Fixed assets and depreciation
D   Gearing adjustment

A   *Cost of sales Adjustment and Stock*
    A1   The average age of stock is 2 months. The company prepares its own stock price index which moved as follows:

Year 9		Year 10		
Oct 31	Dec 31	Average	Oct 31	Dec 31
126	130	142	154	156

The company uses the FIFO convention in its historical cost accounts.

    A2   The unrealized revaluation surplus on opening stock is:

$$£K90 \times \frac{130}{126} - £K90 = £K2·9$$

    A3   The cost of sales adjustment for year 10:

$$COSA = \frac{\text{FIFO opening stock}}{\text{Av. price of opening stock}} \left(\text{Av. price of purchases} - \text{Av. price of opening stock} \right)$$

$$+ \frac{\text{FIFO closing stock}}{\text{Av. price of closing stock}} \left(\text{Av. price of closing stock} - \text{Av. price of purchases} \right)$$

$$= \frac{£K90}{126}(142 - 126) + \frac{£K110}{154}(154 - 142) = £K11·4 + £K8·6 = £K20·0$$

    A4

The current replacement cost of the closing stock is £K110 $\left(\frac{156}{154} \right)$ = £K111·4 and the unrealized revaluation surplus at the end of the year is £K1·4.

A5 The net transfer to the current cost reserve account in respect of stock is then:

	£000
Cost of sales adjustment i.e. the realized revaluation surplus (A3)	20·0
Add: Unrealized revaluation surplus on closing stock (A4)	1·4
	21·4
Less: Unrealized revaluation surplus on opening stock (A2)	2·9
	£18·5

B **Monetary Working Capital**

B1 The following assumptions will be made:

(i) That the stock price index can be used for both debtors and creditors
(ii) That the profit element in debtors can be ignored i.e. the adjustment will be made on the gross figure
(iii) That the ages of debtors and creditors can be ignored i.e. that no material difference will result from the use of index numbers at the year ends as opposed to the use of the indices applicable to the average ages of debtors and creditors
(iv) That part of the overdraft fluctuates in sympathy with the level of stock and monetary working capital. It will be assumed that £5,000 of the overdraft can be regarded as providing a medium term source of finance and that the difference between the overdraft and £5,000 will be included with monetary working capital; £5,000 will therefore be included in the company's net borrowing. The overdraft element of monetary working capital can be calculated by reference to the stock price index.

B2 On the basis of the above assumptions the monetary working capital balances at the beginning and end of the year are:

	£000	£000	£000	£000
Debtors		30·0		40·0
Less:				
Creditors	50·0		66·0	
Overdraft (less £5,000)	22·0	72·0	8·0	74·0
Monetary Working Capital		£(42·0)		£(34·0)

Note that in each case the negative balances are less than the stock subject to the COSA.

B3 The following price indices will be used to calculate the MWCA

	Year 10	
1 Jan	Average	31 Dec
130	142	156

B4 The MWCA will be calculated by using the same formula as used for the COSA i.e.

$$MWCA = \frac{\text{Open. bal}}{\text{Open Index}} \text{ (A. Index} - \text{Open Index)} + \frac{\text{Clos. bal}}{\text{Close Index}} \left(\frac{\text{Clos. Index}}{-\text{Av. Index}} \right)$$

Thus, substituting the figures from B3 we have:

$$MWCA = \frac{-£42,000}{130}(142 - 130) + \frac{-£34,000}{156}(156 - 142) = -£6,928$$

The adjustment is negative since the company's monetary liabilities exceeded its monetary assets in a period of increasing prices. The adjustment of £6,928 will hence be credited to the current cost profit and loss account and debited to the current cost reserve account.

C   *Fixed Assets and Depreciation*

Freehold Land

C1   Let us assume that the freehold land is revalued at £58,000 as at 31 December year 10. Since freehold land is not subject to depreciation the whole of the difference between the new and the former valuation £8,000 (£58,000 − £50,000) is credited to the current cost reserve account as an unrealized revaluation surplus.

Freehold Buildings

C2   We must first examine the position as at 1 January year 10. The value to the business of the freehold buildings at that date was £160,000 and we will assume that the estimated remaining life of the buildings as at that date was 18 years. Let us now assume that the buildings had been revalued at the end of year 10 and that the new valuation is £180,000 and that the estimated remaining life of buildings measured from 31 December year 10 was 20 years*.

It is clear that the buildings are regarded as non-specialized (if they had been treated as specialized buildings the current cost balance sheet would have shown the gross current replacement and accumulated depreciation of the buildings). We will assume that the buildings are depreciated on a straight line basis.

C3   Using the method described on page 420 the depreciation charge in the current cost accounts is:

$$\frac{\text{Value to the business of the asset at year end}}{\text{Remaining life of the asset as at the year end}}$$

$$= \frac{£180,000}{20} = £9,000$$

The depreciation adjustment is then:

	£
CCA Depreciation	£9,000
Less: Historical cost depreciation (from the historical cost P & L account)	4,000
Depreciation Adjustment	£5,000

---

*It would be sensible, but not necessary, to revise the period over which the asset is to be written off in the historical cost accounts in line with the estimates made for the current cost accounts. For the sake of simplicity we will not alter the historical cost accounts in this example.

C4   The value to the business of the buildings as at 31 December year 10 *before* depreciation is:

	£
Valuation of buildings at the end of year 10 on the basis of their condition as at that date	180,000
Add: Depreciation for year 10 (from C3)	9,000
	£189,000

The revaluation surplus for year 10 which will be credited to the current cost reserve account is then:

	£
Value before depreciation (from above)	189,000
Value at the beginning of the year	160,000
Revaluation surplus	£ 29,000

Fixtures and Fittings

C5   It is first necessary to analyse the company's holdings of fixtures and fittings as at 1 January, Year 10. The assets are depreciated on a straight line basis over 10 years assuming a zero scrap value.

	Current Cost			Historical Cost		
	GC RC	Acc Depr	NC RC	Cost	Acc Depr	NBV
Purchased on 1 Jan Year 7	40,000	12,000	28,000	30,000	9,000	21,000
Purchased on 1 Jan Year 8	60,000	12,000	48,000	50,000	10,000	40,000
	£100,000	£24,000	£76,000	£80,000	£19,000	£61,000

C6   Let us assume that the price index applicable to fixtures and fittings increased from 100 to 118 over the year. Thus the gross current replacement cost at the year end is:

$$£100,000 \times \frac{118}{100} = £118,000$$

Thus the increase in the gross current replacement cost is £18,000 (£118,000 − £100,000)

C7   We will assume that the CCA depreciation is based on average values and hence the depreciation charge for the year is:

$$\frac{\frac{1}{2}£(100,000 + 118,000)}{10} = £10,900$$

C8   The depreciation adjustment is then:

	£
CCA Depreciation (C7)	10,900
Historical Cost Depreciation	8,000
Depreciation Adjustment	£ 2,900

C9   The backlog depreciation can be found as follows:

	£
Assets purchased on 1 January Year 7 Gross current replacement cost at the end of Year 10 £40,000 × 118/100	47,200
Net current replacement cost at the end of Year 10 i.e. 60% of Gross current RC	28,320
Required balance on accumulated depreciation	£18,880

	£
Assets purchased on 1 January Year 8 Gross current replacement cost £60,000 × 118/100	70,800
Net current replacement cost 70% of Gross current RC	49,560
Required balance on accumulated depreciation	£21,240

Required balance on accumulated depreciation as at the end of Year 10	£	£
Year 7 purchases		18,880
Year 8 purchases		21,240
		40,120
Less: Balance of accumulated depreciation at 1 January Year 10	24,000	
CCA depreciation charge for Year 10	10,900	34,900
Backlog depreciation		£5,220

C10   The net credit to the current cost reserve is then:

	£
Increase in gross current replacement cost (from C6)	18,000
Less: Backlog depreciation (from C9)	5,220
Net revaluation surplus	£12,780

Motor Vehicles

C11   The vehicles owned on 31 December Year 9 were purchased on 1 January Year 9. An additional vehicle costing £4,000 was purchased on 1 January Year 10. Vehicles are depreciated at 25% using the straight line method. The appropriate price index increased from 110 to 121 in Year 10.

C12   The gross current replacement cost at 31 December Year 10 is then:

	£
Year 9 purchases, £18,000 × 121/110	19,800
Year 10 purchases, £4,000 × 121/110	4,400
	£24,200

The increase in the gross current replacement cost is £24,200 − £22,000 = £2,200.

C13   The CCA depreciation charge, based on average values is:

25% of $\frac{1}{2}$£(22,000 + 24,200) = £5,775

C14   The depreciation adjustment is:

	£
CCA depreciation (C13)	5,775
Historical cost depreciation	5,000
Depreciation adjustment	£ 775

C15   Backlog depreciation can be found as follows:

		£
Vehicles purchased in Year 9		
Required balance on accumulated depreciation at 31 December Year 10 50% of £19,800		9,900
Vehicles purchased in Year 10		
Required balance on accumulated depreciation at 31 December Year 10 25% of £4,400		1,100
		11,000
Accumulated depreciation 1 January Year 10	4,500	
CCA depreciation charge Year 10 (C13)	5,775	10,275
Backlog depreciation		£ 725

C16   The net credit to the current cost reserve account is then:

	£
Increase in gross current replacement cost (from C12)	2,200
Less: Backlog depreciation (from C15)	725
Net revaluation surplus	£1,475

D   *Gearing Adjustment*
   D1   The gearing proportion is found by taking the average values, derived from the opening and closing CCA balance sheets, of net borrowing and shareholders' interest. The opening CCA balance sheet is available and so our task consists of little more than rearranging the figures. There is, how-

ever, one complication that must be borne in mind, that is the point that the overdraft has in part been included in monetary working capital (see B1 (iii)). It has been assumed that the difference between the actual amount of the overdraft and £5,000 fluctuates in sympathy with stock and monetary working capital. Thus the difference is included in monetary working capital and £5,000 is to be regarded as an element of net borrowing. It is also worth repeating the point that dividends payable are counted as part of shareholders' interest.

The CCA balance sheet at 1 January Year 10 can therefore be analysed as follows:

Shareholders' Interest

	£
Share Capital	50,000
Current Cost Reserve	187,400
Retained Earnings	38,000
Dividends Payable	10,000
	£285,400

Net Borrowing

Overdraft	5,000
Debentures	60,000
	£65,000

D2   We next require the figures from the closing balance sheet which has yet to be produced. However, we have already completed sufficient workings to be able to determine both the shareholders' interest and the net borrowing.

Retained Earnings		£	£
	Working		
We start with the historical cost profit for Year 10			25,000
From the above must be deducted the current cost operating adjustments, viz:			
Cost of Sales	A3	20,000	
Monetary Working Capital	B4	(6,928)	
Depreciation:			
Freehold Buildings	C3	5,000	
Fixtures & Fittings	C8	2,900	
Motor Vehicles	C14	775	21,747
			3,253
The dividends for the year must be deducted			6,000
			(2,747)
The retained earnings from the CCA balance sheet at 31 December Year 9 are then added			38,000
Thus, the retained earnings at 31 December Year 10 (before crediting the gearing adjustment) are			£35,253

Current Cost Reserve

	Workings	£
Balance 1 January Year 10		187,400
Add:		
Stock	A5	18,500
MWCA	B4	(6,928)
Freehold Land	C1	8,000
Freehold Buildings	C4	29,000
Fixtures & Fittings	C10	12,780
Motor Vehicles	C16	1,475
Balance 31 December Year 10		
before debiting the gearing adjustment		£250,227

The gearing adjustment represents a transfer between retained earnings and the current cost reserve and hence the total of the shareholders' interest as at 31 December, Year 10 can be found

Shareholders' Interest as at 31 December Year 10

	£
Share Capital	50,000
Retained Earnings	
(before the gearing adjustment)	35,253
Current Cost Reserve	
(before the gearing adjustment)	250,227
Dividends Payable	6,000
	£341,480

Net Borrowing as at 31 December Year 10

	£
Overdraft	5,000
Debentures	60,000
	£65,000

D3   The average values can now be calculated:

	1 January	31 December	Average
	£	£	£
Shareholders' Interest (S)	285,400	341,480	313,440
Net Borrowing (L)	65,000	65,000	65,000

The gearing proportion is thus given by:

$$\frac{L}{L+S} = \frac{65,000}{65,000 + 313,440} = 0.17$$

The sum of the current cost operating adjustments is £21,747 debit (see D2) and hence the gearing adjustment is $0.17 \times £21,747 = £3,697$ which is credited to the current cost profit and loss account and debited to the current cost reserve account.

D4   The balance on the current cost reserve account as at 31 December, Year 10 is then:

	£
Balance before gearing adjustment (see D2)	250,227
Less: Gearing adjustment (see D3)	3,697
Balance at 31 December, Year 10	£246,530

D5   The retained earnings at 31 December, Year 10 are:

	£
Balance before gearing adjustment (see D2)	35,253
Add: Gearing Adjustment (see D3)	3,697
Balance at 31 December, Year 10	£38,950

Before preparing the current cost accounts it will be helpful if we summarized the adjustments in the form of a worksheet. The use of this approach reduces the risk of arithmetical and other errors. The worksheet is shown in Figure 12.1.

The worksheet shows the adjustments required to convert the historical cost balance sheet as at 31 December Year 10 into a current cost balance sheet as at the same date. The historical cost balance sheet is shown in column (i). The first task is to incorporate the current cost reserve at 1 January, Year 10 which is done in column (ii). The balance (item (b)) is £187,400 which represents the various unrealized revaluation surpluses at 1 January and these are debited to the appropriate asset accounts (items (a)) while the total of the current cost adjustments which have been transferred from the profit and loss account to the current cost reserve account; £60,000, is debited to retained earnings (item (c)). Column (iii) shows the adjustments made in respect of stock and cost of goods sold expense. The COSA of £20,000 is debited to retained earnings (item (f)) while the current cost reserve is credited with the £18,500 (item (e)). It may be thought strange that the stock account is debited with £1,500 (item (d)) but this adjustment simply reflects the fact that the unrealised revaluation surplus on stock at the year end is £1,500 less than the corresponding figure at the beginning of the year. Column (iv) deals with the MWCA of £6,928 which is debited to current cost reserve and credited to retained earnings. The fixed assets adjustments are the subject of column (v). The individual net surpluses on revaluation are debited to the appropriate asset account and, in total, credited to the current cost reserve (items (h)) while the depreciation adjustments are credited to the asset accounts and debited to retained earnings (items (i)). The penultimate column (vi) simply shows the gearing adjustment which is debited to the current cost reserve and credited to retained earnings. The current cost balance sheet which is summarized in the final column (vii) can now be found.

The current cost accounts are given below:

TAN LIMITED

CURRENT COST PROFIT AND LOSS ACCOUNT
Year ended 31 December, Year 10

	£	£	Workings
Profit before interest on the historical cost basis		31,000	
Less: Current cost operating adjustments (Note 1)		21,747	
Current Cost Operating Profit *b/f*		9,253	

Figure 12.1

	(i) Historical Cost Bal Sheet @ 31 Dec Year 10	(ii) Current Cost Reserve @ 1 Jan Year 10	(iii) Stock Adjustments	(iv) MCW Adjustment	(v) Fixed Assets Adjustments	(vi) Gearing Adjustment	(vii) Current Cost Bal Sheet as @ 31 Dec Year 10
Freehold land	30,000 (a)	20,000			8,000 (h)		58,000
Fixtures and fittings	53,000 (a)	15,000		}	(2,900) (i) / 12,780 (h)		77,880
Motor Vehicles	11,000 (a)	1,500		}	(775) (i) / 1,475 (h)		13,200
Freehold Buildings	68,000 (a)	88,000		}	(5,000) (i) / 29,000 (h)		180,000
Stock	110,000 (a)	2,900 (d)	(1,500)				111,400
Debtors	40,000						40,000
	£312,000	£127,400	£(1,500)	—	£42,580	—	£480,480
Share Capital	50,000						50,000
Current Cost Reserve	(b)	187,400 (e)	18,500 (g)	(6,928) (h)	51,255 (h)	(3,697) (j)	246,530
Retained earnings	117,000 (c)	(60,000) (f)	(20,000)	6,928 (i)	(8,675) (i)	3,697 (j)	38,950
Debentures	60,000						60,000
Current Liabilities	85,000						85,000
	£312,000	£127,400	£(1,500)	—	£42,580	—	£480,480

	£	£	*Workings*
c/f		9,253	
Less:			
Gearing Adjustment	(3,697)		D3
Interest payable	6,000	2,303	
Current Cost Profit attributable to shareholders		6,950	
Dividends		6,000	
Retained current cost earnings for the year		£ 950	

Statement of retained earnings/reserves

Retained current cost earnings for the year	950
Movements on the current cost reserve (Note 2)	66,058
	67,008
Retained reserves at the beginning of the year	225,400
Retained reserves at the end of the year	£292,408

Current Cost Balance Sheet as at 31 December, Year 10

	Gross Current Replacement Cost	*Accumulated Depreciation*	*Net Current Replacement Cost*	*Workings*
	£	£	£	
Fixed Assets				
Freehold Land	58,000	—	58,000	C1
Fixtures & Fittings	118,000	40,120	77,880	C6 and C9
Motor Vehicles	24,200	11,000	13,200	C12 and C15
	£200,200	£ 51,120	149,080	
Freehold Buildings			180,000	C2
			329,080	
Current Assets				
Stock		111,400		A4
Trade Debtors and Prepayments		40,000		
		151,400		
Current Liabilities				
Trade Creditors and accruals	66,000			
Dividends payable	6,000			
Overdraft	13,000	85,000	66,400	
			£395,480	
Share Capital				
Ordinary Shares of £1 each			50,000	
Current Cost Reserve			246,530	D4
Retained Earnings			38,950	D5
			335,480	
10% Debentures			60,000	
			£395,480	

Notes

1. *Current Cost Operating Adjustments*

Cost of Sales	20,000
Monetary Working Capital	(6,928)
Depreciation	8,675
	£21,747

2. *Current Cost Reserve*

Balance at 1 January Year 10			187,400
Revaluation surpluses reflecting price changes:			
Fixed Assets	51,255		
Stock	18,500	69,755	
Monetary Working Capital			
Adjustment		(6,928)	
Gearing Adjustment		(3,697)	59,130
			£246,530
of which – realized			78,050
unrealized			168,480
			£246,530

The unrealized element of the balance can be found from a comparison of the amounts at which the assets are stated in the current cost and historical cost balance sheets.

SSAP16 specifies a number of other notes – some compulsory and some voluntary – which can be appended to the published accounts. These notes include statements showing details of the bases and methods used to prepare the current cost accounts and an analysis of the current cost balance sheet in terms of the net operating assets, shareholders' interest and net borrowing. It is not necessary to illustrate these notes in a text which is concerned with basic principles and readers who wish to gain further information should refer to the Standard. One of the voluntary statements – the statement of changes in shareholders' equity interest after allowing for changes in the general purchasing power of money – will, however, be discussed later in this chapter.

Current Cost Accounting and General Price Level Changes

Strictly current cost accounting permits no adjustments for changes in the general price level. The only price changes which are recorded are those which affect the goods and services used by the business and the Index of Retail Prices is only used when it is considered to be the best available proxy for the price changes affecting all or part of the business.

In order to understand the reason for this it is necessary to return to the recommendations of the Sandilands Committee which very firmly rejected both CPP accounting itself and a combined system which would allow adjustments for changes in the general purchasing power of money to be incorporated into a system which was based on current values.

This aspect of the Sandilands Report caused a good deal of controversy. We do not have enough space to summarize all the various arguments that have been advanced but we will attempt to touch on some of the main themes and try to clear away some matters which we see as being irrelevant.

Much of Sandilands' criticisms of CPP accounting concerned the treatment of the valuation of assets. The committee suggested that the publication of the 'value to the business' of assets is likely to be of more relevance to the users of the accounts than the presentation of CPP's restated historical cost. We accept this, and believe that the view is generally held, subject to the reservations that many people have about the possibility of overcoming the practical problems of producing current valuations.

Thus, we believe that the points at issue are not those concerning the treatment of assets and liabilities in the balance sheet but are centred on the owners' equity section. However, that still means that we have a large field in which to pursue the arguments and we shall have to consider such matters as the nature of profit, and whether a company can make a loss or gain by holding monetary items.

It is possible to develop a system of accounting that includes the use of current values but that still takes account of changes in the general price level.

It will be convenient if, when discussing the various views, we use a phrase such as 'general price men' to describe those men, and women, who believe that general price level accounting should be combined with current cost accounting.

Let us first take a broad view of the differences between the two schools of thought. A general price man might say that the Sandilands Committee, which described itself as the 'Inflation Accounting Committee', failed because its proposals only took account of changes in individual prices and ignored changes in the general price level (which is what inflation is all about). The Sandilands reply to this point is essentially that it is not possible to measure inflation and hence account for it, because inflation is a personal matter depending on a person's own particular pattern of consumption of goods and services.

They wrote:

'Inflation does not exist as a quantifiable phenomenon independent of the price movement in any specific group of goods and services or of the spending pattern of any specific group of individuals or entities and is not a phenomenon capable of independent and objective measurement, affecting individuals and entities in the same way. The rate of inflation will vary for different individuals and entities in the country according to the selection of goods and services which they buy.'*

Report of the Inflation Accounting Committee, Cmnd. 6225, page 13. The authors are striving hard to adopt a neutral tone when describing the various views. However, as battered victims of inflation, they cannot resist saying that they believe that the rate of inflation disclosed by the index of retail prices in recent years provides a better estimate of their personal rates of inflation than an estimate of zero.

Another reason why the Sandilands Committee disliked the use of the index of retail prices is that it is based on the goods and services used by final consumers and does not cover the goods and services used by companies. The argument here is very much bound up with the question whether the accounts should be constructed from the point of view of the company or the owners of the company or indeed whether there is any difference between the two. This enigmatic remark merits an illustration.

Suppose that K Limited is owned by Messrs A and B but is managed by Mr P. On 1 January 1985 K Limited starts business by purchasing 100 widgets at £1 each. It holds the widgets for a year during which time the price of widgets increases to £1·50 each. We will assume that the difference between the net realizable value and replacement cost of the widgets is negligible. We will assume that the general price index increased by 30 per cent during the year. Mr P is employed because of his skill and experience as a widget trader and he might well, from his standpoint, explain the results for the year in the following way.

'The company did not make any sales and hence would not have made a profit – which I define as an excess of revenue over the current cost of the inputs used up in earning the revenue. The company has an unrealized holding gain of £50, but this does not mean that it is any better off, because the gain represents the additional investment that will have to be made if it is to be able to maintain its present level of activity in the future.'

On the other hand, a general price man might advance the following argument: 'A and B sacrificed £100 of purchasing power on 1 January and would need to have £130 (£100 × 130/100) on 31 December to maintain their original purchasing power. Since the value of the business at that date is £150, they are better off by £20, and this figure should be disclosed in the accounts. This £20 is a profit, for I define the profit for a period as the increase of the purchasing power represented by the owners' investment in the business. The fact that it is their intention to use the cash raised from the sale of the widgets to purchase replacements at a higher price does not detract from my view of the nature of profit. The accounts should show that they have made a profit which may or may not reinvest in the business'.

It can be seen that the views of P are in line with the Sandilands proposals. He thinks in terms of the assets of the business, and not the purchasing power they represent; he therefore believes that changes in the general price level are irrelevant in measuring the increase in the value of the company. He would say that it is up to the owners to make their own judgement about their own increase in well-offness, which will depend on their personal rate of inflation, and that this job cannot be done for them in the accounts.

Development of the Sandilands Model

In the Sandilands version of current cost accounting the only adjustments required to convert an historical cost profit and loss account into a current cost profit and loss account were the cost of sales and depreciation adjustments. The monetary working capital and gearing adjustments appeared in

the course of the development of current cost accounting. These adjustments were included to deal with certain criticisms of the Sandilands model,
i.e. its failure to show the impact of price changes on the business' investment in monetary working capital or show the gain that accrues to debtors in
periods of rising prices. In fact these developments have to some extent
narrowed the differences between CPP and current cost accounting in that
the MWC and gearing adjustments can be regarded as being equivalent to
the loss or gain on holding net monetary assets in CPP accounting.

The MWCA is similar to the CPP loss or gain on the short term
monetary position in that both are based on the business' holding of net
monetary assets. The essential difference is that with the CCA the adjustment is calculated by reference to the price changes of the items which give
rise to the need to invest in net monetary assets while the CPP adjustment
depends on movements of the retail price index. The CCA adjustment is to
be preferred in that it does attempt to show the additional sums that have to
be invested in monetary working capital in order to cope with price
increases. While both the gearing adjustment in CCA and CPP's gain* on
holding long term monetary liabilities attempt to measure the same thing –
the gain to the shareholders from holding long term monetary liabilities –
they do so in very different ways. The CPP adjustment relates to the liability
itself in that it measures the gain in purchasing power which follows from the
reduction in the 'real value' of the liability. In contrast the CCA gearing
adjustment is calculated by reference to the assets which have been partly
financed by the liability. Thus the credit to the current cost profit and loss
account is an appropriate proportion of the realized revaluation surpluses
(including the MWCA). The proportion depending on the ratio between
shareholders' funds and long term finance (or net borrowing) (see page
405).

It can therefore be seen that the development of current cost accounting from the original Sandilands version has narrowed the differences
between the CCA and CPP methods in that the monetary working capital
and gearing adjustment share certain common features with the CPP loss or
gain on the business' net monetary position. One major difference does,
however, remain in that with CCA the adjustments are made from the point
of the business while with CPP the measurements are based on the position
of the shareholders.

The failure of CCA to make specific adjustments has at least two
serious consequences. First comparability over time is lost in that the figures
of profit over, say, a five year interval will not be comparable if there has
been a change in the general price level. The ASC is considering this matter
and it is expected that a standard on the matter will be issued in due course.
In the meantime companies are encouraged to provide comparative figures
adjusted to a common price level with the results of the period and to adjust
any five or ten year summaries of results in a similar way.

---

* By assuming that prices are increasing and that the business does not hold any long term
monetary assets we can confine our attentions to long term monetary gains.

The second consequence is that shareholders are given no indication of whether their interest in the business has been maintained in real terms i.e. after adjusting for changes in the general price level. In order to overcome this difficulty SSAP 16 includes a 'statement of changes in shareholders' equity interest after allowing for changes in the general purchasing power of money'. Companies are not required to publish this statement in order to comply with SSAP 16; it is produced on a voluntary basis. The statement is illustrated in example 12.5 which is based on the figures included in example 12.4.

Example 12.5

Facts as in example 12.4. In addition it is assumed that the Index of Retail Prices was 120 on 1 January Year 10 and 135 on 31 December Year 10.

TAN LIMITED

Statement of change in shareholders' equity
interest after allowing for the change in the
general purchasing power of money for
the year ended 31 December Year 10

	£
Equity interest at the beginning of the year, as shown in the current cost accounts	275,400
Amount required to compensate for the change in the general purchasing power of money during the year (see working 1)	34,425
	309,825
Equity interest before dividends at the end of the year, as shown in the current cost accounts (see working 2)	341,480
Excess	£ 31,655

Workings

		£
1.	Amount required £275,400 $\left\{ \dfrac{135-1}{120} \right\} =$	£34,425
2.	Equity interest per CCA balance sheet as at 31 December Year 10	335,480
	Add: Dividends payable	6,000
		£341,480

Note
Dividends payable at the year end are added back so that shareholders can see whether the increase in equity interest has been sufficient to compensate them for the fall in the value of money. The statement would have to be modified if there had been an increase in share capital during the year.

CCA and the Valuation of a Business

Current cost accounting is based on the valuation of individual assets and liabilities and hence the information shown in a current cost balance sheet are not intended to provide an estimate of the current economic value of the business as a whole. In other words the problem of goodwill which bedevils a number of areas in historical cost accounting did not disappear with the introduction of current cost accounting. However, since current cost accounting generally places higher values on the assets than does historical cost accounting the difference between the sum of the book values of the assets less liabilities and the value of the business as a whole is usually less with current cost accounting than with historical cost accounting.

Since it is not the objective of either current cost or historical cost accounting to disclose the value of the business as a whole it means that the impact of events which lead to a reduction in the value of the business are not recorded unless they effect the book value of a particular asset or assets. Thus a change in technology which adversely affects a business will partially be recognized insofar that the book values of certain items of plant and machinery will be written down if they have become obsolete, while the loss of a very major customer, which may well have a greater impact on the future profits of the business, will not be reflected in the balance sheet since no particular asset has been effected by the change.

The practical consequences of the above defect in current cost and historical cost accounting are not very serious when the adverse events simply reduce, but do not eliminate, goodwill. The problem becomes greater after the disappearance of goodwill. In this case the incidence of an adverse event will mean, unless it is reflected in the write down of a particular asset or assets, that the value of the business will be less than the sum of the book values of the assets less liabilities. Of course if the event is so significant that it can no longer be assumed that the business is a 'going concern' the balance sheet will be drawn up on the basis of the realizable value of the assets. However, the abandonment of the assumption that the business is a going concern is comparatively rare and does not at all cover all those instances where the sum of the book value of the assets less liabilities is greater than the value of the business. Now it could be argued that since it is not an objective of accounting to produce balance sheets which show the value of the business no problem exists. To argue in this way, however, ignores the fact that users of accounts generally believe that the figures shown in the balance sheet do provide a lower limit of the value of the business and would consider that they had been seriously misled if they found that this was not the case.

Instances where the sum of the book values of the assets less liabilities exceeds the value of the business are comparatively rare in historical cost accounting because with this system the book values of assets are generally less than their current values. These differences are not present in current cost accounting and it therefore follows that situations where the sum of the book values of the assets less liabilities exceeds the value of the business will occur more frequently. In addition current cost accounting can produce further problems in this area which arise from the difficulties of dealing with interdependent assets.

Interdependent Assets

SSAP 16 states that assets should be valued at their net current replacement cost unless 'a permanent diminution to below net current replacement cost has been recognized'*. The problem is that if an individual asset is considered in isolation it may not be apparent that there has been a 'permanent diminution'.

For example, suppose that a company has a small department which uses three machines and manufactures a single product. Assume that the replacement costs (RC) and net realisable values (NRV) of the machines are:

	RC	NRV
Machine	£	£
A	100	40
B	200	15
C	300	20

Let us assume that the present value of the net cash flow that will be generated by the sale of the product is £500. It is clear that if the company were deprived of all three machines it would not replace them, since the total replacement cost of £600 exceeds their economic value of £500 which is the value to the business of the group of assets. However, if the company were deprived of any one of the machines it would be replaced.

Suppose that machine C is destroyed by fire. The company is then faced with the choice of selling A and B or replacing C. If it did the first it would receive £55. If it selected the second alternative it would have to spend £300 in order to restore a positive cash flow with a present value of £500. It would thus replace machine C. Similarly, it would replace machines A or B.

If each asset were viewed in isolation it is unlikely that a permanent diminution would be recognised and hence each asset would be valued by reference to its net current replacement cost. If the group of machines were treated as one asset, however, a permanent diminution would be recognized.

The business as a whole could be viewed as an interdependent group of assets in respect of which a permanent diminution should be recognized. However, SSAP 16 does not require this adjustment to be made. We are thus left with our original unsatisfactory position that reductions in value which can be related to individual assets will be recorded but those which relate to the business as a whole will usually not be reflected in the accounts.

EXPOSURE DRAFT 35 'ACCOUNTING FOR THE EFFECTS OF CHANGING PRICES'

SSAP 16 was not regarded by the ASC, or anyone else, as the last word in current cost accounting. Thus, although the ASC announced that there

---

*SSAP 16, paragraph 42

would be no modifications in the three years following the publication of the standard, the Committee commissioned a number of studies focusing both on the problems of preparing current cost accounts and the extent to which they were used by shareholders, investment analysts and other interested groups.

Following these studies and their own further reflections, the ASC published in July 1984, Exposure Draft 35 – 'Accounting for the effects of changing prices' which would, if it became a standard, replace SSAP 16. In the preamble to ED35 the ASC firmly restated its belief that for publicly accountable companies the benefit of providing current cost information exceeds the cost of providing that information. Thus the basic principles of current cost accounting as expressed in SSAP 16 are retained but there are some material changes in the way in which the information should be presented and the scope of the proposed standard.

Scope of ED35

SSAP 16 applies, with certain exceptions, to all listed companies and other large profit seeking entities. The proposed standard would allow the same exemptions, i.e. wholly owned subsidiaries and, so called value-based companies such as Banks and Insurance Companies, but would change the main focus in that ED35 proposes that current cost information should be published by all public companies. All listed companies have by definition to be public companies so they would still be covered by the standard. However, larger private companies which exceeded the size criteria laid down in SSAP 16 would no longer be required to publish current cost information while smaller public, but unlisted, companies would come within the scope of the standard. This change would reduce the number of entities which would have to provide current cost information and would mean that only those companies where there is generally a separation between the ownership and management of the enterprise would be covered by the standard.

Method of Presenting Current Cost Information

In practice those companies which complied with SSAP 16 did so by publishing, along with the main historical cost accounts, a set of supplementary current cost accounts. However, as a result of their studies the ASC concluded that the inclusion of two separate sets of accounts prepared on different bases in published reports did not commend general support. Hence, ED35 proposes that only one set of accounts should be produced. If these accounts are prepared under the historical cost convention the required current cost information should be disclosed in a note to the accounts. Companies could base their single set of accounts on the current cost convention, in which the required information would automatically be disclosed but it is likely that only a tiny minority of companies would chose this option.

In particular the ASC noted that current cost balance sheets are often taken to show the current value of the business which, of course, they do not. Thus the proposed standard would only require the current cost of fixed assets and stocks to be included in the note to the historical cost accounts.

The Required Current Cost Information

It is proposed that the financial statements should show the effects of changing prices on the operating capability and financing of the company by giving the following current cost information:

(a)   a depreciation adjustment;
(b)   a cost of sales adjustment;
(c)   a monetary working capital adjustment;
(d)   a gearing adjustment;
(e)   any other material adjustments to the profit or loss on ordinary activities consistent with the current cost convention (showing each separately);
(f)   the effect of the above current cost adjustments on the profit or loss on ordinary activities;
(g)   the current cost adjustment or adjusted amount in respect of minority interests;
(h)   the current cost adjustment or adjusted amount in respect of extra-ordinary items; and
(i)   the effect of all the above current cost adjustments on the profit or loss for the financial year.

The cost of sales and monetary working capital adjustments may be combined as a working capital adjustment.

In addition the note should include the gross and net current cost of fixed assets together with the accumulated current cost, depreciation and the current cost of stocks.

The exposure draft does not specify the way in which the information should be presented although a number of possible methods are illustrated in an appendix.

Changes to the Basic Method Specified in SSAP 16

Whilst it is proposed to make slight changes to the way in which terms are defined in SSAP 16, ED35 retains, with one exception, the basic principles of the approach to current cost accounting as specified in SSAP 16.

The exception relates to the gearing adjustment. This was one of the less satisfactory elements of SSAP 16 and there is, as yet no agreement as to the way in which it should be calculated. Hence the ED35 proposals would allow companies to select one of three possible options. One alternative is the form of gearing adjustment required by SSAP 16 (see page 433). The second alternative would be to apply the gearing ratio to the total of the realized and unrealized gains or losses for the year*. The third alternative does appear to represent a departure from the basic principles of current cost accounting in that it is, in effect, the loss or gain on holding monetary items which is a feature of CPP accounts (see page 380). This third form of gearing adjustment is calculated by applying the rate of increase in general prices to the average net borrowing during the year.

CONCLUSION

Whilst there are those who still believe that historical cost accounting serves well enough, the general view is that it is desirable that accounts should show the effects of changing prices.

There is, however, no unanimity as to the way this should be done. As we have discussed in this chapter there are a number of weaknesses in the SSAP 16 version of current cost accounting and it does not appear that this defect would be remedied by the adoption of proposals contained in ED35. Indeed, the exposure draft itself came under strong attack from a number of quarters. Some believe that it is wrong to relegate current cost information to the notes to the accounts while others believe that companies should be allowed greater freedom to decide the way in which they would account for the effect of changing prices.

The criticisms of ED 35 were of such a weight that the Exposure Draft was withdrawn and, at the time this book went to press, the ASC was having to reassess its position. Whatever the outcome of these deliberations it is unlikely that the accounting profession will revert to a total reliance on historical cost accounts. Changing prices are of great significance to the operations and financial situation of businesses and any set of accounts which does not attempt to reflect their effects and can only present an incomplete and distorted picture.

EXERCISES

12.1 'A business is a mere abstraction and the only price changes that really matter are those which affect its owners'.
'The change in the prices faced by an individual is a matter that cannot be measured in the accounts of a business'.

Comment on the above.

12.2 Use the information provided in Exercise 11.2 (page 391) and assume that all appropriate price indices have increased in 19X5. For each pair of companies compare (a) the current cost operating profits and (b) the total credits to the current cost reserve account for 19X5.

12.3 Assume that a future SSAP extends current cost accounts to all sizes of business enterprises. A client, who owns a small engineering company which

*The SSAP 16 method applies the gearing ratio to the realised gains only.

produces components for the motor industry, has written to you in the following terms.

"Will you please explain the differences between current cost and historical cost accounting and outline the additional information you will require to prepare my current cost accounts. As you know my wife owns an antique store and I would be grateful if you could tell me whether there are any special problems which might arise when preparing current cost accounts for her business."

Required
A reply to the above request. You may assume that your client is familiar with the principles of historical cost accounting but you should avoid the use of technical terms.

12.4 Francine Limited started business buying and selling widgets on 1 January 19X3 with a capital, in the form of cash, of £200. Purchases and sales for the two years ended 31 December 19X4 were as follows:

	Purchases	*Sales*
19X3		
January	34 @ £5	
March		10 @ £8
June		12 @ £8
July	12 @ £6	
November	10 @ £7	
December		8 @ £10
19X4		
January		8 @ £12
March	10 @ £8	
August		12 @ £12
November	10 @ £10	
December		10 @ £15

The replacement cost of the widgets:

Increased from £5 to £6 per unit on 1 April 19X3

Increased from £6 to £7 per unit on 1 August 19X3

Increased from £7 to £8 per unit on 1 February 19X4

Increased from £8 to £9 per unit on 1 July 19X4

Increased from £9 to £10 per unit on 1 October 19X4

Sundry expenses for 19X3 were £80 and for 19X4, £100

All trading was for cash. Assume that cash is not included in monetary working capital.

Required:
CCA accounts for the years ended 31 December 19X3 and 31 December 19X4. (Do not use the averaging method).

12.5 Bush Limited started business on 1 January 19X4. Capital of £3,500 (in the form of cash, £500, a delivery van, £2,000 and fixtures and fittings £1,000) was introduced on that date.

Sales for 19X4 were 1,000 units @ £10 each. Bush Limited purchased 1,200 units at an average cost of £6 per unit, the last 200 units purchased had an average cost of £8 each. The replacement cost at the year-end was £9 each. Expenses for 19X4 were £1,800.

Bush Limited estimates that its vehicles will last for 4 years and its fixtures for 10 years. No changes are made in these estimates in 19X4 and 19X5.

On 1 January 19X5 Bush Limited traded in its van in part exchange for a larger van; £1,500 was allowed in part exchange and £2,600 was paid in cash.

19X5 sales were 1,200 units at £15 per unit and 1,300 units were purchased, the purchase price being constant at £11 per unit. Expenses for 19X5 were £2,000.

All trading was for cash. Cash is not regarded as being part of monetary working capital.

Suitable price indices for motor vehicles and fixtures and fittings are:

	Motor Vehicles	*Fixtures and Fittings*
1 Jan 19X4	100	100
31 Dec 19X4	120	110
31 Dec 19X5	132	121

Required:
Bush Limited's CCA profit and loss and appropriation accounts for the years ended 31 December 19X4 and 31 December 19X5 and its balance sheets as at those dates.

12.6 Tate Limited's current cost balance sheet as at 31 December 19X2 is summarized below:

	£		£	£
Share Capital	900	Stock		3,366
Current Cost Reserve	500	Trade Debtors		2,800
Retained Earnings	666			6,166
	2,066	*Less:*		
		Trade Creditors	1,400	
		Overdraft	1,100	
10% Debentures	1,000	Proposed Dividends	600	3,100
	£3,066			£3,066

The company's *historical cost* profit and loss account for the year ended 31 December 19X3 is:

	£	£
Sales		43,000
Less: Opening Stock	3,300	
Purchases	27,700	
	31,000	
Less: Closing Stock	4,000	27,000
		16,000
Less: Overheads (including debenture interest)		10,000
		6,000
Less: Proposed Dividend		800
		£ 5,200

During 19X3 Tate Limited paid all its overheads for cash, paid its suppliers £27,000 and paid the dividend for 19X2. It received £42,500 from its customers.

The average age of stock was two months.

A suitable price index which can be applied to stock and monetary working capital moved as follows:

1 November 19X2	100
31 December 19X2	102
Average for 19X3	118
1 November 19X3	130
31 December 19X3	134

Assume that the balance at bank/overdraft should be included in monetary working capital.

Required:

(a) Tate Limited's current cost profit and loss account for the year ended 31 December 19X3 and its current cost balance sheet as at that date.

(b) The balances on the current cost reserve account and current cost retained earnings as at 31 December 19X3 if the balance at bank/overdraft is not included in monetary working capital.

12.7 Jim Limited started business on 1 January 19X2 and its purchases and sales of fixed assets for the three years to 31 December 19X4 are given overleaf:

                                                                                £

Freehold Land
Purchases, 1 January 19X2   200,000

Freehold Buildings
Purchases, 1 January 19X2   400,000

Plant and Machinery
Purchases, 1 January 19X2 Machine A   20,000
                1 January 19X2 Machine B   10,000
                1 January 19X3 Machine C   30,000
         Sales   30 June 19X4   Machine A for   22,000

Motor Vehicles
Purchases, 1 January 19X2 Vehicle P   2,000
                1 January 19X3 Vehicle Q   5,000

Initially it is estimated that all items of plant and machinery will last for 10 years and all motor vehicles for 5 years.

The land and buildings were professionally valued on 31 December 19X2 and 19X4 and the following valuations were reported.

	Land	Buildings	Expected useful life of the buildings from the date of valuation
	£	£	
31 December 19X2	220,000	416,000	40
31 December 19X4	216,000	478,000	36

The directors estimated that the value to the business of the land and buildings increased by 5% and 8% respectively in 19X3.

The following estimates, based on expert opinion, of the gross replacement costs of the machinery were obtained.

	31 Dec 19X2	*31 Dec 19X3*	*31 Dec 19X4*
	£	£	£
Machine A	28,000	30,000	—
Machine B	15,000	12,000	10,000
Machine C		34,000	36,000

It was agreed that as at 31 December 19X4, the net replacement cost of machine B had fallen below its recoverable value of £8,000 and that the machine should be valued on the latter basis. A reassessment of the remaining life of machine C made as at 31 December 19X4 resulted in an estimate of 6 years.

Motor vehicles are valued with reference to a price index which moved as follows:

1 Jan 19X2	*31 Dec 19X2*	*31 Dec 19X3*	*31 Dec 19X4*
100	125	130	120

It was decided towards the end of December 19X4 that vehicle P should be sold and not replaced. It was expected that the vehicle would fetch £800. The vehicle was sold on 3 January 19X5.

Required:

A table setting out for each of the years 19X2 to 19X4 and for each class of fixed asset:

(i) The depreciation charge.
(ii) Any other amounts charged or credited to the profit and loss account in respect of the assets.
(iii) Backlog depreciation.
(iv) Surplus or deficit on revaluation.

12.8 Violet Limited started business on 1 January 19X2; its historical cost balance sheets and profit and loss accounts for the first two years of operation are given below:

Profit and Loss Accounts

	19X2		*19X3*	
	£000	*£000*	*£000*	*£000*
Sales		200		240
less Opening stock	—		50	
Purchases	160		146	
	160		196	
less Closing stock	50	110	60	136
Gross Profit		90		104
less Depreciation	11		12	
Other expenses	49	60	60	72
Profit for the year		30		32
less Dividends		5		6
		25		26
Opening retained earnings		—		25
		£ 25		£ 51

Balance Sheets

	19X2		19X3	
	£000	£000	£000	£000
Land, at cost		80		80
Other fixed assets, at cost	120		120	
accumulated depreciation	11	109	23	97
		189		177
Stock, at cost (FIFO)		50		60
Monetary working capital		(14)		14
		£225		£251
Share capital		200		200
Retained earnings		25		51
		£225		£251

(a)   The land, which was purchased on 1 January 19X2, was revalued as follows:

	£
31 Dec 19X2	85,000
31 Dec 19X3	82,000

(b)   The 'other fixed assets' were purchased as follows:

	£
1 Jan 19X2	100,000
30 Jun 19X2	20,000
	£120,000

It is estimated that these assets will last for 10 years from the date of purchase.

A suitable price index for 'other fixed assets' moved as follows:

1 Jan 19X2	100
30 Jun 19X2	108
31 Dec 19X2	112
31 Dec 19X3	128

(c)   The average age of items in stock is 2 months. A suitable stock price index moved as follows:

Average for 19X2	100
31 Oct 19X2	105
31 Dec 19X2	108

Average for 19X3	110
31 Oct 19X3	118
31 Dec 19X3	121

(d) The following price index may be used for monetary working capital:

31 Dec 19X2	100
Average for 19X3	106
31 Dec 19X3	112

(e) The index of retail prices moved as follows:

1 Jan 19X2	31 Dec 19X2	31 Dec 19X3
100	128	150

(f) All the share capital was subscribed on 1 January 19X2

Required:

Violet Limited's

  (i) CCA profit and loss accounts for each of the two years ended 31 December 19X2 and 19X3
 (ii) CCA balance sheets as at 31 December 19X2 and 19X3
(iii) Statements of change in shareholders' equity interest after allowing for changes in the general purchasing power of money for each of the two years.

SECTION D

13 | *Financial Statement Analysis*

The purpose of financial statement analysis is to provide data for decision-making. The financial statements disclose the results of the activities of an entity and are prepared to help interested persons decide on questions such as whether to lend it money or invest in its shares. Financial statement analysis can be seen as part of the link between the financial statements and the decision-making process.

In this chapter we shall concentrate on the analysis of the traditional historical cost accounts but we will, from time to time, refer to changes that would be made in the analysis if current value accounts were available. We shall also point out some of the limitations that are inherent in the use of historical cost for the purposes of analysis. It is worth stressing however that the analyses described in this chapter will still be the relevant ones when using current cost accounts, the only difference being that the resulting figures will be a good deal more meaningful!

We would immediately stress the point that the financial statements give a representation of the past activities of the entity but that, with the possible exception of tax-gatherers, decision-makers will be interested in the results that the entity will be capable of achieving in the future. Thus, when examining financial statements the analyst must continually ask himself the extent to which the information that he is deriving will help him in forming expectations about the future.

It is being increasingly recognized that the users of financial statements extend beyond present and potential shareholders and creditors, and include such groups as employees, government bodies and society at large. We will not attempt to deal with the possible decision needs of each class of user – such a discussion would require a book of its own. Instead we will concentrate on two aspects of the entity that are relevant to all groups of users, namely, its profitability and solvency. We will discuss the topics in terms of limited companies, but it should be realized that most of the points will be relevant when examining the accounts of other business entities.

Financial statement analysis is not a fully developed science and comparatively little is known about the information needs of decision-makers, either by accountants or by decision-makers themselves. Our justification for the second part of this statement is the lack of formal decision models, and, correspondingly, the need for decision-makers to bring significant amounts of subjectivity and intuition to their work. For example, there is no generally agreed formula (or model) for calculating the value of a share, despite the large number of such models that have been suggested in the accounting and business finance literature. The aims of this chapter will therefore be severely limited and we shall confine ourselves to a discussion of those techniques that can be used to help increase the decision-maker's awareness of the state of the company. We shall not attempt to provide data which, if plugged into some formula, would enable the decision-maker to compute the answer to a question such as whether a share was worth buying at a given price.

A further caveat needs to be made at this stage. Although we are not certain of the exact needs of decision-makers, we can state, with some confidence, that they make considerable use of 'non-accounting' data, i.e. information which is not disclosed in a company's accounts. Thus, when deciding whether to lend money to a motor manufacturer, a bank or a government will consider the present and possible future state of the economy and the motor industry in general, besides the circumstances of the particular company. Further, even when considering the particular company, the potential lender normally wishes to have information about many matters that would not be disclosed in the company's accounts, such as details of new models and the state of its industrial relations. Thus, the information that can be obtained from an analysis of companies' financial statements only provides part of the information used by decision-makers.

The above may well seem to be the most negative introduction to a chapter that our readers have had to endure. We recognize this, but we are unrepentant since we believe it essential that readers should be fully aware that, although the topics discussed in this chapter are important, they do not, in themselves, provide all the answers. In fact, as we shall show, the importance of many topics is that they raise important questions in the mind of the analyst, which will suggest aspects of the company that call for further study.

FINANCIAL RATIOS

Much of this chapter will be devoted to a discussion of financial ratios. A financial ratio may be defined as an expression of the relationship between two accounting measurements; for example the current ratio, see page 472, expresses the relationship between current assets and current liabilities.

A ratio is usually evaluated by reference either to the ratios that the company itself has generated in the past, or to ratios currently achieved by other companies in the same industry. The first type of ratio evaluation is called *time-series analysis* and the second type is known as *cross-sectional analysis*. We will return to these points after describing the ratios which are most commonly used in financial statement analysis.

Ratio analysis is useful in that it provides guidance and discipline to the analyst's approach. It provides information about a number of different relationships that are not highlighted in the company's accounts. An analyst who includes the examination of financial ratios in an appraisal which also includes a review of the actual accounts, the flow of funds statements and relevant 'non-accounting' information would generally gain a useful insight into the activities of the company. He should then be in a position to make an *informed judgement* about the prospects of the company's surviving and, if it does, its future levels of profitability.

To demonstrate the calculations of the various ratios we will make use of the hypothetical retailing company, Owl Limited, whose accounts for 19X8 are shown below:

OWL LIMITED
Balance Sheet as at 31 December 19X8

31 December 19X7				Cost	Accumulated depreciation	Net book value
£000	*£000*			*£000*	*£000*	*£000*
		Fixed assets				
		Freehold land and				
57		buildings		60	4	56
187		Fixtures and fittings		290	132	158
244				£350	£136	214
		Current assets				
	116	Inventory			136	
	24	Trade debtors			28	
	1	Prepaid expenses			2	
147	6	Balance at bank			41	
391					207	
		less: Current liabilities				
	88	Trade creditors		93		
	4	Accrued expenses		5		
	22	Corporation tax payable		25		
119	5	Dividend payable		6	129	78
£272						£292
100		Share capital, £1 shares				100
52		Retained earnings				72
152						172
120		10 per cent Debentures				120
£272						£292

A summary of Owl Limited's profit and loss account for the year ended 31 December 19X8 is given below:

	£000	£000
Turnover		£1,260
Profit before tax after charging the item shown in Note 1		55
less Taxation		
Corporation tax, at 52 per cent based on the profits for the year		25
Profit after taxation		30
less Dividends – paid	4	
– proposed	6	10
		20
Retained earnings 1 January 19X8		52
Retained earnings 31 December 19X8		£72

Note 1

The profit for the year is stated after charging the following:

	£000
Directors' emoluments	20
Debenture interest	12
Depreciation	30

The amount of detailed information that will be included in the published profit and loss account will depend on the format statement used (the cost of goods sold expense is shown in formats 1 and 3 but not in formats 2 and 4) whilst small companies are not required to publish profit and loss accounts.

For the purposes of our explanation, we will assume that the following more detailed profit and loss account is available. Such information can often be obtained by financial analysts working for banking and lending firms, i.e. if a firm requires financial support it may have to give detailed accounting information and other 'non-accounting' data to the prospective lender. For other financial analysts the position is more difficult; they will not have access to detailed profit and loss accounts, and so some of the ratios described in the chapter will have to be based on estimates or omitted altogether.

	£000	£000
Sales		1,260
less Opening inventory	116	
Purchases	800	
c/f	916	

	£000	£000
b/f	916	1,260
less: Closing inventory	136	780
Gross profit (38 per cent)		480
less Selling and administrative expenses	363	
Directors' emoluments	20	
Depreciation	30	
Debenture interest	12	425
Profit before tax		55
less Taxation		25
Profit after tax		30
less Dividends		10
		20
Retained earnings, 1 January 19X8		52
Retained earnings, 31 December 19X8		£72

Liquidity and Solvency Ratios

These ratios are concerned with a company's ability to generate sufficient cash to continue in existence. The ratios can be considered as giving some indication of the risks associated with the company's future cash flows, i.e. they help the analyst make a judgement about the probability that the company will be able to generate sufficient cash inflows to cover the necessary cash outflows.

We can conveniently divide our attention between the short and long-run measures. Some writers refer to the short-run indicators as measures of liquidity and the long-run indicators as measures of solvency.

Short Run Indicators

Current Ratio

The *current ratio* is defined as $\dfrac{\text{Current assets}}{\text{Current liabilities}}$

Owl Limited's current ratio at 31 December 19X8 is $\dfrac{£207,000}{£129,000} = 1 \cdot 60$

The current ratio was the first financial ratio to be developed. It was used towards the end of the last century by prospective creditors as an indication of the creditworthiness of a company. The rationale for its use is the view that a company must have sufficient assets which can be converted into cash within a reasonably short period (i.e. current assets) to cover those liabilities that are due for payment either immediately or in the near future (current liabilities). The current ratio can, therefore, be said to provide an indication of the company's short-term financial strength.

When the ratio was first used there was a tendency for prospective creditors to expect companies to have a current ratio of two, and one still finds statements such as 'the ideal current ratio is two'. One argument for expecting the current assets to be larger than the current liabilities is that, if a company ceased to trade, it would be unlikely that the current assets could be sold for their book values, and so it would be prudent to require a potential borrower to have a substantial excess of current assets over current liabilities. This reasoning is, in part, sound, for if the financial statements are prepared by using the going concern concept, then, for example, the book value of the inventory will be shown at the lower of cost or net realizable value in the normal course of business. If the company ceased to trade, its inventory would have to be sold either immediately or in the very near future. It is likely that in such circumstances the company would have to sell its inventory for a price lower than its net realizable value in the normal course of business, and that this lower amount might be less than the cost. In particular, work in progress may often realize a very low price if it has to be sold in its partially completed condition.

The above is an argument in favour of saying that a company's current assets should be greater than its current liabilities, but it is not, of course, a justification for requiring the current ratio to be two. Nowadays it is recognized that the application of an arbitrarily derived rule about the desired level of a company's current ratio is less useful than the information provided by time series and cross-sectional analyses.

Quick Ratio

There is a further problem associated with inventory which has to be considered, even if it can be assumed that the company under review will continue to trade. It often takes a fairly considerable time for inventory to be converted into cash and hence be available to help pay creditors. Thus, another ratio is often used to help assess a company's short-term financial health – this is the *quick* (or quick assets) *ratio*. This is the ratio of quick assets, usually taken to be current assets less inventory, to current liabilities, i.e.

$$\text{Quick ratio} = \frac{\text{Current assets less inventory}}{\text{Current liabilities}}$$

for Owl Limited,

$$\text{Quick ratio} = \frac{£K207 - £K136}{£K129} = \frac{£K71}{£K129} = 0.55$$

Some analysts use a refinement of the above in that they exclude from quick assets such items as prepaid expenses which cannot be directly converted into cash. They would only include as quick assets, cash, bank balances, debtors and bills receivable. However, since published balance sheets usually do not differentiate between trade debtors and prepaid expenses it is often not possible to calculate this variant of the quick ratio.

In those cases where there is a long debtors collection period, it may be appropriate to exclude debtors from the definition of quick assets. This would show us whether the company has sufficient cash to pay its creditors at that immediate point in time. In most cases this is not a very useful ratio as all it discloses is that most companies do not have sufficient cash since they rely on the working capital cycle (see page 317) making the cash available. The terminology of ratio analysis becomes, we fear, somewhat confusing here. Some writers use the phrase *acid test* to mean the ratio of cash to current liabilities while others use the phrase as an alternative description of the quick ratio.

We shall return to our consideration of the quick ratio. The 'ideal' quick ratio is usually considered to be one on the grounds that the company should be able to generate sufficient cash (without waiting for the inventory to be converted into cash) to discharge its liabilities as they fall due. However, reasonable as this view seems, care must still be taken when interpreting this ratio. One of the main causes of difficulty is bank overdrafts.

The existence of a bank overdraft distorts both the current and quick ratios. Since bank overdrafts are, legally, repayable on demand (as opposed to bank loans which are repayable on agreed dates) they are treated as current liabilities. However, many companies, with the agreement of their banks, use overdrafts as a medium-term, if not a long-term, source of finance. Thus for the purposes of the short-term analysis, the analyst should deduct from the actual overdraft shown in the balance sheet, the level of overdraft which the bank would be prepared to see maintained for a period of two or three years or even longer. That is, the current liabilities should include only that part of the overdraft which the bank requires to be repaid in the near future. This would not be disclosed by the financial statements, and an analyst would have to estimate this amount unless he had access to the appropriate 'non-accounting' information.

A further point is that the company may have agreed an overdraft limit with its bank, and this facility is not used or not used fully at the balance sheet date. For example, Owl Limited's quick ratio is 0·55 which appears to show a dangerous position, but its condition depends on the attitude of its bankers. If they are not prepared to grant Owl Limited an overdraft, then unless the company is able to take other remedial action, it might well run into cash flow problems in the very near future. On the other hand, if the bank has agreed to allow the company an overdraft of up to say, £200,000, the company's short-term financial strength is sound despite its 'poor' quick ratio.

The state of the relationship between a company and its bankers is an important factor is assessing its ability to pay its creditors, but no information about this is contained or supplied with a company's financial statements. It is interesting to note, in this context, that one of the recommendations of the Sandilands Committee was that directors of all companies should include in their annual report a statement of the adequacy of the cash resources likely to become available to meet the company's requirements in the ensuing year. Such a statement would make the analyst's work easier but not unnecessary, for the directors might well be wrong.

The current and quick ratios are particularly susceptible to certain manipulations which are often referred to as 'window-dressing' or 'cosmetic reporting'. These terms cover those devices which enable a company to manipulate its current assets and liabilities at its balance sheet date so as to disclose 'better ratios'.

This sort of manipulation can take a number of forms. The company might, for instance, borrow money from another company with which it shares common ownership (a subsidiary, fellow subsidiary or parent company). The cash would increase its current assets while the liability would be shown as a non-current liability (see Chapter 8).

In general, the changing of the classification of a non-current asset into a current asset and a current liability into a non-current liability will improve (increase) the ratios. The auditor should prevent such manipulations, but, as the distinctions between current and non-current items are not always clear, he might not always be successful.

Another possible ploy can best be understood if it is realized that if one starts with a ratio greater than 1, say A/B, and then subtracts the same amount, x, from both numerator and denominator the new ratio of $\dfrac{A-x}{B-x}$ will be larger than A/B.

Suppose that $A = £100$, $B = £60$ and $x = £10$

$$\text{Then } \frac{A}{B} = \frac{£100}{£60} = 1 \cdot 67 \text{ and } \frac{A-x}{B-x} = \frac{£90}{£50} = 1 \cdot 80$$

Thus if a company was able to arrange its affairs so that its current assets and current liabilities were both reduced at the balance sheet date from their 'normal' levels by the same amount, it would increase its current ratio.

Suppose that Owl Limited had arranged to delay the delivery of goods costing £50,000 so that they were received and purchased in January 19X9 instead of December 19X8. Subtracting, £50,000 from both the current assets and liabilities would mean that the current ratio would increase from 1·60 to 1·99 (£K157/£K79).

It should be noted that if the original ratio is less than one, i.e. if $A < B$ then the addition of the same amount to the numerator and denominator will increase the ratio, i.e. if $A < B$, $\dfrac{A+x}{B+x} > \dfrac{A}{B}$.

If Owl Limited was more concerned about its 'poor' quick ratio, which is less than one, than about its current ratio, it might decide to delay the payment of creditors of, say, £60,000 until January 19X9. The addition of that amount to both its quick assets and current liabilities would increase its quick ratio from 0·55 to 0·69 (£K131/£K189).

The above discussion of window-dressing highlights what is the major limitation of the use of the current and quick ratios in the assessment of the short-term financial condition of a company, i.e. that ratios are based on a position at a single point in time. The position revealed by the balance sheet may be a satisfactory one but, as was explained in Chapter 9, the company may be experiencing considerable difficulties in the course of the year, owing to such factors as seasonal variations in cash flows.

While it is true that the larger the current and quick ratios the safer the company's position, it is not true to say that the larger the ratios the better. High ratios often indicate that the company has made an excessive investment in working capital; it may be carrying excessive inventories, debtors or cash balances or it may be paying its creditors too quickly. We shall return to this point in the section of this chapter devoted to profitability.

As we have already indicated, modern practice is to pay less attention to the absolute values of the ratios, e.g. whether the current ratio is two or not, and to pay more attention to any divergences from the past trend of the company's ratios and from the ratios disclosed by similar companies. In addition, more stress is nowadays paid to the concept of matching the cash flows in and out. In other words, regard is given to the time taken in converting the current assets into cash and to the period of credit granted by the creditors.

In order to illustrate the importance of the latter aspects we will examine Owl Limited under two alternative sets of assumptions.

We will first suppose that the company will have to pay all its trade creditors in January 19X9 unless it is to lose its source of supply but that it will only collect 50 per cent of its year-end debtors and will, in January, sell only 20 per cent of its year-end inventory for cash. It will be seen from the following cash budget for January 19X9 that the cash flows out exceed the cash flows in and that when the opening bank balance is used up the company will, unless it can borrow some money, be in severe difficulties:

Cash Budget for January 19X9 (1)

	£000	£000
Receipts		
50 per cent of debtors at 1 January 19X9		14·0
20 per cent of inventory sold for cash	27·2	
add Mark-up of 61 per cent (a gross profit of 38 per cent is equivalent to a mark-up of 61 per cent)	16·6	43·8
		57·8
less Payments		
Creditors	93·0	
Overheads, cash overheads for 19X8 ÷ 12 $\dfrac{£K425 - £K30}{12}$	32·9	125·9
Excess of cash flows out over cash flows in January 19X9		£68·1

Let us now suppose that all the year-end debtors will be collected in January, that 50 per cent of the year-end inventory will be sold for cash and that only 80 per cent of the trade creditors will have to be paid in the month.

Cash Budget for January 19X9 (2)

	£000	*£000*
Receipts		
Debtors		28·0
50 per cent of inventory sold for cash	68·0	
add Mark-up of 61 per cent	41·5	109·5
		137·5
Payments		
Creditors, 80 per cent of £K93	74·4	
Overheads	32·9	107·3
Excess of cash flows in over cash flows out		£30·2

With the first set of pessimistic assumptions there appears to be every chance of the company's running out of cash, but if the actual situation is closer to the second set of assumptions it is likely that the company is achieving a satisfactory matching of cash flows in and out.

The above discussion suggests that an analyst will be particularly interested in examining the speed at which the current assets are converted into cash and the credit period granted by trade creditors. We will now examine these.

Inventory Turnover Ratio

The inventory turnover ratio is the ratio of the cost of goods sold to the average stock held during the year:

$$\text{Inventory turnover ratio} = \frac{\text{Cost of goods sold}}{\text{Average inventory}}$$

Since the average inventory figure cannot be determined from the company's accounts, it is often the practice to use, as an approximation, the average of the opening and closing inventory figures. Thus:

$$\text{Inventory turnover ratio} = \frac{\text{Cost of goods sold}}{\text{Average of the opening and closing inventory}}$$

Owl Limited's ratio for 19X8 is:

$$\frac{£K780}{\frac{1}{2}(£K116 + £K136)} = 6·19$$

This ratio represents the number of times the inventory has been 'turned over' and replaced during the year, i.e. if we made the unlikely assumption that the company waited until its inventory fell to zero before making any purchases it would, on average, make just over six purchases per year.

As we indicated when presenting the information about Owl Limited, the cost of goods sold figure may not be disclosed in the published accounts and, so, the sales figure is sometimes used as the numerator when calculating the ratio. This is unsatisfactory, because the figures are not comparable; sales are based on selling prices while the inventory is stated at cost price. However, it might be helpful to use the sales figure if the purpose of the calculation of the ratio is to compare it with the ratios achieved by similar companies which, in particular, earn the same gross profit ratios.

If the sales figure were used the ratio would be larger; in the case of Owl Limited the inventory turnover ratio (based on sales) would be

$$\frac{£K1,260}{\frac{1}{2}(£K116 + £K136)} = 10{\cdot}0$$

However, in many cases, analysts may feel they can estimate the gross profit ratios fairly accurately. If so, they should use their estimate to adjust the sales figure disclosed by the accounts and arrive at the cost of goods sold.

We shall discuss the importance of this ratio in connection with a company's profitability, on page 490 and we shall, at this stage, concentrate on its implications for a company's liquidity. For this purpose it is more helpful to measure the inventory turnover ratio in terms of the average inventory holding period.

This is done by dividing the number of days in the year by the inventory turnover ratio. It is often the practice, for ease of calculation, to assume that there are 360 days in a year. A seemingly more fundamental question is whether to use the number of working days in a year, approximately 250 if there is a five-day week. It does not matter whether 360 or 250 days are taken, so long as the measures with which the company's results are being compared are calculated on the same basis. We shall use a 360-day year.

The average inventory holding period is:

$$\frac{360}{\text{Inventory turnover ratio}} \text{ days}$$

For Owl Limited the average period is:

$$\frac{360}{6{\cdot}19} = 58 \text{ days}$$

Obviously the larger the inventory turnover ratio and, correspondingly, the shorter the inventory holding period, the faster the inventory will be converted into cash or debtors.

When reviewing the above measures the analyst must consider the extent to which he can accept the assumption that the average of the opening and closing inventories is a reasonable estimate of the average inventory held during the year. If the opening and closing inventory figures are unusually high or low, the measures will be distorted. When comparing the measures with those reported by other companies, the analyst must take into account any effects of the different methods of accounting for inventory, and any differences due to their having different year ends (as with seasonal businesses such as fireworks manufacturers).

Debtors' Collection Period

The debtors' collection period is calculated in the same way as the average inventory holding period except that the debtors are based on the year-end balance because the opening debtors' figure depends on the sales of the previous year.

The period is calculated in two steps:

$$\text{Debtors' turnover ratio} = \frac{\text{Credit sales}}{\text{Year-end debtors}}$$

$$\text{Debtors' collection period} = \frac{360}{\text{Debtors' turnover ratio}}$$

An alternative method is to calculate first the average daily credit sales:

$$\text{Average daily credit sales} = \frac{\text{Credit sales}}{360}$$

and then to divide the year-end debtors by the average daily credit sales:

$$\text{Debtors' collection period} = \frac{\text{Year-end debtors}}{\text{credit sales}/360}$$

If we calculated the above measure by using the figures shown in Owl Limited's accounts we would arrive at a period of $\frac{£K28}{£K1,260/360}$ or eight days. This is a very low figure, which indicates that we have probably made the mistake of including cash sales with the credit sales. If a company has only a small proportion of cash sales, it would not greatly matter if we used the company's total sales in the calculations. But, when considering a retail establishment such as Owl Limited, which has a high proportion of cash sales, the use of the total sales figure would result in a meaningless answer. We must, therefore, attempt to find out, or estimate, the proportion of sales made on credit.*

We will assume that we have managed to discover that 25 per cent of Owl Limited's sales are made on credit. We can now calculate Owl Limited's debtors collection period.

---

* The analyst may be able to make some sort of estimate of the proportion of cash and credit sales on the basis of his knowledge of the business.

$$\text{Debtors' turnover ratio} = \frac{25 \text{ per cent of } \pounds K1,260}{\pounds K28} = 11\cdot25$$

$$\text{Debtors' collection period} = \frac{360}{11\cdot25} = 32 \text{ days}$$

These measures are particularly vulnerable to seasonal variations or other changes in the pattern of sales, for the year-end debtors will depend on the credit sales of the last few months of the year. Thus, if the monthly sales at the end of the year are greater than the average for the year the measure calculated above will overstate the average collection period.

Creditors' Payment Period

This is calculated in exactly the same way as the debtors' collection period and the same comments must be made about the problems caused if the year-end position does not reflect the position for the year as a whole.

The creditors' payment period is calculated as follows:

$$\text{Creditors' turnover ratio} = \frac{\text{Credit purchases}}{\text{Year-end creditors}}$$

$$\text{Creditors' payment period} = \frac{360}{\text{Creditors' turnover ratio}}$$

If we assume that all Owl Limited's purchases were on credit its creditors payment period at the year end is given by

$$\frac{360}{\pounds K800/\pounds K93} = 41\cdot8 \text{ days}$$

The Matching of Cash Flows

We shall now try to see how well Owl Limited matches its cash flows. We shall repeat the procedures outlined on page 476, but this time we shall use the various measures of the speed of the conversion of the assets into cash and the creditors payment period that we calculated above.

We shall assume:

1. That sales and purchases take place evenly over each month.

2. That the various ratios and measures calculated above will be maintained in January 19X9.

3. That the overhead expenses for January 19X9 will be equal to the monthly average for 19X8 and that the expenses are paid in cash, i.e. we shall ignore prepaid and accrued expenses.

4. That there are 30 days in each month.

Cash Budget for January 19X9 (3)

Notes	Receipts	£000	£000
(a)	Debtors 30·0/32·0 of £K28		26·2
(b)	Cash sales		85·0
			111·2
	Payments		
	Creditors 30·0/41·8 of £K93	66·7	
	Cash overheads	32·9	99·6
	Excess of cash flows in over cash flows out		£11·6

Notes

(a) If we assume that the sales take place evenly, and ignore bad debts, then on average 30/32 of the debtors outstanding at the start of the month will be collected in January.

	£000
(b) Inventory sold in January 30/58 of £K136	£70·3
Proportion sold for cash, 75 per cent of £K70·3	52·8
add Mark-up of 61 per cent	32·2
	£85·0

It appears that, subject to factors of which we are not aware, such as the variability of the cash flows, Owl Limited's matching of cash flows is satisfactory.

The above analysis can be developed, with the necessary additional assumptions, to cover the rest of the year, and the analyst could produce a cash budget for 19X9 in the form described in Chapter 9. This budget could take account of the dividend and tax payments as well as other cash receipts and payments, e.g. the purchase of fixed assets, which might be expected to take place.

The analyst could also use the above framework to evaluate the position of the company under various alternative assumptions. For example, he could investigate the company's ability to expand its operations from internally generated funds or he could consider the effect of, say, a reduction in the period of credit allowed by its suppliers.

We believe that the above approach affords a much better insight into the short-term financial strength of a company than the basic current and quick ratios. However, these ratios are useful in so far as they provide indicators which are quickly and easily calculated.

Medium and Long-Term Measures of Solvency

We shall now consider the longer term.

Coverage Ratios

If a company has any long-term debt in its capital structure, it must ensure that the interest can be paid. A measure of a company's capacity to pay interest is the cover provided by its profit. This measure is known as 'times interest covered' and is usually calculated as follows:

$$\frac{\text{Profit before tax and interest}}{\text{Interest expense}}$$

Clearly, the higher the cover the better the company's ability to pay the interest and the safer the position of the creditors.

Owl Limited's interest cover for 19X8 was:

$$\frac{£K55 + £K12}{£K12} = 5 \cdot 6$$

The ratio tells us that the profits available for paying the interest are 5·6 times bigger than the interest.

In a way this is not a very sensible measure, but it is generally considered to be a reasonable rule of thumb for the purposes of analysis. A more satisfactory method would be to use in the numerator the funds generated by operations (basically profit plus depreciation) instead of profit, since interest is paid out of funds not out of profit.

A similar coverage ratio may be calculated in respect of the company's dividends. This is taken to be a measure of the company's ability to maintain dividends at their current level. It is not strictly a measure of solvency because the non-payment of dividends does not give the shareholders the right to force the company into liquidation. However, since it is closely related to the 'times interest covered' ratio we will introduce it at this stage.

$$\text{Dividend cover} = \frac{\text{Profit available to ordinary shareholders}}{\text{Dividend}}$$

The measure for Owl Limited in 19X8 was:

$$\frac{£K30}{£K10} = 3 \cdot 0$$

The lower the cover the more likely it is that a reduction in profit will result in a reduction in the dividend.

If the company had preference shares in issue, a similar measure could be calculated, i.e.

$$\frac{\text{Profit available to preference shareholders}}{\text{Preference dividend}}$$

The effect of any change from historical cost accounting to current value accounting on the above coverage ratios should be noted. To the extent that 'current value' profits are less than historical cost profits, the use of the former in the calculations will mean that much lower ratios will be disclosed. In addition, as we explained in Chapter 12, the differences between the two measures of profit will vary as between companies. Thus, analysts have had to become used to interpreting different values of these ratios. Using current cost figures it has been found that many companies are not covering their dividends and only narrowly covering their interest payments with current cost profits.

Debt to Equity Ratio

The relationship between a company's long-term debt and its equity is known as the company's gearing (UK) or leverage (USA). A company which has a large amount of debt when compared to its equity is said to be highly geared.

There are a number of ways of expressing a company's gearing. Perhaps the most commonly used measure is:

$$\frac{\text{Book value of long-term debt}}{\text{Book value of owners' equity}}$$

Owners' equity consists of the company's share capital and reserves. Owl Limited's debt to equity ratio as at 31st December 19X8 was:

$$\frac{£K120}{£K172} = 0.70$$

For some purposes the market values of debt and equity are used (i.e. the market values of the company's debentures and shares) but we will concentrate on the use of book values. The use of the market value of equity is advocated on the basis that it more closely represents the economic value of the entity.

The debt to equity ratio can be considered as giving an indication of the risk, due to gearing, faced by both the long-term creditors (debenture holders) and shareholders. The higher the ratio the more risky the position of both classes.

From the point of view of the debenture holders, the smaller the ratio the greater the chance that they would be repaid even if the borrowing company were to be liquidated. Consider the different circumstances of A Limited and B Limited:

	A Ltd £	B Ltd £
Sundry assets *less* Liabilities	£100	£100

Share capital and reserves	10	90
Debentures	90	10
	£100	£100

If both companies went into liquidation there is more chance that the sale of the assets, even if sold for less than their book values, would realize enough to repay B debenture holders' as compared to the holders of A's debentures.

Similarly, the lower the ratio the greater the likelihood that the company will be able to generate sufficient funds each year to pay the interest. This, of course, makes it less likely that the firm will be forced into liquidation in the first instance. The reader should be able to recognize that the 'times interest covered' ratio, presented on page 482, is also a gearing ratio, since it is a measure of the effect of a given quantity of long-term debt on the profit of the company.

The debt to equity ratio is also a measure of the risk faced by the shareholders. There are two aspects of this risk. Highly geared companies run a greater risk of failing to pay the interest and, hence, of being forced into liquidation.

The second aspect is that the profit attributable to the shareholders is subject to greater variability than is the attributable profit of a company with no, or a low, gearing. The reason is that the interest payments remain constant and thus the whole of the variability of the profits earned by the assets is borne by the profits accruing to shareholders. Thus, if there is, say, a 10 per cent fall in the profit before interest the shareholders in a geared company would experience a decrease of more than 10 per cent in their attributable profit – the decrease in the attributable profits of the shareholders of a company with no gearing would be 10 per cent.

For example, suppose that we have two companies C Limited and D Limited whose balance sheets are as follows:

	C Ltd £	D Ltd £
Sundry assets *less* Liabilities	£800	£800

	C Ltd £	D Ltd £
Owners' equity	800	400
10 per cent debentures	—	400
	£800	£800
Debt to equity ratio	0	1

Suppose that both companies generate the same earnings on their assets, i.e. that each year the profits, before interest, of C and D are equal. We shall assume the profits, before interest, for three years are as follows:

Year 1	Year 2	Year 3
£100	£80	£112
	Decrease of 20 per cent	Increase of
		40 per cent over year 2 or
		12 per cent over year 1

Since C Limited has no debt, the above series also shows the profit attributable to the shareholders.

In contrast, the shareholders of D will face a greater variability in their attributable profits.

	Year 1	Year 2	Year 3
	£	£	£
Profit before interest	100	80	112
less			
Debenture interest	40	40	40
Profit attributable to shareholders	£60	£40	£72

	Decrease of	Increase of
	33·3 per cent	80 per cent over year 2 and
		20 per cent over year 1

The risk faced by the shareholders of a geared company by virtue of its gearing is known as the *financial risk*. This is in contrast with the risk associated with the earnings generated by the assets which is called the *business risk*. Thus C and D seem to have the same business risk in that their profits before interest are the same, but only D's shareholders experience financial risk.

When reviewing the position of ordinary shareholders in a company which has preference shares in issue, the definition of gearing is changed. This is done to take account of the fact that the claims of the preference shareholders have priority over those of the ordinary shareholders. The debt to equity ratio used for this purpose is normally:

$$\frac{\text{Book values of long term debt} + \text{Preference share capital}}{\text{Book value of ordinary shareholders' equity}}$$

The equity of the ordinary shareholders consists of the ordinary share capital plus the reserves.

When reviewing the current and quick ratios on page 473 we discussed the problem caused by bank overdrafts which, because of their legal status, have to be classified as current liabilities but which may be in effect a source of long-term funds. The same problem arises in connection with the debt to equity ratio. If the analyst believes that all, or part, of the overdraft represents a form of long-term debt, he might include all or part of the overdraft in the numerator of the debt to equity ratio.

We shall now consider the effect of using current values as opposed to historical costs in the calculation of the gearing ratios. In general, the use of current values will result in a lower debt to equity ratio. For example, let us consider the SSAP16 approach. The recognition of the enhanced value of fixed assets would generally result in the creation of a revaluation reserve which increases owners' equity. Hence the denominator of the debt to equity ratio will be increased, while the numerator will be unchanged. The decrease in the ratio simply reflects the fact that the current values of the assets are, in general, greater than their historical costs, and hence the protection afforded by the existence of the assets is greater than that indicated by the 'values' disclosed by the historical cost accounts. Our readers may recall that on page 483 we observed that the use of current value accounting would, under present circumstances, result in the disclosure of worse 'times interest covered' ratios. Thus, we have a paradoxical situation. Using current value accounting, instead of historical cost accounting, would mean the disclosure of lower measures of gearing based on the balance sheet (the debt to equity ratio) but larger measures of gearing based on the profit and loss account (the 'times interest covered' ratio). The reason for the paradox is the use of profit instead of funds in the 'times interest covered' ratio. The meaning of a current cost loss is that the company is not generating sufficient revenue to cover the 'value to the business' of the assets used up during the period. However, a company disclosing such a loss may yet be generating sufficient funds to cover its interest payments.

When considering the possible consequences of liquidating the company, we should recognize that the relevant amounts are the net realizable values of the assets which may, in the case of fixed assets, be less than their 'value to the business', or even their depreciated historical costs. A useful measure of the risk borne by the long-term creditors is, then, a comparison of the value of the debt and the sum of the net realizable values of the assets.* However, the net realizable value of the assets is not disclosed in the accounts, and is hence part of the 'non-accounting' data.

Profitability

The second part of the analysis of the financial statements is the consideration of the profit earned by the company. The figure of profit is meaningless unless it is compared to the resources which have been employed in the earning of the profit. The basic approach to measuring the profitability of a company is, therefore, based on a formula of the following form:

$$\frac{\text{A measure of profit}}{\text{A measure of the resources employed}}$$

Before proceeding to consider the various measures of profit and resource, we should discuss the objective behind the calculation of a company's

---

* If the debt is secured against a particular asset the net realizable value of that asset is obviously the significant factor. Similarly, unsecured creditors must pay regard to the assets which have been charged.

profitability. The objective has both what might be described as passive and active aspects. The passive aspect is concerned with forecasting the future, i.e. extrapolating past profitability to help make judgements about the company's future profitability. The active aspect is bound up with the making of suggestions about ways of improving the profitability of the company under review.

This topic is bedevilled by a lack of consistency and many variations of the ratios which we shall describe will be found in practice. We shall not attempt to describe all of them but shall concentrate on one set of measures that are in fairly common use in the United Kingdom.

Perhaps the most commonly used main measure of profitability is called the return on assets (or capital) employed. This is given by

$$\frac{\text{Profit before tax and interest}}{\text{Average total assets used in the business}} \times 100$$

The reason for stating the profit before tax is to make the measure a more suitable basis for cross-sectional and time-series analysis. The tax charge demands on the particular circumstances of a company, e.g. whether it had tax losses brought forward from previous periods, and on the current state of tax legislation. If the profit was stated after taxation the first factor would militate against cross-sectional analysis while both factors would make time-series analysis less effective.

The profit is stated before interest so that we can differentiate between the way a company uses its assets and the way it finances those assets. Stating the profit in this way is also useful in cross-sectional analysis for it enables us to compare the efficiency with which companies with different capital structures use their assets.

The profit is the result of activities over a period, and so it is reasonable to include in the denominator the average of the assets employed. Normally, the best possible estimate of this value is the average of the total assets at the start and end of the period. However, some analysts use the total assets at the end of the year.

We have specified total assets, i.e. fixed assets plus current assets. Net assets (fixed plus current assets less current liabilities) are sometimes taken, but there is then the disadvantage of mixing up the use and the financing of the assets.

If we apply the above formula based on total assets, Owl Limited's return on capital employed for 19X8 is:

$$\frac{£K55 + £K12}{\frac{1}{2}(£K244 + £K147 + £K214 + £K207)} \times 100$$

$$= \frac{£K67}{£K406} \times 100$$

$$= 16 \cdot 50 \,\text{per cent}$$

We can analyse the above rate of return by observing that the overall rate of return depends on two factors, the company's profit margin on sales and its rate of asset turnover, i.e.

$$\frac{\text{Profit}}{\text{Assets}} \times 100 = \frac{\text{Profit}}{\text{Sales}} \times 100 \times \frac{\text{Sales}}{\text{Assets}}$$

We can illustrate the effect of this decomposition of the main ratio by presenting a simple example. Suppose that we have two merchants, A and B, who both sell cinema organs. Cinema organs are large, and A and B have small shops so they can only stock one organ at a time. The organs cost £10,000 each and immediately A and B sell an organ they withdraw any surplus cash left after replacing it. Thus, the average total assets employed for the period are £10,000 in each case. We shall ignore overheads and suppose that A sold 6 organs during the period for £10,500 each while B sold 15 organs for £10,200 each. Thus, they both earned a profit of £3,000 and their rate of return on assets employed was

$$\frac{£3,000}{£10,000} \times 100 = 30 \text{ per cent.}$$

So for A:
$$\frac{\text{Profit}}{\text{Assets}} \times 100 = \frac{\text{Profit}}{\text{Sales}} \times 100 \times \frac{\text{Sales}}{\text{Assets}}$$

i.e. 30 per cent $= \dfrac{£3,000}{£63,000} \times 100 \times \dfrac{£63,000}{£10,000}$

$$= 4{\cdot}76 \text{ per cent} \times 6{\cdot}3$$

While for B:
30 per cent $= \dfrac{£3,000}{£153,000} \times 100 \times \dfrac{£153,000}{£10,000}$

$$= 1{\cdot}96 \text{ per cent} \times 15{\cdot}3$$

The above illustrates that a company can earn a 'reasonable' profit by either obtaining a high margin on a low turnover or a low margin on a high turnover, and, of course, can earn a 'large' profit if it can obtain a high margin on a high turnover!

Given the above analysis, we can see how, for example, we might start examining the results of a company which had a rate of return that was below the industrial average. We could see whether the company had a low profit margin, or a low turnover or both.

Owl Limited's profit margin for 19X8 was:

$$\frac{£K67}{£K1,260} \times 100 = 5{\cdot}32$$

per cent while its rate of asset turnover was: $\dfrac{£K1,260}{£K406} = 3\cdot10$

Note that $5\cdot32 \times 3\cdot10 = 16\cdot5$ per cent.
We now examine the two components of the main ratio in a little more detail.

Profit to Sales

The ratio of profit to sales is, in itself, a useful ratio which can be used directly in time-series and cross-sectional analysis. Assuming that we have been provided with a detailed trading and profit and loss account, we can also examine the composition of the profit to sales ratio. The main subratio is the gross profit ratio.* This is the ratio of gross profit (sales less the cost of goods sold) to sales. Although it is described as a ratio, the measure is usually expressed as a percentage. Owl Limited's gross profit percentage for 19X6 was 38 per cent $\left(\dfrac{£K480}{£K1,260} \times 100 \right)$, and this figure was shown, as is sometimes done in practice, on the face of the trading account.

The cost of goods sold in the case of a manufacturing company is the cost of production (see Chapter 2). In the case of trading companies it is the cost of bringing the goods to the point of sale, i.e. the cost of the goods and carriage in, and, possibly, storage costs.

The preparation of a trading account, and hence the disclosure of gross profit, enables the analyst to approach his task by examining the company's mark-up and level of overheads. He could, for example, see whether it was the policy of the company to set a low mark-up while incurring low overheads (e.g. a discount store) or set a high mark-up accompanied by higher overheads (e.g. a specialist shop).

An examination of the gross profit ratio permits him to isolate certain changes in the company's policy or circumstances. In order to illustrate this point, we will assume that Owl Limited's gross profit percentage in 19X7 was 45 per cent. The factors an analyst might consider when examining the possible reasons for the reduction in the ratio from 45 to 38 per cent are:

1. There may have been a change in the method used to value inventory or an error in computing the book value of the inventory.
    For example, if the inventory at the end of 19X7 had been overstated, the error would serve both to increase the gross profit of 19X7 and decrease the gross profit of 19X8.

2. There may have been a change in the 'sales mix', i.e. the company may have sold a higher proportion of goods which earn a low mark-up in 19X8 as compared with 19X7. It must be noted that the gross profit percentage is an average and that some types of goods sold by the company will earn a higher mark-up than others.

---

* See Volume 1, page 126.

3.   The company may have reduced its selling prices either to counter competition or to encourage a greater volume of sales. A reduction in the gross profit percentage is, after all, not necessarily bad. All other things being equal, it is better to earn a gross profit of 20 per cent on sales of £m1·0 than a gross profit of 25 per cent on sales of £m0·5.

4.   The company may not have been able to pass on the full amount of an increase in its costs because of competitive pressures or government legislation.

The analyst would also consider the overheads in some detail. He might find it useful to prepare a 'percentage profit and loss account', i.e. he would express the items in the profit and loss account as percentages of sales as shown below.

OWL LIMITED
'Percentage' Profit and Loss Account
Year ended 31 December 19X8

	£000	£000	per cent	per cent
Sales		1,260		100·0
less Cost of goods sold		780		61·9
Gross profit		480		38·1
less				
Selling and administrative expenses	363		28·8	
Directors' emoluments	20		1·6	
Depreciation	30		2·4	
Debenture interest	12	425	1·0	33·8
Net profit		£55		4·3

Care must be taken when interpreting the various percentages because of the difference between *fixed* and *variable* costs. This distinction plays an important part in management accounting, but it is also relevant in financial statement analysis. Basically, fixed costs are those costs, or expenses, which remain constant irrespective of the company's level of output or sales, while variable costs are those costs which move in sympathy with changes in the level of activity. The rent of premises is an example of a fixed cost and packaging costs and salesmen's commissions are examples of variable costs. Thus, if the volume of sales were reduced, an increase in the ratio of, say, rent to sales would be expected, but the ratio of commission to sales might be expected to remain constant.

Asset Turnover Rates

We saw earlier that the rate of asset turnover indicated the amount of assets which the company employed in order to support a given level of sales. We also saw that a company's rate of return on capital employed would be increased if its rate of asset turnover were increased. This could be achieved either by increasing sales for a given level of assets or by maintaining the current level of sales with the use of fewer assets, or both.

The analyst can examine the total asset turnover rate by considering the rates of turnover of the individual assets. We have already looked at the turnover of inventory and debtors, and we should now introduce the fixed asset turnover rate. The rate can be calculated as follows:

$$\frac{\text{Sales}}{\text{Net book value of fixed assets}}$$

If we use the net book value of the assets at the year end, Owl Limited's fixed asset turnover rate for 19X8 is:

$$\frac{\pounds K1,260}{\pounds K214} = 5 \cdot 89 \text{ times}$$

However, the effect of depreciation can easily distort the above calculation. Let us suppose that Owl Limited's sales for 19X9 are the same as for 19X8 (£K1,260), that the company neither purchases nor sells any fixed assets in 19X9 and that its depreciation charge for 19X9 is £K30. Owl Limited's fixed asset turnover ratio for 19X9 is then:

$$\frac{\pounds K1,260}{\pounds K184} = 6 \cdot 85 \text{ times}$$

Thus it appears that the company is making more efficient use of its fixed assets, but this is not really a sensible interpretation since the change is simply due to the charging of a further year's depreciation. Thus, using the cost of fixed assets, instead of their net book value, would make the rate of turnover disclosed more suitable for the purposes of comparison. Comparing the fixed asset turnover ratio of a firm with those of its competitors can be very hazardous when using historical costs as the valuation basis. The use of current cost accounting would make interfirm comparisons of this ratio much more valid.

At this stage, we should warn against naive interpretations of the results of the above calculations. The key is the phrase 'all other things being equal'. For example, Company A may have a lower rate of inventory turnover than the industrial average but that does not necessarily mean that the company is holding too much inventory. It may be that Company A, by buying inventory in larger quantities, is able to obtain substantial discounts (and make greater profits in times of rapidly rising prices). The question of fixing the optimum level of inventory is a complex one that depends on a number of factors, such as the cost of placing orders and the losses that the company would suffer if it ran out of inventory. This point reinforces the observation we made earlier that financial statement analysis tends to produce questions rather than answers. Thus, to continue the example, the first reaction of an analyst on finding that the company's rate of inventory turnover is lower than average should be to ask why, rather than to assert that the company is holding too much inventory.

Companies Engaged in More than One Industry

One or more of a company's assets may not be used in the main activity of the company, e.g. an investment in the shares of another company. In such cases, it will usually be desirable to attempt to measure the rate of return earned in the main business of the company. This can be done by removing the relevant assets from the denominator of the ratio and, correspondingly, the profit earned on the assets from the numerator.

It would be useful if this principle could be extended to the analysis of those companies that are engaged in a number of distinct main activities so that the analyst could compute the rates of return earned from each one. In order to do this he would need to know the profit earned from each activity and the assets employed in it. The problem here is that although some indication of the breakdown of the total profit will be provided in the published accounts, it is not often possible to apportion the company's assets between the various activities.* Thus, in general, the analyst can only calculate the company's overall rate of return. This gives rise to some difficulties in both cross-sectional and time-series analysis. The problem in the former is that the analyst would have to find other companies which are engaged, in similar proportions, in the same range of activities. The lessons that can be drawn from time-series analysis will be less useful if the company has, over time, substantially changed the proportions of its different activities.

Return on Shareholders' Equity

The return on the equity of the ordinary shareholders is usually defined as:

$$\frac{\text{After tax profit attributable to ordinary shareholders}}{\text{Book value of ordinary share capital and reserves}} \times 100$$

This formula is stated in terms of ordinary shareholders since, in respect of most of the topics discussed in this section, preference shares have the same effect as debentures on the position of the ordinary shareholders. The formula could easily be modified to disclose the return earned on the total of shareholders' funds.

The rate of return on the equity of the ordinary shareholders of Owl Limited for 19X8 is:

$$\frac{£K30}{\frac{1}{2}\{£K(152 + 172)\}} \times 100 = 18 \cdot 52 \text{ per cent}$$

---

* Many firms set up separate limited company subsidiaries for their different activities. As these subsidiaries have to file accounts with the Registrar of Companies, an analyst can gain some idea of the importance of these activities.

We used the average of the opening and closing book values of ordinary shareholders' equity above, but the closing book value is often used in practice.

We have already discussed the possible distorting effects of taxation on such ratios and, indeed, we used the profit before tax in calculating the overall rate of return on the total assets employed. In some cases it would be useful to calculate the return on equity by using the profit before tax. In particular, the choice would depend on the measure with which the calculated rate of return is to be compared.

It might be helpful if, at this point, we summarized the various ratios that we have discussed so far. The summary is given in the following table which also shows some of the main alternatives.

FINANCIAL RATIOS

	Ratio	*Alternatives*
Short-run liquidity		
1. Current ratio	$\dfrac{\text{Current assets}}{\text{Current liabilities}}$	
2. Quick ratio	$\dfrac{\text{Current assets less inventory}}{\text{Current liabilities}}$	(i) Prepaid expenses may be deducted from the numerator.
		(ii) Prepaid expenses and debtors may be deducted from the numerator.
		(iii) Part, or all, of the overdraft may be excluded from denominator.
Asset turnover rates and collection periods		
3. Inventory turnover ratio	$\dfrac{\text{Cost of goods sold}}{\text{Average inventory held}}$	(i) Numerator may be sales for period (if we cannot estimate the cost of sales with any degree of accuracy).
		(ii) Denominator may be year-end inventory.
4. Debtors' collection period	$\dfrac{\text{Year-end debtors}}{\text{Average daily credit sales}}$ days	
5. Creditors' payment period	$\dfrac{\text{Year-end creditors}}{\text{Average daily credit purchases}}$ days	
Medium and long-run measures of solvency		
6. Times interest covered	$\dfrac{\text{Profit before tax and interest}}{\text{Interest expense}}$	

7. Dividend (ordinary shares) cover	$$\dfrac{\text{Profit attributable to}}{\text{ordinary shareholders}}{\text{Ordinary dividend}}$$	A similar formula may be used for other classes of share capital
8. Debt equity	$$\dfrac{\text{Book value of long-term debt}}{\text{Book value of owners' equity}}$$	(i) Prior charge capital (e.g. preference shares) may be treated as long-term debt. (ii) Market values may be used.

Profitability

9. Return on assets employed	$$\dfrac{\text{Profit before interest and tax}}{\text{Average total assets employed}} \times 100\%$$	There are numerous alternatives, amongst which are: (i) Profit may be stated after tax. (ii) Current liabilities may be deducted from total assets. (iii) Fixed assets might be included at cost or valuation rather than net book value. (iv) Assets, and the associated profit, not employed in the main business of the company may be excluded.
10. Net profit to sales	$$\dfrac{\text{Profit before interest and tax}}{\text{Sales}} \times 100\%$$	Profit may be stated after interest and/or tax.
11. Gross profit percentage	$$\dfrac{\text{Sales less cost of goods sold}}{\text{Sales}} \times 100\%$$	
12. Total asset turnover rate	$$\dfrac{\text{Sales}}{\text{Average total assets employed}}$$	See 9 (ii), 9 (iii) and 9 (iv).
13. Fixed asset turnover rate	$$\dfrac{\text{Sales}}{\text{Net book value of fixed assets}}$$	See 9 (iii) and 9 (iv).

CROSS-SECTIONAL AND TIME-SERIES ANALYSIS OF RATIOS

Many of the ratios that we have introduced above have little meaning in themselves. In general, it is more appropriate to use them as a basis for comparing companies and posing such questions as 'why is A Limited's return on assets employed 25 per cent when B Limited, a similar company, earns 30 per cent?'. The first point that we need to make is that the comparison should be made with a similar company. There would be little point in comparing the return earned on the assets employed by, say, a firm of chartered accountants and a motor manufacturer. Most of the assets of a firm of chartered accountants consists of such things as its staff, reputation and knowledge – assets that are not recorded in the balance sheet. By contrast, the main assets of a motor manufacturer consist of tangible items – plant, stock, etc. – which will appear in the balance sheet. A further factor is that companies in different industries experience different degrees of 'business risk' (see page 485) and it is to be expected that companies facing greater risks would, in compensation, tend to earn greater expected returns.

The ideal basis for comparison is, then, the results of a company engaged in the same industry, but even if one believes that such a company has been found, the following factors must also be considered:

1. The companies may use different accounting policies.

2. Historical cost accounts will not be comparable; see Chapter 10.

3. The companies may have different patterns of asset ownership, e.g. one company may own its buildings while the other company may rent its premises.

4. Most large companies operate in more than one industry and the analyst may not be able to obtain an adequate quantitative break down of the activities.

Some of these difficulties can be partially overcome by using interfirm comparison services. The principle here is that the companies taking part (the subscribers) make their detailed financial statements available to the body making the comparison (the centre). The centre can then make certain adjustments to the accounts in order to make them more comparable. The centre might, for example, rework the depreciation charges on a consistent basis. It could also impute a rental expense for those companies that own their own premises. The centre then calculates a large number of ratios. It supplies each subscriber with its own ratios and the average for the group of companies. However, the information is usually treated as confidential to the subscribers and is not available to an external analyst.

The best-known service of this type in the United Kingdom is provided by the Centre for Interfirm Comparisons which is associated with the British Institute of Management. This service covers a wide range of industries. In addition, other bodies carry out similar surveys for specific industries; for example, the Institute of Chartered Accountants in England and Wales provides such a service for firms of chartered accountants.

The other main use of ratios is in a time-series comparison. Here the ratio of a company for one year is compared with the same ratios calculated from its accounts in prior years. The analyst can examine the recent trends of various ratios, and predictions of these into the future can be made (see below). As an example of the usefulness of the time-series approach, it may be found that a firm has a very poor quick assets ratio – if this ratio has existed for many years, however, and the company has been earning a 'respectable' return on its assets, then it indicates that although the quick assets ratio is low on a traditional or even industrial basis, it is nevertheless suitable for the firm in question.

In using time-series analysis, we need to consider the effect of price changes. It is clear that, if there have been significant price changes over a period, little meaning can be attached to the changes disclosed by a series of unadjusted money values. For example, a company chairman may proudly claim in his annual statement that 'sales and profits have, once again, increased and are at record levels for the third year running'; such a statement is of limited value in the absence of any information about general and relative price changes. However, we should consider the effect of changing prices on a series of ratios. Would it be reasonable to say that as financial ratios express the relationship between two money values at a point in time or over a period, a series of financial ratios, even if based on historical costs, is not distorted by price changes? The answer is 'to some extent, yes'. For example, the stock turnover ratio disclosed by historical cost accounts will often be reasonably close to the ratio that would be produced by using current value accounts. On the other hand, the same cannot be said of, say, the sales to fixed assets ratio. In a period of increasing prices, and all other things being equal, the sales figures would increase year by year but the book value of the fixed assets would not increase immediately (the net book value of the fixed assets would in fact fall because of depreciation, and this further distorts the ratio). The increase would be delayed until the fixed assets were replaced. Thus, if based on historical costs, the fixed asset turnover ratios would increase over time. This would be solely due to the price increases and would not mean that the greater physical volume of sales was being achieved with the same level of fixed assets. Thus, the distorting effect of price changes on historical cost accounts cannot be ignored when subjecting the financial ratios to time-series analysis.

The ratios that are likely to be most distorted by price changes are those concerned with debt to equity, return on capital employed, total asset turnover and fixed asset turnover.

Many analysts extrapolate ratios or absolute accounting figures into the future, i.e. if profits have increased by 10 per cent per annum in each of the past three years, the analyst may predict that profits in the forthcoming year will rise by 10 per cent. These types of mechanically produced forecasts have been extensively analysed, especially in the United States. The results from these studies have shown that in general such predictions are of little value and that time series of profitability measures are characterized by a high degree of randomness. Some analysts have also utilized financial ratios and accounting data in formal prediction models for forecasting such occurrences as takeovers and bankruptcies. The more sophisticated of these models have attempted to explain and predict events on the basis of considering several ratios and variables jointly. A greater degree of success has been claimed for some of these models than for those concerned with the prediction of profitability. *

* The accounting data and financial ratios used in formal prediction models have been based on historical cost accounts. It will be interesting to see if the models predict any more successfully under current cost accounting.

The analyst should take care in interpreting certain ratios when there has been a large increase in the assets of the business. As an example, the investments in new oil fields will take some time to become revenue earning – in the meantime, the return on capital employed ratio will be zero or even negative.

EARNINGS PER SHARE

This is a widely used indicator of a company's performance. The numerator is the profit attributable to ordinary shareholders, i.e. profit less tax, interest and preference dividends, while the denominator is the average number of ordinary shares in issue during the year.

$$\text{Earnings per share} = \frac{\text{Profit attributable to ordinary shareholders}}{\text{Average number of ordinary shares}}$$

Thus, Owl Limited's earnings per share for 19X8 was:

$$\frac{\pounds K30}{K100} = 30 \text{ pence per share}$$

A measure of a firm's performance can be obtained by comparing the rate of change in earnings per share against other companies' earnings per share. In doing so, however, the analyst should try to account for the effect of the firm's increase in retained earnings. Most companies retain a significant proportion of the funds they generate, and hence their earnings per share may be expected to increase even if there has been no increase in the company's profitability. Suppose, for example, that Owl Limited's profitability is the same in 19X9 as in 19X8. Then it will earn 16·5 per cent on the increased assets due to the retention of £20,000 which after tax of, say, 50 per cent will increase its profits by £1,650, and its earnings per share will increase from 30 pence to 31·65 pence. Thus one drawback to the earnings per share figure is that it takes no account of the investment base. The analyst will also have to use some judgement in interpreting earnings per share statistics when there has been a large increase in the capital (the assets acquired may not produce revenue for a number of years).

Earnings per share figures are in fact a primary company performance statistic cited in the stock market and the financial press. The *Financial Times* and other leading financial newspapers quote daily price/earnings ratios for all but the smallest quoted companies. The price/earnings ratio is given by the expression

$$\frac{\text{Share price}}{\text{Earnings per share}}$$

In general, firms that the market believes have better prospects have higher price/earnings ratios.

Earnings per Share (*Statement of Standard Accounting Practice 3, Issued 1972, Revised August 1974*)

The main objective of the Standard is to require quoted companies to publish, on the face of the profit and loss account, earnings per share figures that are comparable both between one company and another and between one financial period and another.

A factor that must be considered when calculating a company's earnings per share is whether the company has made any contractual arrangements under which it might, at some future date, issue additional shares. For example, many companies have issued convertible loan stock. The question relevant to the earnings per share calculation is whether the number of shares used in the denominator should be the average number of shares in issue during the year or whether it should be based on the total number that would be in issue if the various rights to acquire shares were exercised. The issue of the additional shares would dilute the future earnings per share, and hence the result of a calculation made on the latter basis is known as fully diluted earnings per share.

We can now summarize the actual Standard:

1. The earnings per share for all quoted companies, other than banks and discount companies should be shown on the face of the profit and loss account for the period under review and for the previous period.

2. The basis of calculating earnings per share should be disclosed. In particular, the amount of the earnings and the number of equity shares used in the calculation should be shown.

3. In addition to the basic earnings per share, the fully diluted earnings per share should also be shown in the following circumstances:

    (a) where the company has issued a separate class of equity shares which do not rank for dividend in the period under review, but which will do so in the future;

    (b) where the company has issued debentures, loan stock or preference shares convertible into equity shares of the company;

    (c) where the company has granted options or issued warrants* to subscribe for equity shares of the company.

In each case:

   (i) the basis of calculation of fully diluted earnings per share should be disclosed;

---

* A warrant is an option to buy a specified number of shares at a stated price. It is issued by the firm whose shares are the subject of the option.

(ii) the fully diluted earnings per share need not be given unless the dilution is material, i.e. if the dilution amounts to more than 5 per cent of the basic earnings per share;

(iii) fully diluted earnings per share for the previous period should not be shown unless the assumptions on which the calculation was based still apply;

(iv) equal prominence should be given to basic and fully diluted earnings per share.

A CASE STUDY

We shall finish by presenting a case study, the purpose of which is to compare the financial affairs of two companies, Exe Limited and Wye Limited. Their balance sheets as at 31 December 19X6, their trading and profit and loss accounts for the year ending on that date, and summaries of their balance sheets as at 31 December, 19X5 are presented below. The two companies are engaged in the same business. The analysis will generally be on a comparative basis, and in the absence of information about industrial averages, etc. we shall not be able to say very much about the absolute values.

Balance Sheets as at 31 December 19X6

	Exe Limited £	Exe Limited £	Wye Limited £	Wye Limited £
Fixed assets				
Freehold property at cost		105,000		188,000
Other fixed assets, at cost	63,000		84,000	
less Accumulated depreciation	21,000	42,000	66,000	18,000
		147,000		206,000
Current assets				
Inventory	70,875		79,800	
Debtors and prepayments	44,075		42,420	
	114,950		122,220	
less: Current liabilities				
Creditors and accrued expenses	32,030		81,720	
Bank overdraft	1,420		42,000	
Corporation tax payable	20,000		3,500	
Proposed dividend	8,500		16,000	
	61,950	53,000	143,220	(21,000)
		£200,000		£185,000

Ordinary shares of £1 each	84,000	128,000
Retained earnings	63,500	57,000
	147,500	185,000
8 per cent debentures	52,500	
	£200,000	£185,000

Summaries of the companies' balance sheets as at 31 December 19X5:

	Exe Limited		*Wye Limited*
	£		£
Fixed assets, net book value	156,000		213,500
Current assets (Inventory £60,000)	108,000	(Inventory	
		£70,000)	132,000
	264,000		345,500
less Current liabilities	67,500		169,500
	£196,500		£176,000
Owners' equity	144,000		176,000
Debentures	52,500		
	£196,500		£176,000

Trading and Profit and Loss Accounts for the year ended
31 December 19X6

	Exe Limited		*Wye Limited*	
	£	£	£	£
Sales		420,000		315,000
less Cost of goods sold		336,000		236,250
Gross profit		84,000		78,750
less				
Administrative expenses	14,300		12,950	
Selling and distribution expenses	13,500		12,800	
Directors' emoluments	11,000		14,000	
Depreciation	9,000		7,500	
Interest on overdraft	500		3,000	
Debenture interest	4,200	52,500	—	50,250
Profit for the year before tax		31,500		28,500
less Corporation tax		20,000		3,500
Profit for the year after tax		11,500		25,000

Proposed dividends	8,000	16,000
	3,500	9,000
Retained earnings at 1 January 19X6	60,000	48,000
	£63,500	£57,000

Note to Wye Limited's profit and loss account:
The taxation charge for the year has been reduced by virtue of tax losses which existed at the start of the year.

Short-run Liquidity Measures

		Exe Limited	Wye Limited
Current ratio	19X6	$\dfrac{£114,950}{£61,950} = 1\cdot86$	$\dfrac{£122,220}{£143,220} = 0\cdot85$
	19X5	$\dfrac{£108,000}{£67,500} = 1\cdot60$	$\dfrac{£132,000}{£169,500} = 0\cdot78$
Quick ratio	19X6	$\dfrac{£44,075}{£61,950} = 0\cdot71$	$\dfrac{£42,420}{£143,220} = 0\cdot30$
	19X5	$\dfrac{£48,000}{£67,500} = 0\cdot71$	$\dfrac{£62,000}{£169,500} = 0\cdot37$

Exe Limited's position at 31 December 19X6 is marginal. Its quick ratio is less than one but a significant proportion of the current liabilities consists of corporation tax which will not be due to payment for at least nine months. If we exclude tax the quick ratio is $\dfrac{£44,075}{£41,950} = 1\cdot05$. However, the tax will have to be paid and it appears that Exe's liquidity position very much depends on the attitude of its bankers. The current ratio has increased as compared with the previous year while the quick ratio has remained constant. This appears to be due to an increase in inventory.

Wye Limited's liquidity position is very weak. Its quick ratio at the year end is only 0·30 and it appears that the company only survives by virtue of the overdraft and by delaying paying its creditors. The quick ratio discloses a deterioration from the already weak position at 31 December 19X5. The company survived through 19X5 but one must question how much longer it can rely on the goodwill of its bankers and creditors.

We will now examine how quickly the companies appear to be able to convert their current assets into cash and the credit period granted by their suppliers.

| *Exe Limited* | *Wye Limited* |

Inventory turnover ratio

$$\frac{£336,000}{\frac{1}{2}(£60,000 + £70,875)} = 5{\cdot}13 \qquad\qquad \frac{£236,250}{\frac{1}{2}(£70,000 + £79,800)} = 3{\cdot}15$$

Debtors' collection period

Average daily credit sales,

$$\frac{£420,000}{360} = £1,167 \qquad\qquad\qquad \frac{£315,000}{360} = £875$$

Collection period $\dfrac{£44,075}{£1,167} = 37{\cdot}8$ days $\qquad\qquad \dfrac{£42,420}{£875} = 48{\cdot}5$ days

Creditors' payment period

19X6 purchases* £336,000 + £70,875   £236,250 + £79,800
$\qquad\qquad\qquad$ −£60,000 = £346,875   −£70,000 = £246,050

Daily average $\qquad \dfrac{£346,875}{360} = £964 \qquad\qquad \dfrac{£246,050}{360} = £683$

Payment period $\qquad \dfrac{£32,030}{£964} = 33{\cdot}2$ days $\qquad\qquad \dfrac{£81,720}{£683} = 119{\cdot}6$ days

For the purposes of the above calculations, we have assumed that all sales and purchases were on credit and that the accrued and prepaid expenses are immaterial.

Exe has a markedly higher inventory turnover ratio. This may be due to a number of reasons, but there is a strong presumption that Wye is carrying an excessive level of inventory. The low inventory turnover ratio adds to the problems indicated by Wye's low current ratio, since it appears that some considerable time will elapse before its inventory is converted into cash.

Wye's debtors' collection period is longer than Exe's. This suggests that Wye may be less efficient in collecting its debts or it may have to allow its customers better credit terms in order to obtain orders.

The creditors' payment period confirms, and quantifies, our earlier observation that Wye is surviving because of the forbearance of its creditors.

We shall now present a cash flow budget for January 19X7 of the form introduced earlier in the chapter.

| *Exe Limited* | *Wye Limited* |

Cash from customers

$$£44,075 \times \frac{30{\cdot}0}{37{\cdot}8} = \underline{£34,980} \qquad\qquad £42,420 \times \frac{30{\cdot}0}{48{\cdot}5} = \underline{£26,239}$$

---

* Purchases = Cost of goods sold during the year + closing inventory − opening inventory.

less
Cash paid to suppliers

$$£32,030 \times \frac{30 \cdot 0}{33 \cdot 2} = £28,943 \qquad £81,720 \times \frac{30 \cdot 0}{119 \cdot 6} = £20,498$$

Cash overheads
19X6 total divided by 12

$$\frac{£39,300^*}{12} = \underline{£\ 3,275} \qquad \frac{£42,750}{12} = \underline{£\ 3,562}$$
$$£32,218 \qquad\qquad £24,060$$

Reduction in overdraft   £2,762   £2,179

Thus, so long as Wye can continue to pay its suppliers in its present tardy fashion, both companies will generate positive net cash flows. However, the above ignores the payment of dividends. It appears that Exe's dividend policy is a trifle ambitious in that it will probably have to increase its overdraft in order to pay its shareholders. Wye's dividend decision appears ludicrous and it seems difficult to believe that its bankers will be prepared to indulge the company by allowing it to increase its overdraft for this purpose in the future.

Coverage Ratio

Exe Limited's 'times interest' covered ratio is $\frac{£35,700}{£4,200} = 8 \cdot 5,$ which appears reasonable. As stated in the chapter, a more useful measure would be one based on funds generated from operations, less tax, i.e. $\frac{£44,700}{£4,200}$ $= 10 \cdot 64.$ This of course discloses an even better position.

Profitability

Wye Limited's low tax charge, due to the tax losses in existence at the start of the year, illustrates the argument, based on comparability, for using profit before taxation in the calculation of the rate of return on assets employed.

The returns are:**

Exe Limited

$$\frac{£31,500 + £4,200 + £500}{\frac{1}{2}(£147,000 + £114,950 + £156,000 + £108,000)} \times 100$$

$$= \frac{£36,200}{£262,975} \times 100 = 13 \cdot 8 \text{ per cent}$$

* Excluding debenture interest, and, of course, depreciation.

** The definition used is, profits before debenture interest and bank interest ÷ average total assets employed.

Wye Limited

$$\frac{£28,500 + £3,000}{\frac{1}{2}(£206,000 + £122,220 + £213,500 + £132,000)} \times 100$$

$$= \frac{£31,500}{£336,860} \times 100 = 9·4 \text{ per cent}$$

It appears that Exe is earning a much better return on assets employed than Wye. However, we should approach this comparison with some caution. The cost of Wye's freehold premises is substantially greater than Exe's and we should consider the reasons for this. It may be that Wye is only able to maintain its level of sales by using 'better' premises, i.e. it might have to use large premises or be located in a more expensive area. However, it may be that Wye limited does not need more expensive premises but has acquired them through bad management. A third possible reason for the difference is that Exe might have purchased its premises some years before Wye and the difference between cost and market value is greater in the case of Exe. If the third factor is significant, a major cause of the difference is due to the distortions caused by the use of historical cost accounts.

We should also note that the ratio of accumulated depreciation to the cost of other fixed assets is higher for Wye than for Exe. This suggests that Wye's assets may be older than Exe's, a point to which we shall return later, and that if Wye replaced its assets the rate of return would fall, owing to the increase in book value of the investment base.

We shall now break down the main profitability ratio into the two components of profits to sales and sales to total assets. In order to make the measures comparable we will use profit before interest and tax.

Exe Limited	*Wye Limited*

Profit before tax and interest over sales

$\frac{£36,200}{£420,000} \times 100 = 8·6 \text{ per cent}$	$\frac{£31,500}{£315,000} \times 100 = 10 \text{ per cent}$

Sales over total assets

$\frac{£420,000}{£262,975} = 1·60$	$\frac{£315,000}{£336,860} = 0·94$

Thus we can see that Wye's profit to sales ratio is higher than Exe's, but that its return on assets employed is lower because of its slower rate of asset turnover. We have already discussed the latter point in some detail, and it appears that Wye turns over all its assets at a slower rate than Exe, with the possible exception of 'other fixed assets'. The rates of turnover of 'other fixed assets' based on year-end net book values are:

Exe Limited	*Wye Limited*

$$\frac{£420,000}{£42,000} = 10{\cdot}0 \qquad\qquad \frac{£315,000}{£18,000} = 17{\cdot}5$$

However, this difference may be due to the effect of depreciation, for if we calculate the rates by using cost instead of net book values we obtain a different result:

Exe Limited	*Wye Limited*

$$\frac{£420,000}{£63,000} = 6{\cdot}7 \qquad\qquad \frac{£315,000}{£84,000} = 3{\cdot}8$$

The main sub-measure of profitability is the gross profit percentage and we should calculate these for 19X6:

Exe Limited	*Wye Limited*

$$\frac{£84,000}{£420,000} \times 100 = 20 \text{ per cent} \qquad\qquad \frac{£78,750}{£315,000} \times 100 = 25 \text{ per cent}$$

Wye is earning a significantly higher rate of gross profit than Exe. There are, as we explained earlier, a number of possible reasons for the difference. However, a pattern is emerging. It may be that Wye is able to sell its goods at higher prices by giving a better service to its customers – a greater availability of goods due to its larger stock, its longer period of credit or because of its use of more desirable premises. However, although this pattern is consistent with the results that have so far been obtained we should realize that there are other possible scenarios which match our results.

It is interesting to note that, on the surface, it does appear that the cavalier fashion in which Wye treats its suppliers has not affected its gross profit, i.e. there is no evidence that they have been forced to purchase from more expensive suppliers. But, since we have not been provided with any information about the physical volumes involved, this might, in fact, have occurred and Wye's gross profit might have been higher if it had been able to obtain its goods on the same terms as Exe.

Overheads

We can see, without the aid of a percentage profit and loss account that Wye's overheads expressed as a percentage of sales, are higher than Exe's. However, since we do not know the pattern of fixed to variable costs in this industry we cannot say whether the difference is due to Exe's greater sales or greater efficiency.

Wye's directors receive a higher remuneration than their counterparts in Exe. Directors' remuneration is often a difficult figure to interpret in the case of smaller companies, especially when the directors are the principal shareholders. This is because it is not obvious what proportion of the remuneration represents a reasonable charge for management services and how much, in effect, is a withdrawal of profit. It may be that a part of Wye's directors' remuneration represents a withdrawal of profits, which would mean that its profit is somewhat higher than is indicated by the accounts. However, if this were the case, it would also mean that, taken with the large dividend, a significant proportion of Wye's profits had been withdrawn.

Wye's depreciation expense is lower than Exe's both in absolute terms and when expressed as a percentage of the cost of the fixed assets, and as we have noted, the ratio of accumulated depreciation to cost is higher for Wye than for Exe. It may be that Wye's assets are older than Exe's, and that some of the assets have been fully written off. On the other hand, it may be that Wye writes off its assets at a faster rate than Exe. It may, for example, use an accelerated method of depreciation. If the first explanation is correct, Wye will probably have to replace its fixed assets before Exe, possibly in the near future, and this will add to its severe liquidity problems. If the latter explanation holds, then it may be that the difference between the profitabilities of the two companies is greater than indicated by the accounts.

SUMMARY

1.   Wye's short-term liquidity position is exceptionally weak. Exe's position is fair, depending on the attitude of its bankers.

2.   Wye's position may be even worse in the medium term, if it will have to replace a significant proportion of its fixed assets.

3.   Wye's cash flow will be less favourable in the future because it has used up its tax losses.

4.   Wye is adding to its problems by distributing a high proportion of its profits by way of dividends and, possibly, directors' remuneration.

5.   In general Wye appears to be attempting to sustain too high a level of activity with too low a pool of net current assets, a situation which is known as *overtrading*.

6.   Wye achieves a significantly higher gross profit ratio than Exe, but this advantage is reduced because of the structure of overheads and the difference between the two companies' profit to sales ratios is smaller.

7.   Wye's advantage in the above respect is more than outweighed by its proportionately higher assets, i.e. its lower asset turnover ratio.

EXERCISES

13.1 Describe how an investment or credit analyst may use ratios in analysing a firm. In your answer discuss possible limitations in the use of ratios.

13.2 Discuss the ways in which current value accounting may allow better interpretations of company accounts.

13.3 The following statistics relate to a company:

	per cent		*per cent*
Equity capital employed:		Fixed Assets	20
Ordinary share capital	10	Inventory	30
Share premium account	5	Debtors	30
Retained earnings	25	Cash	20
	40		
Debentures	20		
Current liabilities	40		
	100		100

Debenture interest	= £40,000
Inventory turnover	= 6*
Debtors' turnover	= 5† (75 per cent of sales are made on credit)
Return on capital employed	= 8 per cent‡
Earnings per share	= 18p
Number of shares in existence	= 1,000,000
Tax rate	= 50 per cent of pre-tax profits

Required:

Draft the balance sheet and the profit and loss account of the company, inserting as necessary a balancing figure for expenses other than purchases.

13.4 The following are summarized balance sheets of Boutique Supplies Ltd at 31 December 1973 and 31 December 1974:

	1973 £	1974 £		1973 £	1974 £
Issued share			Equipment at		
capital	20,000	45,000	cost	10,000	13,000
Reserves	17,600	8,300	*less* Depreciation	4,000	5,300
Loan from a					
director	4,000	4,300		6,000	7,700
Corporation tax			Goodwill	—	2,000
currently due	3,000	3,800	Stock-in-trade	30,000	40,000
Trade creditors	30,000	40,000	Trade debtors	37,500	50,000
			Bank	1,100	1,700
	£74,600	£101,400		£74,600	£101,400

* Calculated on year-end inventory
† Calculated on year-end debtors
‡ Defined as profit before interest and tax ÷ equity capital employed.

The company's profit and loss accounts included the following information:

| | 1973 | | 1974 | |
	£	£	£	£
Sales		300,000		350,000
Net profit before taxation		7,000		9,500
after charging:				
Depreciation	1,000		1,300	
Rent	4,000		5,000	
Directors' emoluments	7,200		9,100	
Corporation tax on profits of year		3,000		3,800

Boutique Supplies Ltd manufactures a range of women's clothes for sale to a variety of retail outlets.

On 29 June 1974 the company capitalized £15,000 of its reserves for a bonus issue of shares to existing shareholders. On 30 June, 1974, the company acquired all the assets and goodwill of Trendtex, a firm in a similar line of business. The acquisition was made in exchange for the issue of 10,000 ordinary shares in Boutique Supplies Ltd. The former proprietor of Trendtex became a director of Boutique Supplies Ltd which now has three directors.

No dividends were paid by Boutique Supplies Ltd in either 1973 or 1974.

Early in 1975 the directors of Boutique Supplies Ltd, approached the company's bankers for an overdraft limit of £25,000 for 12 months. The directors explained:

'As is well known to the bank, our business is subject to seasonal fluctuations. We are seeking the current borrowing facilities to finance our trading operations. The bank has helped us for similar purposes in the past, although the increased volume of trading obviously involves a substantial increase in the financing request on this occasion'.

'For your guidance the quarterly sales figures for 1973 and 1974, with estimates for 1975, are appended below. Separate figures for Trendtex are shown for the first two quarters of 1974 only; thereafter that firm's sales were, of course, incorporated with those of Boutique Supplies Ltd.'

| | | Quarter ending: | | | Total |
| | 31 Mar | 30 Jun | 30 Sep | 31 Dec | Sales |
	£	£	£	£	£
1973 Boutique Supplies	75,000	102,000	48,000	75,000	300,000
1974 Boutique Supplies	80,000	106,000	64,000	100,000	400,000
Trendtex	20,000	30,000			
1975 Boutique Supplies	110,000	150,000	70,000	110,000	440,000

You are provided with the following calculations, which can be accepted as arithmetically accurate, but may or may not be relevant:

	1973	1974
$\dfrac{\text{Net profit before tax}}{\text{Share capital + reserves}}$	0·19	0·18
$\dfrac{\text{Net profit before tax}}{\text{Sales}}$	0·02	0·03
$\dfrac{\text{Share capital + reserves}}{\text{Total assets}}$	0·50	0·53
$\dfrac{\text{Stock-in-trade}}{\text{Share capital}}$	1·5	0·89
$\dfrac{\text{Stock + debtors + bank}}{\text{Tax liability + trade creditors}}$	2·08	2·09
$\dfrac{\text{Debtors + bank}}{\text{Tax + trade creditors}}$	1·17	1·18

Required:

A full discussion of the financial position and prospects of Boutique Supplies Ltd from the viewpoint of the company's bank.

(Institute of Bankers, Banking Diploma Examination, Part II, Accountancy, April 1975)

13.5 The draft accounts of Suppliers Ltd for the year to 30 June 1975 are as follows:

Balance Sheet as on 30 June

	1975 £000	1974 £000
Freehold property, as revalued	370	325 (cost)
Debtors	600	400
Stock	500	485
	£1,470	£1,210
Ordinary shares of £1 each fully paid	300	200
Share premium account	150	100
15 per cent Debentures (secured)	300	300
Bank overdraft	90	50
Profit and loss account	252	220
Undistributable reserves	275	230
Creditors	103	110
	£1,470	£1,210

Profit and Loss Account for the year to 30 June

	£000	£000
Sales	£2,500	£2,000

	£000	£000	£000	£000
Trading profit		125		115
less Debenture interest	45		45	
Dividends paid	48	93	40	85
Unappropriated profits		£32		£30

The draft accounts were presented to a meeting of directors and the following points were raised:

1. 'There seems little point in making profits when our bank overdraft position goes from bad to worse'.

2. 'What is the return on capital employed for our company and what is its significance?'

3. 'The balance sheet ignores our most valuable asset – the goodwill arising from the reputation of our products.'

4. 'I am told that our 1975 trading position has deteriorated in comparison with 1974. Is this correct?'

5. 'Is the surplus on valuation of the property included in the trading profit?'

6. 'Do you think our shareholders will be satisfied with the dividend for 1975?'

You are required, as the accountant of Suppliers Ltd, to draft your reply to each of the points raised.

(The Institute of Chartered Accountants in England and Wales, Foundation Examination, October 1975).

13.6 Given the following financial statements, historical ratios, and industry averages calculate the Zeta Company's financial ratios for the most recent year. Analyse its overall financial situation from both a time-series and a cross-sectional view point. Your analysis should cover the firm's liquidity, solvency and profitability.

Profit and Loss Account for the year ended 31 December 1975

	£	£
Net sales		
Cash		30,000
Credit		9,700,000
Total		10,000,000
less: Cost of goods sold*		7,500,000
Gross profit		2,500,000
less: Operating expenses		
Selling expense	300,000	
General and administration	700,000	
Depreciation	200,000	1,200,000
Operating profit		1,300,000
less: Interest expense		200,000
Profits before taxes		1,100,000
less: Taxes (50 per cent)		550,000
Profit after taxes		550,000
less: Preference dividends		50,000
Earnings available for ordinary shareholders		500,000
less: Ordinary share dividends		200,000
To retained earnings		£300,000

Balance Sheet as at 31 December 1975

	£	£	£
Fixed assets, at cost		12,000,000	
less: Accumulated depreciation		3,000,000	9,000,000
Other assets			1,000,000
Current assets			
Inventories	950,000		
Debtors	800,000		
Investments	50,000		
Cash	200,000	2,000,000	
less: Current liabilities			
Trade creditors	900,000		
Other creditors and accruals	100,000		
Short-term loans	200,000	1,200,000	800,000
			£10,800,000

*credit purchases = £6,200,000

5 per cent Preference shares	1,000,000
Ordinary shares of 75p	3,000,000
Share premium account	2,800,000
Retained earnings	1,000,000
	7,800,000
Long-term debt	3,000,000
	£10,800,000

Zeta Co Ltd

	Historical Data		Industry Average
Date	1973	1974	1975
Current ratio	1·40	1·55	1·85
Net working capital	£760,000	£720,000	£1,600,000
Quick ratio	1·00	0·92	1·05
Average age of debtors	45·0 days	36·4 days	35·0 days
Inventory turnover	9·52	9·21	8·60
Creditors' payment period	58·53 days	60·75 days	45·75 days
Debt-equity ratio	0·25	0·27	0·39
Gross profit ratio	0·30	0·27	0·25
Operating profit to sales	0·12	0·12	0·10
Net profit to sales	0·056	0·056	0·048
Total asset turnover	0·74	0·80	0·74
Return on capital employed*	0·11	0·12	0·10
Earnings per share	70p	90p	60p
Dividends per share	21p	30p	20p
Book value per share	140p	150p	175p
Times interest covered	8·2	7·3	8·0

* Profit before tax attributable to ordinary shareholders ÷ ordinary shareholders' equity.

EPILOGUE

INTRODUCTION

In this last section we shall deal with a number of matters. We shall first develop the discussion of the objectives of accounting that we started in Chapter 1, and then compare the historical cost and current value methods of accounting in the light of these objectives. We shall also indicate some of the main developments which may be expected to take place in the reasonably near future. We shall discuss the possible impact of the recognition that accounts should be prepared for user groups other than shareholders and creditors. Lastly, we shall look across the English Channel and describe the effect that membership of the European Economic Community (EEC) has had on accounting practice in the United Kingdom.

OBJECTIVES

In Chapter 1 we outlined a number of objectives that financial accounting might be expected to serve – stewardship, the consumption decision, measurement of success, and taxation. While the information provided by companies' accounts is used for all these purposes, there has, until recently, been surprisingly little attention paid to the objectives of accounting and how they should be served. One reason is that for many years accounting was done by, or was under the direct control of, the owner of the business, and so long as the accounting system satisfied the owner's perceived needs, such as helping him keep track of his assets, there were few problems. The troubles started with the separation of management and ownership and, more generally, with the increasing complexity of the economy which made this separation necessary. The owners were no longer able to exercise effective control of the business and the accounting methods used. Extra strains were placed on accounting and we are still trying to come to terms with them. However, this is not the whole story, for although the separation of ownership and management and the need for a clear statement of objectives have been with us since the end of the last century, discussion of the purpose of accounting has only come to the fore in the last twenty or so years.

A possible reason for this long delay was that for much of the relevant period accounting was seen, especially in the United Kingdom, as a purely practical subject. Very little basic research was carried out and the contributions of the few accounting academics were at first treated with scant regard.* Accounting was not seen as an area of concern worthy of academic study, and the first full-time chair of accounting in the United Kingdom was not established until 1946. The position was different in other countries, and the subject has been taught in American universities since the start of the century.

The trouble with practical men is that, although they may be superb when dealing with the perceived problems of the day, they often fail to recognize some of the problem areas which exist, especially those that have arisen from changes in circumstances since they received their professional training. Further, when the changes in circumstances are so great that they can no longer be ignored, practical men may well not have the necessary techniques for dealing with the new situation. The chaos surrounding CPP and current cost accounting is a good example of this.

The situation has now changed and a number of studies concerning the objectives of accounting has been carried out both in the United Kingdom and abroad, for example in the United States and Australia. In 1974, the ASC set up a working party which reported, in July 1975, in a document entitled *The Corporate Report*. We shall discuss the main proposals of the working party later. It should be noted that the status of the report is that of a discussion paper, and that the ASC has yet to issue a statement of the objectives of accounting. None the less, it has issued statements on specific issues. It could be argued that these statements should be seen as short-term reactions to what the ASC believes to be the more immediate issues; they will need to be reviewed if and when the Committee agrees on an operational statement of the objectives of accounting.

The general drift of opinion can be seen from the following quotations drawn from the report of the study group set up by the American Institute of Certified Public Accountants (AICPA) and *The Corporate Report*.

The American view is that 'the basic objective of financial statements is to provide information useful for making economic decisions'.† The following statement is made in *The Corporate Report:* 'In our view the fundamental objective of corporate reports is to communicate economic measurements of, and information about, the resources and performance of the reporting entity useful to those having reasonable rights to such information'.‡

---

* However, the contribution of a number of academics did have an important long-term effect in areas such as current value accounting.
† *Objectives of Financial Statements*, Report of the Study Group on Objectives of Financial Statements, AICPA, 1973.
‡ *The Corporate Report*, ASC, 1975.

The emphasis placed in the above on 'economic decisions' and 'economic measurements' should be noted. They are, of course, fairly vague phrases, but they do indicate a departure from the narrow view that accounts should be confined to the presentation of a picture of the past drawn up in terms of historical costs.

A COMPARISON OF HISTORICAL COST AND CURRENT VALUE

We shall now compare the two systems in the light of the above discussion. Actually, as we have shown, there is no one system of current value accounting. We shall concentrate on current cost accounting in our discussion, but most of the points will be relevant to other forms of current value accounting.

Success

We will attempt to explain what we mean by success, by modifying the parable of the talents. Suppose that a master (M) gives two servants (A and B) £1,000 each and asks them to start businesses rather than, as in the original version, engage in a one-off activity. Let us now consider how, at the end of the first year of activity, M might judge the relative success of his two servants, given that his judgement is to be based purely on economic measurements. He would consider the cash that he had received from the two businesses during the year and the cash that he would expect to receive in the future. As this is a sophisticated parable, we will assume that M knows his discount rate and can calculate the present value of the future cash flows.

The point, we hope, is clear. Even when measuring past performance, M will have to consider the future, i.e. the state of their businesses as at the end of the year, and this ideally would be measured in terms of the present value of the future cash flows. The practical problems of measuring present values are too great for the problem to be tackled directly; so we must consider how well the accounting methods will serve as proxies for the present value of future cash flows.

The historical cost method can be easily dealt with, for it does not attempt to serve as a proxy. No account is taken of current values of assets, except in those circumstances where an asset's current value falls below cost. As we showed in Chapter 10, a current value balance sheet also does not attempt to show the value of the business, though in many circumstances it is likely to be a better proxy than an historical cost balance sheet.

We shall therefore consider how far changes in the present value of future cash flows will be reflected in a current cost balance sheet. Suppose that there is a sharp increase in the demand for a product of a given industry and that this results in an increase in the present value of future cash flows of companies in the industry. Will this be reflected in a current value balance sheet? It will if the increased demand for the product results in an increase in the value to the business of the fixed assets used by the companies in the industry; this will depend, among other things, on the specific nature of the assets. The more specific their nature, the closer the relationship between the increase in the demand for the product of an industry and the increase in the 'value to the business' of the asset. Consider, as an example, a corner shop in an area where a local council decides to site a large housing estate. Very probably this decision will increase the market value of the commercial property in the area, and so the increase in the present value of future cash flows will be accompanied by an increase in the 'value to the business' of the shop. The change will thus be reflected to some extent in the current value balance sheet. In contrast, consider a car rental firm operating in a country area where it is decided to establish a large new factory. The increase in activity in the area will probably enable the car rental firm to increase its future net cash flows, but since the change will have no effect on the 'value to the business' of the cars, it will not be reflected in the current value balance sheet.

The above are extreme examples, but they do illustrate the main point that although there may be a relationship between changes in value of the business (as we have defined it) and changes in 'value to the business' of the individual assets, the relationship will not be direct and will depend on the circumstances.

We can summarize this section by observing that the measurement of past performance depends on the state of the entity at the end of the period under review. An historical cost balance sheet will not disclose much information that will help assess the state of the entity. A current value balance sheet, although not designed to disclose the value of the business, will yield more useful information than the historical cost balance sheet for the objective under review.

Consumption

To what extent is the information revealed in a company's financial accounts helpful when deciding how much should be paid to the owners? We should first think about the nature of the consumption decision. When someone decides whether to spend a pound on current consumption or invest it, he will compare the satisfaction that he would receive from current consumption with the satisfaction that he expects to obtain from consumption in the future. For investment is basically a process of delaying consumption in such a way that, if the investment is worth while, the investor will receive greater satisfaction from delayed consumption than he would from current consumption.

Intuitively it seems reasonable that there should be some connection between the periodic profit and the consumption decision. Such a link is clearly seen in the well-known definition of income, or profit, formulated by Sir John Hicks. He defined income as:

'the maximum value which (a man) can consume during a week and still expect to be as well off at the end of the week as he was at the beginning'.*

* *Value and Capital*, J. R. Hicks, Oxford University Press, 1948.

This concept of income is often referred to as 'economists' income' and tends to be compared favourably (especially by economists) with 'accountants' income or profit' which, at least in the past, was not concerned with changes in well-offness or value.

Let us for the moment ignore the problems of measuring well-offness. If accountants could produce a profit figure based on the Hicksian approach, the decision-maker would be presented with information that would be highly relevant to the consumption decision.

Now it is clear that the historical cost profit does not attempt to measure the increase in well-offness and is thus a long way from the Hicksian concept. The current cost profit proposed by Sandilands is much closer to the Hicksian approach, for the current cost profit does show the profit which is achieved after charging the 'value to the business' of the assets used up. Thus, this profit does show the increase of well-offness, assuming that well-offness can be measured in terms of the 'value to the business' of the assets of the company. Of course, as we discussed in Chapters 10–12, there are a number of ways of measuring the well-offness of a company and its owners. However, it does seem that the profit figure disclosed by any variant of current cost accounting will be of more help for the consumption decision, than an historical cost profit.

Stewardship

Perhaps we have been a little unfair to historical cost accounting. We may have built up a straw man to blow down, for it can be argued that historical cost accounting is not supposed to produce information that is relevant to measuring the success of the business or to deciding the amount that can be consumed. This view was expressed by the Institute of Chartered Accountants in England and Wales in 1952 when it stated that:

'The Council cannot emphasize too strongly that the significance of accounts prepared on the basis of historical cost is subject to limitations, not the least of which is that the monetary unit in which the accounts are prepared is not a stable unit of measurement. In consequence, the results shown by accounts prepared on the basis of historical cost are not a measure of increase or decrease in wealth in terms of purchasing power; nor do the results necessarily represent the amount which can prudently be regarded as available for distribution, having regard to the financial requirements of the business. Similarly the results shown by such accounts are not necessarily suitable for purposes such as price fixing, wage negotiations and taxation, unless in using them for these purposes due regard is paid to the amounts of profit which have been retained in the business for its maintenance'.*

The Recommendation from which the above quotation was taken has now been withdrawn but it does show how historical cost accounting was regarded in that period and makes an interesting contrast to the more recent

---

* ICAEW, *Recommendations on Accounting Principles*, N.15, issued 1952.

statements of the objectives of accounting which we introduced on page 513. The quotation lists the objectives which historical cost accounting should *not* be expected to serve. It does not say what objective *is* served but it is clear that it must be the only thing that is not specifically excluded – stewardship.

The Sandilands committee devoted some attention to an examination of what is meant by stewardship and reported:

'It is a traditional tenet of accounting that the main objective of published financial statements is to enable the directors to give an account of their 'stewardship' of the shareholders' funds to the shareholders. We have not found any agreed definition of this term, but it is clear that it is generally used by accountants in relation to the shareholder's role as part-owner of the Company and subscriber of funds, rather than to the shareholder's role as an investor, who is looking for ways to maximize the return on his investment'.*

The above quotation suggests that there are two aspects of stewardship. One, which may be termed the 'legal aspect', is the need for directors to demonstrate that shareholders' funds have been used for the purposes of the business and not used illegally.

The second aspect, the 'economic aspect' is concerned with the provision of information that will enable shareholders to judge the efficiency of management. The first aspect, which the committee suggests has been given greater emphasis, is to show whether the funds have been used legally, whilst the second aspect is concerned with whether they have been used sensibly.

We will first concentrate on the legal aspect. The mere publication of accounts will not be of much help. If the directors have acted illegally, they are hardly likely to disclose this fact in the accounts. The rights of shareholders under this head are protected by the requirement that the accounts should be audited by an independent qualified auditor. The method of accounting employed is not important; what is important is the quality of the audit and the publication of the audit report.

Let us now consider the economic aspect of stewardship – 'how well have the directors used the resources entrusted to them?' We are inevitably drawn to a consideration of the state to which the directors have brought the company and the discussion will follow exactly the same lines as our earlier discussion concerning the measurement of the success of a company. Thus, so long as we do not confine stewardship to the legal aspect, we must conclude that statements of stewardship should also be expressed in terms of current values.

Objectivity

We have attempted to demonstrate that current value accounts are likely to be more useful than historical cost accounts in the context of the objectives reviewed. However, we cannot leave the comparison between

---

* *Report of the Inflation Accounting Committee* (Cmnd 6225) HMSO, 1975, page 44.

the two methods without considering the argument that the greater objectivity of historical cost overweighs the greater relevance for decision-making of current value accounting.

Objectivity is the quality of a measure which is concerned with its verification by the use of evidence that is independent of the observer. A completely objective measure is one on which all qualified observers would agree. The opposite of objectivity is subjectivity, and a completely subjective measurement is one where the only basis of measurement is personal opinion – 'it's anyone's guess'.

It is difficult to think of many measures which are either completely objective or completely subjective. Most measures lie somewhere in between the two extremes.

Of course no one would suggest that historical cost accounting is completely objective; you have only to think of such measurements as depreciation and the provision against doubtful debts. The choice between two or more acceptable methods, e.g. between the FIFO and average cost methods of computing inventory cannot be made in the absence of personal opinion as to what is the most appropriate method to use in the circumstances. The argument in favour of historical cost is that although such financial statements consist of a number of measurements of different degrees of objectivity or subjectivity they are, on average, more objective than current value financial statements.

The choice between a method which is more objective and less relevant and one which is less objective and more relevant must itself be a very subjective one in the absence of clear knowledge of the information needs of the users of financial statements. However, it seems that the increasing emphasis that is being placed on the use of accounting statements for decision-making is shifting the balance of opinion away from objectivity towards relevance.

THE CORPORATE REPORT

The Corporate Report is a discussion paper prepared by a working party of the ASC. It was issued in July 1975 just before the publication of the Sandilands Report. As a result, *The Corporate Report* was overshadowed by the later publication and has not received the attention which it deserves.

The working party's terms of reference included the following:

'The purpose of the study is to re-examine the scope and aims of published financial reports in the light of modern needs and conditions' (page 1).

The report does not provide a detailed framework for accounting but it does propose some fundamental changes in attitudes. Perhaps the most far-reaching proposal is that published accounts should no longer be prepared solely in the interest of shareholders and creditors but that regard should be paid to the needs and rights of other user groups. This is not a new idea for there has been, for some time, a view that the primacy given to the interest of shareholders and creditors by the originators of company law is no longer appropriate. In particular, there has been considerable discussion about the rights of employees and their representatives to receive financial information.

The basic philosophy underlying the report can be seen in the following quotation:

> 'In our view there is an implicit responsibility to report publicly (whether or not required by law or regulation) incumbent on every economic entity whose size or format renders it significant. By economic entity we mean every sort of organization in modern society, whether a department of central government, a local authority, a co-operative society, an unincorporated firm, a limited company, or a non-profit-seeking organization, such as a trade union or a charity. By significant we mean that the organization commands human or material resources on such a scale that the results of its activities have significant economic implications for the community as a whole, (page 15).

This proposal represents a radical change from the present position. This is that the owners of an entity – e.g. partners and shareholders – are entitled to receive its accounts while, of the various forms of commercial profit-making entities, only those which take advantage of limited liability have to publish their accounts.

The working party's justification for its proposal that all significant economic entities should make their accounts publicly available is:

> 'The public's right to information arises not from a direct financial or human relationship with the reporting entity but from the general role played in our society by economic entities. Such organizations, which exist with the general consent of the community are afforded special legal and operational privileges; they compete for resources of manpower, materials and energy and they make use of community owned assets such as roads and harbours' (page 25).

Although the point is not developed in the report, it is interesting to note that arguments in favour of this view can be advanced both from the point of view of those who favour private enterprise and those who believe in greater government control over the economy.

The first group might well argue that it is in the general interest of the community for resources to be diverted to those areas where they will earn the greater return and that the provision of additional information will help bring about the desired re-allocation of resources. The second group would no doubt take the view that all entities should be accountable to the state, and that the publication of financial information about all economically significant entities would help the government identify those that are not acting in a socially acceptable manner, so that it could take the necessary corrective action.

In addition to its recognition of the desirability that all economically significant entities should report to the public, the working party identified a number of other specific user groups. These were:

1. The equity investor group,
   which includes both existing and potential owners.

2. The loan creditor group.

3. The analyst-adviser group,
   which includes financial analysts and journalists, researchers and other providers of advisory services. Analysts and advisers act on behalf of other user groups and their information needs are likely to be at least as great as the needs of those being advised. However, the existence of the adviser group may justify the provision of more elaborate information than might otherwise be required.

4. The business contact group,
   this includes customers, trade creditors, suppliers and competitors.

5. The government,
   including tax authorities and those government agencies concerned with the supervision of commerce and industry and local authorities.

6. The public.

Clearly, the conventional package of financial statements produced as it is for owners and creditors is not likely to satisfy the needs of all the user groups identified by the working party. Indeed, it does not appear that the conventional package provides all the information that may be useful to owners and creditors, for 'the reporting of profit and loss and balance sheet figures only will be insufficient to impart a comprehensive picture of economic activities' (page 47). Accordingly, it is suggested that entities should publish a more comprehensive package of information – this extended package is described by the working party as the entity's *Corporate Report*. It is proposed that the composition of the package should depend on the nature of the entity. The following list, taken from Appendix 2 of the report, shows the suggested composition of the Corporate Report of a limited company.

1. Chairman's statement
2. Directors' report

3. Statement of accounting policies
4. Auditor's report
5. Profit and loss account
6. Statement of changes in retained earnings
7. Statement of value added*
8. Source and application of funds statement
9. Balance sheet
10. Employment report*
11. Statement of money exchanges with the government*
12. Statement of transactions in foreign currency*
13. Statement of future prospects*
14. Statement of corporate objectives*
15. Summary, for at least the previous five years of:
    (a) Profit and loss account
    (b) Balance sheet
    (c) Source and application of funds statement.*

Of the above statements, the following merit special mention.

(a) Statement of Value Added

A statement of value added discloses the value added by an enterprise for a period and the way in which the 'value added' is divided between the different groups which are deemed to comprise the enterprise.

The *Value Added* is defined as the difference between the market value of the goods, or services, sold by the enterprise in the period (the sales revenue) and the cost (either historical or current depending on the accounting method used) of goods and services acquired from outsiders and used during the period. This definition may not appear to be any different from the normal definition of profit but there is a vital distinction which derives from the different view which is taken of the groups which comprise the enterprise. The concept of value added is based on the view that a business enterprise is comprised of a number of groups – employees, suppliers of long-term credit and the government as well as the shareholders. In contrast to the profit and loss account which shows the residual profit, or loss, available to ordinary shareholders, the statement of value added shows the income of the larger entity and how this has been divided between the various groups comprising the larger entity. This change in emphasis accords with the current organizational theories which view companies as existing to serve the interests of a wider group of people than just the ordinary shareholders.

The differences between a statement showing the profit for the period and one showing the value added for the same period can be illustrated by the following simple example:

---

* These statements are not, at present, commonly published by companies.

Statements showing derivation of:

	Profit for the period			Value added for the period	
	£	£		£	£
Sales		1,000	Sales		1,000
Less Materials	250		*Less* Materials	250	
Wages	450				
Overheads	100	800	Overheads	100	350
Profit before tax		200	Value added		£650
Less Tax		80			
Profit available to ordinary shareholders		£120			

A value added statement also shows the way in which the value added during the period is divided between the different groups comprising the larger entity. In this case the value added of £650 is divided as follows:

	£
To employees	450
To the government	80
To shareholders	120
	£650

To a large degree the statement of value added can be constructed from the information already provided in the annual accounts and hence it could be argued that the statement's information value is low. The counter argument is the way in which the data contained in the statement are presented provides a much better understanding of the relative positions of the groups concerned with the company and of the role and contribution of the company to society at large. For example, in the case of many, especially manufacturing, companies the dividends paid to shareholders represent only a small fraction of the total value added, while in contrast salaries and wages often represent a very large fraction of the application of the value added. Thus the value added statement, by revealing that dividends are relatively small compared to wages (and to other applications of value added, such as taxes paid to the Government), may help improve industrial relations in those industries where the concept of profits may be under attack.

The measure of value added, which has on the whole been neglected by accountants, provides useful information about the performance of a company. For example, there has, recently, been considerable discussion about the relative productivity of various motor manufacturers expressed in terms of the number of vehicles produced per employee. The difficulty with this basis of comparison is that, at one extreme, some companies buy in all their components and act simply as assemblers of those components (low value added companies) while others produce many of their own components from the basic raw materials (high value added companies). A value added statement would help users differentiate between the two types of company.

The statement of value added is normally divided into two parts, the first of which shows the value added by the organization. The second part of the statement shows how the value added has been applied between the various contributors to the firm. The following example of a value added statement is taken from The Corporate Report:

A MANUFACTURING COMPANY
Statement of Value Added

Preceding Year £000		Year to 31 December 19X4 £000	
102·3	Turnover	103·9	
72·1	Bought-in materials and services	67·6	
£30·2	Value added	£36·3	

Applied the following way:

	To pay employees Wages, pensions and			
17·3	fringe benefits		25·9	71·3%
	To pay providers of capital			
0·6	Interest on loans	0·8		
0·9	Dividends to shareholders	0·9		
1·5			1·7	4·7%
	To pay government			
3·1	Corporation tax payable		3·9	10·8%
	To provide for maintenance and expansion of assets			
1·8	Depreciation	2·0		
6·5	Retained profits	2·8		
8·3			4·8	13·2%
£30·2	Value added		£36·3	100·0%*

A few features of the above layout of the value added statement need some comment. Firstly, depreciation is treated as an amount to provide for maintenance and expansion of assets. However there is a strong body of opinion which advocates treating depreciation as a deduction in arriving at

* The percentage column was not included in the statement illustrated in The Corporate Report.

value added. This is based on the idea that a fixed asset is a bought-in item and it is only because it has a long life that depreciation is charged. An alternative format for a statement of value added might therefore show both 'Bought-in materials and services' and depreciation as deductions in arriving at value added.

Under the heading of 'to pay providers of capital' the gross amounts of interest payable on loans and dividends payable on shareholders' capital should be shown. If the company is required to deduct tax from interest and dividend payments the gross amount must still be shown, as the firm is merely accounting for the provider of capital's tax liability at the basic rate.

Under the heading of 'to pay government' many firms include only Corporation Tax. Other companies, however, have gone further and included payments such as PAYE, National Insurance Contributions, tax on interest and dividends (in spite of the comments made in the preceding paragraph), V.A.T., Customs and Excise duties, as well as Corporation Tax. It is this heading which has provided the greatest degree of diversity between companies in their presentations of the statement.

Statements of Value Added althought not compulsory, have become very popular in the last few years and most large companies now incorporate them in their annual reports. As it is still a fairly recent development some further experimentation and variation in report formats is likely before a general consensus of layout and presentation emerges.

(b) Employment Report

The working party pointed out that, as a result of nineteenth century attitudes that still prevail in the field of corporate reporting, the only reference to employees in most sets of annual accounts is the disclosure, in the directors' report, of the average number of employees and their aggregate remuneration. It was proposed that this omission could be rectified by the publication of an employment report. An example of such a statement is provided in the *Corporate Report* but it is too long to reproduced here. Its main points include the following.

1. Employees. The number, broad reasons for changes in the size of the workforce, the age and sex distribution of the workforce, and the functions of employees.

2. The hours scheduled and actually worked with as much detail as possible about the reasons for the difference – sickness, strikes, etc.

3. Details concerning pension schemes, cost of, and time spent on, training, trade unions recognized by the entity, and safety and health factors.

The proposed report is extremely detailed, but it is not clear how well it will satisfy the specific information needs of employees and their representatives. However, it does appear that it will provide useful information to a number of user groups about the personnel policies and the industrial relations record of the entity.

Basis of Accounting Measurements

The view was stated that no one system of measurement can satisfy all the various needs, and the working party called for further research into the preparation of financial statements based on more than one method of accounting. For example, there might be a multi-column balance sheet showing, say, both the net realizable value and 'value to the business' of the assets. The virtues of current value accounting were recognized, but it was suggested that this method should not be adopted until a 'workable and standardized system of current value accounting is developed'. In the meantime, it was suggested that the accounts be based on historical cost adjusted for changes in the general price level. However, Sandilands appeared within a few months of the publication of the *Corporate Report*, and the adoption, in principle, of current cost accounting by the accounting profession meant that the last proposal was soon made redundant.

THE EUROPEAN ECONOMIC COMMUNITY (EEC)

The EEC was established, under the Treaty of Rome, in 1957. One of its main objectives is to bring about the free movement of people and capital between member countries. In order to achieve this, and other aims, the parties to the treaty agreed to modify their own national laws.

The idea behind the free movement of capital is that an investor living in Birmingham should be as willing to purchase the shares of a German company on the Paris Stock Exchange as the shares of ICI on the London Stock Exchange. The intention, so far as the activities of companies is concerned, is that eventually, when a company is deciding where to site a new plant, it will consider economic factors and national boundaries will play no part in its decision.

The total abolition of the barrier to the free movement of people and capital means that, ultimately, companies in, say, Sicily and the Shetlands should be regulated by the same company law and accounting requirements. The breaking down of barriers and the consequent establishment of a common legal and economic environment is known as the process of *harmonization*.

A significant factor which has hindered harmonization in the area with which we are concerned is that two, very different, approaches to company law as it affects accounting practice can be identified in EEC countries. One is the Anglo-Saxon approach, which is followed in Ireland and Holland as well as in the United Kingdom. This is a permissive approach. The overriding objective is that accounts should show a 'true and fair view' and accounting methods are not laid down by law but are left to the accounting profession.

The alternative which is found in its most extreme form in France and West Germany is a prescriptive approach. The concept of 'true and fair' is not central, or particularly evident, in West German practice. For example, it is believed that there should be no difference between the taxable profit and the profit shown in the accounts. Thus, if a West German company wishes to take advantage of the accelerated depreciation methods allowed by tax law, it must use this method in the accounts even if, as a result, the assets are written off at an excessive rate.

The position in France is much the same; all limited companies must follow a model set of accounts, and accounting methods are considered to be the direct concern of the government rather than of the accounting profession. Government control of accounting in France is more extensive than in West Germany for the government controls the accounting system used within companies by means of the 'Le plan compatible general'. This consists of a detailed chart, or list, of specified numbered ledger accounts. Thus, one would find that all French companies controlled by the plan have a ledger account, number 64, for transportation and travel expenses. The plan has some variation to suit particular industries. There are, currently, about 75 variations of the general plan and the intention is that there should be a variation for each main industry. It is interesting to note that this system of uniform accounting was imposed on the French by Germany during the Second World War. At the end of the war, the Germans abandoned the system, although it is used on a voluntary basis in a number of German industries, but it was retained in France.

France and West Germany are founder members of the EEC while the United Kingdom and Ireland did not join until 1973. Thus, it is not surprising to find that the French/German approach has had a far greater impact on the harmonization proposals than the Anglo-Saxon view.

Harmonization is effected by means of *directives*. These are formulated by the European Commission and if and when they are agreed by the Community's Council of Ministers, they would become binding on member countries. The first directive, which has been accepted by the Council of Ministers, is concerned with the validity of contracts entered into by companies and has had a significant effect on the application of the doctrine of *ultra vires* in the United Kingdom. The second directive is concerned with the formation of public limited liability companies and the maintenance and alteration of their share capital. The third directive deals with mergers.

The fourth directive deals with the annual accounts of limited companies. The fifth directive deals with the management, structure and audit of public limited companies and calls for the adoption of the 'two-tier' board system on the West German and Dutch lines. Under this system there are two boards; one, the management board, is responsible for the day-to-day operations of the company, while the supervisory board oversees the activities of the management board and appoints its members. The seventh directive deals with consolidated accounts. It calls for the publication of such accounts by most groups – at present consolidated accounts are not widely used in a number of EEC countries – and sets out rules for their preparation.

The Commission has also produced a proposed directive on prospectuses, i.e. the statements that have to accompany invitations to the public to

528 *Foundation in Accounting*

purchase securities. There also exists a draft regulation for a European
Company (Societas Europea). These companies would be incorporated by,
and come under the control of, the EEC itself and not one of its member
countries.

The Companies Acts 1980 and 1981 carry the major proposals from the
Second and Fourth Directives into British company law.

FURTHER READINGS

SECTION A (Chapters 1–4) – General

BIRD, P. A., 1979, *Understanding Company Accounts*, London, Pitman.
EDEY, H.C., 1966, *An Introduction to Accounting*, London, Hutchinson.
JOHNSON, H. and WHITTAM, A., 1984, *A Practical Foundation in
Accounting,* 2nd Edition, London, George Allen and Unwin.
LEE, G.A., 1981, *Modern Financial Accounting*, 3rd Edition, Woking-
ham, Van Nostrand Reinhold.
WOOD, F., 1984, *Business Accounting, Vs 1 and 2*, 4th Edition, London,
Longman.

Chapter 2 – The Accounts of Manufacturing Firms
HORNGREN, C. T., 1982, *Cost Accounting: A Managerial Emphasis*, 5th
Edition, Englewood Cliffs, N.J., Prentice-Hall Inc.
SIZER, J., 1979, *An Insight into Manufacturing Accounting*, 2nd Edition,
London, Penguin Books.

Chapter 3 – Incomplete Records and Club Accounts
The Preparation of Accounts by Computer from Incomplete Records,
Accountants Digest No 20, London, Institute of Chartered Accountants
in England and Wales.

Chapter 4 – Partnership Accounts
DRAKE, C. D., 1972, *Partnership Law*, London, Sweet & Maxwell.

SECTION B (Chapters 5–9) – General

BIRD, P. A., 1979, *Understanding Company Accounts*, London, Pitman.
LEE, G. A., 1981, *Modern Financial Accounting*, 3rd Edition, Wokingham,
Van Nostrand Reinhold.
LEE, T. A., 1982, *Company Financial Reporting – Issues and Analysis*, 2nd
Edition, Wokingham, Van Nostrand Reinhold.
PARKER, R. H., 1982, *Understanding Company Financial Statements*, 2nd
Edition, London, Penguin Books.

WOOD, F., 1984, *Business Accounting, Vs 1 and 2*, 4th Edition, London, Longman.

Chapter 6 – Taxation in Accounts
PINSON, B., *Revenue Law* (updated annually), London, Sweet & Maxwell.
PRITCHARD, W. E., *Corporation Tax*, Stockport, Polytech Publishers.

Chapter 7 – Limited Companies – 2 Annual Accounts
Form and Content of Company Accounts, 1982, London, Financial Training Publications Limited.
Survey of Published Accounts (published annually). London, Institute of Chartered Accountants in England and Wales.
Accounting Standards (published annually), London, Institute of Chartered Accountants in England and Wales.

Chapter 8 – Consolidated Accounts
SHAW, J. C., 1973, *Bogie on Group Accounts*, 3rd Edition, Bristol, Jordan & Sons Limited.
WILKINS, R. M., 1979, *Group Accounts: The Fundamental Principles, Form and Content*, 2nd Edition, London, Institute of Chartered Accountants in England and Wales.
EEC Seventh Directive on Consolidated Accounts, 13 June 1983, Published in the Official Journal of the European Communities, Vol L 193/1, 18 July 1983.

Chapter 9 – Funds Flow Statements and Cash Budgeting
JAEDICKE, R. K. and SPROUSE, R. T., 1965, *Accounting Flows: Income Funds and Cash*, Englewood Cliffs, N.J., Prentice-Hall Inc.
KNOX, R. W., 1977, *Statements of Source and Application of Funds: A Practical Guide to SSAP10*, London, Institute of Chartered Accountants in England and Wales.
LEE, T. A., 1974, *The Funds Statement*, Edinburgh, Institute of Chartered Accountants in Scotland.

SECTION C (Chapters 10–12) – General

BAXTER, W. T., 1984, *Inflation Accounting*, Oxford, Philip Allan.
LEE, T. A., 1980, *Income and Value Measurement: Theory and Practice*, 2nd Edition, London, Nelson.
LEWIS, R. and PENDRILL, D., 1985, *Advanced Financial Accounting*, 2nd Edition, London, Pitman.
MYDDLETON, 1984, *On a Cloth Untrue*, Cambridge, Woodhead-Faulkner.
REVSINE, L., 1973, *Replacement Cost Accounting*, Englewood Cliffs, N.J., Prentice-Hall Inc.
TWEEDIE, D., 1979, *Financial Reporting, Inflation and the Capital Maintenance Concept*, ICRA Occasional Paper 19.

WHITTINGTON, G., 1984, *Inflation Accounting – An Introduction to the Debate*, Cambridge, Cambridge University Press.

Chapter 12 – Current Cost Accounting

MALLINSON, D., 1980, *Understanding Current Cost Accounting*, London, Butterworth.

Guidance Notes on SSAP16 1980, London, Accounting Standards Committee.

SECTION D

Chapter 13 – Financial Statement Analysis

FIRTH, M.A., 1975, *Investment Analysis*, New York, Harper & Row.

FIRTH, M.A., 1977, *The Valuation of Shares and the Efficient Markets Theory*, London, Macmillan & Co.

FOSTER, G., 1978, *Financial Statement Analysis*, Englewood Cliffs, N.J., Prentice-Hall Inc.

HEFFERT, E. A., 1972, *Techniques of Financial Analysis*, Homewood, Illinois, Irwin.

LEV, B. L., 1974, *Financial Statement Analysis: a New Approach*, Englewood Cliffs, N.J., Prentice-Hall Inc.

Epilogue

FITZGERALD, R. D., STICKLER, A. D., and WATTS, T. R., 1980, *International Survey of Accounting Principles and Reporting Practices*, London, Butterworth.

LAFFERTY, M., 1975, *Accounting in Europe*, Cambridge, Cambridge, Woodhead-Faulkner.

LAFFERTY, M., 1975, *Accounting in Europe*, Cambridge, Woodhead-Faulkner.

GRAY, S. J., and MAUNDERS, K. T., 1980, *Value Added Reporting: Uses and Measurement*, London, Association of Certified Accountants.

RENSHELL, M., ALLAN, R., and NICHOLSON, K., 1979, *Added Value in External Financial Reporting*, London, Institute of Chartered Accountants in England and Wales.

INDEX

A

accounting profession   11
accounting bases   240
   concepts   218
   cycle   318
   exemptions   235–237
   history of   1
   policies   218, 236, 240
   principles   218
   principals and rules as specified in The
      Companies Acts   217
   principles, early influences   4
   rules in Companies Acts   218
Accounting Standards Committee (ASC)
   12, 209
accruals concept   218, 240, 246
Accumulated (or General) Fund   61
acid test   474
acquisition and mergers, accounting for
   262–308
acquisition of own shares by public companies
   153
ACT – see Advanced Corporation Tax
administration expenses   16
Advanced Corporation Tax   185–189
   on dividends paid   199
   on proposed dividends   188
   recoverable and irrecoverable   189,
   199
   surplus of   187
allocation of costs   19
allotment of shares   223
alternative accounting rules in Companies Act
   218, 221
Ammonia Soda Co. Ltd. v Chamberlain (1918)
   149

analysis of financial statements   470–506
Annual General Meeting (AGM)   136
annual returns   171
application and allotment account   141
application of funds   321
apportionment of costs   19
articles of association   134
ASC – see Accounting Standards Committee
asset turnover rate   490
assets, economic value   358
   market value   358
   nature and valuation of   357
auditors ʼ   253
auditors' statuatory responsibilities
   253–254
authorised share capital   134, 223
averaging method   423

B

back duty investigation   54
backlog depreciation   414–419
Bonbright, J C   360
books of accounts   170
bonus issues   163
British Institute of Management   495
budgeted financial statements   342–346
business risk   495

C

call accounts   141
capital allowances   181, 184
capital gains   182
capitalization issues   163–164

capital losses   185
capital profits   150
capital redemption reserve fund   149, 152, 153, 154, 163
capital reserve   196
capital reserve on consolidation   272, 273
cash accounts   141
cash flow   363
cash flow accounting   338, 339
CCA – see Current Cost Accounting
chartered companies   4, 5
centre for interfirm comparisons   495
classification of costs   16–19
clawback   190, 197
close company   135
clubs, societies and associations, accounting for   66–69
    special funds   62
    subscriptions and Entry Fees   66
COMA rule   380
comprehensive tax allocation   192
conservatism (see prudence concept)   7
consistency   218, 240
consolidated accounts, disclosure requirement   296
    legal provisions   294
    reasons for excluding subsidiaries   296
consolidated balance sheets, example of   278
Consultative Committee for Accounting Bodies (CCAB)   13
consumption decision   513, 516
contingencies   250
contingencies, accounting for (see SSAP 18)
contingent gains   250
contract accounts   27
contracts accounting   243
contract work in progress   241
convertible loan stock   144, 222
"Corporate Report", The   519–526
Corporation Tax, general   180–207
    mainstream payment   185
    payable   183
    small company rate   181, 183
    tapering relief   183
cost accounting   16
cost of control   265
cost of funds   363
cost of living index   378
cost of production   16
cost of sales adjustment   400, 422–429
cosmetic reporting   475
coverage ratios   482, 503
CPP (see Current Purchasing Power)
creditors   7, 146, 148, 164
creditors' payment period   480, 493, 502
creditors' turnover ratio   480
cross-section analysis   469, 473
cumulative preference shares   130
current cost accounting (see SSAP 16)

balance sheet   397
general price level changes   449
net operating assets   398
operating adjustments   400
operating profits   398, 430
profit and loss account   398
profit attributable to shareholders   398, 403, 409
reserve account   398
unit of account   397
current ratio   472, 493, 501
current value account (CVA) – liabilities valuation of   363
    treatment of gains   365
current values, use permitted by company legislation   221
current year backlog depreciation   414
customs and excise (VAT)   179
CVA (see Current Value Accounting)

D

debenture holders   148
debenture stock   145–146, 223
debentures, redemption of   166
debentures, redemption by purchasing in the open market   168
debt to equity ratio   483, 494
debtors' collection period   479, 493, 502
debtors' turnover ratio   479
deferred shares   138
deferred tax – account   196, 197
    accounting for, (see SSAP 15)
    asset revaluation   196
    deferral method   193, 197–198
    liability method   193
    timing differences and   191
depreciation – general   27, 181
    accounting for, (see SSAP 12)
    adjustment in CCA   400, 403, 457
    change in method   245
    in funds flow statements   323
    need to depreciate   245
    of plant and machinery in SSAP16   414
deprival value   360–362, 397, 410
direct expenses   20
direct labour   36
direct manufacturing expenses   18
direct materials inventory   21
directors   145, 146, 209–210, 227
director's meeting   170
directors' service contracts   170
dirty surplus method   243
disclosure of accounting policies (see SSAP 2)
disclosure requirements of Companies Acts   264
    accounting policies   222
    auditor's remuneration   232

disclosure requirements – *cont*
current assets   220
comparative figures   233
depreciation   217
details of indebtedness   226
development costs   220
difference between market and book value
of land   234
directors' signatures on balance sheet
238
directors' remuneration   228
dividends in arrears   226
extraordinary and exceptional items
233
foreign currencies   233
fixed assets   219, 223
goodwill   220
guarantees made by company   226
hire of plant and machinery   231
income from listed investments   231
interest expense   230
investments   224
items relating to preceeding year   233
likely future development of business
235
other financial commitments   227
particulars of staff   229
pension commitments   227
political and charitable donations   235
principal activities of company   234
proposed capital expenditure   227
proposed dividends   227
redemption of share capital and loan
capital   231
rental income   231
research and development expenditure
233
reserves and provisions   225
share capital and debentures   222
significant changes in the fixed assets
234
taxation   225, 232
turnover   227
discount, share issued at   134
discount rates, for use in present value
calculations   359
disposal of fixed assets in CCA   421
distributable profits   154
dividends   135, 145, 150, 153
dividend cover   482, 494
dividends payable   164
dividends received   199
double-entry bookkeeping, evolution of   2

E

earnings per share (see SSAP 16)   497–499
economic entities   279

ED – (see Exposure Draft)   12–13
ED 8 – accounting for changes in purchasing
power of money   374
ED 35 – accounting for the effect of changing
prices   455–458
treatment of fixed assets   457
withdrawal of   458
ED 30 – accounting for goodwill   271, 274,
301, 302
EEC (European Economic Community)
526
EEC directives   527
EEC Fourth Directive   208, 235, 270
employees, information for   11
employment report   525
entity concept   279, 285
examination techniques
general   123
incomplete records   55
existing resources   399
exposure draft (see ED)
extraordinary general meeting (EGM)
149
extraordinary items and prior years
adjustments (see SSAP 6)   241, 242,
368
extraordinary profit or loss   232
equity shares   274
equity share capital and reserves, treatment in
CPP accounts   384

F

final dividend   136
financial expenses   16
financial ratios   469–494
financial resources   336
financial risk   485
financial statements
formats   210–217
purposes and users   8–11, 515–521
"Financial Times"   497
finished goods inventory   21, 36
First in First Out (FIFO)   221
fixed asset
replacement reserve   162
treatment in SSAP 16   414
turnover ratio   491, 494
fixed charge   146
floating charge   146
floating debentures   146
foreign currency translation (see SSAP 20)
237
forfeited share account   141
forfeiture of shares   141
format
P and L account   209
balance Sheet   209
format statements   210–217
need for consistency   210

Fourth Directive (EEC)   528
Franked Investment Income (FII)   181, 186
fundamental accounting concepts   239
fungible assets   211
fully diluted earnings per share   498

G

gains and profits – CCA treatment   368
"Garner v Murray" (1904)   102, 104
general (or accumulated) fund   61
general reserve   163
gearing   483, 485
gearing adjustment   404, 407, 409, 433–436,
    457
gearing ratio   409, 484
Gibson, J C   102
going concern concept   218, 240, 254
goodwill   270, 272, 364
goodwill on consolidation   265, 266, 268,
    269, 278, 421
goodwill, valuation of   87
government grants   202
    accounting treatment of (see SSAP 4)
Gower, Prof. L. C. B.   16
gross current costs   457
gross profit   25
gross profit percentage   494
gross replacement cost   411, 414
group accounts – (see SSAP 14)
group of companies – definition   262

H

harmonization   527
Hicks, Sir J   516
historical cost   221, 495
historical cost accounting – limitations
    354–356, 496, 515
historical cost accounting rules   218–219
holding and operating gains – distinction
    between   370
holding company   262, 269
holding gains in CCA   366, 368
H.M. Stationery Office   412

I

IACS – see International Accounting
    Standards Committee   13
imputation system of tax   199
income and expenditure accounts   61, 66
income tax   177
    basic rates   178
    marginal rates   178
incomplete records   47–60

drawings   49
    unidentified payments   49
index numbers   377
index of retail prices   378, 449
indirect manufacturing expenses   18
inflation accounting committee report (see
    Sandiland's Report)
inflation accounting steering group   375
Institute of Chartered Accountants in England
    and Wales   11, 12
Institute of Chartered Accountants of Scotland
    11
inter-company balances and trading   281
interdependent assets, problems in CCA
    455
interest   145
interfirm comparisons   495
interfirm comparisons, centre for   495
interim dividends   136, 150
International Accounting Standards
    Committee (IACS)   13
inventories   21
    cost of   22
    valuation of   27
inventory, holding period   478
    turnover   491
    turnover ratio   477, 493, 502
investing company   262
investment incentives and government grants
    207
investment properties   257
    accounting for (see SSAP 19)
investment revaluation reserves   250
investors   146
issued share capital   157
issue of shares   134

J

job order cost sheets   19
joint stock companies   4
Joint Stock Companies Act   5
joint ventures   3, 104–107

L

Last in, First out (LIFO)   221
leverage   483, 485
liabilities   145
liability method   197
liability or deferral method   198
limitation of historical cost accounting   190,
    354–356
limited companies   6, 9
    accounting for   208
    appropriation account   132

limited companies – *cont*
  formation   133
  memorandum   133
  objects   132
  owner's equity   147
  right to purchase own shares   153
limited liability   135
limited liability, act of 1855   5
limited partnerships   4, 7
liquidation   135
liquidity and solvency ratios   472–486
listed companies   135
loan capital   145
loan stock   145
long term loans   144, 484

M

manufacturing accounts   24, 25
  limitations   24
manufacturing costs, flow of   35
manufacturing expenses, 16, 17, 20
manufacturing overheads   20, 21, 36
mainstream tax payments   188
market purchase   159, 166
mark up   51
matching convention   193, 203, 271
matching of cash flows   476, 480
medium sized companies, criteria   236
  exemptions   237
  modified accounting for   237
merger method of accounting   279
  criteria for   301
memorandum   134, 150
memorandum joint venture account   105
minority interest shareholders   283
minority interests   275, 278, 279, 286
minute books   170
mixed ledger system   35
modern equivalent asset   413
monetary assets and liabilities in CPP
    Accounting   380
monetary working capital   400, 430
Monetary Working Capital Adjustments
    (MWCA)   430, 432–433, 457
monetary working capital, excess of liabilities
    over assets   430
monthly digest of statistics   378

N

naked debentures   146
negative goodwill   272
net book value   269
net borrowing (SSAP 16 definition)   436
net current cost   457
net current replacement cost   411, 414, 421

net liquid funds   332
net monetary assets   337
net profit to sales ratio   494
net realizable value   243, 257
  indication of flexibility of business   364
nominal or par value of shares   134
non-cumulative preference shares   137
non-distributable reserve   157
non-statuatory reserves   163

O

objectives of financial accounting   8, 513,
    515–518
objectivity   28
objects clause – limited companies   133
off market purchase   159, 160
operating capability of the business
    398–399
operating gains   366, 368
opportunity cost of funds   359
ordinary shares   136, 138, 144
owner's equity   53
owner's equity, treatment in group accounts
    262
owner's rate of time preference   359
overdraft, problems in financial analysis
    474, 485
overhead applied account   36
overhead expenses account   36
overhead recovery rate   20
overheads   17, 505

P

Pacioli, Luca   2
par value   134
parent or holding company   8, 262
participating preference shares   137
partly owned subsidiary companies
    275–284
partly paid shares   134
partnership
  absence of accounts at date of change of
      partnership arrangements   98
  accounts, presentation of   82
  admission of partner   85, 90
  agreements   78
  appropriation of profit   79
  capital account   78, 102
  change in profit sharing ratio   85, 94
  current account   78
  definition   77
  discharge by payment of annuity   97
  dissolution and the Partnership Act of
      1890   99
  drawings   78

partnership – *cont*
   early form, of   4, 5
   goodwill   86, 90
   interest on capital   79
   lack of agreement   84, 98
   loan accounts   84
   Partnership Act 1890   77, 98
   piecemeal realization and interim
      distribution   103
   profit sharing ratio   79
   realization account   99, 102
   restriction on number of partners   77
   retirement or death of partner   85, 95
   salaries   81
PAYE – (Pay As You Earn)   177
permanent diminution   410
permissable capital payment   157
perpetual inventory system   34
plant and machinery – treatment in SSAP 16
   411
pooling method of accounting for business
   combinations   264, 297
post balance sheet events   240, 241
   accounting for (see SSAP 17)
preceeding year basis for tax assessment
   178
prediction of bankruptcy   496
preference shareholders   145, 146
preference shares   136
preferential creditors   146
premium arising on consolidation   246
present value   358, 515
   example of calculation   370
   table   370
price earnings ratio   497
prime costs   20, 21
prior years' adjustments   241, 242
prior year backlog depreciation   415
private companies   135
production costs   221
profit and loss account   25
profit to sales ratio   489, 504
profitability, measure of   468, 486–489, 503
profits available for dividends, legal position
   149
progress payments   28
projected cash flow   339
property companies   251
proposed dividends   136
proprietory concept   279
prospectus   140
provisions   34, 225
provisional SSAP 7   374
prudence concept   34, 218, 240, 250
public companies   135
purchase method of accounting for business
   combinations   264
purchase of own shares by company   162
purchasing power of money – measuring
   changes in   375

purchase price   221
pure ledger system   35–40

Q

qualified audit report   254
quick ratio   473, 493, 498

R

realization convention   28
realized capital profits   150
realized profits   218
reasonable probability (see SSAP 15)   197
receipts and expenditure accounts   61
receipts and payments accounts   60, 61
recommendations on accounting principles
   12
recommended dividends   234
recoverable amount in CCA   410
redeemable shares   138
redemption and purchase of shares – distinction
   between   153
redemption of debentures   163
reduction of subscribed capital   147, 160
register of debenture holders   170
register of directors' interest in shares and
   debentures of the company   170
register of charges   170
register of members   169
register of substantial share holdings in public
   companies   169
Registrar of Companies   134, 150, 171, 236
relief for stock appreciation   189–191
replacement costs   221, 357, 423
research and development, accounting for (see
   SSAP 13)
research, applied   246
research expenditure, accounting for   246
research, pure   246
reserve accounting   242
reserve funds   163, 225
Retail Price Index (RPI)   378, 449
retentions   28
Return on assets (or capital) employed
   (ROCE)   487, 491, 494, 503, 504
return on shareholders' equity   492
revaluation of fixed assets   147
revaluation reserve   157
revaluation reserve account   222
revaluation surpluses and deficits   398
ROCE – see return on assets (or capital)
   employed

S

sales to total assets ratio   504
Sandilands, Francis   375

Sandilands's Committee   449
    model, Development of   451–452
    report   450, 475
    view that it is not possible to measure
        inflation in accounts   450
scrip issues   163
secret reserve   7
selling and distribution expenses   16–17
share, application   140, 141
share capital   134
share capital – different types   136
shareholder   7
share premium account   134, 141, 149, 151,
    154, 169
shares, allotment of   146
shares in limited companies   6
shares issued at discount   134
share issue – oversubscription   140
shares, nominal value   136
    of no par value   139
    partly paid   134
    purchased (or redeemed) at a premium
        154
    purchase of own shares by private
        company   157, 162
"*Shearer v Bercain*" (1980)   301, 302
significant economic entities   520
sinking fund   163
sinking fund account   169
sinking fund investments   169
small companies
    criteria   236
    exemptions   236
    modified accounts for   237
    tax rate   183
Societas Europa   528
societies, accounting for   60–69
sole traders   3
solvency   468
solvency measures   482
• source and application of funds statements (see
    SSAP 10)
    dividends, treatment of   333
    preparation of   324–329
    taxation, treatment of   335
    uses and limitations   329
Sprouse, R. T. and Moonitz, M   357
SSAP – see Statements of Standard Accounting
    Practice
stabilized accounting   390
statement of affairs   48
Statements of Standard Accounting Practice
    (SSAP)
SSAP   1 – Accounting for Associated
        Companies   303
    2 – Disclosure of Accounting Policies
        218, 239, 250
    3 – Earnings per Share   438
    4 – Accounting Treatment of
        Government Grants   202

    5 – Accounting for Value Added
        Tax   180
    6 – Extraordinary items and prior year
        adjustments   241, 252
    7 – Withdrawn
    8 – Treatment of Taxation under
        imputation system in the accounts of
        Companies   198
    9 – Stocks and Work-in-Progress
        22, 29, 31, 243
    10 – Statements of Source and
        Application of Funds   332–335
    11 – Withdrawn – replaced by SSAP 15
        196, 197, 198
    12 – Accounting for Depreciation
        243–246, 251, 252
    13 – Accounting for Research and
        Development   242–248
    14 – Group Accounts   270, 273, 302,
        304, 421
    15 – Accounting for Deferred Taxation
        196, 197, 198
    16 – Current Cost Accounting   219,
        221, 396, 406
    17 – Accounting for post Balance Sheet
        Events   248–250
    18 – Accounting for contingencies
        250–251
    19 – Accounting for Investment
        Properties   251–252
    20 – Foreign Currency Translation
        253
statement of value added   522–525
statuatory books   169
statuatory declaration   161
statuatory reserves   151
stewardship
    definitions   146
    function   513, 515, 517
stock   139
stock profits   190
stock relief   188, 189, 197
stock valuation   181, 221
Stock Exchange   135, 136, 146, 159
stock exchange regulations   238
stock not subject to COSA   437
stock, treatment in SSAP 16   422–429
stock, treatment of, in ED35   457
stocks and works-in-progress (see SSAP 9)
subsidiary company   8, 262, 274
super profits   89, 271
Sweeny, Henry   390

T

tangible fixed assets   226
taxation, currently payable   184
taxation, treatment of (see SSAP 8)
tax credit   185, 186

tax losses   184
time lags, impact on CPP Accounts   387
times interest covered ratio   482, 484, 493
Time-series analysis   469
timing differences   197
total asset turnover rate   494
trading accounts   25
trading profit   150
transfer to reserves   234
true and fair view   209, 210, 217, 253, 254, 297

U

ultra vires   133, 527
uncompleted contracts, profits on   29
unlimited companies   132
unlisted companies   135
unqualified audit report   254
unrealized profits   25, 163, 279
unrealized profit, on inter company sales   285
unrealized surpluses on revaluation of fixed assets   242
users of accounts   9, 468, 522

V

value added   522
Value Added Tax (VAT)   179–181

W

wasting and intangible assets, treatment in SSAP 16   420
weighted average price   221
wholly owned subsidiary   270
window dressing   249, 475
working capital   317
working capital cycle   317–320
working capital, flow of   320
work in progress   21, 29, 36, 243
works or factory costs   21

Z

zero rating   179